An Introduction to Programming with *Mathematica*®

An Introduction to Programming with Mathematica® is designed to introduce the *Mathematica* programming language to a wide audience. Since the last edition of this book was published, significant changes have occurred in *Mathematica* and its use worldwide. Keeping pace with these changes, this substantially larger, updated version includes new and revised chapters on numerics, procedural, rule-based, and front end programming, and gives significant coverage to the latest features up to, and including, version 5.1 of the software.

Mathematica notebooks, available from www.cambridge.org/0521846781, contain examples, programs, and solutions to exercises in the book. Additionally, material to supplement later versions of the software will be made available. This is the ideal text for all scientific students, researchers, and programmers wishing to deepen their understanding of *Mathematica*, or even those keen to program using an interactive language that contains programming paradigms from all major programming languages: procedural, functional, recursive, rule-based, and object-oriented.

An Introduction to

Programming

with

Mathematica®

Third Edition

Paul R. Wellin | Richard J. Gaylord | Samuel N. Kamin

PUBLISHED BY THE PRESS SYNDICATE OF THE UNIVERSITY OF CAMBRIDGE
The Pitt Building, Trumpington Street, Cambridge, United Kingdom

CAMBRIDGE UNIVERSITY PRESS
The Edinburgh Building, Cambridge CB2 2RU, UK
40 West 20th Street, New York, NY 10011–4211, USA
477 Williamstown Road, Port Melbourne, VIC 3207, Australia
Ruiz de Alarcón 13, 28014 Madrid, Spain
Dock House, The Waterfront, Cape Town 8001, South Africa

http://www.cambridge.org

First published 2005
Reprinted 2005

Printed in the United Kingdom at the University Press, Cambridge

Typeface Janson 10/12 pt   *System* Mathematica®   [Typeset by author]

A catalog record for this book is available from the British Library

Library of Congress Cataloging in Publication data

Wellin, Paul R.
    An introduction to programming with Mathematica / Paul R. Wellin, Richard J. Gaylord,
Samuel N. Kamin – 3rd ed.
       p.   cm
    First-2nd eds. under Richard J. Gaylord.
    Includes bibliographical references and index.
    ISBN 0 521 84678 1
       1. Mathematica (Computer program language)   I. Title: Programming with
Mathematica.   II. Gaylord, Richard J.   III. Kamin, Samuel N.   IV. Gaylord, Richard J.
Introduction to programming with Mathematica.   V. Title.

    QA76.73.M29W45 2004
    510′.285′53 – dc22   2004056143

ISBN 0 521 84678 1 hardback

Contents

Preface

Technical computing environments

Computers are now an essential component of research and education in science, engineering, and almost all technical fields. Experimentalists routinely use computers to collect and analyze data while theoreticians use computers to manipulate equations numerically and symbolically. For both, computer simulation and modeling have become indispensable investigative tools. In response, technical education has changed to incorporate the use of computers into the curriculum both as a topic and as a medium for the presentation of technical material.

Advances in computer hardware have progressed to the point where researchers and students now have spectacularly powerful machinery at their fingertips. It is not uncommon for a first-year engineering student to have their own laptop which contains more raw computing power than most researchers could even dream of five years ago.

Oftentimes, the spectacular gains in processing power have not been met with similar advances in software. It often seems as if the power and utility of software are inversely proportional to their ease of use. Fortunately, for those who do technical computing, *Mathematica* has long provided a fully integrated environment, including a programming language suitable for individuals who are not full-time programmers but who need to create programs to carry out their work. It includes:

- Built-in mathematical and graphical capabilities that are both powerful and flexible.

- A programming language that can be used to extend its capabilities virtually without limit. That language is interactive, has the capability to perform both numeric and symbolic manipulation, makes broad use of pattern matching, and supports a functional style of programming favored by many computer scientists (while incorporating constructs for more conventional programming styles).

- Extensive online help facilities that make it easy to learn about built-in functions and get their syntax correct.

- The ability to connect *Mathematica* to other computing environments and other languages.

- A programmable interface in which all of the above elements are seamlessly integrated.

In this book, we focus on the *Mathematica* programming language. While there are many books, including the reference manual by Stephen Wolfram, *The Mathematica Book* (Wolfram 2003), that discuss various aspects of *Mathematica*, there has been a need for a text explaining how to use the underlying programming language so that *Mathematica*'s capabilities can be fully utilized. This book explains *Mathematica*'s programming language for the beginning programmer, first discussing the syntax and structure of the language and then focusing on how to use different programming styles to solve problems.

The audience for this book

This book was written for two distinct groups of readers:

- Users who are familiar with *Mathematica* but wish to deepen their understanding of the program and go beyond the most basic kinds of computations. This book introduces you to the syntax and structure of the *Mathematica* programming language, thus helping you to see the bigger picture of how *Mathematica* works.

- Those who want to learn to program and would like a friendly and useful language to start with. Most low-level languages, like C and Fortran, require many lines of complicated code in order to do something interesting, while many high-level languages, like Lisp, are a bit esoteric and difficult to master. Each of these traditional languages require an edit-compile-run cycle every time you wish to check your program. *Mathematica*, on the other hand, has a more natural syntax and provides very high-level built-in operations with which you can do a lot of interesting things right away. Since it is an interactive environment, you can prototype and test your code immediately, all in the same environment.

If you already have programming experience in one of the more traditional languages, you will often write *Mathematica* programs in a procedural style, producing code that looks like "Fortran in *Mathematica*" for example. By understanding how *Mathematica* programs can be constructed using the functional and rule-based styles of programming, much simpler and more efficient code can often be written.

Changes in the new edition

Since the last edition of this book was published, significant changes have occurred both in *Mathematica* and in its use throughout the world. Several new major versions of *Mathematica* have been released (as of the publication date of this book, *Mathematica* 5.1 is the current version) and, with them, quite a few new functions and features, and some changes to existing functions. This new edition of *An Introduction to Programming with Mathematica* has kept pace, including information and examples throughout the book on the most important new features and functions.

Some of the new functions which are now discussed in this book include: `Array`, `Depth`, `ArrayPlot`, `ArrayQ`, `ArrayRules`, `BitAnd`, `BitOr`, `BitXor`, `ButtonBox`, `ButtonFunction`, `ColumnAlignments`, `DisplayForm`, `Element`, `Evaluation`, `Monitor`, `Export`, `FindFit`, `GridBox`, `Import`, `MakeBoxes`, `MakeExpression`, `Mean`, `NestWhile`, `NestWhileList`, `Norm`. `NotebookGet`, `NotebookPut`, `Numeric`, `icQ`, `PadLeft`, `PadRight`, `Pick`, `PieceWise`, `RegularExpression`, `RowAlign`, `ments`, `RowBox`, `SelectionEvaluate`, `SelectionMove`, `Sequence`, `SparseAr`, `ray`, `Split`, `StepMonitor`, `StringExpression`, `StringCases`, `StyleForm`, `Subsets`, `ToFileName`, `TraditionalForm`.

We have reorganized the structure of the chapters to make it easier to find information on broad topics of interest to the reader. There is a new chapter (Chapter 2) devoted specifically to the syntax and structure of the *Mathematica* language that has culled material from several chapters of the earlier edition. The old chapters on iteration and conditional definitions have been incorporated into a new chapter on procedural programming. Rule-based programming now gets its own chapter. The chapter on numerics has been extensively rewritten to take into account the many changes to numerics over the past several versions of *Mathematica*. The chapter on applications has also been reorganized and rewritten to better explain application development. And we have added an entirely new chapter on front end programming, something that was not feasible prior to *Mathematica* 3. See the section below, "Book contents," for details on each chapter.

Throughout this new edition, many new examples have been worked into the text, in particular in Chapters 4, 5, 9, and 11. Exercises have been expanded over the previous edition, as have the solutions to the exercises. In addition to the printed solutions to exercises at the end of this book, they are also available as a *Mathematica* notebook online in several locations (see below).

Readers of the first two editions found a handful of mistakes, which have been corrected in this edition. We welcome further communication from our readers.

How to use this book

There are several ways in which this book should be useful:

- As a primary text in an introductory course on programming. Perhaps the most obvious use would be in an introductory computer science course for students in science, engineering, or mathematics, who would solve technical problems of interest to them, while at the same time learning to program. The *Mathematica* programming language supports many programming styles that are present in other programming languages, so programming skills learned using *Mathematica* can be readily transferred to these languages.

- As a supplemental text in a course in which *Mathematica* is being used as a tool for studying another technical subject. In these kinds of courses, the principles of *Mathematica* programming can be introduced as needed during the course, although we have found that a structured introduction to *Mathematica* programming at the beginning of the semester works best.

- As a self-study book, particularly for *Mathematica* users who need to use its programming capabilities more fully or who are interested in understanding how the *Mathematica* programming language works.

As educators, we strongly believe in the axiom that one learns by doing. Hence we have not only included hundreds of exercises to this book, but have tried hard to make sure that the exercises are interesting and instructive. You will learn how to program in the *Mathematica* language best by trying to solve problems. We strongly encourage you to try the examples in the text on your own, modifying them as you see fit, but also you should try to do as many of the exercises at the end of each section as you can. Quite a few concepts and features are explained in the exercises and their solutions so it is well worthwhile spending some time on those aspects of the book.

When you work with *Mathematica*, you will generally find that you work with several different programming styles, deal with numerical issues as well as symbolics, crunch numbers but also use graphics, etc. Although topics such as functional programming, procedural programming, and rule-based programming are presented in separate chapters, you should not view such a division as ironclad. In fact, it is merely a convenience to enable us to discuss the various topics that make up the body of this book. We have tried to make the materials self-contained and have everything flow logically from beginning to end, but in some instances, this is quite difficult and, in fact, arbitrary. After digesting the first two or three chapters, you should feel free to jump around from chapter to chapter as you work through the materials in this book.

Conventions

All input and output in this book appear in a different font from the regular text. This is true for examples that appear in the middle of text, such as Expand[(a + b)^4], as well as displayed *Mathematica* code. So, for example, lines of input (what you type at your computer) appear as

    In[1]:= 3 + 5

whereas all output (what *Mathematica* prints on your computer screen) appears in a slightly lighter font than the input.

    Out[1]= 8

You do not have to type the prompts *In[1]:=* or *Out[1]=*; *Mathematica* will do that for you automatically.

All of the programs that are defined in this book can be located in the index under the heading **Programs**. So, for example, the function runEncode defined in Section 7.3 is listed in the index under **Programs**, runEncode.

Book contents

We should perhaps start with what is *not* in this book, namely, a complete list and explanation of the hundreds of operations built into *Mathematica*. For that list, the indispensable reference is *The Mathematica Book* (Wolfram 2003).

This book is also not a complete or advanced treatment of programming in *Mathematica*, nor is it a book about using *Mathematica* to solve problems from one particular discipline. So, for example, the reader will not find a discussion of object-oriented programming in *Mathematica*, nor of databases, nor a formal discussion of data types. Fortunately, there are other excellent sources of information on such topics, including books such as *The Mathematica Programmer I* and *II*, or *Computer Science with Mathematica: Theory and Practice for Science, Mathematics, and Engineering*, all by Roman Maeder.

This book is about teaching you how to program with *Mathematica*. We assume that you have little, if any, programming experience (though you may already be a *Mathematica* user), and we take you step by step through the various programming styles that are available in *Mathematica* and explain when to use what style.

The chapter structure is as follows:

- Chapter 1 An introduction to *Mathematica*. For the reader who has little or no knowledge of *Mathematica*, we have included a brief overview of some of its built-in capabilities, including graphics and numerical and symbolic computations. In addition, this chapter contains some of the fundamentals of *Mathematica*, such as how to use the *Mathematica* interface and how to enter expressions. Experienced *Mathematica* users should feel free to skim this material.

- Chapter 2 The *Mathematica* language. This chapter gives an introduction to the syntax and structure of the *Mathematica* programming language. It introduces the basic construct in the *Mathematica* language, an expression, and then discusses some of the building blocks that you will use over and over again in constructing your programs.

- Chapter 3 Lists. The heart of the book begins here, with a discussion of this most important of data types. Aside from numbers, no other data type is more useful in programming. We describe the use of built-in functions to create and manipulate lists. This chapter also discusses strings and characters as their manipulation is so similar to that for lists.

- Chapter 4 Functional programming. This chapter introduces functional programming, a style quite distinct from what is available in traditional languages. We discuss nested function calls, iterating functions, and introduce some of the more important higher-order functions, such as Map, Apply, and Thread. A section on pure functions introduces this important construct borrowed from the lambda calculus. The chapter concludes with a section demonstrating how to construct "one-liners," short programs that solve a particular problem in one line.

- Chapter 5 Procedural programming. Procedures can be thought of as recipes. They spell out a sequence of steps to follow. They often include control structures that determine what action to take depending upon some property of an input. This programming style is more characteristic of conventional languages like C than it is of *Mathematica*, but is still important. This chapter introduces the concepts of loops, iteration, flow control, and conditional definitions, using some traditional problems such as Newton's method and the Sieve of Eratosthenes to demonstrate these concepts.

- Chapter 6 Rule-based programming. This chapter, new to the third edition of this book, explains how rules can be used to transform expressions. Blanks, pattern matching, string patterns, and alternatives are discussed extensively and some classical problems from computer science are examined using rule-based approaches: encoding and sorting.

- Chapter 7 Recursion. This method of programming, in which a function is defined in terms of itself, is heavily used in mathematics and computer science and has a natural implementation in *Mathematica*. For those with little experience programming recursively, we give a gentle introduction to thinking recursively and then use several well-known problems such as merge sort, Gaussian elimination, tree representation, and Huffman encoding to implement the ideas in this chapter. The chapter also includes discussions of dynamic programming (or caching).

- Chapter 8 Numerics. *Mathematica* contains a variety of types of numbers, both exact and approximate. This chapter discusses working with exact vs. inexact numbers and machine-precision vs. high-precision numbers. Efficiency issues are also presented including a discussion of packed arrays and sparse arrays, two data formats that are optimized for both speed and memory. The chapter concludes with a discussion of how to write programs that best take advantage of the numerical capabilities in *Mathematica*.

- Chapter 9 Graphics programming. This chapter introduces the basic concepts of *Mathematica* graphics. It uses some of the techniques of the previous chapters to create graphics-based programs and to solve problems that are inherently graphical in nature. It also demonstrates how to include options in your programs.

- Chapter 10 Front end programming. The front end is the graphical user interface to *Mathematica*. Beginning in Version 3, many aspects of the front end became programmable and this functionality was further extended in Versions 4 and 5. This new chapter introduces the structure of the objects in the front end that can be manipulated using the techniques discussed in earlier chapters. It includes sections on notebooks and cells, cell data types, box structures, and buttons (a special kind of box).

- Chapter 11 Examples and applications. *Mathematica* is used to solve larger-scale programming problems. Included are an application to manipulate and visualize data, as well as *Mathematica* implementations of the Game of Life using functional and rule-based programming, random walks, and finally the creation of a mini picture-description language. Options and default values and documentation implementations are also discussed.

- Chapter 12 Writing packages. The last chapter introduces the method of organizing libraries of *Mathematica* functions into convenient units called packages. Discussion of options, error-trapping, and messages are included.

Supplemental packages and solutions

Materials for this book have been made available in electronic form. *Mathematica* notebooks containing most of the examples, exercises, and solutions are included in an archive appropriate for several platforms: IPM3.zip for Windows, IPM3.tgz for Unix, and IPM3.hqx for Macintosh OS X. The file names correspond directly to the chapter structure. So, for example, the notebook for the first chapter is 01Introduction.nb.

The archive also contains files with *Mathematica* programs that can be loaded into your *Mathematica* sessions as needed. These files (normally called packages), have a file-name extension ending with .m.

Archives for this book have been placed in two locations:

- Cambridge University Press website: www.cambridge.org/0521846781

- Wolfram Research website: library.wolfram.com/infocenter/Books/5169/

The recommended way to use the notebooks and packages is to first unpack the archive on your computer. This will leave you with two directories/folders, one called IPM3 and the other RandomWalks. Move each of these folders and their contents inside one of the *Mathematica* Applications directories on your computer. The recommended location is inside either $BaseDirectory or $UserBaseDirectory as files in these two directories will continue to be found even after you upgrade *Mathematica*.

Here is the recommended location for where to install applications. The output will look different on different operating systems; the following was run in Windows XP.

```
ToFileName[{$BaseDirectory, "Applications"}]

C:\Documents and Settings\All Users\
    Application Data\Mathematica\Applications\
```

Once you have installed the directories in the above location, start up *Mathematica* and, from the Help menu, select Rebuild Help Index. Once this is done, you will find the notebooks in the Help Browser by choosing the Add-ons & Links category.

To load packages from the book, you need only to specify the directory and package name. For example, this loads the package `RandomWalks.m`:

```
<< IPM3`RandomWalks`
```

Further information

While the basic aspects of *Mathematica* programming are discussed in this book, there are a great many more things that can be said about *Mathematica* and the *Mathematica* programming language. The most comprehensive reference source is the manual that comes with each copy of the software: *The Mathematica Book* (Wolfram 2003).

The *Mathematica* Information Center (library.wolfram.com/infocenter) contains thousands of programming examples and notebooks from all areas of science and engineering. It is organized by collection (articles, courseware, demos, etc.), by subject, or you can simply search on any phrase that you wish.

An Internet newsgroup exists that is devoted to all aspects of *Mathematica*: `comp.soft-sys.math.mathematica`. This moderated newsgroup has been in existence for many years and users have come to rely on the collective wisdom of the hundreds of contributors from around the world who respond to any question that is posed. An archive going back to 1989 exists and can easily be browsed or searched in a web browser by going to forums.wolfram.com/mathgroup/.

The Mathematica Journal is a quarterly journal that publishes articles about all aspects of *Mathematica*. For subscription information, or to view issues online, go to the website www.mathematica-journal.com.

Finally, there are now over 300 books about *Mathematica* or that use *Mathematica* to teach a subject. Some of these can be found in the bibliography at the end of this text. See store.wolfram.com/catalog/books/ for a complete up-to-date publications list.

Colophon

The third edition of this book was produced from original *Mathematica* notebooks. *Mathematica* 5 and 5.1 were used throughout. A *Mathematica* style sheet was customized containing page layout information consistent with the page layout as specified by a book designer. The *Mathematica* notebooks were output to PostScript files and then distilled to PDF files which were sent to the printer electronically.

Acknowledgments

Many people have contributed to our understanding of the *Mathematica* programming language over the years. At Wolfram Research these include Lou D'Andria, Harry Calkins, Andy Hunt, Rob Knapp, Dan Lichtblau, John Novak, Robby Villegas, and Dave Withoff. Also Roman Maeder has answered several esoteric questions about the patterns and the ordering of rules in *Mathematica*.

Thanks to Dana Scott for permission to use his material on sorting (Chapter 6) and Klaus Sutner for permission to use his material on encryption (also in Chapter 6) as well as interesting discussions on the pattern matcher in *Mathematica*.

Paul Wellin would like to thank his wife Sheri for her support, understanding, and sense of humor throughout this project.

Richard J. Gaylord would like to thank Shawn Sheridan who was his guru for both *Mathematica* and the Macintosh.

Samuel Kamin would like to acknowledge the Computer Science Department of the University of Illinois for its excellent working environment and the support of his colleagues there. Above all, he would like to thank Judy and Rebecca for their love and patience.

Paul R. Wellin
wellin@wolfram.com

Richard J. Gaylord
gaylord@uiuc.edu

Samuel N. Kamin
kamin@cs.uiuc.edu

Ocotober 2004

1 An introduction to *Mathematica*

Mathematica is a very large and seemingly complex system. It contains hundreds of functions for performing various tasks in science, mathematics, and engineering, including computing, programming, data analysis, knowledge representation, and visualization of information. In this introductory chapter, we introduce the elementary operations in *Mathematica* and give a sense of its computational and programming breadth and depth. In addition, we give some basic information that users of *Mathematica* need to know, such as how to start *Mathematica*, how to get out of it, how to enter simple inputs and get answers, and finally how to use *Mathematica*'s documentation to get answers to questions about the system.

1.1 A brief overview of *Mathematica*

Numerical computations

Mathematica has been aptly described as a sophisticated calculator. With it you can enter mathematical expressions and compute their values.

$$\textit{In[1]:=}\ \ \texttt{Sin[.86] - Log[}\pi\texttt{]}\ \left(1 + \frac{.08}{12}\right)^{12}$$

$$\textit{Out[1]}=\ -0.481899$$

You can store values in memory.

$$\textit{In[2]:=}\ \ \texttt{rent = 350}$$

$$\textit{Out[2]}=\ 350$$

$$\textit{In[3]:=}\ \ \texttt{food = 175}$$

$$\textit{Out[3]}=\ 175$$

$$\textit{In[4]:=}\ \ \texttt{heat = 83}$$

$$\textit{Out[4]}=\ 83$$

In[5]:= **rent + food + heat**

Out[5]= 608

Yet *Mathematica* differs from calculators and simple computer programs in its ability to calculate exact results and to compute to an arbitrary degree of precision.

In[6]:= $\dfrac{1}{15} + \dfrac{1}{35} + \dfrac{1}{63}$

Out[6]= $\dfrac{1}{9}$

In[7]:= 2^{500}

Out[7]= 3273390607896141870013189696827599152216642046043064789483291
36809613379640467455488327009232590415715088668412756007100 9
21725654588539305332 8527589376

In[8]:= **N[π, 500]**

Out[8]= 3.14159265358979323846264338327950288419716939937510582097494
45923078164062862089986280348253421170679821480865132823066 4
70938446095505822317253594081284811174502841027019385211055 5
96446229489549303819644288109756659334461284756482337867831 6
52712019091456485669234603486104543266482133936072602491412 7
37245870066063155881748815209209628292540917153643678925903 6
00113305305488204665213841469519415116094330572703657595919 5
30921861173819326117931051185480744623799627495673518857527 2
48912279381830119491

Symbolic computations

One of the more powerful features of *Mathematica* is its ability to manipulate and compute with symbolic expressions. For example, you can factor polynomials and simplify trigonometric expressions.

In[9]:= **Factor[x^5 - 1]**

Out[9]= $(-1 + x)\ (1 + x + x^2 + x^3 + x^4)$

In[10]:= **TrigReduce[Sin[θ]^3]**

Out[10]= $\dfrac{1}{4}\ (3\,\text{Sin}[\theta] - \text{Sin}[3\,\theta])$

You can simplify expressions using assumptions about variables contained in those expressions. For example, if k is assumed to be an integer, $\sin(2\pi k + x)$ simplifies to $\sin(x)$.

In[11]:= **Simplify[Sin[2 π k + x], k ∈ Integers]**

Out[11]= Sin[x]

This computes the conditions for which a general quadratic polynomial will have both roots equal to each other.

In[12]:= **Reduce[$\exists_{x,\,a x^2 + b x + c == 0}$ ($\forall_{y,\,a y^2 + b y + c == 0}$ x == y), {a, b, c}]**

Out[12]= $(a == 0 \,\&\&\, b \neq 0)\;||\;(a == 0 \,\&\&\, b\,c \neq 0)\;||\;\left(a \neq 0 \,\&\&\, c == \dfrac{b^2}{4\,a}\right)$

You can create functions that are defined piecewise.

In[13]:= **Piecewise[{{1, x == 0}}, Sin[x] / x]**

Out[13]= $\begin{cases} 1 & \text{x == 0} \\ \frac{\text{Sin[x]}}{\text{x}} & \text{True} \end{cases}$

The knowledge base of *Mathematica* includes algorithms for solving polynomial equations, and computing integrals.

In[14]:= **Solve[x^3 - a x + 1 == 0, x]**

Out[14]= $\left\{\left\{x \to \dfrac{\left(\frac{2}{3}\right)^{1/3} a}{\left(-9 + \sqrt{3}\,\sqrt{27 - 4\,a^3}\right)^{1/3}} + \dfrac{\left(-9 + \sqrt{3}\,\sqrt{27 - 4\,a^3}\right)^{1/3}}{2^{1/3}\,3^{2/3}}\right\},\right.$

$\left\{x \to -\dfrac{\left(1 + i\,\sqrt{3}\right) a}{2^{2/3}\,3^{1/3}\left(-9 + \sqrt{3}\,\sqrt{27 - 4\,a^3}\right)^{1/3}} - \right.$

$\left.\dfrac{\left(1 - i\,\sqrt{3}\right)\left(-9 + \sqrt{3}\,\sqrt{27 - 4\,a^3}\right)^{1/3}}{2\,2^{1/3}\,3^{2/3}}\right\},$

$\left\{x \to -\dfrac{\left(1 - i\,\sqrt{3}\right) a}{2^{2/3}\,3^{1/3}\left(-9 + \sqrt{3}\,\sqrt{27 - 4\,a^3}\right)^{1/3}} - \right.$

$\left.\left.\dfrac{\left(1 + i\,\sqrt{3}\right)\left(-9 + \sqrt{3}\,\sqrt{27 - 4\,a^3}\right)^{1/3}}{2\,2^{1/3}\,3^{2/3}}\right\}\right\}$

In[15]:= $\displaystyle\int \dfrac{1}{1 + x^4}\,dx$

Out[15]= $\dfrac{1}{4\,\sqrt{2}}\left(-2\,\text{ArcTan}\left[1 - \sqrt{2}\,x\right] + 2\,\text{ArcTan}\left[1 + \sqrt{2}\,x\right] - \right.$

$\left.\text{Log}\left[-1 + \sqrt{2}\,x - x^2\right] + \text{Log}\left[1 + \sqrt{2}\,x + x^2\right]\right)$

Graphics

The ability to visualize functions or sets of data often allows us greater insight into their structure and properties. *Mathematica* provides a wide range of graphing capabilities. These include two- and three-dimensional plots of functions or data sets, contour and density plots of functions of two variables, bar charts, histograms and pie charts of data sets, and many packages designed for specific graphical purposes. In addition, the *Mathematica* programming language allows you to construct graphical images "from the ground up" using primitive elements, as we will see in Chapter 9.

Here is a simple two-dimensional plot of the function $\sin(x + \sqrt{2}\, \sin(x^2))$.

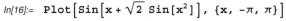

$In[16]:=$ `Plot[Sin[x + `$\sqrt{2}$` Sin[x`^{2}`]], {x, -`π`, `π`}]`

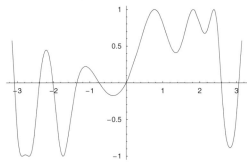

$Out[16]=$ `- Graphics -`

You can combine two or more plots in a single graphic by enclosing them inside curly braces.

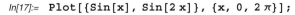

$In[17]:=$ `Plot[{Sin[x], Sin[2 x]}, {x, 0, 2 `π`}];`

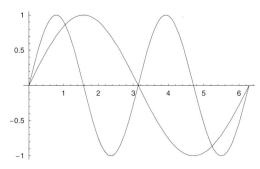

Here is a plot of the sinc function, given in the previous section.

In[18]:= `Plot[Piecewise[ {{1, x == 0}}, Sin[x] / x], {x, -2 π, 2 π}];`

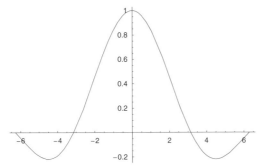

Here is a surface of constant negative curvature, represented parametrically by the three functions ρ, σ, and τ. This surface is often referred to as Dini's surface.

In[19]:= `ρ = Cos[φ] Sin[θ];`
`σ = Sin[φ] Sin[θ];`

$$\tau = 0.2\, \phi + \text{Cos}[\theta] + \text{Log}\left[\text{Tan}\left[\frac{\theta}{2}\right]\right];$$

In[22]:= `ParametricPlot3D[{ρ, σ, τ}, {φ, 0, 4 π}, {θ, .05, 1}, Axes → False,`
`Boxed → False, PlotPoints → 30, AspectRatio → 1.75];`

Working with data

The ability to plot and visualize data is extremely important in engineering and all of the social, natural, and physical sciences. *Mathematica* can import and export data from other applications, plot the data in a variety of forms, and be used to perform numerical analysis on the data.

The file `dataset.m` contains pairs of data points, in this case representing body mass vs. heat production for 13 different animals. The data are given as (m, r), where m represents the mass of the animal and r the heat production in *kcal* per day. First we set up a platform independent path to the file and then import that file.

```
In[23]:= datafile = ToFileName[{$BaseDirectory,
            "Applications", "IPM3", "DataFiles"}, "dataset.m"]
```

```
Out[23]= C:\Documents and Settings\All Users\Application Data\
            Mathematica\Applications\IPM3\DataFiles\dataset.m
```

```
In[24]:= data = Import[datafile, "Table"]
```

```
Out[24]= {{0.06099, 6.95099}, {0.403, 28.189},
            {0.62199, 41.1}, {2.50999, 120.799},
            {2.95999, 147.9}, {3.33, 182.8}, {8.19999, 368.8},
            {28.1999, 981.299}, {57.4, 1303.29}, {72.2999, 1512.5},
            {340.199, 7100.29}, {711, 10101.1}, {5000., 29894.9}}
```

You can immediately plot the data using the `ListPlot` function.

```
In[25]:= ListPlot[data, PlotStyle → PointSize[.02]];
```

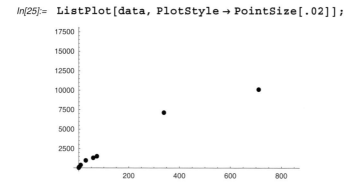

This plots the data on log–log axes.

In[26]:= `logplot = ListPlot[Log[data], PlotStyle → PointSize[.02]];`

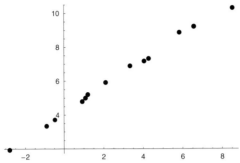

You can then fit a straight line to the log-data by performing a linear least squares fit. In this example, we are fitting to the model $a + m\,x$, where a and m are the parameters to be determined in the model with variable x.

In[27]:= `f = FindFit[Log[data], a + m x, {a, m}, x]`

Out[27]= {a → 4.15437, m → 0.761465}

Here is a plot of the linear fit function.

In[28]:= `fplot = Plot[a + m x /. f, {x, -3, 9}];`

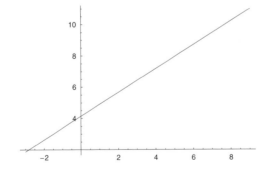

Finally, you can see how well the fitted function approximates the log plot by combining these last two graphics.

In[29]:= `Show[fplot, logplot];`

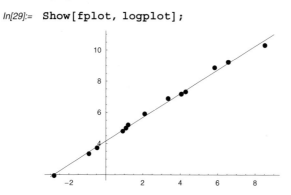

Programming

With a copy of *The Mathematica Book* (Wolfram 2003) or one of the many tutorial books (see, for example, Glynn and Gray 1999) describing the vast array of computational tasks that can be performed with *Mathematica*, it would seem you can compute just about anything you might want. But that impression is mistaken. There are simply more kinds of calculations than could possibly be included in a single program. Whether you are interested in computing bowling scores or finding the mean square distance of a random walk on a torus, *Mathematica* does not have a built-in function to do everything that a user could possibly want. What it *does* have – and what really makes it the amazingly useful tool it is – is the capability for users to define their own functions. This is called *programming*, and it is what this book is all about.

Sometimes, the programs you create will be succinct and focused on a very specific task. *Mathematica* possesses a rich set of tools that enable you to quickly and naturally translate the statement of a problem into a program. For example, the following program defines a test for perfect numbers, numbers that are equal to the sum of their proper divisors.

In[30]:= `PerfectQ[n_] := Apply[Plus, Divisors[n]] == 2 n`

We then define another function that selects those numbers from a range of integers that pass this `PerfectQ` test.

In[31]:= `PerfectSearch[n_] := Select[Range[n], PerfectQ]`

This then finds all perfect numbers less than 1,000,000.

```
In[32]:= PerfectSearch[10^6]

Out[32]= {6, 28, 496, 8128}
```

Here are two functions for representing regular polygons. The first defines the vertices of a regular *n*-gon, while the second uses those vertices to create a polygon graphics object that can then be displayed with the built-in Show function.

```
In[33]:= vertices[n_Integer, r_ : 1] :=
           Table[{r Cos[(2 α π)/n], r Sin[(2 α π)/n]}, {α, 0, n - 1}]

In[34]:= RegularPolygon[n_] :=
           Graphics[Line[vertices[n] /. {a_, b__} → {a, b, a}],
             AspectRatio → Automatic]

In[35]:= Show[RegularPolygon[5]]
```

```
Out[35]= - Graphics -
```

As another example of a succinct program, here is an iterative function that implements the well-known Newton method for root finding.

```
In[36]:= NewtonZero[f_, xi_] := NestWhile[(# - f[#]/f'[#]) &, xi, Unequal, 2]

In[37]:= g[x_] := x^3 - 2 x^2 + 1

In[38]:= NewtonZero[g, 2.0]

Out[38]= 1.61803
```

Of course, sometimes the task at hand requires a more involved program, stretching across several lines (or even pages) of code. For example, here is a slightly longer program to compute the score of a game of bowling, given a list of the number of pins scored by each ball.

```
In[39]:=  BowlingScore[pins_] :=
           Module[{score}, score[{x_, y_, z_}] := x + y + z;
            score[{10, y_, z_, r___}] := 10 + y + z + score[{y, z, r}];
            score[{x_, y_, z_, r___}] :=
             x + y + z + score[{z, r}] /; x + y == 10;
            score[{x_, y_, r___}] := x + y + score[{r}] /; x + y < 10;
            score[If[pins[[-2]] + pins[[-1]] ≥ 10, pins, Append[pins, 0]]]]]
```

Here is the computation for a "perfect" game – 12 strikes in a row.

```
In[40]:=  BowlingScore[{10, 10, 10, 10, 10, 10, 10, 10, 10, 10, 10, 10}]
```

```
Out[40]=  300
```

These examples use a variety of programming styles: functional programming, rule-based programming, the use of anonymous functions, and more. We do not expect you to understand the examples in this section at this point – that is why we wrote this book! What you should understand is that in many ways *Mathematica* is designed to be as broadly useful as possible and that there are many calculations for which *Mathematica* does not have a built-in function, so, to make full use of its many capabilities, you will sometimes need to program. The main purpose of this book is to show you how.

Another purpose is to teach you the basic principles of programming. These principles – making assignments, defining rules, using conditionals, recursion, and iteration – are applicable (with great differences in detail, to be sure) to all other programming languages.

Symbolic and interactive documents

In addition to the computational tools that *Mathematica* provides for what many professionals associate with technical computing, it also contains tools for creating and modifying the user interface to such tasks. These tools include hyperlinks for jumping to other locations within a document or across files, buttons to perform tasks that you might normally associate with a command-line interface, and tools to modify and manipulate the appearance and functionality of your *Mathematica* notebooks directly. In this section we will give a few short examples of what is possible, waiting until Chapter 10 for a methodical look at how to program these elements.

The first example takes the code necessary to display a polyhedron and puts it in a button. The two lines of code that could be evaluated normally in a notebook first load a package and then display an icosahedron in the notebook.

```
In[41]:=  Needs["Graphics`Polyhedra`"]
```

In[42]:= `Show[Stellate[Polyhedron[Icosahedron]]]`

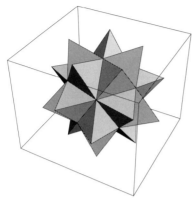

Out[42]= `- Graphics3D -`

Here is a short program that creates a button containing the above two expressions.

```
Cell[BoxData[
    ButtonBox[
      RowBox[{"Stellate", " ", "Icosahedron"}],
      ButtonFunction:>CompoundExpression[
          Needs[ "Graphics`Polyhedra`"],
          Show[Stellate[Polyhedron[Icosahedron]]]
          ],
      ButtonEvaluator->Automatic],
  "Input",
  Active->True]
```

The formatted version of the above cell can be displayed by choosing Show Expression from the Format menu. When you do that, it will look like the following:

Stellate Icosahedron

Clicking the button will cause the *Mathematica* code in the `ButtonFunction` to be immediately evaluated and the following graphics will then be displayed in your notebook.

Functions are available to jump around to different parts of a *Mathematica* notebook and perform various actions. Here is a short piece of code that creates a button which, upon being clicked, moves the selection to the next cell and then evaluates that cell.

```
Cell[TextData[{
  Cell[BoxData[
      ButtonBox["EVALUATE",
        ButtonFunction:>FrontEndExecute[ {
            FrontEnd`SelectionMove[
              ButtonNotebook[ ], All, ButtonCell],
            FrontEnd`SelectionMove[
              ButtonNotebook[ ], Next, Cell],
            FrontEnd`SelectionEvaluate[
              ButtonNotebook[ ]]}],
        Active->True]]],
  StyleBox[" MATHEMATICA INPUT"]
}], "Text"]
```

The formatted version of the above cell can be displayed by choosing **Show Expression** from the **Format** menu. When you do that, it will look somewhat like the following (although we have removed some of the text formatting above to improve readability of the code). Clicking the **EVALUATE** button will cause the input cell immediately following to be selected and then evaluated.

> **EVALUATE *MATHEMATICA INPUT***

In[43]:= **3 (4 + 5)**

Out[43]= 27

The following example demonstrates how you can use *Mathematica* functions to perform some of the user interface actions that you would normally associate with keyboard and mouse events. By using such techniques, you can create a specific set of actions that will follow certain evaluations. For example, if you were creating an electronic quiz for your students, you could include "hint" buttons within your class notebooks that would open a new notebook with hints and suggestions upon clicking.

This creates a new notebook that contains three cells – a Section cell, a Text cell, and an Input cell. Upon evaluation, the NotebookPut command below will cause a new notebook to appear, containing the three specified cells. The screen shots below show what appears in the user interface after evaluating each of the preceding inputs.

In[44]:= `nb = NotebookPut[`
      `Notebook[{`
        `Cell["Symbolic and Interactive Documents", "Section"],`
        `Cell["Cells and notebooks are Mathematica expressions.",`
         `"Text"],`
        `Cell["Integrate[Sin[x]/Cos[x],x]", "Input"]`
      `}]]`

Out[44]= `NotebookObject[ «Untitled-1» ]`

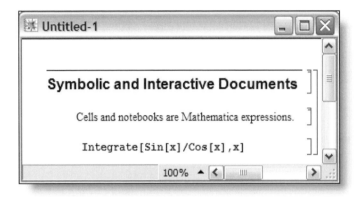

This moves the selection bar past the last cell in the above notebook.

In[45]:= `SelectionMove[nb, Next, Cell, 4]`

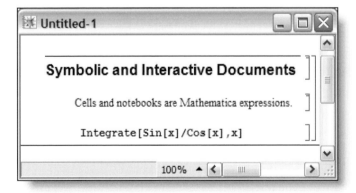

We then select the most previous cell.

In[46]:= **SelectionMove[nb, Previous, Cell]**

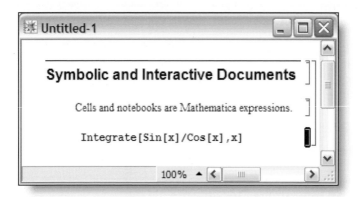

Finally, we evaluate the selected cell.

In[47]:= **SelectionEvaluate[nb]**

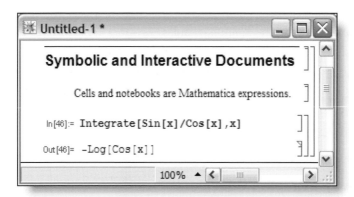

In Chapter 10 we will give a detailed discussion of how to modify and manipulate the user interface through the use of the symbolic programming techniques that are discussed throughout this book.

1.2 Using *Mathematica*

Before you can do any serious work, you will need to know how to get a *Mathematica* session started, how to stop it, and how to get out of trouble when you get into it. These procedures depend somewhat on the system you are using. You should read the system-specific information that came with your copy of *Mathematica*; and you may need to consult a local *Mathematica* guru if our advice here is not applicable to your system.

Getting into and out of Mathematica

The most commonly used interface is often referred to as a notebook interface in which the user creates and works in interactive documents. Personal computers running Windows, Macintosh operating systems, Linux, and most flavors of Unix all support this graphical user interface, which normally starts up automatically when you begin your *Mathematica* session.

There are some situations where you may want to start up *Mathematica* from a command prompt and issue commands directly through that interface, bypassing the notebook interface entirely. For example, you may have a very long computation that you need to run in batch mode. Typically, *Mathematica* is started up on these systems by typing math at a command prompt. We will not discuss using *Mathematica* through a command prompt any further. If you are interested in this mode you should consult the documentation that came with your copy of *Mathematica*.

Starting *Mathematica* and first computations

To start *Mathematica* you will have to find and then double-click on the *Mathematica* icon on your computer, which will look something like this:

The computer will then load parts of *Mathematica* into its memory and soon a blank window will appear on the screen. This window is the visual interface to a *Mathematica* notebook and it has many features that are useful to the user.

Notebooks allow you to write text, perform computations, write and run programs, and create graphics all in one document. Notebooks also have many of the features of common word processors, so those familiar with word processing will find the notebook interface easy to learn. In addition, the notebook provides features for outlining material which you may find useful for giving talks and demonstrations.

When a blank notebook first appears on the screen (either from just starting *Mathematica* or from selecting New in the File menu), you can start typing immediately. For example, if you type N[Pi,200] press SHIFT-ENTER (hold down the Shift key while pressing the Enter key) to evaluate an expression. *Mathematica* will evaluate the result and print the 200-decimal digit approximation to π on the screen.

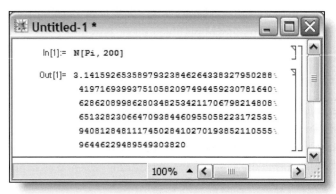

Notice that when you evaluate an expression in a notebook, *Mathematica* adds input and output prompts. In the example notebook above, these are denoted In[1]:= and Out[1]=. These prompts can be thought of as markers (or labels) that you can refer to during your *Mathematica* session.

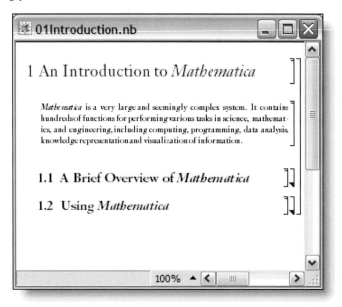

You should also note that when you started typing *Mathematica* placed a *bracket* on the far right side of the window that enclosed the *cell* that you were working in. These *cell brackets* are helpful for organizational purposes within the notebook. Double-clicking on cell brackets will open any collapsed cells, or close any open cells as can be seen in the previous screen shot.

Double-clicking on the cell bracket containing the **1.1 A Brief Overview of *Mathematica*** cell will open the cell to display its contents:

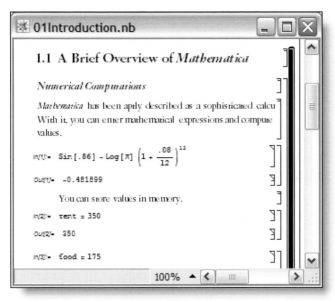

Using cell brackets in this manner allows you to organize your work in an orderly manner, as well as to outline material. For a complete description of cell brackets and many other interface features, you should consult the documentation that came with your version of *Mathematica*.

For information on other features such as saving, printing, and editing notebooks, consult the manuals that came with your version of *Mathematica*.

Entering input

New input can be entered whenever there is a horizontal line that runs across the width of the notebook. If one is not present where you wish to place an input cell, move the cursor up and down until it changes to a horizontal bar and then click the mouse once. A horizontal line should now appear across the width of the window. You can immediately start typing and an input cell will be created.

Input can be entered exactly as it appears in this book. To get *Mathematica* to evaluate an expression that you have entered, press [SHIFT]-[ENTER]; that is, hold down the Shift key and then press the Enter key.

You can enter mathematical expressions in a traditional looking two-dimensional format using either palettes for quick entry of template expressions, or keyboard equivalents. For example, the following expression can be entered by using the Basic Input palette, or through a series of keystrokes. For details of inputting mathematical expressions, read your user documentation or read the section on **2D Expression Input** in the Help Browser.

In[1]:= $\int \frac{1}{1-x^3}\, dx$

Out[1]= $\frac{\text{ArcTan}\left[\frac{1+2x}{\sqrt{3}}\right]}{\sqrt{3}} - \frac{1}{3}\text{Log}[-1+x] + \frac{1}{6}\text{Log}[1+x+x^2]$

As noted previously, *Mathematica* enters the In and Out prompts for you. You do not type these prompts. You will see them *after* you evaluate your input.

You can refer to the result of the previous calculation using the symbol %.

In[2]:= 2^{64}

Out[2]= 18446744073709551616

In[3]:= % + 1

Out[3]= 18446744073709551617

You can also refer to the result of any earlier calculation using its Out [*i*] label or, equivalently, %*i*.

In[4]:= Out[1]

Out[4]= $\frac{\text{ArcTan}\left[\frac{1+2x}{\sqrt{3}}\right]}{\sqrt{3}} - \frac{1}{3}\text{Log}[-1+x] + \frac{1}{6}\text{Log}[1+x+x^2]$

In[5]:= %2

Out[5]= 18446744073709551616

Ending a *Mathematica* session
To end your *Mathematica* session, choose **Exit** from the **File** menu. You will be prompted to save any unsaved open notebooks.

Getting out of trouble

From time to time, you will type an input which will cause *Mathematica* to misbehave in some way, perhaps by just going silent for a long time (if, for example, you have inadvertently asked it to do something very difficult) or perhaps by printing out screen after screen of not terribly useful information. In this case, you can try to "interrupt" the calculation. How you do this depends on your computer's operating system:

- Macintosh: type ⌘[.] (the Command key and the period) and then type a

- Windows 95/98/NT/2000/XP: type [ALT][.] (the Alt key and the period)

- Unix: type [CTRL]–[.] and then type a and then [RET]

These attempts to stop the computation will sometimes fail. If after waiting a reasonable amount of time (say, a few minutes), *Mathematica* still seems to be stuck, you will have to "kill the kernel." (Before attempting to kill the kernel, try to convince yourself that the computation is really in a loop from which it will not return and that it is not just an intensive computation that requires a lot of time.) Killing the kernel is accomplished by selecting **Quit Kernel** from the **Kernel** menu. The kernel can then be restarted without killing the front end by first selecting **Start Kernel ‣ Local** under the **Kernel** menu, or you can simply evaluate a command in a notebook and a new kernel should start up automatically.

The syntax of inputs

You can enter mathematical expressions in a linear syntax using arithmetic operators common to almost all computer languages.

> *In[6]:=* **39 / 13**
>
> *Out[6]=* 3

Alternately, you can enter this expression in the traditional form by typing 39, [CTRL][/], then 13.

> *In[7]:=* $\dfrac{39}{13}$
>
> *Out[7]=* 3

The caret (^) is used for exponentiation.

> *In[8]:=* **2 ^ 5**
>
> *Out[8]=* 32

You can enter this expression in a more traditional typeset form by typing 2, ⎡CTRL⎤[^], and then 5.

In[9]:= **2⁵**

Out[9]= 32

Mathematica includes several different ways of entering typeset expressions, either directly from the keyboard as we did above, or via palettes available from the File menu. Below is a brief table showing some of the more commonly used typeset expressions and how they are entered through the keyboard. You should read your documentation and become comfortable using these input interfaces so that you can easily enter the kinds of expressions in this book.

Expression	FullForm	Keyboard shortcut
x^2	`SuperscriptBox[x, 2]`	x ⎡CTRL⎤[6], 2
x_i	`SubscriptBox[x, i]`	x ⎡CTRL⎤[–], i
$\frac{x}{y}$	`FractionBox[x, y]`	x ⎡CTRL⎤[/], y
$\sqrt{x}$	`SqrtBox[x]`	⎡CTRL⎤[2], x
$x \geq y$	`GreaterEqual[x, y]`	x ⎡ESC⎤ >= ⎡ESC⎤, y

Table 1.1: Entering typeset expressions

You can indicate multiplication by simply putting a space between the two factors, as in mathematics. You can also use the asterisk (*) for that purpose, as is traditional in most computer languages.

In[10]:= **2 5**

Out[10]= 10

In[11]:= **2 * 5**

Out[11]= 10

Mathematica also gives operations the same precedence as in mathematics. In particular, multiplication and division have a higher precedence than addition and subtraction, so that 3 + 4 * 5 equals 23 and not 35.

In[12]:= **3 + 4 5**

Out[12]= 23

Functions are also written as they are in mathematics books, except that function names are capitalized and their arguments are enclosed in square brackets.

In[13]:= **Factor[x⁵ - 1]**

Out[13]= $(-1 + x) (1 + x + x^2 + x^3 + x^4)$

Almost all of the built-in functions are spelled out in full, as in the above example. The exceptions to this rule are well-known abbreviations such as D for differentiation, Sqrt for square roots, Log for logarithms, and Det for the determinant of a matrix. Spelling out the name of a function in full is quite useful when you are not sure whether a function exists to perform a particular task. For example, if we wanted to compute the conjugate of a complex number, an educated guess would be:

In[14]:= **Conjugate[3 + 4 i]**

Out[14]= $3 - 4 i$

Whereas square brackets [and] are used to enclose the arguments to functions, curly braces { and } are used to indicate a *list* or range of values. Lists are a basic data type in *Mathematica* and are used to represent vectors and matrices (and tensors of any dimension), as well as additional arguments to functions such as in Plot and Integrate.

In[15]:= **{a, b, c}.{x, y, z}**

Out[15]= $a x + b y + c z$

In[16]:= **Plot[Sin[x + √2̄ Sin[x]], {x, -2 π, 2 π}];**

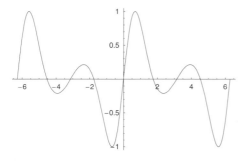

In[17]:= **Integrate[Cos[x], {x, a, b}]**

Out[17]= $-Sin[a] + Sin[b]$

In the Plot example, the list $\{x, -2\pi, 2\pi\}$ indicates that the function $\sin(x + \sqrt{2} \sin(x))$ is to be plotted over an interval as x takes on values from -2π to 2π. The Integrate expression above is equivalent to the mathematical expression $\int_a^b \cos(x)\,dx$.

Mathematica has very powerful list-manipulating capabilities that will be explored in detail in Chapter 3.

When you end an expression with a semicolon (;), *Mathematica* computes its value but does not display it. This is very helpful when the result of the expression would be very long and you do not need to see it. In the following example, we first create a list of the integers from 1 to 10,000, suppressing their display with the semicolon, and then compute their sum and average.

In[18]:= **nums = Range[10000];**

In[19]:= **Apply[Plus, nums]**

Out[19]= 50005000

In[20]:= $\dfrac{\%}{\texttt{Length[nums]}}$

Out[20]= $\dfrac{10001}{2}$

An expression can be entered on multiple lines, but only if *Mathematica* can tell that it is not finished after the first line. For example, you can enter 3* on one line and 4 on the next.

In[21]:= **3 ***

      4

Out[21]= 12

But you cannot enter 3 on the first line and *4 on the second.

In[22]:= **3**
      ***4**

Out[22]= 3

If you use parentheses, you can avoid this problem.

In[23]:= **(3**
      ***4)**

Out[23]= 12

With the notebook interface, you can input as many lines as you like within an input cell; *Mathematica* will evaluate them all when you enter ⸢SHIFT⸥⸢ENTER⸥ still obeying the rules stated above for any incomplete lines.

Finally, you can enter a *comment* – some words that are not evaluated – by entering the words between (* and *).

```
In[24]:= D[Sin[x],      (* differentiate Sin[x]    *)
            {x, 1}]    (* with respect to x once *)

Out[24]= Cos[x]
```

Alternate input syntax

There are several different ways to write expressions in *Mathematica*. Usually, you will simply use the traditional notation, *fun* [*x*], for example. But you should be aware of several alternatives to this syntax that are widely used.

Here is an example using the standard function notation for writing a function with one argument.

```
In[25]:= N[π]

Out[25]= 3.14159
```

This uses a prefix operator.

```
In[26]:= N@π

Out[26]= 3.14159
```

Here is a postfix operator notation.

```
In[27]:= π // N

Out[27]= 3.14159
```

For functions with two arguments, you can use an infix notation. The following expression is identical to N[π, 30].

```
In[28]:= π ~ N ~ 30

Out[28]= 3.1415926535897932384626433 8328
```

Finally, many people prefer to use a more traditional syntax when entering and working with mathematical expressions. You can compute an integral using standard *Mathematica* syntax.

```
In[29]:= Integrate[1 / Sin[x], x]
```

$$Out[29]= -\text{Log}\left[\text{Cos}\left[\frac{x}{2}\right]\right] + \text{Log}\left[\text{Sin}\left[\frac{x}{2}\right]\right]$$

The same integral, represented in a more traditional manner, can be entered from palettes or keyboard shortcuts.

In[30]:= $\int \dfrac{1}{\text{Sin}[x]} \, d x$

Out[30]= $-\text{Log}\left[\text{Cos}\left[\dfrac{x}{2}\right]\right] + \text{Log}\left[\text{Sin}\left[\dfrac{x}{2}\right]\right]$

Many mathematical functions have traditional symbols associated with their operations and when available these can be used instead of the fully spelled-out names. For example, you can compute the intersection of two sets using the `Intersection` function.

In[31]:= `Intersection[{a, b, c, d, e}, {b, f, a, z}]`

Out[31]= `{a, b}`

Or you can do the same computation using more traditional notation.

In[32]:= `{a, b, c, d, e} ⋂ {b, f, a, z}`

Out[32]= `{a, b}`

To learn how to enter these and other notations quickly, either from palettes or directly from the keyboard using shortcuts, refer to the 2D Expression Input section in the Front End category of the Help Browser.

The front end and the kernel

When you work in *Mathematica* you are actually working with two separate programs. They are referred to as the *front end* and the *kernel*. The front end is the user interface. It consists of the notebooks that you work in together with the menu system, palettes (which are really just notebooks), and any element that accepts input from the keyboard or mouse. The kernel is the program that does the calculations. So a typical operation between the user (you) and *Mathematica* consists of the following steps, where the program that is invoked in each step is indicated in parentheses:

- enter input in the notebook (front end)

- send input to the kernel to be evaluated by pressing SHIFT-ENTER (front end)

- kernel does the computation and sends it back to the front end (kernel)

- result is displayed in the notebook (front end)

There is one remaining piece that we have not yet mentioned; that is *MathLink*. Since the kernel and front end are two separate programs, a means of communication is necessary for these two programs to "talk" to each other. That communication protocol is called *MathLink* and it comes bundled with *Mathematica*. It operates behind the scenes, completely transparent to the user.

MathLink is a very general communications protocol that is not limited to communication between the front end and the kernel, but can also be used to set up communication between the front end and other programs on your computer, programs like compiled C and Fortran code. It can also be used to connect a kernel to a word processor or spreadsheet or many other programs.

MathLink programming is beyond the scope of this book, but if you are interested, there are several books and articles that discuss it (see the References at the end of this book).

Errors

In the course of using and programming in *Mathematica*, you will encounter various sorts of errors, some obvious, some very subtle, some easily rectified, and others not. We have already mentioned that it is possible to send *Mathematica* into an infinite loop from which it cannot return. In this section, we discuss those situations where *Mathematica* does finish the computation, but without giving you the answer you expected.

Perhaps the most frequent error you will make is misspelling the name of a function. Here is an illustration of the kind of thing that will usually happen in this case.

```
In[33]:=  Sine[1.5]

          General::spell :
            Possible spelling error: new symbol name "Sine" is
              similar to existing symbols {Line, Sin, Sinh}. More…

Out[33]=  Sine[1.5]
```

Whenever you type a name that is *close* to an existing name, *Mathematica* will print a warning message like the one above. You may often use such names intentionally, in which case these messages can be annoying. In that case, it is best to turn off the warnings.

```
In[34]:=  Off[General::spell]
```

Now, *Mathematica* will not report that function names might be misspelled; and, when it cannot find a definition associated with a misspelled function, it returns your input unevaluated.

```
In[35]:=  Intergate[x², x]

Out[35]=  Intergate[x², x]
```

You can turn these spell warnings back on by evaluating On[General::spell].

In[36]:= **On[General::spell]**

Having your original expression returned unevaluated – as if this were perfectly normal – is a problem you will often run into. Aside from misspelling a function name, or simply using a function that does not exist, another case where this occurs is when you give the wrong number of arguments to a function, especially to a user-defined function. For example, the BowlingScore function takes a single list argument; if we accidentally leave out the list braces, then we are actually giving BowlingScore 12 arguments.

In[37]:= **BowlingScore[10, 10, 10, 10, 10, 10, 10, 10, 10, 10, 10, 10]**

Out[37]= BowlingScore[10, 10, 10, 10, 10, 10, 10, 10, 10, 10, 10, 10]

Of course, some kinds of inputs cause genuine error messages. Syntax errors, as shown above, are one example. The built-in functions are designed to usually warn you of such errors in input. In the first example below, we have supplied the Log function with an incorrect number of arguments (it expects one or two arguments only). In the second example, FactorInteger operates on integers only and so the real number argument causes the error condition.

In[38]:= **Log[2, 16, 3]**

Log::argt : Log called with 3
   arguments; 1 or 2 arguments are expected. More…

Out[38]= Log[2, 16, 3]

In[39]:= **FactorInteger[12.5]**

FactorInteger::facn : Argument 12.5` in
   FactorInteger[12.5] is not an exact number. More…

Out[39]= FactorInteger[12.5]

Getting help

Mathematica contains a vast array of documentation that you can access in a variety of ways. It is also designed so that you can create new documentation for your own functions and program in such a way that users of your programs can get help in exactly the same way as they would for *Mathematica*'s built-in functions.

If you are aware of the name of a function but are unsure of its syntax or what it does, the easiest way to find out about it is to evaluate ?function. For example, here is the usage message for ParametricPlot.

In[40]:= `?ParametricPlot`

```
ParametricPlot[{fx, fy}, {u, umin, umax}] produces a parametric
    plot of a curve with x and y coordinates fx and fy generated
    as a function of t. ParametricPlot[{{fx, fy}, {gx, gy}, ... },
    {u, umin, umax}] plots several parametric curves. More...
```

Also, if you were not sure of the spelling of a command (Integrate, for example), you could type the following to display all built-in functions that start with Integ.

In[41]:= `?Integ*`

System`

```
Integer         IntegerExponent  IntegerQ  Integrate
IntegerDigits   IntegerPart      Integers
```

Clicking on one of these links will produce a short usage statement about that function. For example, if you were to click on the Integrate link, here is what would be displayed in your notebook.

```
Integrate[f, x] gives the indefinite integral of f with respect
    to x. Integrate[f, {x, xmin, xmax}] gives the definite
    integral of f with respect to x from xmin to xmax. Integrate[
    f, {x, xmin, xmax}, {y, ymin, ymax}] gives a multiple
    definite integral of f with respect to x and y. More...
```

Clicking the More... hyperlink would take you directly to the Help Browser where a much more detailed explanation of this function can be found.

You can also get help by highlighting any *Mathematica* function and pressing the F1 key on your keyboard. This will take you directly into the documentation for that function in the Help Browser.

The Help Browser

Mathematica contains a very useful addition to the help system called the Help Browser. The Help Browser allows you to search for functions easily and it provides extensive documentation and examples.

To start the Help Browser, select Help Browser... under the Help menu. You should quickly see something like the following:

Notice the eight category tabs near the top of the Help Browser window. Choosing the Add-ons & Links tab will give you access to all of the packages that come with each implementation of *Mathematica*. Similarly, choosing The *Mathematica* Book tab will give you access to the entire *Mathematica* book that ships with each professional version of *Mathematica*.

Suppose you were looking for information about three-dimensional parametric graphics. First click the Built-in Functions tab, then select Graphics and Sound on the left, then 3D Plots and finally ParametricPlot3D. The Help Browser should look like this:

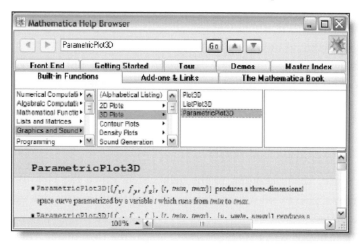

Notice that in the main window, the Help Browser has displayed information about the `ParametricPlot3D` function. This is identical to the usage message you would get if you entered `?ParametricPlot3D`.

Alternatively, you could have clicked the Master Index tab and searched for "ParametricPlot3D" or even simply "parametric" and then browsed through the index to find what you were looking for.

Many additional features are available in the Help Browser and you are advised to consult your documentation for a complete list and description.

2 The *Mathematica* language

Expressions are the basic building blocks from which everything is built. Their structure, internal representation, and how they are evaluated are essential to understanding *Mathematica*. In this chapter we focus on the *Mathematica* language with particular emphasis on the structure and syntax of expressions. We will also look at how to define and name new expressions, how to combine them using logical operators, and how to control properties of your expressions through the use of attributes.

2.1 Expressions

Introduction

Although it may appear different at first, everything that you will work with in *Mathematica* has a similar underlying structure. This means things like a simple computation, a data object, a graphic, the cells in your *Mathematica* notebook, even your notebook itself, all have a similar structure – they are all *expressions*, and an understanding of expressions is essential to mastering *Mathematica*.

Internal forms of expressions

When doing a simple arithmetic operation such as $3 + 4 * 5$, you are usually not concerned with exactly how a system such as *Mathematica* actually performs the additions or multiplications. Yet you will find it extremely useful to be able to see the internal representation of such expressions as this will allow you to manipulate them in a consistent and powerful manner.

Internally, *Mathematica* groups the objects that it operates on into different types: integers are distinct from real numbers; lists are distinct from numbers. One of the reasons that it is useful to identify these different *data types* is that specialized algorithms can be used on certain classes of objects that will help to speed up the computations involved.

The Head function can be used to identify types of objects. For numbers, it will report whether the number is an integer, a rational number, a real number, or a complex number.

In[1]:= $\{$ Head[7], Head$\left[\dfrac{1}{7}\right]$, Head[7.0], Head[7 + 2 i]$\}$

Out[1]= {Integer, Rational, Real, Complex}

In fact, every *Mathematica* expression has a Head that gives some information about that type of expression.

In[2]:= Head[a + b]

Out[2]= Plus

In[3]:= Head[{1, 2, 3, 4, 5}]

Out[3]= List

Atoms

The three basic building blocks of *Mathematica* – the *atoms* – from which every expression is ultimately constructed are, symbols, numbers, and strings.

A symbol consists of a letter followed without interruption by letters and numbers. For example, both f and the built-in Integrate are symbols.

In[4]:= Head[f]

Out[4]= Symbol

In[5]:= Head[Integrate]

Out[5]= Symbol

In *Mathematica*, built-in constants all are Symbols.

In[6]:= {Head[π], Head[e], Head[EulerGamma]}

Out[6]= {Symbol, Symbol, Symbol}

Symbols can consist of one or more concatenated characters so long as they do not begin with a number.

In[7]:= Head[myfunc]

Out[7]= Symbol

The four kinds of numbers – integers, real numbers, complex numbers and rational numbers – are shown in the list below.

In[8]:= $\left\{\texttt{Head[4], Head}\left[\dfrac{5}{7}\right]\texttt{, Head[5.201], Head[3 + 4 i]}\right\}$

Out[8]= {Integer, Rational, Real, Complex}

A string is composed of characters and is enclosed in quotes. They will be discussed in detail in Section 3.5.

In[9]:= `Head["Mathematica"]`

Out[9]= String

The structure of expressions

As mentioned earlier, everything in *Mathematica* is an expression. Expressions are either atomic, as described in the previous section, or they are *normal expressions*, which have a head and contain zero or more elements. Normal expressions are of the following form, where *h* is the head of the expression and the e_i are the elements which may themselves be atomic or normal expressions.

$$h[e_1, e_2, ..., e_n]$$

Although we indicated that you can use Head to determine the type of atomic expressions, this is entirely general. For normal expressions, Head simply gives the head of that expression.

In[10]:= `Head[a + b + c]`

Out[10]= Plus

To see the full internal representation of an expression, use FullForm.

In[11]:= `FullForm[a + b + c]`

Out[11]//FullForm=
    Plus[a, b, c]

In[12]:= `FullForm[{a, b, c}]`

Out[12]//FullForm=
    List[a, b, c]

The important thing to notice is that both of these objects (the sum and the list) have very similar internal representations. Each is made up of a function (Plus and List, respectively), each encloses its arguments in square brackets, and each separates its arguments with commas.

Regardless of how an atomic or normal expression may appear in your notebook, its structure is uniquely determined by its head and parts as seen using `FullForm`. This is important for understanding the *Mathematica* evaluation mechanism which depends on the matching of patterns based on their `FullForm` representation, a subject we will turn to in detail in Chapter 6.

The number of elements in any expression is given by its length.

In[13]:= **Length[a + b + c]**

Out[13]= 3

Here is a more complicated expression.

In[14]:= **expr = Sin[x] (a x² + b x + c)**

Out[14]= $(c + b x + a x^2)$ Sin[x]

Its head is `Times` because it is composed of the product of `Sin[x]` and the quadratic polynomial.

In[15]:= **Head[expr]**

Out[15]= Times

Its length is 2 since it only contains two factors.

In[16]:= **Length[expr]**

Out[16]= 2

Although the `FullForm` of this expression is a little harder to decipher, if you look carefully you should see that it is composed of the product of `Plus[c,Times[b,x]`, Times[a,Power[x,2]]] and Sin[x].

In[17]:= **FullForm[expr]**

Out[17]//FullForm=
         Times[Plus[c, Times[b, x], Times[a, Power[x, 2]]], Sin[x]]

There are several important differences between atomic expressions and nonatomic expressions. While the heads of all expressions are extracted in the same way – using the `Head` function – the head of an atom provides different information than the head of other expressions. For example, the head of a symbol or string is the *kind* of atom that it is.

In[18]:= **Head[Integrate]**

Out[18]= Symbol

In[19]:= **Head["hello"]**

Out[19]= String

The head of a number is the specific kind of number that it is, its data type.

In[20]:= **Head[2]**

Out[20]= Integer

In[21]:= **Head[5.21]**

Out[21]= Real

The FullForm of an atom (except a complex or rational number) is the atom itself.

In[22]:= **FullForm[f]**

Out[22]//FullForm=
   f

In[23]:= **FullForm$\left[\dfrac{5}{7}\right]$**

Out[23]//FullForm=
   Rational[5, 7]

Atoms have no parts (which of course is why they are called atoms). In contrast, nonatomic expressions do have parts. To extract different parts of an expression, use the Part function. For example, the first part of the expression a+b is a.

In[24]:= **Part[a + b, 1]**

Out[24]= a

The second part is b.

In[25]:= **Part[a + b, 2]**

Out[25]= b

This should be clearer from looking at the internal representation of this expression.

In[26]:= **FullForm[a + b]**

Out[26]//FullForm=
      Plus[a, b]

So Part [a+b,1] is another way of asking for the first element of Plus [a,b], which is just a. In general Part [*expr*, *n*] gives the *n*th element of *expr*.

It is worth noting that the 0th part is the Head of the expression.

In[27]:= **Part[a + b, 0]**

Out[27]= Plus

As we stated above, atomic expressions have no parts.

In[28]:= **Part["read my lips", 1]**

> Part::partd : Part specification
>   read my lips〚1〛 is longer than depth of object. More...

Out[28]= read my lips〚1〛

This error message indicates that the string "read my lips" has no first part, since it is atomic. The expression expr[[1]] is shorthand for Part[expr,1].

Similarly, complex numbers are atomic and hence have no parts.

In[29]:= **(3 + 4 i)[[1]]**

> Part::partd : Part specification
>   (3 + 4 i)〚1〛 is longer than depth of object. More...

Out[29]= (3 + 4 i)〚1〛

Because everything in *Mathematica* has the common structure of an expression, most of the built-in functions that are used for list manipulation, such as Part, can also be used to manipulate the arguments of any other kind of expression (except atoms).

In[30]:= **Append[w + x y, z]**

Out[30]= w + x y + z

This result can best be understood by looking at the FullForm of the following two expressions.

In[31]:= **FullForm[w + x y]**

Out[31]//FullForm=
    Plus[w, Times[x, y]]

In[32]:= **FullForm[w + x y + z]**

Out[32]//FullForm=
    Plus[w, Times[x, y], z]

Appending z to w + x y is equivalent to adding z as an argument to the Plus function. More generally:

In[33]:= **Append[f[a, b], c]**

Out[33]= f[a, b, c]

Finally, for more complicated expressions, you might find it useful to display the internal representation with the `TreeForm` function, which shows the "tree structure" of an expression. In the following example, the root node of the tree is `Plus`, which then branches three times at c, bx, and at ax^2, the latter two branching further.

```
In[34]:= TreeForm[a x² + b x + c]
```

```
Out[34]//TreeForm=
        Plus[c,  |                  ,  |                          ]
                 Times[b, x]    Times[a,  |                    ]
                                          Power[x, 2]
```

Exercises

1. Give the full (internal) form of the expression a (b+c).

2. What is the traditional representation of Times [a, Power [Plus [b,c], -1]].

3. What do you expect to be the result of the following operations? Use the FullForm of the expressions to understand what is going on.
   a. ((x^2 + y) z/w) [[2, 1, 2]]

   b. (a/b) [[2, 2]]

4. What is the part specification of the b in the expression a x^2 + b x + c?

2.2 Definitions

Defining variables and functions

One of the most common tasks in any programming environment is to define functions, constants, and procedures to perform various tasks. Sometimes a particular function that you need is not part of the built-in set of functions. Other times, you may need to use an expression over and over again and so it would be useful to define it once and have it available for future reference. Because you want your newly defined expressions to work with all the built-in functions seamlessly, by defining your own functions and constants you essentially expand the range of *Mathematica*'s capabilities.

For example, you might define a constant a to have a certain numeric value.

In[1]:=   **a = N[2 π]**

Out[1]=   6.28319

Then, whenever a is used in a subsequent computation, *Mathematica* will find a rule associated with a and will substitute that value wherever a occurs.

In[2]:=   **Cos[a]**

Out[2]=   1.

To check what definitions are associated with a, use ?a.

In[3]:=   **? a**

Global`a

a = 6.28319

To define a rule for a function f, enclose its arguments in square brackets and use x_ to indicate the variable that will be substituted for x on the right-hand side.

In[4]:=   **f[x_] = $\dfrac{1}{1 + x}$**

Out[4]= $\dfrac{1}{1 + x}$

The expression f[x_] on the left side of this assignment is a *pattern*. It indicates the class of expressions for which this definition should be used. We will have much more to say about patterns and pattern matching in *Mathematica* in Chapter 6, but, for now, it is enough to say that the pattern f[x_] matches f[*any expression*].

You can evaluate f at different values by replacing x with the value you wish to use. These values can be numeric, exact, or symbolic.

In[5]:=   **f[.1]**

Out[5]=   0.909091

In[6]:=   **f[1]**

Out[6]= $\dfrac{1}{2}$

In[7]:=   **f[α^2]**

Out[7]= $\dfrac{1}{1 + \alpha^2}$

We clear the symbols that are no longer needed.

> *In[8]:=* **Clear[a, f]**

Immediate vs. delayed assignments

When you make an assignment to a variable, you are only interested in giving that variable a specific value and then using the variable name to represent that value in subsequent computations. But oftentimes, when you set up definitions for functions, those functions may depend upon the values of previously defined functions or constants. In such instances it us useful to delay the assignment until the function is actually used in a computation. This is the basic difference between immediate and delayed assignments.

An immediate assignment is written Set [*lhs*, *rhs*] or, more commonly:

---

lhs = *rhs*

---

where *lhs* is an abbreviation for "left-hand side" and *rhs* abbreviates "right-hand side".

As an example, consider defining rand1 to be an immediate assignment that generates a uniformly distributed random number between 0 and 1.

> *In[9]:=* **rand1 = Random[]**

> *Out[9]=* 0.668693

Notice that the output of this assignment is the value of the right-hand side and that *Mathematica* evaluates the right-hand side immediately; that is, *when the assignment is made.*

A delayed assignment is set up with the SetDelayed function and is written Set ∶ Delayed [*lhs*, *rhs*] or, in its standard input form:

---

lhs := *rhs*

As an example, consider rand2 to be defined similarly to rand1, but with a delayed assignment.

> *In[10]:=* **rand2 := Random[]**

Notice that the delayed assignment does not return a value when the assignment is made. In fact, the right-hand side will not be evaluated until the function rand2 is called.

Let us call the function `rand1` five times.

In[11]:= **Table[rand1, {5}]**

Out[11]= {0.668693, 0.668693, 0.668693, 0.668693, 0.668693}

Because the right-hand side of `rand1` was evaluated when the definition was made, `rand1` was assigned the value 0.668693. Each subsequent call to `rand1` returns that value.

In[12]:= **? rand1**

Global`rand1

rand1 = 0.668693

On the other hand, creating a table of values using `rand2` produces a very different result.

In[13]:= **Table[rand2, {5}]**

Out[13]= {0.8312, 0.781807, 0.124634, 0.934537, 0.600252}

Each of the five times that `rand2` is called in the `Table`, *Mathematica* looks up the definition of `rand2` (which does not have a numeric value), and sees that it should evaluate `Random[]`. It does this each time it is called, generating a new random number each time.

In[14]:= **? rand2**

Global`rand2

rand2 := Random[]

When a `SetDelayed` function is entered, nothing is returned. When a `Set` function is entered, the value resulting from evaluating the right-hand side is returned. This difference in output is indicative of a more fundamental difference in what happens when the two kinds of functions are entered and rewrite rules are thereby created. To see this, we need to look at the *global rule base*, wherein reside rewrite rules.

The global rule base

The global rule base is composed of two kinds of rewrite rules: the built-in functions, which are part of every *Mathematica* session, and the user-defined rewrite rules, which are entered during a particular session.

We can get information about both kinds of rules in the global rule base by entering *?name*. In the case of a built-in function, the resulting usage message gives information about the syntax for using the function and a brief statement explaining what the function does.

In[15]:= **? Apply**

```
Apply[f, expr] or f @@ expr replaces the head
    of expr by f. Apply[f, expr, levelspec] replaces
    heads in parts of expr specified by levelspec. More...
```

In the case of a user-defined rewrite rule, the rule itself is printed. For the simple examples above, the crucial difference between rewrite rules created with the SetDe＼ layed and Set functions becomes apparent by querying the rule base for the rewrite rules associated with the symbols rand1 and rand2.

In[16]:= **? rand1**

```
Global`rand1

rand1 = 0.668693
```

A rewrite rule created using the Set function has the same left-hand side as the function that created it but the right-hand side of the rule may differ from the right-hand side of the function. This is because the right-hand side of the rule was evaluated at the moment the rule was first evaluated.

In[17]:= **? rand2**

```
Global`rand2

rand2 := Random[]
```

Comparing this with the original SetDelayed function, we see that a rewrite rule created using the SetDelayed function looks exactly like the function that created it. This is because both the left-hand side and right-hand side of a SetDelayed function are placed in the rule base *without being evaluated*.

In view of this difference between the SetDelayed and Set functions, the question is when should you use one or the other function to create a rewrite rule?

When you define a function, you usually do not want either the left-hand side or the right-hand side to be evaluated; you just want to make it available for use when the appropriate function call is made. This is precisely what occurs when a SetDelayed function is entered, so the SetDelayed function is commonly used in writing function definitions.

When you make a value declaration, you do not want the left-hand side to be evaluated; you just want to make it a nickname to serve as a shorthand for a value. This is what happens when a Set function is entered and so the Set function is commonly used to make value declarations, such as assigning a numeric value to a constant or variable.

A new rewrite rule overwrites, or replaces, an older rule with the same left-hand side. However, keep in mind that if two left-hand sides are the same except for the names of their pattern variables, they are considered different by *Mathematica*. Clear [*name*] can be used to remove a rewrite rule from the global rule base.

Piecewise-defined functions

You can set up several definitions for a function and *Mathematica* will apply the definition that applies. In the following example we give a piecewise-defined function *g*, whose values depend upon whether *x* is less than 0, between 0 and 1, or greater than 1. We specify the conditions on *x* by means of the / ; symbol.

```
In[18]:=  g[x_] := x³ /; x ≤ 0
```

```
In[19]:=  g[x_] := x /; 0 < x ≤ 1
```

```
In[20]:=  g[x_] := Sin[x] /; x > 1
```

```
In[21]:=  Plot[g[x], {x, -2, 3}];
```

Defining the function above is more easily accomplished using the new (in Version 5.1) Piecewise function as follows.

```
In[22]:=  Piecewise[{{x³, x ≤ 0}, {x, 0 < x ≤ 1}, {Sin[x], x > 1}}]
```

$$Out[22]= \begin{cases} x^3 & x \le 0 \\ x & 0 < x \le 1 \\ Sin[x] & x > 1 \end{cases}$$

You could plot this expression directly or define a function with this Piecewise object on the right-hand side of your definition and then use that function like any other. We will look at further uses of piecewise-defined objects in later chapters, in particular in the chapter on procedural programming.

Functions with multiple definitions

When you make an assignment, the symbol associated with the evaluation rule is called an *assignment tag*. Assignment tags are used to specify the structure of expressions. So, for example, the expression {a,b,c} is represented internally by List[a,b,c]. Its assignment tag is List. List does not really do anything except serve as a wrapper to specify the structure of this expression. Similarly, the expression 1+2 is represented internally by Plus[1,2]; its assignment tag is Plus.

Occasionally you will encounter the Tag expression when you try to evaluate some incorrect input.

In[23]:= **1 + 2 = 4**

Set::write : Tag Plus in 1 + 2 is Protected. More...

Out[23]= 4

For user-defined functions, the tag basically refers to the name of the function. So, for example, the following assignment associates the rule $1 + x + x^2$ with the tag f.

In[24]:= **f[x_] := 1 + x + x²**

There can be many evaluation rules associated with one tag. The following assignments all associate rules with the symbol f.

In[25]:= **f[x_, y_] := x + y**

In[26]:= **f[x_, y_, z_] :=** $\dfrac{1}{x + y - z}$

To view all of the rules associated with f, use ?f.

In[27]:= **? f**

Global`f

f[x_] := 1 + x + x²

f[x_, y_] := x + y

f[x_, y_, z_] := $\frac{1}{x+y-z}$

The advantages of this structure is that you can use one name for a function that will behave differently depending upon the number or form of arguments you give to that function. Using a different symbol for each of these tasks would require you and those who use your programs to have to remember multiple function names when one might be sufficient.

Let us clear symbols that are no longer needed.

In[28]:= **Clear[f, g]**

Exercises

1. What rewrite rules do each of the following functions create? Check your predictions by entering them and then querying the rule base.

   a. **randLis1[n_] := Table[Random[], {n}]**

   b. **randLis2[n_] := (x=Random[]; Table[x, {n}])**

   c. **randLis3[n_] := (x:=Random[]; Table[x, {n}])**

   d. **randLis4[n_] = Table[Random[], {n}]**

2. Consider the two functions f and g, which are identical except that one is written using an immediate assignment and the other using a delayed assignment.

   In[1]:= **f[n_] = Sum[(1 + x)^j, {j, 1, n}]**

   Out[1]= $\dfrac{(1+x)\ (-1 + (1+x)^n)}{x}$

   In[2]:= **g[n_] := Sum[(1 + x)^j, {j, 1, n}]**

   Explain why the output of these two functions *look* so different. Are they in fact different?

   In[3]:= **f[2]**

   Out[3]= $\dfrac{(1+x)\ (-1 + (1+x)^2)}{x}$

   In[4]:= **g[2]**

   Out[4]= $1 + x + (1+x)^2$

3. Create a piecewise-defined function g(x) based on the following and then plot the function from −2 to 0.

$$g(x) = \begin{cases} -\sqrt{1-(x+2)^2} & -2 \le x \le -1 \\ \sqrt{1-x^2} & x < 0 \end{cases}$$

2.3 Predicates and Boolean operations

Predicates

When working with data sets, you are often presented with the problem of extracting those data points that meet certain criteria. Similarly, when you write programs, oftentimes what to do next at any particular point in your program will depend upon some test or condition being met. Every programming language has constructs for testing data or conditions. Some of the most useful such constructs are called predicates. A *predicate* is a function that returns a value of true or false depending upon whether its argument passes a test. For example, the predicate PrimeQ tests for the primality of its argument.

In[1]:= **PrimeQ[144]**

Out[1]= False

Other predicates are available for testing numbers to see whether they are even, odd, integral, and so on.

In[2]:= **OddQ[21]**

Out[2]= True

In[3]:= **EvenQ[21]**

Out[3]= False

In[4]:= **IntegerQ[5/9]**

Out[4]= False

The NumericQ predicate tests whether its argument is a numeric quantity. Essentially, NumericQ[x] gives True whenever N[x] evaluates to an explicit number.

In[5]:= **NumericQ[π]**

Out[5]= True

In[6]:= **NumericQ[∞]**

Out[6]= False

This is distinct from a related function, NumberQ, which evaluates to True whenever its argument is an explicit number (that is, has head one of Integer, Rational, Real, Complex).

In[7]:= **NumberQ[3.2]**

Out[7]= True

In[8]:= **NumberQ[π]**

Out[8]= False

Many other predicates are available for testing if an expression is an atom, a list, a matrix, a polynomial, and much more.

In[9]:= **AtomQ["string"]**

Out[9]= True

In[10]:= **ListQ[{a, b, c}]**

Out[10]= True

In[11]:= **MatrixQ$\left[\begin{pmatrix} 1 & 0 & 0 \\ 0 & 1 & 0 \\ 0 & 0 & 1 \end{pmatrix}\right]$**

Out[11]= True

In[12]:= **PolynomialQ$\left[\dfrac{1}{x} + \dfrac{1}{x^2} + \dfrac{1}{x^3},\ x\right]$**

Out[12]= False

In[13]:= **IntervalMemberQ[Interval[{3, 4}], π]**

Out[13]= True

Relational and logical operators

Another type of predicate that is commonly used in programming are relational operators. These are used to compare two or more expressions and return a value of True or False. The relational operators in *Mathematica* are Equal (==), Unequal (≠), Greater (>), Less (<), GreaterEqual(≥), and LessEqual (≤). They can be used to compare numbers or arbitrary expressions.

In[14]:= **7 < 5**

Out[14]= False

In[15]:= **Equal** $\left[3, 7 - 4, \dfrac{6}{2}\right]$

Out[15]= True

In[16]:= $\mathbf{x^2 - 1 ==} \dfrac{x^4 - 1}{x^2 + 1}$ **// Simplify**

Out[16]= True

Note that the relational operators have lower precedence than arithmetic operators. The second example above is interpreted as $3 == (7-4)$ and not as $(3==7)-4$. Table 2.1 lists the relational operators and their various input forms.

StandardForm	Functional form	Meaning
$x == y$	Equal[x, y]	equal
$x \, != y$	Unequal[x, y]	unequal
$x > y$	Greater[x, y]	greater than
$x < y$	Less[x, y]	less than
$x \geq y$	GreaterEqual[x, y]	greater than or equal
$x \leq y$	LessEqual[x, y]	less than or equal

Table 2.1: Relational operators

The logical operators (sometimes known as Boolean operators) determine the truth of an expression based on Boolean arithmetic. For example, the conjunction of two true statements is always true.

In[17]:= **4 < 5 && 8 > 1**

Out[17]= True

The Boolean operation "and" is represented in *Mathematica* by And, with shorthand notation && or ∧. Here is a table that gives all the possible values for the And operator. (The function TruthTable is developed in Chapter 10.)

In[18]:= **TruthTable[A ∧ B, {A, B}]**

Out[18]//DisplayForm=

A	B	A ∧ B
T	T	T
T	F	F
F	T	F
F	F	F

The logical "or" operator, represented by Or and with shorthand notation || (or ∨), is true when either of its arguments is true.

In[19]:= **4 == 3 || 3 == $\frac{6}{2}$**

Out[19]= True

In[20]:= **0 == 0.0001 $\bigvee$ π == $\frac{22}{7}$**

Out[20]= False

Note the difference between this Boolean "or" and the common notion of "or." A phrase such as, "It is cold or it is hot," uses the word "or" in an *exclusive* sense; that is, it excludes the possibility that it is *both* cold and hot. The logical Or is inclusive in the sense that if A and B are both true, then A||B is also true.

In[21]:= **True || True**

Out[21]= True

Mathematica also contains an operator for the exclusive or, Xor.

In[22]:= **Xor[True, True]**

Out[22]= False

In[23]:= **Xor[True, False]**

Out[23]= True

Table 2.2 shows the logical operators and their input forms.

StandardForm	Functional form	Meaning
! x	Not[x]	not
x != y	Unequal[x, y]	unequal
x && y	And[x, y]	and
x || y	Or[x, y]	or
(x || y) && ! (x && y)	Xor[x, y]	exclusive or

Table 2.2: Logical operators

Introduced in Version 4 of *Mathematica* are the *bitwise logical operators*. These functions operate on integers as binary bits. For example, BitOr[x,y] gives the integer whose binary representation has 1s wherever the binary representation of x or y has 1s. Here is the bitwise OR of 21 and 19, given in binary form.

```
In[24]:= BaseForm[BitOr[2^^10101, 2^^10011], 2]
```

Out[24]//BaseForm=
    10111_2

Similarly, BitXor[x,y] gives the integer with 1s at positions where either x or y have 1s, but not both.

```
In[25]:= BaseForm[BitXor[2^^10101, 2^^10011], 2]
```

Out[25]//BaseForm=
    110_2

Functional form	Meaning
BitAnd[x, y]	bitwise AND of x and y
BitOr[x, y]	bitwise OR of x and y
BitNot[x]	bitwise NOT of x
BitXor[x, y]	bitwise XOR of x and y

Table 2.3: Bitwise operators

In Chapter 4 we will look at an application of bitwise operators to an example involving error-correcting codes: the computation of Hamming distance.

Exercises

1. Create a predicate function that returns a value of True if its argument is between -1 and 1.

2. Write a predicate function NaturalQ[n] that returns a value of True if n is a natural number and False otherwise; that is, NaturalQ[n] is True if n is among 0, 1, 2, 3, ...

3. Create a predicate function SubsetQ[lis_1, lis_2] that returns a value of True if lis_1 is a subset of lis_2. Remember: the empty set { }, is a subset of every set.

2.4 Attributes

All functions in *Mathematica* have certain properties, called *attributes*. These attributes can make a function commutative or associative, or they may give the function the ability to be threaded over a list. The attributes of any function are displayed with the `Attributes` function.

> *In[1]:=* `Attributes[Plus]`

> *Out[1]=* `{Flat, Listable, NumericFunction,`
>   `OneIdentity, Orderless, Protected}`

The `Flat` attribute indicates that this function (`Plus`) is associative. That is, given three elements to add, it does not matter which two are added first. In mathematics, this is known as *associativity* and is written as $a + (b + c) = (a + b) + c$. In *Mathematica* this could be indicated by saying that the two expressions `Plus[a, Plus[b, c]]` and `Plus[` `Plus[a, b], c]` are equivalent to the flattened form `Plus[a, b, c]`. When *Mathematica* knows that a function has the attribute `Flat`, it writes it in flattened form.

> *In[2]:=* `Plus[Plus[a, b], c]`

> *Out[2]=* `a + b + c`

The `Orderless` attribute indicates that the function is commutative; that is, $a + b = b + a$. This allows *Mathematica* to write such an expression in an order that is useful for computation. It does this by sorting the elements into a *canonical order*. For expressions consisting of letters and words, this ordering is alphabetic.

> *In[3]:=* `t + h + i + n`

> *Out[3]=* `h + i + n + t`

Sometimes a canonical order is readily apparent.

> *In[4]:=* `x^3 + x^5 + x^4 + x^2 + 1 + x`

> *Out[4]=* $1 + x + x^2 + x^3 + x^4 + x^5$

Other times, it is not so apparent.

> *In[5]:=* `x^3 y^2 + y^7 x^5 + y x^4 + y^9 x^2 + 1 + x`

> *Out[5]=* $1 + x + x^4 y + x^3 y^2 + x^5 y^7 + x^2 y^9$

When a symbol has the attribute `Protected`, the user is prevented from modifying the function in any significant way. All built-in operations have this attribute.

Functions with the attribute `OneIdentity` have the property that repeated application of the function to the same argument will have no effect. For example, the expression

Plus [Plus [a, b]] is equivalent to Plus [a, b], hence only one addition is performed.

In[6]:= **FullForm[Plus[Plus[a + b]]]**

Out[6]//FullForm=
    Plus[a, b]

The other attributes for the Plus function, (Listable and NumericFunction) will be discussed in later chapters. Consult the manual (Wolfram 2003) for a complete list of the Attributes that symbols can have.

Although it is unusual to want to alter the attributes of a built-in function, it is fairly common to change the default attributes of a user-defined function. For example, suppose you had a function which you wanted to inherit the Orderless attribute. Without explicitly setting that attribute, the function does not reorder its arguments.

In[7]:= **f[x, a, m]**

Out[7]= f[x, a, m]

The SetAttributes function is used to change the attributes of a function. Explicitly setting f to have the Orderless attribute causes its arguments to be automatically sorted.

In[8]:= **SetAttributes[f, Orderless]**

In[9]:= **f[x, a, m]**

Out[9]= f[a, m, x]

We will see a practical use of SetAttributes in Section 5.3.

3 Lists

The list is the fundamental data structure used in *Mathematica* to group objects together. A very extensive set of built-in functions is provided by *Mathematica* to manipulate lists in a variety of ways, ranging from simple operations, such as moving list elements around, to more sophisticated operations, such as applying a function to a list. We also discuss working with strings, as their structure and manipulation is so similar to lists.

3.1 Introduction

Many computations involve working with a collection of objects. For example, abstract mathematics deals with operations on arbitrary sets, represented notationally, but also conceptually, as lists.

```
In[1]:= {a, b, c} ∪ {c, d, e}
```

```
Out[1]= {a, b, c, d, e}
```

```
In[2]:= {a, b, c} ∩ {c, d, e}
```

```
Out[2]= {c}
```

Data, in *Mathematica*, is represented using lists. A large collection of functions is available for manipulating and analyzing lists of data. For example, you can sort any set of data.

```
In[3]:= Sort[{4, 16, 1, 77, 23}]
```

```
Out[3]= {1, 4, 16, 23, 77}
```

You can extract elements of a dataset based on some criteria. Here we select those numbers from a list that are greater than 0.

```
In[4]:= Select[{4.9239, -1.24441, -0.80388, 3.27761}, Positive]
```

```
Out[4]= {4.9239, 3.27761}
```

Working with such collections of objects requires that the objects (also called *data objects*) be gathered together in some way. There are a variety of structures that can be used to store data objects in a computer. The most often used data structure in *Mathematica* is the *list*. This is created using the built-in `List` function which has the standard input form of a sequence of arguments separated by commas and enclosed in braces.

$\{arg_1,\ arg_2,\ ...,\ arg_n\}$

Lists are used throughout *Mathematica*, not only to represent a collection of data elements, but also to delineate a range of values for some variable or iterator. For example, the second argument to the `Table` function is a list that specifies the iterator variable and the values that it should range over.

In[5]:= `Table[i², {i, 1, 5}]`

Out[5]= `{1, 4, 9, 16, 25}`

Similarly, the plotting functions use lists to specify the range over which a variable should be evaluated.

In[6]:= `Plot[Sin[x], {x, 0, 2 π}];`

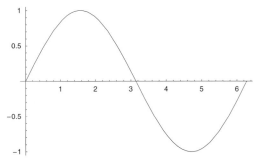

Internally, lists are stored in the functional form using the `List` function with some arbitrary number of arguments.

`List[`$arg_1,\ arg_2,\ ...,\ arg_n$`]`

For example, using `FullForm` we can view the internal representation of the list `{a,b,c}`.

In[7]:= `FullForm[{a, b, c}]`

Out[7]//FullForm=
    `List[a, b, c]`

The arguments of the List function (the *list elements*) can be any type of expression, including numbers, symbols, functions, character strings, and even other lists.

In[8]:= {2.4, f, Sin, "ossifrage", {5, 3}, π, {}}

Out[8]= {2.4, f, Sin, ossifrage, {5, 3}, π, {}}

Elements in lists can be rearranged, sorted, removed, new elements added, and operations performed on select elements or on the list as a whole. In fact, lists are such general objects in *Mathematica* that they can be used to represent a vast array of objects.

In this chapter, we will demonstrate the use of built-in *Mathematica* functions to manipulate lists in various ways. In cases where the operation of a function is relatively straightforward, we will simply demonstrate its use without explanation (the on-line Help system and the *The Mathematica Book* (Wolfram 2003) should be consulted for more detailed explanations of all of the built-in functions). The underlying message here is that almost anything you might wish to do to a list can be accomplished using built-in functions. It is important to have as firm a handle on these functions as possible, since a key to good, efficient programming in *Mathematica* is to use the built-in functions whenever possible to manipulate list structures.

3.2 Creating and measuring lists

List construction

In addition to using the List function to collect data objects, you can also generate lists from scratch by creating the objects and then placing them in a list.

Range [*imin*, *imax*, *di*] generates a list of ordered numbers starting from *imin* and going up to, but not exceeding, *imax* in increments of *di*.

In[1]:= **Range[-4, 7, 3]**

Out[1]= {-4, -1, 2, 5}

If *di* is not specified, a value of one is used.

In[2]:= **Range[4, 8]**

Out[2]= {4, 5, 6, 7, 8}

If neither *imin* nor *di* is specified, then both are given the value of 1.

> *In[3]:=* **Range[4]**

> *Out[3]=* {1, 2, 3, 4}

It is not necessary for *imin*, *imax*, or *di* to be integers.

> *In[4]:=* **Range[1.5, 6.3, .75]**

> *Out[4]=* {1.5, 2.25, 3., 3.75, 4.5, 5.25, 6.}

Table[*expr*, {*i*, *imin*, *imax*, *di*}] generates a list by evaluating *expr* a number of times.

> *In[5]:=* **Table[3 k, {k, 1, 10, 2}]**

> *Out[5]=* {3, 9, 15, 21, 27}

The first argument, 3k in the above example, is the expression that is evaluated to produce the elements in the list. The second argument to the Table function, {*i*, *imin*, *imax*, *di*}, is called the *iterator*. It is a list that specifies the number of times the expression is evaluated and hence the number of elements in the list. The iterator variable may or may not appear in the expression being evaluated. The value *imin* is the value of *i* used in the expression to create the first list element. The value *di* is the incremental increase in the value of *i* used in the expression to create additional list elements. The value *imax* is the maximum value of *i* used in the expression to create the last list element (if incrementing *i* by *di* gives a value greater than *imax*, that value is not used).

> *In[6]:=* **Table[i, {i, 1.5, 6.3, .75}]**

> *Out[6]=* {1.5, 2.25, 3., 3.75, 4.5, 5.25, 6.}

Table[*i*, {*i*, *imin*, *imax*, *di*}] is equivalent to Range[*imin*, *imax*, *di*]. As with the Range function, the arguments to Table can be simplified when the iterator increment is one.

> *In[7]:=* **Table[3 i, {i, 2, 5}]**

> *Out[7]=* {6, 9, 12, 15}

Similarly, both *imin* and *di* can be omitted and are then assumed to be 1.

> *In[8]:=* **Table[i^2, {i, 4}]**

> *Out[8]=* {1, 4, 9, 16}

If the iterator variable does not appear in the expression being evaluated, it may be omitted as well. The expression will then simply be evaluated that many times.

In[9]:= `Table[Random[], {3}]`

Out[9]= `{0.155408, 0.0408563, 0.62081}`

The expression that the `Table` function evaluates can be completely arbitrary. In the following computation, it is used to create tables of formulas.

In[10]:= `Table[Expand[(1 + α)` ^{i} `], {i, 1, 3}]`

Out[10]= `{1 + α, 1 + 2 α + α`^{2}`, 1 + 3 α + 3 α`^{2}` + α`^{3}`}`

`Table` can be used to create a *nested list*; that is, a list containing other lists as elements. This can be done by using additional iterators.

In[11]:= `Table[i + j, {j, 1, 4}, {i, 1, 3}]`

Out[11]= `{{2, 3, 4}, {3, 4, 5}, {4, 5, 6}, {5, 6, 7}}`

When there is more than one iterator, their order of appearance is important, because the value of the outer iterator is varied for each value of the inner iterator In the above example, for each value of `j` (the inner iterator), `i` was varied from 1 to 3, producing a three-element list for each of the four values of `j`. If you reverse the iterator order, you will get an entirely different list.

In[12]:= `Table[i + j, {i, 1, 3}, {j, 1, 4}]`

Out[12]= `{{2, 3, 4, 5}, {3, 4, 5, 6}, {4, 5, 6, 7}}`

You will often find it useful to display nested lists in a matrix or tabular form.

In[13]:= `Table[i + j, {i, 1, 4}, {j, 1, 3}] // TableForm`

Out[13]//TableForm=

```
2   3   4
3   4   5
4   5   6
5   6   7
```

In[14]:= `Table[i + j, {i, 1, 4}, {j, 1, 3}] // MatrixForm`

Out[14]//MatrixForm=

$$\begin{pmatrix} 2 & 3 & 4 \\ 3 & 4 & 5 \\ 4 & 5 & 6 \\ 5 & 6 & 7 \end{pmatrix}$$

The value of the outer iterator may depend on the value of the inner iterator, which can result in a nonrectangular list.

```
In[15]:= Table[i + j, {i, 1, 3}, {j, 1, i}]

Out[15]= {{2}, {3, 4}, {4, 5, 6}}
```

```
In[16]:= TableForm[%]

Out[16]//TableForm=
    2
    3       4
    4       5       6
```

However, the inner iterator may not depend on the outer iterator because, as we have seen, the inner iterator is fixed as the outer one varies.

```
In[17]:= Table[i + j, {i, 1, j}, {j, 1, 3}]

Table::iterb :
    Iterator {i, 1, j} does not have appropriate bounds. More…

Out[17]= Table[i + j, {i, 1, j}, {j, 1, 3}]
```

Measuring lists

Recall from Chapter 2 that Length [*expr*] is used to give the number of elements in *expr*. For a simple unnested (*linear*) list, the Length function tells us how many elements are in the list.

```
In[18]:= Length[{a, b, c, d, e, f}]

Out[18]= 6
```

In a nested list, each inner list is an element of the outer list. Therefore, the Length of a nested list indicates the number of inner lists, and not their sizes.

```
In[19]:= Length[{{{1, 2}, {3, 4}, {5, 6}}, {{a, b}, {c, d}, {e, f}}}]

Out[19]= 2
```

To find out more about the inner lists, use the Dimensions function.

```
In[20]:= Dimensions[{{{1, 2}, {3, 4}, {5, 6}}, {{a, b}, {c, d}, {e, f}}}]

Out[20]= {2, 3, 2}
```

This indicates that there are two inner lists, that each inner list contains three lists, and that the innermost lists each have two elements. MatrixForm may help to see the structure better.

In[21]:= `MatrixForm[{{{1, 2}, {3, 4}, {5, 6}}, {{a, b}, {c, d}, {e, f}}}]`

Out[21]//MatrixForm=

$$\begin{pmatrix} \begin{pmatrix} 1 \\ 2 \end{pmatrix} & \begin{pmatrix} 3 \\ 4 \end{pmatrix} & \begin{pmatrix} 5 \\ 6 \end{pmatrix} \\ \begin{pmatrix} a \\ b \end{pmatrix} & \begin{pmatrix} c \\ d \end{pmatrix} & \begin{pmatrix} e \\ f \end{pmatrix} \end{pmatrix}$$

The number of dimensions of a (possibly nested) list, is given by `ArrayDepth`.

In[22]:= `ArrayDepth[{{{1, 2}, {3, 4}, {5, 6}}, {{a, b}, {c, d}, {e, f}}}]`

Out[22]= 3

This is identical to the number of levels in that expression, as displayed by `TreeForm`.

In[23]:= `TreeForm[{a, {b, {c}}}]`

Out[23]//TreeForm=

$$\text{List}\big[a, \ | \qquad\qquad\qquad \big]$$
$$\text{List}\big[b, \ | \qquad \big]$$
$$\text{List}\,[c]$$

Exercises

1. Generate the list $\{\{0\}, \{0,2\}, \{0,2,4\}, \{0,2,4,6\}, \{0,2,4,6,8\}\}$ in two different ways using the `Table` function.

2. A table containing ten random 1s and 0s can easily be created using `Table[`
   `Random[Integer], {10}]`. Create a ten-element list of random 1s, 0s and -1s.

3. Create a ten-element list of random 1s and -1s. This table can be viewed as a list of the steps taken in a random walk along the x-axis, where a step can be taken in either the positive x direction (corresponding to 1) or the negative x direction (corresponding to -1) with equal likelihood.
   The random walk in one, two, three (and even higher) dimensions is used in science and engineering to represent phenomena that are probabilistic in nature. We will use a variety of random walk models throughout this book to illustrate specific programming points.

4. From a mathematical point of view, a list can be viewed as a vector and a nested list containing inner lists of equal length can be viewed as a matrix (or an array). *Mathematica* has another built-in function `Array` which creates lists. We can use an undefined function `f` to see how `Array` works.

```
In[1]:= Array[f, 5]

Out[1]= {f[1], f[2], f[3], f[4], f[5]}

In[2]:= Array[f, {3, 4}]

Out[2]= {{f[1, 1], f[1, 2], f[1, 3], f[1, 4]},
         {f[2, 1], f[2, 2], f[2, 3], f[2, 4]},
         {f[3, 1], f[3, 2], f[3, 3], f[3, 4]}}
```

Generate both of these lists using the `Table` function.

5. Predict the dimensions of the list {{{1,a},{4,d}},{{2,b},{3,c}}}. Use the `Dimensions` function to check your answer.

3.3 Manipulating lists

Testing a list

The locations of specific elements in a list can be determined using the `Position` function.

```
In[1]:= Position[{5, 7, 5, 2, 1, 4}, 5]

Out[1]= {{1}, {3}}
```

This result indicates that the number 5 occurs in the first and third positions in the list. The extra braces are used to avoid confusion with the case when elements are *nested* within a list.

```
In[2]:= Position[{{a, b, c}, {d, e, f}}, f]

Out[2]= {{2, 3}}
```

The expression f occurs once, in the third position within the second inner list.

There is also a function that picks out the elements in a list that return `True` when a predicate is applied to them. For example, this finds all of the even numbers in a list.

```
In[3]:= Select[{1, 4, 1, 5, 9, 2}, EvenQ]

Out[3]= {4, 2}
```

Other functions exist to select or count the number of elements in a list that match a certain pattern. We will look at these in detail in Chapter 6.

Extracting elements

Elements can easily be extracted from a specific location in a list. For example, this extracts the third element in the list `vec`.

In[4]:= **vec = {2, 3, 7, 8, 1, 4};**

In[5]:= **Part[vec, 3]**

Out[5]= 7

The `Part` function can be abbreviated using a standard input form.

In[6]:= **vec[[3]]**

Out[6]= 7

If you are interested in the elements from more than one location, you can extract them using a list. For example, this picks out the second and fourth elements of `vec`.

In[7]:= **vec[[{2, 4}]]**

Out[7]= {3, 8}

For multi-dimensional lists, you have to specify both the sublist and the position of the element in that sublist that you are interested in.

Here is a sample 3×3 matrix that we will work with.

In[8]:= **(mat = Table[a$_{i,j}$, {i, 3}, {j, 3}]) // MatrixForm**

Out[8]//MatrixForm=
$$\begin{pmatrix} a_{1,1} & a_{1,2} & a_{1,3} \\ a_{2,1} & a_{2,2} & a_{2,3} \\ a_{3,1} & a_{3,2} & a_{3,3} \end{pmatrix}$$

This picks out the first part of the second sublist.

In[9]:= **mat[[2, 1]]**

Out[9]= a$_{2,1}$

For multi-dimensional lists, several options are available to extract subsections of the list. A common operation involves extracting rows or columns from a matrix.

This extracts the entire second column of `mat`.

In[10]:= **mat[[All, 2]] // MatrixForm**

Out[10]//MatrixForm=
$$\begin{pmatrix} a_{1,2} \\ a_{2,2} \\ a_{3,2} \end{pmatrix}$$

And here is the third row of this matrix.

```
In[11]:= mat[[3, All]]

Out[11]= {a_{3,1}, a_{3,2}, a_{3,3}}
```

If you only specify one argument, the second is assumed to be All.

```
In[12]:= mat[[3]]

Out[12]= {a_{3,1}, a_{3,2}, a_{3,3}}
```

In addition to being able to extract elements from specific locations in a list, you can extract consecutively placed elements within the list. You can take elements from either the front or the back of a list.

```
In[13]:= Take[{1, 4, 1, 5, 9, 2}, 2]

Out[13]= {1, 4}
```

```
In[14]:= Take[{1, 4, 1, 5, 9, 2}, -2]

Out[14]= {9, 2}
```

If you take consecutive elements from a list other than from the front and the back, you need to remember that the numbering of positions is different front-to-back and back-to-front.

```
In[15]:= Take[{1, 4, 1, 5, 9, 2}, {2, 4}]

Out[15]= {4, 1, 5}
```

```
In[16]:= Take[{1, 4, 1, 5, 9, 2}, {-5, -3}]

Out[16]= {4, 1, 5}
```

You can mix both positive and negative indices.

```
In[17]:= Take[{1, 4, 1, 5, 9, 2}, {-5, 4}]

Out[17]= {4, 1, 5}
```

You can also take elements in steps. This takes the first through sixth element in increments of 2; that is, it takes every other element.

```
In[18]:= Take[{1, 4, 1, 5, 9, 2}, {1, 6, 2}]

Out[18]= {1, 1, 9}
```

You can discard elements from a list, keeping the rest. Elements can be removed from either end of the list or from consecutive locations.

In[19]:= `Drop[{1, 4, 1, 5, 9, 2}, 2]`

Out[19]= `{1, 5, 9, 2}`

In[20]:= `Drop[{1, 4, 1, 5, 9, 2}, -1]`

Out[20]= `{1, 4, 1, 5, 9}`

In[21]:= `Drop[{1, 4, 1, 5, 9, 2}, {3, 5}]`

Out[21]= `{1, 4, 2}`

You can remove elements at specific locations as well.

In[22]:= `Delete[{1, 4, 1, 5, 9, 2}, 1]`

Out[22]= `{4, 1, 5, 9, 2}`

In[23]:= `Delete[{1, 4, 1, 5, 9, 2}, {{3}, {4}}]`

Out[23]= `{1, 4, 9, 2}`

Certain extractions are used so often that they are given their own functions.

In[24]:= `First[{1, 4, 1, 5, 9, 2}]`

Out[24]= `1`

In[25]:= `Last[{1, 4, 1, 5, 9, 2}]`

Out[25]= `2`

In[26]:= `Rest[{1, 4, 1, 5, 9, 2}]`

Out[26]= `{4, 1, 5, 9, 2}`

Rearranging lists

Every list can be sorted into a canonical order. For lists of numbers or letters, this ordering is usually obvious.

In[27]:= $\mathtt{Sort\left[\left\{3,\ 1.7,\ \pi,\ -4,\ \dfrac{22}{7}\right\}\right]}$

Out[27]= $\left\{-4,\ 1.7,\ 3,\ \dfrac{22}{7},\ \pi\right\}$

Mathematica uses the following canonical orderings: numbers are ordered by numerical value, with complex numbers first ordered by real part and then by absolute value of the imaginary part; symbols and strings are ordered alphabetically, powers and products are ordered in a manner corresponding to the terms in a polynomial; expressions are ordered depth-first with shorter expressions coming first.

You can also sort lists according to an ordering function that you can specify.

In[28]:= $\mathbf{Sort}\left[\{3, 1.7, \pi, -4, \frac{22}{7}\}, \mathbf{Greater}\right]$

Out[28]= $\{\frac{22}{7}, \pi, 3, 1.7, -4\}$

When applied to a nested list, Sort will use the first element of each nested list to determine the order.

In[29]:= `Sort[{{2, c}, {7, 9}, {e, f, g}, {1, 4.5}, {x, y, z}}]`

Out[29]= `{{1, 4.5}, {2, c}, {7, 9}, {e, f, g}, {x, y, z}}`

The order of the elements in a list can be reversed.

In[30]:= `Reverse[{1, 2, 3, 4, 5}]`

Out[30]= `{5, 4, 3, 2, 1}`

All of the elements can be rotated a specified number of positions to the right or the left. By default RotateLeft (and RotateRight) shifts the list one position to the left (right).

In[31]:= `RotateLeft[{1, 2, 3, 4, 5}]`

Out[31]= `{2, 3, 4, 5, 1}`

This rotates every element two positions to the right.

In[32]:= `RotateRight[{1, 2, 3, 4, 5}, 2]`

Out[32]= `{4, 5, 1, 2, 3}`

Partition rearranges list elements to form a nested list. It may use all of the elements and simply divvy up a list. Here we partition the list into nonoverlapping sublists of length two.

In[33]:= `Partition[{1, 4, 1, 5, 9, 2}, 2]`

Out[33]= `{{1, 4}, {1, 5}, {9, 2}}`

You might be interested in only using some of the elements from a list. For example, this takes one-element sublists, with an offset of two; that is, every other one-element sublist.

In[34]:= `Partition[{1, 4, 1, 5, 9, 2}, 1, 2]`

Out[34]= `{{1}, {1}, {9}}`

You can also create overlapping inner lists, consisting of ordered pairs (two-element sublists) whose second element is the first element of the next ordered pair.

In[35]:= `Partition[{1, 4, 1, 5, 9, 2}, 2, 1]`

Out[35]= `{{1, 4}, {4, 1}, {1, 5}, {5, 9}, {9, 2}}`

The `Transpose` function pairs off the corresponding elements of the inner lists. Its argument is a single list consisting of nested lists.

In[36]:= `Transpose[{{1, 2, 3, 4}, {a, b, c, d}}]`

Out[36]= `{{1, a}, {2, b}, {3, c}, {4, d}}`

In[37]:= `Transpose[{{1, 2, 3, 4}, {a, b, c, d}, {i, ii, iii, iv}}]`

Out[37]= `{{1, a, i}, {2, b, ii}, {3, c, iii}, {4, d, iv}}`

For rectangular lists, you might think of `Transpose` as exchanging the rows and columns of the corresponding matrix.

Elements can be added to the front, the back, or to any specified position in a given list.

In[38]:= `Append[{1, 2, 3, 4}, 5]`

Out[38]= `{1, 2, 3, 4, 5}`

In[39]:= `Prepend[{1, 2, 3, 4}, 5]`

Out[39]= `{5, 1, 2, 3, 4}`

In[40]:= `Insert[{1, 2, 3, 4}, 5, 3]`

Out[40]= `{1, 2, 5, 3, 4}`

Elements at specific locations in a list can be replaced with other elements. Here, 5 replaces the element in the second position of the list.

In[41]:= `ReplacePart[{a, b, c, d, e}, 5, 2]`

Out[41]= `{a, 5, c, d, e}`

You can flatten a nested list to various extents. You can remove all of the inner braces, creating a linear list of elements.

In[42]:= `Flatten[{{{3, 1}, {2, 4}}, {{5, 3}, {7, 4}}}]`

Out[42]= `{3, 1, 2, 4, 5, 3, 7, 4}`

You can limit the degree of flattening, removing only some of the inner lists. For example, two inner lists, each having two ordered pairs, can be turned into a single list of four ordered pairs by only flattening down one level deep.

In[43]:= **Flatten[{{{3, 1}, {2, 4}}, {{5, 3}, {7, 4}}}, 1]**

Out[43]= {{3, 1}, {2, 4}, {5, 3}, {7, 4}}

List component assignment

The capability to alter elements of lists merits detailed consideration. The general syntax for modifying a list is:

name[[*integer-valued-expression*]] = *expr*

The *name* must be the name of a list. The *integer-valued-expression* must evaluate to a legal subscript, that is a number whose absolute value is less than or equal to the length of the list. The assignment returns the value of *expr* (as assignments always do), but has the effect of changing the list to which *name* is bound.

Here is a list with five elements.

In[44]:= **L = {0, 1, 2, 3, 4}**

Out[44]= {0, 1, 2, 3, 4}

This replaces the value of the first element of L with the value 10.

In[45]:= **L[[1]] = 10**

Out[45]= 10

We see now that L has changed.

In[46]:= **L**

Out[46]= {10, 1, 2, 3, 4}

Components of nested lists can be modified as well.

name[[*expr*$_1$, *expr*$_2$]] = *expr*

expr$_1$ and *expr*$_2$ are expressions that must evaluate to integers. *expr*$_1$ chooses the sublist of *name*, and *expr*$_2$ the element of that sublist.

Here is a 2×3 nested list.

In[47]:= **A = {{1, 2, 3}, {4, 5, 6}}**

Out[47]= {{1, 2, 3}, {4, 5, 6}}

This assigns the third element in the second sublist the value 20.

In[48]:= **A[[2, 3]] = 20**

Out[48]= 20

In[49]:= **A**

Out[49]= {{1, 2, 3}, {4, 5, 20}}

However, note that assigning one array name to another one makes a copy of the first. In this way, component assignments to either one will not affect the other.

In[50]:= **B = A**

Out[50]= {{1, 2, 3}, {4, 5, 20}}

In[51]:= **B[[1, 2]] = 30**

Out[51]= 30

In[52]:= **B**

Out[52]= {{1, 30, 3}, {4, 5, 20}}

In[53]:= **A**

Out[53]= {{1, 2, 3}, {4, 5, 20}}

In[54]:= **A[[2, 1]] = 40**

Out[54]= 40

In[55]:= **B**

Out[55]= {{1, 30, 3}, {4, 5, 20}}

This behavior is in distinction to languages such as C where aliasing can allow one list to *point* to another; with pointers, changing one array will have an affect on any array that points to it.

Exercises

1. Predict where the 9s are located in the following list.

   {{2, 1, 10}, {9, 5, 7}, {2, 10, 4}, {10, 1, 9}, {6, 1, 6}}

   Confirm your prediction using `Position`.

2. Given a list of $\{x, y\}$ data points

   {{x₁, y₁}, {x₂, y₂}, {x₃, y₃}, {x₄, y₄}, {x₅, y₅}}

   separate the x and y components to get:

   {{x₁, x₂, x₃, x₄, x₅}, {y₁, y₂, y₃, y₄, y₅}}

3. Consider a two-dimensional random walk on a square lattice. (A square lattice can be envisioned as a two-dimensional grid, just like the lines on graph paper.) Each step can be in one of four directions: $\{1,\ 0\}, \{0,\ 1\}, \{-1,\ 0\}, \{0,\ -1\}$, corresponding to steps in the east, north, west and south directions, respectively. Use the list $\{\{1,0\},\{0,1\},\{-1,0\},\{0,-1\}\}$ to create a list of the steps of a ten-step random walk.

4. In three steps, make a list of the elements in even-numbered locations in the list $\{a,b,c,d,e,f,g\}$.

5. Suppose you are given a list S of length n, and a list P containing n different numbers between 1 and n (that is, P is a permutation of Range $[n]$). Compute the list T such that for all k between 1 and n, T[[k]]=S[[P[[k]]]]. For example, if S=$\{a,b,c,d\}$ and P=$\{3,2,4,1\}$, then T=$\{c,b,d,a\}$.

6. Given the lists S and P in the previous exercise, compute the list U such that for all k between 1 and n, U[[P[[k]]]] = S[[k]] (that is, S[[i]] takes the value from position P[[i]] in U). Thus, for S=$\{a,b,c,d\}$ and P=$\{3,2,4,1\}$, U=$\{d,b,a,c\}$. Think of it as moving S[[1]] to position P[[1]], S[[2]] to position P[[2]], and so on. *Hint*: Start by pairing the elements of P with the elements of S.

3.4 Working with several lists

A number of the functions described earlier in this chapter, such as Transpose, work with several lists if they are inside a nested list structure. We can also work directly with multiple lists.

Join concatenates two lists.

In[1]:= **Join[{2, 5, 7, 3}, {d, a, e, j}]**

Out[1]= {2, 5, 7, 3, d, a, e, j}

Here is the union of these two lists.

In[2]:= **{4, 1, 2} ∪ {5, 1, 2}**

Out[2]= {1, 2, 4, 5}

In[3]:= **Union[{4, 1, 2}, {5, 1, 2}]**

Out[3]= {1, 2, 4, 5}

When the Union function is used either on a single list or a number of lists, a list is formed consisting of the original elements in canonical order with all duplicate elements removed. The Complement function gives all those elements in the first list that are not in the other list or lists. Intersection [*list*$_1$, *list*$_2$,...] finds all those elements common to the *list*$_i$. Complement and Intersection also remove duplicates and sort the elements that remain.

In[4]:= **{4, 1, 2} ∩ {5, 1, 2}**

Out[4]= {1, 2}

In[5]:= **Complement[{4, 1, 2}, {5, 1, 2}]**

Out[5]= {4}

These last three functions, Union, Complement, and Intersection, treat lists somewhat like sets in that there are no duplicates and the order of elements in the lists is not respected.

Exercises

1. How would you perform the same task as Prepend [{*x*,*y*},*z*] using the Join function?

2. Starting with the lists {1,2,3,4} and {a,b,c,d}, create the list {2,4,b,d}.

3. Given two lists, find all those elements that are not common to the two lists. For example, starting with the lists, {a,b,c,d} and {a,b,e,f}, your answer would return the list {c,d,e,f}.

3.5 Strings and characters

Characters are the objects that appear on the computer screen like "a", "3", or "!". Uppercase and lowercase letters, numbers, punctuation marks, and spaces form the basic set of characters. A sequence of characters enclosed in double quotes is called a *string*.

> *In[1]:=* **Head["The magic words are squeamish ossifrage."]**
>
> *Out[1]=* String

When *Mathematica* prints out a string, it appears without the quotes.

> *In[2]:=* **"The magic words are squeamish ossifrage."**
>
> *Out[2]=* The magic words are squeamish ossifrage.

You can use the InputForm function to see these quotes.

> *In[3]:=* **InputForm["The magic words are squeamish ossifrage."]**
>
> *Out[3]//InputForm=*
>   "The magic words are squeamish ossifrage."

A string is a value and, like other values (such as numbers and lists), there are built-in functions available to manipulate strings, similar to those for lists. Their operations are indicated by their names.

> *In[4]:=* **StringLength["The magic words are squeamish ossifrage."]**
>
> *Out[4]=* 40

> *In[5]:=* **StringReverse["abcde"]**
>
> *Out[5]=* edcba

> *In[6]:=* **StringTake["abcde", 3]**
>
> *Out[6]=* abc

> *In[7]:=* **StringDrop["abcde", -1]**
>
> *Out[7]=* abcd

In[8]:= `StringPosition["abcde", "bc"]`

Out[8]= `{{2, 3}}`

In[9]:= `StringInsert["abcde", "t", 3]`

Out[9]= `abtcde`

In[10]:= `StringReplace["abcde", "cd" → "uv"]`

Out[10]= `abuve`

New in Version 5.1, you can use regular expressions in the functions you use to manipulate strings.

In[11]:= `StringMatchQ["all in good time", RegularExpression["a.*"]]`

Out[11]= `True`

In[12]:= `StringCases["abc1, abd2, bcd3", RegularExpression["a.+?\\d"]]`

Out[12]= `{abc1, abd2}`

In addition to using built-in functions to manipulate a string, you can convert a string to a list of characters with the built-in `Characters` function.

In[13]:= `Characters["abcde"]`

Out[13]= `{a, b, c, d, e}`

You can then use the list manipulating functions to alter the list or extract elements from the list.

In[14]:= `Take[%, {2, 3}]`

Out[14]= `{b, c}`

Finally, you can change the resulting list back into a string using the built-in `String‐Join` function.

In[15]:= `StringJoin[%]`

Out[15]= `bc`

Another way to manipulate a string is to convert it to a list of character codes and then operate on the codes using mathematical functions. Each character in a computer's character set is assigned a number, called its *character code*. Moreover, by general agreement, almost all computers use the same character codes, called the *ASCII codes*. In this code, the uppercase letters A, B, ..., Z are assigned the numbers 65, 66, ..., 90 while the lowercase letters a, b, ..., z have the numbers 97, 98, ..., 122 (note that the number of an uppercase letter is 32 less than its lowercase version). The numbers 0, 1, ..., 9 are coded as

48, 49, ..., 57 while the punctuation marks period, comma, and exclamation point have the codes 46, 44, and 33, respectively. The space character is represented by the code 32. Table 3.1 shows the characters and their codes.

Characters	ASCII codes
A, B, ..., Z	65, 66, ..., 90
a, b, ..., z	97, 98, ..., 122
0, 1, ..., 9	48, 49, ..., 57
. (period)	46
, (comma)	44
! (exclamation)	33
⎵ (space)	32

Table 3.1: ASCII character codes

Using the character code representation of characters, the following series of computations changes a word from lowercase to uppercase.

```
In[16]:=  ToCharacterCode["darwin"]
Out[16]=  {100, 97, 114, 119, 105, 110}
```

```
In[17]:=  % - 32
Out[17]=  {68, 65, 82, 87, 73, 78}
```

```
In[18]:=  FromCharacterCode[%]
Out[18]=  DARWIN
```

This can be accomplished more succinctly using `StringReplace`.

```
In[19]:=  StringReplace["darwin", x_ → ToUpperCase[x]]
Out[19]=  DARWIN
```

Or simply:

```
In[20]:=  ToUpperCase["darwin"]
Out[20]=  DARWIN
```

Exercises

1. Convert the first character in a string (which you may assume to be a lowercase letter) to uppercase.

2. Given a string containing two digits, convert it to its integer value; so the string "73" produces the number 73.

3. Given a string containing two digits, convert it to its value as an integer in base 8; for example, the string "73" will produce the number 59.

4. Given a string of digits of arbitrary length, convert it to its integer value. (*Hint*: You may find that the Dot function is helpful.)

5. Create a Boolean function OrderedWordQ that returns True or False depending upon whether its argument is in alphabetic order. So OrderedWordQ["best"] would return True but OrderedWordQ["brag"] would return False. Then find all those words in the file dictionary.dat that are ordered according to this function.

    Here is a platform-independent path to the dictionary file.

    ```
    In[1]:= wordfile = ToFileName[{$InstallationDirectory, "Documentation",
                "English", "Demos", "DataFiles"}, "dictionary.dat"]

    Out[1]= C:\Program Files\Wolfram Research\Mathematica\5.1\
                Documentation\English\Demos\DataFiles\dictionary.dat
    ```

    This reads in the file using ReadList, specifying the type of data being read in as a Word.

    ```
    In[2]:= words = ReadList[wordfile, Word];
    ```

6. Create a function PalindromeQ[*str*] that returns a value of True if its argument *str* is a palindrome; that is, if the string *str* is the same forward and backward. For example, "refer" is a palindrome.

4 Functional programming

Programming in *Mathematica* is essentially a matter of writing user-defined functions that work like mathematical functions; when applied to specific values, they perform computations producing results. In fact, these functions can operate on arbitrary expressions, including other functions. This *functional* style of programming distinguishes *Mathematica* from more traditional procedural languages like C and Fortran, and a facility at functional programming is essential for taking full advantage of *Mathematica*'s powerful language to solve your computational tasks.

4.1 Introduction

Functions are objects that operate on expressions and output unique expressions for each input. We can think of functions as mathematicians do. For example, here is a definition for a function of two variables.

In[1]:= `f[x_, y_] := Cos[x] + Sin[y]`

You can evaluate the function for numeric or symbolic values.

In[2]:= `f[π, 1.6]`

Out[2]= `-0.000426397`

In[3]:= `f[θ, ρ]`

Out[3]= `Cos[θ] + Sin[ρ]`

Functions can be significantly more complicated objects. Below is a function that operates on functions. Like the function f above it takes two arguments, but, in this case, its arguments are a function or expression, and a list containing the variable of integration and the integration limits.

In[4]:= `Integrate[Exp[I π x], {x, a, b}]`

Out[4]= $\dfrac{i \left(e^{i a \pi} - e^{i b \pi}\right)}{\pi}$

This particular function can be also be called with a function and a variable.

In[5]:= **Integrate[Exp[I π x], x]**

Out[5]= $-\dfrac{i\, e^{i\pi x}}{\pi}$

Here is a function that also takes two arguments and operates on functions, but it returns a graphical object as its value.

In[6]:= **Plot$\left[\text{Sin}\left[x + \sqrt{2}\ \text{Sin}[x]\right], \{x, 0, 2\pi\}\right]$**

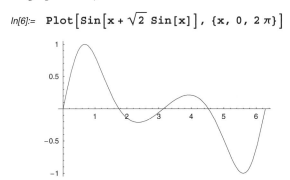

Out[6]= - Graphics -

Programming involves writing a set of instructions to be applied for some appropriate input. Whereas procedural programs provide a step-by-step set of instructions, functional programming involves the application of functions to their arguments. For example, here is a traditional procedural approach to switching the elements in a list of pairs.

In[7]:= **lis = {{α, 1}, {β, 2}, {γ, 3}}**

Out[7]= {{α, 1}, {β, 2}, {γ, 3}}

In[8]:= **temp = lis;**
Do[{temp[[i, 1]], temp[[i, 2]]} = {lis[[i, 2]], lis[[i, 1]]},
** {i, 1, Length[lis]}];**
temp

Out[10]= {{1, α}, {2, β}, {3, γ}}

We first allocate an empty array temp, of the same size as lis; then we put elements into temp one by one as we loop over lis; finally we return the value of temp.

Here is a simpler procedure using a structured iteration.

In[11]:= **Table[{lis[[i, 2]], lis[[i, 1]]}, {i, 1, 3}]**

Out[11]= {{1, α}, {2, β}, {3, γ}}

And here is a functional approach to solving the same problem.

In[12]:= **Map[Reverse, lis]**

Out[12]= {{1, α}, {2, β}, {3, γ}}

This simple example illustrates several of the key features of functional programming. A functional approach often allows for a more direct implementation of the solution to many problems, especially when list manipulations are involved. Notice that the procedural approach required setting up a list structure and then looping over the list as i takes on successive values, whereas the functional approach simply applied the Reverse function to the list directly.

Up to this point, we have described fairly simple functions and stayed focused on the built-in functions present in *Mathematica*. In this chapter we will first take a look at some of the most powerful and useful functional programming constructs in *Mathematica* and then discuss the creation of our own functions, using many of the list and string manipulating functions discussed earlier. It is well worthwhile to spend time familiarizing yourself with these functions by playing around with them; for example, create various lists and apply built-in functions to them. Having a larger vocabulary of built-in functions will not only make it easier to follow the programs and do the exercises here, but will enhance your own programming skills as well.

4.2 Functions for manipulating expressions

Three of the most powerful and commonly used functions by experienced *Mathematica* programmers are Map, Apply, and Thread. They provide very sophisticated ways of manipulating expressions in *Mathematica*. Becoming familiar with them is essential to functional programming in *Mathematica*. In this section we will discuss their syntax and look at some simple examples of their use. We will also briefly look at some related functions (Inner and Outer), which will prove useful in manipulating the structure of your expressions. These higher-order functions will be used throughout the rest of this book.

Map

Map applies a function to each element in a list.

In[1]:= **Map$\left[\text{Head}, \left\{3, \dfrac{22}{7}, \pi\right\}\right]$**

Out[1]= {Integer, Rational, Symbol}

This is illustrated using an undefined function *f* and a simple linear list.

In[2]:= **Map[f, {a, b, c}]**

Out[2]= {f[a], f[b], f[c]}

More generally, mapping a function f over the expression g[a,b,c] essentially wraps the function f around each of the *elements* of g.

In[3]:= **Map[f, g[a, b, c]]**

Out[3]= g[f[a], f[b], f[c]]

So this general computation is identical to Map[f,{a,b,c}], except in that example g is replaced with List (remember that FullForm[{a,b,c}] is List[a,b,c]).

The real power of the Map function is that you can map *any* function across any expression for which that function makes sense. Using the Reverse function with Map, you can reverse the order of elements in each list of a nested list.

In[4]:= **Map[Reverse, {{a, b}, {c, d}, {e, f}}]**

Out[4]= {{b, a}, {d, c}, {f, e}}

The elements in each of the inner lists in a nested list can be sorted.

In[5]:= **Map[Sort, {{2, 6, 3, 5}, {7, 4, 1, 3}}]**

Out[5]= {{2, 3, 5, 6}, {1, 3, 4, 7}}

Often, you will need to define your own function to perform some computation on every element of a list. This is the sort of computation that Map is expressly designed for. Here is a list of three elements.

In[6]:= **vec = {2, π, γ};**

If we wished to square each element and add 1, we could first define a function that performs this computation on its arguments.

In[7]:= **f[x_] := x^2 + 1**

Mapping this function over vec, will then wrap f around each element and evaluate f of those elements.

In[8]:= **Map[f, vec]**

Out[8]= $\{5, 1 + \pi^2, 1 + \gamma^2\}$

Later in this chapter we will look at even simpler ways of performing such computations.

Thread and MapThread

The Thread function exchanges operations with arguments that are lists.

In[9]:= **Thread[g[{a, b, c}, {x, y, z}]]**

Out[9]= $\{g[a, x], g[b, y], g[c, z]\}$

You can accomplish something quite similar with MapThread. It differs from Thread in that it takes two arguments – the function that you are mapping and a list of two (or more) lists as arguments of the function. It creates a new list in which the corresponding elements of the old lists are paired (or zipped together).

In[10]:= **MapThread[g, {{a, b, c}, {x, y, z}}]**

Out[10]= $\{g[a, x], g[b, y], g[c, z]\}$

With Thread, you can fundamentally change the structure of the expressions you are working with. For example, this threads the Equal function over the two lists given as its arguments.

In[11]:= **Thread[Equal[{a, b, c}, {x, y, z}]]**

Out[11]= $\{a == x, b == y, c == z\}$

In[12]:= **Map[FullForm, %]**

Out[12]= $\{Equal[a, x], Equal[b, y], Equal[c, z]\}$

Here is another example of the use of Thread. We start off with a list of variables and a list of values.

In[13]:= **vars = $\{x_1, x_2, x_3, x_4, x_5\}$;**

In[14]:= **values = {1.2, 2.5, 5.7, 8.21, 6.66};**

From these two lists, we create a list of rules.

In[15]:= **Thread[Rule[vars, values]]**

Out[15]= $\{x_1 \to 1.2, x_2 \to 2.5, x_3 \to 5.7, x_4 \to 8.21, x_5 \to 6.66\}$

Notice how we started with a *rule of lists* and `Thread` produced a *list of rules*. In this way, you might think of `Thread` as a generalization of `Transpose`.

Here are a few more examples of `MapThread`. This raises each element in the first list to the power given by the corresponding element in the second list.

In[16]:= **MapThread[Power, {{2, 6, 3}, {5, 1, 2}}]**

Out[16]= {32, 6, 9}

Using `Trace`, you can view some of the intermediate steps that *Mathematica* performs in doing this calculation.

In[17]:= **MapThread[Power, {{2, 6, 3}, {5, 1, 2}}] // Trace**

Out[17]= {MapThread[Power, {{2, 6, 3}, {5, 1, 2}}],
$\qquad$ {2^5, 6^1, 3^2}, {2^5, 32}, {6^1, 6}, {3^2, 9}, {32, 6, 9}}

Using the `List` function, the corresponding elements in the three lists are placed in a list structure (note that `Transpose` would do the same thing).

In[18]:= **MapThread[List, {{5, 3, 2}, {6, 4, 9}, {4, 1, 4}}]**

Out[18]= {{5, 6, 4}, {3, 4, 1}, {2, 9, 4}}

The Listable attribute

Many of the built-in functions that take a single argument have the property that, when a list is the argument, the function is automatically applied to all of the elements in the list. In other words, these functions are automatically mapped on to the elements of the list. For example, the `Log` function has this attribute.

In[19]:= **Log[{a, E, 1}]**

Out[19]= {Log[a], 1, 0}

This is the same result you get using the `Map` function.

In[20]:= **Map[Log, {a, E, 1}]**

Out[20]= {Log[a], 1, 0}

Many of the built-in functions that take two or more arguments have the property that, when multiple lists are the arguments, the function is automatically applied to all of the corresponding elements in the list. In other words, these functions are automatically threaded on to the elements of the list.

In[21]:= **{4, 6, 3} + {5, 1, 2}**

Out[21]= {9, 7, 5}

This gives the same result as using the `Plus` function with `MapThread`.

> *In[22]:=* **MapThread[Plus, {{4, 6, 3}, {5, 1, 2}}]**

> *Out[22]=* {9, 7, 5}

Functions that are either automatically mapped or threaded on to the elements of list arguments are said to be `Listable`. Many of *Mathematica*'s built-in functions have this `Attribute`.

> *In[23]:=* **Attributes[Log]**

> *Out[23]=* {Listable, NumericFunction, Protected}

> *In[24]:=* **Attributes[Plus]**

> *Out[24]=* {Flat, Listable, NumericFunction,
>   OneIdentity, Orderless, Protected}

By default, functions that you define do not have any attributes associated with them. So, for example, if you define a function g, say, it will not automatically be threaded over a list.

> *In[25]:=* **g[{{a, b}, {c, d}}]**

> *Out[25]=* g[{{a, b}, {c, d}}]

If you want your function to have the ability to thread over lists, give it the `Listable` attribute using `SetAttributes`.

> *In[26]:=* **SetAttributes[g, Listable]**

> *In[27]:=* **g[{{a, b}, {c, d}}]**

> *Out[27]=* {{g[a], g[b]}, {g[c], g[d]}}

Note that clearing a symbol only clears values associated with that symbol. It does not clear any attributes associated with the symbol.

> *In[28]:=* **Clear[g]**

> *In[29]:=* **? g**

> Global`g

> Attributes[g] = {Listable}

To clear attributes, you need to use `Remove`.

> *In[30]:=* **Remove[g]**

Now there is no remaining information associated with g.

In[31]:= **? g**

Information::notfound : Symbol g not found. More...

Apply

Whereas Map is used to perform the same operation on each element of an expression, Apply is used to change the structure of an expression.

In[32]:= **Apply[h, g[a, b, c]]**

Out[32]= h[a, b, c]

The function h was applied to the expression g[a,b,c] and Apply replaced the head of g[a,b,c] with h.

If the second argument is a list, applying h to that expression simply replaces its head (List) with h.

In[33]:= **Apply[h, {a, b, c}]**

Out[33]= h[a, b, c]

The following computation shows the same thing, except we are using the internal represen tation of the list {a,b,c} here to better see how the structure is changed.

In[34]:= **Apply[h, List[a, b, c]]**

Out[34]= h[a, b, c]

We see that the elements of List are now the arguments of h. Essentially, you should think of Apply [*h*, *expr*] as replacing the head of *expr* with *h*.

In[35]:= **Apply[Plus, {1, 2, 3, 4}]**

Out[35]= 10

Here, List[1,2,3,4] has been changed to Plus[1,2,3,4] or, in other words, the head List has been replaced by Plus.

Plus[a,b,c,d] is the internal representation of the sum of these four symbols that you would normally write a+b+c+d.

In[36]:= **Plus[a, b, c, d]**

Out[36]= a + b + c + d

This list conversion can be applied to an entire list.

In[37]:= **Apply[h, {{1, 2, 3}, {5, 6, 7}}]**

Out[37]= h[{1, 2, 3}, {5, 6, 7}]

This is just vector addition.

In[38]:= **Apply[Plus, {{1, 2, 3}, {5, 6, 7}}]**

Out[38]= {6, 8, 10}

One important distinction between Map and Apply that you should be aware of concerns the level of the expression at which each operate. By default, Map operates at level 1. That is, in Map [*h, expr*], *h* will be applied to each element at the top level of *expr*. So, for example, if *expr* consists of a nested list, *h* will be applied to each of the sublists, but not deeper, by default.

In[39]:= **Map[h, {{a, b}, {c, d}}]**

Out[39]= {h[{a, b}], h[{c, d}]}

If you wish to apply h at a deeper level, then you have to specify that explicitly using a third argument to Map.

In[40]:= **Map[h, {{a, b}, {c, d}}, {2}]**

Out[40]= {{h[a], h[b]}, {h[c], h[d]}}

Apply, on the other hand, operates at level 0. That is, in Apply [*h, expr*], Apply looks at the part 0 of *expr* (that is, its Head) and replaces it with *h*.

In[41]:= **Apply[f, {{a, b}, {c, d}}]**

Out[41]= f[{a, b}, {c, d}]

Again, if you wish to apply h at a different level, then you have to specify that explicitly using a third argument to Apply.

In[42]:= **Apply[h, {{a, b}, {c, d}}, 1]**

Out[42]= {h[a, b], h[c, d]}

For example, to apply Plus to each of the inner lists, you need to specify that Apply will operate at level 1.

In[43]:= **Apply[Plus, {{1, 2, 3}, {5, 6, 7}}, {1}]**

Out[43]= {6, 18}

If you are a little unsure of what has just happened, consider the following example and, instead of h, think of `Plus`.

In[44]:= **Apply[h, {{1, 2, 3}, {5, 6, 7}}, {1}]**

Out[44]= {h[1, 2, 3], h[5, 6, 7]}

Inner and Outer

The `Outer` function applies a function to all of the combinations of the elements in several lists. This is a generalization of the mathematical *outer product.*

In[45]:= **Outer[f, {a, b}, {2, 3, 4}]**

Out[45]= {{f[a, 2], f[a, 3], f[a, 4]}, {f[b, 2], f[b, 3], f[b, 4]}}

Using the `List` function as an argument, you can create lists of ordered pairs that combine the elements of several lists.

In[46]:= **Outer[List, {a, b}, {2, 3, 4}]**

Out[46]= {{{a, 2}, {a, 3}, {a, 4}}, {{b, 2}, {b, 3}, {b, 4}}}

Using `Inner`, you can thread a function on to several lists and then use the result as the argument to another function.

In[47]:= **Inner[f, {a, b, c}, {d, e, f}, g]**

Out[47]= g[f[a, d], f[b, e], f[c, f]]

This function lets you carry out some interesting operations.

In[48]:= **Inner[Times, {x_1, y_1, z_1}, {x_2, y_2, z_2}, Plus]**

Out[48]= $x_1 x_2 + y_1 y_2 + z_1 z_2$

In[49]:= **Inner[List, {a, b, c}, {d, e, f}, Plus]**

Out[49]= {a + b + c, d + e + f}

Looking at these two examples, you can see that `Inner` is really a generalization of the mathematical dot product.

In[50]:= **Dot[{x_1, y_1, z_1}, {x_2, y_2, z_2}]**

Out[50]= $x_1 x_2 + y_1 y_2 + z_1 z_2$

Exercises

1. Write a function `addPair[{x,y}]` that adds the elements in a pair. Then use your `addPair` function to sum each pair from the following.

   > `data = {{1, 2}, {2, 3}, {3, 4}, {4, 5}, {5, 6}};`

   Your output should look like `{3,5,7,9,11}`.

2. Use `Apply` to add the elements in each pair from a list of pairs of numbers such as in the previous exercise.

3. A matrix can be rotated by performing a number of successive operations. Rotate the matrix `{{1,2,3},{4,5,6}}` clockwise by 90 degrees, obtaining `{{4,1},{5,2},{6,3}}`, in two steps. Use `TableForm` to display the results.

4. While matrices can easily be added using `Plus`, matrix multiplication is more complicated. The `Dot` function, written as a single period, can be used.

   In[1]:= `{{1, 2}, {3, 4}}.{x, y}`

   Out[1]= `{x + 2 y, 3 x + 4 y}`

   Perform matrix multiplication on `{{1,2},{3,4}}` and `{x,y}` without using `Dot`. (This can be done in two or three steps.)

5. `FactorInteger[n]` returns a nested list of prime factors and their exponents for the number *n*.

   In[2]:= `FactorInteger[3628800]`

   Out[2]= `{{2, 8}, {3, 4}, {5, 2}, {7, 1}}`

   Use `Apply` to reconstruct the number from this nested list.

6. Repeat the above exercise but instead use `Inner` to construct the original number *n* from the factorization given by `FactorInteger[n]`.

7. Using `Inner`, write a function `div[vecs, vars]` that computes the divergence of an *n*-dimensional vector field *vecs* = $\{e_1, e_2, \ldots, e_n\}$ dependent upon *n* variables *vars* = $\{v_1, v_2, \ldots, v_n\}$. The divergence is given by the sum of the pairwise partial derivatives.

$$\frac{\partial e_1}{\partial v_1} + \frac{\partial e_2}{\partial v_2} + \ldots + \frac{\partial e_n}{\partial v_n}$$

4.3 Iterating functions

A commonly performed task in computer science and mathematics is to repeatedly apply a function to some expression. Iterating functions has a long and rich tradition in the history of computing. Perhaps the most famous example is Newton's method for root finding. Chaos theory rests on studying how iterated functions behave under small perturbations of their initial conditions or starting values. In this section, we will introduce several functions available in *Mathematica* for function iteration. In later chapters we will apply these and other programming constructs to look at some applications of iteration, including Newton's method.

The Nest function is used to iterate functions. Here, g is iterated (or applied to a) four times.

```
In[1]:= Nest[g, a, 4]

Out[1]= g[g[g[g[a]]]]
```

The NestList function displays all of the intermediate values of the Nest operation.

```
In[2]:= NestList[g, a, 4]

Out[2]= {a, g[a], g[g[a]], g[g[g[a]]], g[g[g[g[a]]]]}
```

Using a starting value of 0.85, this generates a list of ten iterates of the Cos function.

```
In[3]:= NestList[Cos, 0.85, 10]

Out[3]= {0.85, 0.659983, 0.790003, 0.703843, 0.76236, 0.723208,
         0.749687, 0.731902, 0.743904, 0.73583, 0.741274}
```

The list elements above are the values of 0.85, Cos[0.85], Cos[Cos[0.85]], and so on.

```
In[4]:= {0.85, Cos[0.85], Cos[Cos[0.85]], Cos[Cos[Cos[0.85]]]}

Out[4]= {0.85, 0.659983, 0.790003, 0.703843}
```

In fact, the iterates of the cosine function tend towards a fixed point which can be obtained with FixedPoint. This function is particularly useful when you do not know how many iterations to perform on a function whose iterations eventually settle down.

```
In[5]:= FixedPoint[Cos, 0.85]

Out[5]= 0.739085
```

Whereas Nest and NestList operate on functions of one variable, Fold and FoldList generalize this notion by iterating a function of two arguments. In the following example, the function f is first applied to a starting value x and the first element from a list, then this result is used as the first argument of the next iteration, with the second argument coming from the second element in the list, and so on.

In[6]:= **Fold[f, x, {a, b, c}]**

Out[6]= f[f[f[x, a], b], c]

If FoldList is used, then you will see all of the intermediate results of the Fold operation.

In[7]:= **FoldList[f, x, {a, b, c}]**

Out[7]= {x, f[x, a], f[f[x, a], b], f[f[f[x, a], b], c]}

It is easy to see what is going on with the FoldList function by working with an arithmetic operator. This generates "running sums."

In[8]:= **FoldList[Plus, 0, {a, b, c, d}]**

Out[8]= {0, a, a + b, a + b + c, a + b + c + d}

In[9]:= **FoldList[Plus, 0, {1, 2, 3, 4, 5}]**

Out[9]= {0, 1, 3, 6, 10, 15}

Exercises

1. Determine the locations after each step of a ten-step one-dimensional random walk. (Recall that you have already generated the step *directions* in Exercise 3 at the end of Section 3.2.)

2. Create a list of the step locations of a ten-step random walk on a square lattice.

3. Using Fold, create a function fac [*n*] that takes in an integer *n* as argument and returns the factorial of *n*; that is, $n(n-1)(n-2)\cdots3\cdot2\cdot1$.

4.4 Programs as functions

A computer program is a set of instructions (a recipe) for carrying out a computation. When a program is evaluated with appropriate inputs, the computation is performed and the result is returned. In this sense, a program is a mathematical function and the inputs to a program are the arguments of the function. Executing a program is equivalent to applying a function to its arguments or, as it is often referred, making a function call.

User-defined functions

While there are a great many built-in functions in *Mathematica* that can be used to carry out computations, we invariably find ourselves needing customized functions. For example, once we have written a program to compute some values for some particular inputs, we might want to perform the same set of operations on different inputs. We would therefore like to create our own *user-defined* functions that we could then apply in the same way as we call a built-in function – by entering the function name and specific argument values. We will start with the proper syntax (or grammar) to use when writing a function definition.

The function definition looks very much like a mathematical equation: a left-hand side and a right-hand side separated by a colon-equal sign.

$name\ [arg_1\ \_,\ arg_2\ \_,\ ...,\ arg_n\ \_]\ :=\ body$

The left-hand side starts with a symbol. This symbol is referred to as the *function name* (or sometimes just as the function, as in "the sine function"). The function name is followed by a set of square brackets, inside of which are a sequence of symbols ending with *blanks*. These symbols are referred to as the *function argument names*, or just the *function arguments*.

The right-hand side of a user-defined function definition is called the *body* of the function. The body can be either a single expression (a one-liner), or a series of expressions (a compound function), both of which will be discussed in detail shortly. Argument names from the left-hand side appear on the right-hand side without blanks. Basically, the right-hand side is a formula stating what computations are to be done when the function is called with specific values of the arguments.

When a user-defined function is defined with a delayed assignment (: =), nothing is returned. Thereafter, calling the function by entering the left-hand side of the function definition with specific values of the arguments causes the body of the function to be computed with the specific argument values substituted where the argument names occur. In other words, when using delayed assignments, the body of your function is only evaluated when the function is called, not when it is first defined.

A simple example of a user-defined function is `square` which squares a value (it is a good idea to use a function name that indicates the purpose of the function).

In[1]:= `square[x_] := x`^{2}

After entering a function definition, you call the function in the same way that a built-in function is applied to an argument.

In[2]:= `square[5]`

Out[2]= `25`

Building up programs

The ability to use the output of one function as the input of another is one of the keys to functional programming. A mathematician would call this "composition of functions." In *Mathematica*, this sequential application of several functions is known as a *nested function call*. Nested function calls are not limited to using a single function repeatedly, such as with the built-in `Nest` and `Fold` functions.

In[3]:= `Cos[Sin[Tan[4.0]]]`

Out[3]= `0.609053`

To see the above computation more clearly, we can step through the computation.

In[4]:= `Tan[4.0]`

Out[4]= `1.15782`

In[5]:= `Sin[%]`

Out[5]= `0.915931`

In[6]:= `Cos[%]`

Out[6]= `0.609053`

Wrapping the `Trace` function around the computation lets us see all of the intermediate expressions that are used in this evaluation.

In[7]:= `Trace[Cos[Sin[Tan[4.0]]]]`

Out[7]= `{{{Tan[4.], 1.15782}, Sin[1.15782], 0.915931},`
`Cos[0.915931], 0.609053}`

You can read nested functions in much the same way that they are created, starting with the innermost functions and working towards the outermost functions. For example, the following expression determines whether all of the elements in a list are even numbers.

```
In[8]:= Apply[And, Map[EvenQ, {2, 4, 6, 7, 8}]]

Out[8]= False
```

Let us step through the computation much the same as *Mathematica* does, from the inside out.

1. Map the predicate EvenQ to every element in the list {2,4,6,7,8}.

```
In[9]:= Map[EvenQ, {2, 4, 6, 7, 8}]

Out[9]= {True, True, True, False, True}
```

2. Apply the logical function And to the result of the previous step.

```
In[10]:= Apply[And, %]

Out[10]= False
```

Finally, here is a definition that can be used on arbitrary lists.

```
In[11]:= setEvenQ[lis_] := Apply[And, Map[EvenQ, lis]]

In[12]:= setEvenQ[{11, 5, 1, 18, 16, 6, 17, 6}]

Out[12]= False
```

Another, more complicated, example returns the elements in a list of positive numbers that are bigger than all of the preceding numbers in the list.

```
In[13]:= Union[Rest[FoldList[Max, 0, {3, 1, 6, 5, 4, 8, 7}]]]

Out[13]= {3, 6, 8}
```

The Trace of the function call shows the intermediate steps of the computation.

```
In[14]:= Trace[Union[Rest[FoldList[Max, 0, {3, 1, 6, 5, 4, 8, 7}]]]]

Out[14]= {{{FoldList[Max, 0, {3, 1, 6, 5, 4, 8, 7}],
            {Max[0, 3], 3}, {Max[3, 1], Max[1, 3], 3},
            {Max[3, 6], 6}, {Max[6, 5], Max[5, 6], 6},
            {Max[6, 4], Max[4, 6], 6}, {Max[6, 8], 8},
            {Max[8, 7], Max[7, 8], 8}, {0, 3, 3, 6, 6, 6, 8, 8}},
          Rest[{0, 3, 3, 6, 6, 6, 8, 8}], {3, 3, 6, 6, 6, 8, 8}},
          Union[{3, 3, 6, 6, 6, 8, 8}], {3, 6, 8}}
```

This computation can be described as follows:

- The `FoldList` function is first applied to the function `Max`, `0`, and the list
  `{3,1,6,5,4,8,7}` (look at the `Trace` of this computation to see what `Fold⋮`
  `List` is doing here).

  In[15]:= **FoldList[Max, 0, {3, 1, 6, 5, 4, 8, 7}]**

  Out[15]= {0, 3, 3, 6, 6, 6, 8, 8}

- The `Rest` function is then applied to the result of the previous step to remove the
  first element of the list.

  In[16]:= **Rest[%]**

  Out[16]= {3, 3, 6, 6, 6, 8, 8}

- Finally, the `Union` function is applied to the result of the previous step to remove
  duplicates.

  In[17]:= **Union[%]**

  Out[17]= {3, 6, 8}

  Here is the function definition.

  In[18]:= **maxima[x_] := Union[Rest[FoldList[Max, 0, x]]]**

Applying `maxima` to a list of numbers produces a list of all those numbers that are
larger than any number that comes before it.

  In[19]:= **maxima[{4, 2, 7, 3, 4, 9, 14, 11, 17}]**

  Out[19]= {4, 7, 9, 14, 17}

Notice that in each of the nested functions described here, the argument of the first
function was explicitly referred to, but the expressions that were manipulated in the
succeeding function calls were not identified other than as the results of the previous steps
(that is, as the results of the preceding function applications).

Here is an interesting application of building up a program with nested functions –
the creation of a deck of cards. (*Hint*: The suit icons are entered by typing in \ [ClubSuit
], \ [DiamondSuit], etc.)

```
In[20]:=  cardDeck = Flatten[
          Outer[List, {♣, ◊, ♡, ♠}, Join[Range[2, 10], {J, Q, K, A}]], 1]

Out[20]=  {{♣, 2}, {♣, 3}, {♣, 4}, {♣, 5}, {♣, 6}, {♣, 7}, {♣, 8}, {♣, 9}, {♣, 10},
          {♣, J}, {♣, Q}, {♣, K}, {♣, A}, {◊, 2}, {◊, 3}, {◊, 4}, {◊, 5}, {◊, 6},
          {◊, 7}, {◊, 8}, {◊, 9}, {◊, 10}, {◊, J}, {◊, Q}, {◊, K}, {◊, A}, {♡, 2},
          {♡, 3}, {♡, 4}, {♡, 5}, {♡, 6}, {♡, 7}, {♡, 8}, {♡, 9}, {♡, 10},
          {♡, J}, {♡, Q}, {♡, K}, {♡, A}, {♠, 2}, {♠, 3}, {♠, 4}, {♠, 5}, {♠, 6},
          {♠, 7}, {♠, 8}, {♠, 9}, {♠, 10}, {♠, J}, {♠, Q}, {♠, K}, {♠, A}}
```

You might think of `cardDeck` as a name for the expression given on the right-hand side of the immediate definition, or you might think of `cardDeck` as defining a function with zero arguments.

To understand what is going on here, we will build up this program from scratch. First we form a list of the number and face cards in a suit by combining a list of the numbers 2 through 10, `Range[2,10]`, with a four-element list representing the jack, queen, king, and ace, `{J,Q,K,A}`.

```
In[21]:=  Join[Range[2, 10], {J, Q, K, A}]

Out[21]=  {2, 3, 4, 5, 6, 7, 8, 9, 10, J, Q, K, A}
```

Now we pair each of the 13 elements in this list with each of the four elements in the list representing the card suits {♣,◊,♡,♠}. This produces a list of 52 ordered pairs representing the cards in a deck, where the king of clubs, for example, is represented by {♣,K}).

```
In[22]:=  Outer[List, {♣, ◊, ♡, ♠}, %]

Out[22]=  {{{♣, 2}, {♣, 3}, {♣, 4}, {♣, 5}, {♣, 6}, {♣, 7},
            {♣, 8}, {♣, 9}, {♣, 10}, {♣, J}, {♣, Q}, {♣, K}, {♣, A}},
           {{◊, 2}, {◊, 3}, {◊, 4}, {◊, 5}, {◊, 6}, {◊, 7}, {◊, 8},
            {◊, 9}, {◊, 10}, {◊, J}, {◊, Q}, {◊, K}, {◊, A}},
           {{♡, 2}, {♡, 3}, {♡, 4}, {♡, 5}, {♡, 6}, {♡, 7}, {♡, 8},
            {♡, 9}, {♡, 10}, {♡, J}, {♡, Q}, {♡, K}, {♡, A}},
           {{♠, 2}, {♠, 3}, {♠, 4}, {♠, 5}, {♠, 6}, {♠, 7}, {♠, 8},
            {♠, 9}, {♠, 10}, {♠, J}, {♠, Q}, {♠, K}, {♠, A}}}
```

While we now have all of the cards in the deck, they are grouped by suit in a nested list. We therefore un-nest the list:

```
In[23]:=  Flatten[%, 1]

Out[23]=  {{♣, 2}, {♣, 3}, {♣, 4}, {♣, 5}, {♣, 6}, {♣, 7}, {♣, 8}, {♣, 9}, {♣, 10},
          {♣, J}, {♣, Q}, {♣, K}, {♣, A}, {◊, 2}, {◊, 3}, {◊, 4}, {◊, 5}, {◊, 6},
          {◊, 7}, {◊, 8}, {◊, 9}, {◊, 10}, {◊, J}, {◊, Q}, {◊, K}, {◊, A}, {♡, 2},
          {♡, 3}, {♡, 4}, {♡, 5}, {♡, 6}, {♡, 7}, {♡, 8}, {♡, 9}, {♡, 10},
          {♡, J}, {♡, Q}, {♡, K}, {♡, A}, {♠, 2}, {♠, 3}, {♠, 4}, {♠, 5}, {♠, 6},
          {♠, 7}, {♠, 8}, {♠, 9}, {♠, 10}, {♠, J}, {♠, Q}, {♠, K}, {♠, A}}
```

Voila!

The step-by-step construction that we used here, applying one function at a time, checking each function call separately, is a very efficient way to *prototype* your programs in *Mathematica*. We will use this technique again in the next example.

We will perform what is called a *perfect shuffle*, consisting of cutting the deck in half and then interleaving the cards from the two halves. Rather than working with the large list of 52 ordered pairs during the prototyping, we will use a short made-up list. A short list of an even number of ordered integers is a good choice for the task.

```
In[24]:= d = Range[6]

Out[24]= {1, 2, 3, 4, 5, 6}
```

We first divide the list into two equal-sized lists.

```
In[25]:= Partition[d, Length[d] / 2]

Out[25]= {{1, 2, 3}, {4, 5, 6}}
```

We now want to interleave these two lists to form {1,4,2,5,3,6}. The first step is to pair the corresponding elements in each of the two lists above. This can be done using the Transpose function.

```
In[26]:= Transpose[%]

Out[26]= {{1, 4}, {2, 5}, {3, 6}}
```

We now un-nest the interior lists using the Flatten function. We could flatten our simple list using Flatten[...], but, since we know that ultimately we will be dealing with ordered pairs rather than integers, we will use Flatten[...,1] as we did in creating the card deck.

```
In[27]:= Flatten[%, 1]

Out[27]= {1, 4, 2, 5, 3, 6}
```

That does the job. Given this prototype, it is easy to write the actual function to perform a perfect shuffle on a deck of cards. Notice we have generalized this shuffle to lists of arbitrary length.

```
In[28]:= shuffle[lis_] :=
           Flatten[Transpose[Partition[lis, Length[lis] / 2]], 1]
```

```
In[29]:= shuffle[cardDeck]
```

Out[29]= {{♣, 2}, {♡, 2}, {♣, 3}, {♡, 3}, {♣, 4}, {♡, 4}, {♣, 5}, {♡, 5}, {♣, 6},
         {♡, 6}, {♣, 7}, {♡, 7}, {♣, 8}, {♡, 8}, {♣, 9}, {♡, 9}, {♣, 10},
         {♡, 10}, {♣, J}, {♡, J}, {♣, Q}, {♡, Q}, {♣, K}, {♡, K}, {♣, A}, {♡, A},
         {♢, 2}, {♠, 2}, {♢, 3}, {♠, 3}, {♢, 4}, {♠, 4}, {♢, 5}, {♠, 5}, {♢, 6},
         {♠, 6}, {♢, 7}, {♠, 7}, {♢, 8}, {♠, 8}, {♢, 9}, {♠, 9}, {♢, 10},
         {♠, 10}, {♢, J}, {♠, J}, {♢, Q}, {♠, Q}, {♢, K}, {♠, K}, {♢, A}, {♠, A}}

Let us take this example one step further and construct a function that deals cards from a card deck. We will construct this function in stages using the prototyping method we showed earlier.

First we need to define a function that removes a single element from a randomly chosen position in a list.

```
In[30]:=  removeRand[lis_] :=
            Delete[lis, Random[Integer, {1, Length[lis]}]]
```

The function removeRand first uses the Random function to randomly choose an integer *k* between 1 and the length of the list, and then uses the Delete function to remove the *k*th element of the list. For example, if a list has 10 elements, an integer between 1 and 10, say 6, is randomly determined and the element in the sixth position in the list is then removed from the list.

```
In[31]:=  lis = {1, 2, 3, 4, 5, 6, 7, 8, 9, 10};
          removeRand[lis]
```

```
Out[32]=  {2, 3, 4, 5, 6, 7, 8, 9, 10}
```

Now we want to make a function call that applies the removeRand function to the cardDeck list, then applies the removeRand function to the resulting list, then applies the removeRand function to the resulting list, and so on, a total of *n* times. The way to carry out this operation is with the Nest function.

```
Nest[removeRand, cardDeck, n]
```

Lastly, we want the cards that are removed from cardDeck rather than those that remain.

```
Complement[cardDeck, Nest[removeRand, cardDeck, n]]
```

Now, we write this up formally into the user-defined deal function.

```
In[33]:=  deal[n_] := Complement[cardDeck, Nest[removeRand, cardDeck, n]]
```

Let us try it out.

```
In[34]:=  deal[5]
```

```
Out[34]=  {{♣, 3}, {♣, K}, {◊, 2}, {♡, K}, {♠, J}}
```

Not a bad hand!

Exercises

1. One of the games in the Illinois State Lottery is based on choosing *n* numbers, each between 0 and 9, with duplicates allowed; in practice, a selection is made from containers of numbered ping pong balls. We can model this game using a simple user-defined function, which we will call `pick` (after the official lottery names of *Pick 3* and *Pick 4*).

   In[1]:= **pick[n_] := Table[Random[Integer, {0, 9}], {n}]**

   In[2]:= **pick[4]**

   Out[2]= {0, 9, 0, 4}

   This program can be generalized to perform *random sampling with replacement* on any list. Write a function chooseWithReplacement [*lis*, *n*], where *lis* is the list, *n* is the number of elements being chosen and the following is a typical result.

   In[3]:= **chooseWithReplacement[{a, b, c, d, e, f, g, h}, 3]**

   Out[3]= {h, b, f}

2. Write your own user-defined functions using the ToCharacterCode and From: CharacterCode functions to perform the same operations as StringInsert and StringDrop.

3. Create a function distance [*a,b*] that finds the distance between two points *a* and *b* in the plane.

4. Write a user-defined function interleave2 that interleaves the elements of two lists of unequal length. (You have already seen how to interleave lists of equal length using Partition earlier in this section.) Your function should take the lists {1,2,3} and {a,b,c,d} as inputs and return {1,a,2,b,3,c,d}.

5. Write a nested function call that creates a deck of cards and performs a perfect shuffle on it.

6. Write nested function calls using the ToCharacterCode and FromCharacter: Code functions to perform the same operations as the built-in StringJoin and StringReverse functions.

4.5 Auxiliary functions

There are several major drawbacks to the deal function created in the previous section. In order to use deal, the definition of removeRand and the value of cardDeck must be entered before calling deal. It would be much more convenient if we could incorporate these functions within the deal function definition itself. In the next section, we will show how this can be done.

Compound functions

The left-hand side of a *compound function* is the same as that of any user-defined function. The right-hand side consists of consecutive expressions enclosed in parentheses and separated by semicolons.

$name\,[arg_1\,\_,\,arg_2\,\_,\,...,\,arg_n\,\_]\ :=\ (expr_1;\ expr_2;\ ...;\ expr_m)$

The expressions can be user-defined functions (also known as *auxiliary* functions), value declarations, and function calls. When a compound function is evaluated with particular argument values, these expressions are evaluated in order and the result of the evaluation of the last expression is returned (by adding a semicolon after $expr_n$, the display of the final evaluation result can also be suppressed).

We will work with the deal function to illustrate how a compound function is created. We need the following three expressions.

```
In[1]:=  cardDeck = Flatten[Outer[List,
             {♣, ♦, ♡, ♠}, Join[Range[2, 10], {J, Q, K, A}]], 1];
```

```
In[2]:=  removeRand[lis_] :=
             Delete[lis, Random[Integer, {1, Length[lis]}]]
```

```
In[3]:=  deal[n_] := Complement[cardDeck, Nest[removeRand, cardDeck, n]]
```

The conversion to a compound function is easily done. We will first remove the old definitions.

```
In[4]:=  Clear[deal, cardDeck, removeRand]
```

Now we can create and enter the new definition.

```
In[5]:=  deal[n_] := (
           cardDeck = Flatten[Outer[List,
             {♣, ◇, ♡, ♠}, Join[Range[2, 10], {J, Q, K, A}]], 1];
           removeRand[lis_] := Delete[lis,
             Random[Integer, {1, Length[lis]}]];
           Complement[cardDeck, Nest[removeRand, cardDeck, n]]
         )
```

Let us check that this works.

```
In[6]:=  deal[5]
```

```
Out[6]=  {{♣, 3}, {◇, 2}, {♡, 3}, {♡, 4}, {♡, Q}}
```

A couple of things should be pointed out about the right-hand side of a compound function definition. Since the expressions on the right-hand side are evaluated in order, value declarations and auxiliary function definitions should be given *before* they are used and the argument names used on the left-hand side of auxiliary function definitions *must* differ from the argument names used by the compound function itself.

Finally, when we enter a compound function definition, we are entering not only the function but also the auxiliary functions and the value declarations. If we then remove the function definition using Clear, the auxiliary function definitions and value declarations remain. This can cause a problem if we subsequently try to use the names of these auxiliary functions and values elsewhere.

So how does the global rule base treat compound functions? When a compound function definition is entered, a rewrite rule corresponding to the entire definition is created. Each time the compound function is subsequently called, rewrite rules are created from the auxiliary function definitions and value declarations within the compound function.

```
In[7]:=  ? cardDeck
```

```
Global`cardDeck
```

```
cardDeck = {{♣, 2}, {♣, 3}, {♣, 4}, {♣, 5}, {♣, 6}, {♣, 7}, {♣, 8},
  {♣, 9}, {♣, 10}, {♣, J}, {♣, Q}, {♣, K}, {♣, A}, {◇, 2}, {◇, 3}, {◇, 4},
  {◇, 5}, {◇, 6}, {◇, 7}, {◇, 8}, {◇, 9}, {◇, 10}, {◇, J}, {◇, Q}, {◇, K},
  {◇, A}, {♡, 2}, {♡, 3}, {♡, 4}, {♡, 5}, {♡, 6}, {♡, 7}, {♡, 8}, {♡, 9},
  {♡, 10}, {♡, J}, {♡, Q}, {♡, K}, {♡, A}, {♠, 2}, {♠, 3}, {♠, 4}, {♠, 5},
  {♠, 6}, {♠, 7}, {♠, 8}, {♠, 9}, {♠, 10}, {♠, J}, {♠, Q}, {♠, K}, {♠, A}}
```

It is considered bad programming practice to leave auxiliary definitions in the global rule base that are not explicitly needed by the user of your function. In fact, it could interfere with a user's workspace and cause unintended problems.

To prevent these additional rewrite rules from being placed in the global rule base, you can localize their names by using the Module construct in the compound function definition. This is what we discuss next.

Localizing names: Module

When a user-defined function is written, it is generally a good idea to isolate the *names* of values and functions defined on the right-hand side from the outside world in order to avoid any conflict with the use of a name elsewhere in the session (for example, cardDeck might be used elsewhere to represent a pinochle deck). This can be done by wrapping the right-hand side of the function definition in the built-in Module function.

$name [arg_1 \_, arg_2 \_, ..., arg_n \_] :=$ Module $[\{name_1, name_2 = value, ...\},$
    $expr]$

The first argument of the Module function is a list of the names we want to localize. If we wish, we can assign values to these names, as is shown with *name*$_2$ above (the assigned value is only an initial value and can be changed subsequently). The list is separated from the right-hand side by a comma and so the parentheses enclosing the right-hand side of a compound function are not needed.

We can demonstrate the use of Module with the deal function.

In[8]:= **Clear[deal]**

In[9]:= **deal[n_] := Module[{cardDeck, removeRand},**
        cardDeck = Flatten[Outer[List,
            {♣, ◇, ♡, ♠}, Join[Range[2, 10], {J, Q, K, A}]], 1];
        removeRand[lis_] := Delete[lis,
            Random[Integer, {1, Length[lis]}]];
        Complement[cardDeck, Nest[removeRand, cardDeck, n]]]

Briefly, when Module is encountered, the symbols that are being localized (card‐ Deck and removeRand in the above example) are temporarily given new and unique names, and all occurrences of those symbols in the body of the Module are given those new names as well. In this way, these unique and temporary names, which are local to the function, will not interfere with any functions outside of the Module.

It is generally a good idea to wrap the right-hand side of all compound function definitions in the Module function. Another way to avoid conflicts in the use of names of auxiliary function definitions is to use a function that can be applied without being given a name. Such functions are called *pure functions*, which we discuss in Section 4.6.

Localizing values: Block

Occasionally, you will need to localize a *value* associated with a symbol without localizing the symbol name itself. For example, you may have a recursive computation that requires you to temporarily reset the system variable $RecursionLimit. You can do this with Block, thereby only localizing the *value* of $RecursionLimit during the evaluation inside the Block.

```
In[10]:= Block[{$RecursionLimit = 20},
            x = g[x]
         ]

         $RecursionLimit::reclim :
           Recursion depth of 20 exceeded. More…
```

Out[10]= g[g[
            g[g[g[g[g[g[g[g[g[g[g[g[g[g[g[g[g[g[Hold[g[x]]]]]]]]]]]]]]]]]]]]]

Notice the global value of $RecursionLimit is unchanged.

```
In[11]:= $RecursionLimit
```

Out[11]= 256

This construct is similar to what is done for the iterators in Table, Do, Sum, and Prod:uct.

Module, on the other hand, would create an entirely new symbol, $Recursion:Limit$*nn* that would have nothing to do with the global variable $RecursionLimit, and so Module would be inappropriate for this particular task.

Localizing constants: With

Another scoping construct is available when you simply need to localize constants. If, in the body of your function, you use a variable that is assigned a constant once and never changes, then With is the preferred means to localize that constant.

This sets the global variable y to have the value 5.

```
In[12]:= y = 5;
```

Here is a simple function that initializes y as a local constant.

```
In[13]:=  f[x_] := With[{y = x + 1},
              y
          ]
```

We see the global symbol is unchanged and it does not interfere with the local symbol y inside the With.

```
In[14]:=  y
Out[14]=  5
```

```
In[15]:=  f[2]
Out[15]=  3
```

Using With, you can initialize local constants with the values of global symbols. For example:

```
In[16]:=  With[{y = y},
              g[x_] := x + y
          ]
```

This shows that the global value for y was inserted inside g.

```
In[17]:=  ? g
Global`g

g[x$_] := x$ + 5
```

Resetting the global value of y has no effect on the localized y inside the With.

```
In[18]:=  y = 1;
```

```
In[19]:=  g[5]
Out[19]=  10
```

Exercises

1. Write a compound function definition for the location of steps taken in an *n*-step random walk on a square lattice. *Hint*: Use the definition for the step increments of the walk as an auxiliary function.

2. The PerfectSearch function defined in Section 1.1 is impractical for checking large numbers because it has to check all numbers from 1 through *n*. If you already

know the perfect numbers below 500, say, it is inefficient to check all numbers from 1 to 1,000 if you are only looking for perfect numbers in the range 500 to 1,000. Modify `searchPerfect` so that it accepts two numbers as input and computes all perfect numbers between the inputs. For example, `PerfectSearch[a,b]` will produce a list of all perfect numbers in the range from *a* to *b*.

3. Overload the `PerfectSearch` function to compute all *3-perfect* numbers. A 3-perfect number is such that the sum of its divisors equals *three* times the number. For example, 120 is 3-perfect since it is equal to three times the sum of its divisors.

   In[1]:= **Apply[Plus, Divisors[120]]**

   Out[1]= 360

   Find the only other 3-perfect number under 1,000.
   You can overload `PerfectSearch` as defined in Exercise 2 above by defining a three-argument version `PerfectSearch[a,b,3]`.

4. Overload `PerfectSearch` to find the three 4-perfect numbers less than 2,200,000.

5. Redefine `PerfectSearch` so that it accepts as input a number *k*, and two numbers *a* and *b*, and computes all *k*-perfect numbers in the range from *a* to *b*. For example, `PerfectSearch[1,30,2]` would compute all 2-perfect numbers in the range from 1 to 30 and, hence, would output {6,28}.

6. If $\sigma(n)$ is defined to be the sum of the divisors of *n*, then *n* is called *superperfect* if $\sigma(\sigma(n)) = 2n$. Write a function `SuperPerfectSearch[a,b]` that finds all superperfect numbers in the range from *a* to *b*.

7. Often in processing files you will be presented with expressions that need to be converted into a format that can be more easily manipulated inside *Mathematica*. For example, a file may contain dates in the form 20030515 to represent May 15, 2003. *Mathematica* represents its dates as a list {*year*, *month*, *day*, *hour*, *minutes*, *seconds*}. Write a function `convertToDate[n]` to convert a number consisting of eight digits such as 20030515 into a list of the form {2003,5,15}.

   In[2]:= **convertToDate[20030515]**

   Out[2]= {2003, 5, 15}

4.6 Pure functions

A *pure function* is a function that does not have a name and that can be used "on the spot"; that is, at the moment it is created. This is often convenient, especially if the function is only going to be used once or as an argument to a higher-order function, such as Map, Fold, or Nest. The built-in function Function is used to create a pure function.

The basic form of a pure function is Function[x, *body*] for a pure function with a single variable x (any symbol can be used for the variable), and Function[$\{x, y, ...\}$, *body*] for a pure function with more than one variable. The *body* looks like the right-hand side of a user-defined function definition, with the variables x, y, ..., where argument names would be.

As an example, the square function we created earlier can be written as a pure function.

In[1]:= **Function[z, z^2]**

Out[1]= Function[z, z^2]

There is also a standard input form that can be used in writing a pure function which is easier to write than the Function notation but can be a bit cryptic to read. The right-hand side of the function definition is rewritten by replacing the variable by the pound symbol (#) and ending the expression with the ampersand symbol (&) to indicate that this is a pure function.

#^{2} &

If there is more than one variable, #1, #2, and so on are used.

A pure function can be used exactly like more conventional looking functions, by following the function with the argument values enclosed in square brackets. First we show the pure function using Function.

In[2]:= **Function[z, z^2][6]**

Out[2]= 36

Here is the same thing, but using the more cryptic shorthand notation (the parentheses in the following example are purely for readability and can be omitted if you wish).

In[3]:= **(#^{2} &)[6]**

Out[3]= 36

We can, if we wish, give a pure function a name and then use that name to call the function later. This has the same effect as defining the function in the more traditional manner.

In[4]:= **squared = (#^{2}) &;**

In[5]:= **squared[6]**

Out[5]= 36

Pure functions are very commonly used with higher-order functions like Map and Apply, so, before going further, let us first look at a few simple examples of the use of pure functions.

Here is a list of numbers.

In[6]:= **lis = {2, -5, 6.1};**

Now suppose we wished to square each number and then add 1 to it. The pure function that does this is: #^{2} + 1 &. So that is what we need to map across this list.

In[7]:= **Map[#^{2} + 1 &, lis]**

Out[7]= {5, 26, 38.21}

In the next example we will create a set of data and then use the Select function to filter out outliers.

In[8]:= **data = {24.39001, 29.669, 9.321, 20.8856,**
　　　　　23.4736, 22.1488, 24.7434, 22.1619, 21.1039,
　　　　　24.8177, 27.1331, 25.8705, 39.7676, 24.7762}

Out[8]= {24.39, 29.669, 9.321, 20.8856, 23.4736, 22.1488, 24.7434,
　　　　　22.1619, 21.1039, 24.8177, 27.1331, 25.8705, 39.7676, 24.7762}

A plot of the data shows there are two outliers.

In[9]:= **ListPlot[data, PlotStyle → PointSize[.02]];**

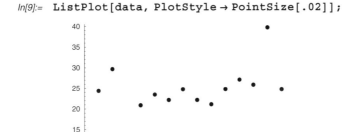

The Select function takes two arguments – the first is the expression from which it will select elements, and the second argument is a function that must return True or False. Select [*expr, test*] will then select those elements from *expr* that return True when *test* is applied to them.

Suppose we wish to exclude all data points that lie outside of the range 20 to 30. Then we need a function that returns True if its argument is in that range.

```
In[10]:= Select[data, 20 ≤ # ≤ 30 &]

Out[10]= {24.39, 29.669, 20.8856, 23.4736, 22.1488, 24.7434,
          22.1619, 21.1039, 24.8177, 27.1331, 25.8705, 24.7762}
```

A good way to become comfortable with pure functions is to see them in action, so we will convert some of the functions we defined earlier into pure functions, showing both the (...#...) & and the Function forms so that you can decide which you prefer to use.

This function tests whether all the elements of a list are even.

```
In[11]:= areEltsEven[lis_] := Apply[And, Map[EvenQ, lis]]

In[12]:= areEltsEven[{2, 4, 5, 8}]

Out[12]= False
```

Here it is written using pure functions.

```
In[13]:= Function[lis, Apply[And, Map[EvenQ, lis]]][{2, 4, 5, 8}]

Out[13]= False

In[14]:= (Apply[And, Map[EvenQ, #1]]) &[{2, 4, 5, 8}]

Out[14]= False
```

This function returns each element in the list greater than all previous elements.

```
In[15]:= maxima[x_] := Union[Rest[FoldList[Max, 0, x]]]

In[16]:= maxima[{2, 6, 3, 7, 9, 2}]

Out[16]= {2, 6, 7, 9}
```

Here it is written using pure functions.

```
In[17]:= Function[x, Union[Rest[FoldList[Max, 0, x]]]][{2, 6, 3, 7, 9, 2}]

Out[17]= {2, 6, 7, 9}

In[18]:= Union[Rest[FoldList[Max, 0, #]]] &[{2, 6, 3, 7, 9, 2}]

Out[18]= {2, 6, 7, 9}
```

We can also create nested pure functions. For example, this maps the pure squaring function over the three-element list {3,2,7}.

```
In[19]:= Map[#² &, {3, 2, 7}]

Out[19]= {9, 4, 49}
```

When dealing with nested pure functions, the shorthand notation can be used for each of the pure functions but care needs to be taken to avoid confusion as to which # variable belongs to which pure function. This can be avoided by using `Function`, in which case different variable names can be used.

In[20]:= `Function[y, Map[Function[x, x²], y]][{3, 2, 7}]`

Out[20]= `{9, 4, 49}`

Exercises

1. Write a function to sum the squares of the elements of a numeric list.

2. Write a function to sum the digits of any integer. You will need the `IntegerDig-its` function (use `?IntegerDigits`, or look up `IntegerDigits` in the Help Browser to find out about this function).

3. Using the definition of the `distance` function from Exercise 3 of Section 4.4, write a new function `diameter` [*pts*] that, given a set of points in the plane, finds the maximum distance between all pairs of points. Try to incorporate the `distance` function into `diameter` without naming it explicitly; that is, use it as a pure function. Consider using `Distribute` to get the set of all pairs of points.

   In[1]:= `pts = {p₁, p₂, p₃};`

   In[2]:= `Distribute[{pts, pts}, List]`

   Out[2]= `{{p₁, p₁}, {p₁, p₂}, {p₁, p₃}, {p₂, p₁},`
   `{p₂, p₂}, {p₂, p₃}, {p₃, p₁}, {p₃, p₂}, {p₃, p₃}}`

4. Take the `removeRand` function defined in Section 4.4 and rewrite it as a pure function.

   In[3]:= `removeRand[lis_] :=`
   `Delete[lis, Random[Integer, {1, Length[lis]}]]`

5. Convert the `deal` function developed earlier into one that uses pure functions. Use the pure function version of the `removeRand` function from the previous exercise in your new `deal` function definition.

6. Create a function `RepUnit` [*n*] that generates integers of length *n* consisting entirely of 1s. For example `RepUnit` [7] should produce 1111111.

7. Create a function chooseWithoutReplacement [*lis*, *n*] that is a generalization of the deal function in that it will work with *any* list.

8. Write a pure function that moves a random walker from one location on a square lattice to one of the four adjoining locations with equal probability. For example, starting at {0,0}, the function should return either {0,1}, {0,-1}, {1,0} or {-1,0} with equal likelihood. Now, use this pure function with NestList to generate the list of step locations for an *n*-step random walk starting at {0,0}.

9. Create a function WordsStartingWith [*lis*, *char*] that outputs all those words in *lis* that begin with the character *char*. As a sample list, you can use the dictionary.dat file that comes with *Mathematica*.

   Here is a platform-independent path to the dictionary file.

   In[4]:= **wordfile = ToFileName[{$InstallationDirectory, "Documentation", "English", "Demos", "DataFiles"}, "dictionary.dat"]**

   Out[4]= C:\Program Files\Wolfram Research\Mathematica\5.1\ Documentation\English\Demos\DataFiles\dictionary.dat

   This reads in the file using ReadList, specifying the type of data we are reading in as a Word.

   In[5]:= **words = ReadList[wordfile, Word];**

10. Modify Exercise 9 above so that WordsStartingWith accepts a string of arbitrary length as its second argument.

11. A naive approach to polynomial arithmetic would require three additions and six multiplies to carry out the arithmetic in the expression $a x^3 + b x^2 + c x + d$. Using Horner's method for fast polynomial multiplication, this expression can be represented as $d + x(c + x(b + a x))$, where there are now half as many multiplies. In general, the number of multiplies for an *n*-degree polynomial is given by:

    In[6]:= **Binomial[n + 1, 2]**

    Out[6]= $\frac{1}{2}$ n (1 + n)

    This, of course, grows quadratically with *n*, whereas Horner's method grows linearly. Create a function Horner [*lis*, *var*] that implements Horner's method for polynomial multiplication. Here is some sample input and the corresponding output that your function should generate.

In[7]:= `Horner[{a, b, c, d}, x]`

Out[7]= $d + x (c + x (b + a x))$

In[8]:= `Expand[%]`

Out[8]= $d + c x + b x^2 + a x^3$

4.7 One-liners

In the simplest version of a user-defined function, there are no value declarations or auxiliary function definitions; the right-hand side is a single nested function call whose arguments are the names of the arguments on the left-hand side, without the blanks. These "one-liners" are fantastically useful and so we will discuss them in the context of three examples, one from electrical engineering (computing Hamming distance), one from ancient history (the Josephus problem), and the last a simple and practical problem (counting change).

Hamming distance

When a code is transmitted over a channel in the presence of noise, errors will often occur. The task of channel coding is to represent the source information in a manner that minimizes the error probability in decoding. *Hamming distance* is used in source coding to represent an information source with the minimum number of symbols. For two lists of binary symbols, the Hamming distance is defined as the number of nonmatching elements and so gives a measure of the how well these two lists match up.

Let us first think about how we might determine if two binary symbols are identical. `SameQ [x,y]` will return `True` if x and y are identical.

In[1]:= `{SameQ[0, 0], SameQ[1, 0], SameQ[1, 1]}`

Out[1]= `{True, False, True}`

So we need to thread `SameQ` over the two lists of binary numbers

In[2]:= `MapThread[SameQ, {{1, 0, 0, 1, 1}, {0, 1, 0, 1, 0}}]`

Out[2]= `{False, False, True, True, False}`

and then count up the occurrences of `False`.

```
In[3]:=  Count[%, False]
```

```
Out[3]=  3
```

So a first definition of `HammingDistance` could be accomplished by putting these last two pieces together.

```
In[4]:=  HammingDistance[lis1_, lis2_] :
            Count[MapThread[SameQ, {lis1, lis2}], False]
```

```
In[5]:=  HammingDistance[{1, 0, 0, 1, 1}, {0, 1, 0, 1, 0}]
```

```
Out[5]=  3
```

We might try to solve this problem by a more direct approach. Since we are dealing with binary information, we could use some of the logical binary operators built into *Mathematica*.

Here is our transposed list again.

```
In[6]:=  lis = Transpose[{{1, 0, 0, 1, 1}, {0, 1, 0, 1, 0}}]
```

```
Out[6]=  {{1, 0}, {0, 1}, {0, 0}, {1, 1}, {1, 0}}
```

`BitXor[x,y]` returns the bitwise XOR of x and y. So if x and y can only be among the binary integers 0 or 1, `BitXor` will return 0 whenever they are the same and will return 1 whenever they are different.

```
In[7]:=  Apply[BitXor, {{0, 0}, {1, 0}, {1, 1}}, {1}]
```

```
Out[7]=  {0, 1, 0}
```

Here then is `BitXor` applied to `lis`.

```
In[8]:=  Apply[BitXor, lis, {1}]
```

```
Out[8]=  {1, 1, 0, 0, 1}
```

And here are the number of 1s that occur in that list.

```
In[9]:=  Apply[Plus, %]
```

```
Out[9]=  3
```

Summing up, our function `HammingDistance2` first pairs up the lists (`Transpose`), then determines which pairs contain different elements (apply `BitXor`), and finally counts up the number of 1s (`Apply[Plus,...]`).

```
In[10]:=  HammingDistance2[lis1_, lis2_] := Apply[Plus,
             Apply[BitXor, Transpose[{lis1, lis2}], {1}]
           ]
```

```
In[11]:=  HammingDistance2[{1, 0, 0, 1, 1}, {0, 1, 0, 1, 0}]
```

Out[11]= 3

Let us compare the running times of these implementations using a large data set, in this case two lists consisting of one million 0s and 1s.

```
In[12]:=  data1 = Table[Random[Integer], {10^6}];
```

```
In[13]:=  data2 = Table[Random[Integer], {10^6}];
```

```
In[14]:=  Timing[HammingDistance[data1, data2]]
```

Out[14]= {1.162 Second, 499801}

```
In[15]:=  Timing[HammingDistance2[data1, data2]]
```

Out[15]= {1.392 Second, 499801}

Although these times do not look too bad, they are in fact too slow for any serious work with signal processing. The exercises ask you to write an implementation of Hamming Distance that runs about two orders of magnitude faster than those presented here.

As an aside, the above computations are not a bad check on the built-in random number generator – we would expect that about one half of the paired up lists would contain different elements.

The Josephus problem

Flavius Josephus was a Jewish historian during the Roman–Jewish war of the first century AD. Through his writings comes the following story:

> *The Romans had chased a group of ten Jews into a cave and were about to attack. Rather than die at the hands of their enemy, the group chose to commit suicide one by one. Legend has it though, that they decided to go around their circle of ten individuals and eliminate every other person until only one was left.*

Who was the last to survive? Although a bit macabre, this problem has a definite mathematical interpretation that lends itself well to a functional style of programming. We will start by changing the problem a bit (the importance of rewording a problem can hardly be overstated; the key to most problem-solving resides in turning something we can not work with into something we can work with). We will restate the problem as follows: n people are lined up. The first person is moved to the end of the line, the second person is removed from the line, the third person is moved to the end of the line, and so on until only one person remains in the line.

The statement of the problem indicates that there is a repetitive action, performed over and over again. It involves the use of the `RotateLeft` function (move the person at the front of the line to the back of the line) followed by the use of the `Rest` function (remove the next person from the line).

In[16]:= **Rest[RotateLeft[#]] &[{a, b, c, d}]**

Out[16]= {c, d, a}

At this point it is already pretty clear where this computation is headed. We want to take a list and, using the `Nest` function, perform the pure function call (Rest[Rotate⸜ Left[#]]) & on the list until only one element remains. A list of *n* elements will need *n* − 1 calls. So we can now write the function, to which we give the apt name `survivor`.

In[17]:= **survivor[lis_] :=**
Nest[Rest[RotateLeft[#]] &, lis, Length[lis] - 1]

Trying out the `survivor` function on a list of ten, we see that the fifth position will be the position of the survivor.

In[18]:= **survivor[Range[10]]**

Out[18]= {5}

Tracing the applications of `RotateLeft` in this example gives a very clear picture of what is going on. The following form of `TracePrint` shows only the results of the applications of `RotateLeft` that occur during evaluation of the expression survivor[⸜ Range[6]].

In[19]:= **TracePrint[survivor[Range[6]], RotateLeft]**

```
RotateLeft

{2, 3, 4, 5, 6, 1}

RotateLeft

{4, 5, 6, 1, 3}

RotateLeft

{6, 1, 3, 5}

RotateLeft

{3, 5, 1}

RotateLeft

{1, 5}
```
Out[19]= {5}

Pocket change

As another example, we will write a program to perform an operation most of us do every day: calculating how much change we have in our pocket. Suppose we have the following collection of coins.

```
In[20]:=  coins = {p, p, q, n, d, d, p, q, q, p}

Out[20]=  {p, p, q, n, d, d, p, q, q, p}
```

Assume *p*, *n*, *d*, and *q* represent pennies, nickels, dimes, and quarters, respectively. Let us start by using the Count function to determine the number of pennies we have.

```
In[21]:=  Count[coins, p]

Out[21]=  4
```

This works. So let us do the same thing for all of the coin types.

```
In[22]:=  {Count[coins, p], Count[coins, n],
            Count[coins, d], Count[coins, q]}

Out[22]=  {4, 1, 2, 3}
```

Looking at this list, it is apparent that there ought to be a more compact way of writing the list. If we Map a pure function involving Count and coins on to the list {p,n,d,q}, it should do the job.

```
In[23]:=  Map[(Count[coins, #1] &), {p, n, d, q}]

Out[23]=  {4, 1, 2, 3}
```

Now that we know how many coins of each type we have, we want to calculate how much change we have. We first do the calculation *manually* to see what we get for an answer (so we will know when our program works).

```
In[24]:=  4 1 + 1 5 + 2 10 + 3 25

Out[24]=  104
```

From the above computation we see that the lists {4,1,2,3} and {1,5,10,25} are first multiplied together element-wise and then the elements of the result are added. This suggests a few possibilities.

```
In[25]:=  Apply[Plus, ({4, 1, 2, 3} {1, 5, 10, 25})]

Out[25]=  104


In[26]:=  {4, 1, 2, 3}.{1, 5, 10, 25}

Out[26]=  104
```

Either of these operations are suitable for the job (to coin a phrase, "there's not a penny, nickel, quarter, or dime's worth of difference"). We will write the one-liner using the first method.

```
In[27]:= pocketChange[x_] :=
           Apply[Plus, Map[(Count[x, #] &), {p, n, d, q}] {1, 5, 10, 25}]

In[28]:= pocketChange[coins]

Out[28]= 104
```

Exercises

1. Write a function to compute the Hamming distance of two binary lists (assumed to be of equal length), using `Select` and an appropriate predicate function.

2. All of the implementations of Hamming distance discussed so far are a bit slow for large datasets. You can get a significant speedup in running times by using functions that are optimized for working with numbers (a topic we discuss in detail in Chapter 8). Write an implementation of Hamming distance using the `Total` function and then compare running times with the other versions discussed in this chapter.

3. One of the best ways to learn how to write programs is to practice reading code. We list below a number of one-liner function definitions along with a very brief explanation of what these user-defined functions do and a typical input and output. Deconstruct these programs to see what they do and then reconstruct them as compound functions without any pure functions.

   a. Determine the frequencies with which distinct elements appear in a list.

   ```
   In[1]:= frequencies[lis_] := Map[({#, Count[lis, #]}) &, Union[lis]]

   In[2]:= frequencies[{a, a, b, b, b, a, c, c}]

   Out[2]= {{a, 3}, {b, 3}, {c, 2}}
   ```

   b. Divide up a list into parts each of whose lengths are given by the second argument.

   ```
   In[3]:= split1[lis_, parts_] :=
            (Inner[Take[lis, {#1, #2}] &, Drop[#1, -1] + 1,
               Rest[#1], List] &)[FoldList[Plus, 0, parts]]
   ```

In[4]:= `split1[Range[10], {2, 5, 0, 3}]`

Out[4]= `{{1, 2}, {3, 4, 5, 6, 7}, {}, {8, 9, 10}}`

This is the same as the previous program, done in a different way.

In[5]:= `split2[lis_, parts_] :=`
` Map[(Take[lis, # + {1, 0}])&,`
` Partition[FoldList[Plus, 0, parts], 2, 1]]`

c. Another game in the Illinois State Lottery is based on choosing *n* numbers, each between 0 and *s* with no duplicates allowed. Write a user-defined function called `lotto` (after the official lottery names of *Little Lotto* and *Big Lotto*) to perform *sampling without replacement* on an arbitrary list. (*Note*: The difference between this function and the function `chooseWithoutReplacement` is that the order of selection is needed here.)

In[6]:= `lotto1[lis_, n_] := (Flatten[`
` Rest[MapThread[Complement, {RotateRight[#], #}, 1]]] &)[`
` NestList[Delete[#, Random[Integer, {1, Length[#]}]] &,`
` lis, n]]`

In[7]:= `lotto1[Range[10], 5]`

Out[7]= `{10, 3, 2, 7, 6}`

This is the same as the previous program, done in a different way.

In[8]:= `lotto2[lis_, n_] := Take[Transpose[Sort[`
` Transpose[{Table[Random[], {Length[lis]}], lis}]]][[2]], n]`

As the `split` and `lotto` programs illustrate, user-defined functions can be written in several ways. The choice as to which version of a program to use has to be based on efficiency. A program whose development time was shorter and which runs faster is *better* than a program which took more time to develop and which runs more slowly. Although concise *Mathematica* programs tend to run fastest, when execution speed is a primary concern (when dealing with very large lists) it is a good idea to take various programming approaches and perform `Timing` tests to determine the fastest program.

4. Use the `Timing` function to determine when (in terms of the relative sizes of the list and the number of elements being chosen) it is preferable to use the different versions of the `lotto` function.

5. Rewrite the `pocketChange` function in two different ways – one, using `Dot`, and the other using `Inner`.

6. Make change with quarters, dimes, nickels, and pennies using the fewest coins.

    In[9]:= **makeChange[119]**

    Out[9]= {4, 1, 1, 4}

7. Write a one-liner to create a list of the step locations of a two-dimensional random walk that is not restricted to a lattice. *Hint*: Each step length must be the same, so the sum of the squares of the x- and y-components of each step should be equal to 1.

8. Write a one-liner version of convertToDate as described in Exercise 7 from Section 4.5. Consider the built-in function FromDigits.

5 Procedural programming

Conventional programming languages like C and Fortran embody a style of programming that has roots in the early days of computing when resource constraints forced programmers to write their code in a step-by-step manner. These procedures, as they came to be known, typically involved certain basic elements: looping over an array, conditional statements that controlled the flow of execution, logical constructs to build up tests, and functions to jump around from one place in a program to another. Although newer languages have introduced many new programming paradigms, procedural programming continues to be used and remains an appropriate style for certain kinds of problems. In this chapter we will look at how procedural programming is used in *Mathematica*, discuss what types of problems it is most appropriate for, and compare *Mathematica*'s implementation with other languages.

5.1 Introduction

A *procedure* is a series of instructions that are evaluated in a definite order. The following program is a procedure.

```
In[1]:=  mat = {{a, b, c}, {d, e, f}, {g, h, k}};
         newmat = mat;
         Do[newmat[[i, j]] = mat[[j, i]],
            {i, Length[mat]}, {j, Length[mat]}];
         newmat
```

```
Out[4]=  {{a, d, g}, {b, e, h}, {c, f, k}}
```

```
In[5]:=  MatrixForm[%]
```

```
Out[5]//MatrixForm=
         ⎛ a  d  g ⎞
         ⎜ b  e  h ⎟
         ⎝ c  f  k ⎠
```

We could look at this procedure as a compound expression consisting of a sequence of four expressions: the first assigns the symbolic 3×3 matrix to the symbol mat; the second is also an assignment copying the matrix to another symbol, newmat; the third expression loops through the matrix, interchanging columns and rows of the original and putting them into the new matrix – essentially performing a transpose operation; the final expression simply outputs the new matrix.

Procedural programs also typically involve some *flow control*. What this means is that, depending upon a certain condition, different steps in the procedure will be followed. Perhaps the simplest example of this is an If statement.

```
In[6]:=  f[x_] := If[20 ≤ x ≤ 30, x,
            Print["The number ", x, " is outside the range."]]
```

```
In[7]:=  f[23]
```

```
Out[7]= 23
```

```
In[8]:=  f[66]
```

```
The number 66 is outside the range.
```

The value of the first argument of the If function determines the direction of the rest of the evaluation. This is a control structure.

These are typical components of procedural programs – a series of expressions to evaluate in some order and functions to control the flow of execution. In this chapter we will explore these topics in addition to conditional definitions which are another form of flow control. All of these features will greatly expand what we can do with *Mathematica* and we will find many applications of these techniques in later chapters on recursion and numerics.

5.2 Loops and iteration

Newton's method

One of the most famous of all numerical algorithms is Newton's method for finding the roots of a function. Even though *Mathematica* includes a built-in function, FindRoot, that implements this method, this is a classic use of iteration and so central to numerical analysis that it is well worth your time learning how to implement it.

Throughout this section we will use the function $x^2 - 50$, whose root is, of course, the square root of 50. Here is the computation using the built-in FindRoot.

```
In[1]:=  FindRoot[x² - 50 == 0, {x, 50}]
```

```
Out[1]= {x → 7.07107}
```

The number 50 in {x, 50} is the initial guess of the root.

So why should you learn to program a root-finder yourself? As we stated above, it is a classical algorithm and the basis of many more advanced root-finding techniques in numerical analysis. But also, with many numerical problems, the built-in operations do not always give you optimal results. This is because the built-in functions are designed to work for the broadest possible set of situations, but might have occasional trouble with certain exceptional cases. An example is the function $f(x) = x^{1/3}$.

In[2]:= **FindRoot[x$^{1/3}$ == 0, {x, 0.1}]**

> FindRoot::lstol :
>> The line search decreased the step size to within tolerance
>> specified by AccuracyGoal and PrecisionGoal but was
>> unable to find a sufficient decrease in the merit
>> function.   You may need more than MachinePrecision digits
>> of working precision to meet these tolerances. More…

Out[2]= $\{x \rightarrow -0.000405502 - 2.29415 \times 10^{-15} \; i\}$

Although this particular function's root can be better approximated using an option (DampingFactor) to FindRoot, we will find it very instructive to program our own root-finding functions that can solve this problem and, in the process, learn about the structure of iterative programming.

In[3]:= **FindRoot[x$^{1/3}$ == 0, {x, 0.1}, DampingFactor → 2]**

Out[3]= $\{x \rightarrow 8.93553 \times 10^{-17}\}$

Do loops

Suppose we are given a function f and can compute its derivative, f'. Then Newton's algorithm works as follows:

- give an initial estimate of the root, say x_0

- keep generating better estimates, x_1, x_2, …, using the following rule until you are done (we will discuss this later):

$$x_{i+1} = x_i - \frac{f(x_i)}{f'(x_i)}$$

The method is illustrated in Figure 5.1. Under the favorable circumstances pictured there the estimates get closer and closer to the root.

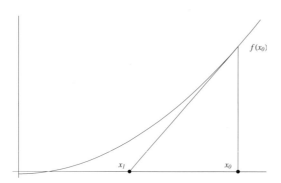

Figure 5.1: Illustration of Newton's method

We will discuss in a moment when to stop, but first let us look at an example. For the function $f(x) = x^2 - 50$, the derivative is $f'(x) = 2x$. This specific case is shown in Figure 5.2, with 50 itself as the initial estimate. Let us see what happens after five iterations of this procedure.

```
In[4]:=  f[x_] := x² - 50
```

```
In[5]:=  x0 = 50;
```

$$In[6]:=\ \ \texttt{x1 = N}\left[\texttt{x0} - \frac{\texttt{f[x0]}}{\texttt{f'[x0]}}\right]$$

```
Out[6]= 25.5
```

$$In[7]:=\ \ \texttt{x2 = N}\left[\texttt{x1} - \frac{\texttt{f[x1]}}{\texttt{f'[x1]}}\right]$$

```
Out[7]= 13.7304
```

$$In[8]:=\ \ \texttt{x3 = N}\left[\texttt{x2} - \frac{\texttt{f[x2]}}{\texttt{f'[x2]}}\right]$$

```
Out[8]= 8.68597
```

$$In[9]:=\ \ \texttt{x4 = N}\left[\texttt{x3} - \frac{\texttt{f[x3]}}{\texttt{f'[x3]}}\right]$$

```
Out[9]= 7.22119
```

$$In[10]:=\ \ \texttt{x5 = N}\left[\texttt{x4} - \frac{\texttt{f[x4]}}{\texttt{f'[x4]}}\right]$$

```
Out[10]= 7.07263
```

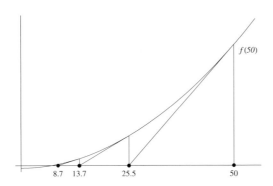

Figure 5.2: Newton's method for $f(x) = x^2 - 50$

As you can see, these values are getting closer and closer to the real square root of 50, which is approximately 7.07107.

We need to discuss how to decide when we are satisfied with the answer we have computed. First, though, note one thing: Wherever we decide to stop, say at the fifth iteration, all the previous values we computed are of no interest. So we could have avoided introducing those new names by instead just writing the following:

In[11]:= **a = 50;**

In[12]:= **a = N[a - $\dfrac{\texttt{f[a]}}{\texttt{f'[a]}}$]**

Out[12]= **25.5**

In[13]:= **a = N[a - $\dfrac{\texttt{f[a]}}{\texttt{f'[a]}}$]**

Out[13]= **13.7304**

In[14]:= **a = N[a - $\dfrac{\texttt{f[a]}}{\texttt{f'[a]}}$]**

Out[14]= **8.68597**

In[15]:= **a = N[a - $\dfrac{\texttt{f[a]}}{\texttt{f'[a]}}$]**

Out[15]= **7.22119**

In[16]:= **a = N[a - $\dfrac{\texttt{f[a]}}{\texttt{f'[a]}}$]**

Out[16]= **7.07263**

To return to the question of when to terminate the computation, one simple answer is: repeat it ten times.

In[17]:= `Do[a = N[a - f[a] / f'[a]], {10}]`

In general, Do [*expr*, {*n*}], evaluates *expr* n times. So, in this case, we can initialize a and perform the ten evaluations as follows:

In[18]:= `a = 50;`

$$Do\left[a = N\left[a - \frac{f[a]}{f'[a]}\right], \{10\}\right]$$

In[20]:= `a`

Out[20]= `7.07107`

Note that the Do loop itself yields no value (or rather, it yields the special value Null, which is a symbol *Mathematica* uses when there is no result from an evaluation; nothing is printed). But the important thing is that the Do loop assigns a value to a that is very close to the square root of 50.

The arguments of Do are the same as those of Table (see Section 3.2; see also Exercise 3 at the end of this section).

Do [*expr*, {*i*, *imin*, *imax*, *di*}]

This form repeats *expr* with variable *i* having values *imin*, *imin* + *di*, and so on, as long as the value of *imax* is not exceeded. The loop is repeated a total of | (*imax* − *imin*) / *di* | times. Furthermore, if *di* is omitted, it is assumed to be 1; and if only *i* and *imax* are given, both *imin* and *di* are assumed to be 1. For example, if we wanted to print each approximation and label it with a number, we could do that by using a compound expression inside the body of the Do loop, in this case, adding a Print statement.

In[21]:= `a = 50;`
`Do[a = N[a - f[a] / f'[a]];`
`  Print["approximation ", i, ": ", a], {i, 1, 6}]`

```
approximation 1: 25.5

approximation 2: 13.7304

approximation 3: 8.68597

approximation 4: 7.22119

approximation 5: 7.07263

approximation 6: 7.07107
```

Example: *Random permutations*

Let us look at another example of a Do loop. We will create a function `random`
`Permutation`[*lis*] that will take a list as an argument and generate a random permutation of its elements.

To build this function up step by step, we first start with a small list of ten elements.

In[23]:= `lis = Range[10]`

Out[23]= `{1, 2, 3, 4, 5, 6, 7, 8, 9, 10}`

The idea will be to choose a position within the list at random and remove the element in that position and put it into a new list `res`.

In[24]:= `rand := Random[Integer, {1, Length[lis]}]`

In[25]:= `x = Part[lis, rand]`

Out[25]= `1`

In[26]:= `res = {};`
`res = Append[res, x]`

Out[27]= `{1}`

We then repeat the above process on the remaining elements of the list.

In[28]:= `lis = Complement[lis, {x}]`

Out[28]= `{2, 3, 4, 5, 6, 7, 8, 9, 10}`

In[29]:= `x = lis[[rand]]`
`res = Append[res, x]`
`lis = Complement[lis, {x}]`

Out[29]= `8`

Out[30]= `{1, 8}`

Out[31]= `{2, 3, 4, 5, 6, 7, 9, 10}`

In this example we know explicitly how many iterations to perform in our Do loop: n times, where n is the length of the list that is being worked on.

First we clear some symbols.

In[32]:= `Clear[lis, res, x, rand];`

Now we just put the pieces of the previous computations together in one input.

```
In[33]:=  lis = Range[10];
          res = {};
          Do[
           x = Part[lis, Random[Integer, {1, Length[lis]}]];
           res = Append[res, x];
           lis = Complement[lis, {x}],
           {i, 1, 10}]
```

When we are done, the result is left in the new list res.

```
In[36]:=  res
```

```
Out[36]=  {7, 1, 2, 5, 8, 10, 4, 3, 9, 6}
```

Here then is our function randomPermutation that takes a list as an argument and generates a random permutation of that list's elements.

```
In[37]:=  Clear[res, rand, x, lis]
```

```
In[38]:=  randomPermutation[lis_] := Module[{res = {}, x, l2 = lis},
            Do[
             x = Part[l2, Random[Integer, {1, Length[l2]}]];
             res = Append[res, x];
             l2 = Complement[l2, {x}],
             {i, 1, Length[lis]}];
            res]
```

Here is a permutation of the list consisting of the first 20 integers.

```
In[39]:=  randomPermutation[Range[20]]
```

```
Out[39]=  {7, 20, 16, 8, 19, 10, 15, 17,
           13, 3, 5, 12, 1, 11, 2, 4, 6, 18, 9, 14}
```

And here is a random permutation of the lowercase letters of the English alphabet.

```
In[40]:=  alphabet = Map[FromCharacterCode, Range[97, 122]]
```

```
Out[40]=  {a, b, c, d, e, f, g, h, i, j, k,
           l, m, n, o, p, q, r, s, t, u, v, w, x, y, z}
```

```
In[41]:=  randomPermutation[alphabet]
```

```
Out[41]=  {i, l, c, s, t, d, j, q, y, f, e,
           k, x, a, h, r, o, g, u, z, v, n, p, w, b, m}
```

While loops

Let us return to Newton's method for finding roots and see how we can use a different control structure for the iteration. In the previous section on Do loops, we explicitly stopped the iteration after ten times through the loop. Ten times is okay for $f(x) = x^2 - 50$, but not always. Consider the function $x - \sin(x)$.

In[42]:= **g[x_] := x - Sin[x]**

It has a root at 0.

In[43]:= **g[0]**

Out[43]= 0

However, ten iterations of Newton's algorithm does not get us very close to it.

In[44]:= **xi = 1.0;**

$$\text{Do}\left[\text{xi = N}\left[\text{xi} - \frac{\text{g[xi]}}{\text{g'[xi]}}\right], \{10\}\right]$$

In[46]:= **xi**

Out[46]= 0.0168228

Twenty-five iterations does a bit better.

In[47]:= **xi = 1.0;**

$$\text{Do}\left[\text{xi = N}\left[\text{xi} - \frac{\text{g[xi]}}{\text{g'[xi]}}\right], \{25\}\right]$$

In[49]:= **xi**

Out[49]= 0.0000384172

In truth, no fixed number of iterations is going to do the trick for all functions. We need to iterate repeatedly until our estimate is close enough to stop. When is that? There are a number of ways to answer that question, none always best, but here is an easy one: when $f(x_i)$ is very close to zero. So, choose ϵ to be a very small number, and iterate until $|f(x_i)| < \epsilon$.

But how can we write a loop that will test some condition and stop when the condition is no longer met? The looping construct Do iterates a number of times that is fixed when the loop is begun. We need a new kind of iterative function. It is While, and it has the following form.

```
While [test, expr]
```

The first argument is the *test* or *condition*, the second the *body*. It works like this: evaluate the test; if it is true then evaluate the body and then the test again. If it is true again, then again evaluate the body and the test. Continue this way until the test evaluates to `False`. Note that the body may not be evaluated at all (if the test is false the first time), or it may be evaluated once, or a thousand times.

This is just what we want: if the estimate is not yet close enough, compute a new estimate and try again.

```
In[50]:=  f[x_] := x² - 50
```

```
In[51]:=  ε = .0001;
          xi = 50;
          While[Abs[f[xi]] > ε,
            xi = N[xi - f[xi]/f'[xi]]]
```

```
In[54]:=  xi
```

```
Out[54]=  7.07107
```

To wrap things up, let us put this all into a function.

```
In[55]:=  findRoot[fun_, init_, ε_] := Module[{xi = init},
            While[Abs[fun[xi]] > ε,
              xi = N[xi - fun[xi]/fun'[xi]]];
            xi]
```

```
In[56]:=  findRoot[f, 50, .0001]
```

```
Out[56]=  7.07107
```

Instead of setting a global variable to the final estimate, this function returns that estimate as its value. (For an explanation of why we introduced the local variable `xi`, see the end of this subsection.)

Let us work with this example a little more. Suppose we would like to know how many iterations were needed to find the answer. One possibility is to insert a `Print` to show the value of `xi` each time through the loop.

```
In[57]:=  findRoot[fun_, init_, ε_] := Module[{xi = init},
            While[Abs[fun[xi]] > ε,
              Print["x = ", xi];
              xi = N[xi - fun[xi]/fun'[xi]]];
            xi]
```

```
In[58]:= findRoot[f, 50, 0.001]

x = 50

x = 25.5

x = 13.7304

x = 8.68597

x = 7.22119

x = 7.07263

Out[58]= 7.07107
```

Counting the lines shows that the function converged after six iterations (note that we were seeing the value of xi at the *beginning* of each execution of the body). A better idea would be to have the function actually count the number of iterations and return it as part of its answer.

```
In[59]:= findRoot[fun_, init_, ε_] :=
           Module[{xi = init, count = 0}, While[Abs[fun[xi]] > ε,
             count = count + 1;
             xi = N[xi - fun[xi]/fun'[xi]]];
             {xi, count}]

In[60]:= findRoot[f, 50, 0.001]

Out[60]= {7.07107, 6}
```

Here is another question: in all these versions of findRoot, f[xi] is computed two times at each iteration, once in the condition and once in the body. In many circumstances, calls to f are very time consuming, and should be minimized. Can we arrange that f[xi] only be computed once in each iteration?

The solution to this is to create a new local variable, funxi, which *always* contains the value of fun[xi] for the current value of xi. We can ensure that it does so by recomputing it whenever xi is reassigned.

```
In[61]:= findRoot[fun_, init_, ε_] :=
           Module[{xi = init, funxi = fun[init]},
             While[Abs[funxi] > ε,
             xi = N[xi - funxi/fun'[xi]];
             funxi = fun[xi]];
             xi]
```

In all our examples, we used Module to introduce a local variable to which we assigned values in the body of the While. We did this to avoid a common error in the use of iteration: *attempting to assign to a function's argument.* For example, the following version of findRoot does not work.

In[62]:= **findRoot[fun_ , x_ , ϵ_] :=**

$$\left(\text{While}\left[\text{Abs}\left[\text{fun}\left[x\right]\right] > \epsilon,\right.\right.$$

$$\left.x = N\left[x - \frac{\text{fun}\left[x\right]}{\text{fun}'\left[x\right]}\right]\right];$$

$$\left.x\right)$$

In[63]:= **findRoot[Sin, .1, .01]**

Set::setraw : Cannot assign to raw object 0.1`. More…

General::stop : Further output of Set::setraw will
    be suppressed during this calculation. More…

Out[63]= $Aborted

What happened can be seen from the trace (of which we have only shown some) of the output.

In[64]:= **TracePrint[findRoot[Sin, .1, .01], findRoot]**

    findRoot

$$\text{While}\left[\text{Abs}\left[\text{Sin}\left[0.1\right]\right] > 0.01,\ 0.1 = N\left[0.1 - \frac{\text{Sin}\left[0.1\right]}{\text{Sin}'\left[0.1\right]}\right]\right];\ 0.1$$

Set::setraw : Cannot assign to raw object 0.1`. More…

General::stop : Further output of Set::setraw will
    be suppressed during this calculation. More…

Out[64]= $Aborted

The x in the body of findRoot is replaced by the argument .1, which is perfectly normal, leaving an expression of the form 0.1 = *something*, which is not possible. There is a way around this, using the HoldFirst attribute, but introducing local variables is much better style. It is very disconcerting, after all, to call a function and find, when it is done, that your global variables have changed values.

NestWhile and NestWhileList

Let us look again at the last version of the findRoot function we just created.

```
In[65]:= findRoot[fun_, init_, ϵ_] :=
           Module[{xi = init, funxi = fun[init]},
             While[Abs[funxi] > ϵ,
               xi = N[xi - funxi/fun'[xi]];
               funxi = fun[xi]];
             xi]
```

The While loop evaluates the body of this function (the two assignments, one to xi and the other to funxi) until the test fails. There is another function we could use to simplify this calculation – it is NestWhile.

NestWhile [*f*, *init*, *test*]

This function iterates *f* with initial value *init*, while *test* continues to be true.

Let us rewrite findRoot using NestWhile. The first argument is the function we are iterating. Here we will use a pure function that represents the Newton iteration. The second argument is the initial guess, the initial value for the iteration. The third argument to NestWhile is the test that will be performed each time through the loop until it returns False. In this case, we are setting an explicit value for ϵ of 0.001 and so our test is $|f(x)| > .001$.

```
In[66]:= f[x_] := x² - 50
```

```
In[67]:= findRoot[fun_, init_] :=
           NestWhile[# - fun[#]/fun'[#] &, N[init], Abs[fun[#]] > .001 &]
```

This computes the square root of 50 with an initial guess of 10.

```
In[68]:= findRoot[f, 10]
```

```
Out[68]= 7.07108
```

We can easily write a function findRootList based on NestWhileList that will output all the intermediate computed values.

```
In[69]:= findRootList[fun_, init_] :=
           NestWhileList[# - fun[#]/fun'[#] &, N[init], Abs[fun[#]] > .001 &]
```

In[70]:= `findRootList[f, 10]`

Out[70]= `{10., 7.5, 7.08333, 7.07108}`

Note: the functions introduced in this section are rather simplistic implementations of Newton's algorithm. At this stage, we are only interested in learning about how to use some of *Mathematica*'s procedural functions to implement the iterations here. In their current form, they have some serious limitations regarding accuracy and precision that we will address in Chapter 8, where we will discuss numerical issues in detail. The exercises at the end of this section also walk the reader through several improvements to these functions.

Exercises

1. Compute the square roots of 50 and 60 simultaneously, that is, with a single Do loop.

2. Compare the use of a Do loop with using the function Nest (see Section 4.3). In particular, compute the square root of 50 using Nest.

3. Do is closely related to Table, the main difference being that Do does not return any value, whereas Table does. Use Table instead of Do in your solution to Exercise 1. What do you get?

4. Compute Fibonacci numbers iteratively. You will need to have two variables, say this and prev, giving the two most recent Fibonacci numbers, so that after the ith iteration, this and prev have the values F_i and F_{i-1}, respectively.

5. One additional improvement can be made to the findRoot program developed in this section. Notice that the derivative of the function fun is computed each time through the loop. This is quite inefficient. Rewrite findRoot so that the derivative is computed only once and that result is used in the body of the loop.

6. Another termination criterion for root-finding is to stop when $|x_i - x_{i+1}| < \epsilon$; that is, when two successive estimates are very close. The idea is that if we are not getting much improvement, we must be very near the root. The difficulty in programming this is that we need to remember the *two* most recent estimates computed. (It is similar to computing Fibonacci numbers iteratively, as in Exercise 4.) Program findRoot this way.

7. The built-in FindRoot function is set up so that you can monitor intermediate computations using the option EvaluationMonitor.

```
In[1]:= xintermed = {};
        FindRoot[x² - 50, {x, 50},
          EvaluationMonitor :→ AppendTo[xintermed, x]];
```

```
In[3]:= xintermed
```

Out[3]= {50., 25.5, 13.7304, 8.68597,
          7.22119, 7.07263, 7.07107, 7.07107}

Modify each of the versions of findRoot presented in the text that use a Do or While loop to produce a *list* of all the estimates computed.

```
        f[x_] := x² - 50;
        findRootList[f, 50, 0.001]
```

{50, 25.5, 13.7304, 8.68597, 7.22119, 7.07263, 7.07107, 7.07107}

8. To guard against starting with a poor choice of initial value, modify findRootList to take, as an argument, a *list* of initial values, and simultaneously compute approximations for each until one converges; then return that one.

9. The *bisection method* is quite useful for finding roots of functions. If a continuous function $f(x)$ is such that $f(a) < 0$ and $f(b) > 0$ for two real numbers a and b, then, as a consequence of the Intermediate Value Theorem of calculus, a root of f must occur between a and b. If f is now evaluated at the midpoint of a and b, and if $f(a + b)/2 < 0$, then the root must occur between $(a + b)/2$ and b; if not, then it occurs between a and $(a + b)/2$. This bisection can be repeated until a root is found to any specified tolerance.
   Define bisect [f, {a, b, ϵ}] to compute a root of f, within ϵ, using the bisection method. You should give it two initial values a and b and assume that $f(a) \cdot f(b) < 0$; that is, one of $f(a)$ and $f(b)$ is positive and the other is negative.

10. Using a While loop, write a function gcd [m, n] that computes the greatest common divisor of m and n. The Euclidean algorithm for computing the gcd of two numbers m and n, assumed to be positive integers, sets $m = n$, and $n = m \bmod n$. It iterates this process until $n = 0$, at which point the gcd of m and n is left in the value of m.

11. Create a procedural definition for each of the following functions, first by creating a new list and filling in the elements. For each function, create a definition using a Do loop and another using Table. For example, the following function first creates an array of the same dimension as mat, but consisting of 0s. Then inside the Do loop it assigns the element in position {j, i} in mat to position {i, j} in matA, effectively

performing a transpose operation. Finally, it returns matA, since the Do loop itself does not return a value.

```
In[4]:=  transpose[mat_] :=
            Module[{matA = Table[Table[0, {n = Length[mat]}],
                {m = Length[mat[[1]]]}]}, Do[matA[[i, j]] = mat[[j, i]],
              {i, 1, m},
              {j, 1, n}];
            matA]
```

```
In[5]:=  mat1 = {{a, b, c}, {d, e, f}, {h, k, l}};
```

```
In[6]:=  MatrixForm[mat1]
```

Out[6]//MatrixForm=
$$\begin{pmatrix} a & b & c \\ d & e & f \\ h & k & l \end{pmatrix}$$

```
In[7]:=  MatrixForm[transpose[mat1]]
```

Out[7]//MatrixForm=
$$\begin{pmatrix} a & d & h \\ b & e & k \\ c & f & l \end{pmatrix}$$

Note this same computation could be performed with what is referred to as a *structured iteration* using Table.

```
In[8]:=  transposeStruc[mat_] :=
            Module[
              {matA = Table[0, {n = Length[mat]}, {m = Length[mat[[1]]]}]},
              Table[matA[[i, j]] = mat[[j, i]], {i, m}, {j, n}]
            ]
```

```
In[9]:=  transposeStruc[mat1] // MatrixForm
```

Out[9]//MatrixForm=
$$\begin{pmatrix} a & d & h \\ b & e & k \\ c & f & l \end{pmatrix}$$

a. Create the function reverse [*vec*], which reverses the elements in the list *vec*.

b. Create a function rotateRight [*vec*, *n*], where *vec* is a vector and *n* is a (positive or negative) integer.

   c. Create a procedural implementation of `rotateRows`, which could be defined in this functional way:

In[10]:= `rotateRows [mat_]  := Map [(rotateRight [mat [[#]], #-1]) &,`
                          `Range [1, Length [mat]]]`

That is, it rotates the *i*th row of mat *i* − 1 places to the right.

   d. Create a procedural function `rotateRowsByS`, which could be defined in this functional way:

In[11]:= `rotateRowsByS[mat_, S_] /; Length[mat] == Length[S] :=`
      `Map [ (rotateRight [mat⟦#1⟧, S⟦#1⟧] &), Range[1, Length[mat]]]`

That is, it rotates the *i*th row of matA by the amount `S [[i]]`.

   e. Create a function `compress [lisA,  lisB]`, where *lisA* and *lisB* are lists of equal length, and *lisB* contains only Boolean values (`False` and `True`), selects out of *lisA* those elements corresponding to `True` in *lisB*. For example, the result of `compress [{a,b,c,d,e},{True,True,False,False,True}]` should be `{a,b,e}`. To know what size list to create, you will first need to count the occurrences of `True` in *lisB*.

5.3 Flow control

Conditional functions

In this section we will look at functions that control the flow of execution of an evaluation. Perhaps the simplest and easiest to understand of these class of functions is the `If` statement. Here is a rather simplistic implementation of the absolute value function, using `If`.

In[1]:= `abs [x_] := If [x ≥ 0, x, -x]`

In[2]:= `abs [-4]`

Out[2]= 4

   The `If` function takes three arguments: the first is a test; if the test evaluates to `True`, then the second argument is evaluated; if the test evaluates to `False`, then the third argument of the `If` is evaluated.

`If` can also be used in conjunction with the higher-order functions discussed in Chapter 4 to achieve greater flexibility. For example, `abs` can now be mapped over a list of numbers.

In[3]:= `Map[abs, {-2, -1, 0, 1, 2}]`

Out[3]= `{2, 1, 0, 1, 2}`

By default, this function will not *automatically* map across lists.

In[4]:= `abs[{-2, -1, 0, 1, 2}]`

Out[4]= `If[{-2, -1, 0, 1, 2} ≥ 0, {-2, -1, 0, 1, 2}, -{-2, -1, 0, 1, 2}]`

If you want `abs` to behave like many of the built-in functions and automatically map across lists when they are given as the argument to `abs`, you need to make the function `Listable` as described in Sections 2.4 and 4.2.

In[5]:= `SetAttributes[abs, Listable]`

In[6]:= `abs[{-2, -1, 0, 1, 2}]`

Out[6]= `{2, 1, 0, 1, 2}`

Here are some additional examples using `If`. Given a list, the following function adds 1 to all the *numeric* quantities occurring in it.

In[7]:= `incrementNumbers[lis_] := Map[If[NumericQ[#1], #+1, #] &, lis]`

In[8]:= `incrementNumbers[{4, f, 6.1 + I, π}]`

Out[8]= `{5, f, 7.1 + i, 1 + π}`

Here is a function that divides 100 by every number in a numerical list, except 0s.

In[9]:= $\texttt{divide100By[lis\_] := Map}\left[\texttt{If}\left[\texttt{\# == 0, \#, } \dfrac{100}{\#}\right] \texttt{ \&, lis}\right]$

In[10]:= `divide100By[{5, π, 0}]`

Out[10]= $\left\{20, \dfrac{100}{\pi}, 0\right\}$

Here is a function to remove consecutive occurrences of the same value.

In[11]:= `removeRepetitions[lis_] :=`
`        Fold[If[#2 == Last[#1], #1, Append[#1, #2]] &,`
`        {First[lis]}, Rest[lis]]`

In[12]:= `removeRepetitions[{0, 1, 1, 2, 2, 2, 1, 1}]`

Out[12]= `{0, 1, 2, 1}`

As a final example of `If`, the function `applyChar` takes a list as an argument. This list must contain, first, a character, which must be one of `"+"`, `"-"`, `"*"`, or `"/"`; that character must be followed by all numbers. `applyChar` applies the function named by the character to the elements of the rest of the list.

```
In[13]:= applyChar[lis_] := Module[{op = First[lis], nums = Rest[lis]},
            If[op == "+", Apply[Plus, nums],
             If[op == "-", Apply[Subtract, nums],
              If[op == "*", Apply[Times, nums],
               If[op == "/", Apply[Divide, nums],
                Print["Bad argument to applyChar"]]]]]]
```

```
In[14]:= applyChar[{"+", 1, 2, 3, 4}]
```

```
Out[14]= 10
```

(Recall the `Module` function, which permits us to introduce local variables. In this case, it saves us from having to write `First [lis]` and `Rest [lis]` several times each.)

Even though the argument list in `applyChar` *must* contain one of the four operators as its first element, it is still best to check for it explicitly; otherwise, if the condition is ever violated, the results may be very mysterious. We have used the `Print` function, which prints all of its arguments (of which it can have an arbitrary number) and then skips to a new line.

```
In[15]:= applyChar[{"^", 2, 5, 10}]
```

```
Bad argument to applyChar
```

Notice that what we have in this code is several nested `If`s, each occurring in the false part of the previous one. Thus, the structure of the computation is a sequence of tests of predicates until one is found to be true, at which point a result can be computed. Such a sequence of *cascading* `If` statements can get quite long, and the indentation can become unmanageable, so it is conventional to violate the usual rule for indenting `If` expressions and indent this type of structure as follows:

```
If [cond₁, result₁,
  If [cond₂, result₂,
    ⋮
    If [condₙ, resultₙ,
            resultₙ₊₁] …]]
```

Conditional definitions can be written using another construct in *Mathematica*, the `Condition` operator, `/;`. For example, the `abs` function can be entered (using several definitions) as follows:

In[16]:= **Clear[abs]**

In[17]:= **abs[x_] := x /; x ≥ 0**

In[18]:= **abs[x_] := -x /; x < 0**

The first definition should be interpreted as "abs [x] is equal to x whenever (or under the condition that) x is greater than or equal to 0" and the second definition as "abs [x] is equal to the opposite of x whenever x is less than 0."

The conditions on the right-hand side of the rules can, in fact, be entered on the left-hand side of these definitions as follows:

In[19]:= **abs[x_ /; x ≥ 0] := x**

In[20]:= **abs[x_ /; x < 0] := -x**

This last notation has the advantage of preventing the right-hand side of our definitions from being evaluated whenever the pattern on the left does not match.

In[21]:= **abs[-4]**

Out[21]= 4

In[22]:= **abs[z]**

Out[22]= abs[z]

This use of multiple rules associated with the symbol abs is a very useful and powerful means of associating rules with symbols under user-defined conditions and we turn to it next.

Multiclause definitions

The abs function defined above is fine for integers and real number arguments, but, since the complex numbers cannot be ordered, the initial test comparing a complex number argument with 0 will fail.

In[23]:= **abs[3 + 4 I]**

        GreaterEqual::nord :
         Invalid comparison with 3 + 4 i attempted. More…

        Less::nord : Invalid comparison with 3 + 4 i attempted. More…

Out[23]= abs[3 + 4 i]

We can solve this problem by providing an additional definition for abs.

```
In[24]:=  Clear[abs];
          abs[x_] := Sqrt[Re[x]² + Im[x]²] /; x ∈ Complexes;
          abs[x_] := x /; x ≥ 0
          abs[x_] := -x /; x < 0
```

The test as the first argument of If on the right-hand side checks to see if x is an element of the domain of complex numbers and, if it is, then $\sqrt{re(x)^2 + im(x)^2}$ is computed. If x is not complex, nothing is done, but then the other definition for abs will be invoked.

```
In[28]:=  abs[3 + 4 I]
```

```
Out[28]=  5
```

```
In[29]:=  abs[-3]
```

```
Out[29]=  3
```

The condition itself can appear on the left-hand side of the function definition, as part of the pattern match. Here is a slight variation on the abs definition.

```
In[30]:=  Clear[abs]
          abs[x_] := If[x ≥ 0, x, -x]
          abs[x_ /; x ∈ Complexes] := Sqrt[Re[x]² + Im[x]²]
```

```
In[33]:=  abs[3 + 4 I]
```

```
Out[33]=  5
```

```
In[34]:=  abs[-3]
```

```
Out[34]=  3
```

We may want to add an additional rule for symbols.

```
In[35]:=  abs[x_ /; Head[x] == Symbol] := x
```

```
In[36]:=  abs[z]
```

```
Out[36]=  z
```

Such a definition is called a *multiclause definition*. In this case we have associated three rules with abs; two are rather specific and will only be applied if the argument to abs passes the conditions specified. If neither of those conditions are met, then the most general rule (the one with no conditions on x) will be used.

Which and Switch

Recall the earlier definition of applyChar defined using cascading Ifs.

```
In[37]:= applyChar[lis_] := Module[{op = First[lis], nums = Rest[lis]},
          If[op == "+", Apply[Plus, nums],
           If[op == "-", Apply[Subtract, nums],
            If[op == "*", Apply[Times, nums],
             If[op == "/", Apply[Divide, nums],
              Print["Bad argument to applyChar"]]]]]]
```

Needless to say, this is a little difficult to read and figure out which clause goes with which If. Fortunately, cascaded Ifs are so common that *Mathematica* provides a more direct way of writing them, using the function Which.

```
Which[cond₁,  result₁,
       cond₂,  result₂,
         ⋮
       condₙ,  resultₙ,
       True,   resultₙ₊₁]
```

This has exactly the same effect as the cascaded If expression above: it tests each condition in turn, and, when it finds an i such that $cond_i$ is true, it returns $result_i$ as the result of the Which expression itself. If none of the conditions turns out to be true, then it will test the final "condition," namely the expression True, which always evaluates to true, and it will then return $result_{n+1}$.

applyChar can now be written more neatly.

```
In[38]:= applyChar[lis_] := Module[{op = First[lis], nums = Rest[lis]},
          Which[op == "+", Apply[Plus, nums],
           op == "-", Apply[Subtract, nums],
           op == "*", Apply[Times, nums],
           op == "/", Apply[Divide, nums],
           True, Print["Bad argument to applyChar"]]]
```

One last form deserves mention. Our use of the Which command is still quite special, in that it consists of a simple sequence of comparisons between a variable and a constant. Since this is also a common form, *Mathematica* again provides a special function for it, called Switch.

```
Switch[expr,
    pattern₁,   result₁,
    pattern₂,   result₂,
      ⋮
    patternₙ,   resultₙ,
    _,   resultₙ₊₁
    ]
```

This evaluates *expr* and then checks each pattern, in order, to see whether *expr* matches; as soon as *expr* matches one, say *patternᵢ*, it returns the value of *resultᵢ*. Of course, if none of the patterns *pattern₁*, ..., *patternₙ* matches, the _ certainly will.

If all the patterns happen to be constants, the Switch expression is equivalent to the following Which expression.

```
Which[expr == pattern₁,   result₁,
      expr == pattern₂,   result₂,
        ⋮
      expr == patternₙ,   resultₙ,
      True,  resultₙ₊₁
      ]
```

Here, then, is our final version of applyChar.

```
In[39]:= applyChar[lis_] := Module[{op = First[lis], nums = Rest[lis]},
           Switch[op,
               "+", Apply[Plus, nums],
               "-", Apply[Subtract, nums],
               "*", Apply[Times, nums],
               "/", Apply[Divide, nums],
               _, Print["Bad argument to ApplyChar"]
           ]
         ]
```

Notice that Switch uses the blank character, _, for the final, or *default* case, just as Which uses the always-true expression True. We will have much more to say about patterns and pattern matching in Chapter 6.

Piecewise

Several of the functions we created in previous sections could be caste as piecewise-defined functions. Although technically not a procedural construct, Piecewise (new in Version 5.1) is designed specifically for such problems. The syntax is Piecewise[{{e_1, c_1}, ..., {e_n, c_n}}] which outputs e_1 if c_1 is true, e_2 if c_2 is true, ... , e_n if c_n is true, and 0 otherwise (the default).

So, for example, here is the definition for the absolute value function given as a piecewise object.

In[40]:= **abspw[x_] := Piecewise[{{x, x ≥ 0}, {-x, x < 0}}]**

Piecewise objects display as you would expect in traditional mathematical notation.

In[41]:= **abspw[x]**

Out[41]=
$$\begin{cases} x & x \geq 0 \\ -x & x < 0 \end{cases}$$

Furthermore, Piecewise is fully integrated with the algebraic, symbolic, and graphical functions in *Mathematica* and so is preferable to other approaches.

In[42]:= **Integrate[abspw[x], {x, -1, 1}]**

Out[42]= 1

In[43]:= **D[abspw[x], x]**

Out[43]=
$$\begin{cases} -1 & x < 0 \\ 1 & x > 0 \\ \text{Indeterminate} & \text{True} \end{cases}$$

In[44]:= **Plot[abspw[x], {x, -2, 2}];**

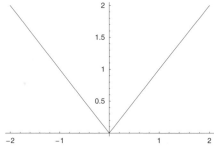

Notice that the definition of the absolute value function given in terms of conditionals is not fully supported by many of the built-in functions.

In[45]:= **Clear[abs]**

In[46]:= **abs[x_] := x /; x ≥ 0**

In[47]:= **abs[x_] := -x /; x < 0**

In[48]:= **Integrate[abs[x], {x, -1, 1}]**

Out[48]= $\int_{-1}^{1} \text{abs}[x]\, dx$

In[49]:= **D[abs[x], x]**

Out[49]= abs′[x]

Argument checking

Often, when we write functions, we know ahead of time that the definitions we give them are valid only for certain kinds of inputs. For example, the following definition for the factorial function only makes sense for positive integers.

In[50]:= **fact[0] = 1;**
　　　　　fact[n_] := n fact[n - 1]

In[52]:= **fact[5]**

Out[52]= 120

If we were to give `fact` an argument that was not a positive integer, the recursion could run away from us.

In[53]:= **fact[3.4]**

　　　　$RecursionLimit::reclim :
　　　　　Recursion depth of 256 exceeded. More…

Out[53]= $-2.729671867921455 \times 10^{494}$ Hold[fact[-250.6 - 1]]

Conditionals are a convenient way of checking that the arguments to our functions pass some criteria. For example, there are several ways that we could make the `fact` function valid only under the condition that its argument is a positive integer. Here is how we might approach it using the `If` construct to test that *n* passes the appropriate criteria.

In[54]:= **Clear[fact]**

In[55]:= **fact[0] = 1;**

In[56]:= **fact[n_] := If[IntegerQ[n] && n > 0, n fact[n - 1]]**

In[57]:= **{fact[5], fact[-3], fact[2.4]}**

Out[57]= {120, Null, Null}

We see that the function works fine for positive integers, but since we did not give an alternative condition to the `If` function, nothing is returned (technically `Null` is returned) when the test condition fails.

Let us define a message that will be output in the case that the argument to `fact` fails the positive integer test.

```
In[58]:= fact::noint = "Argument `1` is not a positive integer.";
```

We then use `Message` as the third argument to our `If`, so that when the condition fails the message will be triggered. Essentially `Message[messname, e₁, e₂, ...]` prints using `StringForm[messg, e₁, e₂, ...]`, where *messg* is the value of the message name and the e_i are substituted in for any expressions of the form `` `i` ``. In the above example, the message name is `noint` and its value is the string beginning with `"Argument..."`. In this example, the value of n will be substituted into the string where the `` `1` `` occurs.

```
In[59]:= fact[n_] := If[IntegerQ[n] && n > 0,
            n fact[n - 1],
            Message[fact::noint, n]]
```

```
In[60]:= fact[-3]

         fact::noint : Argument -3 is not a positive integer.
```

Of course, there are a variety of ways of using conditionals to do argument checking. Here are three more implementations, without the messaging.

```
In[61]:= fact1[0] = 1;
         fact1[n_] := n fact1[n - 1] /; (IntegerQ[n] && n > 0)
```

```
In[63]:= {fact1[5], fact1[2.4]}
Out[63]= {120, fact1[2.4]}
```

```
In[64]:= fact2[0] = 1;
         fact2[n_ /; (IntegerQ[n] && n > 0)] := n fact2[n - 1]
```

```
In[66]:= {fact2[5], fact2[2.4]}
Out[66]= {120, fact2[2.4]}
```

```
In[67]:= fact3[0] = 1;
         fact3[n_ ? IntegerQ /; n > 0] := n fact3[n - 1]
```

```
In[69]:= {fact3[5], fact3[2.4]}
Out[69]= {120, fact3[2.4]}
```

Summary

When writing a function whose result must be computed differently, depending upon the values of its arguments, you have a choice:

1. Use a multiclause definition, where the conditions are optional, and may appear after the right-hand sides.

$f[pattern_1\_] \; / ; \; cond_1 \; := \; rhs_1$

$\vdots$

$f[pattern_n\_] \; / ; \; cond_n \; := \; rhs_n$

2. Use a single-clause definition with a conditional expression.

```
f [x_]  :=  If [cond₁,  rhs₁,
            ⋮
                If [condₙ,  rhsₙ,
                rhsₙ₊₁]  ⋯]
```

In the latter case, if n is greater than two, use the equivalent Which expression; and if all conditions have the form $x \; == \; const_i$, for a given variable x and some constants $const_i$, use the Switch function.

The next section contains several applications that use various combinations of the procedural constructs we have learned in this chapter.

Exercises

1. Write the function signum [x] which, when applied to an integer x, returns -1, 0, or 1, according as x is less than, equal to, or greater than, 0. Write it in three ways: using three clauses, using a single clause with If, and using a single clause with Which.

2. Extend signum from Exercise 1 to apply to both integers and reals; again, write it in three ways (though you may use more than three clauses for the multiclause version).

3. Write applyChar in multiclause form, using pattern matching on the first element of its argument.

4. Use `If` in conjunction with `Map` or `Fold` to define the following functions:

   a. In a list of numbers, double all the positive numbers, but leave the negative numbers alone.

   b. `remove3Repetitions` is like `removeRepetitions` except that it only alters three or more consecutive occurrences, changing them to two occurrences; if there are only two occurrences to begin with, they are left alone. For example, `remove3Repetitions[{0,1,1,2,2,2,1}]` will return `{0,1,1,2,2,1}`.

   c. Add the elements of a list in consecutive order, but never let the sum go below 0.

   In[1]:= `positiveSum[{5, 3, -13, 7, -3, 2}]`

   Out[1]= `6`

   Since the -13 caused the sum to go below 0, it was instead put back to 0 and the summation continued from there.

5. Using `NestWhileList`, write a function `CollatzSequence[n]` that produces the Collatz sequence for any positive integer n. The Collatz sequence is generated as follows: starting with a number n, if it is even, then output $\frac{n}{2}$; if n is odd, then output $3n + 1$. Iterate this process while $n \neq 1$.

5.4 Examples

Sieve of Eratosthenes

One of the oldest algorithms in the history of computing is the Sieve of Eratosthenes. Named after the famous Greek astronomer Eratosthenes (*ca.* 276 – *ca.* 194 BC), this method is used to find all prime numbers below a given number n. The great feature of this algorithm is that it finds prime numbers without doing any divisions – an operation that took considerable skill and concentration before the introduction of the Arabic numeral system. In fact, its only operations are addition and component assignment.

   The algorithm can be summarized as follows: to find all the prime numbers less than an integer n:

   • create a list of the integers 1 through n

   • starting with $p = 2$, cross out all multiples of p

- increment p (that is, add 1 to p) and cross out all multiples of p

- repeat the previous two steps until $p > \sqrt{n}$.

You should convince yourself that the numbers that are left after all the crossings out are in fact the primes less than n. This algorithm lends itself very well to a procedural approach, so let us walk through the steps.

We will use a For structure for this problem. The syntax is For [*start*, *test*, *incr*, *body*], where *start* will first be evaluated (initializing values), and then *incr* and *body* will be repeatedly evaluated until *test* fails.

1. Let lis be a list containing all the integers between 1 and n.

```
In[1]:=  n = 20;
         lis = Range[n]
```

```
Out[2]=  {1, 2, 3, 4, 5, 6, 7, 8, 9, 10,
          11, 12, 13, 14, 15, 16, 17, 18, 19, 20}
```

2. Let $p = 2$. Repeat the following two steps:

   - Starting at position $2p$, "cross out" every pth value in lis. We will assign 1 to lis at positions $2p$, $3p$, and the 1 will represent a crossed out value.

```
In[3]:=  p = 2;
         Do[lis[[i]] = 1, {i, 2 p, n, p}]
```

```
In[5]:=  lis
```

```
Out[5]=  {1, 2, 3, 1, 5, 1, 7, 1, 9, 1, 11, 1, 13, 1, 15, 1, 17, 1, 19, 1}
```

   - While $p \leq \sqrt{n}$, increment p by 1, until lis [[p]] is not 1, or until $p = n + 1$.

```
In[6]:=  n = 20;
         lis = Range[n];
         For[p = 2,
          p ≠ 1 && p ≤ Floor[Sqrt[n]],
          p++,
          Do[lis[[i]] = 1, {i, 2 p, n, p}]]
```

3. The non-1s in lis are all the prime numbers less than or equal to n.

```
In[9]:=  DeleteCases[lis, 1]
```

```
Out[9]=  {2, 3, 5, 7, 11, 13, 17, 19}
```

Let us put these steps together in our function `Sieve`.

```
In[10]:= Clear[n, p, lis]
```

```
In[11]:= Sieve[n_Integer] := Module[{lis = Range[n], p},
           For[p = 2,
            p ≠ 1 && p ≤ Floor[Sqrt[n]],
            p++,
            Do[lis[[i]] = 1, {i, 2 p, n, p}]];
           DeleteCases[lis, 1]
          ]
```

Here are a few simple tests to check the correctness of our function. First we check that `Sieve` produces the correct number of primes less than a large integer.

```
In[12]:= Length[Sieve[10^5]]
```

```
Out[12]= 9592
```

The built-in `PrimePi [x]` gives the number of primes $\pi(x)$ less than or equal to x.

```
In[13]:= PrimePi[10^5]
```

```
Out[13]= 9592
```

Next we do some simple timing tests to check the efficiency of this algorithm against the built-in functions that are optimized for this task.

```
In[14]:= Sieve[10^6]; // Timing
```

```
Out[14]= {13.62 Second, Null}
```

```
In[15]:= Timing[Table[Prime[i], {i, 10^6}];]
```

```
Out[15]= {5.648 Second, Null}
```

```
In[16]:= Timing[Map[Prime, Range[10^6]];]
```

```
Out[16]= {5.628 Second, Null}
```

For numbers in this range (less than about 10^6), sieving is fairly efficient – its speed is within an order of magnitude of the built-in algorithms. But, beyond this range, it does tend to bog down and it would be best to consider specialized algorithms that are asymptotically fast (for large integers, `PrimePi` uses an algorithm due to Lagarias, Miller, and Odlyzko that is based on estimates of the density of primes).

Classifying points

Quadrants in the Euclidean plane are conventionally numbered counterclockwise from quadrant 1 (x and y positive) to quadrant 4 (x positive, y negative). The function `point Loc [{x,y}]` will compute the classification of point (x, y), according to Table 5.1.

Point	Classification
(0, 0)	0
$y = 0$ (on the x-axis)	-1
$x = 0$ (on the y-axis)	-2
Quadrant 1	1
Quadrant 2	2
Quadrant 3	3
Quadrant 4	4

Table 5.1: Quadrant classification

We will use this problem to illustrate the features covered in this chapter, by giving a number of different solutions, using multiclause function definitions with predicates, single-clause definitions with `If` and its relatives, and combinations of the two.

Perhaps the first solution that suggests itself is one that uses a clause for each of the cases above.

```
In[17]:=  pointLoc[{0, 0}] := 0
          pointLoc[{x_, 0}] := -1
          pointLoc[{0, y_}] := -2
          pointLoc[{x_, y_}] := 1 /; x > 0 && y > 0
          pointLoc[{x_, y_}] := 2 /; x < 0 && y > 0
          pointLoc[{x_, y_}] := 3 /; x < 0 && y < 0
          pointLoc[{x_, y_}] := 4  (* /; x>0 && y<0 *)
```

It is a good idea to include the last condition as a comment, rather than as a condition in the code, because *Mathematica* would not realize that the condition has to be true at that point and would check it anyway.

We will use the following list of points as our test cases.

```
In[24]:=  pts =
             {{0, 0}, {4, 0}, {0, 1.3}, {2, 4}, {-2, 4}, {-2, -4}, {2, -4}};

In[25]:=  Map[pointLoc, pts]

Out[25]=  {0, -1, -2, 1, 2, 3, 4}
```

Translated directly to a one-clause definition using If, this becomes:

```
In[26]:=  pointLoc[{x_, y_}] :=
            If[x == 0 && y == 0, 0,
              If[y == 0, -1,
                If[x == 0, -2,
                  If[x > 0 && y > 0, 1,
                    If[x < 0 && y > 0, 2,
                      If[x < 0 && y < 0, 3, 4]]]]]]
```

```
In[27]:=  Map[pointLoc, pts]
```

```
Out[27]=  {0, -1, -2, 1, 2, 3, 4}
```

Actually, a more likely solution here uses Which.

```
In[28]:=  pointLoc[{x_, y_}] := Which[
            x == 0 && y == 0, 0,
            y == 0, -1,
            x == 0, -2,
            x > 0 && y > 0, 1,
            x < 0 && y > 0, 2,
            x < 0 && y < 0, 3,
            True (* x>0&&y<0 *), 4]
```

```
In[29]:=  Map[pointLoc, pts]
```

```
Out[29]=  {0, -1, -2, 1, 2, 3, 4}
```

```
In[30]:=  pointLoc[{-5, -9}]
```

```
Out[30]=  3
```

All of our solutions so far suffer from a certain degree of inefficiency, because of repeated comparisons of a single value with 0. Take the last solution as an example, and suppose the argument is $(-5,-9)$. It will require five comparisons of -5 with 0 and three comparisons of -9 with 0 to obtain this result. Specifically:

1. evaluate $x == 0$; since it is false, the associated $y == 0$ will not be evaluated, and we next

2. evaluate $y == 0$ on the following line; since it is false,

3. evaluate $x == 0$ on the third line; since it is false,

4. evaluate $x > 0$ on next line; since it is false, the associated $y > 0$ will not be evaluated, and we next,

5. evaluate $x < 0$ on the next line; since it is true, we do,

6. the y > 0 comparison, which is false, so we next,

7. evaluate x < 0 on the next line; since it is true, we then evaluate y < 0, which is also true, so we return the answer 3.

How can we improve this? By nesting conditional expressions inside other conditional expressions. In particular, as soon as we discover that x is less than, greater than, or equal to 0, we should make maximum use of that fact without rechecking it. That is what the following pointLoc function does.

```
In[31]:= pointLoc[{x_, y_}] :=
        Which[x == 0, If[y == 0, 0, -2],
          x > 0, Which[y > 0, 1,
                       y < 0, 4,
                       True (* y==0 *), -1],
          True, (* x<0 *)
          Which[y < 0, 3,
                y > 0, 2,
                True (* y==0 *), -1]
        ]
```

Let us count up the comparisons for (−5, −9) this time: (*i*) evaluate x == 0; since it is false, we next, (*ii*) evaluate x > 0; since it is false, we go to the third branch of the Which, evaluate True, which is, of course, true; then, (*iii*) evaluate y < 0, which is true, and we return 3. Thus, we made only three comparisons – a substantial improvement.

When pattern matching is used, as in our first, multiclause solution, efficiency calculations are more difficult. It would be inaccurate to say that *Mathematica* has to compare x and y to 0 to tell whether the first clause applies; what actually happens is more complex. What is true, however, is that it will do the comparisons indicated in the last four clauses. So, even if we discount the first three clauses with argument (−5, −9), some extra comparisons are done. Specifically: (*i*) the comparison x > 0 is done; then, (*ii*) x < 0 and (*iii*) y > 0; then, (*iv*) x < 0 and (*v*) y < 0. This can be avoided by using conditional expressions *within* clauses.

```
In[32]:= pointLoc[{0, 0}] := 0
        pointLoc[{x_, 0}] := -1
        pointLoc[{0, y_}] := -2
        pointLoc[{x_, y_}] := If[x < 0, 2, 1] /; y > 0
        pointLoc[{x_, y_}] := If[x < 0, 3, 4] (* /; y<0 *)
```

Now, no redundant comparisons are done. For (−5, −9), since y > 0 fails, the fourth clause is not used, so the x > 0 comparison in it is not done. Only the single x < 0 comparison in the final clause is done, for a total of two comparisons.

Having done all these versions of pointLoc, we would be remiss if we did not remind the reader of a basic fact of life in programming: your time is more valuable than your computer's time. You should not be worrying about how slow a function is until there is a demonstrated need to worry. Far more important is the clarity and simplicity of the code, since this will determine how much time you (or another programmer) will have to spend when it comes time to modify it. In the case of pointLoc, we would argue that we got lucky and found a version (the final one) that wins on both counts (if only programming were always like that!).

Finally, a technical, but potentially important, point: Not all of the versions of pointLoc work exactly the same. The integer 0, as a pattern, does not match the real number 0.0, since they have different heads. Thus, using the last version as an example, pointLoc[{0.0,0.0}] returns 4.

In[37]:= **pointLoc[{0.0, 0.0}]**

Out[37]= 4

See Section 6.2 for a discussion of alternatives, which allows us to efficiently deal with these various cases.

Exercises

1. Using an If function, write a function gcd[*m*,*n*] that implements the Euclidean algorithm (see Exercise 10 of Section 5.2) for finding the greatest common divisor of *m* and *n*.

2. Use Piecewise to define the pointLoc function given in this section.

3. Extend pointLoc to three dimensions, following this rule: for point (x, y, z), if $z \geq 0$, then give the same classification as (x, y), with the exception that zero is treated as a positive number (so the only classifications are 1, 2, 3, and 4); if $z < 0$, add 4 to the classification of (x, y) (with the same exception). For example, $(1, 0, 1)$ is in octant 1, and $(0, -3, -3)$ is in octant 8. pointLoc should work for points in two or three dimensions.

6 Rule-based programming

The use of rules to transform expressions from one form to another is one of the most powerful and useful tools available in the *Mathematica* programming language. The thousands of rules built in to *Mathematica* can be expanded limitlessly through the creation of user-defined rules. Rules can be created to change the form of expressions, to filter data based on some criteria, and can be set up to apply to broad classes of expressions or limited to certain narrow domains through the use of appropriate pattern matching techniques. These rules can perform many of the tasks normally associated with more traditional programming constructs, such as we have discussed in the chapters on procedural and functional programming. In this chapter we will discuss the structure and application of rules to common programming tasks and look at their application in some concrete examples.

6.1 Introduction

Users of *Mathematica* typically first encounter rules as the output to many built-in functions. For example, the `Solve` function returns its solutions as a list of rules.

$In[1]:=$ **soln = Solve[a x^2 + b x + c == 0, x]**

$Out[1]=$ $\left\{\left\{x \to \dfrac{-b - \sqrt{b^2 - 4\,a\,c}}{2\,a}\right\}, \left\{x \to \dfrac{-b + \sqrt{b^2 - 4\,a\,c}}{2\,a}\right\}\right\}$

They are also used to specify options for functions and replacement rules in many kinds of computations.

$In[2]:=$ **FactorInteger[5, GaussianIntegers → True]**

$Out[2]=$ **{{-i, 1}, {1 + 2 i, 1}, {2 + i, 1}}**

$In[3]:=$ **StringReplace["acgttttccctgagcataaaaacccagcaatacg",**
{"ca" → "CA", "tt" → "TT"}]

$Out[3]=$ **acgTTTTccctgagCAtaaaaaccCAgCAatacg**

When you define a function via an assignment such as the function f below, you are defining a rule that says whenever f is given an argument, it should be replaced with that argument squared. This rule will be applied automatically whenever you evaluate f [*anything*].

In[4]:= **f [x_] := x²**

In[5]:= **f [bob]**

Out[5]= bob²

On the other hand, you can set up rules to be applied on demand by using the replacement operator ReplaceAll, written in shorthand notation as /. . These rules can then be used to transform one expression into another. For example, the following rule is used to extract the real and imaginary parts of a complex number and convert it to an ordered pair.

In[6]:= **3 + 4 i /. Complex[a_, b_] → {a, b}**

Out[6]= {3, 4}

This rule reverses the elements in each ordered pair.

In[7]:= **{{α, 1}, {β, 2}, {γ, 3}} /. {x_, y_} → {y, x}**

Out[7]= {{1, α}, {2, β}, {3, γ}}

And here is a rule that turns each of the superscripts in the polynomial below into a subscript.

In[8]:= **poly = Factor[1 - x¹¹]**

Out[8]= $- (-1 + x) (1 + x + x^2 + x^3 + x^4 + x^5 + x^6 + x^7 + x^8 + x^9 + x^{10})$

In[9]:= **ToBoxes[poly] /. SuperscriptBox → SubscriptBox // DisplayForm**

Out[9]//DisplayForm=

$- (-1 + x) (1 + x + x_2 + x_3 + x_4 + x_5 + x_6 + x_7 + x_8 + x_9 + x_{10})$

Rule-based programming is such a useful construct for manipulating lists and arbitrary expressions that no user of *Mathematica* should be without a working knowledge of this paradigm. This chapter gives a thorough introduction to pattern matching and then proceeds to rule-based programs, many of which were introduced earlier as functional or procedural programs.

6.2 Patterns

Blanks

When you make an assignment to a symbol, like x=4, you are making a rule that should be applied to the literal expression x. Loosely speaking, the rule says, replace x with the value 4 whenever x is encountered. We have seen that you can also define functions of one or more arguments that allow you to substitute arbitrary expressions for those arguments.

In[1]:= **f[x_] := x + 1**

The left-hand side of the above assignment is a pattern. It contains a blank (underscore) which can stand for any expression, not just the literal expression x.

In[2]:= **f[ζ]**

Out[2]= 1 + ζ

In[3]:= **f[bob]**

Out[3]= 1 + bob

While any specific expression can be pattern matched (because any object must match itself), we usually want to be able to pattern match large classes of expressions (for example, a sequence of expressions or expressions having Integer as the head). For this purpose, *patterns* are defined as expressions that may contain *blanks*. That is to say, a pattern may contain one of the following: a single (_) blank, a double (__) blank, or a triple (___) blank.

We will find it useful to identify the pattern to which an expression is matched (for example, on the left-hand side of a function definition) so that it can be referred to by name elsewhere (for example, on the right-hand side of the function definition). A pattern can be labeled by *name_*, or *name__*, or *name___* (which can be read as "a pattern called *name*") and the labeled pattern will be matched by the same expression that matches its unlabeled counterpart. The matching expression is given the name used in the labeled pattern.

You can see what class of expressions match a given pattern by using MatchQ. For example, this tests whether the symbol bob matches any expression because the single underscore can stand for *any Mathematica* expression.

In[4]:= **MatchQ[bob, _]**

Out[4]= True

This tests whether the number 3.14 matches any expression with head `Real`.

```
In[5]:= MatchQ[3.14, _Real]
Out[5]= True
```

Of course 3.14 does not match any expression with head `Integer`.

```
In[6]:= MatchQ[3.14, _Integer]
Out[6]= False
```

If you want to look at a list of expressions and see which ones match a particular pattern, you can use `Cases`. `Cases [expr, patt]` outputs those elements of *expr* that match the pattern *patt*. For example, the only two elements of the list below that have head `Integer` are 3 and 17. Notice the fourth element is a string.

```
In[7]:= Cases[{3, 3.14, 17, "3", 4 + 5 I}, _Integer]
Out[7]= {3, 17}
```

```
In[8]:= Cases[{3, 3.14, 17, "3", 4 + 5 I}, _String]
Out[8]= {3}
```

Remember that the `OutputForm` of strings is to display without the quote characters. If you want to check the structure of this last output, use `FullForm` or check its `Head`.

```
In[9]:= FullForm[%]
Out[9]//FullForm=
        List["3"]
```

Here are some additional examples of pattern matching. This next example matches all those expressions with head g.

```
In[10]:= Cases[{g[x], f[x], g[h[x]], g[a, 0]}, _g]
Out[10]= {g[x], g[h[x]], g[a, 0]}
```

In the following example, the pattern {p_,q_} matches any list with two elements.

```
In[11]:= Cases[{{a, b}, {}, {1, 0}, {c, d, 3}}, {p_, q_}]
Out[11]= {{a, b}, {1, 0}}
```

Let us clear symbols we no longer need.

```
In[12]:= Clear[f]
```

Sequence pattern matching

A *sequence* consists of a number of expressions separated by commas. For example, the arguments of expressions are written as sequences.

A double blank (BlankSequence) represents a sequence of one or more expressions and __*h* represents a sequence of one or more expressions, each of which has head *h*. An expression that matches a blank will also match a double blank.

A triple blank (BlankNullSequence) represents a sequence of zero or more expressions and ___*h* represents a sequence of zero or more expressions, each of which has head *h*. An expression that matches a blank will also match a triple blank and a sequence that matches a double blank pattern will also match a triple blank pattern.

The pattern {p__}, using two _ characters, matches any list containing one or more elements.

In[13]:= **Cases[{{a, b}, {}, {1, 0}, {c, d, 3}}, {p__}]**

Out[13]= {{a, b}, {1, 0}, {c, d, 3}}

The pattern {p___}, using three _ characters, matches any list containing zero or more elements.

In[14]:= **Cases[{{a, b}, {}, {1, 0}, {c, d, 3}}, {p___}]**

Out[14]= {{a, b}, {}, {1, 0}, {c, d, 3}}

A list {a,b,c} is matched by the pattern _ (using Blank), as well as by List[__] (using BlankSequence) and List[___] (with BlankNullSequence). However, the list {a,b,c} is not matched by the pattern List[_] (a list of one expression) because for the purposes of pattern matching, a sequence is not an expression.

In[15]:= **MatchQ[{a, b, c}, _]**

Out[15]= True

In[16]:= **MatchQ[{a, b, c}, {_}]**

Out[16]= False

Here are some other examples of successful pattern matches.

In[17]:= **MatchQ[{a, b, c}, __]**

Out[17]= True

In[18]:= **MatchQ[{a, b, c}, {___}]**

Out[18]= True

In[19]:= **MatchQ[{a, b, c}, x__]**

Out[19]= True

In[20]:= **MatchQ[{a, b, c}, {x___}]**

Out[20]= True

In the last two examples above, the labels on the blanks do not affect the success or failure of the pattern match.

In[21]:= **MatchQ[{a, b, c}, __]**

Out[21]= True

The labels simply serve to identify different parts of the expression. For example, in MatchQ[{a,b,c},x_], x names the list {a,b,c}, but in MatchQ[{a,b,c},{x___}], x names the *sequence* a,b,c which is quite different. This is illustrated further in the section on conditional pattern matching.

Finally, note that the discussion about lists here applies equally to any function. For example, the following returns True, with x naming the sequence a,b,c.

In[22]:= **MatchQ[Plus[a, b, c], Plus[x__]]**

Out[22]= True

Example: Finding subsequences

As an example of sequence pattern matching, consider the problem of finding a particular subsequence within a sequence of numbers. To simplify this problem, consider both the sequence and the subsequence to be given as lists of numbers. As a concrete example, we will find the positions at which the subsequence 3238 occurs in the digits of π.

Here are the digits of π. Initially, we will look at only 50 digits so we can easily inspect the progress of our program.

In[23]:= **pidigs = First[RealDigits[N[π, 50] - 3]]**

Out[23]= {1, 4, 1, 5, 9, 2, 6, 5, 3, 5, 8, 9, 7, 9, 3,
             2, 3, 8, 4, 6, 2, 6, 4, 3, 3, 8, 3, 2, 7, 9, 5, 0,
             2, 8, 8, 4, 1, 9, 7, 1, 6, 9, 3, 9, 9, 3, 7, 5, 1}

Here is our subsequence, given as a list of digits.

In[24]:= **subseq = {3, 2, 3, 8};**

One approach to this problem is to partition the list of digits in `pidigs` into lists of the same length as the list `subseq`, with overlapping sublists of offset 1. This means that we will examine all length 4 sublists from `pidigs`.

```
In[25]:= p = Partition[pidigs, Length[subseq], 1]
```

```
Out[25]= {{1, 4, 1, 5}, {4, 1, 5, 9}, {1, 5, 9, 2},
    {5, 9, 2, 6}, {9, 2, 6, 5}, {2, 6, 5, 3},
    {6, 5, 3, 5}, {5, 3, 5, 8}, {3, 5, 8, 9}, {5, 8, 9, 7},
    {8, 9, 7, 9}, {9, 7, 9, 3}, {7, 9, 3, 2}, {9, 3, 2, 3},
    {3, 2, 3, 8}, {2, 3, 8, 4}, {3, 8, 4, 6}, {8, 4, 6, 2},
    {4, 6, 2, 6}, {6, 2, 6, 4}, {2, 6, 4, 3}, {6, 4, 3, 3},
    {4, 3, 3, 8}, {3, 3, 8, 3}, {3, 8, 3, 2}, {8, 3, 2, 7},
    {3, 2, 7, 9}, {2, 7, 9, 5}, {7, 9, 5, 0}, {9, 5, 0, 2},
    {5, 0, 2, 8}, {0, 2, 8, 8}, {2, 8, 8, 4}, {8, 8, 4, 1},
    {8, 4, 1, 9}, {4, 1, 9, 7}, {1, 9, 7, 1}, {9, 7, 1, 6},
    {7, 1, 6, 9}, {1, 6, 9, 3}, {6, 9, 3, 9}, {9, 3, 9, 9},
    {3, 9, 9, 3}, {9, 9, 3, 7}, {9, 3, 7, 5}, {3, 7, 5, 1}}
```

Now we are ready for the pattern match. From the list p above, we are looking for the positions of any sublist that matches {3,2,3,8}. The `Position` function takes as its first argument, the expression from which we are trying to match. The second argument is the pattern to match. We will use `BlankNullSequence` (___) on either side of our subsequence because zero or one or two expressions may occur before or after it in p.

```
In[26]:= Position[p, Flatten[{___, subseq, ___}]]
```

```
Out[26]= {{15}}
```

So the subsequence 3238 occurs starting at the 15th digit in the sequence given by `pidigs`.

Finally, let us turn this into a function and test it on a much larger example. Note that we use the pattern `_List` on both arguments so that `FindSubsequence` will only match arguments that have head `List`. (In Exercise 5 at the end of this section, you are asked to create a version of `FindSubsequence` that takes numbers instead of lists as its arguments.)

```
In[27]:= FindSubsequence[lis_List, subseq_List] := Module[{p},
        p = Partition[lis, Length[subseq], 1];
        Position[p, Flatten[{___, subseq, ___}]]
    ]
```

We store the first 100,000 digits of π in the symbol `pidigs`.

```
In[28]:= pidigs = First[RealDigits[N[π, 10^5] - 3]];
```

We find that the subsequence $\{3,2,3,8\}$ occurs at the following nine different positions in the first 100,000 digits of π.

```
In[29]:= FindSubsequence[pidigs, {3, 2, 3, 8}]

Out[29]= {{15}, {8990}, {20522}, {20756},
            {28130}, {41865}, {57208}, {86505}, {91936}}
```

The subsequence 31415 occurs once in the first 100,000 digits of π – starting at the 88,008th digit.

```
In[30]:= FindSubsequence[pidigs, {3, 1, 4, 1, 5}]

Out[30]= {{88008}}
```

Conditional pattern matching

Attaching a predicate

In addition to specifying the head of an expression, you can also match expressions against predicate functions. If the blanks of a pattern are followed with *?test*, where *test* is a predicate, then a match is only possible if *test* returns True when applied to the entire expression.

So, to match a class of expressions that have head *h*, you use _*h*. To match a class of expressions that evaluate to True when the predicate *pred* is applied, use _?*pred*.

```
In[31]:= MatchQ[{1, 2, 3}, _?ListQ]

Out[31]= True
```

```
In[32]:= MatchQ[{1, 2, 3}, _?NumberQ]

Out[32]= False
```

Note that in the above example, even though the list $\{1,2,3\}$ consists of numbers, it does not match ?NumberQ because its head (List) does not pass the NumberQ test.

The pattern _?Negative matches any expression that passes the Negative test; that is, it returns true when Negative is applied to it.

```
In[33]:= Cases[{-2, 7, -1.2, 0, -5 - 2 I}, _?Negative]

Out[33]= {-2, -1.2}
```

The following examples use a pure predicate function. In the first example, we are asking if $\{a,b,c\}$ has head List and if the length of $\{a,b,c\}$ is greater than 2. Since it passes both of these conditions, MatchQ returns True.

In[34]:= `MatchQ[{a, b, c}, _List? (Length[#] > 2 &)]`

Out[34]= `True`

Even though the head of {a,b,c} is List, the condition below fails since the list has length less than 4.

In[35]:= `MatchQ[{a, b, c}, _List? (Length[#] > 4 &)]`

Out[35]= `False`

Note that when using a pure function in ?*test*, because of the precedence *Mathematica* gives to evaluating various quantities, it is necessary to enclose the entire function, including the &, in parentheses. We have used *test* to place a constraint on the entire expression.

Here is a simple application of attaching a predicate. This definition of the Fibonacci function tests its argument to see that it is an integer (specifically, this tests that the head of n is Integer).

In[36]:= `f[1] = f[2] = 1;`

In[37]:= `f[n_ ? IntegerQ] := f[n - 1] + f[n - 2]`

Because of the predicate, f will not evaluate for noninteger arguments.

In[38]:= `f[1.2]`

Out[38]= `f[1.2]`

In[39]:= `{f[5], f[10], f[15]}`

Out[39]= `{5, 55, 610}`

We could also check that the arguments to f are both integral and positive.

In[40]:= `Clear[f]`

In[41]:= `f[1] = f[2] = 1;`

In[42]:= `f[n_ ? (IntegerQ && Positive)] := f[n - 1] + f[n - 2]`

In[43]:= `f[-3]`

Out[43]= `f[-3]`

Attaching a condition

If part of a labeled pattern is followed with an expression such as /;*condition*, where *condition* contains labels appearing in the pattern, then a match is possible only if *condition* returns True. We use *condition* to place a constraint on the labeled parts of an expression. The use of labels in *condition* is useful for narrowing the scope of a pattern match.

```
In[44]:= MatchQ[x^2, _^y_ /; EvenQ[y]]
```

```
Out[44]= True
```

```
In[45]:= MatchQ[x^2, _^y_ /; OddQ[y]]
```

```
Out[45]= False
```

We mentioned above that matching a list like {a,b,c} with the pattern x_ is different from matching it with x___ because of the various expressions that are associated with x.

```
In[46]:= MatchQ[{4, 6, 8}, x_ /; Length[x] > 4]
```

```
Out[46]= False
```

```
In[47]:= MatchQ[{4, 6, 8}, {x___} /; Length[x] > 4]
```

```
          Length::argx : Length called with
                3 arguments; 1 argument is expected. More…
```

```
Out[47]= False
```

```
In[48]:= MatchQ[{4, 6, 8}, {x___} /; Plus[x] > 10]
```

```
Out[48]= True
```

In the first example, x was associated with the entire list {4,6,8}; since Length[{4,6,8}] is not greater than 4, the match failed. In the second example, x became the sequence 4,6,8 so that the condition was Length[4,6,8] >4; but Length can only have one argument, hence the error. In the last example, x was again associated with 4,6,8, but now the condition was Plus[4,6,8] >10, which is perfectly legal, and true.

In the following example, the pattern matches all those expressions that are between 2 and 5.

```
In[49]:= Cases[{1, 2, 3, 4, 5, 6, 7, 8}, x_ /; 2 < x < 5]
```

```
Out[49]= {3, 4}
```

Let us try to recast the Fibonacci function example from the previous section in terms of a conditional.

```
In[50]:= Clear[f]

In[51]:= f[1] = f[2] = 1;

In[52]:= f[n_] := f[n - 1] + f[n - 2] /; IntegerQ[n]
```

Because of the predicate, f does not evaluate for noninteger arguments.

```
In[53]:= f[1.2]

Out[53]= f[1.2]

In[54]:= {f[5], f[10], f[15]}

Out[54]= {5, 55, 610}
```

Similarly, we can check that the arguments to f are both integral and positive.

```
In[55]:= Clear[f]

In[56]:= f[1] = f[2] = 1;

In[57]:= f[n_] := f[n - 1] + f[n - 2] /; IntegerQ[n] && Positive[n]

In[58]:= {f[-3], f[10]}

Out[58]= {f[-3], 55}
```

Note that you can alternatively put the condition inside the left-hand side of your definition.

```
In[59]:= Clear[f]

In[60]:= f[1] = f[2] = 1;

In[61]:= f[n_ /; IntegerQ[n] && Positive[n]] := f[n - 1] + f[n - 2]

In[62]:= {f[15], f[1.4], f[-4]}

Out[62]= {610, f[1.4], f[-4]}
```

Alternatives

A final type of pattern uses *alternatives*. Alternatives are denoted $p_1 \mid p_2 \mid \dots \mid p_n$ where the p_i are independent patterns. This pattern will match an expression whenever any one of those independent patterns match it.

In the following example, x^2 matches "an expression which is either the symbol x raised to a real number or the symbol x raised to an integer."

```
In[63]:= MatchQ[x^2, x^_Real | x^_Integer]
```

```
Out[63]= True
```

In this example, x^2 matches "x raised to an expression which is either a real number or an integer."

```
In[64]:= MatchQ[x^2, x^(_Real | _Integer)]
```

```
Out[64]= True
```

Here the pattern matches any expression that has head Integer or Rational or Real.

$$In[65]:= \texttt{Cases}\left[\left\{1,\ 3.1,\ \frac{2}{3},\ x,\ 3+4\,I,\ \texttt{"Hello"}\right\},\right.$$
$$\left.\texttt{\_Integer | \_Rational | \_Real}\right]$$

$$Out[65]= \left\{1,\ 3.1,\ \frac{2}{3}\right\}$$

As a final example, recall the function pointLoc from Section 5.4.

```
In[66]:= pointLoc[{0, 0}] := 0
         pointLoc[{x_, 0}] := -1
         pointLoc[{0, y_}] := -2
         pointLoc[{x_, y_}] := If[x < 0, 2, 1] /; y > 0
         pointLoc[{x_, y_}] := If[x < 0, 3, 4]
```

The integer 0, as a pattern, does not match the real number 0.0, since they have different heads.

```
In[71]:= {Head[0], Head[0.0]}
```

```
Out[71]= {Integer, Real}
```

Thus, using the above version of pointLoc, {0.0,0.0} returns 4, which is, of course, wrong.

```
In[72]:= pointLoc[{0.0, 0.0}]
```

```
Out[72]= 4
```

On the other hand, the single-clause versions using If and Which returned 0, because 0.0 == 0 is true. How can we fix this? There are a number of possibilities. Perhaps the simplest way is to change the rules involving zeroes by means of alternatives.

```
In[73]:= Clear[pointLoc]
```

```
In[74]:=  pointLoc[{0 | 0.0, 0 | 0.0}] := 0
          pointLoc[{x_, 0 | 0.0}] := -1
          pointLoc[{0 | 0.0, y_}] := -2
          pointLoc[{x_, y_}] := If[x < 0, 2, 1] /; y > 0
          pointLoc[{x_, y_}] := If[x < 0, 3, 4]
```

Now the several cases that led to inconsistencies in the previous versions are dealt with properly.

```
In[79]:=  pointLoc[{0, 0.0}]

Out[79]=  0
```

```
In[80]:=  pointLoc[{1, 0}]

Out[80]=  -1
```

String patterns

All of the pattern matching discussed in the previous sections extends to strings in a very powerful manner. You might find it helpful to think of strings as a sequence of characters and use the same general principles on these expressions as you do with lists. Let us look at a few examples to try and make this concrete.

The expression {a, b, c, c, d, e} matches the pattern {__, s_, s_, __} because it is a list that starts with a sequence of one or more elements, it contains an element repeated once, and then ends with a sequence of one or more elements.

```
In[81]:=  MatchQ[{a, b, b, c, d, e}, {__, s_, s_, __}]

Out[81]=  True
```

If we now use a string instead of a list and StringMatchQ instead of MatchQ, we get a similar result using the shorthand notation ~~ for StringExpression, which essentially concatenates strings.

```
In[82]:=  StringMatchQ["abbcde", __ ~~ s_ ~~ s_ ~~ __]

Out[82]=  True
```

```
In[83]:=  "a" ~~ "b"

Out[83]=  ab
```

```
In[84]:=  FullForm[HoldForm["a" ~~ "b"]]

Out[84]//FullForm=
          HoldForm[StringExpression["a", "b"]]
```

StringExpression is quite similar to StringJoin (both can be used to concatenate strings) except that with StringExpression, you can concatenate nonstrings.

The next example also shows the similarity between the pattern matching that we explored earlier and string patterns. Using Cases, we return all those expressions that match the pattern _Symbol; that is, we pick out all those symbols from the list.

```
In[85]:= Cases[{1, f, g, 6, x, t, 2, 5}, _Symbol]
```

```
Out[85]= {f, g, x, t}
```

With the string "1fg6xt25" we can use StringCases whose second argument is a pattern that represents a class of characters to match. For example, LetterCharacter matches a single letter.

```
In[86]:= StringCases["1fg6xt25", LetterCharacter]
```

```
Out[86]= {f, g, x, t}
```

You can match single digits with DigitCharacter.

```
In[87]:= StringCases["1fg6xt25", DigitCharacter]
```

```
Out[87]= {1, 6, 2, 5}
```

Starting in Version 5.1, you can use regular expressions to match string patterns. Regular expressions in *Mathematica* follow a syntax very close to that of the Perl programming language. This syntax is quite compact and powerful but it comes at the cost of readability – regular expressions tend to be quite cryptic to humans. As a result, we will only cover a few examples of their use here and refer the interested reader to the *Mathematica* documentation on string patterns.

The regular expression 1.* will be matched by any string starting with 1, followed by any character repeated zero or more times.

```
In[88]:= StringMatchQ["1a2b3c4d", RegularExpression["1.*"]]
```

```
Out[88]= True
```

The regular expression \\d represents any digit 0 through 9.

```
In[89]:= StringCases["1a2b3c4d", RegularExpression["\\d"]]
```

```
Out[89]= {1, 2, 3, 4}
```

In the following example, we use a regular expression to look for the pattern consisting of the character "a" repeated one or more times, followed by the character "c", followed by any character. The StringReplace function then replaces any expression matching this pattern with a large, bold formatted expression. The "$0" is used to refer to the matched pattern.

```
In[90]:=  StringReplace["acgttttccctgagcataaaaacccagcaatacg",
          RegularExpression["a..c."] :> "\!\(\*StyleBox[
          \"$0\",FontSize->14,FontWeight->\"Bold\"]\)"]
```

Out[90]= acgttttccctgagcataa**aaacc**cagca**atacg**

Exercises

1. Find as many patterns as possible that match the expression x^3 + y z.

2. Find as many pattern matches as possible for the following expression.

   {5, erina, {}, "give me a break"}

3. Using both forms (predicate and condition), write down five conditional patterns that match the expression {4, {a,b}, "g"}.

4. In Exercise 10 of Section 5.2, we developed a procedural implementation of the Euclidean algorithm for finding the greatest common divisor of two numbers. The function given in the solutions does no argument checking and hence can give erroneous output for arguments that are not integers. Rewrite the gcd function given there so that it uses pattern matching to check that each of its two arguments are integers.

5. The function FindSubsequence defined in this section suffers from the limitation that the arguments lis and subseq must both be lists of numbers. Write another definition of FindSubsequence that takes integers as its two arguments. So for example, the following should work:

   ```
   In[1]:=  pi = FromDigits[ RealDigits[N[Pi, 10^5] - 3] [[1]]];
   ```

   ```
   In[2]:=  FindSubsequence[pi, 1415]
   ```

   Out[2]= {{1}, {6955}, {29136}, {45234}, {79687}, {85880}, {88009}}

6. Write a function Collatz that takes an integer n as an argument and returns $3n + 1$ if n is an odd integer and returns $\frac{n}{2}$ if n is even. Your function Collatz should attach a predicate to its argument to check whether it is even or odd.

7. Write the Collatz function from the above exercise, but this time attach a condition instead of a predicate. In addition, your condition should also check that the argument to Collatz is positive.

8. Use alternatives to write a function abs [x] that, whenever x is an integer or a rational, returns x if x ≥ 0, and −x if x < 0. Whenever x is complex, abs [x] should return $\sqrt{re(x)^2 + im(x)^2}$.

9. Create a function swapTwo [lis_List] that returns lis with its first two elements interchanged; for example, swapTwo [{a,b,c,d,e}] is {b,a,c,d,e}. If lis has fewer than two elements, swapTwo just returns it. Write swapTwo using three clauses: one for the empty list, one for one-element lists, and one for all other lists. Then write it using two clauses: one for lists of length zero or one and another for all longer lists.

10. Convert this definition to one that has no conditional parts (/ ;), but instead uses pattern matching in the argument list:

```
f[x_, y_] := x - y /; IntegerQ[x]

f[x_, y_] :=
   x[[1]] + y /; Head[x] == List && IntegerQ[First[x]] && y == 1
```

11. Write a version of the HammingDistance function (described in Section 4.7) that uses Cases instead of Select.

6.3 Transformation rules

Transformation rules are ubiquitous in *Mathematica*. They are used to represent solutions to equations, as a means to specify options for functions, and they form the basis of most of the algebraic manipulation in *Mathematica*. In this section we will look at how to use pattern matching together with replacement rules to transform expressions based on these rules.

A replacement rule is of the form *pattern* → *replacement* or *pattern* :→ *replacement*. Just like traditional function definitions, the left-hand side of each of these rules matches an expression and the right-hand side describes the transformation of that expression.

One of the most common uses for rules is in making substitutions of the form *expr* / . *rule*. Any part of *expr* that matches the pattern in *rule* will be rewritten according to that rule.

In[1]:= **x + y /. y → α**

Out[1]= x + α

A similar rule but using assignments would look like this:

In[2]:=   **f[x_ , y_] = x + y;**

In[3]:=   **f[x, α]**

Out[3]=   x + α

The main difference between the replacement rule and the assignment is that the assignment will automatically be used whenever there is an appropriate pattern match during evaluation. The expression f[x, α] matched the rule for f and the substitution was performed automatically.

If you wish to restrict the use of a rule to a specific expression, you can use the ReplaceAll function (shorthand notation / .) with the expression as the first argument and a user-defined Rule or RuleDelayed function as the second argument. In standard input form, the transformation rule (or local rewrite rule) appears immediately after the expression, as the second argument to ReplaceAll.

In[4]:=   **x + y /. y → α**

Out[4]=   x + α

Here is the standard input form of the above.

In[5]:=   **ReplaceAll[x + y, Rule[y, α]]**

Out[5]=   x + α

When the Rule function is used with an expression, the expression itself is first evaluated. Then *both* the left-hand side and right-hand side of the rule are evaluated, except for those parts of the right-hand side that are held unevaluated by the Hold attribute. Finally, everywhere that the evaluated left-hand side of the rule appears in the evaluated expression, it is replaced by the evaluated right-hand side of the rule.

In[6]:=   **{a, a} /. a → Random[]**

Out[6]=   {0.474439, 0.474439}

Using Trace, we can see the way the transformation rule works. Note in particular, that the right-hand side of the rule is evaluated first.

In[7]:=   **Trace[{a, a} /. a → Random[]]**

Out[7]=   {{{Random[], 0.0883691}, a → 0.0883691, a → 0.0883691},
              {a, a} /. a → 0.0883691, {0.0883691, 0.0883691}}

Just as in the case of assignments, there are immediate rules and delayed rules. In an immediate rule (*pattern→replacement*, with standard input form Rule [*pattern*, *replacement*]), the replacement will be evaluated immediately. For delayed rules (*pattern:→replace-*

ment, with standard input form `RuleDelayed [pattern, replacement]`), the replacement is only evaluated after the substitution is made.

In[8]:= `{a, a} /. a :> Random[]`

Out[8]= `{0.672823, 0.703154}`

Using `Trace`, we can see the way this transformation rule works.

In[9]:= `Trace[{a, a} /. a :> Random[]]`

Out[9]= `{{a :> Random[], a :> Random[]}, {a, a} /. a :> Random[],`
`{Random[], Random[]}, {Random[], 0.174287},`
`{Random[], 0.722288}, {0.174287, 0.722288}}`

Transformation rules can be written using symbols.

In[10]:= `{a, b, c} /. List → Plus`

Out[10]= `a + b + c`

Transformation rules can also be written using labeled patterns.

In[11]:= `{{3, 4}, {7, 2}, {1, 5}} /. {x_, y_} → {y, x}`

Out[11]= `{{4, 3}, {2, 7}, {5, 1}}`

We can use multiple rules with an expression by enclosing them in a list.

In[12]:= `{a, b, c} /. {c → b, b → a}`

Out[12]= `{a, a, b}`

A transformation rule is applied only once to each part of an expression (in contrast to a rewrite rule) and multiple transformation rules are used in parallel. Hence, in the above example, the symbol c is transformed into b but it is not further changed into a. In order to apply one or more transformation rules repeatedly to an expression until the expression no longer changes, the `ReplaceRepeated` function is used.

For example, the product of x and y is replaced by the sum of x and y, but this is only done for the first such occurrence that matches.

In[13]:= `a b c d /. x_ y_ → x + y`

Out[13]= `a + b c d`

Using `ReplaceRepeated`, the rule is applied repeatedly until the expression no longer changes.

In[14]:= `a b c d //. x_ y_ → x + y`

Out[14]= `a + b + c + d`

Let us now look at a few examples of problems that we solved earlier using a functional style of programming but now solve them using a rule-based approach.

Example: Counting coins

Recall the pocket change example from Chapter 4 where a list of coins was given and a function was constructed to count the value of the set of coins. Let us try to do the same thing, but with a rule that gives the values of the coins.

```
In[15]:= coins = {p, p, q, n, d, d, p, q, q, p}
```

```
Out[15]= {p, p, q, n, d, d, p, q, q, p}
```

Here are the values, given by a list of rules.

```
In[16]:= values = {p → 1, n → 5, d → 10, q → 25};
```

This replaces each coin by its value.

```
In[17]:= coins /. values
```

```
Out[17]= {1, 1, 25, 5, 10, 10, 1, 25, 25, 1}
```

And here is the value of the set of coins.

```
In[18]:= Apply[Plus, coins /. values]
```

```
Out[18]= 104
```

Finally, here is a function that wraps up all these steps.

```
In[19]:= CountChange[coins_List] := Module[{values},
            values = {p → 1, n → 5, d → 10, q → 25};
            Apply[Plus, coins /. values]]
```

```
In[20]:= CountChange[{p, q, q, n, d, d, p, q, q, d, d}]
```

```
Out[20]= 147
```

Example: Finding maxima

Our last example employs a sophisticated rewrite rule which demonstrates most of the things discussed in this section: the repeated use of a transformation rule with delayed evaluation, sequence patterns, and conditional pattern matching.

Recall the `maxima` function that we defined in Chapter 4, which returns the elements in a list of positive numbers that are bigger than all of the preceding numbers in the list.

In[21]:= **maxima[x_List] := Union[Rest[FoldList[Max, 0, x]]]**

In[22]:= **maxima[{3, 5, 2, 6, 1, 8, 4, 9, 7}]**

Out[22]= {3, 5, 6, 8, 9}

We can also write this function using a pattern matching transformation rule.

In[23]:= **maximaR[x_List] :=**
x //. {a___, b_, c___, d_, e___} /; d ≤ b :> {a, b, c, e}

Basically, the transformation rule repeatedly looks through the list for two elements (b and d here), separated by a sequence of zero or more elements, such that the second selected element is no greater than the first selected element. It then eliminates the second element. The process stops when there are no two elements such that the second is less than or equal to the first.

In[24]:= **maximaR[{3, 5, 2, 6, 1, 8, 4, 9, 7}]**

Out[24]= {3, 5, 6, 8, 9}

Exercises

1. Using Trace on maxima and maximaR, explain why the functional version is much faster than the pattern matching version of the maxima function.

2. The following compound expression returns a value of 14.

   In[1]:= **z = 11;**
   a = 9;
   z + 3 /. z → a

   Out[3]= 14

   Describe the evaluation sequence that was followed. Use the Trace function to check your answer.

3. Use the Hold function in the compound expression in the previous exercise to obtain a value of 12.

4. The function definition f[x_Plus] := Apply[Times,x] works as follows:

   In[4]:= **Clear[f, a, b, c]**

   In[5]:= **f[x_Plus] := Apply[Times, x]**

In[6]:= **f [a + b + c]**

Out[6]= a b c

The rewrite rule g [x_] := x /.Plus [z___]→Times [z] does not work. Use
Trace to see why and then modify this rule so that it performs the same operation as
the function f above.

5. Create a rewrite rule that uses a repeated replacement to "unnest" the nested lists
within a list.

In[7]:= **unNest[{{a, a, a}, {a}, {{b, b, b}, {b, b}}, {a, a}}]**

Out[7]= {{a, a, a}, {a}, {b, b, b}, {b, b}, {a, a}}

6. Define a function using pattern matching and repeated replacement to sum the
elements of a list.

7. Using the built-in function ReplaceList, write a function cartesianProduct
that takes two lists as input and returns the Cartesian product of these lists.

In[8]:= **cartesianProduct[{x_1, x_2, x_3}, {y_1, y_2}]**

Out[8]= {{x_1, y_1}, {x_1, y_2}, {x_2, y_1}, {x_2, y_2}, {x_3, y_1}, {x_3, y_2}}

8. The function CellularAutomaton [*rule, init, t*] creates a list of the evolution
of a cellular automaton. For example, this generates five iterations of the cellular
automaton rule number 30 starting with the initial condition of a single 1 surrounded
by 0s.

In[9]:= **CellularAutomaton[30, {{1}, 0}, 5]**

Out[9]= {{0, 0, 0, 0, 0, 1, 0, 0, 0, 0, 0}, {0, 0, 0, 0, 1, 1, 1, 0, 0, 0, 0},
{0, 0, 0, 1, 1, 0, 0, 1, 0, 0, 0}, {0, 0, 1, 1, 0, 1, 1, 1, 1, 0, 0},
{0, 1, 1, 0, 0, 1, 0, 0, 0, 1, 0}, {1, 1, 0, 1, 1, 1, 1, 0, 1, 1, 1}}

Write a function CAGraphics [*lis*] that takes as argument, a list generated by
CellularAutomaton and produces a Graphics object that can then be displayed
directly with Show. Your function should use RasterArray and also a set of rules
to transform each 0 and 1 into different color directives such as Hue [.2].

In[10]:= **ca30 = CellularAutomaton[30, {{1}, 0}, 500];**

In[11]:= `Show[CAGraphics[ca30]]`

Out[11]= `- Graphics -`

6.4 Examples

This section focuses on two classical problems in computer science: encryption and sorting. Even though we will only scratch the surface of these two very deep problems, they are so important and ubiquitous in modern computing that it is well worth while learning about them. As it turns out, these problems are well suited to a rule-based approach, at least at an introductory level. We encourage you to investigate further the theory and implementation of modern cipher and sorting algorithms. See, for example, (Sedgewick, 1988) and (Wagon, 1999) for details.

Encoding text

In this example, we will develop functions for coding and decoding strings of text. The particular coding that we will do is quite simplistic compared with contemporary commercial-grade ciphers, but it will give us a chance to see how to combine string manipulation, the use of functional programming constructs, and rule-based programming all in a very practical example that should be accessible to anyone.

The problem in encryption is to develop an algorithm that can be used to encode a string of text and then a dual algorithm that can be used to decode the encrypted message. At first we will just limit ourselves to the 26 lowercase letters of the alphabet.

In[1]:= `alphabet = Map[FromCharacterCode , Range[97, 122]]`

Out[1]= `{a, b, c, d, e, f, g, h, i, j, k,`
`       l, m, n, o, p, q, r, s, t, u, v, w, x, y, z}`

One of the simplest encryption schemes is attributed to Julius Caesar who is said to have used this cipher to encode communications with his generals. The scheme is simply to shift each letter of the alphabet some fixed number of places to the left. Using `Thread`, we can set up rules that implement this shift.

```
In[2]:= CaesarCodeRules = Thread[alphabet → RotateLeft[alphabet]]

Out[2]= {a → b, b → c, c → d, d → e, e → f, f → g, g → h, h → i,
         i → j, j → k, k → l, l → m, m → n, n → o, o → p, p → q, q → r,
         r → s, s → t, t → u, u → v, v → w, w → x, x → y, y → z, z → a}
```

The decoding rules are simply to shift back in the other direction.

```
In[3]:= CaesarDecodeRules = Thread[alphabet → RotateRight[alphabet]]

Out[3]= {a → z, b → a, c → b, d → c, e → d, f → e, g → f, h → g,
         i → h, j → i, k → j, l → k, m → l, n → m, o → n, p → o, q → p,
         r → q, s → r, t → s, u → t, v → u, w → v, x → w, y → x, z → y}
```

To code a string, we will decompose the string into individual characters, apply the code rules, and then join up the resulting characters in a "word."

```
In[4]:= Characters["hello"]

Out[4]= {h, e, l, l, o}
```

```
In[5]:= % /. CaesarCodeRules

Out[5]= {i, f, m, m, p}
```

```
In[6]:= Apply[StringJoin, %]

Out[6]= ifmmp
```

Here is the function to accomplish this.

```
In[7]:= encode[str_String, coderules_] :=
          Apply[StringJoin, Characters[str] /. coderules]
```

Similarly, here is the decoding function.

```
In[8]:= decode[str_String, decoderules_] :=
          Apply[StringJoin, Characters[str] /. decoderules]
```

Let us try it out on a phrase.

```
In[9]:= encode["squeamish ossifrage", CaesarCodeRules]

Out[9]= trvfbnjti pttjgsbhf
```

```
In[10]:= decode[%, CaesarDecodeRules]

Out[10]= squeamish ossifrage
```

Other ciphers can be created using permutations on the letters of the alphabet. We will need the `randomPermutation` function we created in Section 5.2 of the chapter on procedural programming.

```
In[11]:= randomPermutation[lis_] := Module[{x, res = {}, 12 = lis},
         Do[
           x = Part[12, Random[Integer, {1, Length[12]}]];
           res = Append[res, x];
           12 = Complement[12, {x}],
           {i, 1, Length[lis]}];
         res]
```

First we create a random permutation of the letters of the alphabet.

```
In[12]:= p = randomPermutation[alphabet]
```

```
Out[12]= {y, g, r, e, j, h, f, b, t, p, a,
          k, i, m, o, c, u, z, w, d, v, q, s, n, x, l}
```

Then, using `Thread`, we create a rule for each letter paired up with the corresponding letter from the permutation p.

```
In[13]:= PermutationCodeRules = Thread[alphabet → p]
```

```
Out[13]= {a → y, b → g, c → r, d → e, e → j, f → h, g → f, h → b,
          i → t, j → p, k → a, l → k, m → i, n → m, o → o, p → c, q → u,
          r → z, s → w, t → d, u → v, v → q, w → s, x → n, y → x, z → l}
```

The decoding rules are obtained by simply reversing the above rules.

```
In[14]:= PermutationDecodeRules = Thread[p → alphabet]
```

```
Out[14]= {y → a, g → b, r → c, e → d, j → e, h → f, f → g, b → h,
          t → i, p → j, a → k, k → l, i → m, m → n, o → o, c → p, u → q,
          z → r, w → s, d → t, v → u, q → v, s → w, n → x, x → y, l → z}
```

```
In[15]:= encode["squeamish ossifrage", PermutationCodeRules]
```

```
Out[15]= wuvjyitwb owwthzyfj
```

```
In[16]:= decode[%, PermutationDecodeRules]
```

```
Out[16]= squeamish ossifrage
```

Sorting a list

This next example also incorporates several of the concepts discussed in this chapter. It uses a delayed rule, contains a conditional, and has several types of pattern matching.

We will create a rule named `listsort` that, upon repeated application, will put a list of numbers into numerical order. To account for the first and last elements in the list, we use `BlankNullSequence (___)`.

In[17]:= `listsort =`
            `{x___, a_?NumericQ, b_?NumericQ, y___} :→ {x, b, a, y} /; b < a`

Out[17]= `{x___, a_?NumericQ, b_?NumericQ, y___} :→ {x, b, a, y} /; b < a`

The pattern that has to match `{x___,a_,b_,y___}` is a list of at least two elements since `x___` and `y___` will match zero or more elements. The condition on the right-hand side of the rule says that whenever b is less than a, switch the order of a and b in the original list to output `{x,b,a,y}`.

Here is a list of ten real numbers between 0 and 1.

In[18]:= `nums = Table[Random[], {10}]`

Out[18]= `{0.237736, 0.182151, 0.822792, 0.264693, 0.968603,`
            `0.599673, 0.602053, 0.101958, 0.219543, 0.539043}`

In[19]:= `nums //. listsort`

Out[19]= `{0.101958, 0.182151, 0.219543, 0.237736, 0.264693,`
            `0.539043, 0.599673, 0.602053, 0.822792, 0.968603}`

Notice that because we used `?NumericQ` as part of the pattern match, `listsort` will work on expressions that may not be explicit numbers, but are numerical in nature; that is, expressions that return explicit numbers when `N` is applied to them.

In[20]:= `{e, π, EulerGamma, GoldenRatio} //. listsort`

Out[20]= `{EulerGamma, GoldenRatio, e, π}`

This algorithm is far less efficient than many classical sorting algorithms, especially those that employ a divide-and-conquer strategy.

In[21]:= `nums = Table[Random[], {100}];`

In[22]:= `Timing[(nums //. listsort);]`

Out[22]= `{0.942 Second, Null}`

The built-in `Sort` function uses a classical algorithm called "merge sort" (discussed in Section 7.5), which starts by dividing the list into two parts of approximately equal size. It then sorts each part recursively and finally merges the two sorted sublists.

In[23]:= `Timing[Sort[nums];]`

Out[23]= `{0. Second, Null}`

The above implementation of `listsort` only works for numerical arguments. We can overload `listsort` to work on characters of strings by making only two small changes. First, we pattern match a and b with head `String` instead of `?NumericQ`. Second, instead of comparing a < b, we need to compare their character codes.

```
In[24]:= ToCharacterCode["z"][[1]]
```

```
Out[24]= 122
```

Here then is the definition of `listsort` that operates on lists of string characters.

```
In[25]:= listsort = {x___, a_String, b_String, y___} :> {x, b, a, y} /;
          Part[ToCharacterCode[b], 1] < Part[ToCharacterCode[a], 1];
```

```
Out[25]= {x___, a_String, b_String, y___} :>
          {x, b, a, y} /; ToCharacterCode[b][[1]] < ToCharacterCode[a][[1]]
```

Here are ten random characters.

```
In[26]:= chars =
          Table[FromCharacterCode[Random[Integer, {97, 122}]], {10}]
```

```
Out[26]= {c, x, z, e, c, i, d, c, a, l}
```

Here they are sorted.

```
In[27]:= chars //. listsort
```

```
Out[27]= {a, c, c, c, d, e, i, l, x, z}
```

Exercises

1. Modify the Caesar cipher so that it encodes by shifting five places to the right.

2. Modify the alphabet permutation cipher so that instead of being based on single letters, it is instead based on adjacent pairs of letters. Whereas the single letter cipher will have 26! = 403291461126605635584000000 permutations, the adjacent pairs cipher will have 26^2! permutations – a very large number.

```
In[1]:= N[26² !]
```

```
Out[1]= 1.883707684133810 × 10^1621
```

3. You can quickly create a graphics function to plot binary data (0s and 1s) using `Raster`. For example:

```
In[2]:=  data = Table[Random[Integer], {5}, {5}]
```

```
Out[2]=  {{1, 1, 0, 0, 1}, {1, 0, 1, 1, 0},
           {0, 1, 1, 1, 1}, {0, 1, 0, 1, 1}, {0, 1, 1, 1, 0}}
```

```
In[3]:=  Show[Graphics[Raster[Reverse[data]], AspectRatio → Automatic]]
```

```
Out[3]=  - Graphics -
```

If you wanted to color the squares with color directives such as RGBColor or Hue or
GrayLevel, then you need to use RasterArray instead. Create a function
matrixPlot[*mat*, *rules*] that takes a matrix *mat* as its first argument and a list of
rules as the second argument. The list of rules should specify what color directive
each of the values in *mat* should be mapped to. Finally, compare your function with
ArrayPlot (new in Version 5.1).

```
In[4]:=  ArrayPlot[data, ColorRules → {0 → Black, 1 → White}];
```

4. Plot the function sin(*x*) over the interval [−2 π, 2π] and then reverse the *x*- and
   y-coordinates of each point by means of a transformation rule.

5. Plot the function sin(*x y*) with *x* and *y* taking on values from 0 to 3 π / 2. Then use a
   transformation rule to perform a *shear* by shifting the graphic in the *x*-direction by a
   factor of four.

6. Create a function rotatePlot [*gr*, θ] that takes a plot *gr* and rotates it about the origin by an angle θ. For example, to rotate a plot of the sine function, first create the plot:

In[5]:= **plot1 = Plot[Sin[x], {x, 0, 2 π}];**

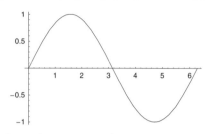

Then perform the rotation of π radians.

In[6]:= **rotatePlot[plot1, π];**

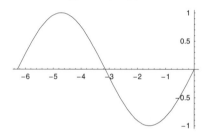

7. Create a function rotatePlot3D [*gr*, ϕ, θ, ψ] that will rotate a Graphics3D object *gr* about the origin by the angles ϕ, θ, and ψ in the *x*, *y*, and *z* directions, respectively.

7 Recursion

Some very important and classical problems in mathematics and computer science are defined, or have solutions in terms of recursive definitions. A function is defined using recursion if in its definition, it makes calls to itself. This programming paradigm is easily implemented in *Mathematica* in a manner that is both natural and quite efficient. In fact, many of the built-in operations of *Mathematica* could be written in *Mathematica* itself using recursion. In this chapter, we will present many examples of recursion and explain how recursive functions are written.

7.1 Fibonacci numbers

Recursive definitions of mathematical quantities were used by mathematicians for centuries before computers even existed. One famous example is the definition of a special sequence of numbers first studied by the thirteenth-century Italian mathematician Leonardo Fibonacci. The *Fibonacci numbers* have since been studied extensively, finding application in many areas; see (Knuth 1997) for a detailed discussion.

The Fibonacci numbers are obtained as follows: write down two 1s, then continue writing numbers computed by adding the last two numbers you have written down.

$$
\begin{array}{cccccccc}
1 & 1 & 2 & 3 & 5 & 8 & 13 & 21 & \ldots \\
F_1 & F_2 & F_3 & F_4 & F_5 & F_6 & F_7 & F_8 & \ldots
\end{array}
$$

The simplest way to define these numbers is with recursion.

$$
\begin{aligned}
F_1 &= 1 \\
F_2 &= 1 \\
F_n &= F_{n-2} + F_{n-1}, \quad \text{for } n > 2
\end{aligned}
$$

If we think of this sequence as a function, we would just change this to a functional definition.

$F(1) = 1$
$F(2) = 1$
$F(n) = F(n - 2) + F(n - 1)$,   for $n > 2$

In this form, we can translate the definition directly into *Mathematica*.

```
In[1]:= F[1] = 1;
        F[2] = 1;
        F[n_] := F[n - 2] + F[n - 1] /; n > 2
```

As it turns out, the condition $/; n > 2$ is unnecessary because *Mathematica* looks up specific rules such as F[1] =1 before more general rules like that for F[n].
Here is a table of the first ten Fibonacci numbers.

```
In[4]:= Table[F[i], {i, 1, 10}]
```

```
Out[4]= {1, 1, 2, 3, 5, 8, 13, 21, 34, 55}
```

It is somewhat amazing that this works, but note that whenever we want to compute F[n] for some $n > 2$, we only apply F to numbers smaller than n. Tracing the evaluation of F[4] makes the point well.

```
In[5]:= TracePrint[F[4], F[_Integer] | F[_] + F[_]]

 F[4]

 F[4 - 2] + F[4 - 1]

  F[2]

  F[3]

  F[3 - 2] + F[3 - 1]

   F[1]

   F[2]
```

```
Out[5]= 3
```

The first two lines indicate that F[4] is rewritten to F[4-2]+F[4-1], and the lines that are indented one space show the calls of F[2] and F[3]. The lines showing calls to F[1] and F[2] do not have any indented lines under them, since those values are computed directly by a single rewrite rule, without making any recursive calls (for a fuller explanation of this use of TracePrint, see Appendix B.

The key thing to understand about recursion is this: you can always apply a function within its own definition, so long as you apply it only to *smaller* values. We will see this principle used repeatedly in this chapter.

There is one other key point as well: we can apply the function to smaller and smaller values, but we must eventually reach a value that can be computed *without* recursion. In the case of the Fibonacci numbers, the numbers that can be computed without recursion – the *base cases* – are $F[1]$ and $F[2]$.

We will return to the Fibonacci numbers later in this chapter, in Section 7.6, where we will see what can be done about a serious inefficiency in our implementation of F (also, see Exercise 2 below).

Exercises

Before doing the exercises in this chapter, you may want to take a look at Appendix B, which discusses some common programming errors, and how to debug recursive functions.

1. For each of the following sequences of numbers, see if you can deduce the pattern and write a *Mathematica* function to compute the ith value.

   a.
   $$2, \quad 3, \quad 6, \quad 18, \quad 108, \quad 1944, \quad 209952, \quad \dots$$
   $$A_1 \quad A_2 \quad A_3 \quad A_4 \quad A_5 \quad A_6 \quad A_7 \quad \dots$$

   b.
   $$0, \quad 1, \quad -1, \quad 2, \quad -3, \quad 5, \quad -8, \quad 13, \quad -21, \quad \dots$$
   $$B_1 \quad B_2 \quad B_3 \quad B_4 \quad B_5 \quad B_6 \quad B_7 \quad B_8 \quad B_9 \quad \dots$$

   c.
   $$0, \quad 1, \quad 2, \quad 3, \quad 6, \quad 11, \quad 20, \quad 37, \quad 68, \quad \dots$$
   $$C_1 \quad C_2 \quad C_3 \quad C_4 \quad C_5 \quad C_6 \quad C_7 \quad C_8 \quad C_9 \quad \dots$$

2. The numbers FA_n represent the number of additions that are done in the course of evaluating F $[n]$.

   $$0 \quad 0 \quad 1 \quad 2 \quad 4 \quad 7 \quad 12 \quad 20 \quad 33 \quad \dots$$
   $$FA_1 \quad FA_2 \quad FA_3 \quad FA_4 \quad FA_5 \quad FA_6 \quad FA_7 \quad FA_8 \quad FA_9 \quad \dots$$

   Write a function FA such that FA $[n]$ $= FA_n$.

7.2 List functions

In Chapter 4, we looked at functional implementations of some list-oriented functions in *Mathematica*. Although some of these functions have more efficient implementations in terms of functional constructs, they provide a nice vehicle for discussing recursion, and so in this section we will use them to introduce some of the basic concepts of recursive programming.

We noted in our discussion of Fibonacci numbers that recursion works if the arguments of recursive calls are smaller than the original argument. The same principle applies to functions on lists. One common case is when the argument in the recursive call is the "tail" (that is, Rest) of the original argument. An example is length, our recursively defined version of the built-in function Length. The idea is that the length of a list is always one greater than the length of its tail.

In[1]:= **length[lis_] := length[Rest[lis]] + 1**

Applying length to a list, however, leads to trouble.

In[2]:= **length[{a, b, c}]**

```
Rest::norest :
 Cannot take Rest of expression {} with length zero. More…

Rest::argx :
 Rest called with 0 arguments; 1 argument is expected. More…

General::stop : Further output of Rest::norest will
    be suppressed during this calculation. More…

General::stop :
 Further output of $RecursionLimit::reclim will
    be suppressed during this calculation. More…
```

Out[2]= 255 + Hold[Hold[length[Rest[Rest[Rest[]]]]]]

Well, perhaps it is already obvious, but what we are experiencing is one of the most common errors in defining functions recursively – we forgot the base cases. For length, there is just one base case, the empty list.

In[3]:= **length[{}] := 0**

Now length works as we had intended it to.

In[4]:= **length[{a, b, c}]**

Out[4]= 3

Here is another simple example (for which we again have better solutions using built-in operations): adding the elements of a list. We know several ways to do this, using functional constructs for example.

In[5]:= `sumElements[lis_] := Apply[Plus, lis]`

In[6]:= `sumElements[lis_] := Fold[Plus, 0, lis]`

But for now we are just trying to get some practice with recursion. Here is the most obvious recursive solution.

In[7]:= `sumElements[{}] := 0`
`sumElements[{x_, r___}] := x + sumElements[{r}]`

In[9]:= `sumElements[{a, b, c}]`

Out[9]= `a + b + c`

A trace of this computation shows the evaluation procedure in detail.

In[10]:= `Trace[sumElements[{a, b, c}]]`

Out[10]= `{sumElements[{a, b, c}], a + sumElements[{b, c}],`
`    {sumElements[{b, c}], b + sumElements[{c}],`
`      {sumElements[{c}], c + sumElements[{}],`
`        {sumElements[{}], 0}, c + 0, c}, b + c}, a + (b + c), a + b + c}`

We can use recursion for functions with multiple arguments as well. add
Pairs $[lis_1, lis_2]$ is given two lists of numbers of equal length and returns a list containing the pairwise sums.

Here, the idea is to apply `addPairs` recursively to the tails of both lists.

In[11]:= `addPairs[{}, {}] := {}`
`addPairs[{x1_, r1___}, {x2_, r2___}] :=`
`    Join[{x1 + x2}, addPairs[{r1}, {r2}]]`

In[13]:= `addPairs[{1, 2, 3}, {4, 5, 6}]`

Out[13]= `{5, 7, 9}`

In[14]:= `addPairs[{x_1, y_1, z_1}, {x_2, y_2, z_2}]`

Out[14]= `{x_1 + x_2, y_1 + y_2, z_1 + z_2}`

The recursive calls do not always have to be on the tail of the original argument. Any smaller list will do. The function `multPairwise` multiplies together every pair of elements in a list. The trick is to make the recursive call on the tail of the tail.

In[15]:= `multPairwise[{}] := {}`
`multPairwise[{x_, y_, r___}] := Join[{x y}, multPairwise[{r}]]`

In[17]:= `multPairwise[{3, 9, 17, 2, 6, 60}]`

Out[17]= `{27, 34, 360}`

As a last simple example, consider the function `deal` defined in Chapter 4. The function `deal [n]` produces a list of *n* playing cards randomly chosen from a 52-card deck (stored as the value of `cardDeck`, a 52-element list). Here is how we might write this function recursively.

First, dealing zero cards is easy.

In[18]:= `deal[0] := {}`

Now, suppose we have dealt *n* − 1 cards; how do we deal *n*? Just randomly deal a card from the remaining $52 - (n - 1) = 53 - n$. To do this, randomly choose an integer *r* between 1 and $53 - n$, remove the *r*th card, and add it to the list of cards already dealt.

In[19]:= `deal[n_] := Module[{dealt = deal[n - 1]}, Append[dealt,`
         `Complement[cardDeck, dealt][[Random[Integer, {1, 53 - n}]]]]]`

Here again is the `cardDeck` function defined earlier in Chapter 4.

In[20]:= `cardDeck = Flatten[Outer[List,`
         `{♣, ♦, ♡, ♠}, Join[Range[2, 10], {J, Q, K, A}]], 1];`

And here is the recursive `deal`.

In[21]:= `deal[5]`

Out[21]= `{{♠, 7}, {♠, 5}, {♠, J}, {♦, 2}, {♡, A}}`

Exercises

1. Write a recursive function `sumOddElements` [*lis*] that adds up only the elements of the list *lis* that are odd integers. *lis* may contain even integers and nonintegers. (Use `IntegerQ` to determine if a given element is an integer.)

2. Write a recursive function `sumEveryOtherElement` [*lis*] that adds up `lis[[1]], lis[[3]], lis[[5]]`, etc. Each of these elements is a number. *lis* may have any number of elements.

3. Write a function `addTriples` [*lis*$_1$, *lis*$_2$, *lis*$_3$] that is like `addPairs` in that it adds up the corresponding elements of the three equal-length lists of numbers.

4. Write a function `multAllPairs` [*lis*] that multiplies every consecutive pair of integers in the numerical list *lis*.

    In[1]:= **multAllPairs[{3, 9, 17, 2, 6, 60}]**

    Out[1]= {27, 153, 34, 12, 360}

5. Write the function `maxPairs` [*lis*$_1$, *lis*$_2$] which, for numerical lists of equal length, returns a list of the greater value in each corresponding pair.

6. The function `interleave` [*lis*$_1$, *lis*$_2$], which merges two lists of equal length, can be defined as follows:

    In[2]:= **interleave[lis1_, lis2_] := Flatten[Transpose[{lis1, lis2}]]**

    In[3]:= **interleave[{a, b, c}, {x, y, z}]**

    Out[3]= {a, x, b, y, c, z}

    Rewrite `interleave` using recursion.

7.3 Thinking recursively: examples

The manner in which expressions are rewritten during *Mathematica*'s evaluation process completely explains how recursion works, and it can be seen using `Trace` or `Trace` `Print`, as we did above. But that knowledge is of only limited usefulness in writing recursive functions.

Indeed, the real trick is to *forget* the evaluation process and simply *assume* that the function you are defining will return the correct answer when applied to smaller values. Suspend disbelief – you will begin to see how simple recursion really is.

Finding maxima

Recall the function `maxima` (from Section 4.4 of the Functional Programming chapter), which, given a list of numbers, produces a list of those numbers greater than all those that precede them.

    In[1]:= **maxima[{9, 2, 10, 3, 14, 9}]**

    Out[1]= {9, 10, 14}

We again start by assuming that we can easily compute maxima [Rest [*lis*]] for any list *lis*, and then ask ourselves: how can we compute maxima [*lis*] starting from maxima [∵ Rest [*lis*]] ?

```
In[2]:=  maxima[Rest[{9, 2, 10, 3, 14, 9}]]

Out[2]=  {2, 10, 14}
```

The answer is to remove any values not greater than First [*lis*], then put First [*lis*] at the beginning of the result.

```
In[3]:=  Select[%, # > 9 &]

Out[3]=  {10, 14}
```

```
In[4]:=  Join[{9}, %]

Out[4]=  {9, 10, 14}
```

Again, the base case needs to be accounted for, and we end up with the following:

```
In[5]:=  maxima[{}] := {}

In[6]:=  maxima[{x_, r___}] := Join[{x}, Select[maxima[{r}], # > x &]]

In[7]:=  maxima[{3, 6, 2, 1, 8, 7, 12}]

Out[7]=  {3, 6, 8, 12}
```

The lesson of this section (and it is an important one) is not to worry about how the recursive cases are computed – *assume* that they work, and just think about how to compute the value you want from the result of the recursive call.

Subsets

The second problem we will tackle is to generate a list of k-element subsets of any given set. Our sets will be represented by lists in *Mathematica*, so this amounts to a recursion on the elements of this list. The syntax of our function will be subsets [*lis*, k], so if $k = 2$, for example, this would generate all 2-element subsets of *lis*.

Let us apply the basic principle we have just learned. Given *lis*, we *assume* that subsets [Rest [*lis*], k-1] will give the correct result, and call that result res. How can we then compute subsets [*lis*] ?

A possible approach to defining subsets is to take subsets [Rest [*lis*], k] together with the result of joining {First [*lis*] } to all the elements in subsets [∵ Rest [*lis*], $k - 1$] .

We need to first define the base cases: subsets of length 0 and the subsets of an empty set.

```
In[8]:=  subsets[lis_, 0] := {{}}
         subsets[{}, k_] := {}
```

Here then is the recursion.

```
In[10]:=  subsets[lis_, k_] :=
           Module[{res = subsets[Rest[lis], k - 1]}, Join[
             Map[(Join[{First[lis]}, #] &), res], subsets[Rest[lis], k]]
           ]
```

Here are a few tests.

```
In[11]:=  subsets[Range[5], 1]
```

```
Out[11]=  {{1}, {2}, {3}, {4}, {5}}
```

```
In[12]:=  subsets[Range[5], 2]
```

```
Out[12]=  {{1, 2}, {1, 3}, {1, 4}, {1, 5},
           {2, 3}, {2, 4}, {2, 5}, {3, 4}, {3, 5}, {4, 5}}
```

```
In[13]:=  subsets[Range[5], 4]
```

```
Out[13]=  {{1, 2, 3, 4}, {1, 2, 3, 5},
           {1, 2, 4, 5}, {1, 3, 4, 5}, {2, 3, 4, 5}}
```

The recursion is fairly deep, so this function is not terribly efficient for large values. This computes all of the 5-element subsets from the 30-element set given by Range[30].

```
In[14]:=  Timing[xx = subsets[Range[30], 5];]
```

```
Out[14]=  {6.189 Second, Null}
```

There are $\binom{30}{5} = 142{,}506$ of them.

```
In[15]:=  Length[xx]
```

```
Out[15]=  142506
```

We should check that our function at least produced the correct number of subsets.

```
In[16]:=  Binomial[30, 5]
```

```
Out[16]=  142506
```

Comparing our subsets with the built-in Subsets, we can see that the built-in function is clearly superior in terms of speed, being more than two orders of magnitude faster.

In[17]:= **Timing[yy = Subsets[Range[30], {5}];]**

Out[17]= {0.03 Second, Null}

In[18]:= **Length[yy]**

Out[18]= 142506

The exercises at the end of this section include a problem to modify the subsets function so that it behaves more like the built-in Subsets, which allows you to also generate subsets of *all* lengths up to a given size.

Run-length encoding

We now turn to another, somewhat more involved example – programming run-length encoding. runEncode implements a method commonly used to compress large amounts of data in those cases where the data are likely to contain long sequences ("runs") of the same value. A good example is the representation of video images in a computer as collections of color values for the individual dots, or "pixels," in the image. Since video pictures often contain large areas of a single color, this representation may lead to lists of hundreds, or even thousands of occurrences of the identical color value, one after another. Such a sequence can be represented very compactly using just two numbers, the color value and the length of the run.

runEncode compresses a list by dividing it into runs of occurrences of a single element, and returns a list of the runs, each represented as a pair containing the element and the length of its run. So the following list,

{9, 9, 9, 9, 9, 4, 3, 3, 3, 3, 5, 5, 5, 5, 5, 5}

should produce the following runs once encoded.

{{9, 5}, {4, 1}, {3, 4}, {5, 6}}

Given list *lis*, we just assume that runEncode [Rest [*lis*]] gives the compressed form of the tail of *lis* (call it *res*), and ask ourselves: given the list *lis* and the list *res*, how can we compute runEncode [*lis*] ? Let *x* be *lis* [[1]] , and consider the cases:

1. First we define what runEncode should do in the two base cases: when the list is empty and when the list consists of only one element.

In[19]:= **runEncode [{}] := {}**
        runEncode [{x_}] := {{x, 1}}

2. res might be { }, if lis has one element. In this case, *lis* = {x} and run·
   Encode [*lis*] } = {x, 1}.

3. If the length of lis is greater than 1, res has the form { {y, k} , ...}, and there
   are two cases:

   - y = x: runEncode [*lis*] = { {y, k + 1} , ...}

   - y ≠ x: runEncode [*lis*] = { {x, 1} , {y, k} , ...}

In[21]:= `runEncode[{x_, res___}] := Module[{R = runEncode[{res}], p},`
   `p = First[R];`
   `If[x == First[p],`
   `Join[{{x, p[[2]] + 1}}, Rest[R]],`
   `Join[{{x, 1}}, R]]]`

In[22]:= `runEncode[{9, 9, 9, 9, 9, 4, 3, 3, 3, 3, 5, 5, 5, 5, 5, 5}]`

Out[22]= `{{9, 5}, {4, 1}, {3, 4}, {5, 6}}`

This can be made a lot clearer by replacing the last clause above with a transformation rule.

In[23]:= `runEncodeT[{x_, res___}] := runEncodeT[{res}] /.`
   `{{y_, k_}, s___} → If[x == y, {{x, k + 1}, s}, {{x, 1}, {y, k}, s}]`

In[24]:= `runEncodeT[{}] := {}`
   `runEncodeT[{x_}] := {{x, 1}}`

In[26]:= `runEncodeT[{9, 9, 9, 9, 9, 4, 3, 3, 3, 3, 5, 5, 5, 5, 5, 5}]`

Out[26]= `{{9, 5}, {4, 1}, {3, 4}, {5, 6}}`

Incidentally, a program for this problem, due to Frank Zizza of Willamette College, won an honorable mention in the programming contest at the 1990 *Mathematica* Conference. It uses no recursion, just repeated substitution.

In[27]:= `runEncodeZ[lis_] := Map[{#, 1} &, lis] //.`
   `{x___, {y_, i_}, {y_, j_}, z___} → {x, {y, i + j}, z}`

In[28]:= `runEncodeZ[{9, 9, 9, 9, 9, 4, 3, 3, 3, 3, 5, 5, 5, 5, 5, 5}]`

Out[28]= `{{9, 5}, {4, 1}, {3, 4}, {5, 6}}`

Impressively clever, and quite similar conceptually to the `listsort` function we created in Section 6.4, but our recursive version is much more efficient on most examples. *Mathematica* contains a function `Split` which effectively does run length encoding, although it represents the output slightly different from our `runEncode` functions.

```
In[29]:= Split[{9, 9, 9, 9, 9, 4, 3, 3, 3, 3, 5, 5, 5, 5, 5, 5}]

Out[29]= {{9, 9, 9, 9, 9}, {4}, {3, 3, 3, 3}, {5, 5, 5, 5, 5, 5}}
```

You could easily convert the output of Split to that produced by our runEncode functions by mapping the appropriate pure function.

```
In[30]:= Map[{First[#], Length[#]} &, %]

Out[30]= {{9, 5}, {4, 1}, {3, 4}, {5, 6}}
```

We leave it as an exercise to go in the other direction – that is, convert the output of our runEncode function to that produced by Split.

Finally, we should mention some efficiency issues. Each of the run-length encoding implementations presented in this section are reasonably fast for relatively small inputs, vectors of length less than a few hundred. But for larger vectors and for certain cases, they get quite bogged down, mostly due to the deep recursion needed in these cases. This can be seen quite plainly as follows:

```
In[31]:= data = Range[300];

In[32]:= runEncode[data]

        $RecursionLimit::reclim :
         Recursion depth of 256 exceeded. More...

        General::stop :
         Further output of $RecursionLimit::reclim will
          be suppressed during this calculation. More...

        Join::heads : Heads List and If at positions
         1 and 2 are expected to be the same. More...

        General::stop : Further output of Join::heads will
          be suppressed during this calculation. More...

Out[32]= If[1 == {2, 1}, Join[{{1, p$178481[[2]] + 1}}, Rest[R$178481]],
         Join[{{1, 1}}, R$178481]]
```

A possible solution would be to recognize that there is quite a deep recursion here and hence to increase the built in recursion limit; and this seems to work.

```
In[33]:= Block[{$RecursionLimit = ∞},
         Timing[runEncode[data];]]

Out[33]= {0.01 Second, Null}
```

But trying a larger example shows that the underlying algorithm, although mostly linear in the size of the input, is quite slow for input as small as about 10,000 in length.

```
In[34]:= Block[{$RecursionLimit = ∞},
            Table[Timing[runEncode[Range[2^k 10^3]];][[1]], {k, 0, 3}]]
```

```
Out[34]= {0.07 Second, 0.18 Second, 0.671 Second, 2.413 Second}
```

In such cases it is best to rethink your algorithm and either try to refine it or find a different and better implementation. In the case of run-length encoding, a more direct, functional approach proves to be much more efficient. Although the following code does not use recursion, we present it here anyway so the reader can compare it with the recursive functions and perform some efficiency tests on the various implementations.

Here is an example list we will use to develop the prototype code.

```
In[35]:= vec = {9, 9, 9, 9, 9, 4, 3, 3, 3, 3, 5, 5, 5, 5, 5, 5};
```

We first take overlapping pairs from vec.

```
In[36]:= Partition[vec, 2, 1]
```

```
Out[36]= {{9, 9}, {9, 9}, {9, 9}, {9, 9}, {9, 4}, {4, 3}, {3, 3}, {3, 3},
          {3, 3}, {3, 5}, {5, 5}, {5, 5}, {5, 5}, {5, 5}, {5, 5}}
```

Each run ends at the position at which a pair from the above partition contains different elements.

```
In[37]:= end = Flatten[Position[%, {a_, b_} /; a ≠ b]]
```

```
Out[37]= {5, 6, 10}
```

We have to add the positions at the beginning and end of the list.

```
In[38]:= end = Join[{0}, end, {Length[vec]}]
```

```
Out[38]= {0, 5, 6, 10, 16}
```

Creating pairs again shows the ending position paired up with the next ending position for each run.

```
In[39]:= Partition[end, 2, 1]
```

```
Out[39]= {{0, 5}, {5, 6}, {6, 10}, {10, 16}}
```

To indicate where the run starts, not where the previous run ended, we add 1 to each first coordinate.

```
In[40]:= runs = Map[Plus[#, {1, 0}] &, %]
```

```
Out[40]= {{1, 5}, {6, 6}, {7, 10}, {11, 16}}
```

Now each pair from runs consists of the starting position and the run length. We can use these pairs as the second argument to Take as in the following example.

```
In[41]:= Take[{a, b, c, d, e}, {3, 5}]
```

```
Out[41]= {c, d, e}
```

So, finally, here is the list of runs.

```
In[42]:= Map[Take[vec, #] &, runs]
```

```
Out[42]= {{9, 9, 9, 9, 9}, {4}, {3, 3, 3, 3}, {5, 5, 5, 5, 5, 5}}
```

Here then is the function split that produces output identical to the built-in Split.

```
In[43]:= split[lis_] := Module[{end, t, runs},
            end =
             Flatten[Position[Partition[lis, 2, 1], {a_, b_} /; a ≠ b]];
            t = Partition[Join[{0}, end, {Length[lis]}], 2, 1];
            runs = Map[Plus[#, {1, 0}] &, t];
            Map[Take[lis, #] &, runs]]
```

```
In[44]:= split[vec]
```

```
Out[44]= {{9, 9, 9, 9, 9}, {4}, {3, 3, 3, 3}, {5, 5, 5, 5, 5, 5}}
```

This implementation is extremely efficient.

```
In[45]:= data = Range[10^5];
```

```
In[46]:= Timing[split[data];][[1]]
```

```
Out[46]= 0.641 Second
```

```
In[47]:= data = Table[Random[Integer], {10^5}];
```

```
In[48]:= Timing[split[data];][[1]]
```

```
Out[48]= 0.591 Second
```

By comparison, we see that our split is only about one order of magnitude slower than the built-in function, which is optimized for such tasks.

```
In[49]:= Timing[Split[data];][[1]]
```

```
Out[49]= 0.04 Second
```

Exercises

1. Write the function prefixMatch [lis_1, lis_2] that finds the starting segments of lis_1 and lis_2 that match.

   In[1]:= **prefixMatch[{1, 2, 3, 4}, {1, 2, 5}]**

   Out[1]= {1, 2}

2. Modify runEncode so that it leaves single elements as they are.

   In[2]:= **runEncode2[{9, 9, 9, 4, 3, 3, 5}]**

   Out[2]= {{9, 3}, 4, {3, 2}, 5}

   For this version, you need to assume that the argument is a list of atoms, otherwise the output would be ambiguous.

3. Modify one of the runEncode functions so that it produces output in the same form as the built-in Split function.

   In[3]:= **Split[{9, 9, 9, 9, 9, 4, 3, 3, 3, 3, 5, 5, 5, 5, 5, 5}]**

   Out[3]= {{9, 9, 9, 9, 9}, {4}, {3, 3, 3, 3}, {5, 5, 5, 5, 5, 5}}

4. A slightly more efficient version of runEncode uses a three-argument auxiliary function.

   ```
   runEncode [{}]  := {}
   runEncode [{x_, r___}]  := runEncode [x, 1, {r}]
   ```

   runEncode [$x, k, \{r\}$] computes the compressed version of $\{x, x, x, ..., x, r\}$, where the xs are given k times. Define this three-argument function. (Note that it is legal to have a function be defined for different numbers of arguments; rules in which runEncode appears on the left-hand side with two arguments will only be applied when runEncode is called with two arguments, and likewise for the three-argument version.) Using the Timing function, compare the efficiency of this version with our earlier version; be sure to try a variety of examples, including lists that have many short runs and ones that have fewer, but longer runs. You will need to use Table to generate lists long enough to see any difference in speed.

5. maxima can also be computed more efficiently with an auxiliary function.

   ```
   maxima [{}] := {}
   maxima [{x_, r___}] := maxima [x, {r}]
   ```

The two-argument version has this meaning: maxima [x, *lis*] gives the maxima of the list Join [{x}, *lis*]. Define it. (*Hint*: the key point about this is that maxima [x, *lis*] is equal to maxima [x, Rest [*lis*]] if $x \geq$ First [*lis*].) Compare its efficiency with the version in the text.

6. Write the function runDecode, which takes an encoded list produced by runEn `code and returns its unencoded form.

> In[4]:= **runDecode[{{9, 5}, {4, 1}, {3, 4}, {5, 6}}]**

> Out[4]= {9, 9, 9, 9, 9, 4, 3, 3, 3, 3, 5, 5, 5, 5, 5, 5}

7. The code we developed to compute the *k*-element subsets of any given list differs from the built-in Subsets function in that the latter has a mechanism for generating all subsets of length less than or equal to *k*.

> In[5]:= **A = {a, b, c, d};**
> **Subsets[A, 2]**

> Out[6]= {{}, {a}, {b}, {c}, {d}, {a, b},
>   {a, c}, {a, d}, {b, c}, {b, d}, {c, d}}

If you want to get *only* two-element subsets you use a slightly different form.

> In[7]:= **Subsets[A, {2}]**

> Out[7]= {{a, b}, {a, c}, {a, d}, {b, c}, {b, d}, {c, d}}

Modify the function subsets developed in this section to take either form: subsets [*lis*, k] or subsets [*lis*, {k}] so that it mimics the behavior of the built-in Subsets.

7.4 Recursion and symbolic computations

Chapters 2 and 6 emphasized the idea that expressions and data are really the same things in *Mathematica*. All that distinguishes an expression like $2 + 3$ from one like $x + y$ is that *Mathematica* has rules for rewriting $2 + 3$ but not for $x + y$.

Symbolic computations are those that transform expressions into other expressions. Programming symbolic computations is no different from any other type of computation: you write rewrite rules, and use local transformations, built-in operations, and recursion.

We will illustrate symbolic computation with what may be the most famous recursive definition of them all: the differential calculus. Every elementary calculus book includes rules for finding derivatives of functions. Generally, they assume that there are expressions *u* containing the variable *x* and they show how to find the derivative of *u* with respect to *x*, $\frac{du}{dx}$, by giving rules like the following.

$$\frac{d(c)}{dx} = 0, \quad \text{for } c \text{ a constant}$$

$$\frac{d(x^n)}{dx} = n\,x^{n-1}$$

$$\frac{d(u+v)}{dx} = \frac{du}{dx} + \frac{dv}{dx}$$

If we think of *du/dx* as a function $\frac{d}{dx}$ being applied to an expression *u*, then these rules would be written in the following notation.

$$\frac{d}{dx}(c) = 0, \quad \text{for } c \text{ a constant}$$

$$\frac{d}{dx}(x^n) = n\,x^{n-1}$$

$$\frac{d}{dx}(u+v) = \frac{d}{dx}(u) + \frac{d}{dx}(v)$$

In this form, it is clear that $\frac{d}{dx}$ is just a recursively defined function from expression to expression, and we can render this function in *Mathematica* directly.

```
In[1]:=  ddx[c_] := 0
         ddx[x^n_] := n x^n-1
         ddx[u_ + v_] := ddx[u] + ddx[v]

In[4]:=  ddx[x² + x³]

Out[4]=  2 x + 3 x²
```

So far, so good, but there are two problems with this, one big and the other bigger. The bigger one is that this function gives completely wrong answers for many expressions.

```
In[5]:=  ddx[5 x³]

Out[5]=  0
```

We have not been careful enough about our base cases. Specifically, the first rule handles *all* expressions not specifically treated elsewhere, instead of just those for which it was intended: constants. This is easily remedied, by replacing that rule with one that makes sure its argument is a number.

First we remove the original definition we gave above for the derivative of a constant.

```
In[6]:=  ddx[c_] =.
```

```
In[7]:=  ddx[c_ ?NumericQ] := 0
```

Now, ddx always gives an answer that is correct, but it still misses a lot of cases.

In[8]:= **ddx [5 x³]**

Out[8]= ddx [5 x³]

At this point, we need to take a close look at the cases we want to cover; that is, the precise set of expressions we want ddx to differentiate. We can define this set using recursion.

An expression (that ddx can differentiate) is one of the following:

- a number

- the variable x

- a sum $u + v$, where u and v are expressions

- a difference $u - v$ of two expressions

- a product $u\,v$ of two expressions

- a quotient u/v of two expressions

- a power u^n of an expression and a number

Now, let us start from scratch, dealing systematically with all the cases.

In[9]:= **Clear[ddx]**
        ddx [c_ ? NumericQ] := 0
        ddx [x] := 1
        ddx [u_ + v_] := ddx [u] + ddx [v]
        ddx [u_ - v_] := ddx [u] - ddx [v]
        ddx [u_ v_] := u ddx [v] + v ddx [u]
        $$\mathbf{ddx\left[\frac{u\_}{v\_}\right] := \frac{v\,ddx[u] - u\,ddx[v]}{v^2}}$$
        ddx [u_ ^c_?NumericQ] := c u^(c-1) ddx [u]

In[17]:= **ddx [5 x³]**

Out[17]= 15 x²

Note the use of NumericQ (as opposed to NumberQ). NumberQ returns a value of True only if its argument is explicitly a number. It returns False for symbols that are numeric though.

In[18]:= **NumberQ[π]**

Out[18]= False

NumericQ, on the other hand, returns true for any expression that is numeric, including symbols such as π, e, and i.

In[19]:= **ddx[π]**

Out[19]= 0

One interesting point to note here is that one of the cases from our first definition, x^n, does not appear here in that form. Still, this case is handled correctly, as we have just seen. A Trace makes it clear why.

In[20]:= **Trace[ddx[x³], ddx]**

Out[20]= {ddx[x³], 3 x³⁻¹ ddx[x], {ddx[x], 1}}

In other words, it is handled as part of a more general case, namely u^n for arbitrary u. Our new rule works in additional cases.

In[21]:= **ddx$\left[(x + 2 x^2)^4\right]$**

Out[21]= 4 (1 + 4 x) (x + 2 x²)³

It is very common to make the mistake of covering cases in more ways than one. For example, many calculus books include both the case $c\,x^n$ and, separately, the cases for c, x, u^n, and $u\,v$, which together can handle expressions of the form $c\,x^n$. It is harmless, but a more systematic treatment of the cases avoids giving extra rules, while also ensuring that all cases are covered.

Finally, we might want to make use of simple algebraic identities to simplify this code. For example, the rule for quotients is already covered by the rules for products and powers, since $\frac{u}{v} = u\,v^{-1}$. Similarly, $u - v = u + (-1)\,v$.

In[22]:= **ddx[u_ - v_] := ddx[u - v]**

        ddx$\left[\dfrac{u\_}{v\_}\right]$:= ddx$\left[\dfrac{u}{v}\right]$

Trying these new definitions out on an example still fails.

In[24]:= **ddx$\left[\dfrac{x^2}{x-1}\right]$**

        $IterationLimit::itlim :
            Iteration limit of 4096 exceeded. More…

Out[24]= Hold$\left[\text{ddx}\left[\dfrac{x^2}{-1 + x}\right]\right]$

In other words, this computation was going on forever. Alas, here *Mathematica*'s own simplification rules defeated us, as we can see by looking at the rules for ddx.

In[25]:= **?ddx**

Global`ddx

ddx[x] := 1

ddx[c_?NumericQ] := 0

ddx[u_ - v_] := ddx[u - v]

ddx[u_ + v_] := ddx[u] + ddx[v]

ddx$\left[\frac{u\_}{v\_}\right]$:= ddx$\left[\frac{u}{v}\right]$

ddx[u_ v_] := u ddx[v] + v ddx[u]

ddx[u_$^{c\_?NumericQ}$] := c u^{c-1} ddx[u]

When we entered the new rules, *Mathematica* rewrote the right-hand sides, so that the rules just say, in effect, "rewrite ddx[u-v] to ddx[u-v]" and "rewrite ddx[u/v] to ddx[u/v]." This fails to satisfy our rule that recursive calls can only be made to *smaller* values.

On the other hand, let us try just deleting those rules entirely and see what happens.

In[26]:= **ddx[u_ - v_] =.**

ddx$\left[\dfrac{u\_}{v\_}\right]$ =.

In[28]:= **Simplify$\left[\text{ddx}\left[\dfrac{x}{x-1}\right]\right]$**

Out[28]= $-\dfrac{1}{(-1+x)^2}$

Again, we need to take into account what *Mathematica* is doing with the expressions we enter. It turns out that it actually reads expressions of the form u/v as $u(v^{-1})$ and expressions of the form $u - v$ as $u + (-1)v$.

In[29]:= **FullForm$\left[\dfrac{u}{v}\right]$**

Out[29]//FullForm=
            Times[u, Power[v, -1]]

In[30]:= **FullForm[u - v]**

Out[30]//FullForm=
    Plus[u, Times[-1, v]]

When we entered ddx[x/(x-1)], *Mathematica* read it as ddx[x(x + 1)$^{-1}$]. In this form, the existing rules apply.

In[31]:= **FullForm[Hold[ddx[$\frac{x}{x - 1}$]]]**

Out[31]//FullForm=
    Hold[ddx[Times[x, Power[Plus[x, -1], -1]]]]

Exercises

1. Add rules to ddx for the trigonometric functions sine, cosine, and tangent.

2. When variables other than *x* are present in an expression, the rules for differentiation with respect to *x* actually do not change. That is, expressions that have no occurrences of *x* are treated like constants. So there should be a rule that says ddx[*u*] = 0, if *x* does not occur anywhere in *u*. Define the function nox[*e*] to return True if *x* does not occur within *e*, then add the new rule for those expressions. You will need to use the comparison function = ! =, called UnsameQ, which tests whether two symbols are unequal; the usual Unequal comparison (! =) cannot be used to compare symbols.

3. Define a two-argument version of ddx whose second argument is the variable with respect to which the derivative of the expression is to be computed. Thus, ddx[*u*, *x*] will be the same as our current ddx[*u*]. You will need to determine when an expression has no occurrences of a variable; you can use the built-in function FreeQ.

7.5 Classical examples

Merge sort

Sorting the elements of a list is one of the most important tasks in computer science. There are quite a few well-studied algorithms that have been developed for performing various types of sorting. These include selection sort, insertion sort, bubble sort, quick sort, heap sort, merge sort, and many others. We have already looked at a rather primitive list sorting algorithm in Section 6.4. In this section, we will develop an algorithm for merge sort, which is a classical divide-and-conquer algorithm.

The procedure for merge sort consists of three basic steps:

- first, split the original list into two parts of roughly equal size

- sort each part recursively

- finally, merge the two sorted sublists

We will start with the last step first – creating a function `merge` that takes two lists, each assumed to be sorted, and produces a single merged, sorted list. Using pattern matching we can set this up as a recursion. First we deal with the cases of when either of the two lists is empty.

```
In[1]:=  merge[lis_List, {}] := lis
         merge[{}, lis_List] := lis
```

The recursion then is on the tail of the sublists. We use the triple-blank to pattern match `ra` and `rb` here so that they can represent zero, one, or more arguments.

```
In[3]:=  merge[{a_, ra___}, {b_, rb___}] :=
           If[a ≤ b,
             Join[{a}, merge[{b}, {ra, rb}]],
             Join[{b}, merge[{a, ra}, {rb}]]
           ]
```

Here are several test cases.

```
In[4]:=  merge[{1, 4, 7}, {2, 6, 9, 14}]
```

```
Out[4]=  {1, 2, 4, 6, 7, 9, 14}
```

```
In[5]:=  merge[{14}, {2, 5, 7, 8}]
```

```
Out[5]=  {2, 5, 7, 8, 14}
```

Now we turn to the sorting function. This too will be defined recursively by first dividing the list into two sublists, performing the sort on each sublist and then merging these two sorted sublists using the above `merge` function.

Here are the two base cases; the empty list and a list with a single element in it.

In[6]:= `MergeSort[{}] := {};`
`MergeSort[{x_}] := {x};`

Here is the recursion.

In[8]:= $\texttt{MergeSort[lis\_List]} := \texttt{Module}\Big[\Big\{\texttt{div} = \texttt{Floor}\Big[\dfrac{\texttt{Length[lis]}}{2}\Big]\Big\},$

$\qquad \texttt{merge[}$
$\qquad\quad \texttt{MergeSort[Take[lis, div]], MergeSort[Drop[lis, div]]]}\Big]$

Let us look at a few test cases to get a sense of the efficiency of our program.

In[9]:= `dataInt = Table[Random[Integer, {1, 100}], {20}]`

Out[9]= `{84, 83, 58, 8, 30, 99, 72, 29, 77,`
`    95, 63, 67, 47, 40, 95, 71, 14, 57, 57, 24}`

In[10]:= `MergeSort[dataInt]`

Out[10]= `{8, 14, 29, 30, 58, 72, 77, 83, 84,`
`    95, 24, 40, 47, 57, 63, 67, 57, 71, 95, 99}`

In[11]:= `dataReal = Table[Random[], {1000}];`

In[12]:= `Timing[`
`    Block[{$RecursionLimit = ∞}, MergeSort[dataReal];]]`

Out[12]= `{0.16 Second, Null}`

Notice the need to increase the built-in recursion limit for larger computations. This limitation in our current definitions is due to the fact that both `merge` and `MergeSort` use recursion and that `MergeSort` has a double recursive call in it.

In comparison, the built-in `Sort` function, which uses a modified merge sort, is optimized for dealing with large arrays of numbers and is much, much faster.

In[13]:= `Timing[Sort[dataReal];]`

Out[13]= `{0. Second, Null}`

Here we see that `Sort` can perform this computation in about the same time it took our `MergeSort` to sort a dataset that was two orders of magnitude smaller.

In[14]:= `Timing[Sort[Table[Random[], {10^5}]];]`

Out[14]= `{0.08 Second, Null}`

The exercises will give you a chance to refine the MergeSort and improve its efficiency.

Gaussian elimination

An extremely common problem in mathematical computation is to solve a linear system S of the following form.

$$E_1 : \; a_{11} x_1 + a_{12} x_2 + \cdots + a_{1n} x_n = b_1$$
$$E_2 : \; a_{21} x_1 + a_{22} x_2 + \cdots + a_{2n} x_n = b_2$$
$$\vdots$$
$$E_n : \; a_{n1} x_1 + a_{n2} x_2 + \cdots + a_{nn} x_n = b_n$$

The values of the variables $x_1, \ldots, x_n$ are called the *unknowns*, and the a_{ij} and b_i are constants.

Mathematica has a built-in function LinearSolve that will usually give the correct answer. For example, here is a simple 2×2 system, two equations in two unknowns.

$$x_1 + 2 x_2 = 3$$
$$4 x_1 + 5 x_2 = 6$$

With a little work, you can see that the solution is $x_1 = -1$, $x_2 = 2$. Here is how to solve this system using the built-in LinearSolve.

```
In[15]:=  m = ( 1 2
              4 5 );

          b = {3, 6};
```

```
In[17]:=  LinearSolve[m, b]
```

```
Out[17]=  {-1, 2}
```

So why learn to program it yourself? Because LinearSolve, like any algorithm, may run into trouble on certain kinds of input, and when confronted with a system for which it fails, your only recourse will be to write your own program.

The Hilbert matrices, containing elements $h_{ij} = 1/(i+j-1)$, cause problems for LinearSolve.

```
In[18]:=  HilbertMatrix[n_] := Table[ 1/(i + j - 1), {i, n}, {j, n}]
```

Here is a random 1×10 vector.

```
In[19]:=  b = Table[Random[], {10}];
```

In[20]:= **xsoln = LinearSolve[HilbertMatrix[10], b]**

> LinearSolve::luc :
>   Result for LinearSolve of badly conditioned
>   matrix {{1., 0.5, ≪6≫, 0.111111, 0.1},
>   ≪8≫, {0.1, ≪8≫, ≪20≫}} may
>   contain significant numerical errors. More…

Out[20]= {1.56074 × 10⁶, -1.28819 × 10⁸, 2.64644 × 10⁹,
   -2.33592 × 10¹⁰, 1.08702 × 10¹¹, -2.92604 × 10¹¹,
   4.71438 × 10¹¹, -4.48426 × 10¹¹, 2.32154 × 10¹¹, -5.04243 × 10¹⁰}

Using this last result in the original system should give all 0s, but it does not.

In[21]:= **HilbertMatrix[10].xsoln - b**

Out[21]= {-0.0000109427, -3.52143 × 10⁻⁶, -0.0000175983,
   8.07756 × 10⁻⁶, 9.30083 × 10⁻⁶, 6.04337 × 10⁻⁶, -1.22291 × 10⁻⁶,
   1.89195 × 10⁻⁶, -8.85718 × 10⁻⁶, -7.31392 × 10⁻⁶}

In this section, we will show how to program a simple and classic method, called *Gaussian elimination*, to solve linear systems. Our method, unfortunately, will also fail on the Hilbert matrix, but we will revisit the problem in Chapter 8 and show how a variant of this method can solve it.

For now, consider that we have the system shown above. By the principle of recursion, we can assume the ability to solve any smaller system – in particular, any system of $n - 1$ equations in $n - 1$ unknowns, and ask our usual question: How can the ability to solve smaller systems be used to solve this system?

The idea behind Gaussian elimination is to *eliminate* all occurrences of x_1 from the equations $E_2, \ldots, E_n$. For example, here is how to eliminate x_1 from E_2:

1. Multiply the first equation E_1 by a_{21} / a_{11}.

$$\frac{a_{21}}{a_{11}} (a_{11} x_1 + a_{21} x_2 + \cdots + a_{1n} x_n) = \left(\frac{a_{21}}{a_{11}}\right) b_1$$

This simplifies to:

$$a_{21} x_1 + \left(\frac{a_{21}}{a_{11}}\right) a_{12} x_2 + \cdots + \left(\frac{a_{21}}{a_{11}}\right) a_{1n} x_n = \left(\frac{a_{21}}{a_{11}}\right) b_1$$

2. Subtract this modified equation from E_2.

$$a_{21} x_1 + a_{22} x_2 + \cdots + a_{2n} x_n = b_2$$
$$-\left(a_{21} x_1 + \left(\frac{a_{21}}{a_{11}}\right) a_{12} x_2 + \cdots + \left(\frac{a_{21}}{a_{11}}\right) a_{1n} x_n = \left(\frac{a_{21}}{a_{11}}\right) b_1\right)$$
$$\left(a_{22} - \frac{a_{21}}{a_{11}} a_{12}\right) x_2 + \cdots + \left(a_{2n} - \frac{a_{21}}{a_{11}} a_{1n}\right) x_n = b_2 - \frac{a_{21}}{a_{11}} b_1$$

We have obtained an equation having only $n - 1$ variables. Now do this for every equation: Transform E_i, for all $2 \le i \le n$, to $E_i' = E_i - \left(\frac{a_{i1}}{a_{11}}\right) E_1$. Call this new system of equations S'.

We are almost there. We can (recursively) find the solution to the system S', obtaining the values of x_2, ..., x_n. Then x_1 is found by computing the following.

$$x_1 = \frac{b_1 - (a_{12} x_2 + \cdots + a_{1n} x_n)}{a_{11}}$$

In programming this procedure, the system will be represented by the $n \times n$ matrix of coefficients, together with the vector of the b_i. In fact, it is somewhat more convenient to represent the entire system as an $(n + 1) \times n$ matrix (called the *augmented matrix*), with the b_i included as the last column. We will define solve [*s*], where *s* is such an $(n + 1) \times n$ matrix, to return a list of the values of the n unknowns x_1, ..., x_n. Once we understand the algorithm, the programming is simply a lot of list manipulation.

```
In[22]:=  solve[s_] := Module[{E1 = First[s], x2toxn = solve[elimx1[s]]},
            Join[
              {(Last[E1] - Drop[Rest[E1], -1].x2toxn) / First[E1]}, x2toxn]]
```

We need to define elimx1 [*s*], which produces the smaller system. But first, let us not forget the base case, $n = 1$ (that is, $a_{11} x_1 = b_1$), which is trivial to solve.

```
In[23]:=  solve[{{a11_, b1_}}] := { b1/a11 }
```

Again the elimination phase takes each row $a_{i1}, a_{i2}, ..., a_{in}, b_i$ and transforms it to the following.

$$a_{i2} - \left(\frac{a_{i1}}{a_{11}}\right) a_{12}, \ ..., \ a_{in} - \left(\frac{a_{i1}}{a_{11}}\right) a_{1n}, \ b_i - \left(\frac{a_{i1}}{a_{11}}\right) b_1$$

Here then is the code that implements these steps.

```
In[24]:=  elimx1[s_] := Map[subtractE1[s[[1]], #] &, Rest[s]]
```

```
In[25]:=  subtractE1[E1_, Ei_] := Rest[Ei] - (Ei[[1]])/(E1[[1]]) Rest[E1]
```

Finally, we will overload this version of solve so that it works like the built-in LinearSolve; that is, it accepts a matrix of coefficients and a column vector as arguments. This will avoid having to compute the transposition manually.

```
In[26]:=  solve[A_, b_] := solve[Transpose[Join[Transpose[A], {b}]]]
```

```
In[27]:=  solve[{{1, 2}, {4, 5}}, {3, 6}]
```

```
Out[27]=  {-1, 2}
```

Trees

Mathematica expressions can be visualized as *upside-down trees*; for example, f [x,y+1] could be expressed using TreeForm.

In[28]:= **TreeForm[f[x, y + 1]]**

Out[28]//TreeForm=

$$f\left[x, \quad \underset{\text{Plus}[1, y]}{\big|}\right]$$

A common visualization of such an expression is by means of a picture like this.

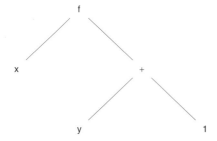

Such structures are called *trees*, drawn upside-down, and they have many uses in programming. In this section, we will discuss a way of representing trees in *Mathematica*, develop some basic functions on trees, and, in the next section, give a well-known application, Huffman encoding.

First, some terminology: Trees consist of *nodes*, which have *labels* (the symbols f, x, +, y, and 1 in the example above) and some number of *children*, which are themselves nodes (that is, the nodes labeled x and + are the children of the node labeled f). If a node has no children, it is called a *leaf*; otherwise, it is an *interior node*. The node at the top of the tree is called the *root* of the tree. In the example above, the interior nodes are the ones labeled f and +, and the root is the node labeled f.

More specifically, we will be discussing *binary trees* – trees in which every interior node has two children, called the *left child* and *right child*.

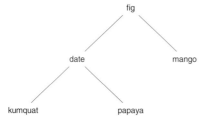

We will be interested in trees whose labels are data values like numbers and strings. The simplest way to represent them in *Mathematica* is to use lists: an interior node is represented by a three-element list containing the node's label and its two children; a leaf node by a one-element list containing the label. For example, the tree above is represented as follows:

```
{"fig", {"date", {"kumquat"}, {"papaya"}}, {"mango"}}
```

Many – in fact, most – algorithms that operate on trees are recursive. It is natural, because simply "visiting" every node in a tree is a recursive process. For example, suppose we have a tree of strings like the fruit tree above, and we want to find the alphabetically smallest string in the tree; that is, the first string in the lexicographic ordering of strings.

```
In[29]:=  fruittree =
            {"fig", {"date", {"kumquat"}, {"papaya"}}, {"mango"}};
```

As usual, we should try not to think about exactly how the function works, but just ask this question: given the minimum strings in the children of a node, how can we find the minimum for the entire tree? Just pick the minimum among the label of this node and the minima (recursively computed) of its children. The easiest way to find the minimum of a collection of strings is to sort them and take the first element.

```
In[30]:=  minInTree[{lab_}] := lab
          minInTree[{lab_, lc_, rc_}] :=
            Sort[{lab, minInTree[lc], minInTree[rc]}][[1]]
```

```
In[32]:=  minInTree[fruittree]
```

```
Out[32]=  date
```

It will be useful to have a function that determines the height of a tree, given by the distance from the root to the farthest leaf node.

```
In[33]:=  height[{lab_}] := 0
          height[{lab_, lc_, rc_}] := 1 + Max[height[lc], height[rc]]
```

It would be nice to have a better way to display trees than as lists. In Chapter 9, we will discuss the graphical display of trees, but for now we can at least print them in a nicely indented style. To do so, we need an auxiliary function: printTree[t, k] prints t in indented form, with the entire tree moved over k units. To put it another way, it prints t, assuming it occurs k levels down. We have chosen, arbitrarily, to indent three spaces for each level in the tree.

```
In[35]:=  printTree[t_] := printTree[t, 0]
```

```
In[36]:= printTree[{lab_}, k_] := printIndented[lab, 3 k]
         printTree[{lab_, lc_, rc_}, k_] :=
           (printIndented[lab, 3 k];
             Map[printTree[#, k + 1] &, {lc, rc}];)
         printIndented[x_, spaces_] :=
           Print[Apply[StringJoin, Table["  ", {spaces}]], x]

In[39]:= printTree[fruittree]
       fig

          date

              kumquat

              papaya

          mango
```

Huffman encoding

Computers represent textual information such as lists of characters, as *bit strings*, which are sequences of 0s and 1s. Especially in the transmission of large amounts of data, it is important to minimize the number of bits used to encode the text.

Character	ASCII Codes Decimal	8 – Bit Binary
A	65	01000001
B	66	01000010
E	69	01000101
H	72	01001000
N	78	01001110
O	79	01001111
S	83	01010011
T	84	01010100
(space)	32	00100000

For simplicity, most of the time strings are represented using *fixed-length* codes, those in which each character is represented by a bit string of the same length. The most common such code, as discussed in Section 3.5, is ASCII. Each character has a number that can be represented in 8 bits, as given in the ASCII codes table.

For example, the string "HONEST ABE" is represented as the following binary code:

```
01001000010011110100111001000101010101011
```

```
01010100001000000100000101000010010000101
```

However, this representation is far from being optimally compact. Better codes are *variable-length codes*, using shorter bit strings for more common characters (just as Morse code uses the shortest code – a single dot – for the most common letter in English, *e*. Given a list of characters and their relative frequencies, the most compact encoding of strings that respect those frequencies is called the *Huffman encoding*. David Huffman showed how to construct this code and represent it using a tree (see Knuth 1997 or Sedgewick 1988 for more information). We will define what Huffman encoding trees are and show how to use them to encode and decode strings, and then show how to construct them.

Simply put, a Huffman encoding tree is a binary tree with characters labeling the leaf nodes. An example is shown in Figure 7.1. Note that the space (B) appears in the tree as an ordinary character, just as it does in the ASCII code.

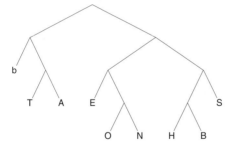

Figure 7.1:   A Huffman encoding tree

To use the tree to find the code for a character, look for the character in the tree and record the sequence of branches going from the root to the character. For example, for H, the trip is: right branch, then right, then left, and left again. Recording a 1 for a right branch and a 0 for a left, this gives the code for H: 1100. Here, then, are the codes for all the characters given in this tree.

Character	Code	Character	Code	Character	Code
b	00	*E*	100	*O*	1010
A	011	*H*	1100	*S*	111
B	1101	*N*	1011	*T*	010

Note how the most common characters have shorter codes; for example, the space, which occurs very often, uses only two bits. Of course, if we included the entire alphabet, our tree would be much bigger, and many letters would have longer codes.

With this code, the string "HONEST ABE" is represented by:

```
1100101010111001110100000111101100
```

We need to put some more information in our tree. To allow for efficiently finding where a character occurs in the tree, we need to label every interior node with the set of characters labeling leaves below it, as shown in Figure 7.2. Now we can give two programs: one to encode character strings, and one to decode bit strings. The programs we write will assume that Htree contains the tree in Figure 7.2.

```
In[40]:= Htree = {" ABEHONST", {" AT", {" "}, {"AT", {"T"}, {"A"}}},
                  {"BEHONS", {"EON", {"E"}, {"ON", {"O"}, {"N"}}},
                  {"BHS", {"BH", {"H"}, {"B"}}, {"S"}}}}

Out[40]= { ABEHONST, { AT, { }, {AT, {T}, {A}}},
          {BEHONS, {EON, {E}, {ON, {O}, {N}}}, {BHS, {BH, {H}, {B}}, {S}}}}
```

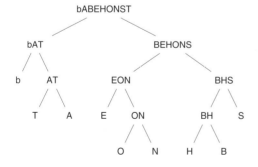

Figure 7.2: A Huffman encoding tree, with interior labels

We consider encoding character strings first. What we really need is the function to give the bit-string encoding of a single character. Given that function – call it encode. Char – we can easily encode an entire string.

In[41]:= **encodeString[str_] := Flatten[Map[encodeChar, Characters[str]]]**

In[42]:= **encodeString["HONEST ABE"]**

Out[42]= {encodeChar[H], encodeChar[O], encodeChar[N],
           encodeChar[E], encodeChar[S], encodeChar[T],
           encodeChar[ ], encodeChar[A], encodeChar[B], encodeChar[E]}

So how do we encode a single character? The method is essentially recursive: find whether the character occurs in the left or the right subtree, recursively find its code in that subtree, and then prepend a 0 if it was in the left or a 1 if it was in the right. For example, consider H again: we can tell from Htree that H occurs in the right subtree; within that subtree, its code is 100 (right, left, left); since it was in the right subtree, we prepend a 1, to get 1100. To do this we give encodeChar two arguments, the character and the Huffman tree.

In[43]:= **encodeChar[c_, {_, lc_, rc_}] := If[stringMemberQ[First[lc], c],
           Join[{0}, encodeChar[c, lc]], Join[{1}, encodeChar[c, rc]]]**

Here is the auxiliary function stringMemberQ.

In[44]:= **stringMemberQ[str_, char_] :=
           Length[StringPosition[str, char]] ≥ 1**

In[45]:= **stringMemberQ["ABE", "B"]**

Out[45]= True

The base case is when we reach a leaf; of course, if the character is in the tree at all – which we are assuming – then it *must* be the label on this leaf, so we do not have to check.

In[46]:= **encodeChar[_, {_}] := {}**

Finally, we can give a one-argument version of encodeChar that uses Htree.

In[47]:= **encodeChar[c_] := encodeChar[c, Htree]**

Decoding of messages works similarly. We use the list of bits to guide our path down the tree, and when we get to a leaf we "emit" that character and start over at the root. Again, we will use a function with two arguments: the list of bits, and the tree. There are two cases: when we are at a leaf, we have reached the end of the encoding of a character; otherwise, we choose the left or right subtree, depending upon the next bit in the code.

```
In[48]:= decode[code_, {ch_}] := StringJoin[ch, decode[code, Htree]]
         decode[{0, r___}, {_, lc_, _}] := decode[{r}, lc]
         decode[{1, r___}, {_, _, rc_}] := decode[{r}, rc]
         decode[{}, _] := ""
```

As usual, we can then give the desired one-argument form.

```
In[52]:= decode[code_] := decode[code, Htree]
```

There is an important point to notice here: in Huffman codes, we always know when a character's code ends. But how? The decode function breaks up the code into characters in some way, but how do we know it is the only possible way?

In fact, a bit of thought will convince you that it must be, because Huffman codes have an interesting property: no character's code can be extended to be the code of another character. For example, no character's code begins with 00, which is the code for space, except space itself; and none begins with 100 except letter Es. This property implies that our decoding algorithm finds the *unique* decoding of a string of bits.

Finally, we discuss how Huffman trees are constructed. This is actually very simple – and not really recursive – so we will describe the method and leave the programming as an exercise.

Keep in mind that the code for a character should be based on a set of *frequencies* of the characters, given at the outset. For example, these might be the frequencies of the characters in our example, based on their occurrences in a large body of English writing (not just our sample phrase).

Characters	Frequency
space	6
E	5
S, T, A	3
H, O, N	2
B	1

So now suppose we are given the list of characters along with their frequencies. For purposes of the algorithm, it is better for us to think that what we have obtained is a list of *trees*, each of which has only a single node, which is labeled by a letter and its frequency.

```
{ {{{b}, 6}}, {{{A}, 3}}, {{{B}, 1}}, {{{E}, 5}}, ...}
```

Still thinking of this as a list of trees, the frequency of each character is called the *weight* of the node containing that character. What we want to do is to combine these single-node trees into larger trees, and keep doing it until they have all been joined into one big tree. So repeatedly perform the following operation on the list of trees:

- Suppose `t1={{cl1,w1},...}` and `t2 = {{cl2,w2},...}` are the trees in the list with the lowest weights (that is, `w1` and `w2` are as small as possible)

- Remove them from the list, and replace them by the single tree `t={{` `Join[cl1,cl2],w1+w2},t1,t2}`

This operation always reduces the number of trees in the list by one. When there is only one tree in the list, that is the Huffman encoding tree for these characters. Or rather it is *a* Huffman encoding tree. The algorithm does not specify how to choose when there are more than two trees of minimal weight, nor in which order to place those two trees once they are chosen, so there are actually many trees that might result. Huffman proved that they all give equally compact representations of bit strings.

Let us see how this works for our example. To make it easier to read, we will draw the trees instead of writing them in *Mathematica* list notation:

1. Start with

    {   b,6   A,3   B,1   E,5   H,2   N,2   O,2   S,3   T,3   }

2. Pick H and B (we could have picked N or O instead of H, but we picked H).
    {   b,6   A,3   BH,3   E,5   N,2   O,2   S,3   T,3   }

    H B

We have dropped the weights from the H and B nodes, since they will not contribute any more to the algorithm.

3. Now we have to choose N and O (although we can put them in either order).
    {   b,6   A,3   BH,3   E,5   NO,4   S,3   T,3   }

    H B   O N

4. We have four trees of weight 3. We (arbitrarily) choose T and A.
    {   b,6   BH,3   E,5   NO,4   S,3   AT,6   }

    H B   O N   T A

5. Now we join the BH tree with the S tree.

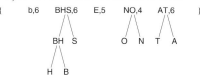

6. Join E with NO.

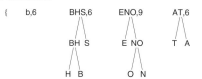

7. And b with AT.

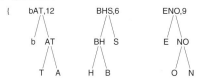

8. BHS with ENO.

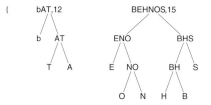

Finally, we join the last two trees, yielding the tree shown in Figure 7.2.

Exercises

1. The Gaussian elimination procedure can fail for a variety of reasons. We have already mentioned that it will not give good results for the Hilbert matrix, but the reason for this is quite subtle and we will postpone our explanation to Section 8.5. Another reason it can fail is that there may be no unique solution at all; consider, for example, the following system.

$$x_1 + x_2 = 0$$
$$2\,x_1 + 2\,x_2 = 0$$

Here, the two equations are essentially the same, so we do not have enough information to determine x_1 and x_2 uniquely. This problem is inherent in this system and cannot be solved, no matter how sophisticated an algorithm we devise.

There is, however, another kind of problem that we should be able to overcome. It is illustrated by the following system.

$$x_1 + x_2 + x_3 = 1$$
$$x_1 + x_2 + 2\,x_3 = 2$$
$$x_1 + 2\,x_2 + 2\,x_3 = 1$$

Our elimination procedure will produce the smaller system corresponding to the call `solve[{{0,1,1},{1,1,0}}]`.

$$x_3 = 1$$
$$x_2 + x_3 = 0$$

This system obviously does have a solution, but `solve` will fail because, in attempting to eliminate x_2, it will compute the new coefficient of x_3 as $1 - \frac{1}{0}$, which involves a division by 0.

The solution to this problem is easily found by observing that in any system of equations, changing the order of the equations does not change the solution. Thus, the above system is equivalent to:

$$x_2 + x_3 = 0$$
$$x_3 = 1$$

`solve` has no difficulty with this system at all.

Modify `solve` such that it reorders the rows of its argument to ensure that a_{11} is non-0. (If *every* row has 0 as its first element, the system cannot be solved.) This process of reordering the equations is called *pivoting*.

2. In Exercise 1 above, suppose A is known to be *upper triangular*, meaning it has 0s below the diagonal (formally, $a_{ij} = 0$ for all $i > j$). Define `solveUpper`, having the same arguments as `solve`, but under the assumption that A is upper triangular. (This is much simpler than `solve`, since it requires no elimination.) Then define `solveLower`, with the same arguments, but for the case where A is *lower triangular* (has 0s *above* the diagonal). `solveLower` should work by manipulating A so as to make it upper triangular, and then calling `solveUpper`.

3. Suppose we could find lower triangular and upper triangular matrices, L and U, such that $A = L U$. Then for any vector B, we could easily compute `solve [A,B]` by computing `solveUpper [U, solveLower [L, B] ]`. (Note that a vector X is a solution to the original system when $AX = B$. But this implies that $L U X = B$, which implies that there is a vector Y such that $L Y = B$ and $U X = Y$; `solveLower [L, B]` is Y, and `solveUpper [U, Y]` is X.)

So, given a square matrix A, if we can find such a decomposition of A, then we can efficiently solve $AX = B$ for any given B. In fact, finding this so-called *LU-decomposition* of A is very similar to doing Gaussian elimination. Specifically, suppose that A' is the smaller matrix produced by the elimination process (that is, the coefficients in the system S'), and suppose further that $A' = L' U'$, where L' is lower triangular and U' is upper triangular (so L' and U' can be computed recursively). Then consider the following two matrices U and L.

- U is U' with the first row of coefficients of A added as the top row, and 0s added as the left column:

$$U = \begin{matrix} a_{11} & a_{12} & \cdots & a_{1n} \\ 0 & & & \\ \vdots & & U' & \\ 0 & & & \end{matrix}$$

U is, of course, upper triangular.

- L is L' with the following changes: add the row $(1, 0, 0, \ldots, 0)$ as the top row. For the left column, add the *multipliers* computed in the elimination process; that is, the quotients a_{i1} / a_{11}:

$$L = \begin{matrix} 1 & 0 & \cdots & 0 \\ \frac{a_{21}}{a_{11}} & & & \\ \vdots & & L' & \\ a_{n1} & & & \end{matrix}$$

It can be shown that, when this construction works, as it does in the same situations in which `solve` works, $L U = A$.

Program two versions of LU-decomposition:

a. `LUdecomp1 [A]` returns two matrices L and U, as just described. That is, it returns a list containing these two matrices.

b. `LUdecomp2` [*A*] returns one matrix which contains both *L* and *U*, specifically, the matrix $(L - I) + U$, where *I* is the identity matrix. In other words, forget the diagonal elements of *L* (which are all 1s) and just place the elements of *L* below the diagonal and the elements of *U* at or above the diagonal in a single matrix.

4. Suppose you have a tree all of whose labels are numbers. Write a function to sum all the labels.

```
In[1]:=  numbertree = {4, {5}, {6, {7}, {9, {10}, {11}}}};

In[2]:=  sumNodes[numbertree]

Out[2]=  52
```

5. Assume now that your tree's labels are all strings. Write a function to concatenate the strings in *depth-first* order. This is the order you get by following the leftmost children of any node as far as possible before visiting their siblings on the right.

```
In[3]:=  fruittree =
             {"fig", {"date", {"kumquat"}, {"papaya"}}, {"mango"}};

In[4]:=  catNodes[fruittree]

Out[4]=  figdatekumquatpapayamango
```

6. A tree is said to be *balanced* if, for every node, the heights of its children differ from one another by no more than 1; that is, the difference in height between the taller child and the shorter is 0 or 1. (`fruittree` is balanced, but `numbertree` from Exercise 4 is not.) Note that the condition must hold at *all* nodes, not just the root. Here is a function to test whether a tree is balanced.

```
In[5]:=  balanced[{_}] := True
         balanced[{_, lc_, rc_}] :=
           balanced[lc] && balanced[rc] && Abs[height[lc] - height[rc]] ≤ 1
```

This is very expensive due to the computing of heights of subtrees. For example, it first checks the height of the two children of the root (which involves visiting every node in the tree except the root itself), and then it calls `balanced` on those two children, which then computes the height of *their* children *for the second time*.

To avoid this extra cost, define a function `balancedHeight` [*t*] that returns a list of two elements: the first is the height of *t*, and the second is a Boolean value saying whether *t* is balanced. Then you can define `balanced` by

```
In[7]:=  balanced[t_] := balancedHeight[t][[2]]
```

7. Write a function `listLevel [`*tr*`,`*n*`]` which gives a list of all the labels in tree *tr* at level *n*, where the root is at level 0, its children are at level 1, its grandchildren at level 2, and so on.

    In[8]:= `listLevel[numbertree, 2]`

    Out[8]= `{7, 9}`

8. In trees of arbitrary degree, one node can have any (finite) number of children. Represent such a tree by a list containing the label of the root and its children. For example, consider the following tree:

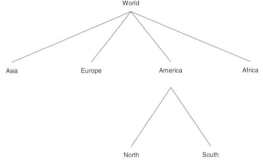

   It can be represented as a list:

`{World, {Asia}, {Europe}, {America, {North}, {South}}, {Africa}}`

   Write functions `minInTree`, `height`, and `printTree` for trees of any degree.

9. Program the function that constructs a Huffman encoding tree, as shown in the last part of this section.

10. Write a more efficient version of `encodeString` that creates a table of all the encodings of all the characters in a given tree, then applies the table to the list of characters. This table can be represented as a list of rewrite rules, like `"a"→ {0,1,1}`, which can then be applied to the list of characters using `ReplaceAll` (`/.`).

11. The `MergeSort` function defined in this section becomes quite slow for moderately sized lists. Perform some experiments to determine if the bottleneck is caused mostly by the auxiliary `merge` function or the double recursion inside `MergeSort` itself. Once you have identified the cause of the problem, try to rewrite `MergeSort` to overcome the bottleneck issues.

7.6 Dynamic programming

Term rewriting can be used to dynamically create rewrite rules *during* evaluation. In a process known as *dynamic programming*, a SetDelayed function whose right-hand side is a Set function of the same name is defined.

$f[x\_] := f[x] = \texttt{right-hand side}$

When an expression is pattern matched to this rewrite rule, term rewriting creates a Set function with the specific argument value which, upon evaluation of the right-hand side, becomes a rewrite rule. Since the global rule base is always consulted during evaluation, storing results as rewrite rules can cut down on computation time, especially in recursive computations.

In this way, "dynamic programming" can be described as a method in which rewrite rules are added to the global rule base *dynamically*; that is, during the running of a program. A well-known application of this is to speed up the computation of Fibonacci numbers.

The function F defined in Section 7.1 is simple, but quite "expensive" to execute. For example, here is a table giving the number of additions needed to compute F[n] for various values of n (these are the values FA_n from Exercise 2 in Section 7.1).

n	5	10	15	20	25
F[n]	5	55	610	6765	75025
number of additions	7	88	986	10945	121392

Here is some code to count the number of additions in the computation of the Fibonacci function. First, define the Fibonacci function.

```
In[1]:=  fib[1] = fib[2] = 1;
         fib[n_] := fib[n - 1] + fib[n - 2]
```

The following code initializes a counter (PlusCount), and then traces the computation of fib[10] incrementing the counter whenever the pattern Plus[___fib] is encountered; in other words, the counter is incremented for each computation of the form fib[x]+fib[y].

```
In[3]:=  Module[{PlusCount = 0},
            TraceScan[++PlusCount &, fib[10], Plus[___fib]]; PlusCount]
```

```
Out[3]=  54
```

The reason for this excessive cost is easy to see – in the course of computing F [*n*], there are numbers *m* < *n* for which F [*m*] is computed many times. For instance, F [*n* – 2] is computed twice (it is called from F [*n*] and also from F [*n* – 1], F [*n* – 3] three times, and F [*n* – 4] five times. This continual recalculation can be eliminated easily by memorizing these values as they are computed – that is, by dynamic programming.

The following definition of function FF is just like the definition of F, but it adds a rule FF [*n*] = F_n to the global rule base the first time the value is computed. Since *Mathematica* always chooses the most specific rule to apply when rewriting, whenever a future request for FF [*n*] is made, the new rule will be used instead of the more general rule in the program. Thus, for every *n*, FF [*n*] will be *computed* just once; after that, its value will be found in the rule base.

```
In[4]:=  FF[1] := 1;  FF[2] := 1
         FF[n_] := FF[n] = FF[n - 2] + FF[n - 1]
```

We can see the change in the trace of FF [4] as compared with that in Section 7.1 Specifically, there is only one evaluation of FF [2] now, since the second evaluation of it is just a use of a global rewrite rule.

```
In[7]:=  TracePrint[FF[4], FF[_Integer] | (FF[_] = FF[_] + FF[_])]

FF[4]

FF[4] = FF[4 - 2] + FF[4 - 1]

  FF[2]

  FF[3]

  FF[3] = FF[3 - 2] + FF[3 - 1]

    FF[1]

    FF[2]

   FF[3]

  FF[4]

Out[7]=  3
```

Another way to understand what is going on is to look at the global rule base *after* evaluating FF [4].

In[8]:= **?FF**

Global`FF

FF[1] := 1

FF[2] := 1

FF[3] = 2

FF[4] = 3

FF[n_] := FF[n] = FF[n - 2] + FF[n - 1]

The cost of executing this version of F is dramatically lower.

n	5	10	15	20	25
number of additions of FF[n]	4	9	14	19	24

Furthermore, these costs are only for the first time FF [n] is computed; in the future, we can find FF [*n*] for free, or rather, for the cost of looking it up in the global rule base.

Dynamic programming can be a useful technique, but needs to be used with care. It will entail some increased cost in memory, as the global rule base is expanded to include the new rules.

Exercises

1. Using dynamic programming is one way to speed up the computation of the Fibonacci numbers, but another is to use a different algorithm. A much more efficient algorithm than F can be designed, based on the following identities.

$$F_{2n} = 2 F_{n-1} F_n + F_n^2, \quad \text{for } n \geq 1$$
$$F_{2n+1} = F_{n+1}^2 + F_n^2, \qquad \text{for } n \geq 1$$

    Program F using these identities.

2. You can still speed up the code for generating Fibonacci numbers by using dynamic programming. Do so, and construct tables, like those in this section, giving the

number of additions performed for various *n* by the two programs you have just written.

3. Calculation of the Collatz numbers, as described in Exercise 5 from Section 5.3, can be implemented using recursion and sped up by using dynamic programming. Using recursion and dynamic programming, create the function `collatz [n, i]`, which computes the *i*th iterate of the Collatz sequence starting with integer *n*. Compare its speed with that of your original solution.

7.7 Higher-order functions and recursion

As a final wrap-up on recursion, we note that many of the built-in functions discussed in Chapter 4 could be written as user-defined functions using recursion. Although they may not be as efficient as the built-in functions, creating them will give you good practice with recursion and should also give you some insight into how these functions operate.

Our first example of programming some built-in functions in a recursive style is Map. We will call our version map. map [*f*, *lis*] applies *f* to each element of the list *lis*. This is a simple recursion on the tail of *lis*: if we assume that `map[f,  Rest[lis]]` works, map [*f*, *lis*] is easily obtained from it by joining `f [First [lis]]` to the beginning.

```
In[1]:=  map[f_, {}] := {}
         map[f_, {x_, y___}] := Join[{f[x]}, map[f, {y}]]
```

We can quickly check that our map does what it was intended to.

```
In[3]:=  map[f, {1, 2, 3}]
```

```
Out[3]=  {f[1], f[2], f[3]}
```

Like many of the functions in Chapter 4, this function has a function as an argument. This is the first time we have seen *user-defined* higher-order functions.

We will give one more example of a built-in function that can be defined using recursion, and leave the rest as exercises.

Nest [*f*, *x*, *n*] applies *f* to *x*, *n* times. The recursion is, obviously, on *n*.

```
In[4]:=  nest[f_, x_, 0] := x
         nest[f_, x_, n_] := f[nest[f, x, n - 1]]
```

Here is an example of the use of this function.

```
In[6]:=  nest[Sin, θ, 4]
```

```
Out[6]=  Sin[Sin[Sin[Sin[θ]]]]
```

Before leaving this topic, we note that, beyond a basic exercise in recursion, it is sometimes quite useful to write your own higher-order functions. Given a function f whose argument must be an integer in the range 1, ..., 1000, and whose result is also in that range, answer the following question: on average, for a number n_1, how many times can f be applied before it repeats itself? That is, on average, if we form the sequence $n_1, n_2 = f(n_1), n_3 = f(n_2), ...$, what is the smallest i such that $n_i = n_j$ for some $j < i$? Assume f is so "expensive" to compute that we prefer to approximate this average by just checking ten randomly chosen numbers. This technique, known as *random sampling*, is used in many areas where statistical analysis of data is required.

If we had a function `repeatCount [n]` to answer this question for a particular n, then we might answer the question in this way:

$$\frac{\text{Sum[repeatCount[Random[Integer,\{1,1000\}]],\{10\}]}}{10}$$

So how do we write `repeatCount`? We will define our own higher-order function.

In[7]:= `repeat[f_ , lis_ , pred_] := lis /; pred[Drop[lis, -1], Last[lis]]`

In[8]:= `repeat[f_ , lis_ , pred_] :=`
         `    repeat[f, Append[lis, f[Last[lis]]], pred]`

`repeat` takes an argument list *lis*, and repeatedly applies f to its last element, and adds that new value to the end, until the predicate *pred* returns `True`. `repeatCount` becomes:

In[9]:= `repeatCount[f_ , n_] := repeat[f, {n}, MemberQ]`

In[10]:= `plus4mod20[x_] := Mod[x + 4, 20]`

In[11]:= `repeatCount[plus4mod20, 0]`

Out[11]= `{0, 4, 8, 12, 16, 0}`

Exercises

1. Write recursive definitions for `Fold`, `FoldList`, and `NestList`.

2. Recall the notion of a random walk on a two-dimensional lattice from Chapter 3. Use `repeat` to define a special kind of random walk, one which continues until it steps on to a location it had previously visited. That is, define `landMineWalk` as a function of no arguments which produces the list of the locations visited in such a random walk, starting from location (0, 0).

8 Numerics

Of the many data types that are available in *Mathematica* – numbers, strings, symbols, lists – numbers are perhaps the most familiar. You can work with all kinds of numbers in *Mathematica*, but, most importantly, what distinguishes it from traditional programming languages and other computational systems is that with it you can operate on numbers of any size and to any degree of precision. In this chapter we will explore some of the issues related to working with numerical quantities and show how you can incorporate some of these ideas into any programs that involve numerical computations.

8.1 Introduction

One of the first things that users of *Mathematica* notice when they begin to use it is how different is its treatment of numbers from other systems including calculators, traditional programming languages, and other technical computing systems. In most traditional programming languages, you must declare the type of number your functions can take as an argument. Although *Mathematica* automatically handles such details for you, an understanding of the different number types and how they invoke different algorithms will be helpful for taking full advantage of *Mathematica*'s capabilities and writing efficient programs.

Although you can work with both exact and approximate numbers, *Mathematica* operates differently depending upon the type of input you give it.

In[1]:= $\texttt{Sin}\left[\dfrac{\pi}{4}\right]$

Out[1]= $\dfrac{1}{\sqrt{2}}$

In[2]:= $\texttt{Sin}\left[\dfrac{\pi}{4.0}\right]$

Out[2]= 0.707107

It is important to understand that not only are different kinds of output returned in such cases, but *Mathematica* uses entirely different algorithms for these two computations.

In the first case, *Mathematica* looks up identities involving the sin function and multiples of $\pi/4$ and applies the appropriate transformation rule to give an algebraic result. In the second example, because a floating point number is involved in the input, a numerical routine (a series expansion for sin) is used and the computation is carried out to insure a result with the same precision as the input.

Another feature that is important to understand involves computations with high-precision numbers. By default, *Mathematica* operates on approximate numbers using a fixed precision that is determined by the machine on which you are working.

In[3]:= **N[π] // Precision**

Out[3]= MachinePrecision

The number of decimal digits of precision for machine numbers is approximately 16 (we will discuss precision in detail in Section 8.3).

In[4]:= **$MachinePrecision**

Out[4]= 15.9546

When you need to, you can raise the number of digits of precision of the numbers you are working with. For example, this computes π to 200 digit precision.

In[5]:= **N[π, 200]**

Out[5]= 3.1415926535897932384626433832795028841971693993751058209749445923078164062862089986280348253421170679821480865132823066470938446095505822317253594081284811174502841027019385211055596446229489549303820

You can extend such arbitrary-precision computations to *Mathematica*'s built-in functions. As a simple, but illuminating example, consider the numerical solution of the van der Pol equation $x''(t) - \frac{1}{5}(1 - x^2(t))\,x'(t) + x(t) = 0$ with the given initial conditions.

In[6]:= **soln = NDSolve$\left[\left\{\text{x}''\text{[t]} - \dfrac{1}{5}\,(1 - \text{x[t]}^2)\,\text{x}'\text{[t]} + \text{x[t]} == 0,\right.\right.$**

$\left.\left.\text{x[0]} == 1,\ \text{x}'\text{[0]} == 0\right\}, \text{x}, \{\text{t, 0, 30}\}\right]$

Out[6]= {{x → InterpolatingFunction[{{0., 30.}}, <>]}}

The solution is represented as an interpolating function, one that passes through the solution over the range for t from 0 to 30. Here is a plot of the original function evaluated at this numerical solution, essentially giving a visual picture of the error in the numerical solution.

In[7]:= `Plot[Evaluate[x''[t] -` $\frac{1}{5}$ `(1 - x[t]²) x'[t] + x[t] /. soln],`

   `{t, 0, 30}, PlotRange → {-10⁻⁵, 10⁻⁵}];`

By increasing the precision of the internal algorithms used to solve this differential equation, we can get a more precise solution.

In[8]:= `soln24 = NDSolve[`

   `{(x')'[t] -` $\frac{1}{5}$ `(1 - x[t]²) x'[t] + x[t] == 0, x[0] == 1, x'[0] == 0},`

   `x, {t, 0, 30}, WorkingPrecision → 27, PrecisionGoal → 24]`

Out[8]= `{{x → InterpolatingFunction[`
   `{{0, 30.000000000000000000000000000}}, <>]}}`

The plot of the original function evaluated at this higher precision solution clearly shows the higher degree of precision obtained with `soln24`.

In[9]:= `Plot[Evaluate[x''[t] -` $\frac{1}{5}$ `(1 - x[t]²) x'[t] + x[t] /. soln24],`

   `{t, 0, 30}, PlotRange → {-10⁻⁷, 10⁻⁷}];`

Working with numbers and understanding issues of precision and accuracy and the interplay between your machine's hardware and the software are essential to working with any computational system or programming language. In this chapter we will discuss all these issues and look at how to make your numeric computations as efficient as possible.

8.2 Numbers

Types of numbers

There are four kinds of numbers represented in *Mathematica* – integer, rational, real, and complex. In addition, mathematical constants like π and e are treated as a special type of number. Integers are considered to be exact and are represented without a decimal point; rational numbers are quotients of integers and are also considered to be exact.

As mentioned in Chapter 2, numbers are atomic expressions, meaning they cannot be broken down into smaller parts. Use the Head function to identify the type of number you are working with.

In[1]:= $\text{Map}\left[\text{Head}, \left\{3, \frac{3}{9}, 0.33333, 4 + 3.1\,\text{I}, \pi\right\}\right]$

Out[1]= {Integer, Rational, Real, Complex, Symbol}

Using FullForm we can see how *Mathematica* represents these objects internally.

In[2]:= $\text{Map}\left[\text{FullForm}, \left\{3, \frac{3}{9}, 0.33333, 4 + 3.1\,\text{I}, \pi\right\}\right]$

Out[2]= {3, Rational[1, 3], 0.33333`, Complex[4, 3.1`], Pi}

As can be seen in the above example, *Mathematica* simplifies rational numbers to lowest terms and leaves them as exact numbers. (We will have more to say about the seemingly strange internal form of real numbers when we discuss their representation in Section 8.3.)

This representation of rational (and complex) numbers as a pair of integers has one more consequence. If you need to pattern match with rational numbers, you should be aware of their internal representation. For example, trying to pattern match with x_/y_ will not work.

In[3]:= $\frac{3}{4} \,/.\, \frac{x\_}{y\_} \rightarrow \{x, y\}$

Out[3]= $\frac{3}{4}$

But pattern matching instead with Rational works fine.

In[4]:= $\frac{3}{4} \,/.\, \text{Rational}[x\_, y\_] \rightarrow \{x, y\}$

Out[4]= {3, 4}

Any number containing a decimal point is classified as a real number in *Mathematica*. These numbers are not considered exact and are hence often referred to as *approximate numbers*. This often leads to confusion for new users of *Mathematica*. You may know that the number 6.0 is identical to the number 6, *from a mathematical perspective*, but from the perspective of the floating point unit (FPU) of your computer and as we saw in the example above, they are quite different both in terms of their representation and in terms of the algorithms that are used to do arithmetic with them. We will have much more to say about this in Section 8.3.

Complex numbers are of the form $a + bi$, where a and b are any numbers – integer, rational, or real. *Mathematica* represents $\sqrt{-1}$ by the symbol I or i.

Mathematica views complex numbers as a distinct data type, different from integers or real numbers.

```
In[5]:=  z = 3 + 4 i
```

```
Out[5]=  3 + 4 i
```

```
In[6]:=  Head[z]
```

```
Out[6]=  Complex
```

You can add and subtract complex numbers.

```
In[7]:=  z + (2 - i)
```

```
Out[7]=  5 + 3 i
```

You can find the real and imaginary parts of any complex number.

```
In[8]:=  {Re[z], Im[z]}
```

```
Out[8]=  {3, 4}
```

The conjugate and absolute value can also be computed. The absolute value of any number is its distance to the origin in the complex plane. The conjugate can be thought of as the reflection of the complex number in the real axis of the complex plane.

```
In[9]:=  {Conjugate[z], Abs[z]}
```

```
Out[9]=  {3 - 4 i, 5}
```

The phase angle is given by the argument.

```
In[10]:=  Arg[4 i]
```

$$Out[10]= \frac{\pi}{2}$$

Each of these properties of complex numbers can be visualized geometrically, as shown in Figure 8.1.

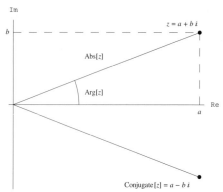

Figure 8.1:   Geometric representation of complex numbers in the plane

For purposes of pattern matching, complex numbers are quite similar to rational numbers. x + I y will not match with complex numbers. A complex number $z = a + bi$ is treated as a single object for many operations, and is stored as Complex[a,b]. So to match a complex number z, use Complex[x_,y_] (or z_Complex and Re[z] and Im[z]) on the right-hand side of any rule you define.

Built-in constants such as π, e, i, and Degree are not treated as real numbers by *Mathematica*.

In[11]:= **{Head[π], NumberQ[π]}**

Out[11]= {Symbol, False}

Although *Mathematica* does not consider constants like π and e like real numbers, it does recognize that they are numerical in nature and thus you can use them more like ordinary numbers.

In[12]:= **Random[Real, {e, π}]**

Out[12]= 2.77033

In[13]:= **Rationalize[π, .0001]**

Out[13]= $\dfrac{333}{106}$

Mathematical constants have an attribute, NumericQ, that essentially alerts *Mathematica* to the fact that they are numeric in nature.

In[14]:= **Map[NumericQ, {π, e, EulerGamma, ∞, i}]**

Out[14]= {True, True, True, False, True}

All mathematical constants and any expressions which are explicit numbers are considered numeric and will return a value of True when NumericQ is applied to them (note in particular that the symbol ∞ is not numeric). When *Mathematica* recognizes that a quantity has this attribute, it converts the symbol to a real number, using what it perceives to be necessary precision.

In[15]:= $e^{\pi} > \pi^{e}$

Out[15]= True

In[16]:= **NumericQ[π^{e}]**

Out[16]= True

If you have to distinguish between explicit numbers and symbols that represent numbers, then use NumberQ.

In[17]:= **Map[NumberQ, {3.14, π}]**

Out[17]= {True, False}

Digits and number bases

A list of the digits of a number can be obtained with the functions IntegerDigits or RealDigits.

In[18]:= **IntegerDigits[1293]**

Out[18]= {1, 2, 9, 3}

In[19]:= **RealDigits[N[EulerGamma]]**

Out[19]= {{5, 7, 7, 2, 1, 5, 6, 6, 4, 9, 0, 1, 5, 3, 2, 9}, 0}

Numbers in base 10 can be displayed in other bases by means of the BaseForm function. For example, the following displays 18 in base 2.

In[20]:= **BaseForm[18, 2]**

Out[20]//BaseForm=
     10010_{2}

The operator $b\verb|^^|n$ takes the number n in base b and converts it to base 10.

In[21]:= **2^^10010**

Out[21]= 18

The letters of the alphabet are used for numbers in bases larger than 10. For example, here are the numbers 1 through 20 in base 16.

In[22]:= `Table[BaseForm[j, 16], {j, 1, 20}]`

Out[22]= $\{1_{16}, 2_{16}, 3_{16}, 4_{16}, 5_{16}, 6_{16}, 7_{16}, 8_{16}, 9_{16}, a_{16},$
$b_{16}, c_{16}, d_{16}, e_{16}, f_{16}, 10_{16}, 11_{16}, 12_{16}, 13_{16}, 14_{16}\}$

Numbers other than integers can be represented in bases different from 10. Here are the first few digits of π in base 2.

In[23]:= `BaseForm[N[`π`, 5], 2]`

Out[23]//BaseForm=
11.00100100010000_2

Recall that *Mathematica* is only displaying six significant *decimal* digits while storing quite a few more. In the exercises you are asked to convert the base 2 representation back to base 10. You will need the digits from the base 2 representation, which are obtained with the `RealDigits` function.

In[24]:= `RealDigits[N[`π`], 2]`

Out[24]= {{1, 1, 0, 0, 1, 0, 0, 1, 0, 0, 0, 0, 1, 1, 1, 1, 1,
1, 0, 1, 1, 0, 1, 0, 1, 0, 1, 0, 0, 0, 1, 0, 0, 0, 1, 0,
0, 0, 0, 1, 0, 1, 1, 0, 1, 0, 0, 0, 1, 1, 0, 0, 0}, 2}

The 2 in this last result indicates where the binary point is placed and can be stripped off this list by wrapping the `First` function around the expression `RealDigits[` `N[`π`],2]`.

Here are the first 16 decimal digits of π given in base 2.

In[25]:= `BaseForm[N[`π`], 2]`

Out[25]//BaseForm=
11.00100100001111111_2

You are not restricted to integral bases such as in the previous examples. The base can be any real number greater than 1. For example:

In[26]:= `RealDigits[N[`π`], N[GoldenRatio]]`

Out[26]= {{1, 0, 0, 0, 1, 0, 0, 1, 0, 1, 0, 1, 0, 0, 1, 0, 0, 0, 1,
0, 1, 0, 1, 0, 1, 0, 0, 0, 0, 0, 1, 0, 1, 0, 0, 1, 0, 0,
0, 0, 1, 0, 0, 1, 0, 1, 0, 0, 0, 1, 0, 0, 0, 0, 0, 1, 0, 1,
0, 1, 0, 1, 0, 1, 0, 0, 0, 0, 0, 0, 1, 0, 0, 0}, 3}

Random numbers

Statistical work and numerical experimentation often require random numbers to test hypotheses. You use the Random function to generate random numbers in various ranges, domains, and distributions.

Using Random without any arguments will generate a uniformly distributed random real number between 0 and 1.

In[27]:= **Random[]**

Out[27]= 0.0691989

Random takes two optional arguments. The first indicates the type of number to generate and the second argument specifies the range. For example, this generates a random integer in the range 0 to 100.

In[28]:= **Random[Integer, {0, 100}]**

Out[28]= 69

A good random number generator will distribute random numbers evenly over many trials. For example, this generates a list of 1,000 integers between 0 and 9.

In[29]:= **numbers = Table[Random[Integer, {0, 9}], {1000}];**

Here is a plot of the frequency with which each of the digits 0 through 9 occur. We first load the packages containing the definitions for Frequencies and BarChart.

In[30]:= **Needs["Statistics`DataManipulation`"]**

In[31]:= **Needs["Graphics`Graphics`"]**

In[32]:= **BarChart[Frequencies[numbers]];**

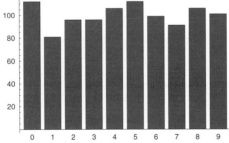

We see each of the numbers 0 through 9 occur *roughly* 1/10 of the time. You would not want these numbers to occur *exactly* 1/10 of the time, as there would be no randomness in this. In fact, for a uniform distribution of the numbers 0 through 9, any sequence of 1,000 digits is equally as likely to occur as any other sequence of 1,000 digits. A sequence of 1,000 numbers that contains exactly 100 occurrences of the digit 0 followed by 100 occurrences of the digit 1, followed by 100 occurrences of the digit 2, etc., is no more likely than the sequence that contains 1000 7s, for example.

In addition to working with uniformly distributed random numbers (the default for Random), you can also work with any of the built-in distributions that are defined in the Add-ons packages, or even your own user-defined distribution. For example, suppose you wished to work with the chi-square distribution (normal random variable with unit variance and mean about 0).

First we load the package in which this distribution is defined.

```
In[33]:= <<Statistics`ContinuousDistributions`
```

Here is a chi-square distribution with four degrees of freedom.

```
In[34]:= ChiSquareDistribution[4]
```

```
Out[34]= ChiSquareDistribution[4]
```

This generates an array of ten random numbers distributed according to this distribution.

```
In[35]:= RandomArray[ChiSquareDistribution[4], 10]
```

```
Out[35]= {9.12669, 3.97231, 3.59231, 8.40731, 0.901804,
          7.79067, 9.37819, 8.14669, 4.44091, 3.01975}
```

Suppose instead of using one of the built-in distributions, you wish to generate random numbers for a continuous distribution based on a small sample of that distribution.

For example, suppose this is the sample from a distribution from which you would like to generate a quantile function.

```
In[36]:= sample = {192, 155, 154, 152, 107, 149, 128, 111, 139,
          108, 127, 130, 189, 119, 200, 178, 116, 180, 108, 129};
```

To construct a quantile function consistent with this sample, we need to generate some probability points, one for each sample point and then pair them up with the sample data points.

To generate a discrete quantile function that is consistent with the above sample, we will first generate some probability values interpolated between the sample points, and then pair them up with the sample points.

$$In[37]:= \texttt{probvals} = \texttt{N}\left[\texttt{Range}\left[0, 1, \frac{1}{\texttt{Length[sample]} - 1}\right]\right]$$

```
Out[37]= {0., 0.0526316, 0.105263, 0.157895, 0.210526,
          0.263158, 0.315789, 0.368421, 0.421053, 0.473684,
          0.526316, 0.578947, 0.631579, 0.684211, 0.736842,
          0.789474, 0.842105, 0.894737, 0.947368, 1.}
```

```
In[38]:=  quantilepts = Transpose[{probvals, Sort[sample]}]

Out[38]=  {{0., 107}, {0.0526316, 108}, {0.105263, 108}, {0.157895, 111},
          {0.210526, 116}, {0.263158, 119}, {0.315789, 127},
          {0.368421, 128}, {0.421053, 129}, {0.473684, 130},
          {0.526316, 139}, {0.578947, 149}, {0.631579, 152},
          {0.684211, 154}, {0.736842, 155}, {0.789474, 178},
          {0.842105, 180}, {0.894737, 189}, {0.947368, 192}, {1., 200}}
```

To generate a continuous quantile function, we need to interpolate through these points.

```
In[39]:=  continuousQuantile = Interpolation[quantilepts]

Out[39]=  InterpolatingFunction[{{0., 1.}}, <>]
```

Here is a plot of this continuous quantile function.

```
In[40]:=  Plot[continuousQuantile[x], {x, 0, 1}];
```

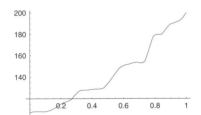

Finally, we generate 20 random numbers that are consistent with the sample.

```
In[41]:=  Table[continuousQuantile[Random[]], {20}]

Out[41]=  {117.556, 118.491, 112.166, 127.481, 120.256, 107.959, 138.437,
          107.926, 120.28, 117.019, 137.763, 118.467, 109.176,
          152.131, 198.151, 199.112, 178., 133.012, 149.839, 179.577}
```

Exercises

1. Define a function complexToPolar that converts complex numbers to their polar representations. Then, convert the numbers $3 + 3\,i$ and $e^{\frac{\pi i}{3}}$ to polar form.

2. Using the built-in Fold function, write a function convert $[lis, b]$ that accepts a list of digits in any base b (less than 20) and converts it to a base 10 number. For example, 1101_2 is 13 in base 10, so your function should handle this as follows:

```
In[1]:=  convert[{1, 1, 0, 1}, 2]

Out[1]=  13
```

3. Write a function sumsOfCubes [*n*] that takes a positive integer argument *n* and computes the sums of cubes of the digits of *n*. This exercise and the next three exercises are excerpted from an article in *The Mathematica Journal*, Sums of cubes of digits, driven to abstraction (Hayes 1992).

4. Use NestList to iterate this process of summing cubes of digits; that is, generate a list starting with an initial integer, say 4, of the successive sums of cubes of digits. For example, starting with 4, the list should look like: $\{4, 64, 280, 520, 133, ...\}$. Note, $64 = 4^3$, $280 = 6^3 + 4^3$, etc. Extend the list for at least 15 values and make an observation about any patterns you notice. Experiment with other starting values.

5. Prove the following statements:
   a. If *n* has more than four digits, then sumsOfCubes [*n*] has fewer digits than *n*.

   b. If *n* has four digits or less, then sumsOfCubes [*n*] has four digits or less.

   c. If *n* has four digits or less, then sumsOfCubes [*n*] $\leq 4 \cdot 9^3$.

   d. If *n* is less than 2,916, then sumsOfCubes [*n*] is less than 2,916.

6. Write a function sumsOfPowers [*n*,*p*] that computes the sums of *p*th powers of *n*.

7. Binary shifts arise in the study of computer algorithms because they often allow you to speed up calculations by operating in base 2 or in bases that are powers of 2. Try to discover what a binary shift does by performing the following shift on 24 (base 10). First get the integer digits of 24 in base 2.

    In[2]:= **IntegerDigits[24, 2]**

    Out[2]= {1, 1, 0, 0, 0}

    Then, do a binary shift, one place to the right.

    In[3]:= **RotateRight[%]**

    Out[3]= {0, 1, 1, 0, 0}

    Finally, convert back to base 10.

    In[4]:= **2^^01100**

    Out[4]= 12

    Experiment with other numbers (including both odd and even integers) and make some conjectures.

8. The survivor[n] function from Chapter 4 can be programmed using binary shifts. This can be done by rotating the base 2 digits of the number n by one unit to the left and then converting this rotated list back to base 10. For example, if $n = 10$, the base 2 representation is 1010_2; the binary shift gives 0101_2; converting this number back to base 10 gives 5, which is the output to survivor[5]. Program a new survivor function using the binary shift.

9. Simulate the throwing of two dice by defining a function rollEm that, when evaluated, displays two integers between 1 and 6.

10. Experiment with creating random two-dimensional images using ListDensity‑Plot.

11. A surprisingly simple pseudorandom number algorithm is the *linear congruential method*. It is quite easy to implement and has been studied extensively. Sequences of random numbers are generated by a formula such as the following:

$$x_{n+1} = x_n b + 1 \pmod m$$

The starting value x_0 is the *seed*, b is the *multiplier*, and m is the *modulus*. Recall that 7 mod 5 is the remainder upon dividing 7 by 5. This is represented in *Mathematica* as

```
In[5]:=  Mod[7, 5]

Out[5]=  2
```

Implement the linear congruential method and test it with a variety of numbers m and b. If you find that the generator gets in a loop easily, try a large value for the modulus m. (See Knuth 1997 for a full treatment of random number generating algorithms.)

12. Write a function quadCong[a, b, c, m, x₀] that implements a *quadratic congruential method*, where a, b, and c are the parameters, m is the modulus, and x_0 is the starting value. The iteration is given by:

$$x_{n+1} = (a x_n^2 + b x_n + c) \bmod m$$

13. Numerous tests are available for determining the effective "randomness" of a sequence. One of the more fundamental tests is known as the χ^2 (chi-square) test. It tests to see how evenly spread out the numbers appear in the sequence and uses their frequency of occurrence. If n is the upper bound of a sequence of m positive num-

bers, then, in a well-distributed random sequence, we would expect about m/n copies of each number. To take into account the actual frequency with which each number occurs, the χ^2 test is implemented by the formula below where the function f_i is the number of copies of i in the sequence. If the χ^2 statistic is close to n, then the numbers are reasonably random. In particular, we will consider the sequence sufficiently random if the statistic is within $2\sqrt{n}$ of n.

$$\chi^2 = \frac{\sum_{1 \leq i \leq n}(f_i - m/n)^2}{m/n}$$

Write a function chiSquare [*lis*] that takes a list of numbers and returns the χ^2 statistic. You will find the built-in Count function helpful for calculating the frequencies.

14. Determine the χ^2 statistic for a sequence of 1000 integers generated with the linear congruential method with $m = 381$, $b = 15$, and a starting value of 0.

15. John von Neumann, considered by many to be the "father of computer science," suggested a random number generator known as the *middle-square* method. Starting with a ten-digit integer, square the initial integer and then extract its middle ten digits to get the next number in the sequence. For example, starting with 1234567890, squaring it produces 1524157875019052100. The middle digits are 1578750190, so the sequence starts out 1234567890, 1578750190, 4521624250, …. Implement a middle square random number generator and then test it on a 1,000-number sequence using the χ^2 test. Was the "father of computer science" a good random number generator?

8.3 Working with numbers

Precision and accuracy

When you work with real numbers in any programming language, you are working with inexact, or approximate quantities. In *Mathematica*, any number which contains a decimal point is considered to be an approximate number. You can specify an approximate number explicitly, such as 1.57, or you can get approximations to exact quantities using N.

```
In[1]:=  e = N[e]

Out[1]=  2.71828
```

Precision of an approximate number is defined as the number of significant decimal digits in that number. You should think of precision as giving a measure of the relative size of the uncertainty in the value of a number. *Accuracy* is defined as the number of these digits to the right of the decimal point. Accuracy can be thought of as a measure of the absolute size of the uncertainty in the value of a number.

In[2]:= **{Precision[e], Accuracy[e]}**

Out[2]= {MachinePrecision, 15.5203}

The symbol `MachinePrecision` (new in Version 5) is used to indicate a machine-precision number. To see the effective precision of any machine number on your computer, evaluate `$MachinePrecision`.

In[3]:= **$MachinePrecision**

Out[3]= 15.9546

The numbers that can be operated with on the hardware (on the floating point unit, or FPU) of your computer are called *machine numbers*. Typically, 64 binary digits (IEEE double floats) are needed to specify a machine number: 1 for the sign, 11 for the exponent, and 52 for the mantissa (actually 53, since the leading one is implicitly taken as 0). A typical value of `$MachinePrecision` is $(64 - 11)\log_{10} 2$, giving machine numbers about 16 *decimal* digits.

In[4]:= **53 Log[10, 2] // N**

Out[4]= 15.9546

To say that a real number x has some uncertainty associated with its value, can be formalized by saying that the value of x lies somewhere inside of an interval $x - \frac{\delta}{2}$ to $x + \frac{\delta}{2}$ for some uncertainty δ. A number with precision p is then defined to have uncertainty $|x|\,10^{-p}$.

In[5]:= **p /. Solve[δ == Abs[x] 10⁻ᴾ, p]**

```
Solve::ifun :
  Inverse functions are being used by Solve, so some
    solutions may not be found; use Reduce
    for complete solution information. More…
```

Out[5]= $\left\{ -\dfrac{\text{Log}\left[\frac{\delta}{\text{Abs}[x]}\right]}{\text{Log}[10]} \right\}$

In other words, the precision of a real number x is given by $-\log_{10}\!\left(\frac{\delta}{|x|}\right)$ for some uncertainty δ. So we could manually compute the precision of e above using an uncertainty of 10^{-15}, which is approximately what *Mathematica* assumes for machine-precision numbers.

$$In[6]:= \ -\text{Log}\left[10, \ \frac{10^{-15}}{\text{Abs[e]}}\right]$$

Out[6]= 15.4343

On the other hand, a number with accuracy a will have uncertainty $\delta = 10^{-a}$ and hence accuracy can be expressed as $-\log_{10}(\delta)$.

Before discussing accuracy and precision of non-machine numbers, let us first look at a few examples.

InputForm can be used to see how you would have to input the full number as it is represented internally in *Mathematica*. The Accuracy indicates there are approximately 16 decimal digits to the right of the decimal point. The Precision indicates that this is a machine-precision number.

```
In[7]:= x = N[EulerGamma];
        {InputForm[x], Accuracy[x], Precision[x]}
```

Out[8]= {0.5772156649015329, 16.1933, MachinePrecision}

The number 123.456 is a machine-precision number, but its accuracy is reduced because it has three digits to the left of the decimal point.

```
In[9]:= x = 123.456;
        {InputForm[x], Accuracy[x], Precision[x]}
```

Out[10]= {123.456, 13.8631, MachinePrecision}

You can see more clearly how *Mathematica* computes Accuracy by looking at the following example.

```
In[11]:= {Accuracy[1.23], Accuracy[12.3], Accuracy[123.]}
```

Out[11]= {15.8647, 14.8647, 13.8647}

Each addition of a digit to the left of the decimal point has the effect of reducing the number of significant digits to the right of the decimal point by 1.

Representation of approximate numbers

Usually, when *Mathematica* displays numbers, it does so in a form that is as close to traditional mathematics as possible, printing six digits for example.

```
In[12]:= pi = N[π]
```

Out[12]= 3.14159

Do not assume that typing in what is displayed will result in the same value.

In[13]:= **pi**

Out[13]= 3.14159

In[14]:= **pi - 3.14159**

Out[14]= 2.65359×10^{-6}

This seemingly strange behavior – the fact that pi does not appear to be equal to 3.14159 – can be explained by looking at the internal representation of pi.

In[15]:= **FullForm[pi]**

Out[15]//FullForm=
     3.141592653589793`

The command N[π] causes *Mathematica* to first convert π to a machine-precision number, and then to display only six digits. Any computations with this number occur using the machine precision.

Note that a number mark ` was printed at the end of the above number. This is a machine-independent mark used to indicate that this is a machine-precision number. When you work with numbers that are not at machine precision, this will be indicated by a number following the number mark. For example, here is a high-precision number.

In[16]:= **N[π, 35]**

Out[16]= 3.1415926535897932384626433832795029

The following shows the full internal representation of this number with the precision indicated by the 35 following the number mark.

In[17]:= **FullForm[%]**

Out[17]//FullForm=
     3.1415926535897932384626433832795028841971693 99375`35.

Finally, note that *Mathematica*, in a sense, treats all machine real numbers as having the same precision.

In[18]:= **Precision[1.23]**

Out[18]= MachinePrecision

Although this last result may seem odd at first, it is a consequence of how *Mathematica* represents real numbers internally. A Precision of 16 (on a computer with $Ma chinePrecision of 16) indicates that the number 1.23 is viewed as a machine-precision real number which will allow *Mathematica* to perform arithmetic with it using the efficient machine-precision arithmetic routines. *Mathematica* views the number 1.23 as a machineprecision real by effectively padding with 0s out to 16 significant digits. If you are uncertain about the precision of the numbers you are working with, it is best to check with `Precision`.

Exact vs. approximate numbers

As stated earlier, all integers and rational numbers are considered *exact*. You can see this by examining the `Precision` of any integer or rational number.

$In[19]:=$ $\{\texttt{Precision[7]}, \texttt{Precision}\left[\frac{1}{9}\right]\}$

$Out[19]=$ $\{\infty, \infty\}$

Mathematica represents complex numbers similarly to rational numbers. If both the real and imaginary parts are exact, then the complex number is treated as exact.

$In[20]:=$ `Precision[3 + 4 I]`

$Out[20]=$ ∞

Exact numbers have more precision than any approximate number. Representing a number with infinite precision is another way of saying that it is exact.

$In[21]:=$ $\texttt{Map}\left[\texttt{Precision}, \left\{4, \frac{1}{9}, 3 + 4 \texttt{ I}\right\}\right]$

$Out[21]=$ $\{\infty, \infty, \infty\}$

As we saw in the example at the beginning of this chapter, this allows *Mathematica* to operate on such a number differently than if the number were only approximate.

$In[22]:=$ $\left\{\texttt{Cos}\left[\frac{\pi}{4}\right], \texttt{Cos}\left[\frac{\pi}{4.0}\right]\right\}$

$Out[22]=$ $\left\{\frac{1}{\sqrt{2}}, 0.707107\right\}$

But, in fact, more is true. As far as *Mathematica* is concerned, all integers are not created equal.

In stark contrast to programming languages, such as C or Pascal that typically restrict computations with integers to 16 or 32 bits (this restricts integers to a magnitude of 2^{16} in the case of 16-bit integers, or to a magnitude of 2^{32} in the case of 32-bit integers), *Mathematica* allows you to compute with integers and rational numbers of arbitrary size.

If two numbers are to be added, $3 + 6$ for example, *Mathematica* checks to see if the numbers can be added as *machine integers*. A machine integer is an integer whose magnitude is small enough to fit into your machine's natural word size, and to be operated on by the machine's instructions, generally on its floating point processor. *Word size* means the number of bits used to represent integers. On many computer systems, the most common word size is 64 bits.

Arithmetic operations on integers within this range can be performed using the machine's own instructions (that is, on the that machine's floating point unit), whereas operations on integers out of that range must be done by programs, which can be less efficient.

If the two numbers to be added are machine integers and *Mathematica* can determine that their sum is a machine integer, then the addition is performed at this low level.

If, on the other hand, the two integers to be added are large and either the integers themselves or their sum is larger than the size of a machine integer, then *Mathematica* performs the arithmetic using special algorithms. Integers in this range are referred to as *extended-precision integers*. For example, the following computation, although impossible to execute on most machine floating point units, is handled by *Mathematica*'s arithmetic algorithms for operating on extended-precision integers.

In[23]:= $2^{256} + 2^{1024}$

Out[23]= 179769313486231590772930519078902473361797697894230657273430081157732675805500963132708477322407536021120113879871393357658789768814416622492847430639474124377767893424865485276302219601246094119453082952085005768838150682342462881589705199778143432586921495693274206093217230604120280344292940337537353777152

Rational numbers are treated somewhat similarly to integers in *Mathematica* since the rational number a/b can be thought of as a pair of integers, and, in fact, as we saw earlier, it is represented as `Rational[a,b]`. In this way, algorithms for exact rational arithmetic will use integer arithmetic (either machine or extended) to perform many of the necessary computations.

High precision vs. machine precision

Real numbers (often referred to as "floating point numbers") contain decimal points, and, as mentioned above, although they can contain any number of digits, they are not considered exact.

In[24]:= `{Head[1.61803], Precision[1.61803]}`

Out[24]= `{Real, MachinePrecision}`

In[25]:= **{Head[1.4987349873487454511],**
         Precision[1.4987349873487454511]}

Out[25]= {Real, 19.1757}

    In a manner similar to how integers are treated *Mathematica* uses different internal algorithms to do arithmetic on real numbers, depending upon whether you are using very high precision reals or not. Whenever possible arithmetic operations on real numbers are performed using machine-precision (fixed) reals. Real numbers that can be computed at the hardware level of the machine are referred to as *fixed precision reals*, and, as stated above, the number of digits that each machine uses for fixed-precision real numbers is given by the system variable $MachinePrecision.

In[26]:= **$MachinePrecision**

Out[26]= 15.9546

    One fact to keep in mind when working with machine-precision numbers is that any computations of expressions containing machine-precision numbers will be done at the machine precision level.

In[27]:= **2.0^{100}**

Out[27]= 1.26765×10^{30}

In[28]:= **Precision[%]**

Out[28]= MachinePrecision

    So, if a machine-precision number is added to a high-precision number, *Mathematica* will perform the computation at the lower, machine precision.

In[29]:= **Precision[2.1 + 3.111111111111111111111]**

Out[29]= MachinePrecision

    Here are the limits on the size of machine numbers that you can work with.

In[30]:= **{$MaxMachineNumber, $MinMachineNumber}**

Out[30]= $\{1.79769 \times 10^{308}, 2.22507 \times 10^{-308}\}$

    To get a sense of the limit given by $MaxMachineNumber, note that this limit is essentially given by $2^{1023} * 1.1111\ldots 11$ (53 total binary digits), a number just smaller than 2^{1024}. The number 53 comes from the number of binary digits that are used to specify the mantissa for any floating point number.

In[31]:= **N[2^{1024}]**

Out[31]= $1.797693134862316 \times 10^{308}$

In[32]:= `1.1111111111111111111111111111111111111111111111111111* 2 ^ 1023`

Out[32]= `9.9871840825684217096072510599390262978776498830128l4× 10`^{307}

In[33]:= **`$MaxMachineNumber`**

Out[33]= `1.79769× 10`^{308}

Although there is a limit to the magnitude of the machine-precision numbers on any given computer, you can still compute with numbers outside of this range. Real numbers larger than machine-precision reals are referred to as *multiple precision reals* and arithmetic on such numbers is called *multiple precision arithmetic* or *variable precision floating point arithmetic*. So, for example, on a machine whose `$MachinePrecision` is 16 decimal digits, computations involving real numbers with greater than 16 significant digits will be performed using multiple-precision algorithms.

When doing exact arithmetic – multiplying two integers, for example – *Mathematica* first checks that both numbers are in fact integers (actually, *machine integers*). If they are small and do not overflow the machine's arithmetic registers, then it goes ahead and multiplies them at the hardware level. If they are large (on most machines, integers are 32 bits long), then *Mathematica* goes to its extended-precision algorithms and multiplies the integers there. In either case, all work done is *exact*.

When doing computations on inexact numbers, *Mathematica* uses two different types of arithmetic, depending upon the precision of the numbers involved. *Fixed precision* floating point arithmetic is used whenever the numbers can be handled in the machine's hardware routines. Sometimes, this arithmetic is referred to as *machine precision* arithmetic. In the previous section, we gave the following example.

In[34]:= **`{Precision[1.23], Accuracy[1.23]}`**

Out[34]= `{MachinePrecision, 15.8647}`

Mathematica has converted 1.23 to a machine floating point number and will use machine arithmetic on it whenever possible. The `Accuracy` of 16 in this example indicates that there are implicit trailing 0s in this number. In the following example, n has smaller accuracy due to the fact that there are an explicit number of numbers to the right of the decimal point and roughly speaking, for machine-precision numbers, the number of digits to the right of the decimal plus the number of digits to the left of the decimal should add up to the number of decimal digits given by `$MachinePrecision`.

In[35]:= **`n = 12345.6789101112`**

Out[35]= `12345.7`

In[36]:= {**Precision[n], Accuracy[n]**}

Out[36]= {MachinePrecision, 11.8631}

You can adjust the precision of numbers with SetPrecision, although you should note that this function will not make an inexact number more exact. Consider the following example.

In[37]:= **a = SetPrecision$\left[\frac{1}{3}, 30\right]$**

Out[37]= 0.333333333333333333333333333333

When SetPrecision is used with exact numbers, such as integers and rational numbers, it creates a few more bits than were asked for, 30 in this case. You can see this by trying to increase the precision.

In[38]:= **b = SetPrecision[a, 50]**

Out[38]= 0.33333333333333333333333333333333333333333333333311

When the number a was first created, the extended-precision number was represented as a finite number of binary bits, followed by infinitely many (implicit) trailing 0s. Increasing the precision of this number uncovered the decimal digits which are not 0s. We can see this by converting 1/3 to a binary representation and then taking a finite number of the binary digits to convert back to base 10.

In[39]:= **RealDigits$\left[N\left[\frac{1}{3}\right], 2\right]$**

Out[39]= {{1, 0, 1, 0, 1, 0, 1, 0, 1, 0, 1, 0, 1, 0, 1, 0, 1,
            0, 1, 0, 1, 0, 1, 0, 1, 0, 1, 0, 1, 0, 1, 0, 1, 0, 1, 0,
            1, 0, 1, 0, 1, 0, 1, 0, 1, 0, 1, 0, 1, 0, 1}, -1}

In[40]:= **2^^.01010101 // FullForm**

Out[40]//FullForm=
            0.33203125`

Let us clear unneeded symbols.

In[41]:= **Clear[a, b, n, x]**

Roundoff errors

Precision and accuracy are affected by performing computations with inexact numbers in ways that can be quite surprising. One such situation concerns a magnification of error due to roundoff. This can be seen with a simple example.

Here is a machine-precision approximation to $\sqrt{2}$ raised to a large power.

In[42]:= $\mathbf{N}\left[\sqrt{2}\,\right]^{200}$

Out[42]= 1.26765×10^{30}

Working with approximations necessarily introduces some error. Comparing the machine-precision result with the exact result gives a measure of how the error is magnified.

In[43]:= $\% - \sqrt{2}^{-200}$

Out[43]= 1.74514×10^{16}

That is an error of over 17 thousand trillion! This loss of accuracy is typically referred to as *roundoff error*. You can see how this loss gets progressively worse by repeating the above example for larger and larger exponents.

In[44]:= $\mathbf{Table}\left[\mathbf{N}\left[\sqrt{2}\,\right]^{j} - \sqrt{2}^{-j}, \ \{j, \ 100, \ 1000, \ 100\}\right]$

Out[44]= $\{7.75, \ 1.74514 \times 10^{16}, \ 2.9156 \times 10^{31},$
$\quad 4.38879 \times 10^{46}, \ 6.18671 \times 10^{61}, \ 8.36779 \times 10^{76}, \ 1.1 \times 10^{92},$
$\quad 1.4105 \times 10^{107}, \ 1.78821 \times 10^{122}, \ 2.23866 \times 10^{137}\}$

In[45]:= $\mathbf{Map[Accuracy, \ \%]}$

Out[45]= $\{15.0653, \ -0.287242, \ -15.5101, \ -30.6878, \ -45.8369,$
$\quad -60.968, \ -76.0868, \ -91.1948, \ -106.298, \ -121.395\}$

Recall that `Accuracy`[x] gives the number of significant digits to the right of the decimal point in x. The negative values indicate that the significant digits are to the *left* of the decimal point.

Of course, if you need to work with such numbers, you can increase the precision with either `N` or `SetPrecision`. Since almost all of the digits in this particular number are to the right of the decimal point, this effectively increases its accuracy.

In[46]:= $\mathbf{N}\left[\sqrt{2}, \ 100\right]^{200}$

Out[46]= $1.2676506002282294014967032053760000000000000000000000000000000000$
$\quad 0000000000000000000000000000000000000000000 \times 10^{30}$

Now the result has much greater accuracy.

In[47]:= $\left(\sqrt{2}\,\right)^{200} - \%$

Out[47]= $0. \times 10^{-68}$

In[48]:= **Accuracy[%]**

Out[48]= 67.596

Computing with different number types

When doing computations with numbers, *Mathematica* tries to work with the most general type of number in the expression at hand. For example, when adding two rational numbers, the sum is a rational number, unless of course it can be reduced to an integer.

In[49]:= $\dfrac{34}{21} + \dfrac{2}{11}$

Out[49]= $\dfrac{416}{231}$

In[50]:= $\dfrac{3}{4} + \dfrac{9}{4}$

Out[50]= 3

But, if one of the terms is a real number, then all computations are done using real-number arithmetic – *Mathematica* works at the lowest precision of the numbers in the expression.

In[51]:= **Precision[10^{100} + 1.3]**

Out[51]= MachinePrecision

One point to keep in mind is that when a symbol is present in the expression to be computed, *Mathematica* does not convert the symbol to a machine number. This ability to perform *symbolic* computations is an extremely important feature that separates *Mathematica* from most other computer languages.

In[52]:= **Simplify[Sin[n π], n $\in$ Integers]**

Out[52]= 0

In[53]:= **Simplify[Sin[n N[π]], n $\in$ Integers]**

Out[53]= Sin[3.14159 n]

When two extended-precision approximate numbers are multiplied, the precision of the result will be the minimum of the precision of the two factors.

In[54]:= **Precision$\left[N\left[\sqrt{2}, 50\right] N\left[\sqrt{3}, 80\right]\right]$**

Out[54]= 50.

In fact, whenever two numbers are multiplied, the precision of the product will be the minimum of the precision of the factors, even if one factor is a machine precision real number and the other factor is a high precision real number.

In[55]:= **a = N[2];**

In[56]:= **b = N[2^{99}, 30];**

In[57]:= **{Precision[a], Precision[b], Precision[a b]}**

Out[57]= {MachinePrecision, 30., MachinePrecision}

For addition of real numbers, it is their *accuracy* that counts most. Recall, Accuracy gives the number of significant digits to the right of the decimal point. In essence, Accuracy[x] measures the absolute error in the number x.

In[58]:= **{Accuracy[1.23], Accuracy[12.5]}**

Out[58]= {15.8647, 14.8577}

For machine-precision numbers, adding a digit to the left of the decimal point essentially removes one digit from the right of the decimal point. These numbers have a fixed number of digits. This is not the case though for extended-precision numbers, where all the digits to the right of the decimal can be considered significant.

In[59]:= **Accuracy[123.44444444444444444444444444]**

Out[59]= 28.

In[60]:= **Accuracy[12321.44444444444444444444444444]**

Out[60]= 28.

In an analogous manner to the use of Precision with multiplication, the Accuracy of an addition will be the minimum of the accuracies of the summands.

In[61]:= **Accuracy[1.23 + 12.3]**

Out[61]= 14.8233

In[62]:= **Accuracy[12.3]**

Out[62]= 14.8647

This last point can lead to some unexpected results if you are not careful.

In[63]:= **1.0 + 10^{-25}**

Out[63]= 1.

In[64]:= **Accuracy[%]**

Out[64]= 15.9546

The number 1.0 is a machine number, so this computation was performed using machine accuracy, hence the 1 in the 25th decimal place to the right in the number 10^{-25} was lost when this computation was performed in machine arithmetic. You can avoid machine arithmetic and get the intended result by extending the precision of 1.0 to 25 digits.

In[65]:= **1.0`25 + 10^{-25} // FullForm**

Out[65]//FullForm=
        1.0000000000000000000000001`25.

In[66]:= **Accuracy[%]**

Out[66]= 25.

Exercises

1. Explain why *Mathematica* is unable to produce a number with 100 digits of precision in the following example.

   In[1]:= **N[1.23, 100]**

   Out[1]= 1.23

   In[2]:= **Precision[%]**

   Out[2]= MachinePrecision

2. Determine what level of precision is necessary when computing $N\left[\sqrt{2}, prec\right]^{200}$ to produce accuracy in the output of at least 100 digits.

3. Explain why the following computation produces an unexpected result (that is, why the value 0.000000000001 is not returned).

   In[3]:= **1.0 - 0.999999999999**

   Out[3]= 9.99978×10^{-13}

4. How close is the number $e^{\pi\sqrt{163}}$ to an integer? Use N, but be careful about the precision of your computations.

8.4 Working with arrays of numbers

Scientists, engineers, and anyone who works with numbers typically do so in the context of arrays of data. In many applications these arrays can become quite large and hence pose special problems when computing with them. *Mathematica* uses two special data types to make computations with arrays faster and more efficient – sparse arrays and packed arrays. In this section we will introduce each of these data types and see how a working knowledge of them can help you work with very large sets of data.

Sparse arrays

In many applications, particularly solving ordinary and partial differential equations, optimization problems, and solving large systems of equations, it is not uncommon to work with very large matrices that have mostly 0s as elements. Such matrices or arrays are referred to as *sparse* and many optimized algorithms have been developed for working with such objects. These algorithms allow you to work with arrays that are often several orders of magnitude larger than dense arrays and generally at speeds that are several orders of magnitude faster.

Sparse arrays are created with the `SparseArray` function. The first argument to `SparseArray` specifies the rules to be used to create the non-0 elements and the second argument specifies the dimensions of the array.

For example, this creates a 5×5 sparse array object with elements on the diagonal equal to 1.

In[1]:= `spmat = SparseArray[{i_, i_} → 1, {5, 5}]`

Out[1]= `SparseArray[<5>, {5, 5}]`

Wrapping `Normal` around a sparse array object converts it into a list of lists, which can then be displayed in a traditional form with `MatrixForm`.

In[2]:= `Normal[spmat] // MatrixForm`

Out[2]//MatrixForm=

$$\begin{pmatrix} 1 & 0 & 0 & 0 & 0 \\ 0 & 1 & 0 & 0 & 0 \\ 0 & 0 & 1 & 0 & 0 \\ 0 & 0 & 0 & 1 & 0 \\ 0 & 0 & 0 & 0 & 1 \end{pmatrix}$$

Here are the rules associated with this sparse array object. Notice that in addition to the explicit rules we specified, *Mathematica* uses the rule {_,_}→0 for the default cases; that is, any element not explicitly specified by a rule should be set to 0.

```
In[3]:= ArrayRules[spmat]
```

```
Out[3]= {{1, 1} → 1, {2, 2} → 1, {3, 3} → 1,
         {4, 4} → 1, {5, 5} → 1, {_, _} → 0}
```

Using a third argument to SparseArray, you can specify that the implicit elements are other than 0.

```
In[4]:= spmat2 = SparseArray[{i_, i_} → 1, {5, 5}, 13]
```

```
Out[4]= SparseArray[<5>, {5, 5}, 13]
```

```
In[5]:= Normal[spmat2] // MatrixForm
```

```
Out[5]//MatrixForm=
       ⎛ 1   13  13  13  13 ⎞
       ⎜ 13  1   13  13  13 ⎟
       ⎜ 13  13  1   13  13 ⎟
       ⎜ 13  13  13  1   13 ⎟
       ⎝ 13  13  13  13  1  ⎠
```

Here is a slightly more complicated specification for the rules associated with a sparse array. In this example, the diagonal elements are 1, and the elements whose vertical and horizontal positions differ by 1 will be 2.

```
In[6]:= spmat3 = SparseArray[
          {{i_, i_} → 1, ({i_, j_} /; Abs[i - j] == 1) → 2}, {5, 5}]
```

```
Out[6]= SparseArray[<13>, {5, 5}]
```

```
In[7]:= MatrixForm[Normal[spmat3]]
```

```
Out[7]//MatrixForm=
       ⎛ 1  2  0  0  0 ⎞
       ⎜ 2  1  2  0  0 ⎟
       ⎜ 0  2  1  2  0 ⎟
       ⎜ 0  0  2  1  2 ⎟
       ⎝ 0  0  0  2  1 ⎠
```

Here is a simple pictorial representation of a sparse array using `ArrayPlot`.

In[8]:= **ArrayPlot[spmat3];**

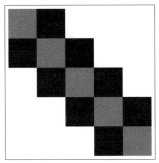

Using a larger array, you can clearly see the nature of the "sparseness" of values.

In[9]:= **ArrayPlot[SparseArray[{i_, j_} /; Abs[i - j] ≤ 2 → 1, {100, 100}]];**

Let us take a look at some computations with sparse arrays to see how speed and memory issues are affected. First we create a 100000×100000 sparse array with random numbers on and just off the diagonal, and 0s everywhere else.

In[10]:= **mat = SparseArray[**
{{i_, j_} /; Abs[i - j] ≤ 2 :→ Random[]}, {10^5, 10^5}]

Out[10]= SparseArray[<499994>, {100000, 100000}]

Here is a vector consisting of 100,000 random numbers.

In[11]:= **b = Table[Random[], {10^5}];**

First, note the difference in size of this sparse array compared with a dense array. The sparse array takes up approximately six megabytes.

In[12]:= **sparseMemory = N[ByteCount[mat]] Byte**

Out[12]= 6.4003×10^6 Byte

The corresponding dense array would require 80 gigabytes to store.

In[13]:= **N[10^5 10^5 8] Byte**

Out[13]= $8. \times 10^{10}$ Byte

Computations involving this sparse linear system are extremely fast.

In[14]:= **Timing[LinearSolve[mat, b];]**

Out[14]= {0.802 Second, Null}

In[15]:= **Timing[mat.mat;]**

Out[15]= {0.09 Second, Null}

Packed arrays

One of the great advantages of the *Mathematica* programming language is that it seamlessly handles the administrative tasks of dealing with a wide variety of data types. So for example, when you perform computations with floating point numbers, *Mathematica* determines the type of numbers you are working with and then chooses to perform the computation either on your machine's floating point processor (if working with numbers that fit there) or does the computation using extended-precision software routines. Similarly computations involving integers will be done in hardware or using special software routines depending upon the size of the integers relative to your machine's hardware constraints.

But all this comes at a cost, and the cost involves the administrative overhead necessary to determine the appropriate routine and whether to perform the computation in hardware or software. For small computations, this overhead is not noticeable, but for large computations involving tens of thousands of rows and columns of a matrix, say, this overhead could start to slow things down.

Fortunately, there is a way to bypass some of this overhead and get significant speed improvements together with a smaller memory footprint. The technology that does this is referred to as *packed arrays* and they are fairly simple to understand. Whenever possible *Mathematica* will represent a list of a single type of machine numbers (integer, real, or complex) as an array, in fact, a packed array object. So a matrix consisting of all machine real numbers will be represented internally as a packed array. This internal representation is transparent to the user.

Here is a 1000×1000 array consisting of random real numbers.

In[16]:= **mat = Table[Random[], {1000}, {1000}];**

Mathematica recognizes that this array consists entirely of machine numbers and so it *packs* the array automatically.

In[17]:= `Developer`PackedArrayQ[mat]`

Out[17]= `True`

Let us also create an array that is not packed. We can do this by replacing one of the elements in `mat` with a number that is not a machine floating point number. Here we replace the element in the first row, second column of `mat` with a 1.

In[18]:= `mat2 = ReplacePart[mat, 1, {1, 2}];`

In[19]:= `Developer`PackedArrayQ[mat2]`

Out[19]= `False`

The first thing to notice is the memory savings obtained by using packed arrays.

In[20]:= `Map[ByteCount, {mat, mat2}]`

Out[20]= `{8000060, 20036032}`

In this example, it takes 60% less memory to store the packed array over the similar unpacked array.

In[21]:= $$\frac{20036032 - 8000060}{20036032} \; \text{// N}$$

Out[21]= `0.600716`

The time to compute the minimum value is roughly an order of magnitude faster for the packed array.

In[22]:= `Map[Timing[Min[#];] &, {mat, mat2}]`

Out[22]= `{{0.01 Second, Null}, {0.15 Second, Null}}`

Simple arithmetic on such objects is also significantly sped up with packed arrays.

In[23]:= `Timing[Do[mat + mat, {100}];]`

Out[23]= `{3.816 Second, Null}`

In[24]:= `Timing[Do[mat2 + mat2, {100}];]`

Out[24]= `{59.685 Second, Null}`

When packed arrays are used in *Mathematica*, the compiler is invoked, thus generally improving the time it takes for the computation to take place. Many of the built-in functions are designed to take advantage of the packed array technology. But they do *not* invoke the compiler whenever the time it takes to compile is close to the running time of the computation itself. There are length limits on many common *Mathematica* functions that determine whether the compiler will be used or not. For example, the length limit for `Table` is 250.

```
In[25]:=  m1 = Table[Random[], {249}];
          Developer`PackedArrayQ[m1]
```

```
Out[26]=  False
```

```
In[27]:=  m2 = Table[Random[], {250}];
          Developer`PackedArrayQ[m2]
```

```
Out[28]=  True
```

For `NestList`, it is 100 (remember that `NestList [f, init, n]` produces a list of $n + 1$ elements because it prepends the initial value to the list of iterates).

```
In[29]:=  n1 = NestList[Sin, .5, 98];
          Developer`PackedArrayQ[n1]
```

```
Out[30]=  False
```

```
In[31]:=  n2 = NestList[Sin, .5, 99];
          Developer`PackedArrayQ[n2]
```

```
Out[32]=  True
```

These length limits are all system parameters that can be set with `SystemOptions`.

```
In[33]:=  Developer`SystemOptions["CompileOptions"]
```

```
Out[33]=  CompileOptions → {ApplyCompileLength → ∞,
             ArrayCompileLength → 250, AutoCompileAllowCoercion → False,
             AutoCompileProtectValues → False,
             AutomaticCompile → False, CompileAllowCoercion → True,
             CompileConfirmInitializedVariables → True,
             CompiledFunctionArgumentCoercionTolerance → 2.10721,
             CompileEvaluateConstants → True,
             CompileReportCoercion → False,
             CompileReportExternal → False, CompileReportFailure → False,
             CompileValuesLast → True, FoldCompileLength → 100,
             InternalCompileMessages → False, MapCompileLength → 100,
             NestCompileLength → 100, NumericalAllowExternal → True,
             SystemCompileOptimizations → All, TableCompileLength → 250}
```

So how do you best take advantage of packed arrays when you write your code? First, it is important that you insure that your lists and arrays consist of machine numbers *all of the same type* – integer, real, or complex. In addition, whenever possible, try to operate on lists and arrays all at once instead of looping through your arrays. Listable operations with packed array input will use the compiler and will produce packed array output. Fortunately, many of the commonly used functions have this attribute.

```
In[34]:=  names = Select[Names["System`*"],
             MemberQ[Attributes[#], Listable] &];
```

Here we display a representative sample of the symbols that have this attribute.

```
In[35]:=  Take[names, {1, Length[names], 10}]
```

```
Out[35]=  {Abs, ArcCsc, Attributes, BitNot, Conjugate, Csch, EllipticPi,
          ExpIntegralE, Fibonacci, Hypergeometric0F1, IntegerDigits,
          LegendreQ, MathieuCharacteristicExponent, NonNegative,
          PolyLog, Quotient, Sign, StringLength, ToUpperCase}
```

Exercises

1. Create a function `RandomSparseArray [n]` that generates an $n \times n$ sparse array with random numbers along the diagonal.

2. Create a function `tridiagonalMatrix [n,p,q]` that creates an $n \times n$ matrix with the integer p on the diagonal, the integer q on the upper and lower subdiagonals, and 0s everywhere else.

3. Create a vector `vec` consisting of 100,000 random real numbers between 0 and 1. Check that it is indeed a packed array by using `Developer`PackedArrayQ`. Then replace one element in `vec` with an integer. Check that this new vector is not a packed array. Finally, perform some memory and timing tests on these two vectors.

8.5 Numerical computations

Mathematica's built-in numerical functions are designed to guarantee the accuracy of their results as much as possible and they are optimized to minimize the work done to generate those results. Functions such as N, FindRoot, NDSolve, NMinimize, and NIntegrate use options to allow you to adjust their behavior and get finer control over precision, accuracy, and other internal aspects of the underlying numerical routines.

In this section we will first look at how to use these options to control the precision and accuracy of your results. We will then discuss how to incorporate these options into your own numerical functions. Finally, we will look at a numerical problem that is mathematical in nature, Gaussian elimination, and see how adjusting the underlying algorithms can help avoid roundoff and division-by-0 errors.

Working with precision and accuracy

When you do computations with *Mathematica*'s numerical functions, results are returned at the default machine precision.

In[1]:= **NIntegrate$\left[\text{Sin}[\ \text{x}^2]\,,\ \left\{\text{x, 0, }\sqrt{\pi}\right\}\right]$**

Out[1]= 0.894831

In[2]:= **Precision[%]**

Out[2]= MachinePrecision

When you need results with higher precision you will need to change the option `PrecisionGoal`, which essentially sets the desired precision of the result (similarly for accuracy, with `AccuracyGoal`).

Here is the same computation as above, but asking for 30 digits of precision in the result.

In[3]:= **NIntegrate$\left[\text{Sin}[\text{x}^2]\,,\ \left\{\text{x, 0, }\sqrt{\pi}\right\}\text{, PrecisionGoal} \rightarrow 30\right]$**

```
NIntegrate::tmap :
 NIntegrate is unable to achieve the tolerances specified
    by the PrecisionGoal and AccuracyGoal options
    because the working precision is insufficient.   Try
    increasing the setting of the WorkingPrecision option.
```

Out[3]= 0.894831

Mathematica is complaining that it is unable to produce a result with the requested precision. If you look at the default value of `WorkingPrecision`, you will see that it is set to `MachinePrecision`. This means that the internal algorithms will work at machine precision. But, in this example, that was not sufficient to guarantee a result with much higher precision.

In[4]:= **Options[NIntegrate]**

Out[4]= {AccuracyGoal $\rightarrow \infty$, Compiled $\rightarrow$ True,
EvaluationMonitor $\rightarrow$ None, GaussPoints $\rightarrow$ Automatic,
MaxPoints $\rightarrow$ Automatic, MaxRecursion $\rightarrow$ 6, Method $\rightarrow$ Automatic,
MinRecursion $\rightarrow$ 0, PrecisionGoal $\rightarrow$ Automatic,
SingularityDepth $\rightarrow$ 4, WorkingPrecision $\rightarrow$ MachinePrecision}

To insure that the `PrecisionGoal` is met, we need to increase the `WorkingPrecision` a bit above the `PrecisionGoal`.

In[5]:= `NIntegrate[Sin[x²], {x, 0, √π},`
        `PrecisionGoal → 30, WorkingPrecision → 36]`

Out[5]= `0.894831469484144958801022013417`

In[6]:= `Precision[%]`

Out[6]= `30.3742`

How much to increase the value of `WorkingPrecision` above that of `PrecisionGoal` is a bit dependent upon the problem at hand, but a good rule of thumb is to start by setting `WorkingPrecision` about 10–15% higher than your `PrecisionGoal`.

Another option to numerical functions that is important to understand is `MaxIterations`. As its name implies, this is the maximum number of iterations that a given iterative function will perform in doing its computation. For example, the default value of `MaxIterations` in `FindRoot` is 100.

In[7]:= `Options[FindRoot]`

Out[7]= `{AccuracyGoal → Automatic, Compiled → True,`
        `DampingFactor → 1, EvaluationMonitor → None,`
        `Jacobian → Automatic, MaxIterations → 100,`
        `Method → Automatic, PrecisionGoal → Automatic,`
        `StepMonitor → None, WorkingPrecision → MachinePrecision}`

For many computations, this limit will be sufficient. But with root finding for example, a function that is very flat near the desired zero may need a higher number of iterations to find that zero. For example, the function x^{11} has a root at 0 of course, but `FindRoot` has difficulty locating it and is unable to guarantee its precision and accuracy using the default settings.

In[8]:= `FindRoot[x¹¹, {x, 0.5}]`

        `FindRoot::cvmit :`
          `Failed to converge to the requested accuracy`
            `or precision within 100 iterations. More…`

Out[8]= `{x → 0.0000362829}`

If you increase the value of `MaxIterations`, you will get a more accurate result.

In[9]:= `FindRoot[x¹¹, {x, 0.5}, MaxIterations → 1000]`

Out[9]= `{x → 9.84816 × 10⁻⁸}`

To get even more accuracy, try increasing `AccuracyGoal`. As discussed above, you should increase the value of the `WorkingPrecision` option as well.

In[10]:= **FindRoot[x^{11}, {x, 0.5}, AccuracyGoal → 30,**
            WorkingPrecision → 36, MaxIterations → 1000]

Out[10]= {x → 9.38526423859658090604961544893338306× 10^{-30}}

One final option to *Mathematica*'s numerical functions that we will explore is `EvaluationMonitor`. This option can be used to evaluate an expression during the computation of the function for which it is an option. For example, suppose you would like to see all of the intermediate values that `FindRoot` comes up with during its computation.

You could simply print the values that x takes on throughout the computation using a `Print` statement.

In[11]:= **FindRoot[Sin[x], {x, 2.0}, EvaluationMonitor :→ Print[x]]**

  2.

  4.18504

  2.46789

  3.26619

  3.14094

  3.14159

  3.14159

Out[11]= {x → 3.14159}

This approach suffers from the fact that the `Print` expression produces no output and so there is no direct way to access these intermediate values. A better approach would be to append the intermediate values to a list. In the following example we initialize an empty list `xtemp` and use `EvaluationMonitor` to append values of x to that list throughout the course of the root-finding computation.

In[12]:= **xtemp = {};**
            FindRoot[Sin[x], {x, 2.0},
              EvaluationMonitor :→ AppendTo[xtemp, x]]

Out[13]= {x → 3.14159}

The intermediate values are now stored in `xtemp`.

In[14]:= **xtemp**

Out[14]= {2., 4.18504, 2.46789, 3.26619, 3.14094, 3.14159, 3.14159}

Note the use of the delayed rule above with `EvaluationMonitor`. This ensures that the right-hand side of the rule is not evaluated before `FindRoot` starts its computation.

Newton's method revisited

In Section 5.2 we wrote a program to implement Newton's method for finding roots of equations.

```
In[15]:=  findRoot[fun_ , init_ , e_] :=
            Module[{xi = init, funxi = fun[init], df = fun'},
             While[Abs[funxi] > e,
                          funxi
              xi = N[xi - ───── ];
                         df[xi]
              funxi = fun[xi]];
             xi]
```

One of the limitations of this implementation is that the user has little control over the precision or accuracy of the results. In addition, although the loop will continue until values are within ϵ of the root, there is no mechanism for automatically adjusting this tolerance, nor for controlling the number of iterations that are performed. In this section we will rewrite this root-finding function to take advantage of the options for numerical functions that control precision and accuracy.

First we will change the iterative structure from a `While` loop to a fixed point iteration. The first argument to `FixedPoint` is the function that we are iterating, so that will be the same as the function above, namely, $x_i - \frac{f(x_i)}{f'(x_i)}$. The second argument to `Fixed`-`Point` is the initial value for the iteration. The third argument is the number of iterations. So, using a pure function for the first argument, the Newton iteration will look like this:

```
FixedPoint[# - fun[#]/fun'[#] &, initx, maxIterations]
```

Let us set up the needed options with some default values. We will call our new program `newton`.

```
In[16]:=  Options[newton] =
            {
             MaxIterations :> $RecursionLimit,
             PrecisionGoal → Automatic,
             WorkingPrecision → Automatic
            };
```

We have set the default value of `MaxIterations` to be `$RecursionLimit` (normally 256) using a delayed rule so that `$RecursionLimit` is not evaluated until the option is called. `PrecisionGoal` and `WorkingPrecision` are set to `Automatic`, which, at the moment, has no value associated with it. In the body of our function, we will take a value of `Automatic` for `PrecisionGoal` to mean a precision that is equal to the precision of the initial value passed to `newton`.

```
If[precisionGoal===Automatic, precisionGoal = Precision[init]];
```

As we saw in the previous section, we will need to bump up the value of `Working`. `Precision` to something a little bigger than `PrecisionGoal`. We will set it to be ten more digits than the precision goal.

```
If[workingPrecision === Automatic,
    workingPrecision = precisionGoal + 10];
    initx = SetPrecision[init, workingPrecision];
```

Here then is the definition of `newton` with these added pieces.

```
In[17]:= newton[fun_, init_?NumericQ, opts___?OptionQ] :=
         Module[{maxIterations, precisionGoal,
           workingPrecision, initx, df = fun'},
           {maxIterations, precisionGoal, workingPrecision} =
            {MaxIterations, PrecisionGoal, WorkingPrecision} /.
             Flatten[{opts}] /. Options[newton];
           If[precisionGoal === Automatic,
            precisionGoal = Precision[init]];
           If[workingPrecision === Automatic,
            workingPrecision = precisionGoal + 10];
           initx = SetPrecision[init, workingPrecision];
           SetPrecision[
```

$$\text{FixedPoint}\left[\# - \frac{\text{fun}[\#]}{\text{df}[\#]} \ \&, \ \text{initx}, \ \text{maxIterations}\right],$$

```
           precisionGoal]]
```

Let us use `newton` to find the roots of various functions.

```
In[18]:= f[x_] := x^2 - 2
```

```
In[19]:= newton[f, 1.0]
```

```
Out[19]= 1.41421
```

The precision of this result is the same as the precision of the initial guess.

In[20]:= **Precision[%]**

Out[20]= MachinePrecision

Setting PrecisionGoal higher generates a high-precision result.

In[21]:= **newton$\left[\text{Sin}, \dfrac{14}{10}, \text{PrecisionGoal} \to 40\right]$**

Out[21]= 3.141592653589793238462643383279502884197

In[22]:= **% − π**

Out[22]= 0. × 10^{-40}

   There are still a number of problems that can arise with our implementation of Newton's method. First is the possibility that the derivative of the function we are working with might be equal to 0. This will produce a division-by-0 error. Another type of difficulty that can arise in root finding occurs when the derivative of the function in question is either difficult or impossible to compute. As a very simple example, consider the function $|x + 3|$, which has a root at $x = -3$. Both the built-in function FindRoot and our user-defined newton will fail with this function since a symbolic derivative cannot be computed.

In[23]:= **D[Abs[x + 3], x]**

Out[23]= Abs′ [3 + x]

   One way around such problems is to use a numerical derivative (as opposed to an analytic derivative). The *secant method* approximates $f'(x_k)$ using the difference quotient:

$$\frac{f(x_k)-f(x_{k-1})}{x_k-x_{k-1}}$$

   Although this will require two initial values to start, it has the advantage of not having to compute symbolic derivatives. Here is a simple implementation using a While loop.

In[24]:= **secant[f_, a_, b_] :=**
   Module$\left[\{x1 = a, x2 = b, df\}, \text{While}\left[\text{Abs}[f[x2]] > \dfrac{1}{10^{10}},\right.\right.$
   df = $\dfrac{f[x2] - f[x1]}{x2 - x1}$;
   $\{x1, x2\} = \left\{x2, x2 - \dfrac{f[x2]}{df}\right\}\right]$;
   x2$\Big]$

In[25]:= **f[x_] := Abs[x + 3]**

In[26]:= **secant[f, -3.1, -1.8]**

Out[26]= -3.

In the exercises, the reader is asked to refine this program by writing it in a functional style and including mechanisms to gain finer control over precision and accuracy in a manner similar to what we did with the `newton` function earlier in this section.

Gaussian elimination revisited

When solving the linear system $A x = b$ by numerical techniques, several types of problems may arise. One problem, roundoff error, sometimes occurs when using machine numbers as opposed to exact numbers. For many matrices A, there is little propagation of roundoff error. But for some matrices the error tends to magnify in a startling way and can lead to highly inaccurate results. Such matrices are called *ill-conditioned*, and, in this section, we will identify ill-conditioned matrices and discuss what to do about them when doing numerical linear algebra.

Another type of problem that can occur was first mentioned in Section 7.5 where we used Gaussian elimination to solve the system $A x = b$. In the exercises at the end of that section, we gave a very brief discussion of the conditions under which the method might fail, namely, division by 0. In this section we will give a more detailed treatment of the potential pitfalls with Gaussian elimination.

Since the method of Gaussian elimination is essentially list manipulation involving additions, subtractions, multiplications, and divisions, clearly one avenue of failure would be if we were to divide by 0. We formed what are commonly called *multipliers* ($\frac{Ei[[1]]}{E1[[1]]}$, in the example below) as follows:

```
subtractE1[E1_, Ei_] := Rest[Ei] - Ei[[1]]/E1[[1]] Rest[E1]
```

If the element `E1[[1]]` were ever equal to 0, the method would fail. Recall the example from the exercises at the end of Section 7.5.

In[27]:= **m = {{0, 3}, {3, 0}};**
          b = {5, 6};

This simple linear system *m.x* = *b* has solution vector $x = \{2, \frac{5}{3}\}$.

In[29]:= $\mathbf{m.\left\{2, \dfrac{5}{3}\right\}}$

Out[29]= {5, 6}

Unfortunately, the `solve` command we developed earlier in Section 7.5 will fail on this linear system.

In[30]:= **solve [m, b]**

Power::infy : Infinite expression $\dfrac{1}{0}$ encountered. More...

∞::indet :
 Indeterminate expression 0 ComplexInfinity encountered. More...

Power::infy : Infinite expression $\dfrac{1}{0}$ encountered. More...

Out[30]= {Indeterminate, Indeterminate}

It is pretty clear that our `solve` command has not been written to take this situation into account. The problem can be remedied as suggested in Exercise 1 in Section 7.5, by interchanging rows (equations) so that the 0 element is not in this pivoting position. Interchanging rows is equivalent to swapping equations, so this will not change the solution of the system in any way.

However, there is another problem that can arise when solving systems containing finite precision coefficients. The imprecision of the coefficients tends to become magnified in performing the necessary arithmetic. We can see this more clearly with an example.

Suppose we were using six-digit rounded arithmetic on the following system.

$$\begin{pmatrix} 0.000001 & 1.0 \\ 1.0 & 1.0 \end{pmatrix}\begin{pmatrix} x \\ y \end{pmatrix} = \begin{pmatrix} 1.0 \\ 2.0 \end{pmatrix}$$

The augmented matrix would look like the following.

$$\begin{pmatrix} 0.000001 & 1.0 & 1.0 \\ 1.0 & 1.0 & 2.0 \end{pmatrix}$$

Gaussian elimination would start solving this system by multiplying the first row by 10^6 (which contains seven digits) and subtracting from the second row. But six-digit rounded arithmetic would then produce:

$$\begin{pmatrix} 0.0000001 & 1.0 & 1.0 \\ 0.0 & -1000000. & -1000000 \end{pmatrix}$$

Dividing the second row by $-1000000.$ gives the solution for y.

$$\begin{pmatrix} 0.000001 & 1.0 & 1.0 \\ 0.0 & 1. & 1. \end{pmatrix}$$

The second part of the back substitution gives the solution for x; that is, $(-1.\times 1.0)/0.000001$.

$$\begin{pmatrix} 1.00000 & 0.0 & 0.0 \\ 0.0 & 1. & 1. \end{pmatrix}$$

This "solution" $\{x, y\} = \{0, 1\}$, is in fact, not the least bit close to the correct answer. A much more accurate solution is given by the ordered pair $\{x, y\} = \{1.000001000001, 0.999998999999\}$.

What has gone wrong? In general, accuracy is lost when the magnitude of the pivoting position is small compared with the remaining coefficients in that column. Pivoting can be used to avoid two situations. First, it is used to avoid a 0 element, when the matrix is nonsingular. A square matrix A is said to be *nonsingular* if it has an inverse; that is, if there exists a matrix B such that $A B = I$.

Pivoting is also used to minimize the potential for roundoff errors. It does this by selecting the element from the remaining rows (equations) that is the maximum in absolute value. This will make the multiplier small and will have the effect of reducing possible roundoff errors. The following code selects this pivot and reorders the rows of the system accordingly.

```
In[31]:= pivot[S_] := Module[{p, ST1},
          ST1 = Abs[Transpose[S][[1]]];
          p = Position[ST1, Max[ST1]][[1, 1]];
          Join[{S[[p]]}, Delete[S, p]]
          ]
```

Now the original `solve` function can be rewritten to pivot on this non-0 element. The new function is called `solvePP` (for "partial pivot").

```
In[32]:= subtractE1[E1_, Ei_] := Rest[Ei] - Ei[[1]] Rest[E1]/E1[[1]] ;
```

```
In[33]:= elimx1[T_] := Map[subtractE1[T[[1]], #1] &, Rest[T]];
```

```
In[34]:= solvep[{{a11_, b1_}}] := {b1/a11};
```

```
In[35]:= solvep[S_] := Module[{S1 = pivot[S], E1, a12toa1n, x2toxn},
            x2toxn = solvep[elimx1[S1]];
            E1 = First[S1];
            a12toa1n = Drop[Rest[E1], -1];
            Join[{(Last[E1] - a12toa1n.x2toxn)/First[E1]}, x2toxn]];
```

```
In[36]:= solvePP[mat_, b_] :=
            solvep[Transpose[Append[Transpose[mat], b]]]
```

As we did in Section 7.5, we set things up so that the user can simply pass the matrix *mat* and column vector *b* as arguments, and `solvePP` will form the augmented matrix in the call to `solvep` on the last line above.

We can quickly see how partial pivoting solves our first problem of division by 0. Solving the system given earlier with this new function now gives the correct result.

```
In[37]:= m = {{0, 3}, {3, 0}};
         b = {5, 6};
```

```
In[39]:= solvePP[m, b]
```

$$Out[39]= \left\{2, \frac{5}{3}\right\}$$

The problem with roundoff error can best be seen by constructing a matrix that would tend to produce quite large intermediate results relative to its original elements. One such class of matrices are referred to as *ill-conditioned* matrices, a complete study of which is outside the scope of this book. The reader is encouraged to consult Skeel and Keiper 1993 or Burden and Faires 2000 for a comprehensive discussion of ill-conditioning.

A set of classically ill-conditioned matrices are the *Hilbert matrices* which arise in numerical analysis in the solution of what are known as *orthogonal polynomials*. Recall the definition of the *n*th degree Hilbert matrix that we gave in Section 7.5.

```
In[40]:= HilbertMatrix[n_] := Table[1/(i + j - 1), {i, n}, {j, n}]
```

```
In[41]:= HilbertMatrix[3] // MatrixForm
```

Out[41]//MatrixForm=

$$\begin{pmatrix} 1 & \frac{1}{2} & \frac{1}{3} \\ \frac{1}{2} & \frac{1}{3} & \frac{1}{4} \\ \frac{1}{3} & \frac{1}{4} & \frac{1}{5} \end{pmatrix}$$

We will use the Hilbert matrices, but, instead of working with exact arithmetic, we will work with floating point numbers.

```
In[42]:= N[HilbertMatrix[3]] // MatrixForm
```

Out[42]//MatrixForm=

$$\begin{pmatrix} 1. & 0.5 & 0.333333 \\ 0.5 & 0.333333 & 0.25 \\ 0.333333 & 0.25 & 0.2 \end{pmatrix}$$

To compare the simple solver `solve` and the partial pivoting solver `solvePP` along with the built-in `LinearSolve` we first construct a 25×25 Hilbert matrix and a random 25×1 column vector (and, of course, suppress the display of the 625 elements of the matrix and 25 elements of the column vector).

```
In[43]:= h25 = N[HilbertMatrix[25]];
```

```
In[44]:= b25 = Table[Random[], {25}];
```

Now let us use each of these three methods to find the solution vector *x* of the system `h25.x = b25`. We also give a measure of the total error involved in each case by computing the difference between `h25.x` and `b25`.

`LinearSolve` fails on this linear system.

```
In[45]:= xLS = LinearSolve[h25, b25];
```

```
        LinearSolve::luc :
          Result for LinearSolve of badly conditioned
            matrix {{1., 0.5, 0.333333, 0.25, 0.2, <<20>>,
              0.142857, 0.125, 0.111111, 0.1, <<15>>}, <<10>>}
            may contain significant numerical errors. More...
```

The `solve` function (without pivoting) solves the system and produces a total error of about 161 (this result will vary depending upon the random vector b25).

```
In[46]:= xGE = solve[h25, b25];
```

```
In[47]:= totalerrorGE = Total[Abs[h25.xGE - b25]]
```

Out[47]= 161.552

Here we compute the solution to this system using partial pivoting.

```
In[48]:= xPP = solvePP[h25, b25];
```

```
In[49]:= totalerrorPP = Total[Abs[h25.xPP - b25]]
```

Out[49]= 12.8731

It is no surprise that our initial implementation of Gaussian elimination, `solve`, had a greater total error than `solvepp`. As we mentioned above, the Hilbert matrices are very ill-conditioned and so we would expect that roundoff error would be more significant without pivoting. (As noted above, results will vary from machine to machine and from session to session since each evaluation of b25 above will produce a different column vector.)

The importance of these numbers is that they tell us that there can be a significant increase in error in using Gaussian elimination without pivoting. We have to be a bit careful in reading too much into that though. Quite a bit of roundoff error is present in these results. You should check that this is in fact the case by running the examples with smaller Hilbert matrices. The exercises outline a method to help reduce such potential roundoff error.

Exercises

1. The newton function developed in this section suffers from several inefficiencies. One of them is that if the precision goal is no more than machine precision, all intermediate computations should be done at the more efficient machine precision as well. Modify newton so that it will operate at machine precision if the precision goal is at most machine precision.

2. In the newton program, we added SetPrecision[result,precisionGoal] at the very end to return the final result at the precision goal, but we have done no test to insure that the result meets the required precision. Add a test to the end of the newton function so that, if this condition is not met, an error message is generated and the current result is output.

3. Some functions tend to cause root-finding methods to converge rather slowly. For example, the function $f(x) = \sin(x) - x$ requires over ten iterations of Newton's method with an initial guess of $x_0 = 0.1$ to get three-place accuracy. Implement the following acceleration of Newton's method and determine how many iterations of the function $f(x) = \sin(x) - x$, starting with $x_0 = 0.1$, are necessary for six-place accuracy.

$$\text{accelNewton}(x) = \frac{f(x)f'(x)}{[f'(x)]^2 - f(x)f''(x)}$$

This accelerated method is particularly useful for functions with multiple roots.

4. Write a functional implementation of the secant method. Your function should accept as arguments the name of a function and two initial guesses. It should maintain the precision of the inputs and it should output the root at the precision of the

initial guess, and the number of iterations required to compute the root. Consider using the built-in functions `FixedPoint` or `Nest`.

5. The *norm* of a matrix gives some measure of the size of that matrix. The norm of a matrix A is indicated by $\|A\|$. There are numerous matrix norms, but all share certain properties. For $n \times n$ matrices A and B:

    (i) $\|A\| \geq 0$

    (ii) $\|A\| = 0$ if and only if A is the zero matrix

    (iii) $\|cA\| = |c| \, \|A\|$ for any scalar c

    (iv) $\|A + B\| = \|A\| + \|B\|$

    (v) $\|A B\| \leq \|A\| \, \|B\|$

    One particularly useful norm is the l_∞ norm, sometimes referred to as the *max norm*. For a vector, this is defined as

    $$\|\vec{x}\|_\infty = \max_{1 \leq i \leq n} \left| x_i \right|$$

    The corresponding matrix norm is defined similarly. Hence, for a matrix $A = a_{ij}$, we have

    $$\|A\|_\infty = \max_{1 \leq i \leq n} \sum_{j=1}^{n} \left| a_{ij} \right|$$

    This computes the sum of the absolute values of the elements in each row, and then takes the maximum of these sums. That is, the l_∞ matrix norm is the max of the l_∞ norms of the rows.

    Write a function `norm[mat, Infinity]`, which takes a square matrix as an argument and outputs its $\| \cdot \|_\infty$ norm. Compare your function with the built-in `Norm` function.

6. If a matrix A is nonsingular (that is, is invertible), then its *condition number* $c(A)$ is defined as $\|A\| \cdot \|A^{-1}\|$. A matrix is called *well-conditioned* if its condition number is close to 1 (the condition number of the identity matrix). A matrix is called *ill-conditioned* if its condition number is significantly larger than 1.

    Write a function `conditionNumber[mat]` that uses the `norm` you defined in the previous exercise as an auxiliary function, and outputs the condition number of *mat*. Use `conditionNumber` to compute the condition number of the first ten Hilbert matrices.

7. An additional technique for solving linear systems of equations is known as *scaled pivoting*. Assuming that no column of a matrix *mat* contains all 0s (in which case there

would be no unique solution), then, for each row, a scale factor is determined by selecting the element that is the largest in absolute value; that is, in row i, the scale factor is defined as $s_i = \max_{1 \leq j \leq n} |a_{ij}|$. Now a row interchange is determined by finding the first integer k such that:

$$\frac{|a_{ki}|}{s_k} = \max_{j=1,2,\ldots,n} \frac{a_{ji}}{s_j}$$

Once such a k is found, then the ith row and the kth row are interchanged. The scaling itself is only done for comparison purposes so no additional roundoff error is introduced by the scaling factor.

Write a function `solveSPP` that implements scaled partial pivoting using the above description.

9 Graphics programming

Mathematica contains a rich set of tools for visualizing functions and data. Generally the built-in graphics functions will provide what you need, but, just like the rest of the *Mathematica* programming language, you will periodically find yourself with the need to create your own plotting and visualization routines. In this chapter we will discuss how to construct graphical images using *Mathematica*, and how to write programs that solve problems that are graphical in nature.

9.1 Structure of graphics

All *Mathematica* graphics are constructed from objects called *graphics primitives*. These primitive elements (`Point`, `Line`, `Polygon`, `Circle`, etc.) are used by built-in functions such as `Plot` to create graphics. Although it is quite straightforward to create images using *Mathematica*'s built-in functions, you will frequently find yourself having to create a graphic image for which no *Mathematica* function exists. This is analogous to the situation in programming where you often have to write a specialized procedure to solve a particular problem. We use the basic building blocks and put them together according to the rules governing the structure of the language and the nature of the problem at hand. In this section we will look at the building blocks of graphics programming and at how we put them together to make graphics.

Primitives, directives, and options

Graphics created with functions such as `Plot` and `ListPlot` are constructed of lines connecting points, with options governing the display. We can get some insight into this process by looking at the internal representation of a plot.

Here is a plot of the sin function.

In[1]:= `sinplot = Plot[Sin[x], {x, 0, 2 π}]`

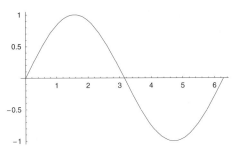

Out[1]= - Graphics -

Mathematica constructs plots by piecing together various graphics elements. The `InputForm` function displays the expression that we could have entered manually to get the same plot. We use `Short` to display an abbreviated listing of that expression. (*Note:* The formatted output from `Short` will vary slightly depending upon the width of your notebook.)

In[2]:= `Short[InputForm[sinplot], 10]`

Out[2]//Short= `Graphics[{{Line[{{2.617993877991494*^-7,`
`2.6179938779914644*^-7}, {0.25488992540742256,`
`0.25213889196341294}, {0.5328694051959508,`
`0.5080069997492929}, {0.7939393140028285,`
`0.7131204212611485}, {1.04500937601917, 0.864929243756943},`
`{1.1741328775392965, 0.9223551787683757},`
`{1.2459531215560486, 0.9477007807106171},`
`{1.3122595300248905, 0.9667651045914426}, {<<2>>},`
`<<69>>, {5.756221700231303, -0.5029111934098898},`
`{6.016521477574974, -0.2635146543573849},`
`{6.266821408128109, -0.016363168748098372},`
`{6.283185045380199, -2.6179938774695577*^-7}}]}}, {<<25>>}]`

This graphic consists of a series of coordinates, or points, in the plane connected by lines of a certain thickness. There are 82 points that are sampled to make this plot – the 13 displayed here together with 69 more indicated by the notation <<69>>.

In[3]:= `Count[InputForm[sinplot],`
`{p_?NumericQ, q_?NumericQ}, Infinity]`

Out[3]= `82`

The `<<25>>` on the bottom indicates options (omitted from this display), such as `PlotRange→Automatic`. Below we can see that some of these options are immediate rules and some are delayed.

```
In[4]:=  Count[InputForm[sinplot], p_Symbol → q_ , Infinity]
```

Out[4]= 21

```
In[5]:=  Count[InputForm[sinplot], p_Symbol :→ q_ , Infinity]
```

Out[5]= 4

We will examine these graphics elements by constructing a graphic using *only* primitive elements. In a later section we will look into how the built-in functions such as `Plot` construct graphics out of the primitive elements.

In Section 8.1 in the numerics chapter, we displayed a graphic that demonstrated some of the properties of complex numbers. Let us show how this graphic was created, using *Mathematica*'s primitive elements.

The following table lists the graphics primitives that we will use in this example (`Point`, `Line`, `Circle`, and `Text`) in addition to several other two-dimensional elements that are available. Note that three-dimensional versions of `Point`, `Line`, `Polygon`, and `Text` are also available for constructing three-dimensional graphics.

Graphics elements	Usage
`Point[{x, y}]`	a point at position $\{x, y\}$
`Line[{{x_1, y_1}, {x_2, y_2}, ...}]`	a line through the points $\{x_i, y_i\}$
`Rectangle[{{x_{min}, y_{min}}, {x_{max}, y_{max}}}]`	a filled rectangle
`Polygon[{{x_1, y_1}, {x_2, y_2}, ...}]`	a filled polygon
`Circle[{x, y}, r, {θ_2, θ_2}]`	a circular arc of radius r
`Disk[{x, y}, r]`	a filled disk of radius r
`Raster[{{x_{11}, x_{12}, ...}, {x_{21}, x_{22}, ...}, ...}]`	a rectangular array of gray levels
`Text[expr, {x, y}]`	text centered at $\{x, y\}$

Table 9.1: Graphics primitives

The graphic we will create will contain the following elements:

- points in the plane at a complex number $a + bi$ and its conjugate $a - bi$

- lines drawn from the origin to each of these points

- an arc, indicating the polar angle of the complex number

- dashed lines indicating the real and imaginary values

- a set of axes in the coordinate plane

- labels for each of the above elements

First we choose a point in the first quadrant and then construct a line from the origin to this point.

In[6]:= `z = 8 + 3 i;`

$\text{Line}[\{\{x_1,y_1\}, \{x_2,y_2\}, ..., \{x_n,y_n\}\}]$ is a graphics primitive that creates a line from the point whose coordinates are (x_1, y_1) to the point (x_2, y_2), etc..

In[7]:= `line1 = Line[{{0, 0}, {Re[z], Im[z]}}];`

Let us also create a point in the plane.

In[8]:= `point1 = {PointSize[.02], Point[{Re[z], Im[z]}]};`

We have added the graphics directive `PointSize` here so that our displayed point will be reasonably large. A *graphics directive* works by changing only those objects within its scope. In this case, that scope is delineated by the curly braces. The form for directives is {*directive*, *primitive*}. Additional primitives can also be placed in the scope of any directive.

{*dir*, *prim*₁, *prim*₂, ..., *prim*ₙ}

The directive *dir* will affect each of the primitives *prim*ᵢ occurring within its scope. You can place as many primitives as you like within the scope of each directive.

A complete list of the two-dimensional graphics directives, together with usage statements, is given in Table 9.2.

To display what we have created so far, we first wrap the `Graphics` function around the points and lines to turn them into *graphics objects*. Then we display the list of objects with the `Show` function.

In[9]:= `Show[Graphics[{line1, point1}]]`

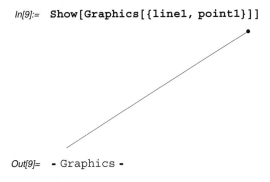

Out[9]= - Graphics -

Admittedly not too exciting, but it is a start. We can add additional graphics elements indicating the conjugate and a set of axes.

```
In[10]:=  cz = Conjugate[z];
          line2 = Line[{{0, 0}, {Re[cz], Im[cz]}}];
          point2 = {PointSize[.02], Point[{Re[cz], Im[cz]}]};
```

```
In[13]:=  Show[Graphics[{line1, point1, line2, point2}]]
```

```
Out[13]=   - Graphics -
```

Directive	Usage
AbsoluteDashing[{d_1, d_2, …}]	dashed line segments using absolute units
AbsoluteThickness[d]	lines of thickness d measured in absolute units
CMYKColor[{c, m, y, b}]	cyan, magenta, yellow, and black of four color process
Dashing[{d_1, d_2, …}]	dashed line segments of length d_1, d_2, …
GrayLevel[d]	gray between 0 (black) and 1 (white)
Hue[h, s, b]	color with hue, saturation, and brightness between 0 and 1
PointSize[r]	points of radius r given as a fraction of the width of the entire plot
RGBColor[r, g, b]	color with red, green, and blue components between 0 and 1
Thickness[d]	lines of thickness d given as a fraction of the width of the entire plot

Table 9.2: *Mathematica* graphics directives

At this point it would be useful to have axes displayed in our graphic. All of *Mathematica*'s graphics functions have options that allow you to modify some attribute of the entire graphic. We can get a complete list of those options relevant to `Graphics` objects by evaluating the following.

In[14]:= `Options[Graphics]`

Out[14]= $\{$`AspectRatio` $\rightarrow \dfrac{1}{\text{GoldenRatio}}$, `Axes` $\rightarrow$ `False`, `AxesLabel` $\rightarrow$ `None`,
`AxesOrigin` $\rightarrow$ `Automatic`, `AxesStyle` $\rightarrow$ `Automatic`,
`Background` $\rightarrow$ `Automatic`, `ColorOutput` $\rightarrow$ `Automatic`,
`DefaultColor` $\rightarrow$ `Automatic`, `DefaultFont` $:\rightarrow$ `$DefaultFont`,
`DisplayFunction` $:\rightarrow$ `$DisplayFunction`, `Epilog` $\rightarrow \{\}$,
`FormatType` $:\rightarrow$ `$FormatType`, `Frame` $\rightarrow$ `False`, `FrameLabel` $\rightarrow$ `None`,
`FrameStyle` $\rightarrow$ `Automatic`, `FrameTicks` $\rightarrow$ `Automatic`,
`GridLines` $\rightarrow$ `None`, `ImageSize` $\rightarrow$ `Automatic`, `PlotLabel` $\rightarrow$ `None`,
`PlotRange` $\rightarrow$ `Automatic`, `PlotRegion` $\rightarrow$ `Automatic`, `Prolog` $\rightarrow \{\}$,
`RotateLabel` $\rightarrow$ `True`, `TextStyle` $:\rightarrow$ `$TextStyle`, `Ticks` $\rightarrow$ `Automatic`$\}$

Notice that each option is specified as a rule with the default value for each option given on the right-hand side of the rule. In particular, note that `Axes` is one of the options for `Graphics` types and that it is set to `False` by default.

Options differ from directives in that they affect the entire graphic. Options to functions are placed after any required arguments and are separated by commas. Since `Axes` is an option to the `Graphics` function, it is placed after the graphics elements $\{line_1,$ $point_1, \ldots\}$. Using the value `Automatic` for the `Axes` option is how we ask *Mathematica* to figure out the best arrangement for the axes placement and labels, given the elements present in the graphic.

In[15]:= `Show[Graphics[{line1, point1, line2, point2}, Axes → Automatic]]`

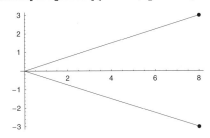

Out[15]= - Graphics -

Next, let us create dashed lines indicating the real and imaginary components of our complex number. We use the `Dashing` directive with `Line` to get the desired effect.

In[16]:= `hline =`
`    {Dashing[{0.04, 0.04}], Line[{{0, Im[z]}, {Re[z], Im[z]}}]};`
`  vline = {Dashing[{0.04, 0.04}],`
`      Line[{{Re[z], 0}, {Re[z], Im[z]}}]};`

Since we were using this graphic to display an arbitrary complex number, we are not interested in the units on the axes, so we suppress the default value and add our own with the `Ticks` option. `Ticks→{{{Re[z],"a"}},{{Im[z],"b"}}}` places tick marks at `Re[z]` on the horizontal axis and at `Im[z]` on the vertical axis and labels them `a` and `b`, respectively. In addition, let us add labels on the axes.

In[18]:= `Show[Graphics[{line1, point1, line2, point2, hline, vline},`
       `Axes → Automatic, AxesLabel → {Re, Im},`
       `Ticks → {{{Re[z], "a"}}, {{Im[z], "b"}}}]];`

Mathematica tries to fit the plot into a region that is similar in shape to your computer screen and uses a ratio of height to width that is known to be pleasing to the eye. This height to width ratio is known as the `AspectRatio` and has a default value of $\frac{1}{\phi}$, where ϕ is the golden ratio. By setting `AspectRatio` to `Automatic`, we will force *Mathematica* to use a ratio that is determined from the actual coordinates in the plot.

In[19]:= `Show[Graphics[{line1, line2, point2, hline, vline},`
       `Axes → Automatic, AxesLabel → {Re, Im}, Ticks →`
       `{{{Re[z], "a"}}, {{Im[z], "b"}}}, AspectRatio → Automatic]];`

We now wish to put labels at the two complex numbers and along the line representing the length `Abs[z]`. We will use another graphics primitive, `Text`, to place text where we need it.

Text[*expr*, {*x*,*y*}] will create a text object of the expression *expr* and center it at (*x*, *y*). So, to create "z = *a* + *bi*" as a piece of text centered at a point a little bit above and to the left of *z*, we use:

```
Text["z = a + b i", {Re[z]-0.75, Im[z]+0.35}]
```

We are going to add one further element to this graphic object. We would like this text to use a different font and a different size than the default of Courier, 10 points. Using StyleForm we can specify any available font and size. In this example we use the Times font family and set the font size at 9 points. (Names of fonts will vary on different computers. Users should check their *Mathematica* documentation for font-naming conventions.)

```
Text[StyleForm["z = a + b i", FontFamily→"Times", FontSize→9]],
    {Re[z] - 0.75, Im[z] + 0.35}]
```

Here then are the labels for the complex number and the length given by the absolute value of the complex number.

```
In[20]:= text1 = Text[StyleForm["z=a+b i",
            FontFamily → "Times", FontSize → 9],
            {Re[z] - .75, Im[z] + .35}];

In[21]:= text2 = Text[StyleForm["Abs[z]",
            FontFamily → "Times", FontSize → 9],
            {4.2, 2}];

In[22]:= Show[Graphics[{line1, line2, point1, point2, hline, vline,
            text1, text2}, Axes → Automatic, AxesLabel → {Re, Im},
        Ticks → {{{Re[z], "a"}}, {{Im[z], "b"}}},
        AspectRatio → Automatic]];
```

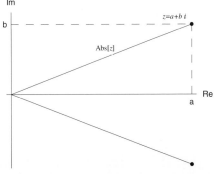

Lastly, we need to add the arc representing the polar angle and label it. The arc can be generated with another graphic primitive. `Circle[{x,y},r,{a,b}]` will draw an arc of a circle centered at (x, y), of radius r, counterclockwise from an angle of a radians to an angle of b radians. The arc that we are interested in will have a radius smaller than `Abs[z]` and will be drawn from the real (horizontal) axis to the line connecting the origin and z. Here is the code for the arc and its label, as well as the graphic containing all of the above elements (we also add the text to label the conjugate).

```
In[23]:= arc = Circle[{0, 0}, Abs[z]/3, {0, Arg[z]}];
```

```
In[24]:= text3 = Text[StyleForm["Conjugate[z]=a-b i",
            FontFamily → "Times", FontSize → 9],
            {Re[cz] - 1.4, Im[cz] - .35}];
```

```
In[25]:= text4 = Text[StyleForm["Arg[z]",
            FontFamily → "Times", FontSize → 9], {3.5, .5}];
```

```
In[26]:= Show[Graphics[{line1, line2, point1, point2,
            hline, vline, text1, text2, text3, text4, arc},
            Axes → True, AxesLabel → {Re, Im}, Ticks →
            {{{Re[z], "a"}}, {{Im[z], "b"}}}, AspectRatio → Automatic]];
```

We have made assignments to many different symbols in this section. Before going on, it would be a good idea to clear the values associated with all of these symbols. In Chapter 12 we will talk about contexts in detail, but, for now, you can clear the values associated with all symbols in the `Global`` ` context by evaluating the following.

```
In[27]:= ClearAll["Global`*"]
```

Exercises

1. Create a primitive color wheel by coloring successive sectors of a Disk according to the Hue directive.

2. Create a graphic that contains one each of a circle, a triangle, and a rectangle. Your graphic should include an identifying label for each object.

3. Create a three-dimensional graphic containing six Cuboid graphics primitives, randomly placed in the unit cube.

4. Create a graphic that consists of 500 points placed randomly in the unit square. The points should be of random radii between .01 and 0.1 units, and colored randomly according to a Hue function.

5. Create a graphic that represents the solution to the following algebraic problem that appeared in Porta, Davis and Uhl, 1994. Find the positive numbers r such that the following system has exactly one solution in x and y.

$$(x - 1)^2 + (y - 1)^2 = 2$$
$$(x + 3)^2 + (y - 4)^2 = r^2$$

Once you have found the right number r, then plot the resulting circles in true scale on the same axes, plotting the first circle with solid lines and the two solutions with dashed lines together in one graphic.

6. Load the package Graphics`Polyhedra` and then display each of the solids defined in the package, including Tetrahedron, Octahedron, Icosahedron, Cuboid, and the Dodecahedron.

7. Create a graphic of the sin function over the interval $(0, 2\pi)$ that displays vertical lines at each point calculated by the Plot function to produce its plot.

9.2 Graphics programming

Up until this point, we have looked at the tools that are available to construct relatively simple graphics in *Mathematica*. This has allowed us to create images by using the graphics building blocks – primitives, directives, and options. In this section we consider problems that are more involved or whose solution requires geometric insight as we construct our programs. We will begin with two examples that create specialized plotting functions, the first for plotting roots on a given interval and the second for plotting data. The second of these will give a good introduction to incorporating error messages and options into your functions. The last two examples are more mathematical in nature. The first is a purely geometric problem on simple closed paths. The last example shows how to construct graphics from programming work we did in Chapter 7, the display of binary trees.

Root plotting

In this section we will use our knowledge of built-in graphics functions together with various programming techniques from previous chapters to write a program that plots a function together with all of its roots in a given interval. The basic idea, using Cases to extract the points in a plot and Split to identify sign changes, is due to Paul Abbott from his article in *The Mathematica Journal* (Abbott 1998).

In Exercise 7 of Section 9.1, we used Cases to extract coordinate pairs from the data in sinplot. In this section, we will use a function with a few more roots in the specified interval to work through the details of the problem.

In[1]:= **sinplot = Plot[Sin[2 x], {x, -1, 7}];**

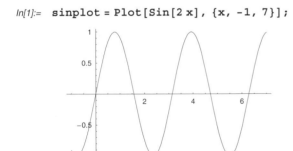

This finds all those Line expressions from sinplot and extracts only their arguments, the point coordinates. Note the need for ∞ as a third argument to Cases so that the pattern matching goes down to the deepest nested expression in sinplot.

In[2]:= **pts = Cases[sinplot, Line[{x__}] → x, ∞];**

In[3]:= **Shallow[pts]**

Out[3]//Shallow= {{-1., -0.909298}, {-0.960965, -0.938983},
       {-0.924601, -0.961495}, {-0.884699, -0.980344},
       {-0.862349, -0.98818}, {-0.842015, -0.993596},
       {-0.831653, -0.995724}, {-0.820668, -0.997513},
       {-0.81129, -0.99866}, {-0.800961, -0.999516}, ≪147≫}

From the above list of points, we select each pair that exhibits a sign change in the *y*-coordinate (Last [...]).

In[4]:= **Select[Split[pts, Sign[Last[#2]] == -Sign[Last[#1]] &],**
    Length[#1] == 2 &]

Out[4]= {{{-0.00256681, -0.0051336}, {0.17505, 0.342993}},
     {{1.32279, 0.475915}, {1.65979, -0.177051}},
     {{3.0015, -0.276542}, {3.34379, 0.39347}},
     {{4.65091, 0.12264}, {4.82866, -0.230455}},
     {{6.01028, -0.519114}, {6.34258, 0.118509}}}

A sign change occurs between each of the first and second points, the third and fourth, the fifth and sixth. FindRoot will use the bisection method if we pass it two initial values, so using the first two *x*-coordinates in each of these three pairs should give us the roots we are after.

In[5]:= **Map[First, %, {2}]**

Out[5]= {{-0.00256681, 0.17505}, {1.32279, 1.65979},
     {3.0015, 3.34379}, {4.65091, 4.82866}, {6.01028, 6.34258}}

In[6]:= **Map[FindRoot[Sin[2 x] == 0, {x, #[[1]], #[[2]]}] &, %]**

Out[6]= {{x → 4.12702 × 10^{-19}}, {x → 1.5708},
     {x → 3.14159}, {x → 4.71239}, {x → 6.28319}}

Now we can turn these roots into graphics objects and combine them with the original plot.

In[7]:= **roots = x /. %**

Out[7]= {4.12702 × 10^{-19}, 1.5708, 3.14159, 4.71239, 6.28319}

In[8]:= **pts = Map[Point[{#, 0}] &, roots]**

Out[8]= {Point[{4.12702 × 10^{-19}, 0}], Point[{1.5708, 0}],
     Point[{3.14159, 0}], Point[{4.71239, 0}], Point[{6.28319, 0}]}

In[9]:= ```Show[sinplot,
    Epilog → {RGBColor[0, 0, 1], PointSize[.02], pts}];```

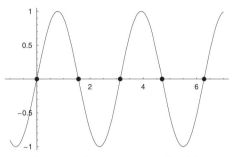

Here then is a function that combines all of these steps.

In[10]:= ```RootPlot[fun_, {x_, xmin_, xmax_}] :=
    Module[{z, fplot, pts, spts, roots,
        points, f = Function[x, Evaluate[fun]]},
      fplot = Plot[f[x], {x, xmin, xmax},
        DisplayFunction → Identity];
      pts = Cases[fplot, Line[{z__}] → z, ∞];
      spts = Map[First,
        Select[Split[pts, Sign[Last[#2]] == -Sign[Last[#1]] &],
          Length[#1] == 2 &], {2}];
      roots = Map[FindRoot[f[x] == 0, {x, #[[1]], #[[2]]}] &, spts];
      points = Map[Point[{#, 0}] &, x /. roots];
      Show[fplot, DisplayFunction → $DisplayFunction,
        Epilog → {RGBColor[0, 0, 1], PointSize[.02], points}];
      roots]```

In[11]:= ```RootPlot[Sin[z + √2 Sin[z]], {z, -π, 3 π}]```

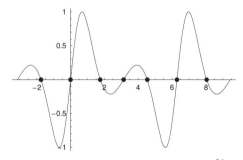

Out[11]= $\{\{z \to -1.75004\}, \{z \to 4.21345 \times 10^{-24}\}, \{z \to 1.75004\},$
$\{z \to 3.14159\}, \{z \to 4.53315\}, \{z \to 6.28319\}, \{z \to 8.03322\}\}$

In[12]:= **Chop[%]**

Out[12]= {{z → -1.75004}, {z → 0}, {z → 1.75004}, {z → 3.14159},
          {z → 4.53315}, {z → 6.28319}, {z → 8.03322}}

The exercises at the end of this section contain suggestions for passing options from
RootPlot to the auxiliary fplot by means of Utilities`FilterOptions`.

Plotting data

In this section we will create a function from graphics primitives that overcomes a minor
inconvenience of ListPlot. ListPlot normally plots a vector or matrix of data, displaying each piece of data as a Point object. When the option PlotJoined is set to True,
the data points are connected by Line primitives, but the original Point primitives are
not displayed. For example, here are ten points in the plane.

In[13]:= **data2D = {{0.043, 0.575},**
              {0.151, 0.120}, {0.234, 0.001}, {0.283, 0.930},
              {0.343, 0.569}, {0.416, 0.768}, {0.465, 0.675},
              {0.539, 0.528}, {0.786, 0.856}, {0.914, 0.794}};

Here is a plot of the points in the plane. We make the points a little larger with the
PlotStyle option.

In[14]:= **ListPlot[data2D, PlotStyle → PointSize[.02]];**

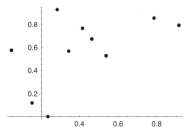

When given the PlotJoined option, ListPlot simply connects the points with
lines, but the points themselves are omitted.

In[15]:= **ListPlot[data2D, PlotJoined → True];**

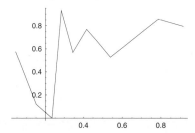

A simplistic first approach would be to make a function that grabs the data and then stuffs them into Point primitives. Note the use of conditional definitions so that Show·Points handles both one- and two-dimensional data sets. In the case of a one-dimensional data vector, each point is "indexed" by its position in the vector. In the case of two-dimensional data input, we assume that each data point maps to its coordinates in the plane.

```
In[16]:= ShowPoints[data_, s_: 0.02] := {PointSize[s],
            MapIndexed[Point[{#2[[1]], #1}] &, data]} /; VectorQ[data];
```

```
In[17]:= ShowPoints[data_, s_: 0.02] :=
            {PointSize[s], Map[Point, data]} /; Dimensions[data][[2]] == 2;
```

Here, Epilog is used to add the points after the data have been plotted.

```
In[18]:= ListPlot[data2D, PlotJoined → True,
            Epilog → ShowPoints[data2D]];
```

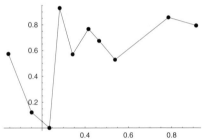

Here is a one-dimensional example of the use of ShowPoints.

```
In[19]:= data1D = Table[Random[Integer, {1, 10}], {8}]
```

```
Out[19]= {8, 7, 5, 9, 1, 8, 9, 2}
```

```
In[20]:= ListPlot[data1D, PlotJoined → True,
            Epilog → ShowPoints[data1D]];
```

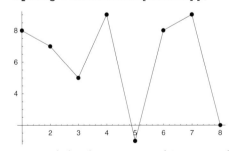

There are several disadvantages to this approach. Epilog is not a commonly used method of modifying graphics and so users might not expect that this would be the way to display the points. Secondly, it is difficult to modify the style of the Point objects with this approach – you would have to make `PlotStyle→PointSize[…]` an available option to `ShowPoints` and that makes things too complicated for the user who would have to think about options to options.

A better approach, more consistent with established *Mathematica* programming style, would be to create a function that plots the data much like `ListPlot`, has a `Plot`-`Joined` option, but does not omit the `Point` graphics objects from the plot. Although a function already exists that does much of this (see the Standard Add-ons package `Graphics`MultipleListPlot``), it is instructive to create such a function from scratch in order to demonstrate how to use graphics primitives, options, and error-checking in writing functions.

First, let us deal with the shape of the data. If the data are given as a two-dimensional list we will assume that each data point, consisting of a pair of numbers, gives the horizontal and vertical coordinates directly. In this case, the data can be passed directly to the graphics primitives.

If the data are given as a one-dimensional list, we will put them into a two-dimensional form by indexing each data point.

```
In[21]:= data1D = Table[Random[Integer, {1, 10}], {8}]

Out[21]= {3, 5, 7, 7, 10, 6, 10, 10}
```

```
In[22]:= pts = MapIndexed[{#2[[1]], #1} &, data1D]

Out[22]= {{1, 3}, {2, 5}, {3, 7}, {4, 7}, {5, 10}, {6, 6}, {7, 10}, {8, 10}}
```

The plot will be constructed of graphics primitives directly. For example to simply plot the points, we could do the following.

```
In[23]:= Show[Graphics[{PointSize[.02], Map[Point, pts]}],
           Axes → Automatic]
```

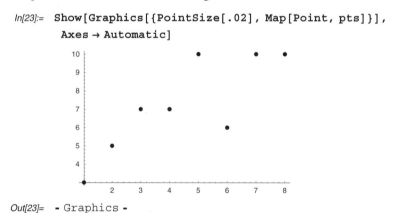

```
Out[23]= - Graphics -
```

Our function will be named `DataPlot`. We start by giving it the same options as those of `ListPlot`.

In[24]:= **Options[DataPlot] = Options[ListPlot]**

Out[24]= $\Big\{$AspectRatio $\rightarrow$ $\dfrac{1}{\text{GoldenRatio}}$, Axes $\rightarrow$ Automatic, AxesLabel $\rightarrow$ None,

AxesOrigin $\rightarrow$ Automatic, AxesStyle $\rightarrow$ Automatic,

Background $\rightarrow$ Automatic, ColorOutput $\rightarrow$ Automatic,

DefaultColor $\rightarrow$ Automatic, DefaultFont :$\rightarrow$ $DefaultFont,

DisplayFunction :$\rightarrow$ $DisplayFunction, Epilog $\rightarrow$ {},

FormatType :$\rightarrow$ $FormatType, Frame $\rightarrow$ False, FrameLabel $\rightarrow$ None,

FrameStyle $\rightarrow$ Automatic, FrameTicks $\rightarrow$ Automatic,

GridLines $\rightarrow$ None, ImageSize $\rightarrow$ Automatic, PlotJoined $\rightarrow$ False,

PlotLabel $\rightarrow$ None, PlotRange $\rightarrow$ Automatic, PlotRegion $\rightarrow$ Automatic,

PlotStyle $\rightarrow$ Automatic, Prolog $\rightarrow$ {}, RotateLabel $\rightarrow$ True,

TextStyle :$\rightarrow$ $TextStyle, Ticks $\rightarrow$ Automatic$\Big\}$

Next, we need a way of passing the option `PlotJoined` to the `DataPlot`. This is accomplished by the following construction.

```
pjQ = PlotJoined /. Flatten[{opts, Options[DataPlot]}]
```

Read from right to left, first the options that are passed to `DataPlot` are combined in a list with the options defined for `DataPlot` above. Then that list is flattened to remove any nested lists of options. Then the value for the rule `PlotJoined→`*val* is extracted and assigned to the symbol `pjQ`. So, for example, if the user evaluates `DataPlot[data, PlotJoined→True]`, then inside the body of `DataPlot`, `pjQ` will be assigned the value `True`.

Finally, here are all the pieces put together in our first construction of `DataPlot`. Note the use of the package `Utilities`FilterOptions``. This allows us to pass the options for `Graphics` directly into our function `DataPlot` inside `Show`. `FilterOptions` will insure that only valid `Graphics` options are passed.

In[25]:= **Needs["Utilities`FilterOptions`"]**

In[26]:= **Options[DataPlot] = Options[ListPlot];**

```
In[27]:= DataPlot[data_, opts___] := Module[{pjQ, pts},
            pjQ = PlotJoined /. Flatten[{opts, Options[DataPlot]}];
            pts = Which[
               VectorQ[data], MapIndexed[{#2[[1]], #1} &, data],
               Dimensions[data][[2]] == 2, data];
            If[pjQ,
             Show[Graphics[{PointSize[.02], Point /@ pts, Line[pts]}],
              FilterOptions[Graphics, opts], Axes → Automatic],
             Show[Graphics[{PointSize[.02], Point /@ pts}],
              FilterOptions[Graphics, opts], Axes → Automatic]]]
```

```
In[28]:= data2D = {{0.043, 0.575}, {0.151, 0.120}, {0.234, 0.001},
           {0.283, 0.930}, {0.343, 0.569}, {0.416, 0.768},
           {0.465, 0.675}, {0.539, 0.528}, {0.786, 0.856},
           {0.914, 0.794}};
```

```
In[29]:= DataPlot[data2D, PlotJoined → True];
```

```
In[30]:= data1D = Table[Random[Integer, {1, 10}], {8}]
```

```
Out[30]= {2, 7, 7, 7, 3, 3, 6, 1}
```

```
In[31]:= DataPlot[data1D];
```

The exercises contain several examples of modifications and improvements to DataPlot.

Simple closed paths

Our next example of a programming problem that involves the use of graphics solves a very simplified variation of what are known as *traveling salesman problems*. A *closed path* is one that travels to every point and returns to the original point. The traveling salesman problem asks for the *shortest* closed path that connects an arbitrary set of points.

The traveling salesman problem is one of great theoretical, as well as practical, importance. Airline routing and telephone cable wiring over large regions are examples of problems that could benefit from a solution to the traveling salesman problem.

From a theoretical point of view, the traveling salesman problem is part of a large class of problems that are known as *NP-complete* problems. These are problems that can be solved in polynomial time using nondeterministic algorithms. A *nondeterministic algorithm* has the ability to "choose" among many options when faced with numerous choices, and then to verify that the solution is correct. The outstanding problem in computer science at present is known as the $\mathcal{P} = \mathcal{NP}$ problem. This equation says that any problem that can be solved by a nondeterministic algorithm in polynomial time ($\mathcal{NP}$) can be solved by a deterministic algorithm in polynomial time ($\mathcal{P}$). It is widely believed that $\mathcal{P} \neq \mathcal{NP}$ and considerable effort has gone into solving this problem. (The interested reader should consult Lawler *et al* 1985 or Pemmaraju and Skiena 2003.)

Our focus will be on a solvable problem that is a substantial simplification of the traveling salesman problem. We will find a *simple closed path* – a closed path that does not intersect itself – through a set of *n* points.

We will demonstrate a graphical solution to the problem by working with a small value of *n* and then generalizing to arbitrary values of *n*. Let us first create a set of ten pairs of points (*n* = 10) in the unit square.

```
In[32]:=  coords = Table[Random[], {10}, {2}]

Out[32]=  {{0.429717, 0.94548}, {0.154498, 0.333952},
          {0.829465, 0.187126}, {0.185409, 0.208253},
          {0.253829, 0.432073}, {0.36397, 0.603652},
          {0.0593643, 0.774766}, {0.804412, 0.766921},
          {0.898828, 0.920331}, {0.858976, 0.829739}}
```

Here we have created a table of ten pairs of numbers (the coordinates of our points in the plane), and then created graphics primitives by mapping `Point` over each pair.

```
In[33]:= points = Map[Point, coords]
```

```
Out[33]= {Point[{0.429717, 0.94548}], Point[{0.154498, 0.333952}],
         Point[{0.829465, 0.187126}], Point[{0.185409, 0.208253}],
         Point[{0.253829, 0.432073}], Point[{0.36397, 0.603652}],
         Point[{0.0593643, 0.774766}], Point[{0.804412, 0.766921}],
         Point[{0.898828, 0.920331}], Point[{0.858976, 0.829739}]}
```

We can show the points alone.

```
In[34]:= Show[Graphics[{PointSize[.02], points}]]
```

```
Out[34]=  - Graphics -
```

Or we can show the points connected by lines.

```
In[35]:= lines = Line[coords]
```

```
Out[35]= Line[{{0.429717, 0.94548}, {0.154498, 0.333952},
         {0.829465, 0.187126}, {0.185409, 0.208253},
         {0.253829, 0.432073}, {0.36397, 0.603652},
         {0.0593643, 0.774766}, {0.804412, 0.766921},
         {0.898828, 0.920331}, {0.858976, 0.829739}}]
```

```
In[36]:= Show[Graphics[{PointSize[.02], points, lines}]]
```

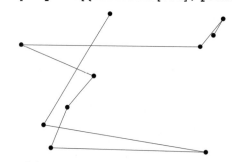

```
Out[36]=  - Graphics -
```

Let us create a utility function for plotting a set of points in the plane together with lines connecting them in order.

```
In[37]:= PointPlot[coords_List] :=
          Show[Graphics[{
             Line[coords],
             PointSize[.02], RGBColor[1, 0, 0], Map[Point, coords]
          }]]
```

```
In[38]:= PointPlot[coords];
```

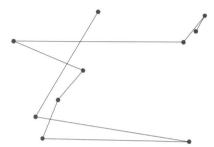

At this stage, it is apparent that there are two problems. First, the path is not closed; that is, the last point visited is not the point we started from. The `Line` primitive connects the first point to the second, the second to the third, etc., in the sequence that the points are presented to it. So we need to connect the last point to the first point to close the path. This can be accomplished by appending the first point to the end of the list of coordinates.

```
In[39]:= path = coords /. {a_, b__} → {a, b, a};
```

```
In[40]:= PointPlot[path];
```

The second problem – the fact that our path is not simple – is geometric in nature. To find an algorithm that will insure that our path does not cross itself for *any* set of points in the plane, we will first pick a point from our set at random and call this the *base* point.

```
In[41]:= base = coords[[Random[Integer, {1, Length[coords]}]]]
```

```
Out[41]= {0.253829, 0.432073}
```

The path problem can be solved by first computing the counterclockwise (polar) angle between a horizontal line and each of the remaining points, using the base point as the vertex of the angle. Then, sorting the points according to this angle and connecting the points in this order will produce the desired result.

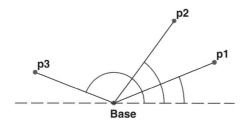

First we compute the angle between two points a and b. (You should verify the trigonometric analysis necessary to find this angle in the various cases. Note that we are computing the polar angle between two points and, hence, we need the ArcTan function.)

```
In[42]:= angle[a_List, b_List] := Apply[ArcTan, (b - a)]
```

We can use this function to compute the angle between our base point and each of the points in the list coords. We need to make sure that we do not try to compute the angle between the base point and itself as this will evaluate to ArcTan[0,0], which is undefined. This situation can be avoided by removing the base point from our list of coordinates when computing the angles.

```
In[43]:= remain = Complement[coords, {base}];
```

```
In[44]:= Map[angle[base, #] &, remain]
```

```
Out[44]= {2.08695, -2.36232, -1.86747, 1.00012,
          1.24074, 0.546405, -0.402315, 0.581378, 0.64796}
```

Instead of computing the angles explicitly, we will just use the angle function as an ordering function on our list of coordinates. Sort [*list*, *rule*] will sort *list* according to *rule*, which is a two-argument predicate. We wish to sort coords according to our ordering function on the angles between each point and the base point. The following code accomplishes this.

```
In[45]:= s = Sort[remain, angle[base, #1] ≤ angle[base, #2] &]
```

```
Out[45]= {{0.154498, 0.333952},
          {0.185409, 0.208253}, {0.829465, 0.187126},
          {0.804412, 0.766921}, {0.858976, 0.829739},
          {0.898828, 0.920331}, {0.36397, 0.603652},
          {0.429717, 0.94548}, {0.0593643, 0.774766}}
```

This is our list of coordinates sorted according to the polar angle between each point and the base point. In order to start and end with the base point, we `Join` three separate lists and then display the graphic.

In[46]:= **path = Join[{base}, s, {base}]**

Out[46]= {{0.253829, 0.432073}, {0.154498, 0.333952},
{0.185409, 0.208253}, {0.829465, 0.187126},
{0.804412, 0.766921}, {0.858976, 0.829739},
{0.898828, 0.920331}, {0.36397, 0.603652}, {0.429717, 0.94548},
{0.0593643, 0.774766}, {0.253829, 0.432073}}

In[47]:= **PointPlot[path];**

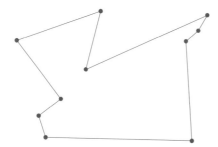

If we collect the above commands into a program `simpleClosedPath`, then we can find such paths for arbitrary sets of coordinates.

In[48]:= **simpleClosedPath[lis_] := Module[{base, angle, sorted},**
    base = lis[[Random[Integer, {1, Length[lis]}]]];
    angle[a_, b_] := Apply[ArcTan, b - a];
    sorted = Sort[Complement[lis, {base}],
        angle[base, #1] ≤ angle[base, #2] &];
    Join[{base}, sorted, {base}]]

Now we can create large sets of points and find the corresponding simple closed path readily.

In[49]:= **data = Table[Random[], {25}, {2}];**

In[50]:= **PointPlot[simpleClosedPath[data]];**

In[51]:= `data = Table[Random[], {100}, {2}];`

In[52]:= `PointPlot[simpleClosedPath[data]];`

Although the algorithm we have developed in this section for computing simple closed paths seems to work fairly well, there are certain conditions under which it will still fail. The exercises at the end of this section investigate some of those conditions and walk you through how best to work around them.

Drawing trees

The trees drawn in Chapter 7 were drawn using a *Mathematica* program. We will develop a simpler version of the program here; the full version is developed in the exercises. Here, trees are drawn without their labels – with just a disk at each node – and, more importantly, the placement of nodes is not as good (aesthetically speaking). Still, it is a good example of using recursion to create a line drawing.

When drawing trees, the central question is: How far should the children of a given node be separated? For example, in Figure 9.1, the separation of the children of node 2 is much greater than that of the children of node 1. That is because the *total width* of the trees below node 2 is so great that they require such a separation; or, rather, the total width of the right side of the left subtree and the left side of the right subtree requires that separation.

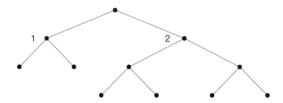

Figure 9.1:   A tree with different separations

To illustrate this point, consider the trees in Figures 9.2(a) and 9.2(b). The subtrees of the root are the same, but in a different order; the result is that in Figure 9.2(a), the children of the root must be separated much more.

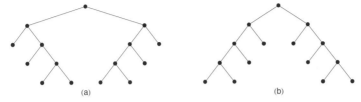

(a)   (b)

Figure 9.2: Trees whose children have different separations

Thus, to properly place subtrees, we need to know, for each one, its total width to the left and to the right of its root. Then, the two trees will be separated by an amount equal to the right width of the left subtree plus the left width of the right subtree, plus some arbitrary additional separation. This is illustrated in Figure 9.3. `lw1` represents the left width of the left subtree, `rw1` the right width of the left subtree, and `lw2` and `rw2` represent the corresponding widths for the right subtree. `minsep` is the additional separation always added between subtrees, and `sep` is the separation eventually computed for these two subtrees.

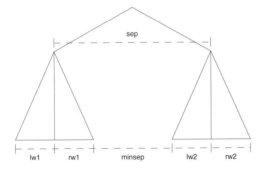

sep

lw1   rw1   minsep   lw2   rw2

Figure 9.3: Calculation of the separation between children

The function `placeTree` is given a binary tree (represented as in Section 7.5) and returns a list of three things:

1. A *separation tree*: a tree having the same shape as the argument, labelled at each interior node with a number, the separation of that node's children.

2. The *left width* of the tree: the distance it extends to the left from its root.

3. The *right width* of the tree.

Now, computing `placeTree[{`*lab*`},` *lc* `,` *rc*`}]` is accomplished in these steps:

- Recursively compute `placeTree[`*lc*`]` and `placeTree[`*rc*`]`; suppose the results are $\{st1, lw1, rw1\}$ and $\{st2, lw2, rw2\}$, respectively.

- The separation of *lc* and *rc* is equal to the right width of *lc* (*rw1*) plus the left width of *rc* (*lw2*), plus the additional separation. Call the total separation thus computed `sep`.

- The left width of the total tree is `sep/2` `+lw1`, and its right width is `sep/2 + rw2`.

This leads to the following code.

```
In[53]:= placeTree[{_}] := {{}, 0, 0}
         placeTree[{_, lc_, rc_}] := Module[{left = placeTree[lc],
            right = placeTree[rc], minsep = 1.0, sep},
           sep = left[[3]] + right[[2]] + minsep;
```
$$\left\{\{sep, left[[1]], right[[1]]\}, left[[2]] + \frac{sep}{2}, right[[3]] + \frac{sep}{2}\right\}]$$

Given a list $\{st, lw, rw\}$ produced by `placeTree`, we no longer need *lw* or *rw* to draw the tree: the separation tree *st* suffices. Transforming *st* into a drawing is straightforward (the `Disk` primitive draws a filled circle with given center and radius).

```
In[55]:= drawSepTree[{}, lev_, xaxis_] :=
           {Disk[{xaxis, lev}, 0.1]}
         drawSepTree[{sep_, lc_, rc_}, lev_, xaxis_] :=
           Join[{Disk[{xaxis, lev}, 0.1],
             Line[{{xaxis, lev}, {xaxis - sep, lev - 1}}],
             Line[{{xaxis, lev}, {xaxis + sep, lev - 1}}]},
             drawSepTree[lc, lev - 1, xaxis - sep],
             drawSepTree[rc, lev - 1, xaxis + sep]
           ]
```

Thus, to draw a tree `tree`, enter:

```
placeTree[tree];
drawSepTree[%[[1]], 0, 0];
Show[Graphics[%]]
```

Alternately, we can create a function to automate this process.

```
In[57]:= showTree[tree_, opts___] :=
           Show[Graphics[drawSepTree[placeTree[tree][[1]], 0, 0], opts]]
```

Here is a simple example.

In[58]:= `tree1 = {a, {b}, {a, {c, {e, {g}, {f}}, {d}}, {b}}};`

In[59]:= `showTree[tree1, AspectRatio → Automatic];`

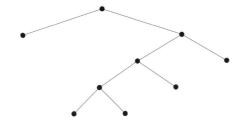

Exercises

1. Create a function `ComplexListPlot` that plots a list of complex numbers using the `ListPlot` function. Set initial options so that the `PlotStyle` is red, the `PointSize` is a little larger than the default, and the horizontal and vertical axes are labeled "Re" and "Im," respectively. Set it up so that options to `ComplexListPlot` are passed to `ListPlot`.

2. Create a function `RootPlot` that plots the complex solutions to a polynomial in the plane. Use your implementation of `ComplexListPlot` that you developed in the previous exercise.

3. Modify the function `RootPlot` so that you can pass the options from `Plot` to the auxiliary function `fplot`. You will need to use the `Utilities`FilterOp`. `tions`` package to pass these options.

4. Add some error checking to `DataPlot` so that a message is returned if the data that are passed are not a one- or two-dimensional list. Your message should be of the following form:

In[1]:= `DataPlot::baddim = "The data used by DataPlot must be`
`             in the form of a one- or two-dimensional list.";`

Then modify the `Which` statement inside `DataPlot` so that it continues to do the right thing if the data that are passed are a one- or two-dimensional list, but, if not, the `baddim` message above is returned. For example, something like the following will work.

```
In[2]:=  pts = Which[
             VectorQ[data], MapIndexed[{#2[[1]], #1} &, data],
             Dimensions[data][[2]] == 2, data,
             True, Message[DataPlot::baddim]; $Failed];
```

5. Although the program simpleClosedPath works well, there are conditions under which it will occasionally fail. Experiment by repeatedly computing simpleClosed∙ Path for a set of ten points until you see the failure. Determine the conditions that must be imposed on the selection of the base point for the program to work consistently.

6. Modify simpleClosedPath so that the point with the smallest x-coordinate of the list of data is chosen as the base point.

7. Modify simpleClosedPath so that the point that has the largest y-coordinate is chosen as the base point.

8. Write a function triangleArea that computes the area of any triangle in the plane given a list of the three coordinate points that describe that triangle.

9. Write a function pointInPolygonQ that tests whether a given point is inside a specified polygon. For example, the origin is inside the polygon formed by joining the four unit vectors:

```
pointInPolygonQ[{{1, 0}, {0, 1}, {-1, 0}, {0, -1}}, {0, 0}]

True
```

10. A polygon is called *convex* if a line connecting any two points inside the polygon lies completely inside the polygon. Most of the simple closed polygons we computed in this section are nonconvex. For a given set of n points, find those points which form a convex polygon that is a boundary for the entire point set. (The smallest such boundary is called the *convex hull* of the set of points.) That is, given a set of points in the plane

write a function `convex` that outputs a graph such as the following.

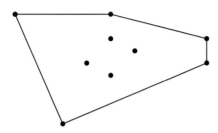

11. Another way of finding a simple closed path is to start with any closed path and progressively make it simpler by finding intersections and changing the path to avoid them. Prove that this process ends, and that it ends with a closed path. Write a program to implement this procedure and then compare the paths given by your function with those of `simpleClosedPath` given in the text.

12. The tree-drawing code we have presented is not the same code we used in drawing the trees in Chapter 7. The two trees drawn in Figure 9.4 show the difference: drawing (a) is the one produced by `placeTree`, and (b) is the one produced by the algorithm used in Chapter 7. That algorithm is due to Reingold and Tilford (1981), and basically what it does is just this: instead of basing the separation of subtrees on their total width, it does a level-by-level comparison, and separates them only as far as needed at any particular level.

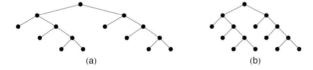

Figure 9.4: Results from different tree-drawing algorithms

Program this tree-drawing algorithm. There is one tricky part to it, which we will leave you to discover for yourself, except to say this: your program should draw the tree shown in Figure 9.5 roughly as you see it here.

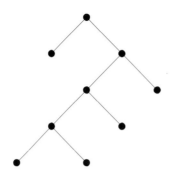

Figure 9.5: A tricky tree to draw

13. Another difference between the tree-drawing code we have shown here and the code that was used in Chapter 7 is that the algorithm there was able to draw trees with labels at the nodes. Extend your algorithm from Exercise 13 to add labels; your trees should have strings as their labels. You need to take the width of the labels into account when computing the separation tree (this is a change to `placeTree`), and make sure the lines do not intersect the labels (this is a change to `drawSepTree`). Unfortunately, there is no way to compute the exact width of a text string as it will appear in a *Mathematica* graphic; just approximate using the number of characters in the label.

9.3 Sound

The sound of mathematics

We hear sound when the air around our ears compresses and expands the air near the eardrum. Depending upon how the eardrum vibrates, different signals are sent to the brain via the auditory nerves in the inner ear. These signals are then interpreted in the brain as various sounds. Musical tones compress and expand the air periodically according to sine waves. The human ear is able to hear these waves when the frequency is between 20 and 20,000 oscillations per second, or hertz.

Recall that one oscillation of sin(*x*) occurs between 0 and 2 π.

In[1]:= **Plot[Sin[x], {x, 0, 2 π}];**

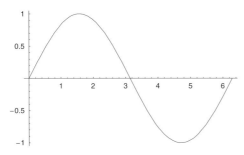

The function sin(4 *x*) oscillates four times in the same interval.

In[2]:= **Plot[Sin[4 x], {x, 0, 2 π}];**

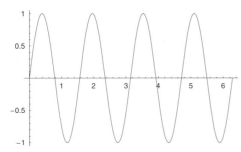

Mathematica is able to take a function such as sin and sample its amplitudes roughly 8000 times per second, and then send corresponding voltages to the speaker on your computer, if it has one, to produce the sound of the sine wave. The function that accomplishes this is `Play`, which has the same syntax as the `Plot` command.

In[3]:= **? Play**

```
Play[f, {t, tmin, tmax}] plays a sound
    whose amplitude is given by f as a function of
    time t in seconds between tmin and tmax. More...
```

The function `Sin[256t]` oscillates 256 times each 2 π units, so, if we want to "play" a function that oscillates 256 times per second, we want `Sin[256 t (2π)]`. This plays the function for two seconds.

In[4]:= **Play[Sin[256 t (2 π)], {t, 0, 2}]**

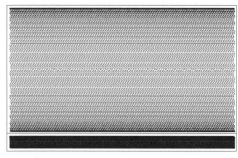

Out[4]= **- Sound -**

If your computer has sound capabilities, you should hear a C, one octave below middle C, played for two seconds. The graphic that *Mathematica* outputs with the Sound object is a somewhat primitive attempt to display the waveform. Since it does not contain very useful information, we will occasionally omit it from the display.

The Play function samples functions at a rate of about 8,000 times per second, or hertz. This is good to keep in mind as anomalies can occur when playing a function whose periodicity is very close to the sample rate. Listen to the quite surprising result that follows (users will have to check the SampleRate on their computers and adjust the following code accordingly).

In[5]:= **Options[Play, SampleRate]**

Out[5]= {SampleRate → 8000}

In[6]:= **Play[Sin[8000 2 π t], {t, 0, 1}]**

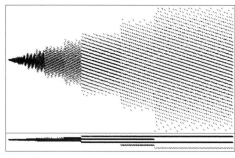

Out[6]= **- Sound -**

Although we would expect a tone at 8,000 hertz, we get something quite different. You are encouraged to try other frequencies that are close to the sample rate on your computer. Play is sampling the function sin(8000 2 π t) 8,000 times. Since the function oscillates 8,000 times on this interval, the samples appear to be about the same and so

Play misses the periodic nature of this function. If Play did adaptive sampling, much like Plot does, then it would avoid this particular problem.

Sounds that are generally thought to be pleasant to the human ear are modeled by periodic functions. Noise consists of random amplitudes. We can use these notions to find periodicity in sequences of numbers.

For example, recall that a rational number can be expressed as a finite or repeating decimal, whereas an irrational number cannot be so represented. If we were to "play" the digits of a rational number, its periodic nature should be apparent as a discernible tone. Playing the digits of an irrational number should result in noise.

The following displays the first 20 digits of the decimal expansion of $\frac{1}{19}$.

In[7]:= **RealDigits$\left[\text{N}\left[\dfrac{1}{19}, \text{20}\right]\right]$**

Out[7]= {{5, 2, 6, 3, 1, 5, 7, 8, 9, 4, 7, 3, 6, 8, 4, 2, 1, 0, 5, 3}, -1}

The -1 at the end of the above list indicates the number of places to the left of the decimal point where the first non-0 digit occurs. Since the first digit of this real number is one place to the *right* of the decimal point, this is indicated with a negative number.

The periodic nature of this number is not apparent from such a short list. We can lengthen the list and pull off only the decimal digits as follows. We suppress the display of the output using the semicolon.

In[8]:= **digits = First[RealDigits[N[1/19, 1000]]];**

Now we can play this list of digits. ListPlay will play a sound where the amplitudes are given by the numbers in our list. (*Mathematica* scales the amplitudes to fit in a range that ListPlay can work with, and that is audible.)

In[9]:= **ListPlay[digits]**

Out[9]= - Sound -

Clearly (from listening to the resulting tone), this sequence is periodic, whereas the following sequence of digits is not.

In[10]:= **irratdigits = First[RealDigits[N[π, 1000]]];**

In[11]:= **ListPlay[irratdigits]**

Out[11]= - Sound -

As the reader is probably well aware at this point, Play and ListPlay are audio analogues of Plot and ListPlot. This analogy will allow us to do "audio programming" in much the same way as we approached graphics programming earlier in this chapter. The next section contains a discussion of some ideas in sound synthesis.

White noise, white music

Imagine playing a recording of a certain sound at different speeds. Normally you would expect the character of the resulting sound to be quite different than the original. Speeding up a recording of your voice makes it sound cartoon-like, and if sped up fast enough, unintelligible. Slowing down a recording of the first few bars of Gershwin's *Rhapsody in Blue* would make the clarinet solo sound like a rumble.

There are some sounds though that sound roughly the same when played at different speeds. Benôit Mandelbrot of the IBM Thomas J. Watson Research Center described these sounds as "scaling noises." White noise is probably the most common example of a scaling noise. If you tuned your radio in between stations, recorded the noise, and then played the recording at different speeds, you would hear roughly the same sound, although you would have to adjust the volume to get this effect.

Mandelbrot additionally characterized white noise as having zero *auto-correlation*. This means that the fluctuations in such a sound at any moment are completely unrelated to any previous fluctuations.

In his book, *Fractal Music, Hypercards, and More ...* Martin Gardner describes an algorithm for generating "white tunes," those having no correlation between notes (Gardner 1992). In this section we will implement his algorithms in *Mathematica* and compose such tunes. We will then see how to generate tunes that have varying degrees of correlation among the notes.

A simple "melody" with no correlation can be generated by randomly selecting notes from a scale. First we generate the frequencies of the 12 semitones from an equal-tempered C major scale. This is just a chromatic scale beginning with middle C.

```
In[12]:= Cmajor = Table[N[261.62558 2^(j/12)], {j, 0, 11}]
```

```
Out[12]= {261.626, 277.183, 293.665, 311.127, 329.628, 349.228,
         369.994, 391.995, 415.305, 440., 466.164, 493.883}
```

This plays the entire scale.

```
In[13]:= Timing[Do[Play[Sin[Cmajor[[j]] 2 π t], {t, 0, 1}],
            {j, 1, Length[Cmajor]}]]
```

```
Out[13]= {1.622 Second, Null}
```

The reader who executes the above code will certainly notice that it is a bit slow. Since we will be generating many sounds below, we will need to speed up the execution of multiple sounds. The reason for the slowness has to do with how Play handles the functions on which it operates. Normally, Play will compile the function that appears as its argument, but it does not do this if what appears is only the name of a function defined elsewhere. Cmajor was defined elsewhere, so it is not compiled. The following function

`PlayTones` will speed the evaluation immensely. Note the time for execution of the same scale as compared with the `Do` loop above. (We have made the `PlayTones` function `Listable` so that it will automatically map across lists of frequencies. Otherwise, we would have to manually `Map` it across such lists.)

```
In[14]:= SetAttributes[PlayTones, Listable]
```

```
In[15]:= PlayTones[freq_, time_ : 0.5] :=
           Play[Sin[2 π t freq], {t, 0, time}]
```

```
In[16]:= Timing[PlayTones[Cmajor, 1];]
```

```
Out[16]= {0.21 Second, Null}
```

Now we can quickly generate the tune. First, we randomly generate 20 frequencies from the list `Cmajor` (we have suppressed the display of the graphics images).

```
In[17]:= randomnotes =
           Table[Cmajor[[Random[Integer, {1,12}]]], {20}]
```

```
Out[17]= {466.164, 311.127, 391.995, 440., 277.183, 293.665, 293.665,
          440., 391.995, 391.995, 329.628, 440., 311.127, 311.127,
          493.883, 369.994, 369.994, 311.127, 261.626, 349.228}
```

This plays the list of frequencies for half-second intervals each.

```
In[18]:= PlayTones[randomnotes, 0.5]
```

```
Out[18]= {- Sound -, - Sound -, - Sound -, - Sound -, - Sound -,
          - Sound -, - Sound -, - Sound -, - Sound -, - Sound -,
          - Sound -, - Sound -, - Sound -, - Sound -, - Sound -,
          - Sound -, - Sound -, - Sound -, - Sound -, - Sound -}
```

A listener would be hard-pressed to find a pattern or any autocorrelation in this "tune" and the music is quite uninteresting as a result. Melodies generated using this scaling are referred to as $1/f^0$, where the 0 loosely refers to the level of correlation.

We leave as an exercise the writing of more sophisticated white melodies – one where the duration of each note varies randomly, and another where the likelihood of a note being chosen obeys a certain probability distribution.

Brownian music

We now move in the other direction and generate melodies that are overly correlated. We will essentially perform a "random walk" through the C major scale. Music generated in such a way is called *Brownian* because it behaves much like the movement of particles suspended in liquid – Brownian motion.

Our melody will be constructed as follows: each note will be generated by randomly moving up or down a few semitones from the previous note. When a sequence gets to one end of the scale, we will simplify matters by having it wrap around to the other end.

We first create a function `step` that will randomly choose an integer from -2 to 2. These steps will determine how many semitones to move up or down.

```
In[19]:= step := Random[Integer, {-2, 2}]
```

Instead of alternating between choosing a step size and moving up and down the scale, we will first create a list of the steps in entirety. We will choose 20 steps corresponding to 20 notes.

```
In[20]:= SeedRandom[0];
         s20 = Table[step, {20}]
```

```
Out[21]= {1, -1, 1, -2, 0, 0, -2, 2, -1, 0, 2, 1, -1, 0, 1, -2, -2, 2, 1, -1}
```

This list will correspond to first moving one step up, then two steps down, then two steps up, etc. So, starting (arbitrarily) with the sixth element of the list `Cmajor`, the following gives the positions of the notes to play.

```
In[22]:= FoldList[Plus, 6, s20]
```

```
Out[22]= {6, 7, 6, 7, 5, 5, 5, 3, 5, 4, 4, 6, 7, 6, 6, 7, 5, 3, 5, 6, 5}
```

There is one problem with this approach. If we get to the end of the list (12th position), and have to add two steps say, we would be stuck.

```
In[23]:= Cmajor[[14]]
```

```
         Part::partw :
           Part 14 of {261.626, 277.183, 293.665, <<6>>, 440., <<2>>}
             does not exist. More…
```

```
Out[23]= {261.626, 277.183, 293.665, 311.127, 329.628, 349.228,
           369.994, 391.995, 415.305, 440., 466.164, 493.883}[[14]]
```

The way around this is to use modular arithmetic. This will have the effect of wrapping around to the opposite end of the list whenever you reach one boundary. Since the list `Cmajor` is 12 elements long, we will use mod 11 and add 1. This will give us positions 1 through 12, as opposed to 0 through 11 if we used mod 12 alone. (Recall that `Part [list, 0]` gives the `Head` of *list*.)

```
In[24]:= pos = Mod[FoldList[Plus, 4, s20], 11] + 1
```

```
Out[24]= {5, 6, 5, 6, 4, 4, 4, 2, 4, 3, 3, 5, 6, 5, 5, 6, 4, 2, 4, 5, 4}
```

Finally, we create a list of those frequencies from Cmajor at the positions given by the above list pos.

```
In[25]:=  brown = Cmajor[[pos]]
```

```
Out[25]=  {329.628, 349.228, 329.628, 349.228, 311.127, 311.127, 311.127,
          277.183, 311.127, 293.665, 293.665, 329.628, 349.228, 329.628,
          329.628, 349.228, 311.127, 277.183, 311.127, 329.628, 311.127}
```

Here, then, is a function for generating the tones from a Brownian walk across the C major scale. This function is set up so that the default range of steps is −2 to 2 (r_:2).

```
In[26]:=  BrownMusic[n_Integer, r_:2] := Module[{cmajor, steps},
            cmajor = Table[N[261.62558 2^(j/12)], {j, 0, 11}];
            steps = Table[Random[Integer, {-r, r}], {n}];
            cmajor[[Mod[FoldList[Plus, 4, steps], 11] + 1]]]
```

This plays the tones with half-second intervals.

```
In[27]:=  PlayTones[BrownMusic[20], 0.5]
```

```
Out[27]=  {- Sound -, - Sound -, - Sound -, - Sound -, - Sound -,
           - Sound -, - Sound -, - Sound -, - Sound -, - Sound -,
           - Sound -, - Sound -, - Sound -, - Sound -, - Sound -,
           - Sound -, - Sound -, - Sound -, - Sound -, - Sound -}
```

This melody has a different character from the $1/f^0$ melody produced above. In fact, it is so over-correlated that it is often referred to as $1/f^2$ music as a result of a computed spectral density of $1/f^2$. Although different in character from $1/f^0$ music, it is just as monotonous. The melody meanders up and down the scale aimlessly without any central theme. The exercises contain a discussion of $1/f$ music (or noise); that is, music that is moderately correlated. $1/f$ noise is quite widespread in nature and is intimately tied to areas of science that study fractal behavior. John Casti, in his book *Reality Rules: I, Picturing the World in Mathematics* gives the following characterization of $1/f$ noise: "If an electrical engineer were to compute the power spectrum (the squared magnitude of the Fourier transform) $f(x)$ of the relative frequency intervals x between successive notes in Bach's *Brandenburg Concerto*, it would be found that over a large range $f(x) = c/x$, where c is some constant. Thus Bach's music is characterized by the kind of 'noise' that engineers call $1/f$ noise." (The interested reader should consult Casti 1992 or Mandelbrot 1982.)

Exercises

1. Evaluate `Play[Sin[1000/x],{x,-2,2}]`. Explain the dynamics of the sound generated from this function.

2. Experiment with the `Play` function by creating arithmetic combinations of sin functions. For example, you might try the following.

   In[1]:= `Play[`$\frac{\text{Sin[440 2 π t]}}{\text{Sin[660 2 π t]}}$`, {t, 0, 1}]`

   Out[1]= - Sound -

3. Create a tone that doubles in frequency each second.

4. A *square wave* consists of the addition of sine waves, each an odd multiple of a fundamental frequency; that is, it consists of the sum of sine waves having frequencies f_0, $3 f_0$, $5 f_0$, $7 f_0$, etc. Create a square wave with a fundamental frequency of 440 hertz. The more overtones you include, the "squarer" the wave.

5. Create a square wave consisting of the sum of sine waves with frequencies f_0, $3 f_0$, $5 f_0$, $7 f_0$, etc., and amplitudes 1, $\frac{1}{3}$, $\frac{1}{5}$, $\frac{1}{7}$, etc. This is actually a truer square wave than that produced in the previous exercise.

6. Create a square wave consisting of overtones that are randomly out of phase. How does this wave differ from the previous two?

7. A *sawtooth wave* consists of the sum of both odd- and even-numbered overtones (f_0, $2 f_0$, $3 f_0$, $4 f_0$, etc. with amplitudes in the ratios 1, $\frac{1}{2}$, $\frac{1}{3}$, $\frac{1}{4}$, etc.) Create a sawtooth wave and compare its tonal qualities with the square wave.

8. A wide variety of sounds can be generated using *FM (frequency modulation) synthesis*. The basic idea of FM synthesis is to use functions of the form

   $$a \sin(2 \pi F_c, t + \text{mod} \sin(2 \pi F_m t))$$

   where a is the peak amplitude, F_c is the carrier frequency in hertz, mod is the modulation index, and F_m is the modulating frequency in hertz.
   Determine what effect varying the parameters has on the resulting tones by creating a series of FM synthesized tones. First, create a function `FM[Amp,Fc,mod, Fm,time]` that implements the above formula and generates a tone using the `Play` function. Then you should try several examples to see what effect varying the parameters has on the resulting tones. For example, you can generate a tone with strong

vibrato at a carrier frequency at middle A for one second by evaluating
`FM[1,440,45,5,1]`.

9. Write a function `pentatonic` that generates $1/f^2$ music choosing notes from a five-tone scale. A pentatonic scale can be played on a piano by beginning with C♯, and then playing only the black keys: C♯, E♭, F♯, A♭, C♯. The pentatonic scale is common to Chinese, Celtic, and Native American music.

10. Modify the routine for generating $1/f^0$ music so that frequencies are chosen according to a specified probability distribution. For example, you might use the following distribution that indicates a note and its probability of being chosen: C – 5%, C♯ – 5%, D – 5%, E♭ – 10%, E – 10%, F – 10%, F♯ – 10%, G – 10%, A♭ – 10%, A – 10%, B♭ – 5%, B – 5%, C – 5%. (*Hint*: Try the `Which` function.)

11. Modify the routine for generating $1/f^0$ music so that the *durations* of the notes obey $1/f^0$ scaling. Write a function `tonesAndTimes` that creates a two-dimensional list of frequencies and time durations. Consider using the function `MapThread`.

12. If you read musical notation, take a musical composition such as one of Bach's *Brandenburg Concertos* and write down a list of the frequency intervals x between successive notes. Then find a function that interpolates the power spectrum of these frequency intervals and determine if this function is of the form $f(x) = c/x$ for some constant c. (*Hint*: To get the power spectrum, you will need to square the magnitude of the Fourier transform: take `Abs[Fourier[...]]^2` of your data.) Compute the power spectra of different types of music using this procedure.

13. Modify the routine for generating $1/f^2$ music so that the *durations* of the notes obey $1/f^2$ scaling.

14. The following series of exercises are designed to create $1/f$ music – music that is mildly correlated.

 a. Write a function `Cmajor16` that extends `Cmajor` to 16 consecutive semitones.

 b. Write three functions `red`, `green`, and `blue` that simulate rolling 3 six-sided dice. The first note from `cmajor16` is picked by rolling the dice and choosing the note in the position given by the sum (mod 16) + 1.

 c. To generate the next eight notes, think of the numbers 0 through 7 in binary. Let `red` correspond to the 1s digit, `green` to the 2s digit, and `blue` to the 4s digit. Starting from 0, and going to 1, only the 1s digit changes. So only the red die is retossed, the blue and green are left alone. This new sum (mod 16) of the red, green and blue is the next position from the list `Cmajor16`. The third roll is obtained by noticing that in going from 1 to 2, both the 1s digit and the 2s digit change. Hence, reroll the `red` and `green` die, leaving the `blue` alone. The new sum of the three dice is the position of the next note. Continue in this fashion, rolling only those dice that correspond to digit changes when moving through the numbers 0–7, base 2. Finally, generate the tones corresponding to these frequencies.

d. Extend the above algorithm to include four dice to produce 16 notes from a 21-tone scale. If you have a sufficiently powerful computer with lots of memory and disk space, try ten dice to produce 1,024 notes from a 55-tone scale.

10 Front end programming

In this chapter we extend the programming concepts we have covered thus far to the objects that comprise the user interface, or front end. Because the objects that the *Mathematica* user interacts with are themselves *Mathematica* expressions, all of the tools that you use to do computations can also be used to create, manipulate, and alter cells and notebooks themselves. We will first look at the underlying structure of these objects and then discuss ways of manipulating them directly from within *Mathematica*.

10.1 Introduction

Up until this point, we have been primarily concerned with learning about programming constructs and styles so that we can write programs to manipulate data or solve problems from science, engineering, or mathematics. We have taken for granted that the space in which we do our experimenting, prototyping, and documenting has been the *Mathematica* notebook, an interface that has some similarities to a word processor document.

It is not uncommon now to add interactive elements to your documents to make them more useful for yourself or the intended reader of your documents. With programs, documentation, and papers all being created and used in electronic format, *Mathematica* provides a seamless and well-integrated interface to these elements.

Another tool that is useful, especially for educators, are buttons that allow you to hide your program code behind a familiar and easy-to-use interface element – the button. The user clicks on a button and an action happens that is determined by the underlying code. For example, you might want to have calculus students quickly plot Taylor polynomial approximations to a function together with the original function but do not want them to spend time learning the syntax of such commands in *Mathematica*. You could easily program an interface that would only require them to fill in a few parameters before clicking a button to produce the desired plot.

In this chapter we will discuss the structure of cell and notebook expressions, look at a few basic functions for manipulating these expressions, and then create several simple examples that give a flavor of the kind of things that can be done with front end programming.

Before we begin we should mention that this chapter is not intended as a complete discussion of front end programming. An entire book could certainly be written on this topic alone. This book is intended to give you an introduction to the many aspects of programming with *Mathematica* and front end programming is certainly an appropriate topic for that introduction. But there are several areas that cannot be included here, either because of space limitations or because they do not fit under the introductory nature of this book. These topics include front end options and front end tokens. An understanding of each of these topics is quite important for more advanced front end programming. The interested reader can delve further into this subject by looking in the Front End category of the Help Browser or by searching the *Mathematica* Information Center online at library.wolfram.com/infocenter.

10.2 The structure of cells and notebooks

We have spent a lot of time in this book focusing on the structure of *Mathematica* expressions. In Chapter 2 we indicated that *Mathematica* expressions are of the form h $[e_1, e_2, ...]$ where h is the head of the expression and the e_i are the elements which may themselves be *Mathematica* expressions. We even went so far as to say that everything in *Mathematica* is an expression. In this section we will learn that this statement extends to elements of the front end, specifically to notebooks and cells.

Notebook expressions

Notebooks are ASCII files, meaning that you can open them in a text editor and view their contents directly. If you were to do that, you would see that the underlying expression is a *Mathematica* function called a Notebook. The notebook would look like this:

```
Notebook[{
        Cell[string, style, options],
        Cell[string, style, options],
        ...
        },
    options]
```

In other words, the Notebook is a function whose first argument is a list of one or more Cell objects, followed by some options. The *Mathematica* kernel does not do anything with this practically. It is the *Mathematica* front end that knows how to render this expression as the familiar notebook.

For example, here is a very simple notebook that you could write in a text editor (of course there is no reason to do that).

```
Notebook[{
    Cell["Demo notebook", "Section"],
    Cell["This is a text cell.","Text"],
    Cell["1+2+3", "Input"]
    }]
```

The *Mathematica* front end renders this expression in the familiar manner, a window.

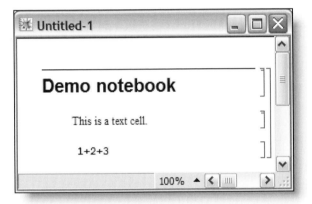

Let us create the notebook from scratch using a kernel command, NotebookPut. NotebookPut [*expr*] will create a notebook corresponding to *expr* in the front end and make it the currently selected notebook.

```
In[1]:=  nb = NotebookPut[
            Notebook[{
              Cell["Demo notebook", "Section"],
              Cell["This is a text cell", "Text"],
              Cell["1+2+3", "Input"]
              }]
            ]

Out[1]=  NotebookObject[ <<Untitled-1>> ]
```

Here is the notebook as viewed in the front end.

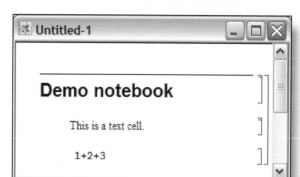

There is actually quite a lot going on behind the scenes here in terms of the interaction between the kernel and the front end. As stated in Chapter 1, the kernel and the front end are two separate programs that communicate with each other through a protocol called *MathLink*. For purposes of efficiency, *MathLink* itself does not store the notebook in memory but instead refers to it by means of a *handle*. These handles are called *notebook objects* and are given as NotebookObject [*fe, id*], where *fe* is an object that refers to the entire front end and *id* is an integer that is a unique identifier for that notebook. In the example above, looking at the InputForm displays this information stored with the notebook object.

In[2]:= **InputForm[nb]**

Out[2]//InputForm=
```
NotebookObject[FrontEndObject[LinkObject["3v8_shm",
    1, 1]], 28]
```

Since we have assigned a symbol, nb, to this object, we can refer to it through this symbol. NotebookGet gets the expression corresponding to this notebook and reads it into the kernel. You should think of it as analogous to Get for packages.

In[3]:= **NotebookGet[nb]**

Out[3]= Notebook[
```
    {Cell[CellGroupData[{Cell[Demo notebook, Section], Cell[
        This is a text cell, Text], Cell[1+2+3, Input]}, Open]]},
    FrontEndVersion → 5.0 for Microsoft Windows,
    ScreenRectangle → {{0., 1024.}, {0., 681.}}]
```

Notice that the front end has added two options to this notebook: FrontEndVersion and ScreenRectangle. It has also added some grouping information for the cells.

These are default behaviors of the front end and may vary from one front end to another. They are also user-settable.

Manipulating notebooks

`NotebookPut` and `NotebookGet` are general functions for dealing with entire notebooks at once. There are a host of additional functions for manipulating parts of notebooks. You might first think that we can simply use functions like `Part` to extract a particular part of a notebook we are interested in. There are several reasons why this is not generally practical. First, because a notebook can contain many, many cells, it is often quite difficult to determine precisely which part you want to work on. Secondly, since the notebook resides in the front end, not the kernel, it is often not very efficient to manipulate the notebook directly by the kernel (although, if the notebook is small enough, this is certainly possible).

As it turns out, there is a way around these issues and that is through something referred to as the "current selection," which is essentially a reference to the notebook object. You could then think of the notebook manipulation functions as operating on streams.

To see a list of the open notebooks, use `Notebooks []`.

```
In[4]:=  Notebooks[]
```

```
Out[4]=  {NotebookObject[ «Untitled-1» ],
         NotebookObject[ «10FEProgramming.nb» ],
         NotebookObject[ «Messages» ]}
```

Again, using `InputForm`, you can see the actual handles to each of the notebooks.

```
In[5]:=  Notebooks[] // InputForm
```

```
Out[5]//InputForm=
         {NotebookObject[FrontEndObject[LinkObject["3v8_shm",
             1, 1]], 28], NotebookObject[
           FrontEndObject[LinkObject["3v8_shm", 1, 1]], 27],
           NotebookObject[FrontEndObject[LinkObject["3v8_shm",
             1, 1]], 7]}
```

Let us walk through some of the most common notebook operations you should learn about. The first is `NotebookCreate`. As its name implies, this function will create a new untitled notebook in the front end. We assign `nb` to be the handle to this notebook.

In[6]:= **nb = NotebookCreate[]**

Out[6]= NotebookObject[≪Untitled-2≫]

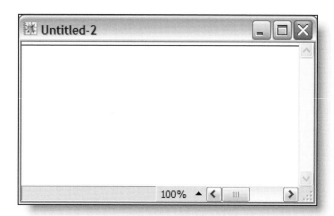

Now let us write to the notebook. NotebookWrite takes two arguments: the first argument is the notebook object that we are writing to; the second argument is what we are writing. We will create a few different examples below.

A Cell is an expression with two arguments. The first argument is the contents of the cell; the second argument is the cell style, a listing of which is under the Format▷Style menu in the front end.

In[7]:= **NotebookWrite[nb, Cell["Here is some text.", "Text"]]**

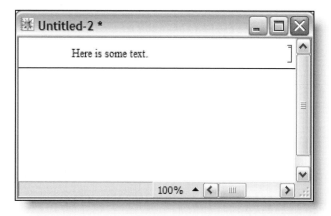

Adding options to `Cell` allows us to change some of the properties of the cell. For example, here are several of the options that you can add.

In[8]:= `Take[Options[Cell], {10, 15}]`

Out[8]= `{Deletable → True, PageWidth → WindowWidth, Visible → True,`
`CellFrame → False, CellDingbat → None, ShowCellBracket → True}`

In[9]:= `NotebookWrite[nb,`
`Cell["Here is some more text.", "Text",`
`CellFrame → True, CellDingbat → ☺]]`

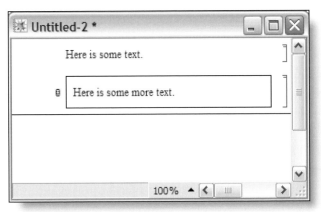

If we simply give a string as the second argument to `NotebookWrite`, *Mathematica* will use the default cell type, `Input`.

In[10]:= `NotebookWrite[nb, "Here is some text."]`

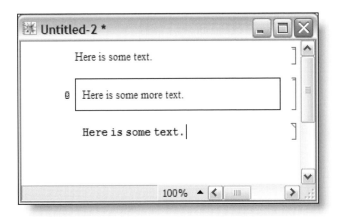

Now suppose we wanted to insert an input cell with the expression 2^{100} in it.

In[11]:= 2^{100}

Out[11]= 1267650600228229401496703205376

If you were to look at the underlying expression of the above cell (under the Format menu, choose Show Expression), it would look like this:

```
Cell[BoxData[
    SuperscriptBox["2", "100"]], "Input"]
```

We will talk about BoxData in just a moment, but we should be able to insert a cell like this directly into our notebook object. Before we do this, notice that the insertion point has been left inside the Input cell after the last NotebookWrite. To move the cell insertion bar after the current cell, we will use SelectionMove which takes three arguments: the notebook we are operating on, the direction to move, and the unit by which we should move. The direction can be any of Next, Previous, After, Before, All. The units are things like Word, Cell, CellGroup, Notebook (see the Help Browser under SelectionMove for a complete description).

So, in our example, we want to move the selection just after the present cell.

In[12]:= **SelectionMove[nb, After, Cell]**

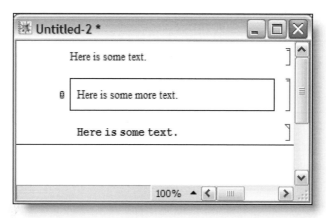

Now we can write the input cell to the notebook.

In[13]:= `NotebookWrite[nb,`
        `Cell[BoxData[SuperscriptBox["2", "100"]], "Input"]]`

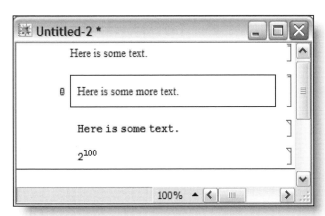

Notice that at the end of each `NotebookWrite`, the cell insertion bar was placed just after the cell that was written, except in the case of writing input cells. Oftentimes, you will need to move around within the notebook or select a particular cell (or other expression) and perform some operation on it. For example, suppose we would like to select the previous cell (the one containing the 2^{100}) in nb and evaluate it. We can do this with the `SelectionMove` function.

In[14]:= `SelectionMove[nb, Previous, Cell]`

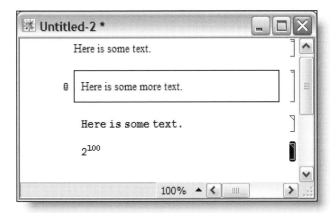

To evaluate the currently selected expression, use `SelectionEvaluate`.

In[15]:= **SelectionEvaluate[nb]**

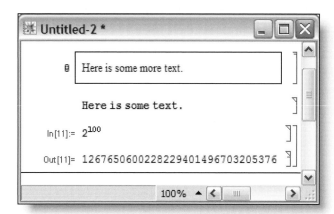

Let us put a few of these pieces together and create a function that will evaluate the next input cell. In Section 10.5 we will turn this code into a button.

For this example we will operate in the current notebook. We can refer to the notebook in which these commands are being evaluated by `EvaluationNotebook[]`. First we select the current unit; that is, the cell in which the following code lives.

```
SelectionMove[EvaluationNotebook[],All,Cell]
```

Then we move the selection insertion to the next cell (at the moment, this code will only work if it is immediately followed by an input cell).

```
SelectionMove[EvaluationNotebook[],Next,Cell]
```

Finally, we evaluate the currently selected input.

```
SelectionEvaluate[EvaluationNotebook[]]
```

Here we bundle this code up into the function `EvaluateNext`.

```
In[16]:=  EvaluateNext := (
             SelectionMove[EvaluationNotebook[], All, Cell];
             SelectionMove[EvaluationNotebook[], Next, Cell];
             SelectionEvaluate[EvaluationNotebook[]];
          )
```

Evaluating the cell containing `EvaluateNext` causes the immediately following cell to be evaluated.

```
In[17]:=  EvaluateNext

In[18]:=  2 + 2

Out[18]=  4
```

Exercises

1. Using `NotebookPut`, create a notebook with one Title cell, one Section cell, one Text cell and two Input cells.

2. Use `NotebookGet` to read the notebook you created in Exercise 1 into the kernel. Then programmatically change the Section cells to Subsection cells either using `Cases` or an appropriate rule.

3. Take either of the notebooks you created in the above exercises and use `Selection‑Move` and `SelectionEvaluate` to evaluate all of the Input cells in the notebook.

10.3 Cell data types

The cells in your notebooks often contain different kinds of data. Sometimes they will only contain text. Other times they may contain formatted mathematical expressions, or possibly a graphical object. Since the `Cell` data object has to handle each one of these kinds of data, there is a mechanism that enables the front end to deal with these objects in a consistent manner – cell data types. We will look at a few of the most important and useful cell data types in the next few sections.

TextData

Let us first look at a text cell that contains no special formatting.

```
Cell["Here is some text.", "Text"]
```

The formatted version of this cell looks like this:

Here is some text.

Adding some formatting to this cell causes a `TextData` wrapper to be added.

```
Cell[TextData[{
   "Here is some ", StyleBox["italicized", FontSlant->"Italic"],
   " text."
}], "Text"]
```

The formatted version of this cell looks like this:

Here is some *italicized* text.

Cells with `TextData` can contain a number of other data objects embedded in the cell. For example, here is a text cell that contains a `ValueBox`. `ValueBox`es provide a means of embedding evaluations inside of your text cells.

```
Cell[TextData[{
   "The current version is: ", ValueBox["$Version"]
}], "Text"]
```

The formatted version of this cell looks like this:

The current version is: 5.1 for Microsoft Windows

A listing of all of the possible `ValueBox` names that can be used can be found choosing **Create Value Display Object** from the **Input** menu. Looking under the list of global variables that can be used as the argument to `ValueBox`, you will see `Date`, for example.

```
Cell[TextData[{
    "The current date is: ",
    ValueBox["DateLong"]
}], "Text"]
```

The formatted version of this cell looks like this:

The current date is: Friday, October 8, 2004

BoxData

Many of your cells in *Mathematica* will contain formatted mathematical expressions. Whenever you work with these two-dimensional typeset objects, a different editor is invoked, called the math editor. This is indicated in the front end by a pink background in Text cell style on the typeset expression (you can enter a math typeset expression by pressing Control-9). This is also indicated in the underlying cell structure by means of the BoxData wrapper. For example, consider the following cell containing a superscript expression.

```
Cell[BoxData[
    RowBox[{
        SuperscriptBox["x", "2"], "+", "y"}]], "Input"]
```

The formatted version of this cell looks like this:

$x^2 + y$

There are several things to note here. First, we see that *Mathematica* has automatically placed the elements x^2, + and y all in something called a RowBox. This is how *Mathematica* represents box objects or a series of strings.

Secondly, the x^2 object is represented internally as another box object, specifically SuperscriptBox[x,2]. You can use DisplayForm to print box expressions in an explicit two-dimensional form.

```
In[1]:= SuperscriptBox[x, 2] // DisplayForm
```
```
Out[1]//DisplayForm=
    x^2
```

There are many different box objects in *Mathematica*. Below are just a few commonly used box objects.

```
Cell[BoxData[
    SqrtBox["2"]], "Input"]
```

The formatted version of this cell looks like this:

$$\sqrt{2}$$

```
Cell[BoxData[
    FractionBox["x", "y"]], "Input"]
```

The formatted version of this cell looks like this:

$$\frac{x}{y}$$

```
Cell[BoxData[
    RowBox[{
        SubsuperscriptBox["∫", "a", "b"],
        RowBox[{"x", " ",
            RowBox[{"d", "x"}]
        }]
    }]
], "Input"]
```

The formatted version of this cell looks like this:

$$\int_a^b x \, dx$$

GraphicsData

Another type of data wrapper that you will encounter is `GraphicsData`, used to indicate a graphical object in the cell. For example, creating a graphics object in the front end displays a plot.

In[2]:= `Plot[Sin[x], {x, 0, 2 π}];`

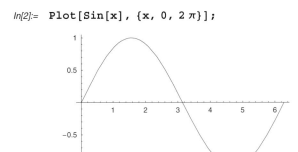

If you unformat the graphics cell, the first few lines would look like the following:

```
Cell[GraphicsData["PostScript", "\<\
%!
%%Creator: Mathematica
%%AspectRatio: .61803
MathPictureStart
. . .
```

Normally you will not create graphics objects from scratch so it would seem as if there is not too much you could do with `GraphicsData` objects manually. But suppose you were interested in displaying your graphics to a notebook other than the one in which you evaluate the graphics input. For example, we could use `NotebookPut` to write out a new notebook containing a graphics cell object as follows:

In[3]:= `MyDisplayChannel[gr_] :=`
       `NotebookPut[Notebook[{Cell[GraphicsData[`
        `"PostScript", DisplayString[gr]], "Graphics"]}]]`

This is now used by giving `MyDisplayChannel` as the value of `DisplayFunc``tion` for any plot you create.

In[4]:= `Plot3D[Sin[x y], {x, 0, 2 π}, {y, 0, 2 π},`
       `DisplayFunction → MyDisplayChannel]`

Out[4]= `NotebookObject[«Untitled-5»]`

Evaluating the above expression will cause a new notebook window to be created in your front end containing just the output of the `Plot3D` command, a graphic of the surface $\sin(x\,y)$.

Exercises

1. Using `NotebookPut`, create a notebook with several Text cells each containing a `ValueBox` such as `$Version`, `$OperatingSystem`, and `$UserName`.

2. Using `NotebookPut`, create a notebook with an Input cell containing the integral $\int \frac{1}{1-x^3}\,dx$. Then evaluate the integral using `SelectionMove` and `SelectionEval`‐uate.

10.4 GridBoxes

ShowTable

Whenever you create a two-dimensional expression consisting of some number of rows and columns, *Mathematica* represents that expression as a `GridBox` object. For example, if you used the BasicInput palette to create a 2×2 matrix, it would be represented as follows:

```
Cell[BoxData[GridBox[{
        {"a", "b"},
        {"c", "d"}
        }]], "Input"]
```

The formatted version of this cell looks like this:

```
a  b
c  d
```

Looking at the `GridBox` object, you should see that it is identical (structurally) to a matrix in *Mathematica*, which is really just a list of lists.

In[1]:= `FullForm[`$\begin{bmatrix} a & b \\ c & d \end{bmatrix}$`]`

Out[1]//FullForm=
    `List[List[a, b], List[c, d]]`

In[2]:= `{{a, b}, {c, d}} // MatrixForm`

Out[2]//MatrixForm=
$$\begin{pmatrix} a & b \\ c & d \end{pmatrix}$$

Using `GridBox`es, let us create a function for displaying arrays of data in a formatted table. First we create some sample data.

```
In[3]:= data = {{"α", "β", "γ"},
       {1.234, 2.3451, 3.4567801}, {SqrtBox["π"], "x/y", "Γ(n)"}};
```

We can put this data into a `GridBox` and immediately print it in a two-dimensional grid using `DisplayForm`.

```
In[4]:= GridBox[data] // DisplayForm
```

Out[4]//DisplayForm=

$$
\begin{array}{ccc}
\alpha & \beta & \gamma \\
1.234 & 2.3451 & 3.4567801 \\
\sqrt{\pi} & \frac{x}{y} & \Gamma(n)
\end{array}
$$

`GridBox` can be given several options that control its appearance.

```
In[5]:= Options[GridBox]
```

Out[5]= {GridBaseline → Axis, RowSpacings → 1., ColumnSpacings → 0.8,
    ColumnWidths → Automatic, RowAlignments → Baseline,
    ColumnAlignments → {Center}, GridFrame → False,
    GridFrameMargins → {{0.4, 0.4}, {0.5, 0.5}},
    RowLines → False, ColumnLines → False, RowMinHeight → 1.,
    RowsEqual → False, ColumnsEqual → False,
    AutoDelete → True, AllowScriptLevelChange → True,
    MultilineFunction → None, GridDefaultElement :→ □}

Let us add a frame, make the margins around each grid element a bit larger than the default, and add some lines between the rows and columns. Usually you will set the values for `GridFrame`, `RowLines`, and `ColumnLines` to either `True` or `False` to enable or disable these elements. Giving an explicit number as the value of each of these options gives the thickness of the line that is drawn for that object.

```
In[6]:= GridBox[data,
       GridFrame → 1.2, GridFrameMargins → {{1, 1}, {1, 1}},
       RowLines → 1, ColumnLines → 1] // DisplayForm
```

Out[6]//DisplayForm=

$$
\begin{array}{|c|c|c|}
\hline
\alpha & \beta & \gamma \\
\hline
1.234 & 2.3451 & 3.4567801 \\
\hline
\sqrt{\pi} & \frac{x}{y} & \Gamma(n) \\
\hline
\end{array}
$$

Now we can bundle up this code and turn all of it into a function, `ShowTable`. If we wish, we can add some formatting, but to do so we have to wrap the `GridBox` in a `Style`

Box. `FontSize`, `FontFamily`, `Background`, and `SingleLetterItalics` are all options to `StyleBox`.

In[7]:= `ShowTable[data_] := DisplayForm[StyleBox[`
    `GridBox[data,`
      `GridFrame → 1.2, GridFrameMargins → {{1, 1}, {1, 1}},`
      `RowLines → 1, ColumnLines → 1],`
    `FontFamily → "Times",`
    `Background → GrayLevel[.8], SingleLetterItalics → True`
    `]]`

In[8]:= `ShowTable[data]`

Out[8]//DisplayForm=

α	β	γ
1.234	2.3451	3.4567801
$\sqrt{\pi}$	$\frac{x}{y}$	$\Gamma(n)$

Sometimes the data you work with will need to be manipulated in some way to display it. The following is another example of the use of `ShowTable`, but one for which we first need to think about the dimensions of our data. Consider displaying a table of reciprocals of rep units, numbers consisting entirely of 1s.

In[9]:= `RepUnit[n_ ? Positive] := Nest[10 #1 + 1 &, 1, n - 1]`

In[10]:= `expr = Map[` $\dfrac{1}{\texttt{RepUnit[#]}}$ `&, Range[12]]`

Out[10]= $\left\{1, \dfrac{1}{11}, \dfrac{1}{111}, \dfrac{1}{1111}, \dfrac{1}{11111}, \dfrac{1}{111111}, \dfrac{1}{1111111}, \dfrac{1}{11111111}, \right.$
$\left. \dfrac{1}{111111111}, \dfrac{1}{1111111111}, \dfrac{1}{11111111111}, \dfrac{1}{111111111111} \right\}$

Since the above output contains 12 expressions, we need to explicitly partition it to be rectangular. First we partition the data into rows of three elements (columns) each.

In[11]:= `ShowTable[Partition[expr, 3]]`

Out[11]//DisplayForm=

1	$\frac{1}{11}$	$\frac{1}{111}$
$\frac{1}{1111}$	$\frac{1}{11111}$	$\frac{1}{111111}$
$\frac{1}{1111111}$	$\frac{1}{11111111}$	$\frac{1}{111111111}$
$\frac{1}{1111111111}$	$\frac{1}{11111111111}$	$\frac{1}{111111111111}$

Here we partition the data into rows of four elements each.

In[12]:= `ShowTable[Partition[expr, 4]]`

Out[12]//DisplayForm=

1	$\frac{1}{11}$	$\frac{1}{111}$	$\frac{1}{1111}$
$\frac{1}{11111}$	$\frac{1}{111111}$	$\frac{1}{1111111}$	$\frac{1}{11111111}$
$\frac{1}{111111111}$	$\frac{1}{1111111111}$	$\frac{1}{11111111111}$	$\frac{1}{111111111111}$

In the above tables, we are manually partitioning the rows and columns into sublists that will be rectangular when they are put into the table. It would be good programming style to take that task from the user and do it automatically. We leave this as an exercise.

TriangleForm

In this section we will use `GridBox` to develop a function for displaying an array in a triangular format. Such a function is quite useful for displaying the elements of Pascal's triangle in the familiar triangular array.

```
                        1
                     1     1
                  1     2     1
               1     3     3     1
            1     4     6     4     1
         1     5    10    10     5     1
      1     6    15    20    15     6     1
   1     7    21    35    35    21     7     1
1     8    28    56    70    56    28     8     1
```

First let us create a function for generating the first *n* rows of Pascal's triangle.

In[13]:= `PascalTable[rows_] :=`
`        Table[Binomial[n, m], {n, 0, rows}, {m, 0, n}]`

Here are the first four rows (including the 0th row).

In[14]:= `expr = PascalTable[3]`

Out[14]= `{{1}, {1, 1}, {1, 2, 1}, {1, 3, 3, 1}}`

If we put empty strings around the elements in the appropriate places we can see what the grid should look like.

```
In[15]:= GridBox[{
            {"", "", 1, "", ""},
            {"", 1, "", 1, ""},
            {1, "", 2, "", 1}
          }] // DisplayForm
```

```
Out[15]//DisplayForm=
            1
         1     1
       1    2    1
```

So we need to develop a function to insert these empty strings between each element in each row and we also need to pad out each row to the length of the longest row in the entire table. First we write the function to pad each row.

```
In[16]:= pad[lis_] := PadLeft[lis, 2 Length[expr] - 1,
            "", Round[(2 Length[expr] - 1 - Length[lis]) / 2]]
```

```
In[17]:= pad[expr[[1]]]
```

```
Out[17]= {, , , 1, , , }
```

```
In[18]:= pad[expr[[2]]]
```

```
Out[18]= {, , , 1, 1, , }
```

Now to insert the appropriate number of empty strings between elements, let us first manually insert space in a few rows.

```
In[19]:= Insert[expr[[2]], "", {{2}}]
```

```
Out[19]= {1, , 1}
```

```
In[20]:= Insert[expr[[3]], "", {{2}, {3}}]
```

```
Out[20]= {1, , 2, , 1}
```

```
In[21]:= Insert[expr[[4]], "", {{2}, {3}, {4}}]
```

```
Out[21]= {1, , 3, , 3, , 1}
```

Here is the function to create the third argument for `Insert`.

```
In[22]:= Map[List, Rest[Range[Length[{1, 3, 3, 1}]]]]
```

```
Out[22]= {{2}, {3}, {4}}
```

Here is the function to add the appropriate amount of space between elements in each row.

```
In[23]:= addspace[lis_] :=
           Insert[lis, "", Map[List, Rest[Range[Length[lis]]]]]
```

```
In[24]:= addspace[expr[[3]]]
```

```
Out[24]= {1, , 2, , 1}
```

```
In[25]:= addspace[expr[[1]]]
```

```
Out[25]= {1}
```

This maps the `addspace` function across each row of the Pascal table.

```
In[26]:= expr = Map[addspace, PascalTable[3]]
```

```
Out[26]= {{1}, {1, , 1}, {1, , 2, , 1}, {1, , 3, , 3, , 1}}
```

Then we pad out each row using our `pad` function developed above.

```
In[27]:= Map[pad, expr]
```

```
Out[27]= {{, , , 1, , , }, {, , 1, , 1, , },
          {, 1, , 2, , 1, }, {1, , 3, , 3, , 1}}
```

Finally we put this expression into a `GridBox` and display it.

```
In[28]:= GridBox[%] // DisplayForm
```

```
Out[28]//DisplayForm=
                1
            1       1
          1     2     1
        1     3     3     1
```

Here is the `TriangleForm` function then consisting of the above pieces.

```
In[29]:= TriangleForm[lis_List] :=
           Module[{addspace, expr, len = Length[lis]},
             addspace[l_] :=
               Insert[l, "", Map[List, Rest[Range[Length[l]]]]];
             expr = Map[addspace, lis];
             DisplayForm[GridBox[Map[PadLeft[#, 2 len - 1,
```

$$\text{"", Round}\left[\frac{1}{2} \ (2 \ len - 1 - Length[\#])\right]\right] \ \&, \ expr\Big]\Big]$$

```
             ]
           ]
```

In[30]:= **PascalTable[5] // TriangleForm**

Out[30]//DisplayForm=

```
                    1
               1         1
          1         2         1
     1         3         3         1
1         4         6         4         1
1    5    10        10        5    1
```

Exercises

1. Modify `ShowTable` so that it can display a user-specified heading in the first row of the grid. Include formatting to set the style of the strings in the heading to be different than the rest of the elements displayed by `ShowTable`.

2. Modify `ShowTable` so that it automatically partitions the list it is passed to be rectangular, with the number of rows and columns as close to each other as possible.

3. Create a function `TruthTable [expr, vars]` that displays the logical expression *expr* together with all the possible truth values for the variables in the list *vars*. For example, here is the truth table for the expression $(A \lor B) \Rightarrow C$.

   In[1]:= **TruthTable[Implies[A || B, C], {A, B, C}]**

   Out[1]//DisplayForm=

A	B	C	$(A \lor B) \Rightarrow C$
T	T	T	T
T	T	F	F
T	F	T	T
T	F	F	F
F	T	T	T
F	T	F	F
F	F	T	T
F	F	F	T

   You will first need to create a list of all possible truth value assignments for the variables, A, B, C in this case. One approach would be to use `Distribute`. So, essentially, this is the left-hand side, or first three columns of the above table (not counting the first row containing the table headings).

```
In[2]:=  vars = {A, B, C};
         len = Length[vars]; ins =
          Distribute[Table[{True, False}, {len}], List, List, List]
```

```
Out[3]=  {{True, True, True}, {True, True, False}, {True, False, True},
          {True, False, False}, {False, True, True}, {False, True, False},
          {False, False, True}, {False, False, False}}
```

You can then create a list of rules associating each of these triples of truth values with
a triple of variables.

```
In[4]:=  Map[Thread[vars → #1] &, ins]
```

```
Out[4]=  {{A → True, B → True, C → True},
          {A → True, B → True, C → False}, {A → True, B → False, C → True},
          {A → True, B → False, C → False}, {A → False, B → True, C → True},
          {A → False, B → True, C → False}, {A → False, B → False, C → True},
          {A → False, B → False, C → False}}
```

Substituting these rules into the logical expression produces a truth value for each of
the above rows.

```
In[5]:=  Implies[A || B, C] /. Map[Thread[vars → #1] &, ins]
```

```
Out[5]=  {True, False, True, False, True, False, True, True}
```

Your task is to put all these pieces together in a `GridBox` with appropriate
formatting.

10.5 Buttons

Buttons are very user-friendly objects whose functionality is familiar to any computer user.
From the programmer's point of view, they allow you to hide your code behind a graphical
element, the button. Instead of writing a function and evaluating it by pressing Shift-Enter
from the keyboard, you pass the mouse cursor over the button and simply click. Whatever
code is hidden underneath the button is then evaluated.

In this section we will first look at the structure of `ButtonBoxes` and then create
some examples to demonstrate the variety of tasks that can be accomplished with buttons.

Making buttons the easy way

The simplest way to create buttons is to select an expression in your *Mathematica* notebook, choose **Create Button** from the **Input** menu, and then activate your button. Let us walk through these steps to create a button that pastes an expression into your notebook.

Suppose you were writing a paper in which you are discussing sequences and you need to use an expression such as the following repeatedly in your notebook: $\{a_1, a_2, ..., a_n\}$. To create a button that would allow you to paste this expression into your notebook by simply clicking that button, we first write down the expression we will work with below in a regular input cell.

      {a₁, a₂, …, aₙ}

Now select the entire expression and choose **Create Button ▷ Paste** from the **Input** menu.

      {a₁, a₂, …, aₙ}

Finally, to activate the button so that you can click it to have an action occur, select the cell in which the button occurs and then choose **Cell Properties ▷ Cell Active** from the **Cell** menu.

      {a₁, a₂, …, aₙ}

Clicking the above button will paste the following at the insertion point: $\{a_1, a_2, ..., a_n\}$.

If you wished, you could create a free-standing palette from this button by choosing **Generate Palette from Selection** from the **File** menu.

Although the above procedure for creating buttons is quite straightforward, it is only convenient for fairly simple buttons. For more complicated buttons you will find that you need a good understanding of the structure of buttons and the various options that control their actions and display. We turn to those topics in the next few sections.

The structure of buttons

Buttons are created with the `ButtonBox` function in *Mathematica*. `ButtonBox` takes one argument and by default, that argument is pasted at the current selection point.

In the examples that follow, we will use `DisplayForm` to display the button as an interactive element. If you were to unformat your button (**Show Expression** from the **Format** menu), you would see essentially all that precedes the `DisplayForm` below.

In[1]:= `ButtonBox["some text", Active → True] // DisplayForm`

Out[1]//DisplayForm=

> some text

Note that we have added the option `Active→True`. This makes the resulting button uneditable, one that is clickable. You will need to add this option to all your buttons to activate them. Clicking this button causes the following to be pasted at the current selection point.

> some text

Let us create a button that can serve as a template for a definite integral.

In[2]:= `ButtonBox["Integrate[fun,{x,xmin,xmax}]", Active->True]`
`//DisplayForm`

Out[2]//DisplayForm=

> Integrate[fun, {x, xmin, xmax}]

Clicking the button causes the following to be pasted in.

> Integrate[fun, {x, xmin, xmax}]

We can use placeholders in our template button so that the user can move from one placeholder to the next by pressing the Tab key. The placeholder character □ can be entered either from the Complete Characters palette (look under Letter-like Forms and then Keyboard Forms), or directly from the keyboard by typing ESC-sp-ESC (pressing the Escape key, then the characters s and then p, and finally the closing Escape key).

In[3]:= `ButtonBox["Integrate[□,{□,□,□}]", Active->True]`
`//DisplayForm`

Out[3]//DisplayForm=

> Integrate[□, {□, □, □}]

Clicking on this button causes the following expression to be pasted. You can move from one placeholder to another by pressing the Tab key.

> Integrate[□, {□, □, □}]

ButtonStyle

Although having buttons that paste their contents at the current selection point is useful, there is much more that buttons can do. For example, they can wrap the contents of the `ButtonBox` around a selected expression and then evaluate that expression. To change the default behavior of buttons from simply pasting their contents to other actions, we have to use the `ButtonStyle` option. `ButtonStyle` is used to control both the style and the actions associated with your buttons. In the following example, `ButtonStyle` is set to `CopyEvaluateCell`.

```
In[4]:=  ButtonBox["Integrate[■,x]", Active → True,
             ButtonStyle → "CopyEvaluateCell"] // DisplayForm
```

The ■ character is entered either from palettes or directly from the keyboard by typing ESC-spl-ESC. Evaluating the above input produces the cell below. Selecting the input cell containing $Cos[x^2] + x^5$ and then clicking the button causes the template to be wrapped around the selected expression and then it is evaluated.

```
Out[4]//DisplayForm=
```

```
Integrate[■, x]
```

```
In[5]:=  Cos[x²] + x⁵
```

```
In[6]:=  Integrate[Cos[x²] + x⁵, x]
```

$$Out[6]= \frac{x^6}{6} + \sqrt{\frac{\pi}{2}}\ \text{FresnelC}\left[\sqrt{\frac{2}{\pi}}\ x\right]$$

If you were to use `ButtonStyle→EvaluateCell` instead of `CopyEvaluate`⸬ `Cell`, the button action would erase the selection and replace it with the new input and the result.

Another very useful `ButtonStyle` is `Hyperlink`. Making a hyperlink is accomplished by creating a button out of some expression and setting the `ButtonStyle` option to `Hyperlink` and adding the `ButtonData` option.

```
Cell [TextData [{
   "Search for button on ",
   ButtonBox ["Google",
      ButtonData:>{
         URL[ "http://www.google.com"], None},
      ButtonStyle->"Hyperlink"]
}], "Text"]
```

The formatted version of this cell looks like this:

Search for button on <u>Google</u>

Setting `ButtonStyle` to `Hyperlink` sets the button action to jump to some location. That location is specified as the value of the option `ButtonData`. In this example, that is set to `URL["http://www.google.com"]`. `ButtonData` set to a URL will cause your web browser to be launched and opened to the location given as the argument to the URL – in this case http://www.google.com.

A list of all the possible `ButtonStyle` values is displayed in Table 10.1.

ButtonStyle values	Action
`Paste`	pastes the contents (default)
`Evaluate`	pastes, then evaluates in place
`EvaluateCell`	paste, then evaluate entire cell
`CopyEvaluate`	copy current selection into new cell, then paste and evaluate
`CopyEvaluateCell`	copy current selection into new cell, then paste and evaluate cell
`Hyperlink`	jump to different location

Table 10.1: Possible `ButtonStyle`s and associated actions

ButtonFunction

Whenever you need to put some *Mathematica* code inside your button, you will need to do so as the value of the option `ButtonFunction`. You will also need to explicitly set the option `ButtonEvaluator` which is set to `None` by default. The `ButtonEvaluator` option tells the front end what program it should communicate with to process the contents of the button function. Setting it to `None` tells the front end to communicate with itself which is fine for operations like copying and pasting. But for operations that need to communicate with a kernel, you will have to specify that explicitly. A value of `Automatic` sends the code to the default kernel for the current notebook. If you had other kernels set up, you could direct the button function at one of those.

```
In[7]:=  ButtonBox["Compute 5!",
            Active → True,
            ButtonFunction :→ Factorial[5],
            ButtonEvaluator → Automatic] // DisplayForm
```

Out[7]//DisplayForm=

> Compute 5 !

Clicking this button will not cause any output to be displayed. This is because these buttons are not evaluated in the kernel in the usual way as part of the main loop. In this case, you can use `Print` to see the side effect of this computation.

```
In[8]:=  ButtonBox["Compute 5!",
            Active → True,
            ButtonFunction :→ Print[Factorial[5]],
            ButtonEvaluator → Automatic] // DisplayForm
```

Out[8]//DisplayForm=

> Compute 5 !

   120

You can use any *Mathematica* function you wish as the value of the `ButtonFunc`‍
`tion` option. But, in addition to the above issue with displaying output, you should be aware of another important issue. As it turns out, the front end does not know how to parse the special shorthand notation we often use for arithmetic and other operations. You will be forced to use the `FullForm` of such expressions inside of your `ButtonFunc`‍
`tion`. So instead of 2+2, use `Plus[2,2]`; instead of `{<<Graphics`; LogPlot[`‍
`Exp[x],{x,1,2}]}` use `CompoundExpression[Get["Graphics`", LogPlot[`‍
`Exp[x],{x,1,2}]]`. Fortunately, the parser for the front end can recognize the shorthand notation for `List`, `Rule`, and `RuleDelayed`, so you can use the shorthand notations { }, →, and :→, respectively.

As a final example, we will create a button that loads a package and then performs a computation with some functions from that package. Here is the code that we want to encapsulate in our button.

```
In[9]:=  Needs["Graphics`Polyhedra`"]
```

In[10]:= **Show[Graphics3D[Stellate[Icosahedron[]]]];**

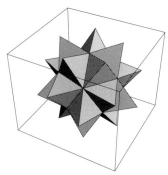

Here is the button code. Note that we have also added an option to ButtonBox to set the background and set the entire cell to use the Times font family.

```
Cell[BoxData[
    ButtonBox[RowBox[{"Stellate"," ","Icosahedron"}],
        ButtonFunction->
          CompoundExpression[Needs["Graphics`Polyhedra`"],
            Show[Graphics3D[Stellate[Icosahedron[]]]]],
        ButtonEvaluator->Automatic,
        Background->GrayLevel[.5]],
      "Input",Active->True,
      FontFamily->"Times",
      FontColor->GrayLevel[1]]
```

And here is the button with a result of clicking it just below.

In[11]:= **Stellate Icosahedron**

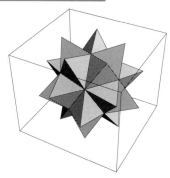

Example: an evaluate button

At the end of Section 10.2 we created a function `EvaluateNext`, which evaluated the immediately following input cell. In this section we will turn the code from that function into a button.

Here was the code we developed in that section.

```
EvaluateNext:=(
    SelectionMove[EvaluationNotebook[],All,Cell];
    SelectionMove[EvaluationNotebook[],Next,Cell];
    SelectionEvaluate[EvaluationNotebook[]];
    )
```

To put this code inside a button, we need to make a few modifications. First, remember that the front end does not know how to parse shorthand notation such as ; . Instead we need to use `CompoundExpression`. Second, instead of `EvaluationNotebook`, we will use `ButtonNotebook`, which gives the notebook in which the current button lives. Finally, we need to use `ButtonCell` to refer to the cell containing the button itself. Putting all these pieces together, here is the `ButtonFunction`.

```
In[13]:=  ButtonFunction :→ CompoundExpression[
            {SelectionMove[ButtonNotebook[], All, ButtonCell],
            SelectionMove[ButtonNotebook[], Next, Cell],
            SelectionEvaluate[ButtonNotebook[]]}];
```

Here then is the code to generate our evaluate button.

```
Cell[TextData[{
  Cell[BoxData[
      ButtonBox["EVALUATE",
        ButtonFunction:>CompoundExpression[ {
            SelectionMove[
              ButtonNotebook[ ], All, ButtonCell],
            SelectionMove[
              ButtonNotebook[ ], Next, Cell],
            SelectionEvaluate[
              ButtonNotebook[ ]]}],
          Active->True]]],
    " MATHEMATICA INPUT"
}], "Text"]
```

And here is the formatted button. Clicking the Evaluate button causes the cell just below the button cell to be evaluated.

EVALUATE MATHEMATICA INPUT

In[14]:= **2 + 2**

Out[14]= 4

Finally, let us add some formatting to make this cell a little nicer looking.

```
Cell[TextData[{
   Cell[BoxData[
      ButtonBox[
         StyleBox["EVALUATE",
            FontFamily->"Helvetica",
            FontSize->10,
            FontWeight->"Bold"],
         ButtonFunction:>CompoundExpression[ {
             SelectionMove[
                ButtonNotebook[ ], All, ButtonCell],
             SelectionMove[
                ButtonNotebook[ ], Next, Cell],
             SelectionEvaluate[
                ButtonNotebook[ ]]}],
         Active->True,
         Background->GrayLevel[0.500008]]]],
   StyleBox[" MATHEMATICA INPUT",
      FontFamily->"Helvetica",
      FontSize->10,
      FontWeight->"Bold",
      FontSlant->"Italic",
      FontColor->GrayLevel[1]]
}], "Text",
   Background->GrayLevel[0.500008]]
```

Here is the formatted version of this code with the result of clicking the button.

EVALUATE *MATHEMATICA INPUT*

In[15]:= **2 + 5**

Out[15]= 7

There is a little inefficiency in our code as we are calling the kernel several times (two instances of `SelectionMove` and one of `SelectionEvaluate`) for what are essentially front end operations, moving and selecting. You can send these sorts of commands directly to the front end by wrapping them in `FrontEndExecute`. To distinguish between the kernel command and the front end command you also need to append the `FrontEnd`` context to the function. So, for example, instead of using `Selection` Move […] in the kernel, you can send it directly to the front end with the following.

```
FrontEndExecute[FrontEnd`SelectionMove[…]]
```

With this in mind, the EVALUATE button can be rewritten by only changing the `ButtonFunction`.

```
ButtonFunction:>FrontEndExecute[ {
    FrontEnd`SelectionMove[
        ButtonNotebook[ ], All, ButtonCell],
    FrontEnd`SelectionMove[
        ButtonNotebook[ ], Next, Cell],
    FrontEnd`SelectionEvaluate[
        ButtonNotebook[ ]]}]
```

Another method of directly accessing front end commands is via front end tokens. These tokens allow you to perform any menu command directly from the kernel. We will not discuss them here, but for a detailed discussion of front end tokens, see the Front End category of the Help Browser.

Exercises

1. Create a button that will serve as a template for the `Plot3D` function.

2. Create a button that will wrap `Expand[]` around any selected expression and evaluate that expression.

3. Using `GridBox`, create a palette of buttons that operate on polynomials like that in Exercise 2. Include in your palette a button for each of `Expand`, `Factor`, `Apart`, and `Together`.

11 Examples and applications

The development of larger-scale *Mathematica* programming projects is discussed and illustrated in this chapter. Each of the examples in this chapter contain numerous tasks that need to work together and also integrate well with *Mathematica*. When you develop such applications, it is important to think about how your functions work with each other as well as how well they integrate with the rest of *Mathematica*. The user's interface to your programs should be as close as possible to the built-in functions of *Mathematica* so that users can more easily learn the syntax and usage. Features such as options, argument checking, messaging, and documentation are all discussed in the context of larger applications that are developed using all of the tools that were developed in earlier chapters.

11.1 Manipulating data files

Introduction

One of the most common tasks for scientists and engineers is working with data sets that have been generated by some external process or collector. If they are lucky, the data are stored in a file that has a standard format and can then be read into other programs such as *Mathematica* with ease using that program's importing functionality. Oftentimes, however, data are stored in files with nonstandard formats and reading that file into a program such as *Mathematica* requires some manual processing of that file to extract the required parts.

In this section we will walk through the steps of reading, manipulating, and visualizing a dataset that consists of solar radiation data collected by the Renewable Resource Data Center, an organization that is managed by the US Department of Energy (interested readers should visit rredc.nrel.gov). A copy of one such dataset has been placed in the IPM3 files that are available for this book (see the Preface for details).

Getting the data into Mathematica

Our first task is to read the data into *Mathematica*. There are several functions that are useful for getting data into *Mathematica*. One of them is `Import`, which is a good function to try if you know your data are in one of the standard file formats supported by `Import`. In this example, we will take a more general approach, one that can be used for somewhat arbitrary file formats, with appropriate modifications.

When working with files that you need to read into *Mathematica*, you have several options for how to deal with file locations. One option is to put your data file anywhere on your system and then point to it in your *Mathematica*. For example, suppose you place a data file testdata.txt in the following directory:

```
C:\Work\Project42\DataFiles\
```

In your notebook you could then create a path to this file as follows. (Note, this does not read the file into *Mathematica*, it simply creates a path to the file.)

```
In[1]:=  file = ToFileName[
            {"C:", "Work", "Project42", "DataFiles"}, "testdata.txt"]

Out[1]=  C:\Work\Project42\DataFiles\testdata.txt
```

Any cells, such as the above, that you need to evaluate before doing any other work in a notebook, can be turned into initialization cells by selecting those cell brackets and then selecting Cell Properties ▷ Initialization Cell from the Cell menu.

Another strategy for setting up your work environment would be to put any *Mathematica* commands such as that above in an init.m file that will then be read into the kernel whenever the kernel is first started up. For more information on this approach, see the subsection "Creating Help Browser documentation" in Section 11.2.

It is a common convention to put user applications and packages in one of several Applications subdirectories. The two places to consider are given by the following. (Although the input will be the same on all operating systems, the output will reflect the directory structure of your operating system.)

```
In[2]:=  ToFileName[{$BaseDirectory, "Applications"}]

Out[2]=  C:\Documents and Settings\All Users\
            Application Data\Mathematica\Applications\
```

In[3]:= **ToFileName[{$UserBaseDirectory, "Applications"}]**

Out[3]= C:\Documents and Settings\Paul Wellin\
  Application Data\Mathematica\Applications\

`$BaseDirectory` is only writable by users who have administrative privileges. Typically you put your applications there if you want to make them available to all users of your computer. `$UserBaseDirectory` is only writable by the currently logged-in user of you computer. This is the place to put your files if you do not have administrative privileges or if you simply wish to keep your files accessible only to yourself.

The full list of the directories on *Mathematica*'s search path is given by `$Path`.

In[4]:= **$Path // TableForm**

Out[4]//TableForm=
```
C:\Program Files\Wolfram Research\Mathematica\5.0\AddOns\JLink
C:\Program Files\Wolfram Research\Mathematica\5.0\AddOns\NETLink
C:\Documents and Settings\Paul Wellin\Application Data\Mathematica\Kernel
C:\Documents and Settings\Paul Wellin\Application Data\Mathematica\Autoload
C:\Documents and Settings\Paul Wellin\Application Data\Mathematica\Applications
C:\Documents and Settings\All Users\Application Data\Mathematica\Kernel
C:\Documents and Settings\All Users\Application Data\Mathematica\Autoload
C:\Documents and Settings\All Users\Application Data\Mathematica\Applications

.

C:\Documents and Settings\Paul Wellin
C:\Program Files\Wolfram Research\Mathematica\5.0\AddOns\StandardPackages
C:\Program Files\Wolfram Research\Mathematica\5.0\AddOns\StandardPackages\StartUp
C:\Program Files\Wolfram Research\Mathematica\5.0\AddOns\Autoload
C:\Program Files\Wolfram Research\Mathematica\5.0\AddOns\Applications
C:\Program Files\Wolfram Research\Mathematica\5.0\AddOns\ExtraPackages
C:\Program Files\Wolfram Research\Mathematica\5.0\SystemFiles\Graphics\Packages
C:\Program Files\Wolfram Research\Mathematica\5.0\Configuration\Kernel
```

The files associated with this book are all stored in a directory IPM3 which should live in the Applications directory in either `$BaseDirectory` or `$UserBaseDirec`tory. Since both are on the path, the following designation sets up a system-independent file name that is relative to the path given by `$Path`.

In[5]:= **datafile = ToFileName[{"IPM3", "DataFiles"}, "23232.txt"]**

Out[5]= IPM3\DataFiles\23232.txt

Now suppose you have looked at this text file 23232.txt in a text editor (see display of the first few lines of this file below) and noted that it contains strings and numbers and that elements are separated by commas.

```
"City:      ","SACRAMENTO                    "
"State:     ","CA"
"WBAN No:   ", 23232
"Lat(N):    ",  38.52
"Long(W):   ",121.50
"Elev(m):   ",      8
"Pres(mb):",   1015
"Stn Type:","Secondary"
"MONTHLY SOLAR RADIATION (kWh/m2/day)"
"COLUMN A: Year"
"COLUMN B: Month"
"COLUMN C: Flat-Plate Collector Facing South at Fixed Tilt=0"
"COLUMN D: Flat-Plate Collector Facing South at Fixed Tilt=Lat-15"
⋮
```

Program Listing 11.1:   Display of first few lines of file 23232.txt

Back in *Mathematica*, you can use ReadList to read the file using some assumptions about the data in the file.

```
In[6]:=  rawdata = ReadList[datafile, Word,
            WordSeparators → ",",
            RecordLists → True,
            RecordSeparators → {"\r\n", "\n", "\r"}];
```

ReadList takes two arguments: the first argument is the file that we are reading, in this case, datafile; the second argument specifies the type of objects that are contained in the file. Since we have a mix of strings and numbers in this file, we will simply assume each entry is of type Word and manipulate the entries afterwards.

In addition to the two arguments to ReadList, we have also used several options that state some assumptions about the form of the data and file. WordSeparators→"," indicates that elements in the file are assumed to be separated by commas. Record⸱ Lists→True indicates that each line of data from the file should be put in a separate sublist in *Mathematica*. RecordSeparators→{"\r\n","\n","\r"} specifies that any of the three ways to end lines in text files (Windows, Unix, and Macintosh Classic) should be considered. This is particularly useful if you do not know the origin of the operating system on which your file was created or if you are unsure of how it has been transported between operating systems.

Examining the data file

Now that we have read the data file into *Mathematica*, let us try to get a sense of its shape and its contents so that we can start to determine in which parts we will be most interested.

Here is an abbreviated view showing the first few lines, an indication that 377 lines are not displayed, and then the last few lines.

```
In[7]:= Short[rawdata, 10]
```

```
Out[7]//Short= {{"City:      ", "SACRAMENTO                  "},
               {"State:    ", "CA"}, {"WBAN No: ",  23232},
               {"Lat(N):   ",  38.52}, {"Long(W): ", 121.50},
               ≪377≫, {90,  9,  5.9,  7.0,  7.1,  6.8,  4.6,  8.7,
                9.6,  9.7,  9.5,  9.7,  5.6,  6.9,  7.7,  7.7},
               {90, 10,  4.3,  5.8,  6.3,  6.4,  5.2,  6.5,  7.6,
                7.9,  8.0,  8.1,  4.8,  4.9,  6.1,  6.2},
               {90, 11,  2.9,  4.2,  4.8,  5.1,  4.5,  4.2,  5.3,
                5.7,  5.9,  6.0,  3.7,  2.9,  4.2,  4.4},
               {90, 12,  2.2,  3.5,  4.1,  4.5,  4.2,  3.3,  4.3,
                4.8,  5.1,  5.2,  3.3,  2.3,  3.5,  3.8}}
```

Note that the data set contains 386 records, or lines. In *Mathematica*, we should think of these records as sublists since `ReadList` reads each record in as a list.

```
In[8]:= Dimensions[rawdata]
```

```
Out[8]= {386}
```

Here are the first nine lines of the data set. They give information about where the solar data were collected. Note that these lines are strings of text.

```
In[9]:= Take[rawdata, 9] // TableForm
```

```
Out[9]//TableForm=
         "City:       "                              "SACRAMENTO
         "State:     "                               "CA"
         "WBAN No:  "                                23232
         "Lat(N):    "                               38.52
         "Long(W):  "                                121.50
         "Elev(m):   "                               8
         "Pres(mb):"                                 1015
         "Stn Type:"                                 "Secondary"
         "MONTHLY SOLAR RADIATION (kWh/m2/day)"
```

The next several lines contain information about each of the columns later in the file that contain the actual data. Again, these lines are strings. Although lines 10 through 25 contain this metadata about the columns, here we only display the first several.

```
In[10]:= Take[rawdata, {10, 16}] // TableForm
```

Out[10]//TableForm=
```
"COLUMN A: Year"
"COLUMN B: Month"
"COLUMN C: Flat-Plate Collector Facing South at Fixed Tilt=0"
"COLUMN D: Flat-Plate Collector Facing South at Fixed Tilt=Lat-15"
"COLUMN E: Flat-Plate Collector Facing South at Fixed Tilt=Lat"
"COLUMN F: Flat-Plate Collector Facing South at Fixed Tilt=Lat+15"
"COLUMN G: Flat-Plate Collector Facing South at Fixed Tilt=90"
```

The 26th record of this file is simply a column identifier for the data that follows.

```
In[11]:= Take[rawdata, {26}]
```

Out[11]= ```
{{"COL A", "COL B", "COL C", "COL D", "COL E",
  "COL F", "COL G", "COL H", "COL I", "COL J", "COL K",
  "COL L", "COL M", "COL N", "COL O", "COL P"}}
```

Starting at row 27, we have our actual data – first the year, then the month, and then several columns with numbers that represent solar radiation collected by different collectors, measured in kilowatt hours per square meter per day.

```
In[12]:= Take[rawdata, {27, 29}]
```

Out[12]= ```
{{61, 1, 1.6, 1.9, 2.0, 2.0, 1.6, 1.7,
   2.0, 2.0, 2.1, 2.1, 0.7, 0.5, 0.8, 0.8},
 {61, 2, 3.0, 4.0, 4.3, 4.4, 3.7, 4.2, 4.9,
   5.2, 5.3, 5.3, 2.8, 2.6, 3.4, 3.5},
 {61, 3, 4.3, 5.1, 5.2, 5.1, 3.7, 5.8, 6.4,
   6.6, 6.5, 6.6, 3.2, 3.6, 4.2, 4.2}}
```

The data in these rows are still strings as a result of using the Word data type in ReadList when we read in the file.

```
In[13]:= Map[Head, Take[rawdata, {27}], {2}]
```

Out[13]= ```
{{String, String, String, String,
  String, String, String, String, String, String,
  String, String, String, String, String, String}}
```

To convert each of these elements to numbers, we need to map ToExpression across each element.

```
In[14]:= Map[ToExpression, Take[rawdata, {27}], {2}]
```

Out[14]= ```
{{61, 1, 1.6, 1.9, 2., 2., 1.6,
  1.7, 2., 2., 2.1, 2.1, 0.7, 0.5, 0.8, 0.8}}
```

In[15]:= `Map[Head, %, {2}]`

Out[15]= `{{Integer, Integer, Real, Real, Real, Real, Real,`
`        Real, Real, Real, Real, Real, Real, Real, Real, Real}}`

Extracting and converting data

We only wish to work with the actual data that represent the solar radiation values collected on various dates. To extract only those rows that contain these numbers, we will
select those rows from `rawdata` that do not begin with a quote character.

In[16]:= `data = Select[rawdata, StringTake[#[[1]], 1] =!= "\"" &];`

Now we can turn each of the elements in `data` into a number using
`ToExpression`.

In[17]:= `cleandata = Map[ToExpression, data, {2}];`

Here we can see the results of these operations by looking at the first two rows of
`cleandata`.

In[18]:= `Take[cleandata, {1, 2}]`

Out[18]= `{{61, 1, 1.6, 1.9, 2., 2., 1.6, 1.7, 2., 2., 2.1,`
`        2.1, 0.7, 0.5, 0.8, 0.8}, {61, 2, 3., 4., 4.3, 4.4,`
`        3.7, 4.2, 4.9, 5.2, 5.3, 5.3, 2.8, 2.6, 3.4, 3.5}}`

In[19]:= `Map[Head, cleandata[[1]]]`

Out[19]= `{Integer, Integer, Real, Real, Real, Real, Real,`
`        Real, Real, Real, Real, Real, Real, Real, Real, Real}`

Each of these rows in `cleandata` represent a year, a month, and a set of solar
radiation values collected during that month. We can use `Select` to pick out the row
whose first element (year) is 61 and whose second element (month) is 2; in other words, to
get the data corresponding to February 1961.

In[20]:= `Select[cleandata, (#[[1]] == 61 && #[[2]] == 2) &]`

Out[20]= `{{61, 2, 3., 4., 4.3, 4.4, 3.7,`
`        4.2, 4.9, 5.2, 5.3, 5.3, 2.8, 2.6, 3.4, 3.5}}`

Here is how we would pick out all records between August 1961 and January 1962.

```
In[21]:= Select[cleandata,
          (#[[1]] == 61 && #[[2]] ≥ 8) || (#[[1]] == 62 && #[[2]] ≤ 1) &]

Out[21]= {{61, 8, 6.7, 7.1, 6.8, 6.2, 3.5, 9.5, 9.9, 9.7,
           9.3, 9.9, 5.4, 7.2, 7.3, 7.6}, {61, 9, 5.8, 6.8, 7.,
           6.8, 4.6, 8.6, 9.4, 9.6, 9.4, 9.6, 5.4, 6.8, 7.5, 7.5},
           {61, 10, 4.1, 5.4, 5.8, 5.9, 4.7, 6., 6.9, 7.3, 7.3,
           7.4, 4.3, 4.3, 5.4, 5.5}, {61, 11, 2.5, 3.6, 4., 4.2,
           3.7, 3.5, 4.3, 4.7, 4.8, 4.9, 2.9, 2.3, 3.2, 3.4},
           {61, 12, 1.6, 2.1, 2.3, 2.3, 2.1, 1.9, 2.3, 2.5, 2.5,
           2.6, 1.2, 0.8, 1.3, 1.4}, {62, 1, 2.3, 3.3, 3.8,
           4., 3.6, 3.2, 4., 4.3, 4.6, 4.6, 2.8, 2., 3., 3.2}}
```

It will be useful to have a more natural interface for selecting data based on this date criteria. Here then is a function that we can use to easily select those records between two dates, each given by a month and year.

```
In[22]:= GetData[dat_, {m1_, y1_}, {m2_, y2_}] := Select[dat,
          (#[[1]] == y1 && #[[2]] ≥ m1) || (#[[1]] == y2 && #[[2]] ≤ m2) &]
```

Using GetData, this picks out the data from August 1970 through January 1971.

```
In[23]:= GetData[cleandata, {8, 70}, {1, 71}]

Out[23]= {{70, 8, 7.4, 7.9, 7.6, 6.9, 3.7, 10.8, 11.2, 11.1,
           10.6, 11.3, 6.6, 8.8, 8.9, 9.2}, {70, 9, 6.1, 7.2, 7.3,
           7.1, 4.8, 9., 9.9, 10., 9.8, 10., 5.8, 7.2, 8., 8.},
           {70, 10, 4.1, 5.4, 5.8, 5.9, 4.7, 6., 6.9, 7.3, 7.3,
           7.3, 4.3, 4.4, 5.4, 5.5}, {70, 11, 2.2, 2.9, 3.2, 3.3,
           2.8, 2.8, 3.4, 3.6, 3.7, 3.7, 1.9, 1.5, 2.1, 2.2},
           {70, 12, 1.4, 1.8, 1.9, 1.9, 1.6, 1.6, 1.9, 2., 2.,
           2., 0.7, 0.5, 0.8, 0.9}, {71, 1, 2.1, 2.9, 3.3, 3.5,
           3.1, 2.8, 3.4, 3.7, 3.9, 3.9, 2.2, 1.6, 2.3, 2.5}}
```

Visualizing the data

The third through 16th columns of rawdata contain solar radiation values that come from different collectors, or perhaps one collector set at a different angle to the sun. Let us take a look at just one of these.

```
In[24]:= Take[rawdata, {15}]

Out[24]= {{"COLUMN F: Flat-Plate
            Collector Facing South at Fixed Tilt=Lat+15"}}
```

Using `GetData` we can extract all those values for this particular collector (the sixth column, referred to as `"COL F"`) taken from January 1980 through December 1980,

In[25]:= `d1 = Part[GetData[cleandata, {1, 80}, {12, 80}], All, 6]`

Out[25]= `{2.7, 3.6, 5.9, 5.7, 5.9, 5.9, 6.1, 6.7, 6.8, 6., 4.7, 3.1}`

and similarly for 1981.

In[26]:= `d2 = Part[GetData[cleandata, {1, 81}, {12, 81}], All, 6]`

Out[26]= `{2.4, 4.3, 4.7, 6.2, 6.2, 6.2, 6.3, 6.8, 6.8, 5.8, 3.7, 2.2}`

Using `MultipleListPlot` (defined in `Graphics`MultipleListPlot``), we can quickly view these two datasets together.

In[27]:= `<< Graphics`MultipleListPlot``

In[28]:= `MultipleListPlot[d1, d2, PlotJoined → True,`
            `AspectRatio → Automatic, AxesLabel → {None, "kWh/m`^{2}`/day"}];`

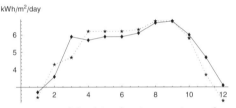

It would be easy to modify this plot in a variety of ways. For example, we could give explicit month text for the horizontal axis tick marks.

In[29]:= `months = {{1, "Jan"}, {2, "Feb"}, {3, "Mar"}, {4, "Apr"},`
            `{5, "May"}, {6, "Jun"}, {7, "Jul"}, {8, "Aug"},`
            `{9, "Sep"}, {10, "Oct"}, {11, "Nov"}, {12, "Dec"}};`

In[30]:= `MultipleListPlot[d1, d2, PlotJoined → True,`
            `AspectRatio → Automatic, Ticks → {months, Automatic},`
            `AxesLabel → {None, "kWh/m`^{2}`/day"}];`

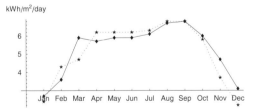

Of course lots of additional information could be added to the plot.

```
In[31]:=  MultipleListPlot[d1, d2, PlotJoined → True,
          AspectRatio → Automatic, Ticks → {months, Automatic},
          AxesLabel → {None, "kWh/m²/day"},
          PlotLegend → {"1980", "1981"}, LegendTextSpace → 5,
          LegendLabel → "Lat(N): 38.52, \nLong(W): 121.50"];
```

The exercises ask you to bundle up the code developed in this section into several functions and also to modify the graphical content and display it in several useful ways.

Exercises

1. Create a function ReadSolarData [*file*, *opts*] that reads in a solar data file such as 23232.txt using ReadList, strips out any line beginning with a quote character, and returns the remaining lines with each element converted to a number. You should set explicit options to ReadSolarData that borrow from ReadList.

2. Create a function that computes the total solar radiation for a given year from one collector (your choice) from the data file 23232.txt. Make a plot comparing these yearly radiation values for the history of the dataset.

3. Create a function PlotSolarData [*dat₁*, *dat₂*, *opts*] that uses MultipleListPlot as in the previous section to plot datasets *dat₁* and *dat₂*. Your function should include customized tick information, axes labels, and a legend that displays the latitude and longitude of the collector in the LegendLabel. In addition, you function should be able to accept options similar to MultipleListPlot and pass them directly to MultipleListPlot.

4. Overload PlotSolarData so that when evaluated as PlotSolarData [*month*, *opts*], and *month* is one of January, February,…, December, it will produce a plot comparing the solar radiation for that month across all years of the dataset.

11.2 Random walks

Introduction

Random walks are widely used to represent random processes in nature; physicists model the transport of molecules, biologists model the locomotion of organisms, engineers model heat conduction, and economists model the time behavior of financial markets, all with the random walk model. This model can be envisioned by thinking of a person taking a succession of steps, which are randomly oriented with respect to one another. It is a good application of *Mathematica* to a problem that involves a diverse set of computing tasks.

In this section, we will develop a program for executing a random walk. Then we will run the program and create a visualization of the walk that is created. In the course of our application development, we discuss options, defaults, messaging, and documentation issues.

The one-dimensional random walk

The simplest random walk model consists of n steps of equal length, back-and-forth along a line. A step increment (or step) in the positive x direction corresponds to a value of 1 and a step increment in the negative x direction corresponds to a value of -1. A list of the successive step increments of an n-step random walk in one dimension is therefore a list of n randomly selected 1s and -1s. This list can be generated in many ways. Here is one straightforward implementation, generating a list of ten steps.

```
In[1]:= Table[(-1)^Random[Integer], {10}]

Out[1]= {1, 1, -1, -1, 1, -1, 1, 1, 1, 1}
```

Using `FoldList`, we can generate a list of the $n+1$ locations of a one-dimensional n-step walk, which starts at the origin.

```
In[2]:= FoldList[Plus, 0, %]

Out[2]= {0, 1, 2, 1, 0, 1, 0, 1, 2, 3, 4}
```

We can now write the program `walk1D` to generate a list of the step locations of an n-step random walk, originating at the origin.

```
In[3]:= walk1D[n_] := FoldList[Plus, 0, Table[(-1)^Random[Integer], {n}]]
```

Here is a ten-step one-dimensional random walk using this `walk1D` program.

```
In[4]:= walk1D[10]

Out[4]= {0, -1, -2, -1, -2, -1, -2, -3, -2, -3, -2}
```

A list of the step locations can also be generated without first creating a list of the step increments, using the nesting operation.

In[5]:= **walk1D2 [n_] := NestList[# + (-1)$^{\text{Random[Integer]}}$ &, 0, n]**

This is just slightly faster than the previous approach.

In[6]:= **n = 10^6;**
          {Timing[walk1D[n];], Timing[walk1D2[n];]}

Out[7]= **{{0.461 Second, Null}, {0.31 Second, Null}}**

Finally, we can plot the random walk using **ListPlot**.

In[8]:= **ListPlot[walk1D[1000], PlotJoined → True];**

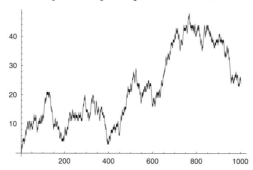

The two-dimensional random walk

The random walk model in two or more dimensions is more complicated than the random walk in one dimension. Although each step of a one-dimensional walk is at 0 degrees (forward) or 180 degrees (backward) with respect to the preceding step, in higher dimensions each step can take a range of orientations with respect to the previous step.

We will first consider a random walk on a lattice. Specifically, we will look at a lattice walk on the two-dimensional square lattice. This walk consists of steps of uniform length, randomly taken in the North, East, South, or West direction. The list of the possible step increments in this walk is given by the compass directions.

In[9]:= **NSEW = {{0, 1}, {1, 0}, {0, -1}, {-1, 0}}**

Out[9]= **{{0, 1}, {1, 0}, {0, -1}, {-1, 0}}**

Here is a list of five step increments.

In[10]:= **n = 5;**
           NSEW[[Table[Random[Integer, {1, 4}], {n}]]]

Out[11]= **{{0, -1}, {0, 1}, {1, 0}, {0, -1}, {-1, 0}}**

Here then is a program, called `walk2D` that generates a list of the step locations of an *n*-step lattice walk starting at the origin {0, 0}.

```
In[12]:= walk2D[n_] :=
         Module[{NSEW = {{0, 1}, {1, 0}, {0, -1}, {-1, 0}}},
           FoldList[Plus, {0, 0},
             NSEW〚Table[Random[Integer, {1, 4}], {n}]〛]]
```

Here is a ten-step lattice walk in two dimensions.

```
In[13]:= walk2D[10]
```

```
Out[13]= {{0, 0}, {1, 0}, {0, 0}, {0, 1}, {-1, 1},
          {0, 1}, {1, 1}, {1, 2}, {2, 2}, {2, 1}, {2, 2}}
```

Finally, here is a short function to generate a two-dimensional off-lattice walk. A random angle, θ, is chosen between 0 and 2π and then a pair consisting of $\{\cos(\theta), \sin(\theta)\}$ is generated. `FoldList` then iterates the process of adding one pair to the previous as above.

```
In[14]:= walk2DOffLattice[n_] :=
         FoldList[Plus, {0, 0},
           Map[{Cos[#], Sin[#]} &, Table[Random[Real, {0, 2 π}], {n}]]]
```

Visualizing the random walk

We will create a snapshot of the path of the two-dimensional walk using the graphics primitive `Line` to draw lines between successive points in the walk.

```
In[15]:= ShowWalk2D[coords_, opts___] :=
         Show[Graphics[Line[coords], opts, AspectRatio → Automatic]]
```

Here we have set the value of the `AspectRatio` option to `Automatic` so that steps in the *x* and *y* directions will appear to have equal lengths in the plot. This option can be overwritten by specifying a different value in the list of options given by `opts`. Note the use of the triple blank in the definition of `ShowWalk2D`. The pattern `opts___` matches any sequence (possibly empty) of rules which are used here to govern the display of the graphic by changing certain options to the `Graphics` function. It is important that `opts` appears *before* the option `AspectRatio`. This will allow you to override this (or any) option value. If *Mathematica* sees an option listed more than once in a list of options, it will only use the first such option. If `opts` had come at the end of this function, you would not be able to change the value for `AspectRatio`.

Here is a 125-step off-lattice walk.

In[16]:= `ShowWalk2D[walk2DOffLattice[125], Axes → Automatic];`

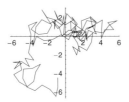

And here is a 25-step two-dimensional lattice walk.

In[17]:= `ShowWalk2D[walk2D[25]];`

A lattice walk repeatedly revisits sites that have been previously visited in the course of its meandering. As a result, it is difficult, and usually impossible, to discern the history of the walk from a snapshot of the path. The best way to see the entire evolution process of the walk in an unobstructed fashion is to create an animation.

Creating an animation of a random walk in *Mathematica* is straightforward. This can be explained using a short lattice walk as an example.

In[18]:= `walk = walk2D[10]`

Out[18]= `{{0, 0}, {-1, 0}, {-1, 1}, {-1, 2}, {0, 2},`
`{0, 1}, {0, 0}, {-1, 0}, {-1, 1}, {-2, 1}, {-1, 1}}`

The animation consists of a sequence of graphics cells where the first cell shows the first step of the walk (consisting of a line drawn between the first two elements in `walk` for example) and each succeeding cell shows one more step than the previous cell. In general then, the *m*th cell is drawn using the `Line` function and the first *m* + 1 elements in `walk`. All of the graphics cells are drawn by mapping `Show` across the `walk` list.

```
Map [ (Show [Graphics [Line [Take [walk, #]]]]) &,
     Range [2, Length [walk] ]]
```

In general, objects in a graphics cell are scaled to fill the monitor screen. Therefore, if we simply create cells, each containing a different number of steps of the walk using the above graphics command, steps in one cell will appear to be of a different length than the same steps in other cells. This will result in a jerky looking animation.

We can make all of the step lengths in all of the graphics cells uniform by using the `PlotRange` option with the ordered pair of the minimum and maximum values of the components of the random walk in each direction, $\{\{xmin, xmax\}, \{ymin, ymax\}\}$. This quantity can be determined by separating the x and y components of the walk using `Transpose` and then mapping an anonymous function containing `Min` and `Max` on to it.

```
In[19]:=  Map[{Min[#], Max[#]} &, Transpose[walk]]
```

```
Out[19]=  {{-2, 0}, {0, 2}}
```

Here then, is the overall program for creating the animation.

```
In[20]:=  AnimateWalk2D[coords_, opts___] :=
            Map[
             Show[Graphics[
                Line[Take[coords, #]]],
               opts, AspectRatio → Automatic,
               PlotRange →
                Map[{Min[#] - 1, Max[#] + 1} &, Transpose[coords]]] &,
             Range[2, Length[coords]]]
```

Note: We have added 1 to the maximum x and y values and subtracted 1 from the minimum x and y values in order to enhance the display by making the graphics a little smaller inside its bounding box. You might also wish to replace `Map[Show[...]]` with `Scan[Show[...]]`. `Scan` is quite similar to `Map` but its main difference is that it does not return an expression, so the `Show` is essentially a side effect of this computation.

While we can not see the random walk animation run in a book, we can look at the graphics cells in the animation by creating a graphics array.

```
In[21]:=  Show[GraphicsArray[Partition[
             AnimateWalk2D[walk, DisplayFunction → Identity], 5]]];
```

The option `DisplayFunction→Identity` is used to suppress the display of the individual graphics cells created by the `AnimateWalk` function (the `GraphicsArray` has its own `DisplayFunction` function option whose default value is `$DisplayFunc` `tion`) and the `Partition` function is used to specify the number of graphics in each row of the `GraphicsArray` picture.

The three-dimensional random walk

For a three-dimensional random lattice walk, we will use the vertices of a cube as our directional vectors. We could input them manually, but they are defined in the Graphics`Polyhedra` package so we may as well use those.

```
In[22]:= <<Graphics`Polyhedra`
```

```
In[23]:= NSEW3 = Vertices[Cube]
```

$$Out[23]= \left\{\left\{\frac{1}{\sqrt{2}}, \frac{1}{\sqrt{2}}, \frac{1}{\sqrt{2}}\right\}, \left\{-\frac{1}{\sqrt{2}}, \frac{1}{\sqrt{2}}, \frac{1}{\sqrt{2}}\right\}, \left\{-\frac{1}{\sqrt{2}}, -\frac{1}{\sqrt{2}}, \frac{1}{\sqrt{2}}\right\},\right.$$
$$\left\{\frac{1}{\sqrt{2}}, -\frac{1}{\sqrt{2}}, \frac{1}{\sqrt{2}}\right\}, \left\{-\frac{1}{\sqrt{2}}, -\frac{1}{\sqrt{2}}, -\frac{1}{\sqrt{2}}\right\},$$
$$\left.\left\{\frac{1}{\sqrt{2}}, -\frac{1}{\sqrt{2}}, -\frac{1}{\sqrt{2}}\right\}, \left\{\frac{1}{\sqrt{2}}, \frac{1}{\sqrt{2}}, -\frac{1}{\sqrt{2}}\right\}, \left\{-\frac{1}{\sqrt{2}}, \frac{1}{\sqrt{2}}, -\frac{1}{\sqrt{2}}\right\}\right\}$$

Here then is the lattice walk in three dimensions.

```
In[24]:= walk3D[n_] := FoldList[Plus, {0, 0, 0},
            NSEW3[[Table[Random[Integer, {1, 8}], {n}]]]]
```

```
In[25]:= walk3D[5]
```

$$Out[25]= \left\{\{0, 0, 0\}, \left\{-\frac{1}{\sqrt{2}}, -\frac{1}{\sqrt{2}}, \frac{1}{\sqrt{2}}\right\}, \{0, 0, 0\}, \left\{\frac{1}{\sqrt{2}}, -\frac{1}{\sqrt{2}}, \frac{1}{\sqrt{2}}\right\},\right.$$
$$\left.\left\{\sqrt{2}, -\sqrt{2}, \sqrt{2}\right\}, \left\{-\frac{1}{\sqrt{2}} + \sqrt{2}, \frac{1}{\sqrt{2}} - \sqrt{2}, \frac{1}{\sqrt{2}} + \sqrt{2}\right\}\right\}$$

We can visualize this with only a slight modification to the ShowWalk2D function.

```
In[26]:= ShowWalk3D[coords_, opts___] :=
            Show[Graphics3D[Line[coords], opts, AspectRatio → Automatic]]
```

```
In[27]:= ShowWalk3D[walk3D[1200]];
```

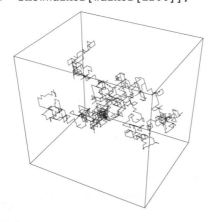

Finally, we create an off-lattice walk in three dimensions.

```
In[28]:= walk3DOffLattice[n_] :=
            FoldList[Plus, {0, 0, 0}, Map[{Cos[#], Sin[#], #/(2 π)} &,
                Table[Random[Real, {-2 π, 2 π}], {n}]]]
```

```
In[29]:= ShowWalk3D[walk3DOffLattice[1000]];
```

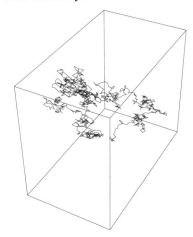

Adding options and defaults

When writing your own programs, it is often difficult to predict how a user will want to use your functions. Programmers usually try to provide a variety of ways to use their functions (allowing for different types of input, for example), or sometimes they write separate functions to handle special cases. The problem with having a separate function for each special case is that the user can soon become overloaded with the variety of functions to learn.

In this section, we will show how to write options for your functions so that they behave like the built-in options in *Mathematica*. (In Chapter 12 we will add some error-trapping and messaging and we will see how to incorporate the use of options into a full-fledged package.)

The use of options and defaults in your programs allows you to minimize the use of many parameters and function names for the user to remember. For example, the built-in function FactorInteger has an option GaussianIntegers, which, when set to True, will factor a number over the Gaussian integers.

```
In[30]:= FactorInteger[5, GaussianIntegers → True]
```

```
Out[30]= {{-i, 1}, {1 + 2 i, 1}, {2 + i, 1}}
```

The alternative to such an option would be to have a separate function, say Factor⁎ GaussianInteger, that the user would have to use. Since the main process here is factorization of numbers, it makes sense to have one function that covers various situations allowing for factorization over different domains by specifying different options.

On the other hand, polynomial factorization is a fundamentally different operation from integer factorization, and so a different function is used for that.

In[31]:= **Factor[27 x⁵ + 81 x⁴ y + 9 x³ y² - 73 x² y³ + 32 x y⁴ - 4 y⁵]**

Out[31]= $(3 x - y)^3 (x + 2 y)^2$

In the previous sections we developed five separate functions, walk1D, walk2D, walk2DOffLattice, walk3D, and walk3DOffLattice that each generated random walks, the only differences being in the dimension of the walk or whether the walk was on the lattice or not. It is not practical to expect the user to remember five different function names for what is essentially the same process. It would be far easier to create only one function RandomWalk and set the dimension or lattice walk through the use of options.

We will define two options to RandomWalk, Dimension and LatticeWalk. The LatticeWalk option will be specified as a rule and when set to True, it will generate a lattice walk; when set to False, it will generate an off-lattice walk. The following definition both defines options for the RandomWalk function and specifies their default values.

In[32]:= **Options[RandomWalk] = {LatticeWalk → True, Dimension → 2}**

Out[32]= {LatticeWalk → True, Dimension → 2}

If you were now to ask for information about the RandomWalk function, you would see these new options listed.

In[33]:= **? RandomWalk**

Global`RandomWalk

Options[RandomWalk] = {LatticeWalk → True, Dimension → 2}

As far as the LatticeWalk option is concerned, we will use this option in the RandomWalk function by branching to either a lattice walk or an off-lattice walk, depending upon the value of this new option. We will need to extract the value of this option inside the RandomWalk function, which we do as follows:

```
latticeQ = LatticeWalk/.Flatten[{opts,Options[RandomWalk]}];
```

From right to left, the values of the options to `RandomWalk` are substituted into `opts`; then these (rules) are substituted to extract the value of `LatticeWalk`. This value is then assigned to the symbol `latticeQ`.

Similarly, we will extract the value of the option `Dimension`. But we want to use the definitions given in the previous sections to branch appropriately, depending upon the value of `Dimension`; that is, depending upon whether we wish a 1D, 2D, or 3D random walk. The `Which` function is perfect for this task.

```
Which[
      dim == 1, use walk1D definition,
      dim == 2, use walk2D definition,
      dim == 3, use walk3D definition]
```

Here then is the full function `RandomWalk`, using this option structure.

```
In[34]:= <<Graphics`Polyhedra`
```

```
In[35]:= RandomWalk[n_Integer, opts___?OptionQ] :=
         Module[{dim, latticeQ},
           {latticeQ, dim} = {LatticeWalk, Dimension} /.
             Flatten[{opts, Options[RandomWalk]}];
           Which[
            dim == 1, walk1D[n],
            dim == 2, If[latticeQ, walk2D[n], walk2DOffLattice[n]],
            dim == 3, If[latticeQ, walk3D[n], walk3DOffLattice[n]]
           ]]
```

Notice that if the `LatticeWalk` option has been set to `True`, then the first branch of the `If` statement is followed, giving the lattice walk. If `LatticeWalk` has any other value (`False` for example), then the off-lattice definition is used.

This uses the default value of `LatticeWalk` and the default value of `Dimension` to create five steps of a two-dimensional lattice walk.

```
In[36]:= RandomWalk[5]
```

```
Out[36]= {{0, 0}, {0, -1}, {-1, -1}, {-1, 0}, {0, 0}, {0, -1}}
```

This creates an off-lattice walk.

```
In[37]:= RandomWalk[4, LatticeWalk → False]
```

```
Out[37]= {{0, 0}, {-0.282568, 0.959247}, {0.584254, 0.460629},
         {1.13491, -0.374105}, {1.82222, -1.10047}}
```

Here is a three-dimensional lattice walk.

In[38]:= **RandomWalk[4, Dimension → 3]**

Out[38]= $\left\{\{0, 0, 0\}, \left\{-\frac{1}{\sqrt{2}}, \frac{1}{\sqrt{2}}, \frac{1}{\sqrt{2}}\right\}, \{-\sqrt{2}, \sqrt{2}, 0\},\right.$

$\left.\left\{\frac{1}{\sqrt{2}} - \sqrt{2}, -\frac{1}{\sqrt{2}} + \sqrt{2}, -\frac{1}{\sqrt{2}}\right\}, \{-\sqrt{2}, 0, 0\}\right\}$

And here is a three-dimensional off-lattice walk.

In[39]:= **RandomWalk[4, LatticeWalk → False, Dimension → 3]**

Out[39]= {{0, 0, 0}, {-0.895264, -0.445536, -0.426506},
        {-1.53545, -1.21375, 0.212921},
        {-1.47703, -2.21204, -0.0277754},
        {-2.30801, -2.76835, 0.566116}}

Just as we have combined our various random walks into one function, so should we combine the functions to visualize these walks, using Which to determine which branch to take.

In[40]:= **ShowWalk[coords_, opts___] := Which[**
        Dimensions[coords][[2]] == 2,
        Show[Graphics[Line[coords], opts, AspectRatio → Automatic]],
        Dimensions[coords][[2]] == 3, Show[
        Graphics3D[Line[coords], opts, AspectRatio → Automatic]]]

Here then are several examples of these functions.

In[41]:= **ShowWalk[RandomWalk[10⁴, Dimension → 2, LatticeWalk → False]];**

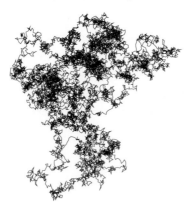

In[42]:= `ShowWalk[RandomWalk[`10^3`, Dimension → 3, LatticeWalk → True]];`

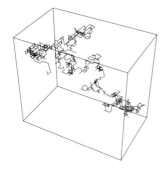

In[43]:= `ShowWalk[RandomWalk[`10^4`, Dimension → 2,`
`Frame → True, Background → GrayLevel[0.9]];`

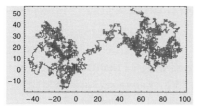

In the next chapter we will see how to bundle up all of these functions into a self-contained package with various implementation details hidden from the user.

Error-trapping and messaging

In addition to error-trapping, messaging, and usage messages, another (even more important) way to make user-defined functions behave like built-in functions is to check the arguments to each function carefully and issue error messages when appropriate.

Good programming practice dictates that we try to anticipate how a user of our programs will interact with them. In particular, it is good programming style to try and catch any errors the user may make and respond with an appropriate message. For example, the built-in `Sin` function will report an error and give you a warning message if you give it the wrong number of arguments.

In[44]:= `Sin[1.2, 3.4]`

```
Sin::argx :
    Sin called with 2 arguments; 1 argument is expected. More…
```

Out[44]= `Sin[1.2, 3.4]`

One of the conditions we might want to check for with our `RandomWalk` function is that the user enters a positive integer as its first argument. Let us first write the warning message.

In[45]:= `RandomWalk::rwn = "Argument `1` is not a positive integer.";`

We can put a simple trap for the condition in the body of `RandomWalk`:

```
If[Not[IntegerQ[n] &&n>0], Message[RandomWalk::rwn,n],...]
```

If the first argument to `RandomWalk` passes the test in this `If` statement (that is, if it fails to be an integer or fails to be greater than 0), then a message will be generated substituting the argument n for `1` in the `rwn` message above.

Here is the rewritten `RandomWalk` function with the error trap included.

In[46]:= `Clear[RandomWalk]`

In[47]:= `Options[RandomWalk] = {LatticeWalk → True, Dimension → 2};`

In[48]:= `<<Graphics`Polyhedra``

In[49]:= `RandomWalk[n_, opts___?OptionQ] := Module[{dim, latticeQ},`
            `    If[Not[IntegerQ[n] && n > 0], Message[RandomWalk::rwn, n],`
            `      {latticeQ, dim} = {LatticeWalk, Dimension} /.`
            `        Flatten[{opts, Options[RandomWalk]}];`
            `      Which[`
            `        dim == 1, walk1D[n],`
            `        dim == 2, If[latticeQ, walk2D[n], walk2DOffLattice[n]],`
            `        dim == 3, If[latticeQ, walk3D[n], walk3DOffLattice[n]]`
            `      ]]]`

Now if we pass a noninteger or negative argument to `RandomWalk`, the warning will be triggered.

In[50]:= `RandomWalk[-6]`

         `RandomWalk::rwn : Argument -6 is not a positive integer.`

In[51]:= `RandomWalk[10.5]`

         `RandomWalk::rwn : Argument 10.5` is not a positive integer.`

Creating Help Browser documentation

Whenever you distribute any *Mathematica* applications, users will appreciate the inclusion of a set of help files that describe your application in some detail. You can incorporate this documentation into *Mathematica*'s Help Browser so that users access your documentation in the same manner as they access the documentation that comes with *Mathematica*. In this section we will describe how to go about doing that.

The directory and file structure of your application is referred to as its *layout*. Your documentation, which will consist of *Mathematica* notebooks, can be viewed in the Help Browser by creating some specific directories and placing certain files in these directories.

The top-level directory name we will use for our random walk application will be RandomWalks. Let us first identify the directory on your computer system where you should place this RandomWalks directory. It is common convention to put user-defined applications in one of several Applications directories. The full path to these directories on your computer can be given as follows:

In[52]:= **ToFileName[{$BaseDirectory, "Applications"}]**

Out[52]= C:\Documents and Settings\All Users\
        Application Data\Mathematica\Applications\

In[53]:= **ToFileName[{$UserBaseDirectory, "Applications"}]**

Out[53]= C:\Documents and Settings\Paul Wellin\
        Application Data\Mathematica\Applications\

$BaseDirectory is writable by anyone with administrative privileges on your computer and is readable by everyone on your computer. $UserBaseDirectory is only writable and readable by the currently logged in user of your computer. For our purposes here we will use $BaseDirectory, but either location is fine.

Inside the base directory there should be an Applications directory. If it does not already exist you will have to create it. Then the following directories for our random walks application should be created inside the applications directory.

```
RandomWalks
    Documentation
        English
    FrontEnd
        Palettes
        StyleSheets
    Kernel
```

So the directory StyleSheets should be created inside the FrontEnd directory which should be a subdirectory of RandomWalks. Any style sheets that you define for your application should go in the FrontEnd/StyleSheets directory. Similarly for any palettes that you want to be associated with your application. The kernel directory can contain an init.m file that may have some *Mathematica* commands that you want to be evaluated every time your application is loaded.

All of the notebooks that you want to appear in the Help Browser need to be placed in the Documentation/English directory. For example, in our random walks application, we have placed the notebook RandomWalks.nb inside of the directory RandomWalks/Documentation/English.

Finally, you must create the text file BrowserCategories.m in the directory Documentation/English. This file will identify precisely how your documentation will appear in the Help Browser. Here is a very simple BrowserCategories.m file from the RandomWalks example.

```
BrowserCategory["Random Walks", None, {
    Item["Introduction", "RandomWalks.nb", CopyTag->"rw:1"],
    Item["The One-Dimensional Random Walk", "RandomWalks.nb",
        CopyTag->"rw:2"],
    Item["The Two-Dimensional Random Walk", "RandomWalks.nb",
        CopyTag->"rw:3"],
    Item["Visualizing the Random Walk", "RandomWalks.nb", CopyTag->"rw:4"],
    Item["The Three-Dimensional Random Walk", "RandomWalks.nb",
        CopyTag->"rw:5"],
    Item["Adding Options and Defaults", "RandomWalks.nb", CopyTag->"rw:6"],
    Item["Error-Trapping and Messaging", "RandomWalks.nb",
        CopyTag->"rw:6"],
    Item["Creating Help Browser Documentation", "RandomWalks.nb",
        CopyTag->"rw:7"]
    }]
```

The opening `BrowserCategory` takes three arguments. The first is the name of the category as it will appear at the top level in the Help Browser. The second argument is the name of the subdirectory in which your notebook source files live. If it is the same as the directory in which the BrowserCategories.m lives (which is typically where it is), then use `None` as the name. Finally, the third argument is a list of `Item` commands. The `Item` function takes the following form: `Item[`*name*, *filename*, *options*`]`. The *name* gives the subcategory name (typically section or subsection names in your source notebook), the *filename* is the file in which the documentation is found, and the *options* typically are tagging commands.

In our example BrowserCategories.m file we have used `CopyTag` to identify the specific set of cells within the RandomWalks.nb notebook that are associated with a particular `Item`. In the notebook itself, you will have to tag the corresponding cells using the Add/Remove Cell Tags command in the Find menu or using a tool such as *AuthorTools* (an application itself that comes with *Mathematica*) to assist you with doing this somewhat automatically.

Once your BrowserCategories.m file is created and placed in the Documentation/English directory of your application, you will need to rebuild the Help index of the Help Browser by choosing that item under the Help menu. The documentation for your application should then appear in the Help Browser under the Add-ons & Links category.

You should feel free to modify the RandomWalk example application that comes with the IPM3 materials by editing the BrowserCategories.m file or using it as a template for your own applications.

Exercises

1. The version of `RandomWalk` developed in this section generates one-dimensional walks of unit step. Modify `RandomWalk` so that the step size is a uniformly distributed random number between -1 and 1.

2. Modify `ShowWalk` so that it produces a `ListPlot` when passed something of the form `RandomWalk[n,Dimension→1]`.

3. The `RandomWalk` program developed in this section is not set up properly to take unit steps in three dimensions on the off-lattice walk. The following formulas can be used to represent a point parametrically on the unit sphere.

$$x(\phi, \theta) = \cos(\theta) \sqrt{1 - \cos^2(\phi)}$$
$$y(\phi, \theta) = \sin(\theta) \sqrt{1 - \cos^2(\phi)}$$
$$z(\phi) = \cos(\phi)$$

Use these formulas to rewrite `walk3DOffLattice` so that off-lattice three-dimensional walks take unit steps.

4. The square end-to-end distance of a two-dimensional walk is defined as $(x_f - x_i)^2 + (y_f - y_i)^2$, where $\{x_i, y_i\}$ and $\{x_f, y_f\}$ are the initial and final locations of the walk, respectively. Assuming the initial point is the origin, then this simplifies to $x_f^2 + y_f^2$. Write a function `SquareDistance` that takes a two-dimensional walk as an

argument and computes the square end-to-end distance. Write a usage message and include this function as a publicly exported function in the RandomWalks.m package.

5. Create a function `AnimateWalk` that takes `RandomWalk [n, Dimension→2]` as an argument and produces a series of graphics that can be animated by displaying in quick succession. Include in your graphics a red disk that moves to the "current position" in the walk. The viewer will then see this red disk moving along on the random walk as the animation is played.

6. Modify `AnimateWalk` from the previous exercise so that it can also accept the output from `RandomWalk [n, Dimension→3]`.

11.3 The Game of Life

A cellular automaton is a system of discrete lattice sites, each of which has a value (usually an integer) associated with it. The values of the sites change simultaneously, in a succession of discrete time steps, by applying rules that depend on the values of a site and the sites in its vicinity.

Cellular automata have been used to model various physical, chemical, biological, and social phenomena (Gaylord and Wellin 1995). In principle, any process that can be described by an algorithm or program can be modeled by a cellular automaton.

The Game of Life, created by the British mathematician John Conway, is the most well-known cellular automaton. It is the forerunner of so-called *artificial life* (or *a-life*) systems and it was the first program run on the first parallel processing computer. It has been estimated that more computer time has been spent (or wasted, depending on your point of view) running the Game of Life program than any other program.

We will show how to program the Game of Life in *Mathematica*, so that it is optimized for efficiency (run speed). This is a good application to work on at this point as its implementation covers many of the topics from earlier chapters of the book: functional vs. procedural programming, rule-based programming, setting attributes, and many more.

The Game of Life is played on a two-dimensional square Boolean lattice where sites have values of either 0 or 1. A site with value 1 is said to be *alive* and a site with value 0 is said to be *dead*. To illustrate the computations involved in the Game of Life program, we will use the following small lattice system.

```
In[1]:=  GameBoard = Table[Random[Integer], {4}, {4}];
         TableForm[GameBoard]
```

Out[2]//TableForm=

```
1   0   0   0
1   0   0   1
0   0   1   1
0   0   1   1
```

In order to update a site of GameBoard, the sum of the values of the sites in its neighborhood must be determined.

The neighborhood of a site in GameBoard consists of the site and the eight nearest neighbor sites lying North, Northeast, East, Southeast, South, Southwest, West, and Northwest of the site.

The neighborhood of a site located in the interior of the lattice is obvious. For example, the nearest neighbor sites to the {2,3} site (which lies in the second row, third column of GameBoard) are the {1,3}, {1,4}, {2,4}, {3,4}, {3,3}, {3,2}, {2,2}, and {1,2} sites.

The neighborhood of a site lying on one of the borders of the lattice is less apparent. Employing what are known as periodic boundary conditions, some of the nearest neighbor sites are taken from the opposing borders. A non-corner site located in the first or last row (column) of the board has the corresponding site in the last or first row (column) as a nearest neighbor site, respectively, and a corner site has the two sites in the opposing corner as two of its nearest neighbor sites. For example, the nearest neighbor sites to the {2,4} site (which lies in the second row, last column of GameBoard) are the {1,4}, {1,1}, {2,1}, {3,1}, {3,4}, {3,3}, {2,3}, and {1,3} sites.

The 16 neighborhoods of the sites in the lattice system can be generated in two steps.

An expanded matrix is created by first copying the first element in each row on to the end of the row and copying the last element in each row on to the front of the row, and then copying the first row on to the end of the list of rows and copying the last row on to the front of the list of rows. The following anonymous function can be used to perform this operation.

```
In[3]:=  wrap = Join[{Last[#1]}, #1, {First[#1]}] &;
```

The application of the `wrap` function to `GameBoard` is shown below.

In[4]:= `wrap[Map[wrap, GameBoard]] // TableForm`

Out[4]//TableForm=

```
1  0  0  1  1  0
0  1  0  0  0  1
1  1  0  0  1  1
1  0  0  1  1  0
1  0  0  1  1  0
0  1  0  0  0  1
```

The expanded matrix created by applying the `wrap` function to the lattice can be partitioned into overlapping three-by-three matrices to create a list of the neighborhoods of the sites in the lattice.

In[5]:= `(Neighborhoods = Partition[`
`        wrap[Map[wrap, GameBoard]], {3, 3}, {1, 1}]) // TableForm`

Out[5]//TableForm=

```
1  0  0  0  0  1  0  1  1  1  1  0
0  1  0  1  0  0  0  0  0  0  0  1
1  1  0  1  0  0  0  1  0  1  1
0  1  0  1  0  0  0  0  0  0  0  1
1  1  0  1  0  0  0  1  0  1  1
1  0  0  0  0  1  0  1  1  1  1  0
1  1  0  1  0  0  0  1  0  1  1
1  0  0  0  0  1  0  1  1  1  1  0
1  0  0  0  0  1  0  1  1  1  1  0
1  0  0  0  0  1  0  1  1  1  1  0
1  0  0  0  0  1  0  1  1  1  1  0
0  1  0  1  0  0  0  0  0  0  0  1
```

Given the neighborhoods of the sites on the lattice, we can determine whether a site is alive or dead and how many of its nearest neighbor sites are alive. These are the two quantities which appear in the rules used to update a site.

The three "life and death" rules for updating a site in the lattice are:

1. A living site (a site with value 1) with exactly two living nearest neighbor sites remains alive (its value is updated to 1).

2. Any site (a site with value 0 or 1) with three living nearest neighbor sites stays alive or is born (its value is updated to 1).

3. Any other site (a site with value 0 or 1) remains dead or dies (its value is updated to 0).

A conditional function which, given the neighborhood of a site, applies the appropriate rule is given below.

```
In[6]:=  LiveOrDie[lis_] := Module[{neighbors},
            neighbors = Count[lis, 1, {2}];
            If[lis[[2, 2]] == 1 && neighbors == 4 || neighbors == 3, 1, 0]]
```

Applying the LiveOrDie function to the neighborhoods of GameBoard yields the updated GameBoard.

```
In[7]:=  Map[LiveOrDie, Neighborhoods, {2}] // TableForm
```

```
Out[7]//TableForm=
        1  1  1  0
        1  1  1  0
        0  1  0  0
        1  1  1  0
```

Finally, the evolution of the lattice over *t* time steps, or until it stops changing, is carried out using FixedPointList.

```
FixedPointList[Map[LiveOrDie,
  Partition[wrap[Map[wrap, #]], {3,3}, {1,1}], {2}] &, GameBoard, t]
```

The code fragments developed above can be used to construct a program for the Game of Life. However, while this program will work, it is unduly slow. A much more efficient (faster running) program for the Game of Life can be developed by following some general *Mathematica* programming guidelines.

The most efficient way to program in *Mathematica* is to utilize the following approaches as much as possible:

- avoid looping

- minimize conditional branching

- manipulate data structures in their entirety

- employ built-in *Mathematica* functions

- use anonymous functions, higher-order functions, and nested function calls

- create look-up tables

The use of these principles is well illustrated in the Game of Life program we will now develop.

A matrix whose elements are the number of living, nearest neighbor sites to the corresponding sites in the Game of Life lattice can be computed directly from the lattice without having to first create the neighborhoods of the lattice, using the following function.

```
In[8]:= liveNeighbors[mat_] :=
            Apply[Plus, Map[RotateRight[mat, #] &, {{-1, -1}, {-1, 0},
                {-1, 1}, {0, -1}, {0, 1}, {1, -1}, {1, 0}, {1, 1}}]]
```

The liveNeighbors function makes use of the fact that *Mathematica* adds lists by vector addition, adding the corresponding elements of the lists. Applying the function to the GameBoard example, we get

```
In[9]:= liveNeighbors[GameBoard]//TableForm
```

```
Out[9]//TableForm=
    3   3   3   5
    3   3   3   4
    4   3   4   5
    3   3   3   4
```

Comparing this output with the Neighborhoods matrix created earlier, we can see that each element in liveNeighbors[GameBoard] is the number of living nearest neighbor sites to the corresponding site in GameBoard.

We can write down site update rules, whose two arguments are the value of a site and the sum of the values of the nearest neighbor sites in its neighborhood. These rules are a direct translation of the life and death rules from words to code.

```
In[10]:= update[1, 2] := 1
         update[_, 3] := 1
         update[_, _] := 0
         SetAttributes[update, Listable];
```

The update rule is given the Listable attribute, so, when it is applied to a matrix of site values and also to a matrix of the number of living neighbors to these sites, a matrix is created whose elements are obtained by applying the update function to the corresponding elements of the two matrices. This behavior can be demonstrated using a general function, g, with the GameBoard and liveNeighbors[GameBoard] matrices.

```
In[14]:= SetAttributes[g, Listable];
```

In[15]:= `g[GameBoard, liveNeighbors[GameBoard]]`

Out[15]= `{{g[1, 3], g[0, 3], g[0, 3], g[0, 5]},`
        `{g[1, 3], g[0, 3], g[0, 3], g[1, 4]},`
        `{g[0, 4], g[0, 3], g[1, 4], g[1, 5]},`
        `{g[0, 3], g[0, 3], g[1, 3], g[1, 4]}}`

Using the `update` rules with the `GameBoard` and `liveNeighbors` matrices, and comparing the result obtained earlier by applying the `LiveOrDie` function to the `Neigh`⸱ borhoods of `GameBoard`, we see that each site in the board has been correctly updated.

In[16]:= `update[GameBoard, liveNeighbors[GameBoard]] // TableForm`

Out[16]//TableForm=
```
1   1   1   0
1   1   1   0
0   1   0   0
1   1   1   0
```

Note: While the three update rules overlap with one another, there is no confusion as to when each rule is used because *Mathematica* applies more specific rules before more general rules. Thus, while a site with value 1 and 2 nearest neighbor sites with value 1 will satisfy both the first and third rules, the first rule is used because it is the most specific applicable rule. Similarly, while a site having three nearest neighbor sites with value 1 will satisfy both the second and third rules, the second rule is used because it is the most specific applicable rule. The third rule is more general than the other two rules and hence is only used if neither of the other rules can be used.

The evolution of the lattice over *t* time steps can be carried out using an anonymous function, where # represents the lattice configuration in `FixedPointList`.

```
update[#, liveNghbrs[#]]&
```

Using the `GameBoard` example and three time steps to illustrate this, gives

In[17]:= `FixedPointList[update[#, liveNeighbors[#]] &, GameBoard, 3]`

Out[17]= `{{{1, 0, 0, 0}, {1, 0, 0, 1}, {0, 0, 1, 1}, {0, 0, 1, 1}},`
        `{{1, 1, 1, 0}, {1, 1, 1, 0}, {0, 1, 0, 0}, {1, 1, 1, 0}},`
        `{{0, 0, 0, 0}, {0, 0, 0, 0}, {0, 0, 0, 0}, {0, 0, 0, 0}},`
        `{{0, 0, 0, 0}, {0, 0, 0, 0}, {0, 0, 0, 0}, {0, 0, 0, 0}}}`

Let us take the `Transpose` of this result in order to interchange rows and columns and facilitate a comparison with our previous results.

In[18]:= `Map[Transpose, %]`

Out[18]= `{{{1, 1, 0, 0}, {0, 0, 0, 0}, {0, 0, 1, 1}, {0, 1, 1, 1}},`
`            {{1, 1, 0, 1}, {1, 1, 1, 1}, {1, 1, 0, 1}, {0, 0, 0, 0}},`
`            {{0, 0, 0, 0}, {0, 0, 0, 0}, {0, 0, 0, 0}, {0, 0, 0, 0}},`
`            {{0, 0, 0, 0}, {0, 0, 0, 0}, {0, 0, 0, 0}, {0, 0, 0, 0}}}`

The code fragments given above are combined into the Game of Life program.

In[19]:=
```
LifeGame[n_Integer?Positive, steps_] :=
  Module[{gameboard, liveNeighbors, update},
    gameboard = Table[Random[Integer], {n}, {n}];
    liveNeighbors[mat_] :=
     Apply[Plus, Map[RotateRight[mat, #] &,
        {{-1, -1}, {-1, 0}, {-1, 1}, {0, -1},
         {0, 1}, {1, -1}, {1, 0}, {1, 1}}]];
    update[1, 2] := 1;
    update[_, 3] := 1;
    update[_, _] := 0;
    SetAttributes[update, Listable];
    FixedPointList[
     update[#, liveNeighbors[#]] &, gameboard, steps]
  ]
```

The input parameters, n and `steps`, are, respectively, the linear size of the lattice and the maximum number of time steps carried out.

Finally, the focus in playing the Game of Life is on identifying various patterns of 1s amongst the 0s, and observing their behaviors. This is best done using a graphical, rather than numerical, display.

First we generate a Game of Life on a 100×100 board, and run it for 150 generations.

In[20]:= `g = LifeGame[100, 150];`

`ArrayPlot` is well-suited for taking arrays of numbers and making plots, explicitly specifying how to color alive and dead sites. This shows only the last frame from the game.

```
In[21]:= ArrayPlot[Last[g], ColorRules → {0 → Black, 1 → Red}];
```

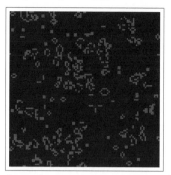

Below is the code to generate an array showing only every 25th iteration.

```
In[22]:= garray = Map[
           ArrayPlot[#, ColorRules → {0 → Black, 1 → Red},
             DisplayFunction → Identity] &,
           Table[g[[i]], {i, 1, 150, 25}]]

Out[22]= {- Graphics -, - Graphics -, - Graphics -,
           - Graphics -, - Graphics -, - Graphics -}
```

```
In[23]:= Show[GraphicsArray[garray]]
```

```
Out[23]= - GraphicsArray -
```

The following generates an animation consisting of 100 iterations of the Game of Life on an initial 75×75 gameboard. We can not show the animation in a printed book, of course, so we just indicate the input to evaluate.

```
In[24]:= AnimateLife[lis_List] :=
           Scan[ArrayPlot[#, ColorRules → {0 → Black, 1 → Red}] &, lis]
```

```
In[25]:= AnimateLife[LifeGame[75, 100]];
```

Exercises

1. Define a new graphics function `LifeGraphics` that creates a raster array of color values. Set it up so that it takes an option `Colors` defined to have default values for 1 and 0 and such that you can give it your own coloring scheme. Then you will display Life games with `Show[LifeGraphics[LifeGame[n, steps]]]`.

2. The Game of Life is most interesting to watch when persistent patterns, known as life-forms, occur during the evolution process. One pattern that has been extensively studied is known as the glider, which is defined by

```
glider[x_, y_] :=
   {{x, y}, {x + 1, y}, {x + 2, y}, {x + 2, y + 1}, {x + 1, y + 2}}
```

Modify the program for the Game of Life so that the lattice can be seeded with life forms and observe the behavior of a glider (it should appear, disappear, and then reappear in a shifted position every fifth generation). To better understand the use of the periodic boundary conditions, note what happens when a glider pattern moves beyond a border of the game board.

11.4 Implementing languages

Introduction to PDL

The *Mathematica* programming language is just one example of a computer language. There are many, many others, including C and Fortran for general-purpose programming, SQL for database queries, TEX and PostScript for typesetting, and on and on. The processing of these languages shares some basic methods, which we will illustrate in this section by implementing a mini Picture-Description Language, *PDL*.

PDL will be used to describe pictures consisting of simple shapes either contained in or next to one another. An example of such a picture is shown in Figure 11.1; it is described by the following picture specification.

```
square (5)
 containing n/n (clear rectangle (5, 2)
      containing w/w (circle (2))
      containing c/c (circle (2))
      containing e/e (circle (2)))
 containing c/n (oval (3, 1)
    connecting sw/ne (square (1))
    connecting se/nw (square (1))
    connecting s/c (circle (1)))
```

The picture in Figure 11.1 contains one large and two small squares, one rectangle (but it is "clear;" that is, invisible), four circles and an oval. The rectangle is contained in the square, and in turn contains three circles; the oval is contained in the square and has the two small squares and a circle connected to it. The numbers in parentheses give the sizes of the shapes, and the odd-looking notations like n/n and se/nw indicate how two shapes are connected.

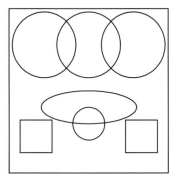

Figure 11.1: A picture produced by PDL

For example, the n/n notation on the second line says that the top (or "north") of the rectangle is positioned next to the top of the square that contains it; the se/nw notation on the second to last line indicates that the upper-left ("northwest") point of the square is placed next to the lower-right ("southeast") point of the oval; on the last line, the south point of the oval connects to the center of the circle.

We will write a function PDL that will take such a description (as a character string) and convert it into *Mathematica* graphics primitives for display.

Syntax

The first property all modern computer languages share is that their syntax can be formally defined. The formal definition guides the implementation in a direct and simple way. The formal definition is given as a *context-free grammar*, in which a set of rules, called *productions*, are used to define both the allowable picture specifications and the syntactic structure of those specifications. The formal syntax of *PDL* is given in Table 11.1.

In the *PDL* grammar, the names given in *slanted* or italic font are called *variables*. The variables generate sets of strings; the legal picture specifications are all the strings generated by the variable *picture*. The items written in `typewriter` font appear literally in specifications. Aside from *integer* (which, by definition, generates all the integers) and *direction* (which, by definition, generates the strings n, e, s, w, c, ne, se, sw, nw), the variables generate strings in the following way: starting with a variable, replace it by the right-hand side of any rule in which it appears on the left-hand side; then continue to replace variables by the right-hand sides of rules for those variables (or, in the case of *integer* and *direction*, by any integer or direction) until a string without variables is obtained. (When production 2 or 8 is applied, the variable just disappears.)

1.	*picture*	$\longrightarrow$	*shape associations*
2.	*associations*		
3.	*associations*	$\longrightarrow$	*connection associations*
4.	*associations*	$\longrightarrow$	*containment associations*
5.	*connection*	$\longrightarrow$	`connecting` *direction* / *direction* (*picture*)
6.	*containment*	$\longrightarrow$	`containing` *direction* / *direction* (*picture*)
7.	*shape*	$\longrightarrow$	*color primitive size*
8.	*color*		
9.	*color*	$\longrightarrow$	`clear`
10.	*primitive*	$\longrightarrow$	`square`
11.	*primitive*	$\longrightarrow$	`circle`
12.	*primitive*	$\longrightarrow$	`oval`
13.	*primitive*	$\longrightarrow$	`rectangle`
14.	*size*	$\longrightarrow$	(*integer size2*)
15.	*size2*	$\longrightarrow$	)
16.	*size2*	$\longrightarrow$	, *integer*)

Table 11.1: Formal syntax of *PDL*

Consider the picture specification which produces the picture shown in Figure 11.2.

```
square (20) containing c/w (oval (9, 18))
```

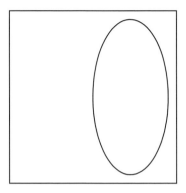

Figure 11.2:   A simpler picture produced by PDL.

It is generated from *picture* in this way (where we have indicated the number of the production being used in each case).

picture $\longrightarrow_1$ *shape associations*

$\longrightarrow_7$ *color primitive size associations*

$\longrightarrow_8$ *primitive size associations*

$\longrightarrow_{10}$ square *size associations*

$\longrightarrow_{14}$ square (*integer size2 associations*

$\longrightarrow$ square (20 *size2 associations*

$\longrightarrow_{15}$ square (20) *associations*

$\longrightarrow_4$ square (20) *containment associations*

...

Parsing

A crucial observation is that the derivation of a string from a variable can be represented as a tree, called a *parse tree*. The derivation above corresponds to the following tree.

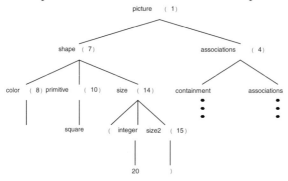

Figure 11.3:   A parse tree

Notice that there is no need to include the variable at each node; the production number immediately determines the variable.

We will use the tree representation of the input – or a very similar representation, omitting uninteresting things like parentheses – extensively. The goal of *parsing* is to transform the sequence of characters in the input into a parse tree. Given that form, we can do the real work: finding the location of each shape and generating the *Mathematica* graphics primitives to draw the picture.

The parsing phase is divided into two steps, *lexical analysis* and *parsing*, and the remainder of the processing is also divided into two steps, computing information about each shape in the picture (especially, its location) and converting this information into graphics primitives. Thus, the function PDL is given by

```
In[1]:=  << IPM3`PDL`

In[2]:=  ShowPicture[p_] := Show[Graphics[p], AspectRatio → Automatic]

In[3]:=  PDL[input_] :=
            ShowPicture[ConvertShapes[ComputeShapes[Parse[Lex[input]]]]]
```

For example, the following produces the graphic in Figure11.2.

In[4]:= `PDL["square (20) containing c/w (oval (9, 18))"];`

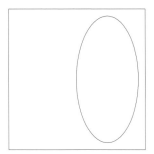

Before delving into programming details, we will finish our brief "user's guide" begun earlier. As we have seen, shapes can be clear, in which case they are not drawn, or regular, in which case they are drawn in black. Each shape has a size (one integer for squares and circles, two for ovals and rectangles) with these meanings:

square :	*length of a side*
circle :	*diameter*
oval :	*horizontal and vertical diameters*
rectangle :	*width and height*

A shape can contain or be connected to any number of other shapes. (Since every shape has an explicit size, a "contained" shape is not necessarily completely contained.) The most complicated aspect of the language is determining where shapes go, depending upon the points at which they are connected. Each shape has a center and eight compass points. These are shown for each shape in Figure 11.4. When a shape is connected to or contained in another shape, the two directions given in the connecting or containing phrase match up. For example, Figure 11.5 shows the picture specified by `square (4) connected se/n (circle (2))`.

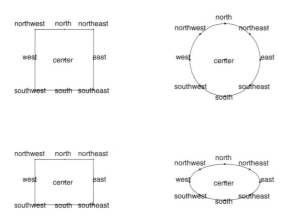

Figure 11.4:   Compass points for the four types of shapes

In[5]:= **PDL["square (4) connecting se/n (circle (2))"];**

The top (north) of the circle is next to the lower-right (southeast) corner of the square. Similarly, Figure 11.6 shows an oval containing a rectangle.

In[6]:= **PDL["oval (10,7) containing n/n (rectangle (1,3))"];**

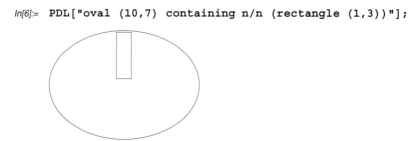

The top of the oval touches the top of the rectangle. However, in both cases, the two figures do not exactly touch; rather, a gap of size 0.1 is left between them. The difference between connecting and containing is simply the direction of the gap.

---

picture$_1$ `connecting` d_1 / d_2 (*picture*$_2$)

In the above code, direction d_2 of *picture*$_2$ is placed at a point determined by finding the d_1 direction of *picture*$_1$ and then moving 0.1 units *away* from the center of *picture*$_1$. If `connecting` is replaced by `containing`, the correction is 0.1 units *toward* the center of *picture*$_1$.

Finally, the rules about correcting by 0.1 do not apply if either direction is c, for center. If the connecting directions are d/c or c/d, whatever d is, it is not adjusted by 0.1 in either direction. (Thus, in this case it does not matter whether *picture*$_2$ is connected or contained.) The reader is urged to try some examples using the code provided in the `IPM3`PDL`` package before continuing.

Lexical analysis

To return to the programming of the *PDL* language processor, we will start with a discussion of the syntactic analysis phase, consisting of *lexical analysis* (or lexing) and *parsing*. This division is conventional and appears in virtually all language processors.

Lexing is the process of dividing up the input (a character string) into significant syntactic units, called *tokens*. (Think of the entire picture specification as a sentence, the characters of the input as the letters, and the tokens as the words; lexing groups the letters into words, and parsing determines the syntactic structure of the sentence.) The function Lex is given a string and produces a list of symbols and numbers.

```
In[7]:=  example = "square (20) containing c/w (oval (9, 18))";
```

```
In[8]:=  Lex[example]
```

```
Out[8]=  {square, lparen, 20, rparen, containing, center, slash, west,
         lparen, oval, lparen, 9, comma, 18, rparen, rparen, eof}
```

```
In[9]:=  Map[Head, %]
```

```
Out[9]=  {Symbol, Symbol, Integer, Symbol, Symbol,
         Symbol, Symbol, Symbol, Symbol, Symbol, Symbol,
         Integer, Symbol, Integer, Symbol, Symbol, Symbol}
```

In the lexed output, we have also replaced special characters like parentheses by symbols and we have added a final symbol, eof (a traditional name meaning "end of file").

Symbols are a little more convenient than strings for what we want to do. However, their use requires that we introduce a new operator for comparing symbols that we have not needed until now, ===. The equality operator == works fine for numbers and strings, and for lists of same, but not for symbols.

In[10]:= **{a, b} == {a, b}**

Out[10]= True

In[11]:= **{a, b} == {a, c}**

Out[11]= {a, b} == {a, c}

Equal (==) can tell when two lists of symbols are identical, but not when they are different. SameQ (===) compares symbols for identity.

In[12]:= **{a, b} === {a, b}**

Out[12]= True

In[13]:= **{a, b} === {a, c}**

Out[13]= False

All the code used by Lex is shown in the following Program Listing 11.1. The basic process is: find the first sequence of characters that form a token, say *t*, recursively lex the remaining characters, and join *t* to the result. Technicalities arise with the treatment of numbers and the desire to ignore blanks.

```
Needs["IPM3`BaseConvert`"]
(* LEXICAL ANALYSIS *)
mainRules = {
  {"(", y___} -> {lparen, y},
  {")", y___} -> {rparen, y},
  {",", y___} -> {comma, y},
  {"/", y___} -> {slash, y},
  {"c", "o", "n", "n", "e", "c", "t", "i", "n", "g", y___}
    -> {connecting, y},
  {"c", "o", "n", "t", "a", "i", "n", "i", "n", "g", y___}
    -> {containing, y},
  {"s", "q", "u", "a", "r", "e", y___} -> {square, y},
  {"c", "i", "r", "c", "l", "e", y___} -> {circle, y},
  {"o", "v", "a", "l", y___} -> {oval, y},
  {"r", "e", "c", "t", "a", "n", "g", "l", "e", y___}
    -> {rectangle, y},
  {"c", "l", "e", "a", "r", y___} -> {clear, y},
```

```
{"n", "e", y___} -> {northeast, y},
{"s", "e", y___} -> {southeast, y},
{"s", "w", y___} -> {southwest, y},
{"n", "w", y___} -> {northwest, y},
{"n", y___} -> {north, y},
{"e", y___} -> {east, y},
{"s", y___} -> {south, y},
{"w", y___} -> {west, y},
{"c", y___} -> {center, y}
};

convertDigits[L_]:= Map[If[DigitQ[#], StringToInteger[#], #]&, L]
numberRule =
  {{m_?NumberQ, n_?NumberQ, y___} -> {10m+n, y}};
removeBlanks = { {" ", y___} -> {y} };Lex[input_]:=
  Module[{inp=FromCharacterCode/@ToCharacterCode[input]},
    Lexaux[Join[convertDigits[inp],{eof}]//.removeBlanks]]
Lexaux[{eof}]:= {eof}
Lexaux[input_]:=
  Module[{lexed = If[NumberQ[First[input]],
            input //. numberRule, input /. mainRules]},
      Join[{First[lexed]}, Lexaux[Rest[lexed] //. removeBlanks]]]
```

Program Listing 11.2:   Code for lexing *PDL*

The first thing Lex does is "explode" the input string into a list of character codes. As we saw in Section 7.5 in the chapter on recursion, we can do whatever we want with that list; however, this would involve looking up a lot of character codes, so a simpler approach is to convert each character code back to a string containing just that character. So, in Lex, inp is a list containing each of the characters in input. convertDigits is applied to change all digit characters to numbers (for example, the string "4" becomes the number 4), using StringToInteger from the BaseConvert package. eof is added to the end of the list. As final preparation before calling Lexaux, the transformation rule removeBlanks is applied repeatedly (//.) to remove all leading blanks. Thus, the argument to Lexaux is a list of one-character strings, numbers, and a final eof symbol, with the first element nonblank. Lexaux repeatedly looks for characters that constitute a token at the start of the list and replaces those characters by the token; it does this either by a single use of a rule in mainRules or by repeated use of numberRule. It recursively lexes the rest of the list and returns its result. We have already shown the result for our running example.

`Parse` takes the list of tokens and, if it is a legal picture specification, returns its parse tree. The parser is the most interesting part of our language processor, as it shows a strong link between the grammar specification (see the section above on *PDL* syntax) and the program.

Our method here is called *top-down*, or *recursive descent*, parsing. The idea is to build the parse tree by starting with a variable and letting the input string guide us in adding nodes to the tree by telling us which production is applicable. For example, consider the following list of tokens.

```
{square, lparen, 20, rparen, containing, center, slash, west,
    lparen, oval, lparen, 9, comma, 18, rparen, rparen, eof}
```

Suppose we wish to create a parse tree for this string from the variable *picture*. The only production from *picture* is production 1, so we could just add it to the tree without even looking at the input. However, we would also like to report any syntactic errors as soon as possible, so we will look at the first token in the input and see if it is legal at this point. It so happens that every string derivable from *picture* must begin with one of the words `square`, `circle`, `oval`, `rectangle`, or `clear`. If the first token is not one of these, we can report an error; if it is, we add *shape* and *associations* to the tree. We continue by trying to use the variable *shape* to match part of the list of tokens. Again, there is only one production for *shape* (production 7), and, after checking, that `square` can be the first token in a string derivable from *shape*, we add production 7 to the tree. The first part of the right-hand side of production 7 is the variable *color*. We have a choice now, production 8 or 9, and we have to choose correctly. However, it is clear that `square` is not the first token in a string derived using production 9, so it must be production 8 and we fill that in. The next unfinished part of the tree is the node containing the variable *primitive*, which has four productions.

A look at the input makes it immediately clear that only production 10 will work here, so we fill it in. Continuing in this way, we eventually get the tree shown in Figure 11.3 and use up all the input. The top-down parsing process is illustrated in the following series of parsing tree figures.

picture

Figure 11.5: Input: {square, lparen, 20, rparen, ...}

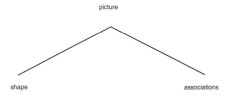

Figure 11.6: Input: {square, lparen, 20, rparen, …}

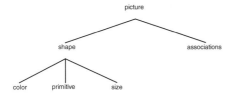

Figure 11.7: Input: {square, lparen, 20, rparen, …}

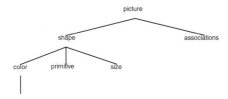

Figure 11.8: Input: {square, lparen, 20, rparen, …}

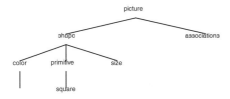

Figure 11.9: Input: {lparen, 20, rparen, …}

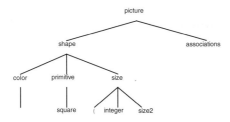

Figure 11.10: Input: {20, rparen, …}

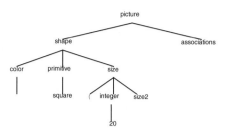

Figure 11.11: Input: {rparen,…}

Parse trees are represented as terms, using function symbols Prod1, Prod2, and so on. Only significant parts of the tree are retained, so that, for example, Prod5 has only three arguments, the two directions and the tree corresponding to the picture. Here is the parse tree for our running example; compare it with the tree in Figure 11.3.

In[14]:= **Parse[Lex[example]]**

Out[14]= Prod1[Prod7[Prod8[], Prod10[], Prod14[20, Prod15[]]],
        Prod4[Prod6[center, west, Prod1[Prod7[Prod8[], Prod12[],
            Prod14[9, Prod16[18]]], Prod2[]]], Prod2[]]]

The Parse function comes in three forms:

- Parse[*tokens_*] returns the parse tree corresponding to the list of tokens. This is the form we just used.

- Parse[*pns_*, *tokens_*], where *pns* is a list of production numbers, derives a string matching part of the *tokens* using one of the productions in *pns*. It returns a pair containing the parse tree and the suffix of *tokens* not derived from the production.

- Parse[*pn_*, *tokens_*], where *pn* is a production number, derives a prefix of tokens from production *pn* and, like the previous form, returns a parse tree and a suffix of *tokens*.

For the tokens in our example, we have:

In[15]:= **Parse[7, Lex[example]]**

Out[15]= {Prod7[Prod8[], Prod10[], Prod14[20, Prod15[]]],
        {containing, center, slash, west, lparen,
            oval, lparen, 9, comma, 18, rparen, rparen, eof}}

In other words, the first four tokens were derived using production 7; the parse tree for production 7 and the remaining tokens are returned.

Parsing is quite simple. We are trying to generate a prefix of the input tokens from a given variable. We call the second form of Parse, passing a list of all the productions for that variable (the function prodsFor, shown in Figure 11.3, gives us the list), and it looks at each one to see which might be usable given the first token (matches, also in Figure 11.3, tells whether a given production might apply for a given token). When it has found the correct production, it calls the third form of Parse, which uses that production to derive a prefix of the list of tokens.

In our example, Parse[1, Lex[ex]] first calls Parse[{7}, Lex[ex]], since 7 is the only production for *shape*, which in turn calls Parse[7, Lex[ex]], returning the pair shown above. It then calls Parse[2,3,4, {containing, center, slash,...}], 2, 3, and 4 being all the productions from *associations*, and containing, center, slash,... being the tokens not matched by *shape*.

The first form of Parse, with one argument, is the one used by PDL. It starts the parsing off by attempting to derive the list of tokens from *picture*; if successful, it discards the {eof} and returns just the parse tree. The code for the three forms of Parse is given in the program listing below.

```
(* PARSING *)

prodsFor[picture] := {1}
prodsFor[associations] := {2, 3, 4}
prodsFor[connection] := {5}
prodsFor[containment] := {6}
prodsFor[shape] := {7}
prodsFor[color] := {8, 9}
prodsFor[primitive] := {10, 11, 12, 13}
prodsFor[size] := {14}
prodsFor[size2] := {15, 16}

matches[1, t_] := MemberQ[{clear, square, circle, oval,
rectangle}, t]
matches[2, t_] := Not[MemberQ[{connecting, containing}, t]]
matches[3, t_] := MemberQ[{connecting}, t]
matches[4, t_] := MemberQ[{containing}, t]
matches[5, t_] := MemberQ[{connecting}, t]
matches[6, t_] := MemberQ[{containing}, t]
matches[7, t_] :=
    MemberQ[{clear, square, circle, oval, rectangle}, t]
matches[8, t_] := MemberQ[{square, circle, oval, rectangle}, t]
```

Program Listing 11.3: Code for prodsFor, matches, and Parse

```
matches[9, t_]  := MemberQ[{clear}, t]
matches[10, t_] := MemberQ[{square}, t]matches[11, t_] :=
    MemberQ[{circle}, t]
matches[12, t_] := MemberQ[{oval}, t]matches[13, t_] :=
MemberQ[{rectangle}, t]
matches[14, t_] := MemberQ[{lparen}, t]
matches[15, t_] := MemberQ[{rparen}, t]
matches[16, t_] := MemberQ[{comma}, t]

Parse[tokens_] := First[Parse[prodsFor[picture], tokens]]

Parse[{}, x_] :=
    (Print["Syntax error:  remaining input is ",
            Take[x, Min[Length[x], 10]], " ..."];
      Abort[])
Parse[{pn_, pns___}, tokens_] :=
    If[matches[pn, First[tokens]],  (* if pn applies *)
        Parse[pn, tokens],          (* parse using it *)
        Parse[{pns}, tokens]]       (* else try other prod's *)

Parse[1, tokens_] :=
Module[{part1 = Parse[prodsFor[shape], tokens], part2},
    part2 = Parse[prodsFor[associations], part1[[2]]];
    {Prod1[part1[[1]], part2[[1]]], part2[[2]]}]

Parse[2, tokens_] := {Prod2[], tokens}

Parse[3, tokens_] := Module[{
    part1 = Parse[prodsFor[connection], tokens], part2},
    part2 = Parse[prodsFor[associations], part1[[2]]];
    {Prod3[part1[[1]], part2[[1]]], part2[[2]]}]

Parse[4, tokens_] :=
Module[{part1 = Parse[prodsFor[containment], tokens],
        part2},
    part2 = Parse[prodsFor[associations], part1[[2]]];
    {Prod4[part1[[1]], part2[[1]]], part2[[2]]}]

Parse[5, tokens_] :=
Module[{part1 = Parse[prodsFor[picture], Drop[tokens, 5]]},
    {Prod5[tokens[[2]], tokens[[4]], part1[[1]]],
Rest[part1[[2]]]}]
```

Program Listing 11.4:   Code for `Parse`

```
Parse[6, tokens_]:=
Module[{part1 = Parse[prodsFor[picture], Drop[tokens, 5]]},
    {Prod6[tokens[[2]], tokens[[4]], part1[[1]]],
Rest[part1[[2]]]}]

Parse[7, tokens_] :=
Module[{part1 = Parse[prodsFor[color], tokens], part2, part3},
    part2 = Parse[prodsFor[primitive], part1[[2]]];
    part3 = Parse[prodsFor[size], part2[[2]]];
    {Prod7[part1[[1]], part2[[1]], part3[[1]]], part3[[2]]}]

Parse[8, tokens_]:= {Prod8[], tokens}
Parse[9, tokens_]:= {Prod9[], Rest[tokens]}
Parse[10, tokens_]:= {Prod10[], Rest[tokens]}
Parse[11, tokens_]:= {Prod11[], Rest[tokens]}
Parse[12, tokens_]:= {Prod12[], Rest[tokens]}
Parse[13, tokens_]:= {Prod13[], Rest[tokens]}
Parse[14, tokens_]:=
    Module[{part1 = Parse[prodsFor[size2], Drop[tokens, 2]]},
        {Prod14[tokens[[2]], part1[[1]]], part1[[2]]}]
Parse[15, tokens_]:= {Prod15[], Rest[tokens]}
Parse[16, tokens_]:= {Prod16[tokens[[2]]], Drop[tokens, 3]}
```

Program Listing 11.5:   Code for `Parse` (cont.)

Computing shapes

With the parse tree in hand, the remaining processing is a fairly routine matter of tree traversal, such as we used in Section 7.5. By computing the characteristics of each shape – its center, size, and compass points – we can compute the characteristics of the shapes it contains or is connected to. The coding has its occasional tricky moments, but is not basically very difficult.

Recall that there are two functions, ComputeShapes and ConvertShapes, in this part of the program. ComputeShapes does the tree traversal; ConvertShapes just converts the list of shapes to a list of *Mathematica* graphics. We take them in order.

ComputeShapes traverses the parse tree and produces a list of "shapes." The key point here is exactly what we mean by "shape." That is, how do we store the information about shapes that we mentioned above (center, size, compass points)? The structure is shown in the code at the top of Figure 11.3. A shape is represented by a seven-element list: its center (a pair of numbers), the primitive shape (a symbol), the color (a production, either `Prod8` for a normal shape or `Prod9` for a clear one), the distance from the center to the east compass point, the distance from the center to the north compass point, the angle of the northeast compass point (in radians), and the distance from the center to the northeast compass point. We have defined functions `center`, `primitive`, `color`, `east`, `north`, `neangle`, and `nedist` to extract these components from a shape.

```
center[{c_, ___}] := c
primitive[{_, p_, ___}] := p
color[{_, _, c_, ___}] := c
east[{_, _, _, e_, ___}] := e
```

```
north[{_, _, _, _, n_, ___}] := n
neangle[{_, _, _, _, _, a_, ___}] := a
nedist[{_, _, _, _, _, _, d_}] := d
angle[s_, north] := Pi/2
angle[s_, south] := -Pi/2
angle[s_, east] := 0
angle[s_, west] := Pi
angle[s_, northeast] := neangle[s]
angle[s_, southeast] := -neangle[s]
angle[s_, southwest] := Pi+neangle[s]
angle[s_, northwest] := Pi-neangle[s]
dist[s_, north] := north[s]
dist[s_, south] := north[s]
dist[s_, east] := east[s]
dist[s_, west] := east[s]
dist[s_, northeast] := nedist[s]
dist[s_, southeast] := nedist[s]
dist[s_, southwest] := nedist[s]
dist[s_, northwest] := nedist[s]

pointOf[s_, d_, delta_] :=
  center[s] + vector[angle[s, d], dist[s, d] + delta]
computeCenter[s_, p_, center] := p
computeCenter[s_, p_, d_] :=
  p + vector[Pi+angle[s, d], dist[s, d]]
vector[theta_, r_] := {r Cos[theta], r Sin[theta]}
```

Program Listing 11.6: Code for dealing with shapes and points

We will need to compute points using angles and distances from the center of a shape. It is convenient to define the following functions, given above in the program listing.

1. `angle` [*shape, direction*] computes the angle from the center of *shape* to the given compass point. East is always 0, north always $\pi/2$, and so on, but the intermediate points depend upon the dimensions of the shape (at least for ovals and rectangles).

2. `dist` [*shape, direction*] computes the distance from the center of a shape to the given compass point. Distances for intermediate points are all the same as the northeast distance.

3. `pointOf` [*shape, direction, delta*] computes the compass point given by *direction* for *shape*, adjusted by *delta*. A positive *delta* moves the point away from the center of the shape, a negative *delta* towards it.

4. `computeCenter` [*shape, point, direction*] , where *shape* does not yet have a center, though it has all its other information, computes its center, given that the compass point named by *direction* is to be at *point*. For example, if s is a square with sides of length 10, `computeCenter` [s, {4, 2}, north] will return {4, -3}; if the square is centered at {4, -3}, its north point will be at {4, 2}.

The tree traversal is initiated by a call to the one-argument form of Compute⸱ Shapes, which is called with a Prod1 tree. It calls the three-argument form of Compute⸱ Shapes, which returns a list of shapes. N is applied to the list to evaluate all numerical formulas and all the "clear" shapes (Prod9) are removed. For our running example (Figure 11.2), we see the result in this session:

```
In[16]:=  ComputeShapes[Parse[Lex[example]]]

Out[16]=  {{{0., 0.}, square, Prod8[], 10., 10., 0.785398, 14.1421},
          {{4.5, 0.}, oval, Prod8[], 4.5, 9., 1.10715, 7.11512}}
```

The main shape, centered at (0, 0), is a 20×20 square (the 10s being the distance from the center to the side and the top). The 9×18 oval is centered at (4.5, 0).

The three-argument form of ComputeShapes takes a tree given in the form Prod1 [*shape, associations*] and computes the shape of *shape* and all the shapes in *associations*, returning a list. The second and third arguments are a point *p* and a direction *d*. First, *shape* is drawn with direction *d* at point *p*. This is done by calling computeShape; shapeInfo computes all the location-independent information, which is everything but the center, and the latter is filled in by a call to computeCenter, discussed above. Then the shapes in *associations* are drawn in positions computed with respect to *shape*. This is accomplished by calling computeAssociatedShapes, passing *associations* as the first argument and the shape computed for *shape* as the second. The *associations* parse tree (Prod2, Prod3, or Prod4) is traversed, and the shapes it contains are computed with respect to that second argument. The auxiliary function compute⸱

Point [*shape*, *dir*$_1$, *dir*$_2$, *relation*] computes the meeting point of *shape* with whatever shape it contains or connects to, given that *dir*$_1$ of *shape* is to meet *dir*$_2$ of the contained shape. The computation also depends upon whether the shape is contained or connected, as given by *relation*.

```
separation = .1;

ComputeShapes[tree_] :=
  Select[N[computeShapes[tree, {0, 0}, center]],
    (color[#] =!= Prod9[]) &]

computeShapes[Prod1[sh_, assoc_], p_, d_] :=
Module[{s = computeShape[sh, p, d], as},
    as = computeAssociatedShapes[assoc, s];
    Join[{s}, as]]

computeAssociatedShapes[Prod2[], _] := {}
computeAssociatedShapes[Prod3[Prod5[d1_,d2_,pic_],assoc_],s_] :=
Module[{p = computePoint[s, d1, d2, connecting], ss},
    ss = computeShapes[pic, p, d2];
    Join[ss, computeAssociatedShapes[assoc, s]]]

computeAssociatedShapes[Prod4[Prod6[d1_,d2_,pic_],assoc_],s_] :=
Module[{p = computePoint[s, d1, d2, containing], ss},
    ss = computeShapes[pic, p, d2];
    Join[ss, computeAssociatedShapes[assoc, s]]]

computePoint[s_, d1_, d2_, relation_] :=
  Which[d1===center, center[s],
     d2===center, pointOf[s, d1, 0],
     relation===connecting, pointOf[s, d1, separation],
     True, pointOf[s, d1, -separation]]

computeShape[s_, p_, d_] := Module[{si = shapeInfo[s]},
    Join[{computeCenter[si, p, d]}, Rest[si]]]

shapeInfo[Prod7[color_, Prod10[], Prod14[i_, _]]] :=
  {0, square, color, i/2, i/2, Pi/4, i/Sqrt[2]}

shapeInfo[Prod7[color_, Prod11[], Prod14[i_, _]]] :=
  {0, circle, color, i/2, i/2, Pi/4, i/2}
ovalNE[a_, b_, theta_] :=
  a b Sqrt[(1 + Tan[theta]^2)/(a^2 + b^2 Tan[theta]^2)]
```

```
shapeInfo[Prod7[color_, Prod12[], Prod14[l_, Prod16[h_]]]] :=
  {0, oval, color, 1/2, h/2, ArcTan[h/l],
  ovalNE[h/2, 1/2, ArcTan[h/l]]}

shapeInfo[Prod7[color_, Prod13[], Prod14[l_, Prod16[h_]]]] :=
  {0, rectangle, color, 1/2, h/2, ArcTan[h/l], Sqrt[h^2 + l^2]/2}
```

Program Listing 11.7: Computing shapes

Finally, the list of shapes is converted to a list of *Mathematica* graphics by mapping
convertShape over the list. The *Mathematica* graphics primitives are well matched to
our representation of shapes, making convertShape easy to write. Here is the final
output of our example.

In[17]:= **ConvertShapes[ComputeShapes[Parse[Lex[example]]]]**

Out[17]= {Line[{{-10., -10.}, {-10., 10.}, {10., 10.}, {10., -10.},
     {-10., -10.}}], Circle[{4.5, 0.}, {4.5, 9.}]}

In[18]:= **Show[Graphics[%]];**

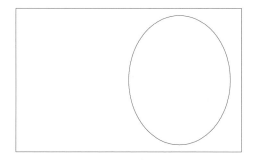

```
makeRectangle[p_, l_, h_] :=
 Line[{p, p+{0,h}, p+{l,h}, p+{l,0}, p}]
convertShape[s_] /; MemberQ[{square, rectangle}, s[[2]]] :=
   makeRectangle[pointOf[s, southwest, 0], 2 east[s], 2 north[s]]
convertShape[s_] /; MemberQ[{circle, rectangle}, s[[2]]] :=
   Circle[center[s], north[s]]
convertShape[s_] /; s[[2]] === oval :=
   Circle[center[s], {east[s], north[s]}]
ConvertShapes[ss_] := Map[convertShape, ss]
```

Program Listing 11.8: Converting shapes to *Mathematica* graphics objects

12 Writing packages

Packages are text files that contain *Mathematica* commands. They are designed to make it easy to distribute your programs to others, but they also provide a mechanism for you to write programs that integrate with *Mathematica* in a seamless manner. In this chapter we will discuss the organization and creation of packages including a discussion of contexts, which are a mechanism for organizing new names and symbols in your *Mathematica* sessions.

12.1 Introduction

When you begin a *Mathematica* session, the built-in functions are immediately available for you to use. There are, however, many more functions that you can access that reside in files supplied with *Mathematica*. In principle, the only difference between those files and the ones you create is that those were written by professional programmers. There is another difference: the definitions in those files are placed in special structures called *packages*. Indeed, these files themselves are often called "packages" instead of "files."

Packages are a *name localizing* construct, analogous to `Module`, but for entire files of definitions. Their purpose is to allow the programmer to define a collection of functions for *export*. These exported functions are for the users of the package to work with and are often referred to as public functions. Other functions, those that are *not for export*, are auxiliary, or private functions, and are not intended to be accessible to users.

In this chapter, you will learn how to write your own packages. Much of the chapter is devoted to an explanation of a more primitive notion, that of *contexts*, which is a prerequisite to understanding packages. We then describe packages and give a simple example, showing the standard and accepted style for writing them. We will also distinguish between functions for export and auxiliary functions that users of your package need not be concerned with.

12.2 Using packages

Mathematica packages have been written for a great variety of problem domains. Many are
provided with each version of *Mathematica* and are referred to as the Standard Packages.
Their documentation is available in the Help Browser. Below, we list some examples of
some of the standard *Mathematica* packages. Note that package names always end with a
back quote (`` ` ``), and often have back quotes within them as well. We will discuss the
meaning of this back quote shortly.

- `Calculus`VectorAnalysis``: This package provides a variety of variables and
  functions for doing calculus in various three-dimensional coordinate systems; for
  example, `SetCoordinates` to set the coordinate system (Cartesian, polar, etc.);
  `CrossProduct` to compute cross products; `Curl` to give the curl of a vector field.

- `Graphics`MultipleListPlot``: Provides functions for superimposing several
  plots on the same graphic. `MultipleListPlot` is the main function in this
  package. It plots lists of data as separate plots on the same axes. Also provided is
  `MakeSymbol` which creates symbols to use in labeling the separate plots, plus a
  number of functions for specifying symbols.

Loading packages

Once you know which package you want to use, you can load it in one of two ways. For
example, to load the package `Calculus`VectorAnalysis``, you can use either `Get` or
`Needs`.

- `<<Calculus`VectorAnalysis`` will read the file and evaluate each expression
  and definition as if it had been typed in. Actually, the argument of `<<` is a string, but
  the quotation marks can be omitted. `<<package`` is shorthand for `Get["package`"]`.

- `Needs["Calculus`VectorAnalysis`"]` will read the package, just like `<<`,
  but only if it has not already been read.

  Here is an example of using the `Calculus`VectorAnalysis`` package.

  In[1]:= **Needs["Calculus`VectorAnalysis`"]**

Here is the usage message for one of the functions defined in the package.

In[2]:= ? **CrossProduct**

```
CrossProduct[v1, v2] gives the cross product (
    sometimes called vector product) of the two vectors v1,
    v2 in three space in the default coordinate system.
    CrossProduct[v1, v2, coordsys] gives the cross product
    of v1 and v2 in the coordinate system coordsys. More…
```

This computes the cross product of two symbolic vectors using the `CrossProduct` function defined in `Calculus`VectorAnalysis``.

In[3]:= **CrossProduct[{x_1, y_1, z_1}, {x_2, y_2, z_2}]**

Out[3]= $\{-y_2 z_1 + y_1 z_2, x_2 z_1 - x_1 z_2, -x_2 y_1 + x_1 y_2\}$

Finding out what is in a package

To use the *Mathematica* packages, you need to know what they provide. In fact, programmers find that even remembering what is in their own packages is not easy, if they have not looked at them for a while. If you know the name of the package and you want to know what it defines, first load it, using *<<package`* or Needs [*"package`"*].

In[4]:= **Needs["DiscreteMath`ComputationalGeometry`"]**

Now you can get a list of hyperlinks of the functions defined in this package as follows.

In[5]:= ? **DiscreteMath`ComputationalGeometry`***

DiscreteMath`ComputationalGeometry`

AllPoints	NearestNeighbor
BoundedDiagram	PlanarGraphPlot
ConvexHull	Ray
DelaunayTriangulation	TileAreas
DelaunayTriangulationQ	TriangularSurfacePlot
DiagramPlot	TrimPoints
Hull	VoronoiDiagram
LabelPoints	

Clicking any of the above links will display the usage message associated with that function.

You can also display a list of the names defined in the package using `Names`.

In[6]:= **Names["DiscreteMath`ComputationalGeometry`*"]**

Out[6]= {AllPoints, BoundedDiagram, ConvexHull, DelaunayTriangulation,
        DelaunayTriangulationQ, DiagramPlot, Hull, LabelPoints,
        NearestNeighbor, PlanarGraphPlot, Ray, TileAreas,
        TriangularSurfacePlot, TrimPoints, VoronoiDiagram}

Once you have loaded the package you can use ? to get the usage message for any of those names.

In[7]:= **? DelaunayTriangulation**

DelaunayTriangulation[{{x1,y1},{x2,y2},...,{xn,
    yn}}] yields the (planar) Delaunay triangulation
    of the points. The triangulation is represented as
    a vertex adjacency list, one entry for each unique
    point in the original coordinate list indicating the
    adjacent vertices in counterclockwise order. More...

If, on the other hand, you forget the name of the package, you can easily browse through the Help Browser which lists all packages, names, and usage messages of any functions defined in these packages. Alternatively, you can find out where the directory of packages is stored on your system, and browse through it in your file system.

Avoiding name collisions

Sometimes, you will read in a package that defines a function f whose name you have already mentioned in your current session. It is very common, for example, to forget to load a package before calling one of its functions. By simply mentioning the function's name you create a symbol in the current context. Then, if you try to make a call to f, *Mathematica* will assume you are talking about the f in the current context rather than the one defined in the package.

For example, suppose we attempted to use a function RandomPermutation that we mistakenly believed was a built-in function.

In[8]:= **RandomPermutation[4]**

Out[8]= RandomPermutation[4]

After a little searching in the Help Browser we discover that RandomPermutation is not a built-in function, but is in fact, defined in the package DiscreteMath`Combina torica`. So let us try to load the package.

```
In[9]:=  << DiscreteMath`Combinatorica`

         RandomPermutation::shdw :
          Symbol RandomPermutation appears in multiple contexts
             {DiscreteMath`Combinatorica`, Global`}; definitions
             in context DiscreteMath`Combinatorica` may
             shadow or be shadowed by other definitions. More…
```

If you try to use the RandomPermutation function defined in the Discrete `
Math`Combinatorica` package, you will not be able to do so in the usual way as its
definition is "shadowed" by the RandomPermutation function that was placed in the
Global` context when we first tried to use it.

```
In[10]:=  RandomPermutation[4]

Out[10]=  RandomPermutation[4]
```

You can still use the RandomPermutation function from the Combinatorica
package but you have to explicitly use its full context.

```
In[11]:=  DiscreteMath`Combinatorica`RandomPermutation[3]

Out[11]=  {2, 1, 3}
```

If, however, you want to be able to call DiscreteMath`Combinatorica`Ran `
domPermutation by its short name, and forget the RandomPermutation you defined
in the Global` context, use the function Remove.

```
In[12]:=  Remove[RandomPermutation]
```

This will make it seem that you had never mentioned the name Global`Random `
Permutation at all as it completely removes the symbol RandomPermutation from
the Global` context. Now you can use the short name for the RandomPermutation
function from the DiscreteMath`Combinatorica` package.

```
In[13]:=  RandomPermutation[3]

Out[13]=  {3, 1, 2}
```

Note that evaluating Clear[RandomPermutation] is not enough; that would
clear values associated with any assignments attached to RandomPermutation, but it
would not "un-mention" the symbol itself; in other words, Clear[*symbol*] clears out the
right-hand side of any definition associated with *symbol*, but it does not remove *symbol* from
the context within which it was first created.

There is a way to minimize this problem, if you have certain packages that you often
use.

DeclarePackage ["*package`*", {"*name*$_1$", "*name*$_2$", ...}]

DeclarePackage tells *Mathematica* that whenever you use one of the names *name*$_1$, *name*$_2$,…, it should load *package* (if it has not already been loaded). It is a good practice to make a file containing a DeclarePackage for each package you frequently use, listing all the names of functions you use from that package. For example, if that file is called mypackage.m then, whenever you start a *Mathematica* session, enter <<mypackage.m as your first input. Alternatively, you could put mypackage.m in one of the init.m files and *Mathematica* will automatically load it whenever you start a session. There are several locations where kernel init.m files can be found:

```
In[14]:= Map[ToFileName,
           {
             {$BaseDirectory, "Autoload", "_", "Kernel", "init.m"},
             {$UserBaseDirectory, "Autoload", "_", "Kernel", "init.m"},
             {$InstallationDirectory,
              "Configuration", "Kernel", "init.m"},
             {$InstallationDirectory, "AddOns",
              "Autoload", "_", "Kernel", "init.m"}
           }]
```

```
Out[14]= {C:\Documents and Settings\All Users\Application
            Data\Mathematica\Autoload\_\Kernel\init.m\,
          C:\Documents and Settings\Paul Wellin\Application
            Data\Mathematica\Autoload\_\Kernel\init.m\,
          C:\Program Files\Wolfram Research\Mathematica
            \5.1\Configuration\Kernel\init.m\,
          C:\Program Files\Wolfram Research\Mathematica
            \5.1\AddOns\Autoload\_\Kernel\init.m\}
```

The first two locations given above are the preferred directories to place your init.m files. The last two are dependent upon the version of *Mathematica* and hence will need to be updated or moved when you upgrade to a newer version of *Mathematica*.

Lastly, you can also put your init.m in a Kernel directory in a package directory in any of the Applications directories. For example, if you have a directory named MathApps that lives inside one of the Applications directories, then put a Kernel directory inside MathApps and an init.m inside that Kernel directory. Your packages will live inside MathApps. So loading a package (<<MathApps`mypackage`) will automatically load the init.m inside the MathApps/Kernel directory.

12.3 Contexts

Every symbol you use in a computation in *Mathematica* has a *full name* consisting of the symbol preceded by the *context* in which the name was first mentioned. The context is a means for organizing symbols. You can think of the context like a namespace – different symbols are in different contexts just like different files on your computer live in different directories.

When you first start your session, the *current context* is Global` (again note the back quote), and any symbol *symbol* you mention now has full name Global`*symbol*. A symbol can be given with its full name or in its regular, short form.

Here is a function created in the Global` context.

In[1]:= **f[x_] := x + 1**

In[2]:= **Context[f]**

Out[2]= Global`

We can use the function with its full name.

In[3]:= **Global`f[3]**

Out[3]= 4

But, of course, it is much more convenient to use the regular, short form.

In[4]:= **f[3]**

Out[4]= 4

Mathematica first searches the current context for definitions associated with any symbols; by default, this is the Global` context. To see a list of the contexts that *Mathematica* uses to search for symbols, use $ContextPath.

In[5]:= **$ContextPath**

Out[5]= {Global`, System`}

As we saw above, symbols you define when your session begins have context Global`. Built-in functions have context System`.

In[6]:= **Map[Context, {Integrate, Plot, π, List}]**

Out[6]= {System`, System`, System`, System`}

You can tell *Mathematica* to use a different context for any new symbols you mention by using the function `Begin`.

In[7]:= `Begin["ContextA`"]`

Out[7]= `ContextA``

In[8]:= `g[x_] := x + 2`

We can use the full name for g:

In[9]:= `ContextA`g[3]`

Out[9]= `5`

Or, since we are currently in the `ContextA`` context, we can use the short name.

In[10]:= `g[3]`

Out[10]= `5`

Here is the current context.

In[11]:= `$Context`

Out[11]= `ContextA``

In this new context, the name g is an abbreviation for `ContextA`g`.

In[12]:= `Map[g, {5, 7, 9}]`

Out[12]= `{7, 9, 11}`

Note that we can still refer to f, even though it was not defined in this context.

In[13]:= `Map[Global`f, {5, 7, 9}]`

Out[13]= `{6, 8, 10}`

In[14]:= `Map[f, {5, 7, 9}]`

Out[14]= `{6, 8, 10}`

After exiting the context using the `End` function, we may define a different g, having context `Global``.

In[15]:= `End[]`

Out[15]= `ContextA``

In[16]:= `g[x_] := x + 3`

In[17]:= `g[3]`

Out[17]= `6`

We now have two definitions of g, or, rather, one definition of Global`g and one of ContextA`g. Since our current context is Global`, when we just say g we get Global`g; but we can still refer to ContextA`g by its full name.

In[18]:= **g[3]**

Out[18]= 6

In[19]:= **ContextA`g[3]**

Out[19]= 5

The question arises: when you enter a symbol *symbol*, how does *Mathematica* decide which version of *symbol* to use? And how can you tell which one it has chosen?

To answer the second question first: the function Context gives the context of a symbol.

In[20]:= **Context[g]**

Out[20]= Global`

In[21]:= **Context[Map]**

Out[21]= System`

In[22]:= **Context[ContextA`g]**

Out[22]= ContextA`

You can also use ?.

In[23]:= **?g**

Global`g

g[x_] := x + 3

How, then, does *Mathematica* decide which definition to use? It maintains two variables, $Context and $ContextPath. $Context contains a context (that is, a string giving the name of a context), which is the current context, and $ContextPath contains a list of contexts. *Mathematica* looks in $Context first, then in the contexts in $Context Path in the order in which they appear there; if it does not find the symbol at all, then it creates it in context $Context. Of course, none of this applies if you give the symbol's full name.

In[24]:= **$Context**

Out[24]= Global`

```
In[25]:=  $ContextPath

Out[25]=  {Global`, System`}

In[26]:=  Begin["ContextA`"]

Out[26]=  ContextA`

In[27]:=  $Context

Out[27]=  ContextA`

In[28]:=  $ContextPath

Out[28]=  {Global`, System`}

In[29]:=  End[]

Out[29]=  ContextA`

In[30]:=  {$Context, $ContextPath}

Out[30]=  {Global`, {Global`, System`}}
```

So the effect of entering a new context using Begin is simply to change the value of $Context; End[] changes it back. In either case, $ContextPath is not changed.

One final point about contexts: contexts can be nested within contexts. That is, you can have context names like A`B`C`. To enter contexts like this, do the following.

```
In[31]:=  Begin["A`"]             (* enter context A` *)

Out[31]=  A`

In[32]:=  Begin["`B`"]            (* enter context A`B` *)

Out[32]=  A`B`

In[33]:=  Begin["`C`"]            (* enter context A`B`C` *)

Out[33]=  A`B`C`

In[34]:=  End[]                   (* back in context A`B` *)

Out[34]=  A`B`C`

In[35]:=  End[]                   (* back in context A` *)

Out[35]=  A`B`
```

In[36]:= **End[]**   (* back in context Global` *)

Out[36]= A`

Note the back quote *before* the context name in the second and third `Begin`. This is used to indicate that the new context should be a sub-context of the current context. We could have also indicated this as follows:

In[37]:= **Begin["A`"]**

Out[37]= A`

In[38]:= **Begin["A`B`"]**

Out[38]= A`B`

In[39]:= **Begin["A`B`C`"]**

Out[39]= A`B`C`

Nested contexts are a way of managing the multiplicity of contexts. You will have noticed how the names of the standard packages we discussed earlier look just like nested contexts. In fact, package names are contexts. *Mathematica* organizes the standard packages into about ten major contexts (for example, `Calculus`` and `Graphics``), each with about ten nested contexts; it is just a way of keeping things organized. Most readers will recognize this as the idea behind hierarchical file systems. In fact, when you load a package using `Needs` or `<<`, *Mathematica* translates the package name directly into a path name in the hierarchical file system on your computer.

For example, you can load the package `mypackage.m` that lives in a directory MathApps as follows:

```
Windows              <<MathApps\mypackage.m
Unix/Linux/OS X      <<MathApps/mypackage.m
Macintosh Classic    <<MathApps:mypackage.m
```

But since *Mathematica* provides a system-independent means of loading packages, you can simply use `Get` with the following syntax and *Mathematica* will automatically translate this into a path name appropriate for your computer.

```
<< MathApps`mypackage`
```

Summary

- Any name mentioned in a *Mathematica* session has a full name, containing a context and the short name.

- When using a name, you may give its full name. If you choose not to (as is customary), *Mathematica* will decide what the full name is; that is, what the context of the name is.

- Here is how *Mathematica* decides on the context:

  - First, it looks in the context given by the variable $Context.

  - Next, it looks in all the contexts given in the variable $ContextPath, in the order in which they appear there.

  - If those searches do not succeed, *Mathematica* assumes this is the first mention of the name, and so gives it the context $Context.

- Begin["*context*`"] and End[] alter the value of $Context (but do not affect $ContextPath). Specifically, Begin["*context*`"] sets $Context to *context*`, and End[] restores it to its prior value before the Begin.

As of now, these functions are the only ways we know to alter the contents of these two variables. In the next section, we will see two other functions that change them in a subtly, but crucially different way.

12.4 The elements of packages

Packages allow you to create an organized collection of function definitions and values, while avoiding collisions with any other definitions of those names. For example, if you load a package that defines functions f and g, and the definition of g contains a call to f, then g should always work – that is, call the f defined in the package – even if you have defined f separately in your session (in the Global` context). Furthermore, packages can define their own auxiliary (or private) functions and constants that the user, or client, of the package will not ordinarily see at all.

All this is achieved using contexts, with two new functions:

- BeginPackage ["*package*`"] sets $Context to *package*`, and $ContextPath to {*package*`, System`}.

- EndPackage [] resets both variables to their values prior to the evaluation of BeginPackage [], and then prepends package` to $ContextPath.

Thus, if you are in a *Mathematica* session, with current context Global`, and you read in a file containing:

```
BeginPackage ["P`"]
    f [x_]  := …
    g [y_]  := …
EndPackage []
```

---

then after it is read, the functions f and g, with full names P`f and P`g, will be defined, and the context P` will be in $ContextPath. If you do not have any other definitions of f, you can refer to it as just f; if you do, then use P`f; and similarly for the function g.

The precise definition of BeginPackage [*package*`] is important as it changes $ContextPath to {*package*`, System`}. Thus, all the names defined in the package will have context *package*`. In our example above, the f and g in the package can be referred to as P`f and P`g, regardless of any other definitions you may have given for them.

It is important to realize, too, that *Mathematica* determines the full name of any name *when it reads it in*. Thus, if g calls f, then the occurrence of f in the body of g becomes P`f when the package is loaded. g will always call this f, even if there is a different f defined in the context in which the call to g is made.

The BeginPackage function can be given multiple arguments. The second and subsequent arguments are the names of other packages that this one uses. They are treated as if they were arguments to the Needs function; that is, they are loaded if they have not already been. Furthermore, they are included in $ContextPath *during the loading* of this package, so its functions can refer to their functions by their short names.

Summary

- BeginPackage ["*package*`"] sets $Context to *package*`, and $ContextPath to {*package*`, System`}, so that any names subsequently mentioned, other than the names of built-in functions and constants, are defined in context *package*`.

- EndPackage[] resets $Context and $ContextPath to their prior values, except that *package`* is added to the front of $ContextPath.

12.5 Writing your own packages

The RandomWalks package

In this section, we list the full RandomWalks.m package, elements of which were developed in earlier chapters. We will add several important user interface elements, such as expressions for options and usage statements. The full package is included in the IPM3 archive as indicated in the Preface.

BeginPackage
First, we set the value of Context`, which causes $ContextPath to be set to {IPM3`, RandomWalks`, System`}.

```
In[1]:= BeginPackage["IPM3`RandomWalks`"]

Out[1]= IPM3`RandomWalks`
```

Importing other packages
You could import a package by using an optional argument to BeginPackage. In that case, you would have BeginPackage["IPM3`RandomWalks`",{Graphics`Arg Colors`,Graphics`Polyhedra`}] above. The argument against this approach is that the two packages Graphics`ArgColors` and Graphics`Polyhedra` will be left on the search path after the RandomWalks` package is read in. It is considered poor programming style to alter the user's environment by simply reading in a package – at least you should try to alter it as little as possible. There is another method of loading a package within a package, and that is to call Needs *after* the call to BeginPackage. Using this mechanism, the Graphics`ArgColors` context will not remain on the context path after the RandomWalks package is read in.

```
In[2]:= Needs["Graphics`ArgColors`"]

In[3]:= Needs["Graphics`Polyhedra`"]
```

Usage statements

Defining usage messages for the functions in your packages creates symbols for the functions in the current context. Each of the functions for which you define a usage message will then be exported for public use; that is, those functions are visible and usable immediately after loading the package. This is in distinction to any functions that are defined in your package for which you do not have usage messages (or, more precisely, for which you have not explicitly exported by mentioning that symbol before the Begin statement). Those functions will be private, unavailable for the user of your package to access.

Making your functions behave much like the built-in functions will make it easier for users of your packages, since they will expect usage messages and general functionality similar to that of *Mathematica*'s functions. It is also a good way for you to document your programs. We would go so far as to suggest that you consider writing your usage messages *before* you write the function definitions in *Mathematica*. This will help you to clearly understand what it is you want your functions to do.

```
In[4]:=  RandomWalk::"usage" =
         "RandomWalk[n] generates an n-step walk in two dimensions.
            The default behavior gives a lattice walk with steps
            in one of the four compass directions. The option
            LatticeWalk takes values True or False. The value
            of the option Dimensions can be any of 1, 2, or 3.";
```

```
In[5]:=  LatticeWalk::"usage" =
         "LatticeWalk→val is an option to RandomWalk
            that determines whether the random walk will
            be a lattice walk or an off-lattice walk.
            Possible values are True and False.";
```

```
In[6]:=  ShowWalk::"usage" =
         "ShowWalk[walk] displays a one, two, or three-dimensional
            random walk connecting each site with a line. Graphics
            options can be passed to ShowWalk. E.g., ShowWalk[walk,
            Background→GrayLevel[0]] to produce a black background.";
```

```
In[7]:=  AnimateWalk::"usage" =
         "AnimateWalk[walk, opts] creates an animation
            of a two-dimensional random walk. A red ball
            will be seen to move to the current position in
            the walk to aid in visualizing the animation.";
```

Warning messages

In[8]:= `RandomWalk::rwn = "Argument `1` is not a positive integer.";`

Options

In[9]:= `Options[RandomWalk] = {LatticeWalk → True, Dimension → 2}`

Out[9]= `{LatticeWalk → True, Dimension → 2}`

Begin private context

The `Begin` command changes the current context without affecting the context path. By starting the argument `` `Private` `` with a context mark `` ` ``, we change to a subcontext of the current context. This new subcontext is `` IPM3`RandomWalks`Private` ``.

In[10]:= `Begin["`Private`"]`

Out[10]= `` IPM3`RandomWalks`Private` ``

The function definitions

In[11]:= `walk1D[n_] := NestList[# + (-1)`$^{\text{Random[Integer]}}$` &, 0, n]`

In[12]:= `walk1DOffLattice[n_] :=`
`   FoldList[Plus, 0, Table[Random[Real, {-1, 1}], {n}]]`

In[13]:= `walk2D[n_] :=`
`   Module[{NSEW = {{0, 1}, {1, 0}, {0, -1}, {-1, 0}}},`
`    FoldList[Plus, {0, 0},`
`     NSEW⟦Table[Random[Integer, {1, 4}], {n}]⟧]]`

In[14]:= `walk2DOffLattice[n_] :=`
`   FoldList[Plus, {0, 0},`
`    Map[{Cos[#], Sin[#]} &, Table[Random[Real, {0, 2 π}], {n}]]]`

In[15]:= `walk3D[n_] := Module[{NSEW3 = √2 Vertices[Cube]}, FoldList[`
`    Plus, {0, 0, 0}, NSEW3⟦Table[Random[Integer, {1, 8}], {n}]⟧]]`

In[16]:= `walk3DOffLattice[n_] :=`
$$\text{FoldList}\left[\text{Plus, } \{0, 0, 0\}, \text{ Map}\left[\left\{\text{Cos}[\#], \text{Sin}[\#], \frac{\#}{2\,\pi}\right\} \&,\right.\right.$$
$$\left.\left.\text{Table}[\text{Random}[\text{Real, } \{-2\,\pi, 2\,\pi\}], \{n\}]\right]\right]$$

```
In[17]:= RandomWalk[n_, opts___?OptionQ] := Module[{dim, latticeQ},
           If[Not[IntegerQ[n] && n > 0], Message[RandomWalk::rwn, n],
           {latticeQ, dim} = {LatticeWalk, Dimension} /.
             Flatten[{opts, Options[RandomWalk]}];
           Which[
             dim == 1, If[latticeQ, walk1D[n], walk1DOffLattice[n]],
             dim == 2, If[latticeQ, walk2D[n], walk2DOffLattice[n]],
             dim == 3, If[latticeQ, walk3D[n], walk3DOffLattice[n]]
           ]]]

In[18]:= ShowWalk[coords_, opts___] :=
           Which[
             Length[Dimensions[coords]] == 1,
               ListPlot[coords, opts, PlotJoined → True],
             Dimensions[coords][[2]] == 2,
               Show[Graphics[Line[coords], opts,
               AspectRatio → Automatic]], Dimensions[coords][[2]] == 3,
               Show[Graphics3D[Line[coords], opts,
             AspectRatio → Automatic]]]

In[19]:= AnimateWalk[coords_, opts___] :=
           Scan[Show[Graphics[{{RGBColor[1, 0, 0], PointSize[0.025],
               Point[coords[[#1]]]}, Line[Take[coords, #1]]}],
             opts, AspectRatio → Automatic, PlotRange →
               ({Min[#1] - 0.2, Max[#1] + 0.2} &) /@ Transpose[coords]] &,
           Range[2, Length[coords]]]
```

End private context

The End[] command closes the Begin[] and puts us back in the context Random
Walks`. Any symbols that were defined in the subcontext IPM3`RandomWalks`Private` can no longer be accessed.

```
In[20]:= End[]
```

```
Out[20]= IPM3`RandomWalks`Private`
```

EndPackage

The EndPackage[] command puts us back in the context we were in prior to the
BeginPackage[] command.

```
In[21]:= EndPackage[]
```

Examples

Starting with a new session, and making sure that the RandomWalks package is in a directory/folder where *Mathematica* can find it, this loads the package.

In[22]:= **Quit[]**

In[1]:= **<< IPM3`RandomWalks`**

Here is the usage message for the RandomWalk function.

In[2]:= **? RandomWalk**

RandomWalk[n] generates an n-step walk in two
    dimensions. The default behavior gives a lattice walk
    with steps in one of the four compass directions. The
    option LatticeWalk takes values True or False. The
    value of the option Dimensions can be any of 1, 2, or 3.

This gives a random walk of length 10 in two dimensions.

In[3]:= **RandomWalk[10, Dimension → 2]**

Out[3]= {{0, 0}, {0, -1}, {0, 0}, {0, -1}, {0, -2},
        {1, -2}, {1, -1}, {1, 0}, {1, -1}, {0, -1}, {0, -2}}

This shows a 250-step off-lattice random walk using the default of two dimensions.

In[4]:= **ShowWalk[RandomWalk[250, LatticeWalk → False]];**

A 500-step two-dimensional random walk with some graphics options.

In[5]:= **ShowWalk[RandomWalk[500], Frame → True];**

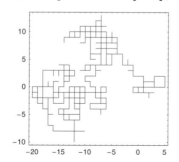

A 100 step off-lattice random walk in three dimensions.

In[6]:= **walk3 =**
     ShowWalk[RandomWalk[10^3, Dimension → 3, LatticeWalk → False]];

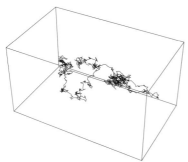

Using a transformation rule, it is straightforward to change the coordinates of each line to a gray point.

In[7]:= **Show[walk3 /. Line[x_] :> {GrayLevel[.5], Map[Point, x]}];**

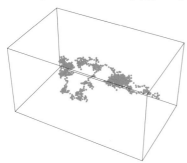

Finally, we should check that RandomWalk does the right thing when passed a bad argument.

In[8]:= **RandomWalk[-5]**

     RandomWalk::rwn : Argument -5 is not a positive integer.

Although we have omitted them here, several additional functions are available in the package IPM3`RandomWalks` for performing numerical analysis on random walks.

Exercises

1. This series of exercises will walk you through the creation of a package `Collatz.m`, a package of functions for performing various operations related to the Collatz problem that we investigated earlier (Exercise 5 of Section 5.3, Exercises 6 and 7 of Section 6.2, and Exercise 3 of Section 7.6). Recall that the Collatz function, for any integer n, returns $3n + 1$ for odd n, and $\frac{n}{2}$ for even n. The (as yet unproven) Collatz Conjecture is the statement that, for any initial positive integer n, the iterates of the Collatz function always reach the cycle 4, 2, 1,... . Start by creating an auxiliary function `collatz[n]` that returns $3n + 1$ for n odd and $n/2$ for n even.

2. Create the function `CollatzSequence[n]` that returns a list of the iterates of the auxiliary function `collatz[n]` from the previous exercise. Here is some sample output of the `CollatzSequence` function.

    In[1]:= `CollatzSequence[7]`

    Out[1]= `{7, 22, 11, 34, 17, 52, 26, 13, 40, 20, 10, 5, 16, 8, 4, 2, 1}`

    In[2]:= `CollatzSequence[111]`

    Out[2]= `{111, 334, 167, 502, 251, 754, 377, 1132, 566, 283, 850, 425,`
    `1276, 638, 319, 958, 479, 1438, 719, 2158, 1079, 3238,`
    `1619, 4858, 2429, 7288, 3644, 1822, 911, 2734, 1367, 4102,`
    `2051, 6154, 3077, 9232, 4616, 2308, 1154, 577, 1732, 866,`
    `433, 1300, 650, 325, 976, 488, 244, 122, 61, 184, 92, 46,`
    `23, 70, 35, 106, 53, 160, 80, 40, 20, 10, 5, 16, 8, 4, 2, 1}`

3. Create a usage message for `CollatzSequence` and warning messages for each of the following situations.
    a. `notint`: the argument to `CollatzSequence` is not a positive integer

    b. `argx`: `CollatzSequence` was called with the wrong number of arguments

4. Modify the definition of `CollatzSequence` that you created in Exercise 2 above so that it does some error trapping and issues the appropriate warning message that you created in Exercise 3.

5. Finally, put all the pieces together and write a package `CollatzSequence.m` that includes the appropriate `BeginPackage` and `Begin` statements, usage messages, warning messages, and function definitions. Put your package in a directory where *Mathematica* can find it on its search path and then test it to see that it returns correct output such as the examples below.

```
In[1]:= << IPM3`Collatz`
```

```
In[2]:= ? CollatzSequence
```

```
CollatzSequence[n] computes the sequence of
   Collatz iterates starting with initial value n. The
   sequence terminates as soon as it reaches the value 1.
```

```
In[3]:= CollatzSequence[37]
```

```
Out[3]= {37, 112, 56, 28, 14, 7, 22, 11, 34,
            17, 52, 26, 13, 40, 20, 10, 5, 16, 8, 4, 2, 1}
```

Here are various cases in which `CollatzSequence` is given bad input.

```
In[4]:= CollatzSequence[-5]
```

```
CollatzSequence::notint : First argument, -5,
      to CollatzSequence must be a positive integer.
```

```
In[5]:= CollatzSequence[4, 6]
```

```
CollatzSequence::argx :
  CollatzSequence called with 2 arguments;
      1 argument is expected. More…
```

```
Out[5]= CollatzSequence[4, 6]
```

Appendix A How expressions are evaluated

Evaluation of expressions

Evaluation takes place whenever an expression is entered. Here is the general procedure followed by *Mathematica* when evaluating an expression (with a few exceptions):

1. If the expression is a number or a string, it is left unchanged.

    In[1]:= **4.58425**

    Out[1]= 4.58425

2. If the expression is a symbol, it is rewritten if there is an applicable rewrite rule in the global rule base; otherwise, it is unchanged.

    In[2]:= **expr**

    Out[2]= expr

    In[3]:= **mysymbol**

    Out[3]= mysymbol

3. If the expression is not a number, string or symbol, its parts are evaluated in a specific order:

    - The head of the expression is evaluated.

    - The arguments of the expression are evaluated in order, except when the head is a symbol with a Hold attribute. In this case, some of its arguments are left in their unevaluated forms.

4. After the head and arguments of an expression are each completely evaluated, the expression consisting of the evaluated head and arguments is rewritten (after making any necessary changes to the arguments based on the Attributes of the head) if there is an applicable rewrite rule in the global rule base.

5. After carrying out the previous steps, the resulting expression is evaluated in the same way and then the result of that evaluation is evaluated, and so on until there are no more applicable rewrite rules.

The term rewriting process done in steps 2 and 4 above can be described as follows:

• pattern match parts of an expression and the left-hand side of a rewrite rule

• substitute the values which match labeled blanks in the pattern into the right-hand side of the rewrite rule and evaluate it

• replace the matched part of the expression with the evaluated result

Both built-in and user-defined rewrite rules are available for use in evaluation. When more than one rewrite rule is found to match an expression, the rule used for term rewriting is selected based on the following priority:

• user-defined rules are used before built-in rules

• more specific rules are used before more general rules

• one rule is more specific than another if its left-hand side matches fewer expressions; for example, the rule `f[0]:=...` is more specific than `f[_]:=....` This is discussed further in Section 5.3.

The evaluation process can be illustrated with a simple case. We first enter a simple rewrite rule into the global rule base.

In[4]:= `square[x_] := x`^{2}

If we now evaluate the following expression, the number 9 is returned as the result.

In[5]:= `square[3]`

Out[5]= 9

We can step through the details of the evaluation process that took place above.

1. The head, `square`, was evaluated first. The global rule base was searched for a rewrite rule whose left-hand side was the symbol `square`. No matching rewrite rule was found and so the symbol was left unchanged.

2. The argument 3 was evaluated. Since 3 is a number, it was left unchanged.

3. The expression `square[3]` was evaluated. The global rule base was searched for a rewrite rule whose left-hand side pattern matched `square[3]`. The pattern `square[3]` was found to match `square[x_]` and so the value of 3 was substi-

tuted for x in the right-hand side of the rewrite rule, Power [x, 2], to give Power [3, 2].

4. Power [3, 2] was then evaluated (by the same general procedure) to give 9.

5. The value 9 was evaluated. Since 9 is a number, it was left unchanged.

6. Since there were no more rules to use, the final value 9 was returned.

These steps can be seen in detail by using Trace with the TraceOriginal option set to True.

In[6]:= **Trace[square[3], TraceOriginal → True]**

Out[6]= {square[3], {square}, {3},
square[3], 3^2, {Power}, {3}, {2}, 3^2, 9}

Appendix B Debugging

Whenever you write programs, much of your time will be spent in *debugging* – figuring out why your program does not work. In this appendix, we offer a few tips on debugging, and also give some examples of common programming errors.

Tracing evaluation

In any programming language, the programmer will, at some point, be faced with an unexpected, and perhaps, mysterious result. You might be expecting one output, but an entirely different one is generated. Or your program may not run to completion and only give error or warning messages that are difficult to decipher. In such situations, you may find it helpful to take a peek at *Mathematica*'s evaluation process. This is most easily done with `Trace` and related functions. For example, using `Trace` on a simple arithmetic operation, you can see that *Mathematica*'s evaluator works from the inside out, following the order of operations for arithmetic.

```
In[1]:=  Trace[2 (3 + 4 (5 + 6))]
```
```
Out[1]=  {{{{5 + 6, 11}, 4 11, 44}, 3 + 44, 47}, 2 47, 94}
```

Similarly, tracing the evaluation of an `If` statement shows that only the first argument to the `If` function is evaluated initially; the `If` function itself returns no value, hence the `Null` at the end of the trace.

```
In[2]:=  Trace[If[4 > 9, Print["true"], Print["false"]]]
```
```
false
```
```
Out[2]=  {{4 > 9, False}, If[False, Print[true], Print[false]],
          Print[false], {MakeBoxes[false, StandardForm], "false"}, Null}
```

`Trace` and `TracePrint` can be especially useful when you know how to use their second argument. If the second argument is just a symbol, then only those parts of the trace that use rewrite rules for that symbol are shown. If it is a pattern, only those lines of the trace that match the pattern will be printed; an example of this was seen in Section 7.1. If the second argument is a transformation rule, then, when the pattern matches a line of the trace, the rule is applied before printing it.

For example, first we trace the evaluation of the Fibonacci function showing all expressions used in the evaluation.

```
In[3]:=  fib[0] := 0
         fib[1] := 1
         fib[n_] := fib[n - 2] + fib[n - 1]
```

```
In[6]:=  Trace[fib[3]]
```

```
Out[6]=  {fib[3], fib[3 - 2] + fib[3 - 1], {{3 - 2, 1}, fib[1], 1},
           {{3 - 1, 2}, fib[2], fib[2 - 2] + fib[2 - 1], {{2 - 2, 0}, fib[0], 0},
            {{2 - 1, 1}, fib[1], 1}, 0 + 1, 1}, 1 + 1, 2}
```

Most of this, you will agree, is not very interesting. We can confine it to only those parts that involve the applications of a fib rule by giving fib as the second argument to Trace.

```
In[7]:=  Trace[fib[3], fib]
```

```
Out[7]=  {fib[3], fib[3 - 2] + fib[3 - 1], {fib[1], 1},
           {fib[2], fib[2 - 2] + fib[2 - 1], {fib[0], 0}, {fib[1], 1}}}
```

Perhaps more useful here would be the pattern fib[_], which includes all lines in the original trace of the form fib[*expr*].

```
In[8]:=  TracePrint[fib[3], fib[_]]
```

```
fib[3]

  fib[3 - 2]

  fib[1]

  fib[3 - 1]

  fib[2]

    fib[2 - 2]

    fib[0]

    fib[2 - 1]

    fib[1]
```

```
Out[8]=  2
```

Using a transformation rule, we can show just the arguments of the various calls that are either `fib` applied to an integer, or the right-hand side of the recursive rule.

In[9]:= **TracePrint[fib[3], fib[n_Integer] → n]**

3

1

2

0

1

Out[9]= 2

Printing variables

The classic debugging method, used in all programming languages, is to insert `Print` statements in the body of a program to show where evaluation is occurring and what the values of variables are at that point. Keep in mind that if *expr* is any expression, the compound expression (`Print` [...] ; *expr*) has the same value as *expr*, so it is easy to insert `Print` statements without changing how the program works.

The most common use of `Print` is to show the values of a function's arguments. A rule f [x_] := *expr* can be changed to f [x_] := (`Print` [x]; *expr*) and it will print the value of the argument in each call.

In[10]:= **F[n_] := (Print[n]; F[n - 2] + F[n - 1]) /; n > 1**

In[11]:= **F[4]**

4

2

3

2

Out[11]= 2 F[0] + 3 F[1]

Reap and Sow

Another way of viewing intermediate results in a computation is to use `Reap` and `Sow`. The arguments to `Sow` will be collected by the nearest `Reap`.

For example, recall the simple procedural program we created in Chapter 5 for implementing Newton's method for root finding.

In[12]:= `f[x_] := x² - 50`

In[13]:= `a = 50;`

$$Do\left[a = N\left[a - \frac{f[a]}{f'[a]}\right], \{7\}\right]$$

At the end of the Do loop, the approximation to the root is in the symbol a.

In[15]:= `a`

Out[15]= `7.07107`

If we Sow a, and then Reap all the values that a took on during the loop, we can see the intermediate values.

In[16]:= `a = 50;`
`Reap[`

$$Do\left[Sow\left[a = N\left[a - \frac{f[a]}{f'[a]}\right]\right], \{7\}\right]$$

`][[2]]`

Out[17]= `{{25.5, 13.7304, 8.68597, 7.22119, 7.07263, 7.07107, 7.07107}}`

Common errors

Many of the errors you will see when programming are obvious. Here is one of the most common ones.

In[18]:= `Part[{x, y, z}, 4]`

`Part::partw :  Part 4 of {x, y, z} does not exist. More…`

Out[18]= `{x, y, z}[[4]]`

Here, you are attempting to extract a part of an expression that does not have that part; that is, trying to extract the fourth element of a list with only three elements.

Another thing you will often see is an entire expression returned instead of a value – sometimes the exact same expression you entered.

In[19]:= `y[n] := Table[i, {i, -n, n}]`

In[20]:= `y[10]`

Out[20]= `y[10]`

What is the problem? The n in the argument list for y is missing the blank. *Mathematica* sees the left-hand side as a pattern that matches the expression y[n] and nothing else – in particular, not y[10]. Of course, when there are no rules to apply to an expression, *Mathematica* is done – it does not even know there is an error!

Another very common case where this occurs is when you fail to supply enough arguments to a function.

```
In[21]:= Clear[f, x, y, r]
```

```
In[22]:= f[{x_, r___}, y_] := If[x < 0, {y, f[{r}]}, f[{r}]]
```

```
In[23]:= f[{}, _] := {}
```

```
In[24]:= f[{-5, 4, 17}, -1]
```

```
Out[24]= {-1, f[{4, 17}]}
```

Similarly, this error occurs when you supply too few arguments.

```
In[25]:= Clear[g]
```

```
In[26]:= g[{x_, r___}, y_] := If[x < 0, {y, g[r, y]}, g[r, y]]
```

```
In[27]:= g[{}, _] := {}
```

```
In[28]:= g[{-5, 4, 17, 12, 21}, -1]
```

```
Out[28]= {-1, g[4, 17, 12, 21, -1]}
```

In the first example, the recursive call to f had just one argument, and there were no rules for this case. In the second, we forgot to put the r in list braces in the recursive call, so g was called with all the elements of r as arguments, giving it too many arguments.

Another very common error is to get your program in a loop where it seems to go on forever. If this happens when you are working with recursive definitions, the chances are that your function is continually making recursive calls and not finishing them. In this case, you will reach *Mathematica*'s limit on the number of recursive calls it allows, which is stored in the variable $RecursionLimit.

```
In[29]:= h[x_] := h[x - 1] + h[x + 1]
```

```
In[30]:= h[0] := 0
```

In[31]:= **h[1]**

> $RecursionLimit::reclim :
> Recursion depth of 256 exceeded. More…
>
> General::stop :
> Further output of $RecursionLimit::reclim will
>   be suppressed during this calculation. More…

Out[31]= $Aborted

Another possibility is to get the same message, but for $IterationLimit, as we saw in Section 7.4.

In either case, *Mathematica* may not stop the computation, but instead continue to give this message. If this occurs, you will have to terminate the program from the keyboard, as described in Section 1.2. There are times when you may want to increase the recursion limit, which you can do by assigning a larger integer to $RecursionLimit, but usually if you exceed it you are in a loop.

When solving problems using iteration, you may go into a loop without doing recursive calls, in which case the program will just go on forever without printing any error messages, or may print an error message indicating that $IterationLimit is exceeded. One option is to terminate the program from the keyboard. You can increase the value of $IterationLimit, but only do that if you are sure there is no error.

References

ABBOTT, P. Finding roots in an interval. *The Mathematica Journal*, **7**(2)108–112, 1998.

BENTLEY, J. L. and FRIEDMAN, J. H. Algorithms for reporting and counting geometric intersections. Technical Report C-28, *IEEE Transactions on Computing*, 1979.

BURDEN, R. L. and FAIRES, J. D. *Numerical Analysis*. Pacific Grove, CA: Brooks/Cole Publishing Co., 7th edition, 2000.

CASTI, J. *Reality Rules I, Picturing the World in Mathematics – The Fundamentals*. New York: John Wiley & Sons, Inc., 1992.

CASTI, J. *Reality Rules II, Picturing the World in Mathematics – The Frontier*. New York: John Wiley & Sons, Inc., 1992.

CRANDALL, R. E. Personal communication, March 1993.

CRANDALL, R. E. *Projects in Scientific Computation*. Santa Clara: TELOS/Springer-Verlag, 1994.

CRANDALL, R. E. *Topics in Advanced Scientific Computation*. Santa Clara: TELOS/Springer-Verlag, 1996.

CRANDALL, R. E. and POMERANCE, C. *Prime Numbers: A Computational Perspective*. New York: Springer-Verlag, 2001

DE BERG, M., VAN KREVELD, M., OVERMARS, and M., SCHWARZKOPF, O. *Computational Geometry, Algorithms and Applications*. Heidelberg: Springer-Verlag, 2nd edition, 2000.

GARDNER, M. *Fractal Music, Hypercards and More…*. New York: W. H. Freeman and Company, 1992.

GAREY, M. and JOHNSON, D. *Computers and Intractability: A Guide to the Theory of NP-Completeness*. San Francisco: W. H. Freeman, 1979.

GAYLORD, R. and WELLIN, P. *Computer Simulations with Mathematica, Explorations in Complex Physical and Biological Systems*. Santa Clara: TELOS/Springer-Verlag, 1995.

GLYNN, J. and GRAY, T. *The Beginner's Guide to Mathematica*, Version 4. Cambridge University Press, 1999.

GOLIN, M. and SEDGEWICK, R. Analysis of a simple yet efficient convex hull algorithm. In *4th Annual Symposium on Computational Geometry*. ACM, 1988.

GOLUB, G. H. and VAN LOAN, C. F. *Matrix Computations*. Baltimore: Johns Hopkins University Press, 3rd edition, 1996.

GRAHAM, R. An efficient algorithm for determining the convex hull of a finite planar set. *Information Processing Letters*, **1**, 1972.

GRAHAM, R., KNUTH, D. E., and PATASHNIK, O. *Concrete Mathematics*. Reading: Addison-Wesley Publishing Company, 2nd edition, 1994.

GRAY, A. *Modern Differential Geometry of Curves and Surfaces with Mathematica*. Boca Raton: CRC Press, 2nd edition, 1997.

GRAY, T. and GLYNN, J. *Exploring Mathematics with Mathematica*. Redwood City: Addison-Wesley Publishing Company, 1992.

HAYES, A. Sums of cubes of digits, driven to abstraction. *Mathematica in Education* **1**(4) 3–11, 1992.

HIBBARD, A. and LEVASSEUR, K. *Exploring Abstract Algebra with Mathematica*. New York: Springer-Verlag, 1999.

HONSBERGER, R. *Mathematical Gems II*. The Dolciani Mathematical Expositions, Number Two. Providence: The Mathematical Association of America, 1976.

JARVIS, R. A. On the identification of the convex hull of a finite set of points in the plane. *Information Processing Letters*, **2**, 1973.

KNUTH, D. E. *The Art of Computer Programming, Volume 1, Fundamental Algorithms*. Reading: Addison-Wesley Publishing Company, 3rd edition, 1997.

KNUTH, D. E. *The Art of Computer Programming, Volume 2, Seminumerical Algorithms*. Reading: Addison-Wesley Publishing Company, 3rd edition, 1997.

KORHFAGE, R. R. *Discrete Computational Structures*. Orlando: Academic Press, Inc., 2nd edition, 1984.

LAGARIAS, J. The $3x + 1$ problem. *The American Mathematical Monthly*, **92** 3–23, 1985.

LAWLER, E., LENSTRA, J. K., RINNOOY KAN, A. H. G., and SHMOYS, D. B. *The Traveling Salesman Problem: A Guided Tour of Combinatorial Optimization*. New York: John Wiley & Sons, Inc., 1985.

LIN, S. Computer solutions of the traveling salesman problem. *Bell System Technical Journal*, **44** 2245–2269, 1965.

MCMAHON, T. A. and BONNER, J. T. *On Size and Life*. New York: Scientific American Books, Inc., 1983.

MAEDER, R. The design of the *Mathematica* programming language. *Dr. Dobbs Journal*, **17**(4) 86, 1992.

MAEDER, R. *The Mathematica Programmer*. Cambridge, MA: Academic Press, Inc., 1994.

MAEDER, R. *Programming in Mathematica*. Reading, MA: Addison-Wesley Publishing Company, 3rd edition, 1997.

MAEDER, R. *Computer Science with Mathematica: Theory and Practice for Science, Mathematics, and Engineering*. Cambridge University Press, 2000.

MANDELBROT, B. *The Fractal Geometry of Nature*. New York: W. H. Freeman and Company, 1988.

The Mathematica Journal. Wolfram Media, Champaign.

MATHEWS, M. V. *The Technology of Computer Music*. Cambridge, MA: MIT Press, 1969.

MIYAJI, C. and ABBOTT, P. *MathLink: Network Programming with Mathematica*. Cambridge University Press, 2001.

NIJENHUIS, A. and WILF, H. *Combinatorial Algorithms*. New York: Academic Press, Inc., 2nd edition, 1978.

O'ROURKE, J. *Computational Geometry in C*. Cambridge University Press, 2nd edition, 1998.

PEMMARAJU, S. and SKIENA, S. *Computational Discrete Mathematics: Combinatorics and Graph Theory with Mathematica*. Cambridge University Press, 2003.

PIERCE, J. R. *The Science of Musical Sound*. New York: W. H. Freeman & Company, 1983.

PLATZMAN, L. K. and BARTHOLDI, J. J. Spacefilling curves and the planar traveling salesman problem. *Journal Assoc. for Computing Machinery*, **36** 719–737, 1989.

POUNDSTONE, W. *The Recursive Universe: Cosmic Complexity and the Limits of Scientific Knowledge*. Oxford: Oxford University Press, 1985.

PREPARATA, F. P. and SHAMOS, M. I. *Computational Geometry: An Introduction*. New York: Springer-Verlag, 1985.

REINGOLD, E. M. and TILFORD, J. S. Tidier drawings of trees. *IEEE Trans. Software Eng*, **SE7** 223–228, 1981.

ROSENKRANTZ, D. J. and STEARNS, R. E. An analysis of several heuristics for the traveling salesman problem. *SIAM Journal of Computing*, **6** 563–581, 1977.

ROSSING, T. D. *The Science of Sound*. Reading: Addison-Wesley Publishing Company, 2nd edition, 1990.

RUST, B. and BURRUS, W. R. *Mathematical Programming and the Numerical Solution of Linear Equations*. New York: American Elsevier Publishing Co., 1972.

SEDGEWICK, R. *Algorithms*. Reading: Addison-Wesley Publishing Company, 1988.

SHAMOS, M. I. and HOEY, D. Closest-point problems. In *16th Annual Symposium on Foundations of Computer Science*. IEEE, 1975.

SHEPARD, R. The analysis of proximities: multidimensional scaling with an unknown distance factor. *Psychometrics*, **27** 125–140, 1962.

SKEEL, R. D. and KEIPER, J. B. *Elementary Numerical Computing with Mathematica*. New York: McGraw-Hill, Inc., 1993.

THOMSEN, D. E. Making music fractally. *Science News*, **117** 187, 1980.

TROTT, M. *The Mathematica Guidebook for Programming*. New York: Springer-Verlag, 2004.

TROTT, M. *The Mathematica Guidebook for Graphics*. New York: Springer-Verlag, 2004.

VOSS, R. F. and CLARKE, J. $1/f$ noise in music and speech. *Nature*, **258** 317–318, 1975.

Voss, R. F. and Clarke, J. 1/f noise in music and speech. *The Journal of the Acoustical Society of America*, **63** 258–263, 1978.

Wagon, S. *Mathematica in Action*. Santa Clara: TELOS/Springer-Verlag, 2nd edition, 1999.

Weiss, G. H. Random walks and their applications. *American Scientist*, **71** 65–71, 1983.

Wickham-Jones, T. *Computer Graphics with Mathematica*. Santa Clara: TELOS/Springer-Verlag, 1994.

Wolfram, S. *The Mathematica Book*. Wolfram Media, Inc., 5th edition, 2003.

Solutions to exercises

2 The *Mathematica* language

2.1 Expressions

1. The expression a (b+c) is given in full form as Times [a, Plus [b, c]].

2. This is simply $\frac{a}{b+c}$ as can be seen by evaluating the full form expression.

    In[1]:= **Times[a, Power[Plus[b, c], -1]]**

    Out[1]= $\dfrac{a}{b+c}$

3. Looking at the internal representation of this expression with FullForm helps to unwind the part specification.

    In[2]:= **FullForm[((x^2 + y) z / w)]**

    Out[2]//FullForm=
        Times[Power[w, -1], Plus[Power[x, 2], y], z]

    In[3]:= **((x^2 + y) z / w) [[2, 1, 2]]**

    Out[3]= 2

4. There are three terms in the expression, with the term b x being the second.

    In[4]:= **expr = a x^2 + b x + c;**

    In[5]:= **FullForm[expr]**

    Out[5]//FullForm=
        Plus[c, Times[b, x], Times[a, Power[x, 2]]]

    The b is the first element of Times [b, x], so the part specification is 2, 1.

    In[6]:= **expr[[2]]**

    Out[6]= b x

    In[7]:= **expr[[2, 1]]**

    Out[7]= b

2.2 Definitions

1. This exercise focuses on the difference between immediate and delayed assignments.

    a. This will generate a list of *n* random numbers.

    In[1]:= `randLis1[n_] := Table[Random[], {n}]`

    In[2]:= `? randLis1`

           Global`randLis1

           randLis1[n_] := Table[Random[], {n}]

    In[3]:= `randLis1[3]`

    Out[3]= `{0.0405431, 0.043554, 0.699358}`

    b. Since the definition for x is an immediate assignment, its value does not change in the body
         of `randLis2`. But each time `randLis2` is called, a new value is assigned to x.

    In[4]:= `randLis2[n_] := (x = Random[]; Table[x, {n}])`

    In[5]:= `? randLis2`

           Global`randLis2

           randLis2[n_] := (x = Random[]; Table[x, {n}])

    In[6]:= `randLis2[3]`

    Out[6]= `{0.651026, 0.651026, 0.651026}`

    c. Because the definition for x is a delayed assignment, the definition for `randLis3` is
         functionally equivalent to `randLis1`.

    In[7]:= `randLis3[n_] := (x := Random[]; Table[x, {n}])`

    In[8]:= `? randLis3`

           Global`randLis3

           randLis3[n_] := (x := Random[]; Table[x, {n}])

    In[9]:= `randLis3[3]`

    Out[9]= `{0.304574, 0.184163, 0.744351}`

    d. Recall that in an immediate assignment, the right-hand side of the definition is evaluated
         first. But in this case, n does not have a value, so `Table` is not able to evaluate properly.

```
In[10]:=  randLis4[n_] = Table[Random[], {n}]
```

Table::iterb : Iterator {n} does not have appropriate bounds. More…

```
Out[10]=  Table[Random[], {n}]
```

```
In[11]:=  ? randLis4
```

Global`randLis4

randLis4[n_] = Table[Random[], {n}]

2.3 Predicates and Boolean operations

1. There are several ways to define this function, using either the relational operator for less than, or with the absolute value function.

```
In[1]:=  f[x_] := -1 < x < 1
```

```
In[2]:=  f[x_] := Abs[x] < 1
```

```
In[3]:=  f[4]
```

```
Out[3]=  False
```

```
In[4]:=  f[-0.35]
```

```
Out[4]=  True
```

2. A number *n* can be considered a natural number if it is an integer and greater than or equal to zero.

```
In[5]:=  Positive[0]
```

```
Out[5]=  False
```

```
In[6]:=  NaturalQ[n_] := IntegerQ[n] && n ≥ 0
```

```
In[7]:=  NaturalQ[0]
```

```
Out[7]=  True
```

```
In[8]:=  NaturalQ[-4]
```

```
Out[8]=  False
```

3. The empty set is a subset of every set. So first we need a definition to cover this case.

```
In[9]:=  SubsetQ[{}, lis2_] := True
```

The intersection of `lis1` and `lis2` will be identical to `lis1` whenever `lis1` is a subset of `lis2`.

In[10]:= `SubsetQ[lis1_, lis2_] := Intersection[lis1, lis2] == lis1`

In[11]:= `A = {a, b, c};`
       `B = {a, b, c, d, e};`

In[13]:= `SubsetQ[A, B]`

Out[13]= `True`

We can also give a definition in terms of the subset character ⊂ which can be entered by typing ESC-sub-ESC or by using one of the palettes.

In[14]:= `lis1_ c lis2_ := Intersection[lis1, lis2] == lis1`

In[15]:= `A c B`

Out[15]= `True`

3 Lists

3.2 Creating and measuring lists

1. You can take every other element in the iterator list, or encode that in the function 2j.

In[1]:= `Table[j, {i, 0, 8, 2}, {j, 0, i, 2}]`

Out[1]= `{{0}, {0, 2}, {0, 2, 4}, {0, 2, 4, 6}, {0, 2, 4, 6, 8}}`

In[2]:= `Table[2 j, {i, 0, 4}, {j, 0, i}]`

Out[2]= `{{0}, {0, 2}, {0, 2, 4}, {0, 2, 4, 6}, {0, 2, 4, 6, 8}}`

2. This is probably the simplest way to generate random − 1s, 0s, and 1s.

In[3]:= `Table[Random[Integer, {-1, 1}], {10}]`

Out[3]= `{1, -1, 1, 1, 1, -1, 1, -1, -1, -1}`

3. Here are three ways to generate the list.

In[4]:= `Table[2 Random[Integer] - 1, {10}]`

Out[4]= `{1, -1, -1, 1, -1, -1, -1, -1, -1, -1}`

In[5]:= `Table[(-1)`$^{\text{Random[Integer]}}$`, {10}]`

Out[5]= `{1, -1, 1, 1, 1, 1, -1, 1, 1, 1}`

The following solution will become clearer in the next section after we have discussed the `Part` function in some detail.

In[6]:= `{1, -1}⟦Table[Random[Integer, {1, 2}], {10}]⟧`

Out[6]= `{1, -1, 1, 1, 1, -1, -1, -1, 1, -1}`

4. These lists can be generated with `Table`, using two iterators in the second example.

In[7]:= `Table[f[i], {i, 5}]`

Out[7]= `{f[1], f[2], f[3], f[4], f[5]}`

In[8]:= `Table[f[i, j], {i, 3}, {j, 4}]`

Out[8]= `{{f[1, 1], f[1, 2], f[1, 3], f[1, 4]},`
`{f[2, 1], f[2, 2], f[2, 3], f[2, 4]}, {f[3, 1], f[3, 2], f[3, 3], f[3, 4]}}`

5. From the top level, there are two lists, each consisting of two sublists, each sublist consisting of two elements.

In[9]:= `Dimensions[{{{1, a}, {4, d}}, {{2, b}, {3, c}}}]`

Out[9]= `{2, 2, 2}`

3.3 Manipulating lists

1. The `Position` function tells us that the 9s are located in the second sublist, first position, and in the fourth sublist, third position.

In[1]:= `Position[{{2, 1, 10}, {9, 5, 7}, {2, 10, 4}, {10, 1, 9}, {6, 1, 6}}, 9]`

Out[1]= `{{2, 1}, {4, 3}}`

2. This is a straightforward use of the `Transpose` function.

In[2]:= `Transpose[{{x1, y1}, {x2, y2}, {x3, y3}, {x4, y4}, {x5, y5}}]`

Out[2]= `{{x1, x2, x3, x4, x5}, {y1, y2, y3, y4, y5}}`

3. Here is one way to do it. First create a list representing the directions.

In[3]:= `NSEW = {{0, 1}, {0, -1}, {1, 0}, {-1, 0}};`

In[4]:= `Table[NSEW[Random[Integer, {1, 4}]], {10}]`

Out[4]= `{{1, 0}, {0, -1}, {0, -1}, {0, 1},`
`{1, 0}, {1, 0}, {0, -1}, {-1, 0}, {0, 1}, {1, 0}}`

4. We first drop the first element in the list, then create a nested list of every other element in the remaining list, and finally unnest the resulting list.

In[5]:= `Rest[{a, b, c, d, e, f, g}]`

Out[5]= `{b, c, d, e, f, g}`

In[6]:= `Partition[%, 1, 2]`

Out[6]= `{{b}, {d}, {f}}`

In[7]:= `Flatten[%]`

Out[7]= `{b, d, f}`

5.

In[8]:= `{a, b, c, d}[[{3, 2, 4, 1}]]`

Out[8]= `{c, b, d, a}`

6.

In[9]:= `Transpose[{{3, 2, 4, 1}, {a, b, c, d}}]`

Out[9]= `{{3, a}, {2, b}, {4, c}, {1, d}}`

In[10]:= `Sort[%]`

Out[10]= `{{1, d}, {2, b}, {3, a}, {4, c}}`

In[11]:= `Transpose[%]`

Out[11]= `{{1, 2, 3, 4}, {d, b, a, c}}`

In[12]:= `%[[2]]`

Out[12]= `{d, b, a, c}`

3.4 Working with several lists

1. `Join` expects lists as arguments.

In[1]:= `Join[{z}, {x, y}]`

Out[1]= `{z, x, y}`

2. The trick here is partitioning the joined list so that you get every other element.

    In[2]:= `expr = Join[{1, 2, 3, 4}, {a, b, c, d}]`

    Out[2]= `{1, 2, 3, 4, a, b, c, d}`

    In[3]:= `Rest[expr]`

    Out[3]= `{2, 3, 4, a, b, c, d}`

    In[4]:= `Partition[%, 1, 2]`

    Out[4]= `{{2}, {4}, {b}, {d}}`

    In[5]:= `Flatten[%]`

    Out[5]= `{2, 4, b, d}`

    This can also be done using the `Take` function.

    In[6]:= `Take[expr, {2, Length[expr], 2}]`

    Out[6]= `{2, 4, b, d}`

3. This is another way of asking for all those elements that are in the union but not the intersection of the two sets.

    In[7]:= `A = {a, b, c, d};`
    `B = {a, b, e, f};`

    In[9]:= `Complement[A⋃B, A⋂B]`

    Out[9]= `{c, d, e, f}`

    In[10]:= `Complement[Union[A, B], Intersection[A, B]]`

    Out[10]= `{c, d, e, f}`

3.5 Strings and characters

1. Here is a test string we will use for this exercise.

    In[1]:= `str = "this is a test string"`

    Out[1]= `this is a test string`

    This extracts the first character from `str`.

    In[2]:= `StringTake[str, 1]`

    Out[2]= `t`

Here is its character code.

In[3]:= `ToCharacterCode[%]`

Out[3]= {116}

For each lowercase letter of the English alphabet, subtracting 32 gives the corresponding uppercase character.

In[4]:= `% - 32`

Out[4]= {84}

Convert back to a character.

In[5]:= `FromCharacterCode[%]`

Out[5]= T

Take the original string minus its first character.

In[6]:= `StringDrop[str, 1]`

Out[6]= his is a test string

Finally, join the previous string with the capital T.

In[7]:= `StringJoin[%%, %]`

Out[7]= This is a test string

2. We first need to extract the character codes from this string.

In[8]:= `numstr = "73"`

Out[8]= 73

In[9]:= `ToCharacterCode[numstr] [[1]]`

Out[9]= 55

In[10]:= `10 (% - 48)`

Out[10]= 70

In[11]:= `ToCharacterCode[numstr] [[2]]`

Out[11]= 51

In[12]:= `% - 48`

Out[12]= 3

In[13]:= % + %%%

Out[13]= 73

Here it is all put together in one line.

In[14]:= 10 (ToCharacterCode[numstr] [[1]] - 48) + (ToCharacterCode[numstr] [[2]] - 48)

Out[14]= 73

There is a built-in function for this task, ToExpression. See the next exercise for details.

3.

In[15]:= numb = ToCharacterCode["73"]

Out[15]= {55, 51}

In[16]:= numb - 48

Out[16]= {7, 3}

In[17]:= 8 Part[%, 1] + Part[%, 2]

Out[17]= 59

Here is another approach that converts the single characters into regular expressions and then operates on those directly.

In[18]:= ToExpression[Characters["73"]]

Out[18]= {7, 3}

In[19]:= 8 First[%] + Last[%]

Out[19]= 59

4. One approach converts the string to character codes.

In[20]:= ToCharacterCode["10495"]

Out[20]= {49, 48, 52, 57, 53}

In[21]:= % - 48

Out[21]= {1, 0, 4, 9, 5}

In[22]:= Reverse[Table[10^j, {j, 0, 4}]]

Out[22]= {10000, 1000, 100, 10, 1}

In[23]:= **%.%%**

Out[23]= 10495

A direct approach uses ToExpression.

In[24]:= **ToExpression["10495"]**

Out[24]= 10495

5. First, consider the character code of a string.

In[25]:= **ToCharacterCode["best"]**

Out[25]= {98, 101, 115, 116}

Then we need only know if this list of codes is in order.

In[26]:= **OrderedQ[%]**

Out[26]= True

So here is our Boolean function OrderedWordQ.

In[27]:= **OrderedWordQ[w_String] := OrderedQ[ToCharacterCode[w]]**

Now we will find all the words in the dictionary file that comes with *Mathematica* that are ordered in this way. First we generate a platform-independent path to the dictionary file.

In[28]:= **wordfile = ToFileName[{$InstallationDirectory, "Documentation",
          "English", "Demos", "DataFiles"}, "dictionary.dat"]**

Out[28]= C:\Program Files\Wolfram Research\Mathematica\5
          .1\Documentation\English\Demos\DataFiles\dictionary.dat

Then we read the file using ReadList, specifying the type of data we are reading in as a Word.

In[29]:= **words = ReadList[wordfile, Word];**

Finally, we select those elements from the list words that pass the OrderedWordQ test.

In[30]:= **Select[words, OrderedWordQ] // Shallow**

Out[30]//Shallow=
          {a, AAA, AAAS, abbe, abbey, abbot, Abbott, abc, Abe, Abel, ≪565≫}

6. Here is the function that checks if a string is a palindrome.

In[31]:= **PalindromeQ[str_String] := StringReverse[str] == str**

In[32]:= `PalindromeQ["mood"]`

Out[32]= False

In[33]:= `PalindromeQ["PoP"]`

Out[33]= True

In[34]:= `PalindromeQ[num_Integer] := PalindromeQ[ToString[num]]`

In[35]:= `PalindromeQ[12522521]`

Out[35]= True

Create a path to the file `dictionary.dat`.

In[36]:= `dictfile = ToFileName[{$BaseDirectory,`
`        "Applications", "IPM3", "DataFiles"}, "dictionary.dat"]`

Out[36]= C:\Documents and Settings\All Users\Application Data\
Mathematica\Applications\IPM3\DataFiles\dictionary.dat

Import the file.

In[37]:= `words = Import[dictfile, "Words"];`

In[38]:= `Select[words, PalindromeQ]`

Out[38]= {a, AAA, ABA, ala, AMA, ana, b, bib, bob, bub, c, CDC, civic, d, dad, deed,
did, DOD, dud, e, eke, ere, eve, ewe, eye, f, g, gag, gig, gog, h, huh, i,
ii, iii, j, k, l, level, m, madam, minim, mum, n, non, noon, nun, o, p, pap,
PDP, peep, pep, pip, poop, pop, pup, q, r, radar, refer, rever, rotor, s,
sis, s's, t, tat, teet, tenet, tit, TNT, toot, tot, u, v, w, wow, x, y, z}

4 Functional programming

4.2 Functions for manipulating expressions

1. Here is a sample set of pairs of numbers.

In[1]:= `data = {{1, 2}, {2, 3}, {3, 4}, {4, 5}, {5, 6}};`

The `pairSum` function can be written simply as:

In[2]:= `addPair[{x_, y_}] := x + y`

Finally we map `pairSum` across data.

In[3]:= **Map[addPair, data]**

Out[3]= {3, 5, 7, 9, 11}

2. Here is a sample set of pairs of numbers.

    In[4]:= **data = {{1, 2}, {2, 3}, {3, 4}, {4, 5}, {5, 6}};**

    Since `Apply` normally works at level 0, we need to give it a third argument to get it to apply `Plus` at level 1.

    In[5]:= **Apply[Plus, data, {1}]**

    Out[5]= {3, 5, 7, 9, 11}

3. First you need to transpose the matrix and then reverse the pairs.

    In[6]:= **lis = {{1, 2, 3}, {4, 5, 6}}**

    Out[6]= {{1, 2, 3}, {4, 5, 6}}

    In[7]:= **Transpose[lis]**

    Out[7]= {{1, 4}, {2, 5}, {3, 6}}

    In[8]:= **Map[Reverse, %]**

    Out[8]= {{4, 1}, {5, 2}, {6, 3}}

    This can also be accomplished using `Thread`.

    In[9]:= **Map[Reverse, Thread[lis]]**

    Out[9]= {{4, 1}, {5, 2}, {6, 3}}

4. This can be done either in two steps, or by using the `Inner` function.

    In[10]:= **Transpose[{{1, 2}, {3, 4}}] {x, y}**

    Out[10]= {{x, 3 x}, {2 y, 4 y}}

    In[11]:= **Apply[Plus, %]**

    Out[11]= {x + 2 y, 3 x + 4 y}

    In[12]:= **Inner[Times, {{1, 2}, {3, 4}}, {x, y}, Plus]**

    Out[12]= {x + 2 y, 3 x + 4 y}

5. To get down to the second level of nested lists, you have to use a second argument to `Apply`.

```
In[13]:=  facs = FactorInteger[3628800]

Out[13]=  {{2, 8}, {3, 4}, {5, 2}, {7, 1}}
```

```
In[14]:=  Apply[Power, facs, 2]

Out[14]=  {256, 81, 25, 7}
```

One more use of `Apply` is needed to multiply these terms.

```
In[15]:=  Apply[Times, %]

Out[15]=  3628800
```

Here is a function that puts this all together.

```
In[16]:=  ExpandFactors[lis_] := Apply[Times, Apply[Power, lis, 2]]
```

```
In[17]:=  FactorInteger[295232799039604140847618609643520000000]

Out[17]=  {{2, 32}, {3, 15}, {5, 7}, {7, 4}, {11, 3},
           {13, 2}, {17, 2}, {19, 1}, {23, 1}, {29, 1}, {31, 1}}
```

```
In[18]:=  ExpandFactors[%]

Out[18]=  295232799039604140847618609643520000000
```

Another approach would be to use `Transpose` to separate the bases from their exponents, then use `MapThread` to raise each base to the corresponding exponent.

```
In[19]:=  Transpose[facs]

Out[19]=  {{2, 3, 5, 7}, {8, 4, 2, 1}}
```

```
In[20]:=  MapThread[Power, %]

Out[20]=  {256, 81, 25, 7}
```

Finally, apply `Times` to the list.

```
In[21]:=  Apply[Times, %]

Out[21]=  3628800
```

```
In[22]:=  ExpandFactors2[lis_] := Apply[Times, MapThread[Power, Transpose[lis]]]
```

6. Here is a factorization we can use to work through this problem.

```
In[23]:=  facs = FactorInteger[10!]

Out[23]=  {{2, 8}, {3, 4}, {5, 2}, {7, 1}}
```

First we extract the prime bases and their exponents.

In[24]:= **bases = Transpose[facs][[1]]**

Out[24]= {2, 3, 5, 7}

In[25]:= **exponents = Transpose[facs][[2]]**

Out[25]= {8, 4, 2, 1}

Here then is the inner product, threading Power over the lists and then multiplying the resulting terms with Times.

In[26]:= **Inner[Power, bases, exponents, Times]**

Out[26]= 3628800

Here is a function that combines these steps.

In[27]:= **ExpandFactors3[lis_] := Module[{facs = Transpose[lis]},**
    Inner[Power, facs[[1]], facs[[2]], Times]]

In[28]:= **ExpandFactors3[facs]**

Out[28]= 3628800

7. If we first look at a symbolic result, we should be able to see how to construct our function. For three vectors and three variables, here is the divergence (think of d as the derivative operator).

In[29]:= **Inner[d, {e1, e2, e3}, {v1, v2, v3}, Plus]**

Out[29]= d[e1, v1] + d[e2, v2] + d[e3, v3]

So for arbitrary-length vectors and variables, we have:

In[30]:= **div[vecs_, vars_] := Inner[D, vecs, vars, Plus]**

As a check, we can compute the divergence of the standard gravitational or electric force field, which should be 0.

In[31]:= **div$\left[\{x, y, z\} / (x^2 + y^2 + z^2)^{3/2}, \{x, y, z\}\right]$**

Out[31]= $-\dfrac{3\,x^2}{(x^2 + y^2 + z^2)^{5/2}} - \dfrac{3\,y^2}{(x^2 + y^2 + z^2)^{5/2}} - \dfrac{3\,z^2}{(x^2 + y^2 + z^2)^{5/2}} + \dfrac{3}{(x^2 + y^2 + z^2)^{3/2}}$

In[32]:= **Simplify[%]**

Out[32]= 0

Finally, we should note that this definition of divergence is a bit delicate as we are doing no argument checking at this point. For example, it would be sensible to insure that the length of the vector list is the same as the length of the variable list before starting the computation. The reader should refer to Chapter 6 for a discussion of how to use pattern matching to deal with this issue.

4.3 Iterating functions

1. First we generate the step directions.

```
In[1]:= Table[(-1)^Random[Integer], {10}]
```

```
Out[1]= {1, 1, 1, -1, -1, -1, 1, -1, 1, 1}
```

Then, starting at 0, the fold operation generates the locations.

```
In[2]:= FoldList[Plus, 0, %]
```

```
Out[2]= {0, 1, 2, 3, 2, 1, 0, 1, 0, 1, 2}
```

2. We can use the method of generating a list of step locations that was shown in an earlier exercise.

```
In[3]:= {{1, 0}, {-1, 0}, {0, 1}, {0, -1}}[[Table[Random[Integer, {1, 4}], {10}]]]
```

```
Out[3]= {{0, -1}, {1, 0}, {0, 1}, {0, -1},
          {0, 1}, {0, 1}, {0, 1}, {0, -1}, {-1, 0}, {-1, 0}}
```

```
In[4]:= FoldList[Plus, {0, 0}, %]
```

```
Out[4]= {{0, 0}, {0, -1}, {1, -1}, {1, 0}, {1, -1},
          {1, 0}, {1, 1}, {1, 2}, {1, 1}, {0, 1}, {-1, 1}}
```

3. Starting with 1, we want to fold the Times functions across the first *n* integers.

```
In[5]:= fac[n_] := Fold[Times, 1, Range[n]]
```

```
In[6]:= fac[10]
```

```
Out[6]= 3628800
```

4.4 Programs as functions

1. The obvious way to do this is to take the list and simply pick out elements at random locations. *Note*: the right-most location in the list is given by Length [*lis*] , using the built-in Part and Random functions.

```
In[1]:= chooseWithReplacement[lis_, n_] :=
          lis[[Table[Random[Integer, {1, Length[lis]}], {n}]]]
```

```
In[2]:= chooseWithReplacement[{a, b, c, d, e, f, g, h}, 3]
```

```
Out[2]= {f, e, c}
```

2. Here is our user-defined `stringInsert`.

```
In[3]:= stringInsert[str1_, str2_, pos_] :=
          FromCharacterCode[Join[Take[ToCharacterCode[str1], pos - 1],
            ToCharacterCode[str2], Drop[ToCharacterCode[str1], pos - 1]]]
```

```
In[4]:= stringInsert["Joy world", "to the ", 5]
```

```
Out[4]= Joy to the world
```

```
In[5]:= stringDrop[str_, pos_] :=
          FromCharacterCode[Drop[ToCharacterCode[str], pos]]
```

3. There are many ways of defining this function. Here we take advantage of the fact that if p and q are each lists of two numbers, then p-q will subtract element-wise.

```
In[6]:= distance[pt1_, pt2_] := √ Apply[Plus, (pt1 - pt2)²]
```

```
In[7]:= distance[{2, 5}, {6, 8}]
```

```
Out[7]= 5
```

4. We assume that `lis1` is longer than `lis2` and pair off the corresponding elements in the lists and then tack on the leftover elements from `lis1`.

```
In[8]:= interLeave2[lis1_, lis2_] :=
          Flatten[Join[Transpose[{lis2, Take[lis1, Length[lis2]]}],
            Take[lis1, Length[lis2] - Length[lis1]]]]
```

```
In[9]:= interLeave2[{a, b, c, d}, {1, 2, 3}]
```

```
Out[9]= {1, a, 2, b, 3, c, d}
```

5. After creating the card deck, we cut it in half and interleave the two halves.

```
In[10]:= cardDeck =
           Flatten[Outer[List, {♣, ♦, ♡, ♠}, Join[Range[2, 10], {J, Q, K, A}]], 1];
```

```
In[11]:= Flatten[Transpose[Partition[cardDeck, 26]], 1]
```

```
Out[11]= {{♣, 2}, {♡, 2}, {♣, 3}, {♡, 3}, {♣, 4}, {♡, 4}, {♣, 5}, {♡, 5}, {♣, 6},
          {♡, 6}, {♣, 7}, {♡, 7}, {♣, 8}, {♡, 8}, {♣, 9}, {♡, 9}, {♣, 10},
          {♡, 10}, {♣, J}, {♡, J}, {♣, Q}, {♡, Q}, {♣, K}, {♡, K}, {♣, A}, {♡, A},
          {♦, 2}, {♠, 2}, {♦, 3}, {♠, 3}, {♦, 4}, {♠, 4}, {♦, 5}, {♠, 5}, {♦, 6},
          {♠, 6}, {♦, 7}, {♠, 7}, {♦, 8}, {♠, 8}, {♦, 9}, {♠, 9}, {♦, 10},
          {♠, 10}, {♦, J}, {♠, J}, {♦, Q}, {♠, Q}, {♦, K}, {♠, K}, {♦, A}, {♠, A}}
```

6. First, here is how we might write our own `StringJoin`.

```
In[12]:= FromCharacterCode[
            Join[ToCharacterCode["To be, "], ToCharacterCode["or not to be"]]]

Out[12]= To be, or not to be
```

And here is a how we might implement a `StringReverse`.

```
In[13]:= FromCharacterCode[Reverse[ToCharacterCode[%]]]

Out[13]= eb ot ton ro ,eb oT
```

4.5 Auxiliary functions

1. In the first definition, we only use one auxiliary function inside the `Module`.

```
In[1]:= latticeWalk1[n_] := Module[{steps},
           steps[m_] := {{1, 0}, {-1, 0}, {0, 1}, {0, -1}}[[
             Table[Random[Integer, {1, 4}], {m}]]]; FoldList[Plus, {0, 0}, steps[n]]]

In[2]:= latticeWalk1[10]

Out[2]= {{0, 0}, {0, 1}, {0, 0}, {-1, 0}, {-1, 1},
         {0, 1}, {1, 1}, {2, 1}, {1, 1}, {0, 1}, {0, 0}}
```

Here we use two auxiliary functions, making the code a bit easier to read.

```
In[3]:= latticeWalk2[n_] :=
          Module[{choices, steps}, choices = {{1, 0}, {-1, 0}, {0, 1}, {0, -1}};
           steps[m_] := choices[[Table[Random[Integer, {1, 4}], {m}]]];
           FoldList[Plus, {0, 0}, steps[n]]]

In[4]:= latticeWalk2[10]

Out[4]= {{0, 0}, {0, 1}, {1, 1}, {2, 1}, {3, 1},
         {4, 1}, {5, 1}, {4, 1}, {5, 1}, {5, 2}, {4, 2}}
```

2. The following function creates a local function `perfectQ` using the `Module` construct. It then checks every other number between *n* and *m* by using a third argument to the `Range` function.

```
In[5]:= PerfectSearch[n_, m_] := Module[{perfectQ},
           perfectQ[j_] := Apply[Plus, Divisors[j]] == 2 j;
           Select[Range[n, m, 2], perfectQ]]

In[6]:= PerfectSearch[2, 1000]

Out[6]= {6, 28, 496}
```

This function does not guard against the user supplying "bad" inputs. For example, if the user starts with an odd number, then this version of PerfectSearch will check every other odd number, and, since it is known that there are no odd numbers below at least 10^{300}, none is reported.

In[7]:= **PerfectSearch[1, 1000]**

Out[7]= {}

You can fix this situation by using the (as yet unproved) assumption that there are *no* odd perfect numbers. This next version first checks that the first argument is an even number.

In[8]:= **Clear[PerfectSearch]**

In[9]:= **PerfectSearch[n_ ? EvenQ, m_] := Module[{perfectQ},**
          perfectQ[j_] := Apply[Plus, Divisors[j]] == 2 j;
          Select[Range[n, m, 2], perfectQ]]

Now, the function only works if the first argument is even.

In[10]:= **PerfectSearch[2, 1000]**

Out[10]= {6, 28, 496}

In[11]:= **PerfectSearch[1, 1000]**

Out[11]= PerfectSearch[1, 1000]

3. This only requires a slight change to the code from the PerfectSearch function from the previous exercise.

In[12]:= **PerfectSearch[n_ , m_ , 3] := Module[{perfectQ},**
           perfectQ[j_] := Apply[Plus, Divisors[j]] == 3 j;
           Select[Range[n, m], perfectQ]]

It appears as if there are only three 3-perfect numbers below 10^6.

In[13]:= **PerfectSearch[1, 10^6, 3]**

Out[13]= {120, 672, 523776}

4. Again, this function only requires a slight modification from that for the PerfectSearch function above.

In[14]:= **PerfectSearch[n_ , m_ , 4] := Module[{perfectQ},**
           perfectQ[j_] := Apply[Plus, Divisors[j]] == 4 j;
           Select[Range[n, m], perfectQ]]

The following computation can be quite time consuming and requires a fair amount of memory to run to completion. If your computer's resources are limited, you should split up the search intervals into smaller units.

```
In[15]:=  PerfectSearch[1, 2200000, 4] // Timing

Out[15]=  {54.769 Second, {30240, 32760, 2178540}}
```

5. This function requires a third argument.

```
In[16]:=  Clear[PerfectSearch];
          PerfectSearch[n_, m_, k_] := Module[{perfectQ},
            perfectQ[j_] := Apply[Plus, Divisors[j]] == k j;
            Select[Range[n, m], perfectQ]]

In[18]:=  PerfectSearch[1, 100, 2]

Out[18]=  {6, 28}
```

6. This function will require two auxiliary functions, the function σ and a predicate to determine whether a number is super-perfect.

```
In[19]:=  SuperPerfectSearch[a_, b_] := Module[{sigma, superQ},
            sigma[n_] := Apply[Plus, Divisors[n]];
            superQ[n_] := Nest[sigma, n, 2] == 2 n;
            Select[Range[a, b], superQ]]
```

Here, then, are all super-perfect numbers less than 100,000.

```
In[20]:=  SuperPerfectSearch[1, 100000]

Out[20]=  {2, 4, 16, 64, 4096, 65536}
```

7. Many implementations are possible for convertToDate. We show here a version that uses string manipulation. First we extract the digits from the 8-digit number.

```
In[21]:=  d = IntegerDigits[20030515]

Out[21]=  {2, 0, 0, 3, 0, 5, 1, 5}
```

The first four digits give us the year.

```
In[22]:=  d[[Range[4]]]

Out[22]=  {2, 0, 0, 3}
```

Here is a function that takes a list of digits, converts them to strings, concatenates them into one string, and then converts that into a number.

```
In[23]:=  convert[str_] := ToExpression[StringJoin[Map[ToString, str]]]

In[24]:=  convert[d[[Range[4]]]]

Out[24]=  2003
```

In[25]:= `Head[%]`

Out[25]= `Integer`

Using `convert`, here are the auxiliary functions to extract the year, month, and day as numbers.

In[26]:= `year[str_] := convert[str[[Range[4]]]]`

In[27]:= `year[d]`

Out[27]= `2003`

In[28]:= `month[str_] := convert[str[[{5, 6}]]]`

In[29]:= `month[d]`

Out[29]= `5`

In[30]:= `day[str_] := convert[str[[{7, 8}]]]`

In[31]:= `day[d]`

Out[31]= `15`

And here are all the pieces put together in the function `convertToDate`.

In[32]:=
```
convertToDate[n_] := Module[{d, convert, year, month, day},
    d = IntegerDigits[n];
    convert[st_] := ToExpression[StringJoin[Map[ToString, st]]];
    year[st_] := convert[st[[Range[4]]]];
    month[st_] := convert[st[[{5, 6}]]];
    day[st_] := convert[st[[{7, 8}]]];
    {year[d], month[d], day[d]}]
```

In[33]:= `convertToDate[20030515]`

Out[33]= `{2003, 5, 15}`

4.6 Pure functions

1. This function adds the squares of the elements in `lis`.

In[1]:= `elementsSquared[lis_] := Apply[Plus, lis`^{2}`]`

In[2]:= `elementsSquared[{3, 29, 2, 17}]`

Out[2]= `1143`

Using a pure function, this becomes:

In[3]:= `Function[lis, Apply[Plus, lis²]][{3, 29, 2, 17}]`

Out[3]= `1143`

or simply,

In[4]:= `Apply[Plus, #²] & [{3, 29, 2, 17}]`

Out[4]= `1143`

2. Here is the function that sums the digits of any integer.

In[5]:= `sumdigits[x_Integer] := Apply[Plus, IntegerDigits[x]]`

In[6]:= `sumdigits[629]`

Out[6]= `17`

Using a pure function, this becomes:

In[7]:= `Function[x, Apply[Plus, IntegerDigits[x]]][629]`

Out[7]= `17`

In[8]:= `Apply[Plus, IntegerDigits[#]] & [629]`

Out[8]= `17`

3. First, here is the distance function.

In[9]:= `distance[pt1_, pt2_] := √Apply[Plus, (pt1 - pt2)²]`

Here are some sample points.

In[10]:= `points = Table[Random[], {5}, {2}]`

Out[10]= `{{0.408123, 0.110529}, {0.640705, 0.227085},`
`{0.605818, 0.074615}, {0.868053, 0.302804}, {0.381267, 0.66605}}`

Just as a check, this computes the distance between the first and second points in our list.

In[11]:= `distance[points[[1]], points[[2]]]`

Out[11]= `0.260153`

Now we need the distance between every pair of points. So we first create the set of pairs.

In[12]:= `pairs = Distribute[{points, points}, List];`

Then we apply the `distance` function and take the `Max`.

```
In[13]:= Max[Apply[distance, pairs, {1}]]
```

```
Out[13]= 0.632628
```

This puts it all together using a pure function in place of the distance function. Since the `diameter` function operates on lists of pairs of numbers, we need to specify them in our pure function by means of #1 and #2.

```
In[14]:= diameter[lis_] :=
            Max[Apply[Sqrt[Apply[Plus, (#1 - #2) ^2]] &,
              Distribute[{lis, lis}, List], {1}]]
```

```
In[15]:= diameter[points]
```

```
Out[15]= 0.632628
```

As a final note, this function is not as efficient as it could be since it computes the distance from every point to itself, as well as computing both the distance from point *a* to point *b* and from point *b* to point *a*, for every pair of points *a* and *b*. In other words, for *n* points, we are computing n^2 distances when we only need to compute $\binom{n}{2}$ distances, highly sub-optimal. We leave the optimization of this function as an exercise to the reader.

4. Using pure functions, `removeRand` becomes:

```
In[16]:= Function[lis, Delete[lis, Random[Integer, {1, Length[lis]}]]][
            {a, b, c, d, e}]
```

```
Out[16]= {a, b, c, e}
```

```
In[17]:= Delete[#1, Random[Integer, {1, Length[#]}]] &[{a, b, c, d, e}]
```

```
Out[17]= {a, c, d, e}
```

5. Here is the `deal` function written using a pure function in place of `removeRand`.

```
In[18]:= deal[n_] := Module[{cardDeck}, cardDeck =
            Flatten[Outer[List, {♣, ◇, ♡, ♠}, Join[Range[2, 10], {J, Q, K, A}]], 1];
          Complement[cardDeck,
            Nest[Delete[#1, Random[Integer, {1, Length[#1]}]] &, cardDeck, n]]]
```

```
In[19]:= deal[5]
```

```
Out[19]= {{♣, A}, {♡, 2}, {♡, 9}, {♠, 2}, {♠, 5}}
```

6. This function is ideally written as an iteration.

```
In[20]:= RepUnit[n_] := Nest[(10 # + 1) &, 1, n - 1]
```

In[21]:= `RepUnit[7]`

Out[21]= `1111111`

In[22]:= `Map[RepUnit[#] &, Range[12]]`

Out[22]= `{1, 11, 111, 1111, 11111, 111111, 1111111, 11111111,`
           `111111111, 1111111111, 11111111111, 111111111111}`

7. Notice that it is not necessary to use the Module function here because the only expressions on the right-hand side of the function definition are pure functions, built-in functions, and the names of the arguments of the function.

In[23]:= `chooseWithoutReplacement[lis_, n_] := Complement[lis,`
           `    Nest[Delete[#1, Random[Integer, {1, Length[#1]}]] &, lis, n]]`

In[24]:= `chooseWithoutReplacement[{a, b, c, d, e}, 4]`

Out[24]= `{a, c, d, e}`

8. Using the list of the step increments in the north, south, east, and west directions, this ten-step walk starts at the origin.

In[25]:= `NestList[#1 + {{1, 0}, {-1, 0}, {0, 1}, {0, -1}}[[Random[Integer, {1, 4}]]] &,`
           `{0, 0}, 10]`

Out[25]= `{{0, 0}, {1, 0}, {1, 1}, {1, 0}, {0, 0},`
           `    {-1, 0}, {-2, 0}, {-3, 0}, {-4, 0}, {-4, 1}, {-4, 2}}`

9. Here is the path to the dictionary file.

In[26]:= `dictfile = ToFileName[{$InstallationDirectory, "Documentation",`
           `    "English", "Demos", "DataFiles"}, "dictionary.dat"]`

Out[26]= `C:\Program Files\Wolfram Research\Mathematica\5`
           `    .1\Documentation\English\Demos\DataFiles\dictionary.dat`

This reads in the file using ReadList specifying the type of data we are reading in as a Word.

In[27]:= `words = ReadList[dictfile, Word];`

Here are three words from the dictionary.

In[28]:= `words[[{5, 55, 555}]]`

Out[28]= `{Aaron, abolish, alder}`

First we need to create a function that takes a string as an argument and returns True if its first character is char. As a first step, here is a pure function that checks if the first character of the argument being passed to it ("abolish") starts with the letter "a".

In[29]:= `(StringTake[#, 1] === "a") &["abolish"]`

Out[29]= True

Now we can use this pure function as the test to select all those words in `lis` that pass this particular test.

In[30]:= `WordsStartingWith[lis_ , char_] :=`
          `Select[lis, StringTake[#, 1] === char &]`

Finally we can check all the words in the dictionary file that start with the letter `"z"` say.

In[31]:= `WordsStartingWith[words, "z"]`

Out[31]= {z, zag, zagging, zap, zazen, zeal, zealot, zealous, zebra, zenith, zero,
          zeroes, zeroth, zest, zesty, zeta, zig, zigging, zigzag, zigzagging,
          zilch, zinc, zing, zip, zircon, zirconium, zloty, zodiac, zodiacal,
          zombie, zone, zoo, zoology, zoom, zounds, z's, zucchini, zygote}

This can also be accomplished using the new (in Version 5.1) `StringMatchQ` together with a wildcard character.

In[32]:= `Select[words, StringMatchQ[#, "z*"] &]`

Out[32]= {z, zag, zagging, zap, zazen, zeal, zealot, zealous, zebra, zenith, zero,
          zeroes, zeroth, zest, zesty, zeta, zig, zigging, zigzag, zigzagging,
          zilch, zinc, zing, zip, zircon, zirconium, zloty, zodiac, zodiacal,
          zombie, zone, zoo, zoology, zoom, zounds, z's, zucchini, zygote}

Or you can get all those words that start with either "z" or "Z" by using the `IgnoreCase` option to `StringMatchQ`.

In[33]:= `Select[words, StringMatchQ[#, "z*", IgnoreCase → True] &]`

Out[33]= {z, Zachary, zag, zagging, Zagreb, Zaire, Zambia, Zan, Zanzibar,
          zap, zazen, zeal, Zealand, zealot, zealous, zebra, Zeiss,
          Zellerbach, Zen, zenith, zero, zeroes, zeroth, zest, zesty,
          zeta, Zeus, Ziegler, zig, zigging, zigzag, zigzagging, zilch,
          Zimmerman, zinc, zing, Zion, zip, zircon, zirconium, zloty, zodiac,
          zodiacal, Zoe, Zomba, zombie, zone, zoo, zoology, zoom, Zorn,
          Zoroaster, Zoroastrian, zounds, z's, zucchini, Zurich, zygote}

Or, using the new (in Version 5.1) `Pick` function:

In[34]:= `Pick[words, StringMatchQ[words, "z" ~~ __]]`

Out[34]= {zag, zagging, zap, zazen, zeal, zealot, zealous, zebra, zenith, zero,
          zeroes, zeroth, zest, zesty, zeta, zig, zigging, zigzag, zigzagging,
          zilch, zinc, zing, zip, zircon, zirconium, zloty, zodiac, zodiacal,
          zombie, zone, zoo, zoology, zoom, zounds, z's, zucchini, zygote}

10. Several modifications to the solution to Exercise 9 are needed. First, we must choose only those words with string length greater than or equal to the string length of the second argument to WordsStartingWith. Secondly, from this modified list, we choose those words whose first several characters match the string we are working with.

```
In[35]:= Clear[WordsStartingWith]
```

```
In[36]:= WordsStartingWith[lis_, str_] := Module[{lis2},
           lis2 = Select[lis, StringLength[#] ≥ StringLength[str] &];
           Select[lis2, StringTake[#, StringLength[str]] === str &]]
```

```
In[37]:= WordsStartingWith[words, "zoo"]
```

```
Out[37]= {zoo, zoology, zoom}
```

Or, using StringMatchQ from Version 5.1, you have to join the string with the wildcard character using ~~.

```
In[38]:= Clear[WordsStartingWith]
```

```
In[39]:= WordsStartingWith[lis_List, str_String] :=
           Select[lis, StringMatchQ[#, str ~~ "*"] &]
```

```
In[40]:= WordsStartingWith[words, "zoo"]
```

```
Out[40]= {zoo, zoology, zoom}
```

Or, using the new (in Version 5.1) Pick function (note the need for the triple-blank here):

```
In[41]:= Pick[words, StringMatchQ[words, "zoo" ~~ ___]]
```

```
Out[41]= {zoo, zoology, zoom}
```

11. Using Fold, this pure function requires two arguments. The key is to start with initial value 0.

```
In[42]:= Horner[list_List, base_] := Fold[base #1 + #2 &, 0, list];
```

```
In[43]:= Horner[{a, b, c, d, e}, x]
```

```
Out[43]= e + x (d + x (c + x (b + a x)))
```

```
In[44]:= Expand[%]
```

$$Out[44]= e + d x + c x^2 + b x^3 + a x^4$$

4.7 One-liners

1. If we map the Mod function with base 2 over a list, it will return 1 for every odd element and 0 for every even element.

In[1]:= `Map[ (Mod[#, 2] &), {1, 1, 0, 2, 1}]`

Out[1]= `{1, 1, 0, 0, 1}`

Taking two lists, if we add them element-wise, we then need to select those that pass the mod test above.

In[2]:= `l1 = {1, 0, 0, 1, 1};`
`l2 = {0, 1, 0, 1, 0};`

In[4]:= `lis = l1 + l2`

Out[4]= `{1, 1, 0, 2, 1}`

In[5]:= `Select[lis, (Mod[#, 2] == 1 &)]`

Out[5]= `{1, 1, 1}`

And finally, we need to know how many elements are in this last list.

In[6]:= `Length[%]`

Out[6]= `3`

In[7]:= `HammingDistance3[lis1_, lis2_] :=`
`    Length[Select[lis1 + lis2, (Mod[#, 2] == 1 &)]]`

Actually this could have been done more cleanly by using the predicate OddQ.

In[8]:= `HammingDistance4[lis1_, lis2_] :=`
`    Length[Select[lis1 + lis2, OddQ]]`

2. Using Total, which simply gives the sum of the elements in a list, Hamming distance can be computed as follows:

In[9]:= `HammingDistance5[lis1_, lis2_] := Total[Mod[lis1 + lis2, 2]]`

In[10]:= `HammingDistance5[l1, l2]`

Out[10]= `3`

Some timing tests show that the implementation with Total is quite a bit more efficient than the previous versions.

In[11]:= `data1 = Table[Random[Integer], {10^6}];`

```
In[12]:=  data2 = Table[Random[Integer], {10^6}];
```

```
In[13]:=  Timing[HammingDistance5[data1, data2]]
```

```
Out[13]=  {0.06 Second, 499016}
```

```
In[14]:=  Timing[HammingDistance4[data1, data2]]
```

```
Out[14]=  {0.691 Second, 499016}
```

```
In[15]:=  Timing[HammingDistance3[data1, data2]]
```

```
Out[15]=  {2.514 Second, 499016}
```

3. *a.*

```
In[16]:=  frequencies[lis_] := Module[{pair},
            pair[x_] := {x, Count[lis, x]};
            Map[pair, Union[lis]]]
```

```
In[17]:=  frequencies[{a, a, b, b, b, a, c, c}]
```

```
Out[17]=  {{a, 3}, {b, 3}, {c, 2}}
```

b.

```
In[18]:=  split1[lis_, parts_] := Module[{lis1, lis2},
            lis1[y_, z_] := Take[lis, {y, z}];
            lis2[x_] := Inner[lis1, Drop[x, -1] + 1, Rest[x], List];
            lis2[FoldList[Plus, 0, parts]]]
```

```
In[19]:=  split1[Range[10], {2, 5, 0, 3}]
```

```
Out[19]=  {{1, 2}, {3, 4, 5, 6, 7}, {}, {8, 9, 10}}
```

```
In[20]:=  split2[lis_, parts_] := Module[{lis1},
            lis1[x_] := Take[lis, x + {1, 0}];
            Map[lis1, Partition[FoldList[Plus, 0, parts], 2, 1]]]
```

```
In[21]:=  split2[Range[10], {2, 5, 0, 3}]
```

```
Out[21]=  {{1, 2}, {3, 4, 5, 6, 7}, {}, {8, 9, 10}}
```

c.

```
In[22]:=  lotto1[lis_, n_] := Module[{lis1, lis2, lis3}, lis1[x_] :=
            Flatten[Rest[MapThread[Complement, {RotateRight[x], x}, 1]]];
            lis2[y_] := Delete[y, Random[Integer, {1, Length[y]}]];
            lis3[z_] := NestList[lis2, z, n];
            lis1[lis3[lis]]]
```

In[23]:= `lotto1[Range[10], 5]`

Out[23]= {2, 5, 4, 6, 8}

In[24]:= `lotto2[lis_, n_] := Take[Transpose[`
`    Sort[Transpose[{Table[Random[], {Length[lis]}], lis}]]][[2]], n]`

In[25]:= `lotto2[Range[10], 5]`

Out[25]= {2, 5, 1, 8, 7}

4.

In[26]:= `{Timing[lotto1[Range[50000], 3];], Timing[lotto2[Range[50000], 3];]}`

Out[26]= {{0.09 Second, Null}, {0.421 Second, Null}}

In[27]:= `{Timing[lotto1[Range[50000], 60];], Timing[lotto2[Range[50000], 60];]}`

Out[27]= {{1.362 Second, Null}, {0.42 Second, Null}}

5. Here are the list of coins.

In[28]:= `coins = {p, p, q, n, d, d, p, q, q, p}`

Out[28]= {p, p, q, n, d, d, p, q, q, p}

In[29]:= `pocketChange2[x_] :=`
`    Dot[Map[(Count[x, #] &), {p, n, d, q}], {1, 5, 10, 25}]`

In[30]:= `pocketChange2[coins]`

Out[30]= 104

In[31]:= `pocketChange3[x_] :=`
`    Inner[Times, Map[(Count[x, #] &), {p, n, d, q}], {1, 5, 10, 25}, Plus]`

In[32]:= `pocketChange3[coins]`

Out[32]= 104

6.

In[33]:= `makeChange[x_] := Module[{coins = {25, 10, 5, 1}},`
`    Quotient[FoldList[Mod, x, Drop[coins, -1]], coins]]`

In[34]:= `makeChange[119]`

Out[34]= {4, 1, 1, 4}

7.

```
In[35]:=  offLattice[n_] :=
            Map[({Sin[#], Cos[#]} &), Table[Random[Real, {0, 2 π}], {n}]]

In[36]:=  offLattice[n_] := Module[{step},
            step[x_] := {Sin[x], Cos[x]};
            Map[step, Table[Random[Real, {0, 2 π}], {n}]]]

In[37]:=  offLattice[3]

Out[37]=  {{0.194181, 0.980966}, {0.956556, -0.291548}, {-0.431374, -0.902173}}
```

8. First, notice what FromDigits does.

```
In[38]:=  ? FromDigits

          FromDigits[list] constructs an integer
              from the list of its decimal digits. FromDigits[
              list, b] takes the digits to be given in base b. More…
```

We use With to create a local constant d, as this expression never changes throughout the body of the function.

```
In[39]:=  convertToDate2[num_] := With[{d = IntegerDigits[num]},
            {FromDigits[Take[d, 4]],
              FromDigits[Take[d, {5, 6}]],
              FromDigits[Take[d, {7, 8}]]}]

In[40]:=  convertToDate2[20030515]

Out[40]=  {2003, 5, 15}
```

5 Procedural programming

5.2 Loops and iteration

1. Using a compound expression inside the Do function, this computes the next approximations of both square roots each time through the loop.

$$In[1]:= next[fun\_, x\_] := N\left[x - \frac{fun[x]}{fun'[x]}\right]$$

In[2]:= a = 50;
         b = 60;
         Do[
           a = next[#² - 50 &, a];
           b = next[#² - 60 &, b],
           {10}]

In[5]:= {a, b}

Out[5]= {7.07107, 7.74597}

2. Notice that to compute the square root of a number r, we need to iterate the following
    expression.

In[6]:= fun[x_] := x² - r;
         $\text{Simplify}\left[x - \dfrac{\text{fun}[x]}{\text{fun}'[x]}\right]$

Out[7]= $\dfrac{r + x²}{2\,x}$

This can be written as a pure function, with a second argument giving the initial guess. Here
we iterate ten times.

In[8]:= $\text{nestSqrt}[r\_,\ \text{init}\_] := \text{Nest}\left[\dfrac{r + \#²}{2\,\#}\ \&,\ \text{N[init]},\ 10\right]$

In[9]:= nestSqrt[50, 10]

Out[9]= 7.07107

3. We need to place the two expressions that were in the body of the Do into a list. Try copying
    the body of the Do exactly as above and see what happens.

In[10]:= $\text{next}[\text{fun}\_,\ x\_] := \text{N}\left[x - \dfrac{\text{fun}[x]}{\text{fun}'[x]}\right]$

In[11]:= a = 50;
          b = 60;
          Table[{
            a = next[(#² - 50) &, a],
            b = next[(#² - 60) &, b]},
            {10}]

Out[13]= {{25.5, 30.5}, {13.7304, 16.2336}, {8.68597, 9.96482}, {7.22119, 7.993},
          {7.07263, 7.74978}, {7.07107, 7.74597}, {7.07107, 7.74597},
          {7.07107, 7.74597}, {7.07107, 7.74597}, {7.07107, 7.74597}}

To mimic the solution to this problem obtained with the Do loop, we need to extract the last set of values obtained.

In[14]:= `Last[%]`

Out[14]= `{7.07107, 7.74597}`

4. Note that this version of the Fibonacci function is much more efficient than the simple recursive version, and is closer to the version that uses dynamic programming.

In[15]:= `fib[n_] := Module[{prev = 0, this = 1, next},`
        `Do[next = prev + this;`
         `prev = this;`
         `this = next,`
         `{n}];`
        `prev]`

In[16]:= `Table[fib[i], {i, 1, 10}]`

Out[16]= `{1, 1, 2, 3, 5, 8, 13, 21, 34, 55}`

Actually, this code can be simplified a bit by using parallel assignments.

In[17]:= `fib2[n_] := Module[{f1 = 0, f2 = 1},`
        `Do[{f1, f2} = {f2, f1 + f2},`
         `{n - 1}];`
        `f2]`

In[18]:= `Table[fib2[i], {i, 1, 10}]`

Out[18]= `{1, 1, 2, 3, 5, 8, 13, 21, 34, 55}`

Both of these implementations are quite fast and avoid the deep recursion of the classical definition.

In[19]:= `{Timing[fib[100000];], Timing[fib2[100000];]}`

Out[19]= `{{0.781 Second, Null}, {0.631 Second, Null}}`

5. We compute the derivative df inside the Module and then use that throughout the body of the function.

In[20]:= `Clear[findRoot]`

In[21]:= `findRoot[fun_, init_, ε_] :=`
    `Module[{xi = init, funxi = fun[init], df = fun'}, While[Abs[funxi] > ε,`

$$xi = N\left[xi - \frac{funxi}{df[xi]}\right];$$

    `funxi = fun[xi]];`
    `xi]`

In[22]:= `findRoot[f, 50, 0.0001]`

Out[22]= `50`

6. The variable b is the current approximation, and the variable a is the previous approximation.

In[23]:= `findRoot[fun_, init_, ε_] := Module[{a = init, b = fun[init]},`
        `While[Abs[b - a] > ε,`
        `a = b;`
        $$b = N\left[b - \frac{fun[b]}{fun'[b]}\right];$$
        `b]`

In[24]:= `f[x_] := x² - 50`

In[25]:= `findRoot[f, 10, .001]`

Out[25]= `7.07107`

7. This solution is based on the solution to Exercise 5 above.

In[26]:= `findRootList[fun_, init_, ε_] := Module[{a = init, b, solns = {init}},`
        $$b = N\left[a - \frac{fun[a]}{fun'[a]}\right];$$
        `While[Abs[b - a] > ε,`
        `a = b;`
        $$b = N\left[b - \frac{fun[b]}{fun'[b]}\right];$$
        `solns = Join[solns, {a}]];`
        `Join[solns, {b}]]`

In[27]:= `f[x_] := x² - 50`

In[28]:= `findRootList[f, 50, 10⁻⁶]`

Out[28]= `{50, 25.5, 13.7304, 8.68597, 7.22119, 7.07263, 7.07107, 7.07107}`

8. We go back to a previous version of `findRoot` and add multiple initial values.

In[29]:= `findRootList[fun_, inits_, ε_] := Module[{a = inits},`
        `While[Min[Abs[Map[fun, a]]] > ε,`
        $$a = Map\left[N\left[\# - \frac{fun[\#]}{fun'[\#]}\right] \&, a\right];$$
        `Select[a, Min[Abs[Map[fun, a]]] == Abs[fun[#]] &]]`

In[30]:= `findRootList[(#² - 50) &, {25, 50, 75, 100}, .001]`

Out[30]= `{7.07107}`

9.

```
In[31]:=  bisect[f_, {a_, b_, ε_}] := Module[
            {low = Min[a, b], high = Max[a, b], mid = N[(a+b)/2], fofMid = N[f[(a+b)/2]]},
            While[Abs[fofMid] > ε,
              If[fofMid < 0, low = mid, high = mid];
              mid = N[(low + high)/2];
              fofMid = N[f[mid]]];
            mid]
```

```
In[32]:=  f[x_] := x^2 - 2
          bisect[f, {0, 2, .001}]
```

```
Out[33]=  1.41406
```

10. Here is a direct implementation of the Euclidean algorithm.

```
In[34]:=  gcd[m_, n_] := Module[{a = m, b = n, tmpa},
            While[b > 0,
              tmpa = a;
              a = b;
              b = Mod[tmpa, b]];
            a]
```

```
In[35]:=  m = 12782;
          n = 5531207;
          gcd[m, n]
```

```
Out[37]=  11
```

We can avoid the need for the temporary variable tmpa by performing a parallel assignment as in the following function. This results in a much cleaner implementation.

```
In[38]:=  gcd[m_, n_] := Module[{a = m, b = n},
            While[b > 0, {a, b} = {b, Mod[a, b]}];
            a]
```

```
In[39]:=  m = 12782;
          n = 5531207;
          gcd[m, n]
```

```
Out[41]=  11
```

11.

a. Create a list rvec of 0s, then use a Do loop to set rvec [[*i*]] to vec [[*n* − *i*]], where *n* is the length of vec.

```
In[42]:= Clear[reverse, a, b, c, d, e]

In[43]:= reverse[vec_] := Module[{vecA = Table[0, {Length[vec]}]},
           Do[vecA[[i]] = vec[[Length[vec] - i + 1]],
            {i, 1, Length[vec]}];
           vecA]

In[44]:= reverse[{a, b, c, d, e}]

Out[44]= {e, d, c, b, a}

In[45]:= reverseStruc[vec_] := Module[{vecA = Table[0, {len = Length[vec]}]},
           Table[vecA[[i]] = vec[[len - i + 1]], {i, len}]
           ]

In[46]:= reverseStruc[{a, b, c, d, e}]

Out[46]= {e, d, c, b, a}
```

b. The key to this problem is to use the Mod operator to compute the target address for any
item from vec. That is, the element vec [*i*] must move to, roughly speaking, position *n* + *i*
mod Length [*vec*]. The "roughly speaking" is due to the fact that the Mod operator returns
values in the range 0, ..., Length [*vec*] − 1, whereas vectors are indexed by values
1, ..., Length [*vec*]. This causes a little trickiness in this problem.

```
In[47]:= rotateRight[vec_, n_] := Module[{vecA = Table[0, {Length[vec]}]},
           Do[vecA[[1 + Mod[n + i - 1, Length[vec]]]] = vec[[i]], {i, 1, Length[vec]}];
           vecA]

In[48]:= rotateRight[{a, b, c, d, e}, 2]

Out[48]= {d, e, a, b, c}

In[49]:= rotateRightStruc[vec_, n_] :=
           Module[{vecA = Table[0, {len = Length[vec]}]},
            Table[vecA[[1 + Mod[n + i - 1, len]]] = vec[[i]], {i, len}];
            vecA
            ]

In[50]:= rotateRightStruc[{a, b, c, d, e}, 3]

Out[50]= {c, d, e, a, b}
```

c. Iterate over the rows of mat, setting row *i* to the result of calling rotateRight.

```
In[51]:= rotateRows[mat_] := Module[{matA = Table[0, {len = Length[mat]}]},
           Do[matA[[i]] = rotateRight[mat[[i]], i],
            {i, 1, len}];
           matA]
```

```
In[52]:= rotateRows[{{a, b, c}, {d, e, f}, {g, h, k}}]

Out[52]= {{c, a, b}, {e, f, d}, {g, h, k}}
```

d.

```
In[53]:= rotateRowsByS[mat_, S_] := Module[{matA = Table[0, {Length[mat]}]},
         Do[matA[[i]] = rotateRight[mat[[i]], S[[i]]],
          {i, 1, Length[mat]}];
         matA]
```

```
In[54]:= rotateRowsByS[{{a, b, c}, {d, e, f}, {g, h, k}}, {1, 2, 3}]

Out[54]= {{c, a, b}, {e, f, d}, {g, h, k}}
```

e. Create a list lisC of correct length, then iterate over lisA and lisB, moving lisA[[i]] to lisC whenever lisB[[i]] is True. The position in lisC that receives this value is not necessarily *i*; we use the variable last to keep track of the next position in lisC that will receive a value from lisA.

```
In[55]:= compress[lisA_, lisB_] :=
         Module[{lisC = Table[0, {Count[lisB, True]}], last = 1},
          Do[If[lisB[[i]], lisC[[last]] = lisA[[i]];
            last = last + 1,
            Null],
           {i, 1, Length[lisB]}];
          lisC]
```

```
In[56]:= compress[{a, b, c, d, e}, {True, True, False, False, True}]

Out[56]= {a, b, e}
```

5.3 Flow control

1. Here are the conditional definitions.

```
In[1]:= signum1[x_ /; x < 0] := -1
        signum1[x_ /; x > 0] := 1
        signum1[0] := 0
```

```
In[4]:= Map[signum1, {-2, 0, 1}]

Out[4]= {-1, 0, 1}
```

Here is the signum function defined using If.

```
In[5]:= signum2[x_] := If[x < 0, -1, If[x == 0, 0, 1]]
```

```
In[6]:= Map[signum2, {-2, 0, 1}]

Out[6]= {-1, 0, 1}
```

Here is the signum function defined using Which.

```
In[7]:= signum3[x_] := Which[x < 0, -1, x == 0, 0, True, 1]

In[8]:= Map[signum3, {-2, 0, 1}]

Out[8]= {-1, 0, 1}
```

Finally, here is the signum function defined using Piecewise.

```
In[9]:= Piecewise[{{-1, x < 0}, {1, x > 0}, {0, x == 0}}]
```

$$Out[9]= \begin{cases} -1 & x < 0 \\ 1 & x > 0 \end{cases}$$

2.

```
In[10]:= signum1[x_ /; x < 0] := -1
         signum1[x_ /; x > 0] := 1
         signum1[0] := 0
         signum1[0.0] := 0

In[14]:= Map[signum1, {-2, 0, 2}]

Out[14]= {-1, 0, 1}

In[15]:= signum2[x_] := If[x < 0, -1, If[x > 0, 1, 0]]

In[16]:= Map[signum2, {-2, 0, 2}]

Out[16]= {-1, 0, 1}

In[17]:= signum3[x_] := Which[x < 0, -1, x > 0, 1, True, 0]

In[18]:= Map[signum3, {-2, 0, 2}]

Out[18]= {-1, 0, 1}
```

3.

```
In[19]:= applyChar[{"+", nums__}] := Apply[Plus, {nums}]
         applyChar[{"-", nums__}] := Apply[Minus, {nums}]
         applyChar[{"*", nums__}] := Apply[Times, {nums}]
         applyChar[{"/", nums__}] := Apply[Divide, {nums}]
         applyChar[_] := Print["Bad argument to applyChar"];
```

4.

  a.

    In[24]:=   `doublePos[lis_] := Map[If[# > 0, 2 #, #] &, lis]`

  b.

    In[25]:=   `remove3Repetitions[lis_] := Fold[`
          `If[Length[#1] > 2 && #2 == #1[[-1]] == #1[[-2]], #1, Join[#1, {#2}]] &, {}, lis]`

  c.

    In[26]:=   `positiveSum[L_] := Fold[If[#1 + #2 < 0, 0, #1 + #2] &, 0, L]`

5. First we define the auxiliary function using conditional statements.

    In[27]:=   `collatz[n_] :=` $\dfrac{n}{2}$ `/; EvenQ[n]`

    In[28]:=   `collatz[n_] := 3 n + 1 /; OddQ[n]`

  Then iterate `Collatz`, starting with n, and continue while n is not equal to 1.

    In[29]:=   `CollatzSequence[n_] := NestWhileList[collatz, n, ! (# == 1) &]`

    In[30]:=   `CollatzSequence[13]`

    Out[30]=   `{13, 40, 20, 10, 5, 16, 8, 4, 2, 1}`

5.4 Examples

1. Here is the gcd function implemented using an `If` structure.

    In[1]:=   `Clear[gcd]`

    In[2]:=   `gcd[m_Integer, n_Integer] := If[m > 0, gcd[Mod[n, m], m], gcd[m, n] = n]`

    In[3]:=   `m = 12782;`
          `n = 5531207;`
          `gcd[m, n]`

    Out[5]=   `11`

2. This is a direct implementation using `Piecewise`.

```
In[6]:= Piecewise[{{0, x == 0 && y == 0}, {-1, y == 0}, {-2, x == 0},
          {1, x > 0 && y > 0}, {2, x < 0 && y > 0}, {3, x < 0 && y < 0}}, 4]
```

$$Out[6]= \begin{cases} 0 & x == 0 \&\& y == 0 \\ -1 & y == 0 \\ -2 & x == 0 \\ 1 & x > 0 \&\& y > 0 \\ 2 & x < 0 \&\& y > 0 \\ 3 & x < 0 \&\& y < 0 \\ 4 & True \end{cases}$$

```
In[7]:= pointLocPW[{x_, y_}] :=
          Piecewise[{{0, x == 0 && y == 0}, {-1, y == 0}, {-2, x == 0},
            {1, x > 0 && y > 0}, {2, x < 0 && y > 0}, {3, x < 0 && y < 0}}, 4]
```

```
In[8]:= Map[pointLocPW, {{0, 0}, {4, 0}, {0, 1.3},
          {2, 4}, {-2, 4}, {-2, -4}, {2, -4}, {2, 0}, {3, -4}}]
```

```
Out[8]= {0, -1, -2, 1, 2, 3, 4, -1, 4}
```

3.

```
In[9]:= pointLoc[{0, 0}] := 0
        pointLoc[{x_, 0}] := -1
        pointLoc[{0, y_}] := -2
        pointLoc[{x_, y_}] := If[x < 0, 2, 1] /; y > 0
        pointLoc[{x_, y_}] := If[x < 0, 3, 4]
        pointLoc[{x_, y_, z_}] := If[x < 0, 2, 1] /; y >= 0 && z >= 0
        pointLoc[{x_, y_, z_}] := If[x < 0, 3, 4] /; y < 0 && z >= 0
        pointLoc[{x_, y_, z_}] := If[x < 0, 6, 5] /; y >= 0 && z < 0
        pointLoc[{x_, y_, z_}] := If[x < 0, 7, 8] /; y < 0 && z < 0
```

```
In[18]:= Map[pointLoc, {{2, 0}, {3, -4}}]
```

```
Out[18]= {-1, 4}
```

6 Rule-based programming

6.2 Patterns

1. Using the `FullForm` of the expression, we can find many pattern matches.

```
In[1]:= FullForm[x^3 + y z]
```

```
Out[1]//FullForm=
        Plus[Power[x, 3], Times[y, z]]
```

In[2]:= `MatchQ[x`^{3}` + y z, _Plus]`

Out[2]= True

In[3]:= `MatchQ[x`^{3}` + y z, _Power + _Times]`

Out[3]= True

There are many more possible matches, including the trivial one.

In[4]:= `MatchQ[x`^{3}` + y z, _]`

Out[4]= True

2. First look at the `FullForm` of this expression.

In[5]:= `FullForm[{5, erina, "give me a break"}]`

Out[5]//FullForm=
    `List[5, erina, "give me a break"]`

In[6]:= `MatchQ[{5, erina, "give me a break"}, _List]`

Out[6]= True

In[7]:= `MatchQ[{5, erina, "give me a break"}, {_Integer, _Symbol, _String}]`

Out[7]= True

3. Again, the `FullForm` should help to guide you.

In[8]:= `FullForm[{4, {a, b}, "g"}]`

Out[8]//FullForm=
    `List[4, List[a, b], "g"]`

In[9]:= `MatchQ[{4, {a, b}, "g"}, x_List /; Length[x] == 3]`

Out[9]= True

In[10]:= `MatchQ[{4, {a, b}, "g"}, _List? (Length[#1] == 3 &)]`

Out[10]= True

In[11]:= `MatchQ[{4, {a, b}, "g"}, {_, y_, _} /; y[[0]] == List]`

Out[11]= True

In[12]:= `MatchQ[{4, {a, b}, "g"}, {x_, y_, z_} /; AtomQ[z]]`

Out[12]= True

In[13]:= `MatchQ[{4, {a, b}, "g"}, {x_, _, _} /; EvenQ[x]]`

Out[13]= True

4. Here is the original solution as from Chapter 5, but, in this case, we check that both m and n have head `Integer`.

In[14]:= `gcd[m_Integer, n_Integer] := Module[{a = m, b = n},`
      `While[b > 0, {a, b} = {b, Mod[a, b]}];`
      `a]`

In[15]:= `gcd[39874, 2868878]`

Out[15]= 2

5. Here is the function `FindSubsequence` as given in the text.

In[16]:= `FindSubsequence[lis_List, subseq_List] := Module[{p},`
      `p = Partition[lis, Length[subseq], 1];`
      `Position[p, Flatten[{___, subseq, ___}]]`
      `]`

This creates another rule associated with `FindSubsequence` that simply takes each integer argument, converts them to lists of integer digits, and then passes that off to the rule above.

In[17]:= `FindSubsequence[n_Integer, subseq_Integer] :=`
      `Module[{nlist = IntegerDigits[n], sublist = IntegerDigits[subseq]},`
      `FindSubsequence[nlist, sublist]`
      `]`

We create the list of the first 100,000 digits of π.

In[18]:= `pi = FromDigits[RealDigits[N[Pi, 10^5] - 3][[1]]];`

This show that the subsequence 1415 occurs seven times at the following locations in the digit expansion of π.

In[19]:= `FindSubsequence[pi, 1415]`

Out[19]= {{1}, {6955}, {29136}, {45234}, {79687}, {85880}, {88009}}

6. The Collatz function has a direct implementation based on its definition.

In[20]:= `Collatz[n_?OddQ] := 3 n + 1`

In[21]:= `Collatz[n_?EvenQ] := `$\dfrac{n}{2}$

In[22]:= `Collatz[4.3]`

Out[22]= Collatz[4.3]

Here we iterate the Collatz function 111 times starting with an initial value of 27.

```
In[23]:= NestList[Collatz, 27, 111]
```

```
Out[23]= {27, 82, 41, 124, 62, 31, 94, 47, 142, 71, 214, 107, 322, 161, 484, 242,
         121, 364, 182, 91, 274, 137, 412, 206, 103, 310, 155, 466, 233, 700,
         350, 175, 526, 263, 790, 395, 1186, 593, 1780, 890, 445, 1336, 668,
         334, 167, 502, 251, 754, 377, 1132, 566, 283, 850, 425, 1276, 638,
         319, 958, 479, 1438, 719, 2158, 1079, 3238, 1619, 4858, 2429, 7288,
         3644, 1822, 911, 2734, 1367, 4102, 2051, 6154, 3077, 9232, 4616, 2308,
         1154, 577, 1732, 866, 433, 1300, 650, 325, 976, 488, 244, 122, 61,
         184, 92, 46, 23, 70, 35, 106, 53, 160, 80, 40, 20, 10, 5, 16, 8, 4, 2, 1}
```

7. Here again is the Collatz function, but this time using a condition on the right-hand side of the definition.

```
In[24]:= Clear[Collatz]
```

```
In[25]:= Collatz[n_] := 3 n + 1 /; OddQ[n] && Positive[n]
```

```
In[26]:= Collatz[n_] := n/2 /; EvenQ[n] && Positive[n]
```

```
In[27]:= Collatz[4.3]
```

```
Out[27]= Collatz[4.3]
```

```
In[28]:= Collatz[-3]
```

```
Out[28]= Collatz[-3]
```

```
In[29]:= NestList[Collatz, 27, 111]
```

```
Out[29]= {27, 82, 41, 124, 62, 31, 94, 47, 142, 71, 214, 107, 322, 161, 484, 242,
         121, 364, 182, 91, 274, 137, 412, 206, 103, 310, 155, 466, 233, 700,
         350, 175, 526, 263, 790, 395, 1186, 593, 1780, 890, 445, 1336, 668,
         334, 167, 502, 251, 754, 377, 1132, 566, 283, 850, 425, 1276, 638,
         319, 958, 479, 1438, 719, 2158, 1079, 3238, 1619, 4858, 2429, 7288,
         3644, 1822, 911, 2734, 1367, 4102, 2051, 6154, 3077, 9232, 4616, 2308,
         1154, 577, 1732, 866, 433, 1300, 650, 325, 976, 488, 244, 122, 61,
         184, 92, 46, 23, 70, 35, 106, 53, 160, 80, 40, 20, 10, 5, 16, 8, 4, 2, 1}
```

8. Using alternatives, this gives the definition for real, integer, or rational arguments.

```
In[30]:= abs[x_Real | x_Integer | x_Rational] := If[x ≥ 0, x, -x]
```

Here is the definition for complex arguments.

```
In[31]:= abs[x_Complex] := √(Re[x]² + Im[x]²)
```

It is probably a good idea to also add a definition for symbolic arguments.

```
In[32]:= abs[x_Symbol] := Abs[x]
```

In[33]:= $\text{Map}\left[\text{abs}, \left\{-3, 3 + 4 \text{ I}, \frac{-4}{5}, a\right\}\right]$

Out[33]= $\left\{3, 5, \frac{4}{5}, \text{Abs}[a]\right\}$

9. We first have to consider the base cases. Given a list with no elements, swapTwo should return the empty list. And, given a list with one element, swapping should give that one element back.

In[34]:= `swapTwo[{}] := {}`
`swapTwo[{x_}] := {x}`

Now, we use the triple-blank to indicate that r could be a sequence of 0 or more elements.

In[36]:= `swapTwo[{x_, y_, r___}] := {y, x, r}`

In[37]:= `Map[swapTwo, {{}, {a}, {a, b, c, d}}]`

Out[37]= `{{}, {a}, {b, a, c, d}}`

Notice in this second definition for swapTwo that the second clause covers both the situation where the argument is the empty list and when it contains only one element.

In[38]:= `swapTwo2[{x_, y_, r___}] := {y, x, r}`
`swapTwo2[x_] := x`

In[40]:= `Map[swapTwo2, {{}, {a}, {a, b, c, d}}]`

Out[40]= `{{}, {a}, {b, a, c, d}}`

10. This one requires the triple blank.

In[41]:= `f[{x1_Integer, ___}, 1] := x1 + 1`
`f[x_Integer, y_] := x - y`

11. Here are two sample lists.

In[43]:= `l1 = {1, 0, 0, 1, 1};`
`l2 = {0, 1, 0, 1, 0};`

First we pair them up.

In[45]:= `ll = Transpose[{l1, l2}]`

Out[45]= `{{1, 0}, {0, 1}, {0, 0}, {1, 1}, {1, 0}}`

Here is the conditional pattern that matches any pair where the two elements are *not* identical.

In[46]:= `Cases[ll, {p_, q_} /; p ≠ q]`

Out[46]= `{{1, 0}, {0, 1}, {1, 0}}`

The Hamming distance is the number of such non-identical pairs.

In[47]:= `Length[%]`

Out[47]= 3

Finally, here is a function that puts this all together.

In[48]:= `HammingDistance[lis1_List, lis2_List] :=`
`Length[Cases[Transpose[{lis1, lis2}], {p_, q_} /; p ≠ q]]`

In[49]:= `HammingDistance[l1, l2]`

Out[49]= 3

The running times of this version of `HammingDistance` are comparable with those from Chapter 4, where we used bit operators.

In[50]:= `HammingDistance2[lis1_, lis2_] := Apply[Plus,`
`Apply[BitXor, Transpose[{lis1, lis2}], {1}]`
`]`

In[51]:= `data1 = Table[Random[Integer], {10^6}];`

In[52]:= `data2 = Table[Random[Integer], {10^6}];`

In[53]:= `Timing[HammingDistance[data1, data2]]`

Out[53]= `{2.905 Second, 500168}`

In[54]:= `Timing[HammingDistance2[data1, data2]]`

Out[54]= `{1.592 Second, 500168}`

6.3 Transformation rules

1. The pattern matched function is slower because it repeatedly applies transformation rules.

In[1]:= `maxima[x_] := Union[Rest[FoldList[Max, -∞, x]]]`

In[2]:= `maximaR[x_List] := x //. {a___, b_, c___, d_, e___} /; d ≤ b :→ {a, b, c, e}`

In[3]:= **Trace[maxima[{3, 5, 2, 6, 1, 8, 4, 9, 7}]]**

Out[3]= {maxima[{3, 5, 2, 6, 1, 8, 4, 9, 7}],
     Union[Rest[FoldList[Max, -∞, {3, 5, 2, 6, 1, 8, 4, 9, 7}]]],
     {{{∞, ∞}, -∞, -∞}, FoldList[Max, -∞, {3, 5, 2, 6, 1, 8, 4, 9, 7}],
       {Max[-∞, 3], Max[3, -∞], 3}, {Max[3, 5], 5},
       {Max[5, 2], Max[2, 5], 5}, {Max[5, 6], 6}, {Max[6, 1], Max[1, 6], 6},
       {Max[6, 8], 8}, {Max[8, 4], Max[4, 8], 8}, {Max[8, 9], 9},
       {Max[9, 7], Max[7, 9], 9}, {-∞, 3, 5, 5, 6, 6, 8, 8, 9, 9}},
     Rest[{-∞, 3, 5, 5, 6, 6, 8, 8, 9, 9}], {3, 5, 5, 6, 6, 8, 8, 9, 9}},
     Union[{3, 5, 5, 6, 6, 8, 8, 9, 9}], {3, 5, 6, 8, 9}}

In[4]:= **Trace[maximaR[{3, 5, 2, 6, 1, 8, 4, 9, 7}]]**

Out[4]= {maximaR[{3, 5, 2, 6, 1, 8, 4, 9, 7}], {3, 5, 2, 6, 1, 8, 4, 9, 7} //.
     {a___, b_, c___, d_, e___} /; d ≤ b :→ {a, b, c, e},
     {{a___, b_, c___, d_, e___} /; d ≤ b :→ {a, b, c, e},
     {a___, b_, c___, d_, e___} /; d ≤ b :→ {a, b, c, e}},
     {3, 5, 2, 6, 1, 8, 4, 9, 7} //.
     {a___, b_, c___, d_, e___} /; d ≤ b :→ {a, b, c, e}, {5 ≤ 3, False},
     {2 ≤ 3, True}, {5 ≤ 3, False}, {6 ≤ 3, False}, {6 ≤ 5, False},
     {1 ≤ 3, True}, {5 ≤ 3, False}, {6 ≤ 3, False}, {6 ≤ 5, False},
     {8 ≤ 3, False}, {8 ≤ 5, False}, {8 ≤ 6, False}, {4 ≤ 3, False}, {4 ≤ 5, True},
     {5 ≤ 3, False}, {6 ≤ 3, False}, {6 ≤ 5, False}, {8 ≤ 3, False},
     {8 ≤ 5, False}, {8 ≤ 6, False}, {9 ≤ 3, False}, {9 ≤ 5, False},
     {9 ≤ 6, False}, {9 ≤ 8, False}, {7 ≤ 3, False}, {7 ≤ 5, False},
     {7 ≤ 6, False}, {7 ≤ 8, True}, {5 ≤ 3, False}, {6 ≤ 3, False}, {6 ≤ 5, False},
     {8 ≤ 3, False}, {8 ≤ 5, False}, {8 ≤ 6, False}, {9 ≤ 3, False},
     {9 ≤ 5, False}, {9 ≤ 6, False}, {9 ≤ 8, False}, {3, 5, 6, 8, 9}}

2. The evaluation sequence can be seen directly from the Trace of this compound expression.

In[5]:= **Trace[y = 11; a = 9; y + 3 /. y → a]**

Out[5]= {y = 11; a = 9; y + 3 /. y → a, {y = 11, 11}, {a = 9, 9}, {{{y, 11}, 11 + 3, 14},
     {{y, 11}, {a, 9}, 11 → 9, 11 → 9}, 14 /. 11 → 9, 14}, 14}

3. First make sure that a and y have no values associated with them.

In[6]:= **Clear[a, y]**

In[7]:= **Hold[y = 11];**
     a = 9;
     y + 3 /. y → a

Out[9]= 12

4. You need to maintain the left-hand side of the transformation rule unevaluated for purposes of pattern matching and the right-hand side of the rule unevaluated until the rule is used.

In[10]:= `Trace[g[x_] = x /. +z___ → Times[z]]`

Out[10]= `{{{{+z___, z___}, {Times[z], z}, z___ → z, z___ → z}, x /. z___ → z, x},`
`g[x_] = x, x}`

In[11]:= `Clear[a, g]`

In[12]:= `g[x_] := x /. Literal[+z___] :> Times[z]`

In[13]:= `g[a + b + c]`

Out[13]= `a b c`

5. The transformation rule unnests lists within a list.

In[14]:= `unNest[lis_] := Map[(# //. {x__List} → x &), lis]`

In[15]:= `unNest[{{a, a, a}, {a}, {{b, b, b}, {b, b}}, {a, a}}]`

Out[15]= `{{a, a, a}, {a}, {b, b, b}, {b, b}, {a, a}}`

6.

In[16]:= `sumList[lis_] := First[lis //. {x_, y___} → x + {y}]`

In[17]:= `sumList[{1, 5, 8, 3, 9, 3}]`

Out[17]= `29`

7. The triple blank is required both before and after the variables x and y.

In[18]:= `cartesianProduct[lis1_, lis2_] :=`
`    ReplaceList[{lis1, lis2}, {{___, x_, ___}, {___, y_, ___}} → {x, y}]`

We should also have a rule for the base case.

In[19]:= `cartesianProduct[{}] := {}`

In[20]:= `Clear[x, y, z, a, b, c]`

In[21]:= `cartesianProduct[{a, b, c}, {x, y, z}]`

Out[21]= `{{a, x}, {a, y}, {a, z}, {b, x}, {b, y}, {b, z}, {c, x}, {c, y}, {c, z}}`

In[22]:= `cartesianProduct[{}]`

Out[22]= `{}`

8. Note that `RasterArray` and `Raster` both display an array of values from bottom to top, hence the need to reverse the argument `lis`.

```
In[23]:= CAGraphics[lis_List] := Module[{colors},
            colors = {1 → Hue[.2], 0 → Hue[.8]};
            Graphics[RasterArray[Reverse[lis] /. colors]]
          ]
```

Here is a larger example of rule 30.

```
In[1]:= ca30 = CellularAutomaton[30, {{1}, 0}, 400];
```

```
In[25]:= Show[CAGraphics[ca30]];
```

Note that this can also be accomplished much more cleanly using `ArrayPlot` (new in Version 5.1).

```
In[26]:= ArrayPlot[ca30, ColorRules → {1 → Hue[.2], 0 → Hue[.8]}];
```

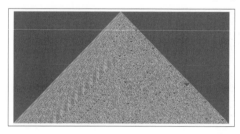

6.4 Examples

1. This is a simple modification of the code given in the text.

```
In[1]:= alphabet = Map[FromCharacterCode, Range[97, 122]]
```

```
Out[1]= {a, b, c, d, e, f, g, h, i, j, k, l, m, n, o, p, q, r, s, t, u, v, w, x, y, z}
```

```
In[2]:= coderules = Thread[alphabet → RotateRight[alphabet, 5]]
```

```
Out[2]= {a → v, b → w, c → x, d → y, e → z, f → a, g → b, h → c,
         i → d, j → e, k → f, l → g, m → h, n → i, o → j, p → k, q → l,
         r → m, s → n, t → o, u → p, v → q, w → r, x → s, y → t, z → u}
```

```
In[3]:=  decoderules = Thread[alphabet → RotateLeft[alphabet, 5]]

Out[3]=  {a → f, b → g, c → h, d → i, e → j, f → k, g → l, h → m,
          i → n, j → o, k → p, l → q, m → r, n → s, o → t, p → u, q → v,
          r → w, s → x, t → y, u → z, v → a, w → b, x → c, y → d, z → e}

In[4]:=  code[str_String] := Apply[StringJoin, Characters[str] /. coderules]

In[5]:=  decode[str_String] := Apply[StringJoin, Characters[str] /. decoderules]

In[6]:=  code["squeamish ossifrage"]

Out[6]=  nlpzvhdnc jnndamvbz

In[7]:=  decode[%]

Out[7]=  squeamish ossifrage
```

3. This version of `matrixPlot` requires a list of rules as the second argument.

```
In[8]:=  matrixPlot[mat_List, rules_] :=
            Show[Graphics[RasterArray[Reverse[mat] /. rules],
               AspectRatio → Automatic]]

In[9]:=  dat = Table[Random[Integer], {50}, {50}];

In[10]:= matrixPlot[dat, {0 → GrayLevel[.2], 1 → GrayLevel[.6]}]
```

```
Out[10]=  - Graphics -
```

You can plot any rectangular array of values with `matrixPlot` so long as you specify the rules for coloring the various elements. For example, the following example generates 100 steps in the evolution of the rule 30 cellular automaton, starting with a single 1 cell and surrounded by 0s.

```
In[11]:= ca30 = CellularAutomaton[30, {{1}, 0}, 100];
```

In[12]:= `matrixPlot[ca30, {1 → Hue[.2], 0 → Hue[.6]}];`

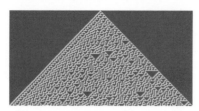

To get `matrixPlot` to produce similar output to the new `ArrayPlot`, you need to make a few changes to the `Frame` and `FrameTicks` options.

In[13]:= `matrixPlot[mat_List, rules_] :=`
`    Show[Graphics[RasterArray[Reverse[mat] /. rules],`
`      AspectRatio → Automatic, Frame → True, FrameTicks → False]]`

In[14]:= `matrixPlot[ca30, {1 → Hue[.2], 0 → Hue[.6]}];`

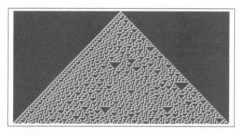

In[15]:= `ArrayPlot[ca30, ColorRules → {1 → Hue[.2], 0 → Hue[.6]}];`

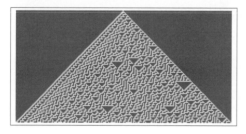

4. Here is the plot of the sine function.

In[13]:= `splot = Plot[Sin[x], {x, -2 π, 2 π}];`

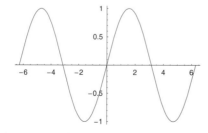

This replacement rule interchanges each ordered pair of numbers.

In[14]:=   `Show[splot /. {x_ ? NumberQ, y_ ? NumberQ} → {y, x}];`

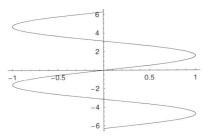

Although this particular example may have worked without the argument checking (_?Num·
berQ), it is a good idea to include it so that pairs of arbitrary expressions are not pattern
matched here. We only want to interchange pairs of numbers, not pairs of options or other
expressions that might be present in the underlying expression representing the graphic.

6. Using the standard rotation matrix, each point is taken to its image under the rotation transformation. Notice that this function first checks that its first argument is in fact a graphics object
   via pattern matching.

In[15]:=   `rotatePlot[p_Graphics, theta_] := Show[p /. {x_ ? NumberQ, y_ ? NumberQ} →`
        `{x, y}.{{Cos[theta], Sin[theta]}, {-Sin[theta], Cos[theta]}}]`

In[16]:=   `plot1 = Plot[Sin[x], {x, 0, 2 π}];`

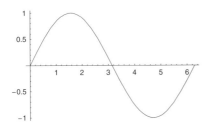

In[17]:=   `rotatePlot[plot1, Pi];`

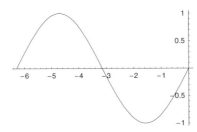

7 Recursion

7.1 Fibonacci numbers

1.

a. This is a straightforward recursion, multiplying the previous two values to get the next.

```
In[1]:=  a[1] := 2
         a[2] := 3
         a[i_] := a[i - 1] a[i - 2]

In[4]:=  Table[a[i], {i, 1, 8}]

Out[4]=  {2, 3, 6, 18, 108, 1944, 209952, 408146688}
```

b. The sequence is obtained by taking the difference of the previous two values.

```
In[5]:=  b[1] := 0
         b[2] := 1
         b[i_] := b[i - 2] - b[i - 1]

In[8]:=  Table[b[i], {i, 1, 9}]

Out[8]=  {0, 1, -1, 2, -3, 5, -8, 13, -21}
```

c. Here we add the previous three values.

```
In[9]:=  c[1] := 0
         c[2] := 1
         c[3] := 2
         c[i_] := c[i - 3] + c[i - 2] + c[i - 1]

In[13]:=  Table[c[i], {i, 1, 9}]

Out[13]=  {0, 1, 2, 3, 6, 11, 20, 37, 68}
```

2. It is important to get the two base cases right here.

```
In[14]:=  FA[1] := 0
          FA[2] := 0
          FA[i_] := FA[i - 2] + FA[i - 1] + 1

In[17]:=  Map[FA, Range[8]]

Out[17]=  {0, 0, 1, 2, 4, 7, 12, 20}
```

7.2 List functions

1.

```
In[1]:=  sumOddElements[{}] := 0
         sumOddElements[{x_, y___}] :=
          x + sumOddElements[{y}] /; IntegerQ[x] && OddQ[x]
         sumOddElements[{x_, y___}] := sumOddElements[{y}]

In[4]:=  sumOddElements[{2, 3, 5, 6, 7, 9, 12, 13}]

Out[4]=  37
```

2.

```
In[5]:=  sumEveryOtherElement[{}] := 0
         sumEveryOtherElement[{x_}] := x
         sumEveryOtherElement[{x_, y_, r___}] := x + sumEveryOtherElement[{r}]

In[8]:=  sumEveryOtherElement[{1, 2, 3, 4, 5, 6, 7, 8, 9}]

Out[8]=  25
```

3.

```
In[9]:=  addTriples[{}, {}, {}] := {}
         addTriples[{x1_, y1___}, {x2_, y2___}, {x3_, y3___}] :=
          Join[{x1 + x2 + x3}, addTriples[{y1}, {y2}, {y3}]]

In[11]:= addTriples[{w₁, x₁, y₁, z₁}, {w₂, x₂, y₂, z₂}, {w₃, x₃, y₃, z₃}]

Out[11]= {w₁ + w₂ + w₃, x₁ + x₂ + x₃, y₁ + y₂ + y₃, z₁ + z₂ + z₃}
```

4.

```
In[12]:= multAllPairs[{}] := {}
         multAllPairs[{_}] := {}
         multAllPairs[{x_, y_, r___}] := Join[{x y}, multAllPairs[{y, r}]]

In[15]:= multAllPairs[{3, 9, 17, 2, 6, 60}]

Out[15]= {27, 153, 34, 12, 360}
```

5.

```
In[16]:= maxPairs[{}, {}] := {}
         maxPairs[{x_, r___}, {y_, s___}] := Join[{Max[x, y]}, maxPairs[{r}, {s}]]

In[18]:= maxPairs[{1, 2, 4}, {2, 7, 2}]

Out[18]= {2, 7, 4}
```

6.

```
In[19]:=  interleave[{}, {}] := {}
          interleave[{x_, r___}, {y_, s___}] := Join[{x, y}, interleave[{r}, {s}]]

In[21]:=  interleave[{a, b, c}, {x, y, z}]

Out[21]=  {a, x, b, y, c, z}
```

7.3 Thinking recursively: examples

1.

```
In[1]:=  prefixMatch[L_, {}] := {}
         prefixMatch[{}, M_] := {}
         prefixMatch[{x_, r___}, {x_, s___}] := Join[{x}, prefixMatch[{r}, {s}]]
         prefixMatch[{x_, r___}, {y_, s___}] := {}
```

2.

```
In[5]:=  runEncode2[{}] := {}
         runEncode2[{x_}] := {x}
         runEncode2[{x_, r__}] := runEncode2[{r}] /.
            {{{y_, k_}, s___} → If[x == y, {{x, k + 1}, s}, {x, {y, k}, s}],
             {y_, s___} → If[x == y, {{x, 2}, s}, {x, y, s}]}
```

3. Perhaps the most straightforward way to do this is to write an auxiliary function that takes the output from runEncode and produces output such as Split would generate.

```
In[8]:=  runEncode[{}]  := {}
         runEncode[{x_}] := {{x, 1}}

In[10]:=  runEncode[{x_, res___}] := Module[{R = runEncode[{res}], p},
             p = First[R];
             If[x == First[p],
               Join[{{x, p[[2]] + 1}}, Rest[R]],
               Join[{{x, 1}}, R]]]
```

Then our split (named to mimic the built-in Split) simply operates on the output of runEncode.

```
In[11]:=  sp[lis_] := Map[Table[#[[1]], {#[[2]]}] &, lis]

In[12]:=  sp[{{3, 2}, {4, 1}, {2, 5}}]

Out[12]=  {{3, 3}, {4}, {2, 2, 2, 2, 2}}

In[13]:=  split[lis_] := sp[runEncode[lis]]
```

```
In[14]:=  split[{9, 9, 9, 9, 9, 4, 3, 3, 3, 3, 5, 5, 5, 5, 5, 5}]

Out[14]=  {{9, 9, 9, 9, 9}, {4}, {3, 3, 3, 3}, {5, 5, 5, 5, 5, 5}}
```

4.

```
In[15]:=  runEncode[{}] := {}
          runEncode[{x_, r___}] := runEncode[x, 1, {r}]
          runEncode[x_, k_, {}] := {{x, k}}
          runEncode[x_, k_, {x_, r___}] := runEncode[x, k + 1, {r}]
          runEncode[x_, k_, {y_, r___}] := Join[{{x, k}}, runEncode[y, 1, {r}]]
```

5.

```
In[20]:=  maxima[{}] := {}
          maxima[{x_, r___}] := maxima[x, {r}]
```

```
In[22]:=  maxima[x_, {}] := {x}
          maxima[x_, {y_, r___}] := maxima[x, {r}] /; x ≥ y
          maxima[x_, {y_, r___}] := Join[{x}, maxima[y, {r}]]
```

6.

```
In[25]:=  runDecode[{}] := {}
          runDecode[{{x_, k_}, r___}] := Join[Table[x, {k}], runDecode[{r}]]
```

7. We will need two sets of rules for the subsets function.

```
In[27]:=  Clear[subsets];
          subsets[lis_, {0}] := {{}}
          subsets[{}, {k_}] := {}
```

```
In[30]:=  subsets[lis_, {k_}] := Module[{ksubs = subsets[Rest[lis], {k - 1}]},
             Join[Map[(Join[{First[lis]}, #] &), ksubs], subsets[Rest[lis], {k}]]]
```

```
In[31]:=  subsets[Range[5], {2}]

Out[31]=  {{1, 2}, {1, 3}, {1, 4}, {1, 5}, {2, 3}, {2, 4}, {2, 5}, {3, 4}, {3, 5}, {4, 5}}
```

The second form simply calls the first.

```
In[32]:=  subsets[lis_, k_] := Flatten[Map[subsets[lis, {#}] &, Range[0, k]], 1]
```

The second form simply calls the first. This gives all subsets up to length 3.

```
In[33]:=  subsets[Range[5], 3]

Out[33]=  {{}, {1}, {2}, {3}, {4}, {5}, {1, 2}, {1, 3}, {1, 4}, {1, 5}, {2, 3},
          {2, 4}, {2, 5}, {3, 4}, {3, 5}, {4, 5}, {1, 2, 3}, {1, 2, 4}, {1, 2, 5},
          {1, 3, 4}, {1, 3, 5}, {1, 4, 5}, {2, 3, 4}, {2, 3, 5}, {2, 4, 5}, {3, 4, 5}}
```

A comparison with the built-in Subsets functions.

In[34]:= **Subsets[Range[5], 3]**

Out[34]= {{}, {1}, {2}, {3}, {4}, {5}, {1, 2}, {1, 3}, {1, 4}, {1, 5}, {2, 3},
        {2, 4}, {2, 5}, {3, 4}, {3, 5}, {4, 5}, {1, 2, 3}, {1, 2, 4}, {1, 2, 5},
        {1, 3, 4}, {1, 3, 5}, {1, 4, 5}, {2, 3, 4}, {2, 3, 5}, {2, 4, 5}, {3, 4, 5}}

The recursion in this definition of subsets can get quite deep.

In[35]:= **Timing[subsets[Range[1000], 2];]**

        $RecursionLimit::reclim : Recursion depth of 256 exceeded. More…

        General::stop : Further output of $RecursionLimit::reclim will
            be suppressed during this calculation. More…

You can temporarily increase the value of $RecursionLimit to let this computation run to
the end.

In[36]:= **Timing[**
        Block[{$RecursionLimit = ∞},
        subsets[Range[1000], 2];]]

Out[36]= {44.855 Second, Null}

But we can see pretty clearly just how inefficient our recursive approach to this problem is for
large computations by comparing with the built-in Subsets function which is more than two
orders of magnitude faster for sets of this size.

In[37]:= **Timing[Subsets[Range[1000], 2];]**

Out[37]= {0.14 Second, Null}

7.4 Recursion and symbolic computations

1.

In[1]:= **ddx[c_ ? NumericQ] := 0**
        ddx[x] := 1
        ddx[u_ + v_] := ddx[u] + ddx[v]
        ddx[u_ - v_] := ddx[u] - ddx[v]
        ddx[u_ v_] := u ddx[v] + v ddx[u]
        $$ddx\left[\frac{u\_}{v\_}\right] := \frac{v\ ddx[u] - u\ ddx[v]}{v^2}$$
        ddx[u_^c_?NumericQ] := c u^{c-1} ddx[u]

In[8]:= `ddx[Sin[u_]] := Cos[u] ddx[u]`
`ddx[ Cos[u_]] := -Sin[u] ddx[u]`

$$\texttt{ddx[Tan[u\_]] := } \frac{1}{\texttt{Cos[u]}^2} \texttt{ ddx[u]}$$

In[11]:= `ddx[Sin[2 x] + Cos[3 x]]`

Out[11]= `2 Cos[2 x] - 3 Sin[3 x]`

In[12]:= `ddx[Tan[3 x⁵]]`

Out[12]= $\texttt{15 x}^4 \texttt{ Sec[3 x}^5\texttt{]}^2$

2.

In[13]:= `Clear[ddx]`

In[14]:= `ddx[c_ ? NumericQ] := 0`
`ddx[x] := 1`
`ddx[u_ + v_] := ddx[u] + ddx[v]`
`ddx[u_ - v_] := ddx[u] - ddx[v]`
`ddx[u_ v_] := u ddx[v] + v ddx[u]`

$$\texttt{ddx}\left[\frac{\texttt{u\_}}{\texttt{v\_}}\right] := \frac{\texttt{v ddx[u] - u ddx[v]}}{\texttt{v}^2}$$

`ddx[u_^c_?NumericQ] := c u^{c-1} ddx[u]`

In[21]:= `ddx[u_] := 0 /; nox[u]`

In[22]:= `nox[c_ ? NumericQ] := True`
`nox[x] := False`
`nox[y_] := True /; Head[y] == Symbol && y =!= x`
`nox[u_ + v_] := nox[u] && nox[v]`
`nox[u_ - v_] := nox[u] && nox[v]`
`nox[u_ v_] := u nox[v] && v nox[u]`

$$\texttt{nox}\left[\frac{\texttt{u\_}}{\texttt{v\_}}\right] := \texttt{nox[u] \&\& nox[v]}$$

`nox[u_^c_?NumericQ] := nox[u]`

3.

In[30]:= `Clear[ddx];`
`ddx[c_ ? NumericQ, y_] := 0`
`ddx[x_, x_] := 1`
`ddx[y_, x_] := 0 /; FreeQ[y, x]`
`ddx[u_ + v_, x_] := ddx[u, x] + ddx[v, x]`
`ddx[u_ - v_, x_] := ddx[u, x] - ddx[v, x]`
`ddx[u_ v_, x_] := u ddx[v, x] + v ddx[u, x]`

$$\texttt{ddx}\left[\frac{\texttt{u\_}}{\texttt{v\_}}, \texttt{x\_}\right] := \frac{\texttt{v ddx[u, x] - u ddx[v, x]}}{\texttt{v}^2}$$

`ddx[u_^c_?NumericQ, x_] := c u^{c-1} ddx[u, x]`

In[39]:=   `ddx[α ζ³ + β ζ² + γ, ζ]`

Out[39]= $2 \beta \zeta + 3 \alpha \zeta^2$

In[40]:= $\mathtt{ddx}\left[\dfrac{\theta}{1+\theta^3},\ \theta\right]$

Out[40]= $\dfrac{1 - 2\,\theta^3}{(1+\theta^3)^2}$

7.5 Classical examples

1. The solution to this problem also appears in Section 8.5. We will call our new function `solvep` (for pivoting).

In[1]:=   `Clear[solve]`

In[2]:=   `solvep[S_] := Module[`
    `{S1 = pivot[S], E1, a12toa1n, x2toxn}, x2toxn = solvep[elimx1[S1]];`
    `E1 = First[S1];`
    `a12toa1n = Drop[Rest[E1], -1];`
    $\mathtt{Join}\Big[\Big\{\dfrac{\mathtt{Last[E1]\ -\ a12toa1n.x2toxn}}{\mathtt{First[E1]}}\Big\},\ \mathtt{x2toxn}\Big]\Big];$

In[3]:= $\mathtt{solvep[\{\{a11\_,\ b1\_\}\}]\ :=\ \left\{\dfrac{b1}{a11}\right\}}$

In[4]:=   `elimx1[S_] := Map[subtractE1[S〚1〛, #] &, Rest[S]]`

In[5]:= $\mathtt{subtractE1[E1\_,\ Ei\_]\ :=\ Rest[Ei]\ -\ \dfrac{Ei〚1〛}{E1〚1〛}\ Rest[E1]}$

In[6]:=   `pivot[Q_] := Module[{p, ST1, pivotrow}, ST1 = Transpose[Q]〚1〛;`
    `p = Position[ST1, x_ /; x ≠ 0];`
    `If[p == {},`
    `Print["Matrix is singular"]; Q,`
    `pivotrow = p〚1〛〚1〛; Join[{Q〚pivotrow〛}, Delete[Q, pivotrow]]]]`

In[7]:=   `solve[A_, B_] := solvep[Transpose[Join[Transpose[A], {B}]]]`

Here are some test examples.

In[8]:=   `mat = Table[Random[], {4}, {4}]`

Out[8]=   `{{0.554127, 0.426593, 0.861278, 0.492521},`
    `{0.572684, 0.477244, 0.690375, 0.88366},`
    `{0.401935, 0.648486, 0.818292, 0.516009},`
    `{0.129603, 0.562562, 0.116779, 0.699194}}`

```
In[9]:=  b = Table[Random[], {4}]

Out[9]=  {0.564681, 0.489887, 0.542515, 0.264061}

In[10]:=  x = solve[mat, b]

Out[10]=  {1.59998, 0.96497, -0.502052, -0.611457}

In[11]:=  mat.x - b
```

$$Out[11]=\ \{-1.11022\times10^{-16},\ -1.66533\times10^{-16},\ -1.11022\times10^{-16},\ -4.44089\times10^{-16}\}$$

```
In[12]:=  Chop[%]

Out[12]=  {0, 0, 0, 0}
```

2. To compute `solveUpper [A, B]`, first recursively compute `solveUpper [A', B']`, where A' is the lower-right square submatrix of A, and B' is the `Rest` of B. This solution gives the values of $x_2, \ldots, x_n$. `B[[1]]` is equal to the dot product of the top row of A (that is, `A[[1]]`) and the vector $x_1, \ldots, x_n$ (that is, `B[[1]]`) is equal to `A[[1]]*`x_1 `+ ... + A[[n]]*`x_n. It is easy to compute x_1 from this formula.

$$In[13]:=\ \texttt{solveUpper[\{\{ann\_\}\}, \{bn\_\}] := }\{\frac{\texttt{bn}}{\texttt{ann}}\}$$

```
In[14]:=  solveUpper[{A1_, rA__}, {b1_, rB__}] :=
             Module[{subsoln = solveUpper[Rest /@ {rA}, {rB}]},
```
$$\texttt{Join}[\{\frac{\texttt{b1 - Rest[A1].subsoln}}{\texttt{First[A1]}}\}, \texttt{subsoln}]]$$

It is easy to show that if you rotate a matrix by 90 degrees, and turn the vector B upside down, the solution to the resulting system is the same as the solution to the original system, but turned upside down.

```
In[15]:=  rotateMatrix[A_] := Reverse[Map[Reverse, A]]

In[16]:=  solveLower[A_, B_] := Reverse[solveUpper[rotateMatrix[A], Reverse[B]]]
```

3.

```
In[17]:=  LUdecomp1[S_] := Module[{mults = multipliers[S[[1, 1]], Rest[S]]}, Module[
             {Sprime = elimx1[mults, Rest /@ S]}, Module[{LU = LUdecomp1[Sprime]},
             {expandL[mults, LU[[1]]], expandU[First[S], LU[[2]]]}]]]

In[18]:=  LUdecomp1[{{a11_}}] := {{{1}}, {{a11}}}

In[19]:=  expandU[S1_, U_] := Join[{S1}, (Join[{0}, #1] &) /@ U]

In[20]:=  expandL[mults_, L_] := Transpose[expandU[Join[{1}, mults], Transpose[L]]]
```

```
In[21]:= elimx1[mults_, subS_] :=
            Table[subS[[i + 1]] - mults[[i]] subS[[1]], {i, 1, Length[mults]}]
```

```
In[22]:= multipliers[S11_, restS_] := Map[ # / S11 &, Transpose[restS][[1]]]
```

```
In[23]:= LUdecomp2[S_] := Module[{soln = LUdecomp1[S]},
            soln[[1]] - IdentityMatrix[Length[S]] + soln[[2]]]
```

4.

```
In[24]:= sumNodes[{lab_}] := lab
         sumNodes[{lab_, lc_, rc_}] := lab + sumNodes[lc] + sumNodes[rc]
```

5.

```
In[26]:= catNodes[{lab_}] := lab
         catNodes[{lab_, lc_, rc_}] :=
           StringJoin[lab, catNodes[lc], catNodes[rc]]
```

6.

```
In[28]:= balanced[t_] := balancedHeight[t][[2]]
         balancedHeight[{lab_}] := {0, True}
```

```
In[30]:= balancedHeight[{lab_, lc_, rc_}] :=
           Module[{lbh, rbh}, lbh = balancedHeight[lc];
             If[lbh[[2]], rbh = balancedHeight[rc]; If[rbh[[2]] && Abs[lbh[[1]] - rbh[[1]]] ≤ 1,
               {Max[lbh[[1]], rbh[[1]]] + 1, True}, {0, False}], {0, False}]]
```

7.

```
In[31]:= listLevel[0, t_] := {t[[1]]}
         listLevel[{lab_}, n_] := {}
```

```
In[33]:= listLevel[{lab_, lc_, rc_}, n_] :=
           Join[listLevel[lc, n - 1], listLevel[rc, n - 1]]
```

8.

```
In[34]:= minInTree[{lab_}] := lab
         minInTree[{lab_, subtrees__}] :=
           Sort[Join[{lab}, Map[minInTree, {subtrees}]]][[1]]
```

```
In[36]:= height[{lab_}] := 0
         height[{lab_, subtrees__}] := 1 + Apply[Max, Map[height, {subtrees}]]
```

```
In[38]:= printTree[t_] := printTree[t, 0]
```

```
In[39]:= printTree[{lab_}, k_] := printIndented[lab, 3 k]
         printTree[{lab_, subtrees__}, k_] :=
           (printIndented[lab, 3 k]; Map[printTree[#, k + 1] &, {subtrees}];)
```

```
In[41]:=  printIndented[x_, spaces_] :=
            Print[Apply[StringJoin, Table[" ", {spaces}]], x]
```

9. We have used a slightly different representation for the list of trees than the one shown in the chapter. Instead of a node's label containing a list of characters and a number, it contains a string and a number. The only reason for this is that it makes the result come out looking like the tree called Htree (shown in Figure 7.1). Note that the algorithm may give different results depending upon how it is programmed, since there are arbitrary choices made at each step. The result of applying our function constructHTree to the initial list of trees shown at the end of the last section (which we have included here as testlist) is different from Htree.

    In our solution, we solve the problem of finding the two trees of smallest weight by keeping the list of trees sorted by weight; then we simply always pick the first two.

```
In[42]:=  HTreeSort[trees_] := Sort[trees, #1[[1, 2]] < #2[[1, 2]] &]
```

```
In[43]:=  joinHTrees[{{{cl_, wt_}, kids___}}] := {cl, kids}
            joinHTrees[{{{cl1_, wt1_}, kids1___},
                {{cl2_, wt2_}, kids2___}, trees___}] := joinHTrees[
                HTreeSort[{{{cl1 <> cl2, wt1 + wt2}, {cl1, kids1}, {cl2, kids2}}, trees}]]
```

```
In[45]:=  constructHTree[t_] := joinHTrees[HTreeSort[t]]
```

```
In[46]:=  htnode[a_, b_] := {{{a, b}}}
```

```
In[47]:=  testlist = Join[htnode[" ", 6], htnode["A", 3],
            htnode["B", 1], htnode["E", 5], htnode["H", 2],
            htnode["N", 2], htnode["O", 2], htnode["S", 3], htnode["T", 3]]
```

```
Out[47]=  {{{ , 6}}, {{A, 3}}, {{B, 1}}, {{E, 5}},
            {{H, 2}}, {{N, 2}}, {{O, 2}}, {{S, 3}}, {{T, 3}}}
```

10. To make the results here comparable to those in the book, we will use Htree from the book as our sample tree. makeTreeTable[tree] produces a list of rules as described in the problem. encodeString[str, rules] decodes the string according to those rules.

```
In[48]:=  Htree = {" ABEHONST", {" AT", {" "}, {"AT", {"T"}, {"A"}}},
            {"BEHONS", {"EON", {"E"}, {"ON", {"O"}, {"N"}}},
            {"BHS", {"BH", {"H"}, {"B"}}, {"S"}}}};
```

```
In[49]:=  makeTreeTable[prefix_, {ch_}] = {ch -> prefix};
```

```
In[50]:=  makeTreeTable[prefix_, {_, left_, right_}] :=
            Join[makeTreeTable[Join[prefix, {0}], left],
            makeTreeTable[Join[prefix, {1}], right]]
```

```
In[51]:=  makeTreeTable[tree_] := makeTreeTable[{}, tree]
```

```
In[52]:=  HtreeRules = makeTreeTable[Htree]
```

Out[52]= { → {0, 0}, T → {0, 1, 0}, A → {0, 1, 1}, E → {1, 0, 0}, O → {1, 0, 1, 0},
          N → {1, 0, 1, 1}, H → {1, 1, 0, 0}, B → {1, 1, 0, 1}, S → {1, 1, 1}}

```
In[53]:=  encodeString[str_, rules_] := Flatten[Characters[str] /. rules]
```

```
In[54]:=  encodeString[str_] := encodeString[str, HtreeRules]
```

7.6 Dynamic programming

1. This implementation uses the identities given in the exercise together with some pattern matching

```
In[1]:=  F[1] := 1
         F[2] := 1
```

$$In[3]:= \quad F[n\_ \,/; \, \text{EvenQ}[n]] := 2 \, F\!\left[\frac{n}{2} - 1\right] F\!\left[\frac{n}{2}\right] + F\!\left[\frac{n}{2}\right]^2$$

$$F[n\_ \,/; \, \text{OddQ}[n]] := F\!\left[\frac{n-1}{2} + 1\right]^2 + F\!\left[\frac{n-1}{2}\right]^2$$

```
In[5]:=  Map[F, Range[10]]
```

Out[5]= {1, 1, 2, 3, 5, 8, 13, 21, 34, 55}

2.

```
In[6]:=  FF[1] := 1
         FF[2] := 1
```

$$In[8]:= \quad FF[n\_ \,? \, \text{EvenQ}] := FF[n] = 2 \, FF\!\left[\frac{n}{2} - 1\right] FF\!\left[\frac{n}{2}\right] + FF\!\left[\frac{n}{2}\right]^2$$

$$FF[n\_ \,? \, \text{OddQ}] := FF[n] = FF\!\left[\frac{n-1}{2} + 1\right]^2 + FF\!\left[\frac{n-1}{2}\right]^2$$

```
In[10]:=  Map[FF, Range[12]]
```

Out[10]= {1, 1, 2, 3, 5, 8, 13, 21, 34, 55, 89, 144}

3.

```
In[11]:=  Clear[collatz]
```

```
In[12]:=  collatz[n_, 0] := n
```

$$In[13]:= \quad \text{collatz}[n\_, \, i\_] := \left(\text{collatz}[n, \, i] = \frac{\text{collatz}[n, \, i-1]}{2}\right) \,/; \, \text{EvenQ}[\text{collatz}[n, \, i-1]]$$

In[14]:= `collatz[n_, i_] :=`
          `(collatz[n, i] = 3 collatz[n, i - 1] + 1) /; OddQ[collatz[n, i - 1]]`

Here is the fifth iterate of the Collatz sequence for 27.

In[15]:= `collatz[27, 5]`

Out[15]= `31`

Here is the Collatz sequence for 27. You can see that it takes a long time for this sequence to settle down to the cycle 4, 2, 1.

In[16]:= `Table[collatz[27, i], {i, 0, 116}]`

Out[16]= `{27, 82, 41, 124, 62, 31, 94, 47, 142, 71, 214, 107, 322, 161, 484, 242, 121,`
          `364, 182, 91, 274, 137, 412, 206, 103, 310, 155, 466, 233, 700, 350,`
          `175, 526, 263, 790, 395, 1186, 593, 1780, 890, 445, 1336, 668, 334,`
          `167, 502, 251, 754, 377, 1132, 566, 283, 850, 425, 1276, 638, 319, 958,`
          `479, 1438, 719, 2158, 1079, 3238, 1619, 4858, 2429, 7288, 3644, 1822,`
          `911, 2734, 1367, 4102, 2051, 6154, 3077, 9232, 4616, 2308, 1154, 577,`
          `1732, 866, 433, 1300, 650, 325, 976, 488, 244, 122, 61, 184, 92, 46, 23,`
          `70, 35, 106, 53, 160, 80, 40, 20, 10, 5, 16, 8, 4, 2, 1, 4, 2, 1, 4, 2}`

7.7 Higher-order functions and recursion

1. First, here is the definition for our user-defined `fold`.

    In[1]:= `fold[f_, x_, {}] := x`
             `fold[f_, x_, {a_, r___}] := fold[f, f[x, a], {r}]`

    In[3]:= `fold[Plus, 0, {a, b, c, d, e}]`

    Out[3]= `a + b + c + d + e`

    In[4]:= `foldList[f_, x_, {}] := {x}`
             `foldList[f_, x_, {a_, r___}] := Join[{x}, foldList[f, f[x, a], {r}]]`

    In[6]:= `foldList[Times, 1, Range[6]]`

    Out[6]= `{1, 1, 2, 6, 24, 120, 720}`

    And here is `nestList`.

    In[7]:= `nestList[f_, x_, 0] := {x}`
             `nestList[f_, x_, n_] := Join[{x}, nestList[f, f[x], n - 1]]`

    In[9]:= `nestList[Sin, θ, 3]`

    Out[9]= `{θ, Sin[θ], Sin[Sin[θ]], Sin[Sin[Sin[θ]]]}`

2. First, here is the recursive `repeat` function from this section.

    In[10]:= `repeat[f_, lis_, pred_] := lis /; pred[Drop[lis, -1], Last[lis]]`

    In[11]:= `repeat[f_, lis_, pred_] := repeat[f, Append[lis, f[Last[lis]]], pred]`

    Then the `MemberQ` function is used to test whether the currently computed point is a member of the existing list of points.

    In[12]:= `landMineWalk[] :=`
    `    repeat[#1 + {{0, 1}, {0, -1}, {1, 0}, {-1, 0}}〚Random[Integer, {1, 4}]〛 &,`
    `    {{0, 0}}, MemberQ[#1, #2] &]`

    Here is a test. On average, these walks will not be terribly long.

    In[13]:= `landMineWalk[]`

    Out[13]= `{{0, 0}, {-1, 0}, {-2, 0}, {-1, 0}}`

8 Numerics

8.2 Numbers

1. This function gives the polar form as a list consisting of the magnitude and the polar angle.

    In[1]:= `complexToPolar[z_] := {Abs[z], Arg[z]}`

    Here are the computations for the examples in the text.

    In[2]:= `complexToPolar[3 + 3 i]`

    Out[2]= $\left\{3\sqrt{2}, \frac{\pi}{4}\right\}$

    In[3]:= `complexToPolar[`$e^{\frac{\pi i}{3}}$`]`

    Out[3]= $\left\{1, \frac{\pi}{3}\right\}$

2. This function uses a default value of 2 for the base. (Try replacing `Fold` with `FoldList` to more clearly see what this function is doing.)

    In[4]:= `convert[digits_List, base_ : 2] := Fold[(base #1 + #2) &, 0, digits]`

    Here are the digits for 9 in base 2:

    In[5]:= `IntegerDigits[9, 2]`

    Out[5]= `{1, 0, 0, 1}`

This converts them back to the base 10 representation.

In[6]:= `convert[%]`

Out[6]= 9

This does the same for the number 129 in base 16.

In[7]:= `IntegerDigits[129, 16]`

Out[7]= {8, 1}

In[8]:= `convert[%, 16]`

Out[8]= 129

This function is essentially an implementation of Horner's method for fast polynomial multiplication.

In[9]:= `Clear[a, b, c, d, e, x]`

In[10]:= `convert[{a, b, c, d, e}, x]`

Out[10]= $e + x (d + x (c + x (b + a x)))$

In[11]:= `Expand[%]`

Out[11]= $e + d x + c x^2 + b x^3 + a x^4$

4. Here is the `sumsOfCubes` function.

In[12]:= `sumsOfCubes[n_Integer] := Apply[Plus, IntegerDigits[n]³]`

Here is the function that performs the iteration.

In[13]:= `sumsOfSums[n_Integer, iter_] := NestList[sumsOfCubes, n, iter]`

We see that the number 4 enters into a cycle.

In[14]:= `sumsOfSums[4, 12]`

Out[14]= {4, 64, 280, 520, 133, 55, 250, 133, 55, 250, 133, 55, 250}

In fact, it appears as if many initial values enter cycles.

In[15]:= `sumsOfSums[32, 12]`

Out[15]= {32, 35, 152, 134, 92, 737, 713, 371, 371, 371, 371, 371, 371}

In[16]:= `sumsOfSums[7, 12]`

Out[16]= {7, 343, 118, 514, 190, 730, 370, 370, 370, 370, 370, 370, 370}

In[17]:= **sumsOfSums[372, 12]**

Out[17]= {372, 378, 882, 1032, 36, 243, 99, 1458, 702, 351, 153, 153, 153}

6. The function sumsOfPowers is a straightforward generalization of the previous cases.

In[18]:= **sumsOfPowers[n_, p_] := Apply[Plus, IntegerDigits[n]^P]**

In[19]:= **sumsOfPowers[123, 5]**

Out[19]= 276

8. Using the number 100 as an example, let us first put it in base 2.

In[20]:= **BaseForm[100, 2]**

 Out[20]//BaseForm=
  1100100_2

Here is the list of its digits.

In[21]:= **IntegerDigits[100, 2]**

Out[21]= {1, 1, 0, 0, 1, 0, 0}

This performs a binary shift of one unit (actually, the 1 in RotateLeft is not needed here as this is the default value to shift by).

In[22]:= **l = RotateLeft[IntegerDigits[100, 2], 1]**

Out[22]= {1, 0, 0, 1, 0, 0, 1}

This converts back from base 2 to base 10 (using the convert function from Exercise 2).

In[23]:= **convert[l, 2]**

Out[23]= 73

Now we can put all of this code together to make the survivor function.

In[24]:= **survivor[n_] :=**
  Module[{p}, p = RotateLeft[IntegerDigits[n, 2]]; Fold[(2 #1 + #2) &, 0, p]]

In[25]:= **survivor[100]**

Out[25]= 73

You could of course do the same thing without the symbol p, but it is just a bit less readable.

In[26]:= **survivor2[n_Integer] :=**
  Fold[(2 #1 + #2) &, 0, RotateLeft[IntegerDigits[n, 2]]]

In[27]:= `survivor2[100]`

Out[27]= 73

9. This function has a straightforward implementation. Each die can be viewed as a random integer between 1 and 6.

In[28]:= `rollEm := {Random[Integer, {1, 6}], Random[Integer, {1, 6}]}`

In[29]:= `rollEm`

Out[29]= {3, 2}

Here are five rolls in a row.

In[30]:= `Table[rollEm, {5}]`

Out[30]= {{6, 4}, {2, 3}, {5, 3}, {4, 3}, {4, 5}}

10. First generate a vector of 100 random real numbers on the interval 0 to 1.

In[31]:= `data = Table[Random[], {100}];`

You could rotate once to the left for each successive row.

In[32]:= `ListDensityPlot[NestList[RotateLeft, data, Length[data]]];`

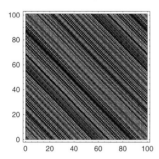

Here are a few other things you can try.

In[33]:= `ListDensityPlot[NestList[#`$^{.75}$` &, data, Length[data]]];`

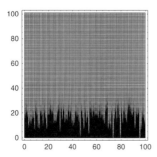

In[34]:= `ListDensityPlot`$\left[\texttt{NestList}\left[\frac{\#1}{1+\#1}\right.\right.$ `&, data, Length[data]]`$\left.\right)$`, Mesh → False];`

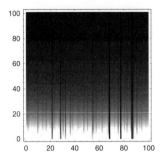

11. Here is the linear congruential generator.

In[35]:= `linearCongruential[x_,m_,b_] := Mod[b x + 1, m]`

With modulus 100 and multiplier 15, this generator quickly gets into a cycle.

In[36]:= `NestList[linearCongruential[#, 100, 15] &, 5, 10]`

Out[36]= `{5, 76, 41, 16, 41, 16, 41, 16, 41, 16, 41}`

With a larger modulus and multiplier, it appears as if this generator is doing better.

Here are the first 60 terms starting with a seed of 0.

In[37]:= `data = NestList[linearCongruential[#, 381, 15] &, 0, 60]`

Out[37]= `{0, 1, 16, 241, 187, 139, 181, 49, 355, 373, 262, 121, 292, 190, 184, 94,`
`268, 211, 118, 247, 277, 346, 238, 142, 226, 343, 193, 229, 7, 106, 67,`
`244, 232, 52, 19, 286, 100, 358, 37, 175, 340, 148, 316, 169, 250, 322,`
`259, 76, 379, 352, 328, 349, 283, 55, 64, 199, 319, 214, 163, 160, 115}`

Sometimes it is hard to see if your generator is getting into a rut. Graphical analysis can help by allowing you to see patterns over larger domains. Here is a `ListPlot` of this sequence taken out to 5,000 terms.

In[38]:= `ListPlot[NestList[linearCongruential[#, 381, 15] &, 0.0, 5000]];`

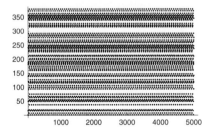

It appears as if certain numbers are repeating. Looking at the plot of the Fourier data shows peaks at certain frequencies, indicating a periodic nature to the data.

```
In[39]:= ListPlot[Abs[Fourier[
          NestList[linearCongruential[#,381,15]&,0.0,5000]]]];
```

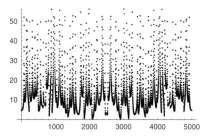

Using a much larger modulus and multiplier (chosen carefully), you can keep your generator from getting in such short loops.

```
In[40]:= ListPlot[
          data = NestList[linearCongruential[#, 2^16, 27421] &, 0.0, 5000]];
```

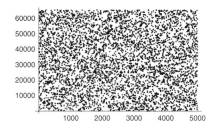

```
In[41]:= ListPlot[Abs[Fourier[data]]];
```

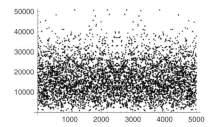

13. First we implement the chi-square test and then use it to run tests on some data in the next exercise.

$$In[42]:= \text{chiSquare[lis\_List]} := \text{Module}\left[\{m = \text{Length[lis]}, n = \text{Max[lis]}\}, \right.$$
$$\left. \frac{\sum_{i=1}^{n} \left(\text{Count[lis, i]} - \frac{m}{n}\right)^2}{\frac{m}{n}}\right]$$

14. Here are some data generated using the linear congruential generator with small modulus and multiplier.

In[43]:= `data = NestList[linearCongruential[#, 381, 15] &, 0, 1000];`

In[44]:= `chiSquare[data]`

Out[44]= $\dfrac{5018521}{1001}$

In[45]:= `N[%]`

Out[45]= `5013.51`

Notice that the statistic is quite far from $2\sqrt{n}$ of n. This is a particularly pathological sequence. You can see a cycle of length 63 within the first 100 iterates.

In[46]:= `NestList[linearCongruential[#1, 381, 15] &, 0, 100]`

Out[46]= `{0, 1, 16, 241, 187, 139, 181, 49, 355, 373, 262, 121, 292, 190, 184,`
`94, 268, 211, 118, 247, 277, 346, 238, 142, 226, 343, 193, 229, 7,`
`106, 67, 244, 232, 52, 19, 286, 100, 358, 37, 175, 340, 148, 316, 169,`
`250, 322, 259, 76, 379, 352, 328, 349, 283, 55, 64, 199, 319, 214,`
`163, 160, 115, 202, 364, 127, 1, 16, 241, 187, 139, 181, 49, 355,`
`373, 262, 121, 292, 190, 184, 94, 268, 211, 118, 247, 277, 346, 238,`
`142, 226, 343, 193, 229, 7, 106, 67, 244, 232, 52, 19, 286, 100, 358}`

Here are those positions that contain the number 1.

In[47]:= `Position[%, 1]`

Out[47]= `{{2}, {65}}`

8.3 Working with numbers

1. The number 1.23 has machine precision.

   In[1]:= `Precision[1.23]`

   Out[1]= `MachinePrecision`

   Asking *Mathematica* to generate 100 digits of precision from a number that only contains about 16 digits of precision would require it to produce 84 digits without any information about where those digits should come from.

2. You could simply produce a table showing the number of digits of precision needed in the input compared with the accuracy of the result.

In[2]:= `Table[{x, Accuracy[N[√2, x]`^{200}` - (√2)`^{200}`]}, {x, 100, 140, 5}] // TableForm`

Out[2]//TableForm=

100	67.596
105	72.596
110	77.596
115	82.596
120	87.596
125	92.596
130	97.596
135	102.596
140	107.596

8.4 Working with arrays of numbers

1. Note the need for a delayed rule in this function.

In[1]:= `RandomSparseArray[n_Integer] := SparseArray[{{i_, i_} :> Random[]}, {n, n}]`

In[2]:= `Normal[RandomSparseArray[5]] // MatrixForm`

Out[2]//MatrixForm=

$$\begin{pmatrix} 0.197227 & 0 & 0 & 0 & 0 \\ 0 & 0.509405 & 0 & 0 & 0 \\ 0 & 0 & 0.965962 & 0 & 0 \\ 0 & 0 & 0 & 0.873469 & 0 \\ 0 & 0 & 0 & 0 & 0.959528 \end{pmatrix}$$

2. Here is the definition of `tridiagonalMatrix`.

In[3]:= `tridiagonalMatrix[n_, p_, q_] :=`
`SparseArray[{{i_, i_} → p, ({i_, j_} /; Abs[i - j] == 1) → q}, {n, n}]`

In[4]:= `tridiagonalMatrix[5, α, β]`

Out[4]= `SparseArray[<13>, {5, 5}]`

In[5]:= `Normal[%] // MatrixForm`

Out[5]//MatrixForm=

$$\begin{pmatrix} \alpha & \beta & 0 & 0 & 0 \\ \beta & \alpha & \beta & 0 & 0 \\ 0 & \beta & \alpha & \beta & 0 \\ 0 & 0 & \beta & \alpha & \beta \\ 0 & 0 & 0 & \beta & \alpha \end{pmatrix}$$

3. First we create the packed array vector.

In[6]:= `vec = Table[Random[], {10⁶}];`

In[7]:= `Developer`PackedArrayQ[vec]`

Out[7]= `True`

Replacing the first element in `vec` with a 1 gives us an expression which is not packed.

In[8]:= `newvec = ReplacePart[vec, 1, 1];`

In[9]:= `Developer`PackedArrayQ[newvec]`

Out[9]= `False`

The size of the unpacked object is about two and a half times larger than the packed array.

In[10]:= `Map[ByteCount, {vec, newvec}]`

Out[10]= `{8000056, 20000032}`

In[11]:= `%[[2]] / %[[1]] // N`

Out[11]= `2.49999`

Sorting the packed object is about four or five times faster than sorting the unpacked object.

In[12]:= `Timing[Do[Sort[vec], {5}]]`

Out[12]= `{4.406 Second, Null}`

In[13]:= `Timing[Do[Sort[newvec], {5}]]`

Out[13]= `{18.777 Second, Null}`

Finding the minimum element is about one order of magnitude faster with the packed array.

In[14]:= `Timing[Min[vec];]`

Out[14]= `{0.01 Second, Null}`

In[15]:= `Timing[Min[newvec];]`

Out[15]= `{0.131 Second, Null}`

8.5 Numerical computations

1. We will overload newton to invoke the secant method when given a list of two numbers as the second argument.

```
In[1]:= Options[newton] = {
            MaxIterations :→ $RecursionLimit,
            PrecisionGoal → Automatic,
            WorkingPrecision → Automatic
        };
```

```
In[2]:= newton[fun_, {x1_ ? NumericQ, x2_ ? NumericQ}, opts___ ? OptionQ] :=
        Module[{maxIterations, precisionGoal,
            workingPrecision, initx, df, next, result},
            {maxIterations, precisionGoal, workingPrecision} =
            {MaxIterations, PrecisionGoal, WorkingPrecision} /. Flatten[{opts}] /.
                Options[newton];
            If[precisionGoal === Automatic, precisionGoal =
                Min[{Precision[x1], Precision[x2]}]];
            If[workingPrecision === Automatic,
                workingPrecision = precisionGoal + 10];
            initx = SetPrecision[{x1, x2}, workingPrecision];
            df[a_, b_] := (fun[b] - fun[a]) / (b - a);
            next[{a_, b_}] := {a, b - fun[b]/df[a, b]};
            result = FixedPoint[next, initx, maxIterations][[2]];
            SetPrecision[result, precisionGoal]
        ]
```

```
In[3]:= f[x_] := x^2 - 2
```

```
In[4]:= newton[f, {1., 2.}]
```

```
Out[4]= 1.41421
```

```
In[5]:= newton[f, {1.0`60, 2.0`50}]
```

```
Out[5]= 1.4142135623730950488016887242096980785696740946953
```

```
In[6]:= Precision[%]
```

```
Out[6]= 50.
```

5. Here is a three-dimensional vector.

```
In[7]:= vec = {1, -3, 2};
```

This computes the l_∞ norm of the vector.

```
In[8]:= norm[v_ ? VectorQ, l_ : Infinity] := Max[Abs[v]]
```

In[9]:= `norm[vec]`

Out[9]= 3

You can compare this with the built-in `Norm` function.

In[10]:= `Norm[vec, Infinity]`

Out[10]= 3

Here is a 3×3 matrix.

In[11]:= `mat = {{1, 2, 3}, {1, 0, 2}, {2, -3, 2}}`

Out[11]= `{{1, 2, 3}, {1, 0, 2}, {2, -3, 2}}`

Here, then, is the matrix norm.

In[12]:= `norm[m_ ? MatrixQ, l_ : Infinity] :=`
           `norm[Apply[Plus, Abs[Transpose[m]]], Infinity]`

In[13]:= `norm[mat]`

Out[13]= 7

Again, a comparison with the built-in `Norm` function.

In[14]:= `Norm[mat, Infinity]`

Out[14]= 7

Notice how we *overloaded* the definition of the function `norm` so that it would act differently depending upon what type of argument it was given. This is a particularly powerful feature of *Mathematica*. The expression `_?MatrixQ` on the left-hand side of the definition causes the function `norm` to use the definition on the right-hand side *only if* the argument is in fact a matrix (if it passes the `MatrixQ` test). If that argument is a vector (if it passes the `VectorQ` test), then the previous definition is used.

6. Here is the function to compute the condition number of a matrix (using the l_∞ norm).

In[15]:= `conditionNumber[m_ ? MatrixQ] :=`
           `norm[m, Infinity] norm[Inverse[m], Infinity]`

In[16]:= `HilbertMatrix[n_] := Table[` $\frac{1}{i+j-1}$ `, {i, n}, {j, n}]`

In[17]:= `conditionNumber[HilbertMatrix[3]]`

Out[17]= 748

Compare this with the condition number of a random matrix.

In[18]:= `conditionNumber[Table[Random[], {3}, {3}]]`

Out[18]= `18.7428`

Here are the condition numbers of the first ten Hilbert matrices.

In[19]:= `Map[conditionNumber[HilbertMatrix[#]] &, Range[10]]`

Out[19]= $\left\{1,\ 27,\ 748,\ 28375,\ 943656,\ 29070279,\ \dfrac{1970389773}{2}\right.$,

$\left.33872791095,\ \dfrac{2199309082685}{2},\ 35357439251992\right\}$

In[20]:= `N[%]`

Out[20]= $\{1.,\ 27.,\ 748.,\ 28375.,\ 943656.,\ 2.90703 \times 10^7,$
$9.85195 \times 10^8,\ 3.38728 \times 10^{10},\ 1.09965 \times 10^{12},\ 3.53574 \times 10^{13}\}$

9 Graphics programming

9.1 Structure of graphics

1. The color wheel can be obtained by mapping the Hue directive over successive sectors of a disk. Note that the argument to Hue must be scaled so that it falls within the range 0 to 1.

In[1]:= `colorWheel[n_] :=`
$\quad$ `Show[Graphics[Map[{Hue[` $\dfrac{\#}{2\pi - n}$ `], Disk[{0, 0}, 1, {#, # + n}]} &,`
$\quad\quad$ `Range[0, 2`π`- n, n]], AspectRatio → Automatic]]`

Here is a color wheel created from 256 separate sectors (hues).

In[2]:= `colorWheel[`$\dfrac{\pi}{256}$`];`

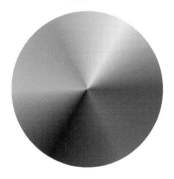

2. Here is the circle graphic primitive together with a text label.

In[3]:= `circ = Circle[{0, 0}, 1];`

In[4]:= `ctext = Text[StyleForm["Circle",`
`FontFamily → "Times", FontSlant -> "Italic", FontSize → 12],`
$\{Cos[\frac{5\pi}{4}] + .25, Sin[\frac{5\pi}{4}]\}];$

This generates the graphics primitive for the triangle and its text label.

In[5]:= `tri = Line[{{-1, 0}, {0, 1}, {1, 0}, {-1, 0}}];`

In[6]:= `ttext = Text[StyleForm["Triangle", FontFamily → "Times",`
`FontSlant → "Italic", FontSize → 12], {0, 0 + .05}];`

Here is the rectangle and label.

In[7]:= `rect = Line[{{-1, -1}, {-1, 1}, {2, 1}, {2, -1}, {-1, -1}}];`

In[8]:= `rtext = Text[StyleForm["Rectangle", FontFamily → "Times",`
`FontSlant → "Italic", FontSize → 12], {1.5, -1 + .05}];`

Finally, this displays each of these graphics elements all together.

In[9]:= `Show[Graphics[{circ, tri, rect, ctext, ttext, rtext}],`
`AspectRatio → Automatic];`

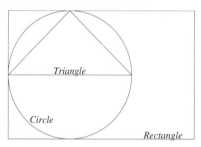

3. First, we need to create the cuboid graphic object. `Cuboid` takes a list of three numbers as the coordinates of its lower-left corner. This maps the object across two such lists.

In[10]:= `Map[Cuboid[#] &, Table[Random[], {2}, {3}]]`

Out[10]= `{Cuboid[{0.177395, 0.551966, 0.857107}],`
`Cuboid[{0.545712, 0.76829, 0.48344}]}`

Here is a list of six cuboids and the resulting graphic. Notice the large amount of overlap of the cubes. You can reduce the large overlap by specifying minimum *and* maximum values of the cuboid.

In[11]:= `cubes = Map[Cuboid[#1] &, Table[Random[], {6}, {3}]];`

In[12]:= `Show[Graphics3D[cubes]];`

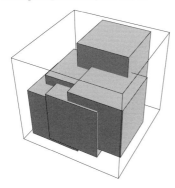

4. First we create the `Point` graphics primitives randomly placed in the unit square.

In[13]:= `randomcoords := Point[{Random[], Random[]}];`

This creates the point sizes according to the specification given in the statement of the problem.

In[14]:= `randomsize := PointSize[Random[Real, {.01, .1}]]`

This will assign a random color to each primitive.

In[15]:= `randomcolor := Hue[Random[]]`

Here then are 500 points. (You may find it instructive to look at just one of these points.)

In[16]:= `pts = Table[{randomcolor, randomsize, randomcoords}, {500}];`

And here is the graphic.

In[17]:= `Show[Graphics[pts, PlotRange → All]]`

Out[17]= - Graphics -

5. The algebraic solution is given by the following steps. First solve the equations for x and y.

In[18]:= `Clear[x, y, r]`

In[19]:= `soln = Solve[{(x - 1)² + (y - 1)² == 2, (x + 3)² + (y - 4)² == r²}, {x, y}]`

Out[19]= $\{\{x \rightarrow \frac{1}{50} \left(-58 + 4\, r^2 - 3\, \sqrt{-529 + 54\, r^2 - r^4}\,\right),$

$y \rightarrow \frac{1}{50} \left(131 - 3\, r^2 - 4\, \sqrt{-529 + 54\, r^2 - r^4}\,\right)\},$

$\{x \rightarrow \frac{1}{50} \left(-58 + 4\, r^2 + 3\, \sqrt{-529 + 54\, r^2 - r^4}\,\right),$

$y \rightarrow \frac{1}{50} \left(131 - 3\, r^2 + 4\, \sqrt{-529 + 54\, r^2 - r^4}\,\right)\}\}$

Then find those values of r for which the x and y coordinates are identical.

In[20]:= `Solve[{(x /. soln[[1]]) == (x /. soln[[2]]),`
           `       (y /. soln[[1]]) == (y /. soln[[2]])}, r]`

Out[20]= $\{\{r \rightarrow -5 - \sqrt{2}\,\}, \{r \rightarrow 5 - \sqrt{2}\,\}, \{r \rightarrow -5 + \sqrt{2}\,\}, \{r \rightarrow 5 + \sqrt{2}\,\}\}$

Here then are those values of r that are positive.

In[21]:= `Cases[%, {r → _ ? Positive}]`

Out[21]= $\{\{r \rightarrow 5 - \sqrt{2}\,\}, \{r \rightarrow 5 + \sqrt{2}\,\}\}$

To display the solution, we will plot the first circle with solid lines and the two solutions with dashed lines together in one graphic. Here is the first circle centered at (1, 1).

In[22]:= `circ = Circle[{1, 1}, √2];`

In[23]:= `Show[Graphics[circ, Axes → Automatic, AspectRatio → Automatic]];`

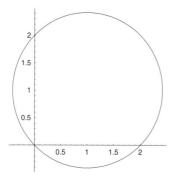

Notice that we have used the Axes and AspectRatio options because we want these commands to apply to the entire graphic.

Here are the circles that represent the solution to the problem.

In[24]:=   r1 = 5 - √2 ;
             r2 = 5 + √2 ;

In[26]:=   Show[Graphics[{circ, Circle[{-3, 4}, r1], Circle[{-3, 4}, r2]},
                Axes → Automatic, AspectRatio → Automatic]];

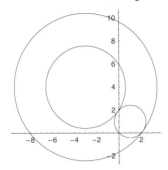

We wanted to display the solutions (two circles) using dashed lines. The graphics directive Dashing[{*x,y*}] directs all subsequent lines to be plotted as dashed, alternating the dash *x* units and the space *y* units. We use it as a graphics directive on the two circles c1 and c2. The important point to note here is that each of the circles inherits only those directives in whose scope they appear.

In[27]:=   dashc1 = {Dashing[{.025, .025}], Circle[{-3, 4}, r1]};
             dashc2 = {Dashing[{.05, .05}], Circle[{-3, 4}, r2]};

In[29]:=   Show[Graphics[{circ, dashc1, dashc2},
                Axes → Automatic, AspectRatio → Automatic]];

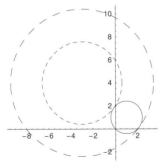

6. This loads the package containing the definitions for the polyhedra.

In[30]:=   Needs["Graphics`Polyhedra`"]

It is often helpful to get a list of the functions defined in a recently loaded package.

In[31]:= **Names["Graphics`Polyhedra`*"]**

Out[31]= {Geodesate, GreatDodecahedron, GreatIcosahedron,
GreatStellatedDodecahedron, OpenTruncate, Polyhedra,
Polyhedron, SmallStellatedDodecahedron, Stellate, Truncate}

First the polyhedra are turned into Graphics3D objects.

In[32]:= **solids = Map[Graphics3D, {Cube[], Dodecahedron[], GreatDodecahedron[],
GreatIcosahedron[], GreatStellatedDodecahedron[], Icosahedron[],
Octahedron[], Tetrahedron[], SmallStellatedDodecahedron[]}];**

We then use Partition to split the list of nine solids into three sublists and then display the
nine polyhedra with GraphicsArray and Show.

In[33]:= **Show[GraphicsArray[Partition[solids, 3]]]**

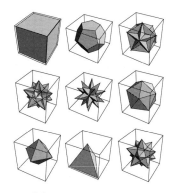

Out[33]= - GraphicsArray -

7. Here is a plot of the sine function.

In[34]:= **sinplot = Plot[Sin[x], {x, 0, 2 π}]**

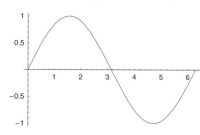

Out[34]= - Graphics -

This solution is essentially that given in *Exploring Mathematics with Mathematica* (Gray and
Glynn 1991). Extracting the points from which *Mathematica* constructs the plot is accomplished by the Nest statement. The Line primitive is then mapped across those points in

such a way as to create lines from the points on the graph to points on the *x*-axis with the same *x*-coordinate.

```
In[35]:= Show[sinplot,
          Graphics[
             {Thickness[.001],
              Map[Line[{{#[[1]], 0}, #}]&,
                 Nest[First, sinplot, 4]]}]]
```

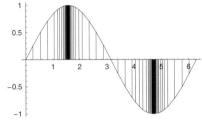

Out[35]= - Graphics -

You could also construct this using pattern matching. Here are the coordinates.

```
In[36]:= (coords = Cases[sinplot, {p_?NumericQ, q_?NumericQ}, Infinity]) // Short
```

Out[36]//Short=
  {{2.61799×10⁻⁷, 2.61799×10⁻⁷}, «80», {6.28319, -«23»}}

Here is what we use to create vertical lines from each coordinate.

```
In[37]:= (lines = Map[Line[{{#[[1]], 0}, #}] &, coords]) // Short
```

Out[37]//Short=
  {Line[{{2.61799×10⁻⁷, 0}, {2.61799×10⁻⁷, «23»}}], «80», Line[«1»]}

Here then is the final graphic.

```
In[38]:= Show[sinplot, Graphics[
             Map[Line[{{#[[1]], 0}, #}] &,
                Cases[sinplot, {p_?NumericQ, q_?NumericQ}, Infinity]]
             ]];
```

9.2 Graphics programming

1. The function `ComplexListPlot` plots a list of complex numbers in the complex plane, with the real part identified with the horizontal axis and the imaginary part identified with the vertical axis. The appropriate options are extracted from `ComplexListPlot` using `Filter` `Options`, given the name `complexOpts`, and then passed to `ListPlot`.

    In[1]:= `<< Utilities`FilterOptions``

    In[2]:= `ComplexListPlot[points_, opts___] :=`
               `   Module[{complexOpts = FilterOptions[ListPlot, opts]},`
               `      ListPlot[Map[{Re[#1], Im[#1]} &, points], complexOpts, PlotStyle →`
               `         {RGBColor[1, 0, 0], PointSize[.025]}, AxesLabel → {"Re", "Im"}]]`

    This plots four complex numbers in the plane.

    In[3]:= `ComplexListPlot[{-1 + I, 2 + I, 1 - 2 I, 0, 1}];`

    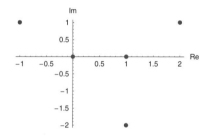

2. The function `RootPlot`, takes a polynomial, solves for its roots, and then uses `ComplexList-` `Plot` from Exercise 1 to plot these roots in the complex plane.

    In[4]:= `RootPlot[poly_, z_, opts___] :=`
               `   ComplexListPlot[z /. NSolve[poly == 0, z], opts]`

    In[5]:= `RootPlot[1 + z + 2 z² + 3 z³ + 5 z⁴ + 8 z⁵ + 13 z⁶, z, AspectRatio → Automatic];`

    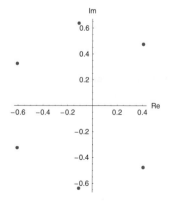

3.

```
In[6]:=  Clear[RootPlot]

In[7]:=  << Utilities`FilterOptions`

In[8]:=  RootPlot[fun_, {x_, xmin_, xmax_}, opts___] := Module[
            {z, fplot, pts, spts, roots, points, f = Function[x, Evaluate[fun]]},
            fplot = Plot[f[x], {x, xmin, xmax}, DisplayFunction → Identity,
               Evaluate[FilterOptions[Plot, opts]]];
            pts = Cases[fplot, Line[{z__}] → z, ∞];
            spts = Map[First, Select[Split[pts, Sign[Last[#2]] == -Sign[Last[#1]] &],
               Length[#1] == 2 &], {2}];
            roots = Map[FindRoot[f[x] == 0, {x, #[[1]], #[[2]]}] &, spts];
            points = Map[Point[{#, 0}] &, x /. roots];
            Show[fplot, DisplayFunction → $DisplayFunction,
             Epilog → {RGBColor[0, 0, 1], PointSize[.02], points}];
            roots]
```

$$In[9]:= \quad \text{RootPlot}\left[\text{Sin}\left[x + \sqrt{2}\ \text{Sin}[x]\right], \{x, -\pi, 4\,\pi\}, \text{PlotStyle} \to \text{Dashing}[\{.02, .02\}]\right];$$

4. Here is the new code for `DataPlot`.

```
In[10]:=  Clear[DataPlot]

In[11]:=  Needs["Utilities`FilterOptions`"]

In[12]:=  Options[DataPlot] = Options[ListPlot];

In[13]:=  DataPlot::baddim = "The data used by DataPlot must
              be in the form of a one- or two-dimensional list.";

In[14]:=  DataPlot[data_, opts___] := Module[{pjQ, pts, lines},
             pjQ = PlotJoined /. Flatten[{opts, Options[DataPlot]}];
             pts = Which[
               VectorQ[data], MapIndexed[{#2[[1]], #1} &, data],
               Dimensions[data][[2]] == 2, data,
               True, Message[DataPlot::baddim]; $Failed];
             If[pts =!= $Failed,
               Show[Graphics[{PointSize[.02],
                  Point /@ pts, If[pjQ, lines = Line[pts], lines = {}]}],
                 FilterOptions[Graphics, opts], Axes → Automatic]]]
```

Here is some sample two-dimensional data.

In[15]:= **data2D = {{0.043, 0.575}, {0.151, 0.120},
              {0.234, 0.001}, {0.283, 0.930}, {0.343, 0.569}, {0.416, 0.768},
              {0.465, 0.675}, {0.539, 0.528}, {0.786, 0.856}, {0.914, 0.794}};**

And here is some sample one-dimensional data.

In[16]:= **data1D = Table[Random[Integer, {1, 10}], {8}]**

Out[16]= {2, 5, 7, 5, 9, 9, 10, 6}

In[17]:= **DataPlot[data1D, PlotJoined → True]**

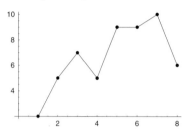

Out[17]= - Graphics -

In[18]:= **DataPlot[data2D, PlotJoined → True]**

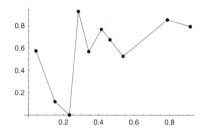

Out[18]= - Graphics -

Here is some data that DataPlot is not designed to deal with.

In[19]:= **DataPlot[{{1, 2, 3}, {2, 3, 4}, {4, 5, 6}}]**

            DataPlot::baddim : The data used by DataPlot
                must be in the form of a one- or two-dimensional list.

5. There are a number of things that could go wrong with the algorithm by just choosing a base
    point randomly and then sorting according to the arctangent. The default branch cut for
    ArcTan gives values between $-\pi/2$ and $\pi/2$. (The reader is encouraged to think about why
    this could occasionally cause the algorithm in the text to fail.) By choosing the base point so
    that it lies at some extreme of the diameter of the set of points, the polar angle algorithm given
    in the text will work consistently. If you choose the base point so that it is lowest and left-most,
    then all the angles will be in the range $(0, \pi]$.

```
In[20]:= simpleClosedPath1[lis_List] := Module[{base, angle, sorted},
           base = Last[Sort[lis, (#2[[2]] < #1[[2]]) &]];
           angle[a_, b_] := Apply[ArcTan, b - a];
           sorted =
            Sort[Complement[lis, {base}], (angle[base, #1] ≤ angle[base, #2]) &];
           Join[{base}, sorted, {base}]
          ]

In[21]:= pts = Table[Random[], {20}, {2}];

In[22]:= PointPlot[coords_List] :=
           Show[Graphics[{
              Line[coords],
              PointSize[.02], RGBColor[1, 0, 0], Map[Point, coords]
             }]]

In[23]:= PointPlot[simpleClosedPath1[pts]];
```

7. A simple change to the program `simpleClosedPath` given in Exercise 5 chooses the base point with the largest *y*-coordinate.

```
In[24]:= simpleClosedPath3[lis_] :=
           Module[{base, angle, sorted}, base = Last[Sort[lis, #2[[2]] > #1[[2]] &]];
             angle[a_, b_] := ArcTan @@ (b - a); sorted = Sort[Complement[lis, {base}],
               angle[base, #1] ≤ angle[base, #2] &]; Join[{base}, sorted, {base}]]

In[25]:= pts = Table[Random[], {20}, {2}];

In[26]:= PointPlot[simpleClosedPath3[pts]];
```

8. The area of a triangle is one-half the base times the altitude. For arbitrary points, the altitude requires a bit of computation that does not generalize.

The magnitude of the cross product of two vectors gives the area of the parallelogram that they determine. Since the vectors we are working with are in two-dimensional space, we embed them in three-dimensional space in the plane $z = 0$ so that we can compute the cross product which, for the purposes of this problem, only makes sense in three dimensions.

```
In[27]:=  << "Calculus`VectorAnalysis`"
```

```
In[28]:=  CrossProduct[{x₂, y₂} - {x₁, y₁}, {x₃, y₃} - {x₁, y₁}] /. {x_, y_} → {x, y, 0}
```

```
Out[28]=  {0, 0, -x₂ y₁ + x₃ y₁ + x₁ y₂ - x₃ y₂ - x₁ y₃ + x₂ y₃}
```

Here are the coordinates for a triangle.

```
In[29]:=  a = {0, 0};
          b = {5, 0};
          c = {3, 2};
```

And here is the computation for the cross product.

```
In[32]:=  CrossProduct[b - a, c - a] /. {x_, y_} → {x, y, 0}
```

```
Out[32]=  {0, 0, 10}
```

So the given area is then just half the magnitude of the cross product.

```
In[33]:=   Apply[Plus, %]
          ───────────────
                 2
```

```
Out[33]=  5
```

Here is a function that computes the area of any triangle using the cross product.

```
In[34]:=  triangleArea[v_List] := 1/2 Apply[Plus,
              (CrossProduct[v[[2]] - v[[1]], v[[3]] - v[[1]]] /. {x_, y_} → {x, y, 0})]
```

This is done more simply using determinants and this method generalizes more easily to higher dimensions.

```
In[35]:=  triangleArea[{v1_, v2_, v3_}] := 1/2 Det[{v1, v2, v3} /. {x_, y_} → {x, y, 1}]
```

```
In[36]:=  triangleArea[{a, b, c}]
```

```
Out[36]=  5
```

9. The key observation is that in computing the area of a triangle using the determinant formulation as in Exercise 9, the area will be a positive quantity if the points are given in counter-clockwise order, and will be negative if in clockwise order. So, for a given point p not on a line ab, the area of $\triangle abp$ will be positive (computed using determinants), if p is to the left of ab. Similarly, for each of the lines in a polygon, relative to the given point p. So, to perform the computation, we first partition the polygon into pairs of points, and then map the triangle area

function with the given point across each pair. If all such areas are greater than or equal to zero, then a value of `True` is returned.

```
In[37]:=  pointInPolygonQ[poly_, p_] := Module[{area},
                          1
              area[{v1_, v2_, v3_}] := ─ Det[{v1, v2, v3} /. {x_, y_} → {x, y, 1}] ≥ 0;
                          2
              Apply[And, Map[area[Join[{p}, #]] &,
                Partition[poly /. {a_, b__} :→ {a, b, a}, 2, 1]]]]
```

Here are the coordinates for a quadrilateral and two distinct points.

```
In[38]:=  quad = {{1, 0}, {0, 1}, {-1, 0}, {0, -1}};
```

```
In[39]:=  p1 = {0, 0};
          p2 = {1, 1};
```

```
In[41]:=  Show[Graphics[{Line[quad /. {a_, b__} :→ {a, b, a}],
              PointSize[.025], Point[p1], Point[p2]}, AspectRatio → Automatic]];
```

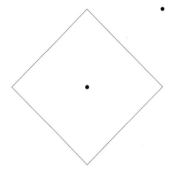

Finally, here are the computations for these points and polygon.

```
In[42]:=  pointInPolygonQ[quad, p1]
```

```
Out[42]=  True
```

```
In[43]:=  pointInPolygonQ[quad, p2]
```

```
Out[43]=  False
```

12. RT (for Reingold–Tilford), replaces the `placeTree` function. In `placeTree`, the result was a separation tree plus two numbers: width of the left side of the tree and width of the right side of the tree. In RT, the result is instead a separation tree plus two lists, the first giving the width of the left side of each level of the tree, the second giving the corresponding widths on the right side. `sep` is calculated by adding the right widths of the left subtree to the left widths of the right subtree at each level, and taking the maximum separation. `drawSepTree` is unchanged.

```
In[44]:=  << IPM3`Trees`
```

```
In[45]:= RT[{_}] := {{}, {}, {}}

In[46]:= RT[{_, lc_, rc_}] :=
           With[{left = RT[lc], right = RT[rc], minsep = 2.0}, With[{sep =
              1
              ─ (Max[0, Max @@ (Plus @@ #1 &) /@ zip[left[[3]], right[[2]]]] + minsep)},
              2
              With[{newtree = {sep, left[[1]], right[[1]]},
                leftedge = Join[{sep}, extend[left[[2]], right[[2]], sep]],
                rightedge = Join[{sep}, extend[right[[3]], left[[3]], sep]]},
                {newtree, leftedge, rightedge}]]]

In[47]:= placeTree[{_}] := {{}, 0, 0}
         placeTree[{_, lc_, rc_}] :=
           Module[{left = placeTree[lc], right = placeTree[rc], minsep = 1.0, sep},
             sep = left[[3]] + right[[2]] + minsep;
                                                    sep                    sep
             {{sep, left[[1]], right[[1]]}, left[[2]] + ───, right[[3]] + ───}]
                                                     2                      2

In[49]:= drawSepTree[{}, lev_, xaxis_] := {Disk[{xaxis, lev}, 0.1]}
         drawSepTree[{sep_, lc_, rc_}, lev_, xaxis_] :=
           Join[{Disk[{xaxis, lev}, 0.1], Line[{{xaxis, lev}, {xaxis - sep, lev - 1}}],
             Line[{{xaxis, lev}, {xaxis + sep, lev - 1}}]},
             drawSepTree[lc, lev - 1, xaxis - sep], drawSepTree[rc, lev - 1, xaxis + sep]]

In[51]:= drawTree[t_] := drawSepTree[RT[t][[1]], 0, 0]
```

The auxiliary functions are `zip` and `extend`. Given the *left* widths of each level of the *right* subtree, and the *right* widths of each level of the *left* subtree, the separation of the two subtrees is determined by adding those numbers at each level and taking the maximum. `zip` is used to join those two lists into a list of pairs; it facilitates this process.

```
In[52]:= zip[{}, _] := {}
         zip[_, {}] := {}
         zip[{x1_, y1___}, {x2_, y2___}] := Join[{{x1, x2}}, zip[{y1}, {y2}]]
```

When the separation of a tree's subtrees is determined, the lists of left and right widths of the combined tree are computed from the corresponding lists for the subtrees. This is simple enough for the most part: the left widths of the tree are obtained mainly by taking the left widths of the left subtree and shifting them left; and similarly for the right widths. There is an exception, though: if the right subtree is taller than the left subtree, the left widths of the bottom part of the tree are obtained from the left widths of the bottom part of the right subtree. Combining the left widths of the two subtrees to create the list of left widths of the combined tree is done by `extend`.

```
In[55]:= extend[edges1_, edges2_, sep_] := Join[edges1 + sep,
             Take[edges2, Min[0, Length[edges1] - Length[edges2]]] - sep]
```

The same reasoning applies to computing the right widths, and `extend` is also used for that.

Here is the "tricky" tree drawn in Figure 9.5.

In[56]:= `Clear[a, b, c, d, e, f, g]`

In[57]:= `t1 = {a, {b}, {a, {c, {e, {g}, {f}}, {d}}, {b}}};`

In[58]:= `Show[Graphics[drawTree[t1]], AspectRatio → Automatic];`

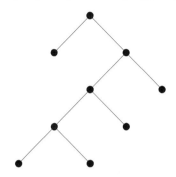

13. RT is modified so that the left widths and right widths of each row take into account the width of the labels.

In[59]:=
$$RT[\{x\_\}] := \{\{\}, \{\frac{width[x]}{2}\}, \{\frac{width[x]}{2}\}\}$$

```
RT[{x_, lc_, rc_}] :=
  With[{left = RT[lc], right = RT[rc], minsep = 0.5}, With[{sep =
      1
      ─ (Max[0, Max @@ (Plus @@ #1 &) /@ zip[left〚3〛, right〚2〛]] + minsep)},
      2
    With[{newtree = {sep, left〚1〛, right〚1〛},
      leftedge = Join[{width[x]/2}, extend[left〚2〛, right〚2〛, sep]],
      rightedge = Join[{width[x]/2}, extend[right〚3〛, left〚3〛, sep]]},
      {newtree, leftedge, rightedge}]]]
  width[t_] := StringLength[t]
```

Drawing the following tree using the new `RT` and the old `drawSepTree` will show the difference in the layout of the trees. However, since `drawSepTree` above only prints disks at each node, a new version of it is required.

In[62]:= `t1 = {"a", {"abcdef"}, {"", {"abcdefghij"}, {"abc"}}};`

The new version of `drawSepTree` draws the labels at each node instead of a disk. A complicating factor is that we can no longer just draw the lines from the center of the disk, since this would collide with the text. So the lines are now drawn in such a way as to leave a gap between the text and the line.

In[63]:= `settext[lab_] := FontForm[lab, {"Helvetica", 9}]`

In[64]:= `drawSepTree[{lab_}, {}, lev_, xaxis_] := {Text[settext[lab], {xaxis, lev}]}`

In[65]:= `drawSepTree[{lab_, lc_, rc_}, {sep_, ls_, rs_}, lev_, xaxis_] :=`
$\quad$`With[{h1 = If[lab == "", 0, .3], h2 = If[lc[[1]] == "", 0, .3],`
$\quad$`h3 = If[rc[[1]] == "", 0, .3]}, Join[{Text[settext[lab], {xaxis, lev}],`
$\quad$`Line[{{xaxis - \frac{sep\ h1}{2}, lev - \frac{h1}{2}}, {xaxis - sep + \frac{sep\ h2}{2}, lev - 1 + \frac{h2}{2}}}],`
$\quad$`Line[{{xaxis + \frac{sep\ h1}{2}, lev - \frac{h1}{2}},`
$\quad$`{xaxis + sep - \frac{sep\ h3}{2}, lev - 1 + \frac{h3}{2}}}]}, drawSepTree[lc, ls,`
$\quad$`lev - 1, xaxis - sep], drawSepTree[rc, rs, lev - 1, xaxis + sep]]]`

In[66]:= `drawTree[t_] := drawSepTree[t, RT[t][[1]], 0, 0]`

In[67]:= `Show[Graphics[drawTree[t1]], PlotRange → All];`

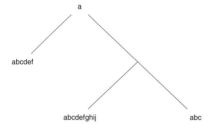

9.3 Sound

1. When x is close to -2, the frequency is quite low. As x increases, the fraction $1000/x$ gets larger, making the frequency of the sine function bigger. This in turn makes the tone much higher in pitch. As x approaches 0, the function is oscillating more and more, and at 0, the function can be thought of as oscillating infinitely often. In fact, it is oscillating so much that the sampling routine is not able to effectively compute amplitudes and, hence, we hear noise in this region.

In[1]:= `Play[Sin[\frac{1000}{x}], {x, -2, 2}]`

$\quad$ `Power::infy : Infinite expression` $\frac{1}{0.}$ `encountered. More...`

Out[1]= `- Sound -`

3. To generate a tone whose rate increases one octave per second, you need the sine of a function whose derivative doubles each second (frequency is a rate). That function is 2^t, so here is the command to produce the tone. You need to carefully choose a range for t that generates tones in a reasonable range.

In[2]:= **Play[Sin[2^t], {t, 10, 14}]**

Out[2]= **- Sound -**

5. Here is a function that creates a square wave with decreasing amplitudes for higher overtones.

In[3]:= $\textbf{SquareWave[freq\_, n\_] := Sum}\left[\dfrac{\textbf{Sin[freq i 2}\,\pi\,\textbf{t]}}{\textbf{i}}\textbf{, \{i, 1, n, 2\}}\right]$

In[4]:= **Plot[SquareWave[440, 17], {t, 0, .01}];**

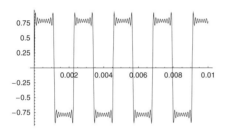

Here then, is an example of playing a square wave.

In[6]:= **Play[SquareWave[440, 17], {t, 0, .5}]**

Out[6]= **- Sound -**

7. This function creates a saw-tooth wave. The user specifies the fundamental frequency and the number of terms in the approximation.

In[7]:= $\textbf{SawtoothWave[freq\_, n\_] := Sum}\left[\dfrac{\textbf{Sin[freq i 2}\,\pi\,\textbf{t]}}{\textbf{i}}\textbf{, \{i, 1, n\}}\right]$

In[8]:= **Plot[SawtoothWave[440, 17], {t, 0, .01}];**

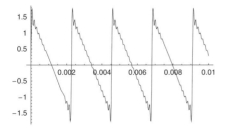

This plays the wave for a half-second duration.

In[9]:= `Play[SawtoothWave[440, 17], {t, 0, .5}]`

Out[9]= - Sound -

Here are definitions for true sawtooth and square waves.

In[10]:= `Fractional[x_] := x - Floor[x]`

In[11]:= `SawtoothWave[x_] := Fractional[-x]`

In[12]:= `SquareWave[x_] :=` $\frac{1}{2}$ `Sign[SawtoothWave[x] -` $\frac{1}{2}$`] + 1`

Here are plots at the fundamental frequency of 440.

In[13]:= `Plot[SawtoothWave[440 t], {t, 0,` $\frac{3}{440}$`}];`

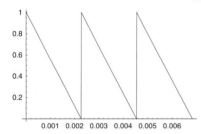

In[14]:= `Plot[SquareWave[440 t], {t, 0,` $\frac{3}{440}$`}];`

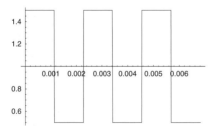

9. Here is a function that picks out frequencies from the pentatonic scale, using essentially brownian motion $1/f^2$ to select notes.

In[15]:=
```
pentatonic[n_Integer, r_ : 2] := Module[{pscale, steps},
    pscale = {277.183, 311.13, 369.99, 415.30, 466.16, 554.37};
    steps = Table[Random[Integer, {-r, r}], {n}];
    pscale[[Mod[FoldList[Plus, 3, steps], 4] + 1]]]
```

You could play a pentatonic "melody" as follows:

In[16]:= `SetAttributes[PlayTones, Listable]`

In[17]:= `PlayTones[freq_, time_ : 0.5] := Play[Sin[2 π t freq], {t, 0, time}]`

In[18]:= `PlayTones[pentatonic[24]]`

Out[18]= {- Sound -, - Sound -, - Sound -, - Sound -, - Sound -, - Sound -, - Sound -,
    - Sound -, - Sound -, - Sound -, - Sound -, - Sound -, - Sound -,
    - Sound -, - Sound -, - Sound -, - Sound -, - Sound -, - Sound -,
    - Sound -, - Sound -, - Sound -, - Sound -, - Sound -, - Sound -}

11. In this function, the notes are randomly chosen from the C major scale $1/f^0$ and the durations
are randomly chosen from the list that represents eighth notes, quarter notes, half notes, and
whole notes (also $1/f^0$). `PlayTones` accepts two arguments, so `MapThread` threads corresponding notes and durations through `PlayTones`.

In[19]:= `tonesAndTimes[n_] := Module[{cmajor, notes, durs},`
    `cmajor = Table[N[261.62558 2^(j/12)], {j, 0, 11}];`
    `notes := Table[cmajor[[Random[Integer, {1, 12}]]], {n}];`
    `durs := Table[` $\dfrac{1}{2^{\text{Random[Integer, \{0, 3\}]}}}$ `, {n}];`
    `MapThread[PlayTones, {notes, durs}]]`

13. Following the implementation in the text, we first create ten steps between -2 and 2 (you can
alter the range of step movements). These steps will determine how to move up or down the
list of tone durations (1/8, 1/4, 1/2, 1).

In[20]:= `d10 = Table[Random[Integer, {-2, 2}], {10}]`

Out[20]= {0, 0, -2, -1, 2, 1, 2, 2, -2, -2}

In[21]:= `Mod[FoldList[Plus, 0, d10], 4] + 1`

Out[21]= {1, 1, 1, 3, 2, 4, 1, 3, 1, 3, 1}

In[22]:= `durs =` $\left\{\dfrac{1}{8}, \dfrac{1}{4}, \dfrac{1}{2}, 1\right\}$ `[[%]]`

Out[22]= $\left\{\dfrac{1}{8}, \dfrac{1}{8}, \dfrac{1}{8}, \dfrac{1}{2}, \dfrac{1}{4}, 1, \dfrac{1}{8}, \dfrac{1}{2}, \dfrac{1}{8}, \dfrac{1}{2}, \dfrac{1}{8}\right\}$

Here are some $1/f^2$ tones.

In[23]:= `s10 = Table[Random[Integer, {-2, 2}], {10}]`

Out[23]= {-2, -2, -1, -2, -1, 1, -2, 2, -1, 1}

In[24]:= `pos = Mod[FoldList[Plus, 0, s10], 13] + 1`

Out[24]= {1, 12, 10, 9, 7, 6, 7, 5, 7, 6, 7}

```
In[25]:=  Cmajor = Table[N[261.62558 2^(j/12)], {j, 0, 12}]
```

```
Out[25]=  {261.626, 277.183, 293.665, 311.127, 329.628, 349.228,
           369.994, 391.995, 415.305, 440., 466.164, 493.883, 523.251}
```

```
In[26]:=  Length[Cmajor]
```

```
Out[26]=  13
```

```
In[27]:=  tones = Cmajor[[pos]]
```

```
Out[27]=  {261.626, 493.883, 440., 415.305, 369.994,
           349.228, 369.994, 329.628, 369.994, 349.228, 369.994}
```

```
In[28]:=  MapThread[PlayTones, {tones, durs}];
```

And finally, here is one function that puts this all together.

```
In[29]:=  tonesAndTimes2[n_] := Module[{cmajor, tones, durs, d, t},
            cmajor = Table[N[261.62558 2^(j/12)], {j, 0, 12}];
            d = Table[Random[Integer, {-2, 2}], {n}];
            durs = {1/8, 1/4, 1/2, 1}[[Mod[FoldList[Plus, 0, d], 4] + 1]];
            t = Table[Random[Integer, {-2, 2}], {n}];
            tones = cmajor[[Mod[FoldList[Plus, 0, t], 13] + 1]];
            MapThread[PlayTones, {tones, durs}]]
```

```
In[30]:=  tonesAndTimes2[12];
```

10 Front end programming

10.2 The structure of cells and notebooks

1. Here is the expression to create the notebook.

```
In[1]:=  nb = NotebookPut[
           Notebook[{
             Cell["Demo Notebook", "Title"],
             Cell["Section 1: Sample Cells", "Section"],
             Cell["This is a text cell", "Text"],
             Cell["2 (3+5)", "Input"],
             Cell["1+2+3", "Input"]}]
         ]
```

```
Out[1]=  NotebookObject[ «Untitled-3» ]
```

2. First we read the notebook from Exercise 1 into the kernel with `NotebookGet`.

```
In[2]:=  nbkernel = NotebookGet[nb]
```

```
Out[2]= Notebook[
          {Cell[CellGroupData[{Cell[Demo Notebook, Title], Cell[CellGroupData[
                {Cell[Section 1: Sample Cells, Section], Cell[This is a text cell,
                   Text], Cell[2(3+5), Input], Cell[1+2+3, Input]}, Open]]},
             Open]]}, FrontEndVersion → 5.1 for Microsoft Windows,
          ScreenRectangle → {{0., 1024.}, {0., 681.}}]
```

Then we do a substitution on cells that contain `"Section"` as their second argument (their style) and finally use `NotebookPut` to display the resulting notebook in the front end.

```
In[3]:=  NotebookPut[nbkernel /. Cell[str_, "Section"] → Cell[str, "Subsection"]]
```

```
Out[3]= NotebookObject[ ≪Untitled-4≫ ]
```

10.3 Cell data types

1. Here is the notebook object with three `ValueBox`es.

```
In[1]:=  nb = NotebookPut[
            Notebook[{
              Cell[TextData[
                {"The current version is ", ValueBox["$Version"]}], "Text"],
              Cell[TextData[{"The operating system is ",
                 ValueBox["$OperatingSystem"]}], "Text"],
              Cell[TextData[{"Current user is ", ValueBox["$UserName"]}], "Text"]
              }]]
```

```
Out[1]= NotebookObject[ ≪Untitled-5≫ ]
```

10.4 GridBoxes

1. There are several ways of approaching this problem. One way is to create a function that contains the formatting rules for the heading.

```
In[1]:=  headstyle[str_] :=
            StyleBox[(MakeBoxes[#, StandardForm] &)[str], FontFamily → "Helvetica",
              FontWeight → "Bold", FontColor → RGBColor[0, 0, 1], FontSize → 10];
```

Here are some sample strings for the heading.

```
In[2]:=  headings = {"first", "second", "third"};
```

```
In[3]:=  data = {{"α", "β", "γ"},
            {1.234, 2.3451, 3.4567801}, {SqrtBox["π"], "x/y", "Γ(n)"}};
```

We now need to create a list of the headings together with their styles and prepend it to the original data. This way the headings will be the first row of the new data set.

In[4]:= `Prepend[data, Map[headstyle, headings]]`

Out[4]= `{{StyleBox["first", FontFamily → Helvetica,`
`        FontWeight → Bold, FontColor → RGBColor[0, 0, 1], FontSize → 10],`
`      StyleBox["second", FontFamily → Helvetica, FontWeight → Bold,`
`        FontColor → RGBColor[0, 0, 1], FontSize → 10],`
`      StyleBox["third", FontFamily → Helvetica, FontWeight → Bold,`
`        FontColor → RGBColor[0, 0, 1], FontSize → 10]},`

$\{\alpha, \beta, \gamma\}$, `{1.234, 2.3451, 3.45678}`, $\left\{\texttt{SqrtBox}[\pi], \frac{x}{y}, \Gamma(n)\right\}\}$

In[5]:= `ShowTable[data_, headings_List] := DisplayForm[StyleBox[`
`        GridBox[Prepend[data, Map[headstyle, headings]],`
`          GridFrame → 2, GridFrameMargins → {{1, 1}, {1, 1}},`
`          RowLines → 1, ColumnLines → 1],`
`        FontFamily → "Times",`
`        Background → GrayLevel[.8], SingleLetterItalics → True`
`      ]]`

In[6]:= `ShowTable[data, {"first", "second", "third"}]`

Out[6]//DisplayForm=

first	second	third
α	β	γ
1.234	2.3451	3.4567801
$\sqrt{\pi}$	$\frac{x}{y}$	$\Gamma(n)$

A cleaner approach would be to set up the headings as an option to `ShowTable`. In addition, the header formatting should be incorporated into `ShowTable`. Here is one approach.

In[7]:= `Options[ShowTable] = {Headings → {}};`

In[8]:= `ShowTable[data_, opts___?OptionQ] := Module[{headstyle, headings},`
`        headstyle[str_] :=`
`          StyleBox[(MakeBoxes[#, StandardForm] &) @ str, FontFamily -> "Helvetica",`
`            FontWeight → "Bold", FontColor → RGBColor[0, 0, 1], FontSize → 10];`
`        headings = Headings /. Flatten[{opts}] /. Options[ShowTable];`
`        DisplayForm[StyleBox[`
`          GridBox[Prepend[data, Map[headstyle, headings]],`
`            GridFrame → 2, GridFrameMargins → {{1, 1}, {1, 1}},`
`            RowLines → 1, ColumnLines → 1],`
`          FontFamily → "Times",`
`          Background → GrayLevel[.8], SingleLetterItalics → True`
`        ]]]`

In[9]:= `ShowTable[data, Headings → {"premier", "deuxieme", "troisieme"}]`

Out[9]//DisplayForm=

premier	deuxieme	troisieme
α	β	γ
1.234	2.3451	3.4567801
$\sqrt{\pi}$	$\frac{x}{y}$	$\Gamma(n)$

3. First, here is the table of all possible truth values for three variables. We will generalize this below.

In[10]:= `ins = Distribute[Table[{True, False}, {3}], List, List, List]`

Out[10]= `{{True, True, True}, {True, True, False},`
`{True, False, True}, {True, False, False}, {False, True, True},`
`{False, True, False}, {False, False, True}, {False, False, False}}`

Here is the logical expression.

In[11]:= `expr = Implies[Or[A, B], C]`

Out[11]= `Implies[A || B, C]`

This creates a set of rules for all possible truth value combinations.

In[12]:= `vars = {A, B, C};`
`Map[Thread[vars → #] &, ins]`

Out[13]= `{{A → True, B → True, C → True}, {A → True, B → True, C → False},`
`{A → True, B → False, C → True}, {A → True, B → False, C → False},`
`{A → False, B → True, C → True}, {A → False, B → True, C → False},`
`{A → False, B → False, C → True}, {A → False, B → False, C → False}}`

And here we substitute these rules into the logical expression we are working with.

In[14]:= `expr /. %`

Out[14]= `{True, False, True, False, True, False, True, True}`

Here then is the TruthTable function.

In[15]:= `TruthTable[expr_, vars_] := Module[{len = Length[vars], n},`
`ins = Distribute[Table[{True, False}, {len}], List, List, List];`
`res = (expr /. Thread[vars → #1] &) /@ ins;`
`DisplayForm[GridBox[Prepend[Transpose[Append[Transpose[ins],`
`(If[! MemberQ[{True, False}, #1], "*", #1] &) /@ res]] /.`
`{True → "T", False → "F"}, Append[vars,`
`TraditionalForm[expr]]], GridFrame → True,`
`RowLines → Prepend[Table[0, {Length[res] - 1}], 2],`
`ColumnLines → Append[Table[0, {Length[vars] - 1}], 2]]]]`

In[16]:= `TruthTable[Implies[A || B, C], {A, B, C}]`

Out[16]//DisplayForm=

A	B	C	$(A \lor B) \Rightarrow C$
T	T	T	T
T	T	F	F
T	F	T	T
T	F	F	F
F	T	T	T
F	T	F	F
F	F	T	T
F	F	F	T

10.5 Buttons

1. Here is the code for the `Plot3D` template button.

In[1]:= `ButtonBox["Plot3D[fun,{x,xmin,xmax},{y,ymin,ymax}]", Active → True] //`
`DisplayForm`

Out[1]//DisplayForm=

```
Plot3D[fun, {x, xmin, xmax}, {y, ymin, ymax}]
```

Alternately, you can use placeholders.

In[2]:= `ButtonBox["Plot3D[□,{□,□,□},{□,□,□}]", Active → True] // DisplayForm`

Out[2]//DisplayForm=

```
Plot3D[□, {□, □, □}, {□, □, □}]
```

2. Here is the code to create the `Expand` button.

In[3]:= `ButtonBox["Expand[■]", Active → True,`
`ButtonStyle → "CopyEvaluateCell"] // DisplayForm`

Out[3]//DisplayForm=

```
Expand[■]
```

Selecting the expression below and then clicking the `Expand` button will cause a new input cell to be created with `Expand` wrapped around the selected expression; then that cell will be evaluated to produce the expanded polynomial below.

In[4]:= $(\alpha + \beta - \gamma)^5$

In[5]:= `Expand[`$(\alpha + \beta - \gamma)^5$`]`

Out[5]= $\alpha^5 + 5\,\alpha^4\,\beta + 10\,\alpha^3\,\beta^2 + 10\,\alpha^2\,\beta^3 + 5\,\alpha\,\beta^4 + \beta^5 - 5\,\alpha^4\,\gamma - 20\,\alpha^3\,\beta\,\gamma -$
$30\,\alpha^2\,\beta^2\,\gamma - 20\,\alpha\,\beta^3\,\gamma - 5\,\beta^4\,\gamma + 10\,\alpha^3\,\gamma^2 + 30\,\alpha^2\,\beta\,\gamma^2 + 30\,\alpha\,\beta^2\,\gamma^2 +$
$10\,\beta^3\,\gamma^2 - 10\,\alpha^2\,\gamma^3 - 20\,\alpha\,\beta\,\gamma^3 - 10\,\beta^2\,\gamma^3 + 5\,\alpha\,\gamma^4 + 5\,\beta\,\gamma^4 - \gamma^5$

3. Here is the code for the palette.

```
Cell[BoxData[GridBox[{
        {
          ButtonBox[
            RowBox[{"Expand", "[", "■", "]"}],
            ButtonStyle->"CopyEvaluateCell",
            Active->True, ButtonEvaluator->Automatic]},
        {
          ButtonBox[
            RowBox[{"Factor", "[", "■", "]"}],
            ButtonStyle->"CopyEvaluateCell",
            Active->True, ButtonEvaluator->Automatic]},
        {
          ButtonBox[
            RowBox[{"Apart", "[", "■", "]"}],
            ButtonStyle->"CopyEvaluateCell",
            Active->True, ButtonEvaluator->Automatic]},
        {
          ButtonBox[
            RowBox[{"Together", "[", "■", "]"}],
            ButtonStyle->"CopyEvaluateCell",
            Active->True, ButtonEvaluator->Automatic]}
        },
      RowSpacings->0,
      ColumnSpacings->0]], "Input"]
```

Here is how the palette looks when the above expression is formatted.

In[6]:=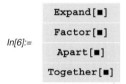

If you wanted to turn this into a free-standing palette, select the above cell and choose **Generate Palette from Selection** from the **File** menu.

Notice that in the code for the palette, each of the buttons used the same three options, `ButtonStyle`, `Active`, and `ButtonEvaluator`, with identical values. Using `ButtonBox`∶ `Options`, we can set each value once at the `GridBox` level and each of the buttons will inherit the option, This cleans up the code considerably.

```
Cell[BoxData[GridBox[{
       {
          ButtonBox[
             RowBox[{"Expand", "[", "■", "]"}]]},
       {
          ButtonBox[
             RowBox[{"Factor", "[", "■", "]"}]]},
       {
          ButtonBox[
             RowBox[{"Apart", "[", "■", "]"}]]},
       {
          ButtonBox[
             RowBox[{"Together", "[", "■", "]"}]]}
       },
     RowSpacings->0,
     ColumnSpacings->0]], "Input",
     ButtonBoxOptions->{ButtonStyle->"CopyEvaluateCell",
          Active->True, ButtonEvaluator->Automatic}
   ]
```

Finally, here is the formatted palette with an input cell and the result of selecting that input cell and clicking the Together [■] button.

In[7]:=

```
Expand[■]

Factor[■]

Apart[■]

Together[■]
```

In[8]:= $\dfrac{1}{x} + \dfrac{1}{y}$

In[9]:= Together$\left[\dfrac{1}{x} + \dfrac{1}{y}\right]$

Out[9]= $\dfrac{x+y}{x\,y}$

11 Examples and applications

11.1 Manipulating data files

1. We first borrow the options from `ReadList` that we wish to pass into `ReadSolarData`.

```
In[1]:= Options[ReadSolarData] = {
            WordSeparators → ",",
            RecordLists -> True,
            RecordSeparators → {"\r\n", "\n", "\r"}
        };
```

```
In[2]:= ReadSolarData[file_, opts___?OptionQ] := Module[{ws, rl, rs, raw, data},
            {ws, rl, rs} = {WordSeparators, RecordLists, RecordSeparators} /.
                Flatten[{opts}] /. Options[ReadSolarData];
            raw = ReadList[file, Word, RecordLists → rl,
                RecordSeparators → rs, WordSeparators → ws];
            data = Select[raw, StringTake[#[[1]], 1] =!= "\"" &];
        Map[ToExpression, data, {2}]
        ]
```

```
In[3]:= datafile = ToFileName[{"IPM3", "DataFiles"}, "23232.txt"]
```

```
Out[3]= IPM3\DataFiles\23232.txt
```

```
In[4]:= data = ReadSolarData[datafile];
```

Now we can use the `GetData` function developed in Section 11.1 to select those records that fall between certain dates.

```
In[5]:= GetData[dat_, {m1_, y1_}, {m2_, y2_}] :=
            Select[dat, (#[[1]] == y1 && #[[2]] ≥ m1) || (#[[1]] == y2 && #[[2]] ≤ m2) &]
```

For example, here are the records between November 1976 and March 1977.

```
In[6]:= GetData[data, {11, 76}, {3, 77}]
```

```
Out[6]= {{76, 11, 2.5, 3.5, 3.9, 4.1, 3.6, 3.5, 4.3,
            4.6, 4.8, 4.8, 2.7, 2.2, 3.1, 3.2}, {76, 12, 2.3, 3.7, 4.4,
            4.7, 4.4, 3.5, 4.6, 5.1, 5.4, 5.5, 3.6, 2.5, 3.8, 4.1},
            {77, 1, 1.9, 2.5, 2.7, 2.8, 2.4, 2.3, 2.8, 3., 3.1, 3.1, 1.5, 1.1, 1.6, 1.7},
            {77, 2, 3.3, 4.5, 4.9, 5.1, 4.3, 4.7,
            5.6, 5.9, 6.1, 6.1, 3.4, 3.1, 4.1, 4.2},
            {77, 3, 4.8, 5.8, 6.1, 6., 4.4, 6.8, 7.6, 7.8, 7.7, 7.8, 4.2, 4.8, 5.6, 5.6}}
```

2. First we need to read the data using the function created in the previous exercise.

```
In[7]:= datafile = ToFileName[{"IPM3", "DataFiles"}, "23232.txt"]
```

```
Out[7]= IPM3\DataFiles\23232.txt
```

In[8]:= **data = ReadSolarData[datafile];**

Here is the first row of the extracted data.

In[9]:= **data[[1]]**

Out[9]= {61, 1, 1.6, 1.9, 2., 2., 1.6, 1.7, 2., 2., 2.1, 2.1, 0.7, 0.5, 0.8, 0.8}

For 1961, we want to extract the elements in the sixth column and add them; then repeat for each of the successive years. For example, this function selects all those rows that start with 61, then pulls off all sixth column elements.

In[10]:= **Part[Select[data, (#[[1]] == 61) &], All, 6]**

Out[10]= {2., 4.4, 5.1, 6.4, 5.7, 6., 6.3, 6.2, 6.8, 5.9, 4.2, 2.3}

In[11]:= **Length[%]**

Out[11]= 12

The total solar radiation for 1961 is the sum of these values.

In[12]:= **Apply[Plus, Part[Select[data, (#[[1]] == 61) &], All, 6]]**

Out[12]= 61.3

Here are the minimum and maximum years (from the first column).

In[13]:= **{ymin, ymax} = Map[{Min[#], Max[#]} &, Part[data, All, 1], {0}]**

Out[13]= {61, 90}

In[14]:= **yearlydata = Table[**
        Apply[Plus, Part[Select[data, (#[[1]] == y) &], All, 6]], {y, ymin, ymax}]

Out[14]= {61.3, 63.1, 56.9, 63.9, 61.2, 63.6, 61.1, 60.7, 63.2,
         62.4, 63.5, 61., 60.7, 63.4, 63.6, 66.6, 62.9, 62.2, 63.4,
         63.1, 61.6, 58.8, 55.7, 63.1, 62., 63., 64.5, 65.3, 64.5, 67.4}

In[15]:= **<< Graphics`MultipleListPlot`**

In[16]:= **MultipleListPlot[yearlydata, SymbolShape → Stem];**

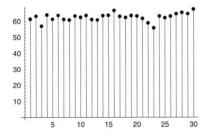

3. We first load the necessary packages.

```
In[17]:= << Graphics`MultipleListPlot`
```

```
In[18]:= << Utilities`FilterOptions`
```

```
In[19]:= PlotSolarData[dat1_, dat2_, opts___?OptionQ] := Module[{months},
            months = {{1, "Jan"}, {2, "Feb"}, {3, "Mar"},
              {4, "Apr"}, {5, "May"}, {6, "Jun"}, {7, "Jul"}, {8, "Aug"},
              {9, "Sep"}, {10, "Oct"}, {11, "Nov"}, {12, "Dec"}};
            MultipleListPlot[dat1, dat2, FilterOptions[MultipleListPlot, opts],
              PlotJoined → True, AspectRatio → Automatic,
              Ticks → {months, Automatic}, AxesLabel → {None, "kWh/m²/day"}]];
```

Read in the file.

```
In[20]:= datafile = ToFileName[{"IPM3", "DataFiles"}, "23232.txt"]
```

```
Out[20]= IPM3\DataFiles\23232.txt
```

Use `ReadSolarData` from the previous exercise to strip out all lines that start with a quote character and insure each element is a number.

```
In[21]:= data = ReadSolarData[datafile];
```

Using `GetData` developed in Section 11.1, we extract the sixth column for all dates between January 1980 and December 1980.

```
In[22]:= d1 = Part[GetData[data, {1, 80}, {12, 80}], All, 6]
```

```
Out[22]= {2.7, 3.6, 5.9, 5.7, 5.9, 5.9, 6.1, 6.7, 6.8, 6., 4.7, 3.1}
```

Similarly for data collected in 1981.

```
In[23]:= d2 = Part[GetData[data, {1, 81}, {12, 81}], All, 6]
```

```
Out[23]= {2.4, 4.3, 4.7, 6.2, 6.2, 6.2, 6.3, 6.8, 6.8, 5.8, 3.7, 2.2}
```

Finally, here is the plot.

```
In[24]:= PlotSolarData[d1, d2]
```

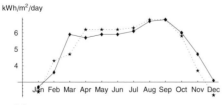

```
Out[24]= - Graphics -
```

11.2 Random walks

1. First defining walk1DOffLattice and then inserting an If statement immediately following dim==1 will do the trick.

```
In[1]:= walk1DOffLattice[n_] :=
          FoldList[Plus, 0, Table[Random[Real, {-1, 1}], {n}]]
```

```
In[2]:= walk1D[n_] := NestList[# + (-1)^Random[Integer] &, 0, n]
```

```
In[3]:= walk2D[n_] :=
          Module[{NSEW = {{0, 1}, {1, 0}, {0, -1}, {-1, 0}}},
            FoldList[Plus, {0, 0},
              NSEW[[Table[Random[Integer, {1, 4}], {n}]]]]]
```

```
In[4]:= walk2DOffLattice[n_] :=
          FoldList[Plus, {0, 0},
            Map[{Cos[#], Sin[#]} &, Table[Random[Real, {0, 2 π}], {n}]]]
```

```
In[5]:= walk3D[n_] := Module[{NSEW3 = √2 Vertices[Cube]},
          FoldList[Plus, {0, 0, 0}, NSEW3[[Table[Random[Integer, {1, 8}], {n}]]]]]
```

```
In[6]:= walk3DOffLattice[n_] := FoldList[Plus, {0, 0, 0},
          Map[{Cos[#], Sin[#], #/(2 π)} &, Table[Random[Real, {-2 π, 2 π}], {n}]]]
```

```
In[7]:= Options[RandomWalk] = {LatticeWalk → True, Dimension → 2}
```

```
Out[7]= {LatticeWalk → True, Dimension → 2}
```

```
In[8]:= RandomWalk[n_, opts___?OptionQ] := Module[{dim, latticeQ},
          If[Not[IntegerQ[n] && n > 0],
            Message[RandomWalk::rwn, n], {latticeQ, dim} =
            {LatticeWalk, Dimension} /. Flatten[{opts, Options[RandomWalk]}];
          Which[
            dim == 1, If[latticeQ, walk1D[n], walk1DOffLattice[n]],
            dim == 2, If[latticeQ, walk2D[n], walk2DOffLattice[n]],
            dim == 3, If[latticeQ, walk3D[n], walk3DOffLattice[n]]
          ]]]
```

2. The output from RandomWalk with the option Dimension set to 1 is a one-dimensional list of integers.

```
In[9]:= RandomWalk[10, Dimension → 1]
```

```
Out[9]= {0, 1, 2, 1, 2, 3, 2, 1, 0, 1, 0}
```

This list can be passed directly to `ListPlot`.

```
In[10]:=  ShowWalk[coords_, opts___] := Which[
              Length[Dimensions[coords]] == 1,
                  ListPlot[coords, opts, PlotJoined → True],
              Dimensions[coords][[2]] == 2,
                  Show[Graphics[Line[coords], opts, AspectRatio → Automatic]],
              Dimensions[coords][[2]] == 3,
                  Show[Graphics3D[Line[coords], opts, AspectRatio → Automatic]]]
```

```
In[11]:=  ShowWalk[RandomWalk[1000, Dimension → 1]];
```

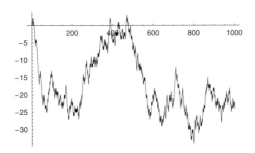

3. First we write down the formulas for representing a point on the unit sphere.

$$In[12]:= x[\phi\_, \theta\_] := \sqrt{1 - Cos[\phi]^2}\ Cos[\theta];$$

$$y[\phi\_, \theta\_] := \sqrt{1 - Cos[\phi]^2}\ Sin[\theta];$$

$$z[\phi\_] := Cos[\phi];$$

This checks that the formulas are correct:

$$In[15]:= Simplify\left[\sqrt{x[\phi, \theta]^2 + y[\phi, \theta]^2 + z[\phi]^2}\right]$$

Out[15]= 1

The next step is to create a pair of angles between 0 and 2π.

```
In[16]:=  ran = Table[Random[Real, {0, 2 π}], {2}]
```

Out[16]= {3.65812, 1.45235}

This applies the functions x, y, and z to this pair of angles.

```
In[17]:=  Apply[{x[#1, #2], y[#1, #2], z[#1]} &, ran]
```

Out[17]= {0.0583615, 0.490403, -0.869539}

Starting at the origin and folding `Plus` across this function gives the following.

```
In[18]:= n = 3;
         FoldList[Plus, {0, 0, 0}, Apply[{x[#1, #2], y[#1, #2], z[#1]} &,
           Table[Random[Real, {0, 2 π}], {n}, {2}], {1}]]
```

```
Out[19]= {{0, 0, 0}, {-0.0583035, 0.166546, 0.984308},
          {0.86393, 0.535037, 1.10136}, {0.64296, 0.540758, 0.126093}}
```

Here then is the rewritten `walk3DOffLattice` with this code inserted.

```
In[20]:= <<Graphics`Polyhedra`
```

```
In[21]:= walk3DOffLattice[n_] := Module[{x, y, z},

           x[φ_, θ_] := √(1 - Cos[φ]²) Cos[θ];

           y[φ_, θ_] := √(1 - Cos[φ]²) Sin[θ];

           z[φ_] := Cos[φ];
           FoldList[Plus, {0, 0, 0}, Apply[{x[#1, #2], y[#1, #2], z[#1]} &,
             Table[Random[Real, {0, 2 π}], {n}, {2}], {1}]]]
```

```
In[22]:= ShowWalk[
           RandomWalk[2500, Dimension → 3, LatticeWalk → False]];
```

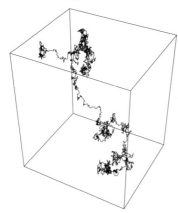

5.

```
In[23]:= AnimateWalk[coords_, opts___] := Scan[
           Show[Graphics[{{RGBColor[1, 0, 0], PointSize[.02], Point[coords[[#1]]]},
             Line[Take[coords, #1]]}], opts, AspectRatio → Automatic,
             PlotRange → Map[{Min[#1] - .2, Max[#1] + .2} &, Transpose[coords]]] &,
           Range[2, Length[coords]]]
```

```
In[24]:= AnimateWalk[RandomWalk[50, LatticeWalk → False]];
```

11.3 The Game of Life

1.

```
In[1]:=  Options[LifeGraphics] =
          Colors → {1 → RGBColor[1, 0, 0], 0 → RGBColor[0, 0, 0]};
```

```
In[2]:=  LifeGraphics[lis_, opts___?OptionQ] := Module[{colors},
          colors = Colors /. Flatten[{opts, Options[LifeGraphics]}];
          Map[
            Graphics[RasterArray[
              Reverse[# /. colors]],
              AspectRatio → Automatic] &, lis]]
```

```
In[3]:=  Options[LifeGraphics]
```

```
Out[3]=  {Colors → {1 → RGBColor[1, 0, 0], 0 → RGBColor[0, 0, 0]}}
```

```
In[4]:=  LifeGame[n_Integer?Positive, steps_] :=
          Module[{gameboard, liveNeighbors, update},
            gameboard = Table[Random[Integer], {n}, {n}];
            liveNeighbors[mat_] := Apply[Plus, Map[RotateRight[mat, #] &,
              {{-1, -1}, {-1, 0}, {-1, 1},
                {0, -1}, {0, 1}, {1, -1}, {1, 0}, {1, 1}}]];
            update[1, 2] := 1;
            update[_, 3] := 1;
            update[_, _] := 0;
            SetAttributes[update, Listable];
            FixedPointList[update[#, liveNeighbors[#]] &, gameboard, steps]
          ]
```

```
In[5]:=  Show[Last[LifeGraphics[LifeGame[10, 5]]]];
```

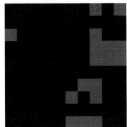

```
In[6]:=  << Graphics`Colors`
```

```
In[7]:=  Show[Last[LifeGraphics[LifeGame[10, 5],
             Colors → {0 → Blue, 1 → Green}]]]
```

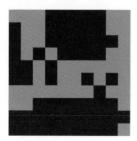

```
Out[7]=  - Graphics -
```

```
In[8]:=  << Utilities`FilterOptions`
```

```
In[9]:=  Options[LifeGraphics] =
             Colors → {1 → RGBColor[1, 0, 0], 0 → RGBColor[0, 0, 0]};
```

```
In[10]:=  AnimateLife[lis_, opts___?OptionQ] :=
             Scan[Show, LifeGraphics[lis, FilterOptions[LifeGraphics, opts]]]
```

2. We will use essentially the same function as before, but we will "overload" the function by providing a definition for the case when a third argument is provided.

```
In[11]:=  LifeGame[n_, steps_, lifeform_List] :=
             Module[{init = Table[0, {n}, {n}], gameboard, liveNeighbors, update},
                gameboard = ReplacePart[init, 1, lifeform];
                liveNeighbors[mat_] := Apply[Plus, Map[RotateRight[mat, #] &, {{-1, -1},
                   {-1, 0}, {-1, 1}, {0, -1}, {0, 1}, {1, -1}, {1, 0}, {1, 1}}]];
                update[1, 2] := 1;
                update[_, 3] := 1;
                update[_, _] := 0;
                Attributes[update] = Listable;
                FixedPointList[update[#, liveNeighbors[#]] &, gameboard, steps]]
```

If LifeGame is called with two arguments, then the definition given earlier will be applied (random initial game board). If LifeGame is called with three arguments, then this definition above will be matched.

Here is a game played on a 50×50 board, starting with a glider object initially at lattice site (20, 20), and played for ten generations.

```
In[12]:=  glider[x_, y_] := {{x, y}, {x + 1, y}, {x + 2, y}, {x + 2, y + 1}, {x + 1, y + 2}}
```

```
In[13]:=  lg50 = LifeGame[50, 10, glider[20, 20]];
```

This game could then be animated by evaluating AnimateLife[lg50].

12 Writing packages

12.5 Writing your own packages

1. Here are the definitions for the auxiliary `collatz` function.

   In[1]:= `collatz[n_ ? EvenQ] := n / 2`

   In[2]:= `collatz[n_ ? OddQ] := 3 n + 1`

2. This is essentially the definition given in the solution to Exercise 5 from Section 5.3.

   In[3]:= `CollatzSequence[n_] := NestWhileList[collatz, n, # ≠ 1 &]`

   In[4]:= `CollatzSequence[7]`

   Out[4]= `{7, 22, 11, 34, 17, 52, 26, 13, 40, 20, 10, 5, 16, 8, 4, 2, 1}`

3. First we write the usage message for `CollatzSequence`, our public function. Notice that we write no usage message for the private `collatz` function.

   In[5]:= `CollatzSequence::usage =`
   `"CollatzSequence[n] computes the sequence of Collatz iterates`
   `   starting with initial value n. The sequence terminates`
   `   as soon as it reaches the value 1.";`

   Here is the warning message that will be issued whenever `CollatzSequence` is passed an argument that is not a positive integer.

   In[6]:= `CollatzSequence::notint =`
   `"First argument, ` `1` `, to CollatzSequence must be a positive integer.";`

4. Here is the modified definition which now issues the warning message created in Exercise 3 whenever the argument *n* is not a positive integer.

   In[7]:= `CollatzSequence[n_] :=`
   `If[IntegerQ[n] && n ≥ 0,`
   `  NestWhileList[collatz, n, # ≠ 1 &],`
   `  Message[CollatzSequence::notint, n]`
   `]`

   The following case covers the situation when CollatzSequence is passed two or more arguments. Note that it uses the built-in `argx` message, which is issued whenever built-in functions are passed the wrong number of arguments.

   In[8]:= `CollatzSequence[_, args__] /; Message[`
   `    CollatzSequence::argx, CollatzSequence, Length[{args}] + 1] := Null`

5. The package begins by giving *usage messages* for every exported function. The functions to be exported are *mentioned* here – *before* the subcontext Private\` is entered – so that name CollatzSequence has context Collatz\`. Notice that collatz is *not* mentioned here and hence will not be accessible to the user of this package.

```
In[9]:= Quit[]
```

```
In[1]:= BeginPackage["IPM3`Collatz`"];
```

```
In[2]:= CollatzSequence::usage =
            "CollatzSequence[n] computes the sequence of Collatz iterates
                starting with initial value n. The sequence terminates
                as soon as it reaches the value 1.";
```

```
In[3]:= CollatzSequence::notint =
            "First argument, `1`, to CollatzSequence must be a positive integer.";
```

A new context IPM3\`Collatz\`Private\` is then begun *within* IPM3\`Collatz\`. All of the definitions of this package are given within this new context. The context IPM3\`Collatz\`: CollatzSequence is defined within the System\` context. The context of collatz, on the other hand, is IPM3\`Collatz\`Private\`.

```
In[4]:= Begin["`Private`"];
```

```
In[5]:= collatz[n_ ? EvenQ] := n / 2
```

```
In[6]:= collatz[n_ ? OddQ] := 3 n + 1
```

```
In[7]:= CollatzSequence[n_] :=
            If[IntegerQ[n] && n ≥ 0,
              NestWhileList[collatz, n, # ≠ 1 &],
              Message[CollatzSequence::notint, n]]
```

```
In[8]:= CollatzSequence[_, args__] /; Message[
            CollatzSequence::argx, CollatzSequence, Length[{args}] + 1] := Null
```

```
In[9]:= End[];
```

```
In[10]:= EndPackage[]
```

After the End[] and EndPackage[] functions are evaluated, $Context and $Context: Path revert to whatever they were before, except that IPM3\`Collatz\` is added to $Con: textPath. Users can refer to CollatzSequence using its short name, but they can only refer to the auxiliary function collatz by its full name. The intent is to discourage clients from using collatz at all, and doing so should definitely be avoided, since the author of the package may change or remove auxiliary definitions at a later time.

Index